D0875364

A Guide to the Best Historical Novels and Tales

✣✣

JONATHAN NIELD

LONGWOOD PRESS
BOSTON

Library of Congress Cataloging in Publication Data

Nield, Jonathan, 1863-
  A guide to the best historical novels and tales.

  Reprint of the 1929 ed. published by Macmillan, New
York.
  Bibliography: p.
  Includes indexes.
  1. Historical fiction--Bibliography. I. Title.
[Z5917.H6N6 1977]   [PN3441]   016.80883'81   76-27529
ISBN 0-89341-051-9

Published in 1977 by LONGWOOD PRESS INC.
P.O.Box 535, Boston, Massachusetts 02148
This Longwood Press book is an unabridged
republication of the edition of 1929.
Library of Congress Catalogue Card Number: 76-27529
International Standard Book Number: 0-89341-051-9
Printed in the United States of America

To

SIR ARTHUR QUILLER-COUCH

IN GRATEFUL RECOGNITION OF HIS KIND AND
ENCOURAGING WORDS WHEN THIS "GUIDE"
FIRST APPEARED AS A VERY SLIGHT
ATTEMPT IN BIBLIOGRAPHY
TWENTY-SEVEN YEARS
AGO

CONTENTS

PREFACE TO THE FIFTH EDITION

THIS edition (1929) is much more than "revised and enlarged" —it is virtually a new book, rewritten and rearranged almost throughout. In the work of preparation I have not only been compelled to cover the last seventeen years' output of historical fiction, but I have also experienced the additional labour of merging into one the third edition list and the large "supplement" list which together formed the fourth edition. Moreover, my annotations are now both more detailed and more accurate; in the period 1900-1910 my literary studies and slight efforts in authorship had to be combined with secretarial and other outside work, so that it was then quite impossible for me to give that undivided attention which the altered circumstances of later life have allowed. Whether success has now been reached after all the pains taken to make the *Guide* far more accurate and helpful, must be left to the judgment of those who may carefully examine, or make regular use of, the book itself.

In this latest edition I have endeavoured, wherever possible, to base each annotation on very careful examination of the *actual novel or tale described;* such a method is, of course, the only one that is entirely adequate to the production of a book of this special kind, but it involves an amount of labour for which few literary workers have either the time or the inclination. Long-continued investigation has shown me that most of the bibliographies of historical fiction (large and small alike) are not to any sufficient extent based on knowledge obtained at first hand; too often the compiler has been satisfied with the information derived from reviews in literary newspapers (old and new), from publishers' announcements and leaflets, from the annotated lists in previous bibliographies, etc. etc. The earlier editions of my own *Guide* contained many serious descriptive errors, due to the comparative shortness of time which I was able to devote to research. If, however, I claim greater accuracy for my fifth edition than that to be found in other bibliographies of the subject, this does not mean that I am ungenerously ignoring the huge amount of valuable material to be found in such works as the "Guide to Historical Fiction" (1914) of Dr. Ernest A. Baker, the "Ireland in Fiction" (1919) of the Rev. Stephen J. Brown, and the "Historical Fiction Chronologically and Historically

Related " (1920) of Dr. James R. Kaye (U.S.A.). In regard to the three important reference books just named, as well as in regard to several smaller contributions, I have—in the *Bibliography* at the end of this volume—offered what praise I could honestly give, after careful examination in each individual case. And I would here express my personal indebtedness to not a few of these compilations (especially Dr. Baker's), in so far as they have prevented my overlooking certain books of merit; as to borrowing their annotations, I invite anybody who may suspect me of being guilty in that respect, to compare my descriptive notes with those appearing in any other previous work of the kind.

During the long interval between my last edition and the present one, I have had plenty of time to give full attention to criticisms made by reviewers. It has been my earnest wish to profit by the suggestions made, but a real difficulty arises when the advice given in two separate quarters is quite contradictory. For example, it was stated by one reviewer in 1911 that I had somewhat spoilt my book by making the lists too comprehensive; another critic was of the opposite opinion that inclusiveness (i.e. the inclusion of as many novels and tales as possible) was the main desideratum. Perhaps it will appease in some degree those people who favour one or other of these opinions, if I tell them that in this latest edition I have with utmost care weeded out over fourteen hundred novels and tales, while, against that large reduction, I have made about eleven hundred and sixty new entries. The fact is that, while I have aimed at choosing the best fiction available for every period, I have always borne in mind that the word " best," as applied to any particular novel, must be interpreted in a wide sense —the sense of being *the best of its kind.* I fully admit that quite a huge number of the books entered in my lists do not belong to that type of historical fiction which attracts me personally; but novels, like different foods, make a varied appeal, and accordingly, in attempting to guide readers, one has to allow for that divergence of taste which is a permanent characteristic of humanity.

The sections (4th edition) respectively headed " Fifty Representative Novels," and " Suggested Courses of Reading," have now been omitted. Sir C. H. Firth's expressed doubts as to the usefulness of any such " Courses " (see Historical Association Leaflet No. 51) have confirmed my own suspicions. On the other hand, an important new feature is the *Subject Index*, which, it is hoped, will add largely to the usefulness of the book. The *Bibliography* has been revised and brought up to date.

I have been obliged once again, in covering such a large province of literature, carefully to weigh the suitability for my lists of this or that book by a writer of established reputation (past or present). Taking, first, a modern instance, I have found what seem to me equally sufficient reasons for including George Moore's " The Brook Kerith," and for omitting his two fictional studies of individual passion: " Héloïse and Abélard " and " Ulick and Soracha." My second example shall be taken from a bygone literary environment. One or two bibliographies of historical fiction have included Walter Savage Landor's deservedly esteemed " Pericles and Aspasia "; as my exclusion of this work may seem to some few readers less reasonable than the omission of such books as those named above, I venture to quote from a Landor authority, who raises just those points which appear to me almost inevitably to rule out the work in question:—" One must not look to find in *Pericles* any strict archæological accuracy, any deep insight into the special conditions of Hellenic life; we must not be surprised to find that on almost every page he is writing with an eye on those English things of his own time that he loved, and especially on those that he hated. . . . Again, there is doubtless a certain connection between the varied episodes " (in these imaginary letters), " but the connection is often of the slightest, and broken up by discursive reflection." As a fine example of English prose literature, Landor's book is, of course, sure of recognition, but the claim for its inclusion among historical novels appears to me unreasonable.

As regards the more or less limited number of novels which were originally chosen to represent Harrison Ainsworth, G. P. R. James, and James Grant respectively, I have not only extended the selections in each case, but I have much more fully described the main historical events which these romancists took for the background of their stories. There have recently been signs of something like a revival in popular taste for these older writers—especially in the case of Ainsworth. Indeed, the last-named novelist has quite lately received enthusiastic support in a distinctly intellectual quarter. In her very interesting volume, " George Eliot and Her Times " (Hodder, 1927), Miss Elizabeth S. Haldane, after referring to the different merits of a few well-known historical novelists (including Kingsley, Lytton and Reade), adds, " though many of us go so far as to prefer Harrison Ainsworth, slipshod, as he often was, to any one of them "; and, still more startling than the tribute just quoted, is the sentence which immediately follows it: " He at least came nearer to that immortal writer of romance, Dumas, whose great novel ' The Three Musketeers,' like Tolstoy's ' War and Peace,' is not of one country, but of all." These remarks by a critic of distinction once more illustrate the need for a wide *catholicity* in the preparation of lists which are to draw the attention of readers to the " best examples " of historical fiction; for it would be easy to quote from eminent literary authorities who, without hesitation, put Ainsworth on a very low level as historical novelist.

Still keeping to mid-nineteenth century authors, I am glad to notice that new editions of Emma Robinson have appeared within a comparatively recent time; her " Whitefriars " had enormous interest for me in my schoolboy days. Miss Yonge, too, continues to attract readers, and here again I venture on a small personal reminiscence: the reading of her " Little Duke " (a tale intended for specially young children) originated that taste for Historical Romance which has remained with me some sixty years later.

But I must turn away from the older writers to glance at some of those historical romancists who—for widely differing reasons—have come specially to the fore in the last two decades (a few of the writers named have, as a matter of fact, reached success more than twenty years ago, but at least their popularity and literary position have since then become more assured).

I will group my authors under separate headings as follows: (I) English and American Novelists; (II) Foreign Novelists; (III) English and American Writers for the Young. It must be understood that, as regards arrangement and selection, there is no finality claimed for these lists: they are merely offered as some indication of more or less recent popular taste in the sphere of Historical Fiction. I am confident that a fair proportion of the names will at once recall to the intelligent reader, stories of such imaginative power and charm that he will see the utter absurdity of a statement often made dogmatically in the past, but rarely, if ever, repeated at the present day: " The Historical Novel is dead! "

(I) *Some recent English and American Novelists :—*

Mrs. F. A. Steel, " Sydney C. Grier," Eden Phillpotts, Neil Munro, Gertrude Atherton, Mary Johnston, Sheila Kaye-Smith, " Marjorie Bowen," Max Pemberton, John Buchan, Rafael Sabatini, H. C. Bailey, Alfred Tresidder Sheppard, William Stearns Davis, Nathan Gallizier, Hamlin Garland, Edward Lucas White, " E. Barrington " (L. Adams Beck), Michael Barrington, Ford Madox Hueffer, Marmaduke Pickthall, Robert Hugh Benson, Violet Jacob, Naomi Mitchison, Miss G. V. McFadden, Warwick Deeping, H. de Vere Stacpoole, Hamilton Drummond, Robert W. Chambers, Margaret L. Woods, Miss Graham Hope, " S. G. Tallentyre," Baroness Orczy (Mrs. Barstow), Halliwell Sutcliffe, J. Huntly McCarthy, J. C. Snaith, " Ashton Hilliers," Bernard Hamilton, Henry Baerlein, Emerson Hough, Irving Bacheller, Randall Parrish, C. G. D. Roberts, H. W. Morrow, Jeffery Farnol, " John Oxenham," Mrs. Evan Nepean, Anthony Armstrong, Crosbie Garstin, Donn Byrne, Miss H. F. M. Prescott, Miss D. K. Broster, Miss J. G. Sarasin, Robert Wm. Mackenna, R. H. Mottram, Stephen Vincent Benét, James Boyd, Ramon Guthrie, Hugh Pendexter.

(II) *Some recent Foreign Novelists :—*

Dmitri Merezhkovsky, Verner von Heidenstam, Louis Couperus, Walter von Molo, Paul and Victor Margueritte, Antoine Baumann,

Blasco-Ibañez, M. A. Aldanov, Fritz Mauthner, Alfred Döblin, Johannes J. Jensen, Selma Lagerlöf, Sigrid Undset, Jacob Wassermann, Louis Bertrand, J. Schlumberger, A. Maurois, Lion Feuchtwanger.

(III) *Some recent English and American Writers for the Young :—*

" Herbert Strang," J. A. Altsheler, E. T. Tomlinson, Tom Bevan, " Morice Gerard," Herbert Hayens, Charles Boardman Hawes, " Harry Collingwood," F. S. Brereton, David Ker, Cyrus T. Brady, Edwin L. Sabin, Escott Lynn, Dorothea Moore, Evaleen Stein, Mrs. E. Knipe, Beulah Marie Dix, Grace I. Whitham, Mary H. Debenham, Gertrude Hollis, John Lesterman, Margaret Baines Reed.

The last name in Section II cannot be left without special remark. Feuchtwanger's wonderful success with his book " Jew Süss," has once more proved the elasticity of the term " Historical Novel "; for, just when there was a disposition in certain literary quarters to ask whether this particular *genre* had not reached its limits of adaptability, there came forward a writer possessed of those two important qualifications of fictional expression and historical knowledge, who showed the world at large that the present demand for analysis and downright out-spokenness, can be met in the shape of historical romance, as well as in that type of fiction which most of us are disposed to class separately as " psychological " and " realistic." Acute literary critics have pointed out that Romance and Realism are not properly antagonistic; but, as to the true relation between them, and as to whether Feuchtwanger's particular method be the ideal one—these are questions which will continue to be debated as time advances. Every age has its own mental atmosphere, and the Historical Novel of the Future will inevitably be adapted to contemporary taste and outlook. Even a genius reflects his period more or less.

I cannot end this Preface without expressing grateful thanks to those authors, publishers, editors, and librarians, who have most kindly furnished me with desired information. Limitations of space compel my making this acknowledgment in general terms. There are, however, a few obligations of a special kind with which I must deal more pre-cisely. Out of many friends in the bookselling business (for, as an inveterate reader and booklover, I have frequented bookshops all my life), there are two whom I wish to mention by name. Mr. Fowler, of Eastbourne, has given me invaluable help; while to Mr. Ernest Cooper (late Commin), of Bournemouth, I owe the encouragement and inspiration which " set me going " at the moment when I was inclined to shirk the big task of a Fifth Edition.

My special thanks are also due to Mr. Arthur I. Ellis and other officials in the British Museum Reading Room; their invariable courtesy, and the great assistance they gave me over a long period, will always remain as a pleasant memory. Miss L. Catharine Thorburn, Secretary of the

Royal Statistical Society, has rendered no little service at a time of unusual stress. To Mr. G. A. Paternoster Brown I am much indebted for the comprehensive Subject Index, the importance of which has already been mentioned. Last of all, though not least, I must acknowledge the extent to which my wife has helped me throughout, more particularly in the tedious, but necessary, work of copying and correcting MSS.

August, 1928.   J.N.

INTRODUCTION

"Those who know very little of the past and care very little for the future, will make but a sorry business of the present. . . . The great Duke of Marlborough said that he had learnt all the history he ever knew out of Shakespeare's historical plays. I have long thought that if we persuaded those classes who have to fight their own little battles of Blenheim for bread every day, to make such a beginning of history as is furnished by Shakespeare's plays and Scott's novels, we should have done more to imbue them with a real interest in the past of mankind than if we had taken them through a course of Hume and Smollett, or Hallam on the English Constitution, or even the dazzling Macaulay."

Lord Morley on " The Great Commonplaces of Reading."

"I take up a volume of Dr. Smollett or a volume of *The Spectator*, and say the fiction carries a greater amount of truth in solution than the volume which purports to be all true."

William Makepeace Thackeray.

"Epitomes are not narratives, as skeletons are not human figures. Thus records of prime truths remain a dead letter to plain folk; the writers have left so much to the imagination, and imagination is so rare a gift. Here, then, the writer of fiction may be of use to the public—as an interpreter."

Charles Reade, in " The Cloister and the Hearth."

"What, after all, can we know about the way in which men felt so long ago— Cavaliers or Crusaders or Romans? But the answer to that is another question. What can we know about the way in which men feel now? The dust of modernity is as thick as the drift of the ages—the only difference is that it has not settled: and still ' we mortal millions live alone.' Every narrative is creation, because understanding is itself a creative act; the strictest history is born dead unless it burns and breathes with imagination from within; if the past *is* only because it *was*, moment by moment that becomes true of the present also; realism and romance are not two different things; the test of any story, scientific, poetic, ancient, modern or futurist, is simply that it convinces."

Gerald Gould in " The English Novel of To-day."

"L'Histoire ne peut prétendre qu'à proposer des hypothèses; c'est dire qu'elle n'a pas grandes concessions à faire pour s'effacer devant le roman."

J. Schlumberger in the Preface to " Le Lion Devenu Vieux."

"Sir Walter Scott is dead. Long live Sir Walter Scott! His great discovery that fiction and history are interchangeable is a basic patent, bound to reappear and reappear in the history of literature. . . . Not psychology, not realism, not the most intense modernism can kill the historical romance."

Henry Seidel Canby in " The Saturday Review of Literature " (New York).

"History to Galdós was the ' novel ' of the human race—a thing inseparable from human passion, human laughter and human tears."

L. B. Walton in " Pérez Galdós and the Spanish Novel."

INTRODUCTION

It is not proposed, in these preliminary remarks, to sketch in detail the origin and growth of the Historical Novel; this has already been amply done by Professor Saintsbury and others. I shall be content to approach the subject on its general side, offering, at the same time, some critical suggestions which will, I hope, not be without value to readers of Romance.

But, first of all, I must explain how the List which follows came to be compiled, and the object I have in offering it. For many years I have been an assiduous reader of novels and tales in which the historical element appeared, supplementing my own reading in this direction by a careful study of all that I could find in the way of criticism on such works and their writers. Only in this way could I venture on a selection involving a survey of several thousand volumes! With the above understanding, I can say that no book has been inserted without *some* reason, while I have made all possible effort to obtain accuracy of description. And this leads me to remark, that just in this process of selection do I claim originality for my List. Nearly twenty years ago* Mr. H. Courthope Bowen's "Descriptive Catalogue" of historical fiction appeared; the general idea of the booklet was excellent, but as an attempt to supply guidance in the formation of "school libraries," it cannot be said to have succeeded. Mr. Bowen's list included all, or nearly all, the works of such uneven writers as G. P. R. James, Ainsworth, Grant, etc., as well as numerous tales by quite third-rate authors; moreover, the descriptive notes were both very meagre and very inaccurate.† It seemed to me that not only was there room for a new list of Historical Novels (Stevenson, Marion Crawford, Conan Doyle, Weyman, Mason, and a number of more or less capable romancists having come forward in the last twenty years), but, also, that more than ever was there a need for some sort of *clue* in the search for such books. In the last year or two there has been an almost alarming influx in this department of Fiction, and teachers in schools,

---

*This Introduction was mostly written in 1901, but in the present edition (1929) it appears with important corrections and additions.

† "A Descriptive Catalogue of Historical Novels and Tales, for the use of School Libraries and Teachers of History" compiled and described by H. Courthope Bowen, M.A. (Edward Stanford, Eng., 1882; and Scribner and Welford, U.S.A., 1884).

besides readers in general, may be glad to be saved a somewhat tedious investigation.

Having thus attempted to justify the existence of my *Guide*, I pass on to deal with the subject of Historical Fiction itself. Most of us, I suppose, at one time or another have experienced a thrill of interest when some prominent personage, whom we knew well by repute, came before us in the flesh. We watched his manner, and noted all those shades of expression which, in another's countenance, we should have passed by unheeded. Well, it seems to me that, parallel with this experience, is that which we gain when, reading some first-rank romance, we encounter in its pages a figure with which History has made us more or less familiar. And I would remark that the great masters do not, as a rule, make that mistake which less skilful writers fall into—the mistake of introducing well-known historical figures too frequently. The Cromwell of " Woodstock " has an element of mystery about him, even while he stands out before our mental vision in bold relief.* Had Scott brought him more prominently into the plot, and thus emphasized the fictional aspect of his figure, our interest in the story, as such, might have been sustained, but we should have lost that atmosphere of *vraisemblance* which, under a more careful reserve, the hand of the master has wrought for us.

But it is not only this introduction of personalities which constitutes a novel " historical "; the mere allusion to real events, or the introduction of dates, may give us sufficient ground for identifying the period with which a novel deals. Of course, the question as to whether a particular person or event is truly historical, is not always an easy one to answer. By the adaptation in it of some purely mythical character or event, a novel is no more constituted " historical " than is a fairy-tale by the adaptation of folk-lore. King Arthur and Robin Hood are unhistorical, and, if I have ventured to insert in my list certain tales which deal with the latter, it is not on *that* account, but because other figures truly historical (*e.g.*, Richard I.) appear. As there has been some dispute on this question of the Historical Novel proper, I offer the following definition:—A Novel is rendered historical by the introduction of dates, personages, or events, to which identification can be readily given. I am quite aware that certain well-known novels which give the *general atmosphere of a period*—such, for example, as Hawthorne's " Scarlet Letter " and Mr. Hewlett's " Forest Lovers " —do not come within the scope of my definition; but this is just why I have added a supplementary list of Semi-Historical tales. And,

* It must, however, be admitted that, while the figure of the Protector does indeed " stand out " well in this particular novel, Scott's depiction shows prejudice, and comes perilously near what Andrew Lang has called the impertinence of attempting to *judge* one of the world's really great men. It is only fair to add that Scott's " Cromwell " was a most favourable presentment compared with the monster of Early Nineteenth Century popular imagination.

I have likewise refrained from giving many tales dealing with Early-Christian times. We are here, it must be admitted, on controversial ground, and under the First Century heading I have endeavoured to insert romances of the highest quality only. For instance, I think that Dr. Abbott's " Philochristus " and Wallace's " Ben Hur " ought to satisfy two different types of readers. And this is the place, doubtless, to say that in my lists will be found books of widely differing merit and aim. School teachers, and others in like capacity, ought to discriminate between authors suitable for juvenile or untrained tastes, and authors whose appeal is specially to those of maturer thought and experience.* Differing as much in method and style as in choice of period and character type, Thackeray's " Vanity Fair " and George Eliot's " Romola " have at least this in common—they require a very high degree of intelligence for their due appreciation. Who, among those of us with any knowledge of such works, would dream of recommending them to a youthful reader fresh from the perusal of Miss Yonge's " Little Duke," or Captain Marryat's " Children of the New Forest? "

Naturally in a list of this kind there is bound to be very great inequality; certain periods have been wholly ignored by writers of the first rank, while in others we have something like an *embarras de richesse*. Consequently, I have been compelled, here and there, to insert authors of only mediocre merit. In other cases, again, I have not hesitated to omit works by writers of acknowledged position when these have seemed below the author's usual standard, and where no gap had to be filled. I would instance the James II.—William III. period. Here " Edna Lyall " might have been represented, but, there being no dearth of good novels dealing with both the above reigns, I did not deem it advisable to call in this popular writer at the point which has been generally considered her lowest. I mention this to show that omissions do not necessarily mean ignorance, though, in covering such an immense ground, I cannot doubt that romances worthy of a place in my list have been overlooked.

I think many will be surprised to find how large a proportion of our best writers (English and American) have entered the domain of Historical or Semi-Historical Romance. Scott, Peacock, Thackeray, Dickens, Hawthorne, George Eliot, Charlotte Brontë, George Meredith, Thomas Hardy, R. L. Stevenson, Charles Kingsley, Henry Kingsley, Charles Reade, George Macdonald, Anthony Trollope, Mrs. Gaskell, Walter Besant, Lytton, Disraeli, J. H. Newman, J. A. Froude, and Walter Pater—these are a few of the names which appear in the following pages; while Tolstoy, Dumas, Balzac, " George Sand," Victor Hugo, " De Stendhal " (Henri Beyle), De Vigny, Prosper Mérimée,

* Since these words were written, I have—in later editions—tried to help in the work of discrimination, by specially marking a large number of books which are more or less likely to appeal to the young. (See Note immediately preceding the Main List, page 1).

Flaubert, Théophile Gautier, Alphonse Daudet, "Anatole France," Freytag, Scheffel, Hauff, Auerbach, Felix Dahn, Georg Ebers, Hausrath, Manzoni, Pérez Galdós, Merezhkovsky, Topelius, Sienkiewicz, and Jókai are, perhaps, the chief amongst those representing Literatures other than our own.

"An Egyptian Princess," "Quo Vadis?," "The Last Days of Pompeii," "The Gladiators," "Hypatia," "Harold," "Ivanhoe," "The Talisman," "Maid Marian," "The Forest Lovers," "Quentin Durward," "Romola," "The Cloister and the Hearth," "The Abbot," "Westward Ho!" "Kenilworth," "The Chaplet of Pearls," "A Gentleman of France," "By Order of the Company," "The Splendid Spur," "John Inglesant," "Under the Red Robe," "The Three Musketeers," "Twenty Years After," "The Viscomte de Bragelonne," "Maiden and Married Life of Mary Powell," "A Legend of Montrose," "John Splendid," "Old Mortality," "John Burnet of Barns," "The Betrothed" (*I Promessi Sposi*), "Lorna Doone," "The Refugees," "The Old Dominion," "The Courtship of Morrice Buckler," "Dorothy Forster," "The Raiders," "Rob Roy," "Esmond," "The Virginians," "Heart of Midlothian," "Waverley," "The Master of Ballantrae," "Kidnapped," "Catriona," "The Chaplain of the Fleet," "The Seats of the Mighty," "Richard Carvel," "Ninety-three" (*L'An '93*), "War and Peace," "The Revolution in Tanner's Lane," "Vittoria" —what visions do these mere titles arouse within many of us! And, though most of the books given in my list cannot be described in the same glowing terms as the masterpieces* just named, yet many " nests of pleasant thoughts " may be formed through their companionship.

Hitherto allusion has been mainly in the direction of modern authors, and I would now say a word or two in regard to those of an earlier period who are also represented. Defoe, Fielding, Richardson, Goldsmith, Smollett, Frances Burney, Mrs. Radcliffe, William Godwin, Maria Edgeworth, Jane Austen, John Galt, Susan Ferrier, Samuel Lover, J. G. Lockhart, Leigh Hunt, Fenimore Cooper, Harriet Martineau, J. L. Motley, W. G. Simms, Horace Smith, Charles Lever, Meadows Taylor and William Carleton—these (in greater or less degree) notable names were bound to have a place; and, coming to less distinguished writers, I may mention John Banim, Gerald Griffin, Mrs. Anne Marsh, Mrs. Bray, Jane Porter, W. H. Maxwell, Sir Arthur Helps, Lewis Wingfield, Thomas Miller, C. Macfarlane, Grace Aguilar, Anne Manning, and Emma Robinson (author of " Whitefriars "). To G. P. R. James, Harrison Ainsworth, and James Grant I have previously alluded. It has been my endeavour to choose the best examples of all the above-named novelists—a task rendered specially difficult in some cases by

---

* " Masterpieces," that is, *in their several degrees;* perhaps I was somewhat rash to invite the criticism that " The Cloister and the Hearth," " Old Mortality," " Esmond," " War and Peace," etc., find themselves in very unequal company.

the fact of immense literary output. Doubtless not a few of the works
so chosen are open to criticism, but they will at least serve to illustrate
certain stages in the growth of Historical Romance. With the exclusion
of Mrs. Gore, Lady Blessington, Lady Fullerton, and Mrs. Child, few
will, I imagine, find fault; but a writer like Miss Tucker (A.L.O.E.)
still finds so many readers in juvenile quarters, that it has required a
certain amount of courage to place her also on my *Index Expurgatorius!*
Turning once again to writers of the sterner sex, I have ruled out
Horace Walpole* and Pierce Egan, Junr.; and (quitting the " sensational " for the " mildly entertaining ") of the Rev. J. M. Neale's many
historical tales, I have selected only two—" Theodora Phranza," and
" Duchenier," both of which have continued to be read, and are good
examples of their kind. Stories possessing a background of History
are to be found in " Tales from Blackwood," as also in " Wilson's Tales
of the Borders," but their extremely slight character seemed scarcely
to justify insertion; while not even the high literary position attained
by him on other grounds reconciled me to either of Allan Cunningham's
novels—" Sir Michael Scott " and " Paul Jones."

Of the Foreign novelists appearing in my list, several have been
already named, but M. Tapparelli-D'Azeglio, F. D. Guerrazzi, Cesare
Cantù, " W. Alexis " (G. Häring), H. Laube, Louise Mühlbach (Klara
M. Mundt), Nicolas Jósika, Viktor Rydberg, Hendrik Conscience,
Amédée Achard, and " Erckmann-Chatrian " here call for notice as
not coming under strictly contemporary classification. In the selection
from Foreign Historical Fiction nothing more has been attempted than
to include the leading examples; most of these, it will be found, have
been translated into English.

Before leaving the subject of older writers, it may be mentioned that
not a few of the works chosen to represent them are, at the moment,
out of print. To anyone objecting that something ought to have been
done to indicate this in each separate case, I would urge that the " out
of print " line can never be drawn with precision in view of constant
reprints as well as of further extinctions.

Perhaps this introduction may be most fitly concluded by something
in the nature of apology for Historical Romance itself. Not only has
fault been found with the deficiencies of unskilled authors in that department, but the question has been asked by one or two critics of standing
—What right has the Historical Novel *to exist at all?* More often than
not, it is pointed out, the Romancist gives us a mass of inaccuracies,
which, while they mislead the ignorant (*i.e.*, the majority), are an un-
pardonable offence to the historically-minded reader. Moreover, the
writer of such Fiction, though he be a Thackeray or a Scott, cannot

---

* Walpole's " The Castle of Otranto " has not unreasonably been described as " the
real starting-point of the English historical novel "; but, whatever interest the book
may have for the careful investigator of literary origins, its absurdities would scarcely
be tolerated by the average reader of fiction to-day.

surmount barriers which are not merely hard to scale, but absolutely impassable. The spirit of a period is like the selfhood of a human being —something that cannot be handed on; try as we may, it is impossible for us to breathe the atmosphere of a bygone time, since all those thousand-and-one details which went to the building up of both individual and general experience, can never be reproduced. We consider (say) the Eighteenth Century from the purely Historical standpoint, and, while we do so, are under no delusion as to our limitations; we know that a few of the leading personages and events have been brought before us in a more or less disjointed fashion, and are perfectly aware that there is room for much discrepancy between the *pictures* so presented to us (be it with immense skill) and the *actual facts* as they took place in such and such a year. But, goes on the objector, in the case of a Historical Romance we allow ourselves to be hoodwinked, for, under the influence of a pseudo-historic security, we seem to watch the real sequence of events in so far as these affect the characters in whom we are interested. How we seem to *live* in those early years of the Eighteenth Century, as we follow Henry Esmond from point to point, and yet, in truth, we are breathing not the atmosphere of Addison and Steele, but the atmosphere created by the brilliant Nineteenth Century Novelist, partly out of his erudite conception of a former period, and partly out of the emotions and thoughts engendered by *that very environment which was his own*, and from which he could not escape!

Well, to all such criticisms it seems to me there are ample rejoinders. In the first place, it must be remembered that History itself possesses interest for us more as the unfolding of certain moral and mental developments than as the mere enumeration of facts. Of course, I am aware that the ideal of the Historian is Truth utterly regardless of prejudice and inclination, but, as with all other human ideals, this one is never fully realised, and there is ever that discrepancy between Fact and its Narration to which I just now alluded. This being so, I would ask—Is not the writer of Fiction justified in emphasizing those elements of History which have a bearing on life and character in general? There is, doubtless, a wise and an unwise method of procedure. One novelist, in the very effort to be accurate, produces a work which —being neither History nor Fiction—is simply dull; while another, who has gauged the true relation between fact and imagination, knows better than to bring into prominence that which should remain only as a background. After all, there are certain root motives and principles which, though they vary indefinitely in their application, underlie Human Conduct, and are common to all ages alike. Given a fairly accurate knowledge as regards the general history of any period, combined with some investigation into its special manners and customs, there is no reason why a truly imaginative novelist should not produce a work at once satisfying to romantic and historical instincts.

Again, if it be true that the novelist cannot reproduce the far past in any strict sense, it is also true that neither can he so reproduce the life and events of *yesterday*. That power of imaginative memory, which all exercise in daily experience, may be held in very different degrees, but its enjoyment is not dependent on accuracy of representation—for, were this so, none of us would possess it. In an analogous manner the writer of Romance may be more or less adequately equipped on the side of History pure and simple, but he need not wait for that which will never come—the power of reproducing *in toto* a past age. If, in reading what purports to be no more than a Novel, the struggle between Christianity and Paganism (for example), or the unbounded egotism of Napoleon, be brought more vividly before our minds— and this may be done by suggestion as well as by exact relation— then, I would maintain, we are to some extent educated historically, using the word in a large though perfectly legitimate sense.

I recently read a work which here presents itself as admirably illustrating my meaning. In her too little known " Adventures of a Goldsmith," Miss M. H. Bourchier has contrived to bring forcibly before us the period when Napoleon, fast approaching the zenith of his power, was known in France as the " First Consul." The " man of destiny " himself—appearing on the scene for little more than a brief moment—can in no sense be described as one of the book's characters, and yet the whole plot is so skilfully contrived as to hinge on his personality. We are made to feel the dominating influence of that powerful will upon the fears and hopes of a time brimming over with revolutionary movement. Whether the Cadoudal-Pichegru conspiracy is in this particular story accurately depicted for us in all its phases, or whether the motives which impelled certain public characters are therein interpreted aright—both in regard to these and other points there may be room for doubt; but at least the general forces of the period are placed before us in such a way as to drive home the conviction that, be the historical inaccuracies of detail what they may in the eyes of this or that specialist, the picture as a whole is one which, while it rivets our attention as lovers of romance, does no injury to the strictest Historic sense.

I know well that numerous novels might be cited which, besides abounding in anachronisms, are harmful in that they present us with a misleading conception of some personality or period; moreover, I acknowledge that this defect is by no means confined to romances of an inferior literary order. That Cromwell has been unreasonably vilified, and Mary Queen of Scots misconceived as a saintly martyr —how often are these charges brought against not a few of our leading exponents of Historical Fiction. Let this be fully granted, it remains to ask—To whom were our novelists originally indebted for these misconceptions? Were not the historians of an *earlier* generation responsible for these wrong judgments? True, the real Science of History—the sifting of evidence, and the discovery and unravelling of ancient documents—may be described as an essentially modern attainment, so it would be unreasonable to blame our older historians for errors which it was largely, if not wholly, beyond their power to overcome. And it is just here that I would emphasize my defence of the Romancist. If Historians themselves have differed (and still differ!) may it not be pleaded on behalf of the Historical Novelist that he also must be judged according to the possibilities of his time? For, while he may have too readily adopted false conceptions in the past, there is no necessity why, in the future, *he also*—profiting by the growth of Critical Investigation—should not have due regard, in the working out of his Historical background, for all the latest "results."* And, I would further add, even though it be true that Scott and others have misled us in certain directions, this does not prevent our acknowledgment that, *given their aspect of a particular period*, it was only fitting that the scheme of their novels should be in harmony with it. If "bloody Mary" was a cruel hypocrite, then our reading of her period will be influenced by that real (or supposed) fact; but, if further investigation reverses this severe judgment on the woman herself, then, in Heaven's name, let us mould our general conception afresh. The fountains of Romance show no sign of running dry, and, though we may look in vain at the moment for a genius of the very highest type, the Future has possibilities within it which the greatest literary pessimist among us cannot wholly deny. If, then, fault can be found with the older Romancists for the spreading here and there of false historical notions, let us look to future workers in the same sphere for adjustment. I believe, however, that one notable critic has pronounced the mischief already done to be quite irreparable, seeing that the only "History" at all widely spread is that derived from those very romances in which errors are so interwoven with the sentimental interest of the plot itself that readers inevitably "hug their delusions!" But I think that this danger need not be contemplated seriously. The Historical Novel *exists primarily as Fiction*, and, even though in our waking moments we may be persuaded of the unreality of that "dream" which a Scott

---

* As these passages were written some twenty-seven years ago, it gives me pleasure to find an authority like Prof. G. M. Trevelyan writing, at a comparatively recent date, on this same question of the historical novelist's proper equipment for his task:—"An historical novelist, if he is to be anything more than a boiler of the pot, requires two qualities: an historical mind apt to study the records of a period, and a power of creative imagination able to reproduce the perceptions so acquired in a picture that has all the colours of life. Some writers, like Charlotte Yonge, Charles Reade, Mr. Stanley Weyman, and Mr. John Buchan . . . can do valuable work each in his own degree by exploiting carefully the results of modern historical scholarship, with the help of the amount of imagination that each has." (Sidgwick Memorial Lecture at Newnham College, Cambridge, 1921).

or a Dumas has produced for us, we shall still be able to place ourselves again and again under the spell of their delightful influence. Moreover, while admitting Dumas' carelessness of exact detail, it would hardly be contended by the most sceptical that his works (still less those of Scott) are without any background of Historic suggestiveness. Scott, indeed, shows signs of having possessed something of that " detachment " which is one important qualification in the Historian proper; there is a fairness and prevision in his historical judgments which we look for in vain when reading the works of his contemporaries. That there was no fundamental antagonism between the Romantic and the Scientific Movements of last Century has been shown by that very brilliant American thinker, Professor Josiah Royce, of Harvard University. " The very spirit," he writes, " that in Great Britain expressed itself in Scott's romances, once wedded to the minuteness of German scholarship, was destined to transform the whole study of history." (*The Spirit of Modern Philosophy*.)

And, having thus touched on what I believe to be the true relation between Romance and History, I may note, as a last word, the use of the Historical Tale to those who have the training of young folk. That " desire to know," which is an essential for all true learning, is sometimes best fostered by methods outside the ordinary School routine. Thus, as regards History, where the textbook fails in arousing interest, the tale may succeed, and, once the spirit of inquiry has been stimulated, half the battle is gained. In saying this, I am far from wishing to imply that the reading of romances can ever take the place of genuine historical study. I know well that such a book as Green's " Short History of the English People " may prove to some young students more fascinating than any novel.* There are, however, cases in which recourse may be had to a high-class work of fiction for the attainment of a truer historic sense; while, taken only as *supplement* to more strictly Academic reading, such a work may prove to have its uses. If, besides being of help to teachers, my recommendations should lead in any degree to further appreciation of the great masters of Romance, the very large amount of labour expended over the preparation of this " Guide " will be amply rewarded.

J.N.

---

* Had this part of my Introduction been written now (1928), I might well have added to my single example of Green's " Short History," books like the recent " History of England," by Prof. G. M. Trevelyan, and the widely-read " Short History of the World," by Mr. H. G. Wells.

PRE-CHRISTIAN ERA

"The picturesqueness of history is largely due to memoirs; and the countries and epochs which have produced them are especially picturesque. Now it is great crises, periods of disruption, great emergencies, which as a rule impress contemporaries and furnish matter for close observation. . . . The Great Rebellion and the French Revolution have furnished endless motives to dramatists, novelists, and painters, because they suggest possibilities of striking contrasts, and afford available situations. The human interest is then most intense, and our sympathies are most easily awakened."—*Dr. Mandell Creighton, on " The Picturesque in History," in Historical Lectures and Addresses.*

"My own view is that English History should be an inheritance of childhood; that its legends and its romance should grow into our thoughts from very early years, and should expand themselves with the expansion of our minds; that we should feel History and dream of it rather than learn it as a lesson."

C. R. L. Fletcher in the Preface to his " Introductory History of England."

"No self-respecting historian would ever dream of suggesting that fiction, however conscientious and erudite, could provide a substitute for genuine historical study. If, however, we bear in mind that we are only in the outer courts of the temple of truth, that it is the privilege, and indeed the duty of the author to give rein to his imagination, and that his object is rather to stimulate interest than to solve problems, there is no reason why we should not take full advantage of the delights which historical novelists in our own and other countries provide for us in rich profusion."

G. P. Gooch in " The Contemporary Review," 1920 (Address to the National Home Reading Union).

"Historical fiction is not history, but it springs from history and reacts upon it. Historical novels, even the greatest of them, cannot do the specific work of history; they are not dealing, except occasionally, with the real facts of the past. They attempt instead to create, in all the profusion and wealth of nature, typical cases imitated from but not identical with, recorded facts. In one sense this is to make the past live, but it is not to make the facts live, and therefore it is not history. Historical fiction has done much to make history popular and to give it value, for it has stimulated the historical imagination. Indeed, a hundred years ago it altered our whole conception of the past, when Scott, by his lays and novels, revolutionised history."

G. M. Trevelyan in his Sidgwick Memorial Lecture, Cambridge, 1921.

"There is a general agreement amongst teachers as to the value of historical novels, however much they may differ concerning the merits of particular specimens. . . . Over-conscientious novelists introduce too many antiquarian details in order to give local colour. . . . Historical facts should furnish the background only, and, as Scott says, we must not let the background eclipse the principal figures. Kings and great men may pass across the stage, but should not fill it for more than a moment. Another reason for this rule is that if the historical personages of the novelist talk and act too much, they generally become less and less like the real men. . . . Other historical novels there are which reduce the historical element to such a minimum that the story becomes a mere chronicle of the fights, escapes, and love-makings of a sentimental swashbuckler, and has so little reference to any particular time or place that it cannot interest anyone in history or help him to understand it."

Sir C. H. Firth on Historical Novels (Historical Association leaflet, 1922).

NOTE.—Books of special worth are marked with an asterisk. The order in which the books are placed is, on the whole, according to the periods illustrated; occasionally the method of special grouping has prevented absolute correctness. Many dates given in the " Pre-Christian Era" section are of course only approximate; the study of early Egyptian History, for instance, has resulted in considerable difference of opinion regarding both the names and dates of the kings. The method adopted of putting Juv. against works which are distinctly Juvenile, obviates the necessity for a separate list of tales suitable for young folk; it need hardly be said, however, that no arbitrary division can be made between romances that are for grown-up people and those which are for more youthful readers. Certain well-known writers for the young are quite worthy of study by parent and child alike, while many of the best historical novels may be read profitably by intelligent boys and girls entering on the " teen" stage. While out-of-print books have been avoided, some that are more or less easily obtainable second-hand have been included: juvenile tales are frequently revived. As, nowadays, cheap reprints at varying prices are continually appearing, I have in most cases given the original publisher only; for current edition and price a good bookseller is the only reliable authority.

PRE-CHRISTIAN ERA

1. QUEEN OF THE DAWN: H. Rider Haggard ; *Hutchinson* [*Eng.*], *Doubleday* [*U.S.A.*].
Egypt in the days of the Shepherd King Apepi, about the 18th Century B.C. A love story.

2. THE CAT OF BUBASTES: G. A. Henty ; *Juv. Blackie* [*Eng.*], *Scribner* [*U.S.A.*].
A tale of Egypt in the time of Thotmes III (the Israelites—Moses " forty years before the Exodus ").

3. THE PANTHER SKIN: W. H. Williamson ; *Holden.*
A decidedly interesting story of Egypt in the time of Amenhotep IV, about 1470 B.C.

4. TUTANKH-ATEN: L. Eckenstein ; *Cape.*
Thebes, etc., during the reign of King Akhen-aten (Eighteenth Dynasty) 14th Century B.C. Moses is introduced. Miss Eckenstein was one of the staff in the Sinaitic researches conducted by Flinders Petrie.

5. *THE BIRTH OF THE GODS.
*AKHNATON, KING OF EGYPT (*sequel*): D. Merezhkovsky (trans.); *Dent* [*Eng.*], *Dutton* [*U.S.A.*].
These two books of the well-known Russian novelist together form one closely linked narrative depicting Crete and Egypt respectively about the 14th Century B.C. The first volume contains six connected tales of the Island of Crete, dealing mainly with

Tutankhamon—Tutankhaton the son-in-law and envoy of King Akhnaton of Egypt, and with a certain Cretan maiden, Dio, priestess of " the Great Mother," whose experiences furnish the main fictional interest in both volumes. The sequel carries on the story of Dio from the point when Tutankhamon had brought her to Egypt as a gift to the King. There is a strange half-mystical element throughout the two volumes, and the author's religious Universalism (embracing his view in regard to " the Christians before Christ ") is emphasized; at the same time, the life, customs, and religious rites of bygone Crete and Egypt are presented in a wonderfully vivid manner. How Dio becomes associated with King Akhnaton the Peace-lover both in life and death, is told with much feeling—the story also illustrating the innovating ideas of Akhnaton in the sphere of religious belief. The closing pages of all show Tutankhamon as King after the death of Akhnaton. Some of the descriptions (notably where an account is given of the " games of the Bulls " in Crete) make painful reading; but such an admission is not intended as serious criticism reflecting on what is undoubtedly—taking the two volumes as one whole—a work of great imaginative power and interest.

---

6. *UARDA: Georg Ebers (trans.); *Sampson Low*, [*Eng.*], *Appleton* [*U.S.A.*].

A romance of Egypt (Thebes) in the time of Rameses II c. 1352 B.C. One of the author's best stories—instructive in its depiction of a bygone civilization, as well as good in the purely fictional sense. Rameses is introduced prominently, while such events as the Battle of Kadesh and the Conspiracy of the Regent furnish a considerable historic background.

---

7. *WHEN NILE WAS YOUNG: Anthony Armstrong; *Hutchinson*.

Egypt about 1330 B.C. A story of the years following the death of Akhenaten, the religious reformer on semi-theistic lines. Depicts the struggle between the old-time worshippers of Amen and the adherents of the single god Aton. An interesting piece of imaginative reconstruction.

---

8. THE HIDDEN TREASURES OF EGYPT: " R. Eustace "; *Simpkin, Marshall*.

Egypt under the Nineteenth Dynasty (Menenptah II, son of Rameses the Great), about 1300 B.C. A story of the Exodus—Moses, the Red Sea, etc.

---

9. MOON OF ISRAEL: H. Rider Haggard; *Murray* [*Eng.*], *Longmans* [*U.S.A.*].

" A Tale of the Exodus." The author identifies the Pharaoh of the Exodus with the usurper Amenmeses (between the death of Meneptah and the accession of Seti II). The period is about the 13th Century B.C.

---

10. THE LOVE OF PRINCE RAMESES: Anthony Armstrong; *Stanley Paul*.

After a brief " modern " prologue (reincarnation suggestions), the author begins his story proper—taking the reader back to Egypt about the year 1100 B.C. (Twentieth Dynasty). A decidedly interesting romance.

---

11. THE PHARAOH AND THE PRIEST (*FARON*): A. Glovatski (trans.); *Sampson Low* [*Eng.*], *Little, Brown* [*U.S.A.*].

Egypt in the 11th Century B.C. (time of Rameses XIII). A story illustrating the struggle between the secular and the ecclesiastical forces.

---

12. MY HEAD! MY HEAD!: Robert Graves; *Secker*.

A good imaginative treatment of an Old Testament theme—Elisha and the Shunamite woman.

---

13. TYRIAN PURPLE: Amy J. Baker; *John Long*.

Tyre and Samaria in the time of Ahab and Jehu—the latter being a prominent figure in the story.

14. *AN EGYPTIAN PRINCESS: Georg Ebers (trans.); *Sampson Low* [*Eng.*], *Appleton* [*U.S.A.*].

Egypt and Persia, 528-522 B.C. This historical romance—generally considered Ebers' best effort in fiction—illustrates the general life, manners, and ideas of the period in a way which only profound study and investigation could render possible. At the same time, the story itself has much interest. Amasis, Cambyses, Croesus, Darius, and Sappho are outstanding historic figures.

15. *THE SPARTAN (The Coward of Thermopylæ): Caroline D. Snedeker; *Juv.* *Hodder & Stoughton* [*Eng.*], *Doubleday* [*U.S.A.*].

Greece, Sparta, and (to a slight extent) Italy, 493 to 479 B.C. A good adventure story, with a half-Spartan, half-Athenian hero. Illustrates the harsh method of training youth in Sparta, as well as depicting in some degree the life and thought of Greece. In the course of the tale Marathon and Thermopylæ are covered, while the book ends with the victory over the Persians at Plataea. A great many historical figures are introduced, including Leonidas, Xerxes, Simonides, Themistokles, Kimon, Aristides, Pausanias, Parmenides, Aeschylus, and Pindar.

16. *A VICTOR OF SALAMIS: W. Stearns Davis; *Macmillan.*

This story—as the title implies—has for its central event the great victory of Themistocles over the Persians, 480 B.C.; Thermopylæ and Plataea (the latter 481 B.C.) are also covered. The Greek and Persian life of the period is here viewed " from the standpoint of an Athenian exile who followed Xerxes." The narrative well illustrates the importance of the Games in ancient Greece. Xerxes, Leonidas, and Themistocles are the chief historical figures.

17. THE LEMNIAN: J. Buchan; In "The Moon Endureth: Tales and Fancies ";—*Blackwood*, also *Nelson.*

A short tale of a man of Lemnos at Thermopylæ. There is a glimpse of Leonidas.

18. THE PERILOUS SEAT: Caroline Dale Snedeker; *Methuen* [*Eng.*], *Doubleday* [*U.S.A.*].

Greece about the time of Thermopylæ and Salamis. Story of a priestess, in which Pindar the poet appears as well as many other historic figures, including Sophocles as a boy.

19. PERSEPHONE OF ELEUSIS: C. W. Harris; *The Stratford Co.* [*Boston, U.S.A.*].

Greece, 480-470 B.C. A story beginning with the Persian invasion (Xerxes), and covering Thermopylæ, Salamis, and Plataea. Later chapters tell of the Eleusinian Mysteries, of the plotting of Pausanias, of the worship of Dionysus in the island of Naxos, and of Themistocles' flight from Athens. Besides Themistocles, several historic figures appear, including Xerxes, Cimon, and Aeschylus.

20. HOW PHIDIAS HELPED THE IMAGE-MAKER: Beatrice Harraden; *Juv.* In " Untold Tales of the Past ";—*Dent* [*Eng.*], *Dutton* [*U.S.A.*].

A short tale of Phidias, the Sculptor; the scene is Athens, 450 B.C.

21. ASPASIA: A ROMANCE OF ART AND LOVE IN ANCIENT HELLAS: Richard Hamerling (trans.); *Gottsberger* [*U.S.A.*].

Athens within the period 445-429 B.C. A novel of Pericles and Aspasia, carefully written, and reflecting Athenian life and thought to a considerable extent. There is a description of the Panathenaic festival, while such events as the Samian War, the Plague, and the beginnings of the Peloponnesian War, are covered. Some of the famous personages introduced into the story are shown discussing Art, Philosophy, etc. The most important figures, besides Pericles and Aspasia, are: Phidias, Socrates, Alcibiades (as a youth), Sophocles, Anaxagoras, and Euripides. There is, also, a glimpse of Cleon. The book ends with the death of Pericles.

22. *THE IMMORTAL MARRIAGE: Gertrude Atherton; Murray [Eng.], Boni [U.S.A.].

Miletus, and (mainly) Athens and district, 445-429 B.C.—Pericles and Aspasia imaginatively treated. Illustrates the period of the Thirty Years' Peace with Sparta, the Samian War, the Peloponnesian War, and the Plague. The golden age of Athens when Arts and Sciences were at their highest. There is much brilliant dialogue in the novel (some of it suggestive of 20th Century developments!) Besides the two principal figures, a host of notabilities appear, including Socrates, Anaxagoras, Sophocles, Euripides, Protagoras, Pheidias, Herodotus, Thucydides, Alcibiades (as boy and youth), and Zeno.

23. THERAS (THERAS AND HIS TOWN): Caroline Dale Snedeker; *Juv.* Dent [Eng.], Doubleday [U.S.A.].

Athens and Sparta in the Age of Pericles. An Athenian schoolboy's experiences, including his escape from Sparta. Pericles and Herodotus appear.

24. *GORGO: Charles Kelsey Gaines; Lothrop [U.S.A.].

Athens and Sparta, mostly in the period of the Peloponnesian War, 431-404 B.C. An historical novel of real merit, reflecting Athenian life on its social, political, and intellectual sides in the years preceding the Spartan supremacy. Covers the plague outbreak in 430, the rise of Alcibiades in the early stages of the War, the deaths of Pericles and Cleon respectively, the leadership of Nicias, the Siege of Syracuse and its disastrous sequel, and the taking of Athens by Lysander. "Gorgo" is a Spartan maiden (daughter of Brasidas) with whom the hero is in love. Several historic figures are introduced—Alcibiades and Socrates in particular; Thrasybulus, Critias, and Nicias are other Athenian notabilities much to the fore, while, on the Spartan side, Brasidas and Lysander are the chief names.

25. *MRS. SOCRATES: Fritz Mauthner (trans.); Eveleigh Nash [Eng.]; International Publishers Co. [U.S.A.].

A tale of Socrates and Xanthippe, which, though it cannot be taken altogether seriously as historic fiction, is much more interesting and suggestive than its rather absurd title might seem to indicate. Covers the period between the death of Pericles and the trial and death of Socrates—the later portions of the book telling of supposed events in the post-Socratic time, when Xanthippe and her son were living in the seclusion of a mountain valley region. Besides the sage and his wife, Aspasia and Alcibiades are prominent, while there are glimpses of Xenophon and Plato.

26. ON THE KNEES OF THE GODS: Anna Bowman Dodds; Dodd, Mead [U.S.A.].

Athens, Corinth, and Syracuse. A romance of the Socratic period, covering Alcibiades' expedition against Sicily in 415 B.C.

27. *CLOUD CUCKOO LAND: Naomi Mitchison; Cape [Eng.], Harcourt, Brace [U.S.A.].

Greece, the islands of the Ægean Sea, and the West Coast of Asia Minor, late 5th Century B.C. A good story—chiefly based on Xenophon—of the Peloponnesian War (later period) and the supremacy of Sparta. Various historical events and persons are introduced.

28. THE STREET OF THE FLUTE-PLAYER: H. de Vere Stacpoole; Murray [Eng.], Duffield [U.S.A.].

Greece about 406 B.C. A tale illustrating the Athens of Socrates and Aristophanes.

29. THE ANCIENT ALLAN: H. Rider Haggard; Cassell [Eng.], Longmans [U.S.A.].

An *Allan Quartermain* novel, which, by a magic "throw-back," takes the reader from modern times to the Egypt of the last native dynasties (roughly about 400 B.C.).

30. THE GARLAND OF WILD OLIVE: Beatrice Harraden; *Juv.* In " Untold Tales of the Past ";—*Dent* [*Eng.*], *Dutton* [*U.S.A.*].
A short tale illustrating the Olympic Games in the year, 400 B.C.

---

31. A TRUE SPARTAN HEART: Beatrice Harraden *Juv.* In " Untold Tales of the Past ";—*Dent* [*Eng.*], *Dutton* [*U.S.A.*].
Tells of a Spartan mother after the death of her son at Leuctra, 371 B.C.

---

32. WISDOM'S DAUGHTER: H. Rider Haggard; *Hutchinson* [*Eng.*], *Doubleday* [*U.S.A.*].
This novel—the last of the *Ayesha*, or *She*, trilogy—depicts " Ayesha's " reincarnation as daughter of an Arab chief, and her experiences in the mid-4th Century B.C. or thereabouts.

---

33. *FOUR SONS: A. H. Gilkes; *Juv. Symcox.*
A tale of Southern Italy in the year 338 B.C. (the Samnite War); also—last chapter—Alexandria 307 B.C.

---

34. THE GOLDEN HOPE: Robert H. Fuller; *Macmillan.*
Various regions in the East, also Egypt, between 336 and 331 B.C. A story covering the period of Alexander the Great's principal victories: at the Granicus River, at Issus, at Tyre (Siege and Capture), and at Arbela. Besides Alexander there are various historic figures including Aristotle, Demosthenes, and Darius III.

---

35. *THE TREASURES OF TYPHON: Eden Phillpotts; *Grant Richards* [*Eng.*], *Macmillan* [*U.S.A.*].
An interesting love tale of Athens about 300 B.C., introducing Epicurus the philosopher, and the poet Menander.

---

36. *SALAMMBO: Gustave Flaubert (trans.); *Grant Richards* [*Eng.*], *Putnam* [*U.S.A.*] *and other publishers.*
A very famous depiction, on realistic lines, of Carthage about the year 240 B.C.: time of Hamilcar and the revolt of the Mercenaries.

---

37. SONNICA: Vicente Blasco-Ibañez (trans.); *John Long* [*Eng.*], *Duffield* [*U.S.A.*].
Saguntum and Rome in the Hannibal period (c. 218 B.C.). This tale of far-away times is stronger on the descriptive side than on the fictional. The author has largely depended upon the historian Livy.

---

38. *KALLISTRATUS: A. H. Gilkes; *Longmans*, also *Froude*—revised and enlarged.
Rhône district, Rome, Capua, etc., mainly in the period 218-216 B.C. A tale in autobiographical form, dealing with the Second Punic War, and covering the Battles of Trasimene and Cannae respectively. Hannibal is prominent, and Scipio Africanus appears. Ends at Athens with the news of Hannibal's death (c. 183 B.C.).

---

39. THE YOUNG CARTHAGINIAN: G. A. Henty; *Juv. Blackie* [*Eng.*], *Scribner* [*U.S.A.*].
The Libyan desert, Carthage, Spain, Italy and Sardinia, mainly in the period 221-216 B.C. Illustrates the Second Punic War and Hannibal's exploits, covering the Siege of Saguntum, the conquest of Catalonia, the crossing of the Rhine and the Alps, and the Battles of Trebia and Lake Trasimene respectively. The tale practically ends with the Battle of Cannae in 216 B.C. The outstanding historical figure is, of course, Hannibal.

c

40. *THE LION'S BROOD: Duffield Osborne; *Heinemann* [*Eng.*], *Doubleday* [*U.S.A.*].
Mainly Rome and Capua, 217-215 B.C. Part I illustrates events in the Second Punic War, beginning with the news of Hannibal's victory, Lake Trasimenus, and ending with an account of the still greater victory at Cannæ. Part II treats of matters at Capua, where Hannibal spent the winter of 216-215; in this section of the novel Hannibal is prominently introduced.

41. PATRIOT AND HERO (formerly *The Hammer*): A. J. Church and R. Seeley; *Juv.* *Seeley* [*Eng.*], *Putnam* [*U.S.A.*].
Jerusalem, Antioch, Joppa, etc., 174-161 B.C. The Maccabees and Antiochus Epiphanes. There are descriptions of the Battles of Bethhoron, Emmaus, etc., and the cleansing of the Temple at Jerusalem. The story ends with the death of Judas Maccabæus.

42. RAPHAEL OF THE OLIVE: Gillard Johnson; *Bennett.*
Jerusalem about 170 B.C. to 164 B.C. A carefully-written story dealing with the period of Antiochus Epiphanes and the Maccabees. Ends with the reconquest of Jerusalem by Judas.

43. DEBORAH: James M. Ludlow; *Juv. Nisbet* [*Eng.*] *Revell* [*U.S.A.*].
Antioch, Jerusalem, etc., in the period 167-165 B.C. A tale of the Maccabees, especially Judas Maccabæus and his victories—Bethhoron, Emmaus, and Bethzur.

44. *THE SISTERS: Georg Ebers (trans.); *Sampson Low* [*Eng.*], *Gottsberger* [*U.S.A.*].
Egypt (Memphis, etc.) 164 B.C. A pleasing story of the period when Egypt was under the united rule of Ptolemy Philometer and Euergetes II—the two hostile brothers. Both the personages just named are brought into the novel.

45. LORDS OF THE WORLD: A. J. Church; *Juv. Seeley* [*Eng.*], *Scribner* [*U.S.A.*].
A story dealing with the fall of the two great commercial cities—Carthage (taken and destroyed by Scipio Africanus Minor in 146 B.C.), and Corinth (destroyed by Mummius in the same year).

46. THE LAST GALLEY: A. Conan Doyle; In "The Last Galley; impressions and tales"—*Smith, Elder* [*Eng.*], *Doubleday* [*U.S.A.*].
Carthage, 146 B.C. A brief imaginative sketch.

47. HOW LIVIA WON THE BROOCH: Beatrice Harraden; *Juv.* In "Untold Tales of the Past"—*Dent* [*Eng.*], *Dutton* [*U.S.A.*].
Rome, 123 B.C. A short tale of the Gladiators in the Circus Maximus.

48. *PRUSIAS: Ernst Eckstein (trans.); *Gottsberger* [*U.S.A.*].
An historical romance illustrating an important period in Roman History. Covers the Third Mithridatic War (begun 74 B.C.), the Rebellion in Spain, and the Slave Revolt (73-71 B.C.). Spartacus, the leader of the revolted slaves and gladiators, is prominent in the story.

49. *TWO THOUSAND YEARS AGO (LUCIUS): A. J. Church; *Juv. Blackie* [*Eng.*], *Dodd, Mead* [*U.S.A.*].
Italy (Sicily) and Asia Minor, etc., 72-63 B.C. A tale of the revolt of Spartacus and the Third Mithridatic War. Adventures by sea (pirates) as well as by land (Tarsus, Antioch, etc.). Pompey and Mithridates both appear—the death of the latter.

50. THE VESTAL VIRGINS: Beatrice Harraden; *Juv.* In "Untold Tales of the Past"—*Dent* [*Eng.*], *Dutton* [*U.S.A.*].
Rome, 62 B.C. A short story dealing with the time of Cicero, and Catalina's conspiracy.

51. THE TIN LAND: M. E. Gullick; *Juv. Pitman.*
A tale of about 60 B.C. Begins Macedonia, but the boy-hero is soon taken (after shipwreck) by the Phœnicians to south-west Britain—the Cornwall of to-day.

52. *THE CONQUERED: Naomi Mitchison; *Cape [Eng.], Harcourt, Brace [U.S.A.].*
A most suggestive and finely-conceived historical romance. Gaul in the period of Cæsar's Wars, between 58 B.C. and 46 B.C. Deals with Vercingetorix and his army, ending with the victory of Rome and the death of Vercingetorix as a prisoner in the Imperial City.

53. *VERCINGETORIX AND THE OTHERS: Naomi Mitchison; In " When the Bough Breaks and Other Stories "—*Cape [Eng.], Harcourt, Brace [U.S.A.].*
A short story illustrating the period of Cæsar's Gallic Wars.

54. A FRIEND OF CÆSAR: W. Stearns Davis; *Macmillan.*
A didactic type of story, depicting life in Rome, Baiae, etc., and Egypt (Alexandria), 50-47 B.C. Julius Cæsar is prominent, while Marcus Antonius and Cleopatra are two of the many other historic figures.

55. THE EVE OF CÆSAR'S "TRIUMPH": Beatrice Harraden; In " Untold Tales of the Past "—*Dent [Eng.], Dutton [U.S.A.].*
Rome, 47 B.C.—the year after the Battle of Pharsalia. Julius Cæsar himself.

56. THE LIFE AND DEATH OF CLEOPATRA: Claude Ferval (trans.); *Hurst & Blackett.*
A carefully-written romance of Cleopatra from girlhood (" hardly yet eighteen ") up to her death in 30 B.C. Julius Cæsar and Mark Antony are, of course, very prominent. The Battle of Actium.

57. CLÉOPÂTRE: " Jean Bertheroy "; *Armand Colin et Cie [France].*
A romance dealing with the latest period of Cleopatra.

58. CLEOPATRA: Georg Ebers (trans.); *Sampson Low [Eng.], Appleton [U.S.A.].*
Alexandria, c. 30 B.C. A novel illustrating the closing episodes in Cleopatra's career. Cæsarion (son of Julius Cæsar and Cleopatra) is one of the many historic figures, and the Emperor Octavianus (Augustus) is prominently introduced in the later chapters. The romance ends with the famous episode of Cleopatra's self-inflicted death (the asp's sting).

FIRST CENTURY

59. THE TOUR: A STORY OF ANCIENT EGYPT: Louis Couperus (trans.); *Thornton Butterworth [Eng.], Dodd, Mead [U.S.A.].*
A wealthy young Roman on a tour in Egypt with his tutor somewhere about A.D. 20 (time of the Emperor Tiberius). More or less detailed accounts are given of Alexandria, Memphis, and other places in the Nile region; indeed, the book is stronger as a piece of descriptive writing than as a work of fiction.

60. *NEÆRA: J. W. Graham; *Macmillan.*
Capreæ and Rome, A.D. 26. A love romance, with somewhat exciting fictional developments (mystery of the heroine's birth, etc.). The historical element is secondary, though there is much in the novel to suggest the life and manners of the time. Moreover, the Emperor Tiberius, who is a prominent figure, is very carefully depicted.

61. *THE STORY OF THE OTHER WISE MAN: Henry Van
    Dyke; *Juv. Harper*.
Persia, Palestine, Egypt, etc., at the beginning of the Christian Era. A finely-conceived extension of the ancient story of the Magi. The general atmosphere of the little
tale, as well as certain allusions to world-events, may fairly be taken as bringing it
under the historical category.

62. JESUS OF NAZARETH: S. C. Bradley; *Sherman, French*
    [*U.S.A.*].
An attempt to fill up imaginatively the twenty formative years of Christ's life between
his childhood and his ministry. This carefully written book is not a romance in the
ordinary sense, but it has at least as much claim to the title as R. Bird's " Jesus, the
Carpenter of Nazareth " (*Juv.*), which is sometimes entered in lists of fiction.

63. KING OF DREAMS: G. R. Warmington; *Methuen*.
Chiefly Egypt and Palestine: the story as a whole (given in the first person) covers
the period between 30 b.c. and a.d. 38, but the events on which it may be said to hinge,
occur a.d. 28-29. A tale of the Rich Young Ruler (New Testament), whom the novelist
chooses to identify with a certain Egyptian of royal descent on his father's side, though
born of a Greek mother. The young man longs to serve the beloved country of his
birth, and the romance tells how his " dreams " become transformed. Christ and
various Scriptural figures are introduced. The book is distinctly interesting, and on
somewhat original lines.

64. *PHILOCHRISTUS: MEMOIRS OF A DISCIPLE OF CHRIST:
    Edwin A. Abbott; *Macmillan*—2nd edition, with special Pre-
    face, 1916.
A Galilean (born in Sepphoris) writes these " memoirs " in Britain about a.d. 80.
The region of the story is Palestine, and the *main* period about a.d. 27 onwards, through
the public ministry of Christ up to, and beyond, the Crucifixion (Christ and his environment sketched in vigorous outline). The supposed narrative is given reverently, yet
freely—the standpoint of the real author being that of a pioneer in liberal scholarship.
Dr. Abbott's stories of Early Christianity are all characterized by a rare combination
of literary charm and spiritual insight. They will probably appeal to the scholarly
and thoughtful reader, for whom the much more popular examples of New Testament
fiction have little or no attraction.

65. BEN HUR: Lew Wallace; *Harper, and other publishers*.
Syria in the time of Christ. The story as a whole covers a long period, but the main
episodes are supposed to occur a.d. 23 onwards at Antioch, etc. Full of dramatic situations, at the same time closely following " orthodox " interpretation where New Testament scenes are introduced. The enormous sales of the book testify to its appealing
quality, but as a literary production its defects are fairly obvious.

66. AS OTHERS SAW HIM: A RETROSPECT A.D. 54: Joseph
    Jacobs; *Heinemann*.
A Jew (one of the Council who voted for the death of Jesus) looks back at events,
and writes to an Alexandrian friend of what he saw in Jerusalem during Jesus' ministry
—beginning with the Money-Changers episode, and ending with the Crucifixion.
Although the standpoint is in some degree critical, the general treatment is reverent,
and largely appreciative, as a single quotation will serve to indicate: " Every Jew
would be wise and good and pious, and that was Jesus."

67. BY AN UNKNOWN DISCIPLE: Anonymous; *Hodder &
    Stoughton* [*Eng.*], *Doran* [*U.S.A.*].
Fictional reminiscences in which portions of the Gospel narrative are re-told and
amplified in a manner likely to make special appeal to thoughtful readers. The standpoint is that of liberal scholarship.

68. THE NAZARENE: W. J. Saunders; *Murray & Evenden*.
Cæsarea, etc., and Jerusalem, early First Century. The hero is a young man in the
service of Pilate. A few New Testament scenes and figures are introduced—Christ,
Pilate, Herod, etc. The standpoint of the story (told in the first person) is somewhat
unconventional.

69. THE STREET OF THE GAZELLE: Dulcie Deamer; *Fisher Unwin.*

Jerusalem in the time of Christ. This highly-coloured tale deals with the Zealots, etc. The Crucifixion is dimly suggested—not described—at the end of the volume.

---

70. VERONICA: Florence M. Kingsley; *Appleton.*

A story dealing largely with the wife of Pilate, as well as with Pilate himself. Judas and Caiaphas are among the other figures introduced. The tale ends at the *time* of the Crucifixion, but actual New Testament scenes are merely suggested to the reader as background. Perhaps the best of the author's several books dealing with the period.

---

71. SIMON OF CYRENE, DIMACHAERUS SPLENDENS: T. H. Shastid; *Wheldon & Wesley* [*Eng.*], *Wahr* [*U.S.A.*].

N. Africa, Syria, etc. An allegorical story of Simon of Cyrene (the sub-title is: " The story of a Man's, and a Nation's, Soul "). There are many experiences and changes of scene, and the book exhibits careful study. The later Gospel incidents (including Simon's bearing of the Cross, etc.) are introduced. Christ, Barabbas, and others appear.

---

72. JUDAS ISCARIOT; BEN TOBIT; AND ELEAZAR—three tales published under the one title " Judas Iscariot ": Leonid Andreev (trans.); *Griffiths.*

These three New Testament tales deal respectively with Judas and his motives; with a certain Jewish merchant's petty experiences on the very day of the Crucifixion; and with Lazarus. The treatment generally is psychological.

---

73. THE AUTOBIOGRAPHY OF JUDAS ISCARIOT: Alfred Tressider Sheppard; *Allen & Unwin.*

Judas from boyhood, and during the period of Christ's ministry. Except in the earlier chapters, the novel takes its main situations from the New Testament, introducing Jesus, Joseph, Mary, St. Peter, etc. This autobiographical romance hardly bears out the promise of its beginning; the later chapters seem more or less devoid of that originality and power which one has learnt to expect from the author. For all that, the story is decidedly above the average of " New Testament " fiction.

---

74. THE TRUMPETS OF GOD (DAWN): Irving Bacheler; *Melrose* [*Eng.*], *Macmillan* [*U.S.A.*].

Colossæ, Jerusalem, Jericho, Damascus, Antioch, Cæsarea, and various other regions, mainly between A.D. 30 and 70. A carefully written tale—autobiographical in form—of early Christian times, covering the later portions of Christ's ministry, the martyrdom of St. Stephen, the conversion and missionary labours of St. Paul, the persecutions under Nero, and the Siege of Jerusalem. There is abundance of fictional incident, but the story, as a whole, is somewhat rambling and disjointed; moreover, at certain points the manner of writing is sensational rather than impressive. Jesus, Nicodemus, Blind Bartimæus, Mary of Magdala, St. Paul, and St. Stephen appear; while—turning to non-Biblical figures—Vespasian is prominent, and there are glimpses of Titus and Josephus.

---

75. *BROTHER SAUL: Donn Byrne; *Sampson Low* [*Eng.*], *Century Co.* [*U.S.A.*].

Tarsus, Jerusalem, Antioch, Damascus, Athens, and Rome (to name only a few of many localities), between c. A.D. 15 and A.D. 65. A fictional study of St. Paul on distinctly original lines, from the time when he was a youth at Tarsus up to his death in Rome. Besides tracing the spiritual and intellectual development of the Apostle, the novel skilfully illustrates certain main episodes in his career. While St. Paul is the dominating figure throughout, quite a host of other New Testament personages appear: Gamaliel, Caiaphas, Stephen, Barnabas, Peter, James, John-Mark, Luke, Timothy, Felix the procurator, Herod Agrippa II, etc. etc.

76. PAUL: THE JEW: by the author of " By an Unknown Disciple "— *Hodder & Stoughton [Eng.], Doran [U.S.A.].*
Jerusalem, Tarsus, and Antioch from the period of Christ's public ministry (later stages) up to the death of St. Stephen. The great apostle is depicted as conversing freely on the subject of religion with men of various nationalities (the modern colloquialism of the dialogue is rather startling at times). The author's evident aim is to trace, in some measure, the mental processes which were carrying St. Paul against his will, in the direction of the Christian faith. Gamaliel, Barnabas, and Stephen are the other principal figures in the story.

77. *THE BROOK KERITH: George Moore; *Werner Laurie [Eng.], Macmillan [U.S.A.].*
This famous romance of Christ—in which Joseph of Arimathea and Paul respectively appear as important figures—is written from the standpoint of one who is altogether outside the sphere of theological belief (whether orthodox or heterodox); at the same time, as Mr. Gerald Bullett well remarks, " only the foolish can regard it as in any sense rationalistic propaganda," and there is nothing flippant or unworthy in the author's presentment of the central figure. To give the merest skeleton outline of the story: Jesus is depicted as, prior to his ministry, a member of the Essene brotherhood. Under John the Baptist's influence he becomes a teacher; then, after passing through stages of hopefulness and despair, he undergoes crucifixion without, however, really dying. Eventually Jesus returns to the Essenes by the Brook Kerith and there meets Paul, with results that must be left for Mr. Moore's own telling. Judged on its merits as imaginative literature, the book is of very high quality.

78. MESSALINA: Vivian Crockett; *Cape.*
After a Prelude depicting the Rome of Caligula, the actual story deals with the infamous Messalina as wife of the Emperor Claudius up to her death by execution in A.D. 48.

79. LYGDUS: Wilfranc Hubbard; In " Orvieto Dust "—*Constable.*
A short tale of Italy in the time of the Emperor Claudius and Messalina.

80. BURENE: E. Durham; *Juv. Drane.*
South Britain, early to mid First Century. The outstanding figure is Caractacus— the story ending with the Battle of Caer Caradoc.

81. BOUDICCA: C. H. Dudley Ward; *Juv. Ousely.*
Roman Britain (Camulodunum), mid First Century. A tale of Boudicca (or Boadicea) from girlhood upwards. Covers her rebellion against Rome—the early successes and the eventual disaster. The romance keeps Boudicca alive after her supposed death, hinting at wedded bliss in the forest.

82. FOR QUEEN AND EMPEROR: Ernest Protheroe; *Juv. Religious Tract Society.*
Britain, Rome, and Palestine, A.D. 61-70. An adventure story illustrating (in about two-thirds of the volume) the events connected with Boadicea's revolt against the Romans. Covers her victories, including the Sack of Camulodunum (Colchester), as well as her ultimate defeat and death. The remaining part of the story has for background the Rome of Nero, and the Wars of Vespasian and Titus in Judæa. Depicts the Circus Maximus and the Christians in Rome; the destruction of Jotapata; and the Zealots, together with the Siege and Capture of Jerusalem by Titus. Suetonius (Roman Governor of Britain), Agricola, Boadicea, Caractacus, Vespasian, Titus, and Josephus all appear.

83. *BERIC THE BRITON: G. A. Henty; *Juv. Blackie [Eng.], Scribner [U.S.A.].*
Eastern Britain and Italy, mostly in the decade A.D. 60-70. A tale illustrating the time of the Roman Invasion, and the warrior-queen, Boadicea. Depicts British life (the Druids, etc.), and covers the Sack of Camulodunum (Colchester) by the Trinobantes and the Iceni. The youthful British hero is eventually taken prisoner by the Romans. Later chapters carry the reader to Rome under Nero—Gladiators, Christians, and the Great Fire; there are, also, adventures with outlaws in Calabria. Ends with Nero's death, the short rule of Galba, and the coming of Vespasian. Boadicea, Suetonius, and Nero are among the most important figures introduced.

84. *ONESIMUS: MEMOIRS OF A DISCIPLE OF ST. PAUL:
EDWIN A. ABBOTT; *Macmillan.*
Various localities including Lystra, Colossæ, Antioch, Athens, Corinth, and Rome—
the main period being, roughly, between A.D. 46 and A.D. 86. A book revealing imaginative power as well as scholarship. Philemon, Epictetus, and St. Paul are, in turn,
prominently introduced.

85. THE TRIUMPH OF FAITH: NAOMI MITCHISON; In "When
the Bough Breaks and Other Stories"—*Cape* [Eng.], *Harcourt,
Brace* [U.S.A.].
A short story of Colossæ in Pauline times. Philemon, Onesimus, and several Scriptural
figures.

86. *QUO VADIS?: H. SIENKIEWICZ (trans.); *Dent* [Eng.], *Little, Brown*
[U.S.A.].
Rome in the period c. A.D. 63 to 68. A celebrated romance of Imperial Rome and
Early-Christian martyrdom. There are thrilling fictional developments, while almost
every type of reader will find something of particular interest in the succession of vivid
pictures illustrating the life and events of the time; especially remarkable are the
chapters describing the Great Fire and the scenes in the amphitheatre (Gladiators and
Christians). Among the numerous historic figures more or less prominently introduced,
one may specify the Emperor Nero, Petronius, Tigellinus, Seneca, Poppæa, St. Peter,
and St. Paul. The novel ends with the death of Nero.

87. THE BURNING OF ROME: A. J. CHURCH; *Juv. Seeley* [Eng.],
Macmillan [U.S.A.].
Nero, Tigellinus, Poppæa, etc. The Great Fire, and the persecution of the Christians.
A feature of the story is the account given of Seneca's death.

88. MYRRHA: JULES LEMAÎTRE (trans.); In "Serenus and Other
Stories"—*Selwyn & Blount.*
A short tale of Rome about the time of Nero's burning of the city. Nero himself
appears.

89. *NERO: A ROMANCE: ERNST ECKSTEIN (trans.); *Gottsberger*
[U.S.A.].
A somewhat unusual picture of Nero as man and as emperor: his marriage with
Poppæa, the Great Fire, etc., down to his death in A.D. 68. Seneca is prominently intro-
duced, while Agrippina, Octavia, and Tigellinus appear more or less frequently. The
romance emphasizes Christian influence.

90. THE HEART OF A SLAVE-GIRL: ANTHONY ARMSTRONG;
Stanley Paul.
An interesting story of Rome under Nero: Christians, Gladiators, and the "Under-
world." The Emperor himself is introduced—the plot turning on his desire for a
beautiful girl (the heroine).

91. CLEOMENES: "MARIS WARRINGTON"; *Jarrolds.*
A love story of Rome in Nero's time, ending with the burning of the city.

92. THE STORY OF PHAEDRUS: NEWELL DWIGHT HILLIS; *Juv.
Duckworth* [Eng.], *Macmillan* [U.S.A.].
A tale of the East, beginning at Ephesus in the time of Nero. Tells of the wanderings
and experiences of a young "literary slave," and purports to describe how the synoptic
gospels first came to be edited.

93. *FOR THE TEMPLE: G. A. HENTY; *Juv. Blackie* [Eng.],
Scribner [U.S.A.].
Lake of Tiberias and other localities in Palestine, A.D. 67-70. An adventure tale,
covering the period of revolt against Rome. The siege and fall of Jotapata, the storming
of Gamala, and the siege and fall of Jerusalem. The story ends in Rome. John of
Gischala, Titus, and Josephus appear.

94. *THE GLADIATORS: G. J. Whyte Melville; *Ward, Lock* [*Eng.*], *Longmans* [*U.S.A.*].

An interesting story, illustrating mainly Rome under Vitellius and Vespasian. The assassination of Vitellius is described (A.D. 69), and there are good general accounts of the school of gladiators, the early Christians, etc. The last part of the book depicts the Siege of Jerusalem by Titus and the destruction of the Temple (A.D. 70). The Zealots are conspicuous in these later chapters.

95. JUDAEUS PROCURATOR: "Anatole France" (trans.); In "Mother of Pearl"; *Lane.*

Pontius Pilate at Baiæ, forty years after the Crucifixion. This imaginative sketch is intended to show the inferior place of Jesus in the life and thought of Roman contemporaries.

96. THE LAST DAYS OF POMPEII: Lord Lytton; *Routledge* [*Eng.*], *Little, Brown* [*U.S.A.*].

A somewhat elaborate and sensational novel of Pompeii just before, and during, the famous eruption of Vesuvius, A.D. 79. Depicts the manners and general life of the time (the amphitheatre, etc.)

97. THE PRIESTESS OF ISIS: Edouard Schuré (trans.); *Rider.*

Pompeii and Egypt, A.D. 79. A somewhat melodramatic story, with an element of sorcery and strange cults, etc. Depicts life in the year of the Vesuvius eruption.

98. DOMITIA: S. Baring Gould; *Methuen* (*Eng.*], *Stokes* [*U.S.A.*].

An imaginative presentment of the Emperor Domitian's wife. Cenchraea, Corinth, etc., and Rome in the period A.D. 76-96, covering the violent deaths of Nero, Vitellius, and Domitian. The story ends with Domitia among the Christians.

99. *SERENUS: Jules Lemaître (trans.). In "Serenus and Other Stories"; *Mathews & Marrot.*

A tale describing how a sceptical patrician, through the circumstances of his death in Rome A.D. 90, came to be regarded as a Christian martyr.

100. ROME: Lilian Hayes; In "The Thirtieth Piece of Silver"— *Fisher Unwin.*

The Emperor Domitian is depicted in this short tale or "episode."

101. THE COMEDIANS: Louis Couperus (trans.); *Cape* [*Eng.*], *Doran* [*U.S.A.*].

The decadent Rome of Domitian. The Emperor himself, the Empress Domitia, the Apostle John, Tacitus, Juvenal, Pliny the Younger, Martial, Quintilian, and a number of historic figures are introduced. Ends with the murder of Domitian A.D. 96. A novel based on careful study—illuminating rather than pleasing.

102. MASTERS OF THE WORLD: Mary M. Hoppus; *Bentley.*

Baiæ, Rome, etc., A.D. 93-96. A praiseworthy attempt to illustrate the ways of life and trend of thought in the Rome of the period: the Amphitheatre, a Christian Assembly, etc., etc. The Emperor Domitian is specially prominent, and such figures as the Empress Domitia, Quintilian, and Martial appear.

103. *QUINTUS CLAUDIUS: Ernst Eckstein (trans.); *Gottsberger* [*U.S.A.*].

Italy (Baiæ, Rome, etc.), A.D. 95-96. A careful picture of Roman life under Domitian —social manners, political plots, the persecution of the Christians, etc. The Emperor and his wife Domitia are prominently introduced, while Martial the poet, Stephanus and others appear. The novel ends with the murder of Domitian.

104. S.P.Q.R.: Peter Hastings; *Robert Holden.*
The title is taken from the beginning of the Edicts: *Senatus populusque Romanus* (The Senate and the Roman People). A sensational novel of considerable interest as fiction, but too " modern " in its general presentment. Rome about A.D. 96 to 98: the period of the Emperor Domitian's assassination, and of Nerva's short rule. The hero is a gladiator of Barbarian parentage, who becomes one of the Prætorian Guard. The Games, the theatre, etc. Both Domitian and Nerva are in turn prominent, while among the other figures, one may specify the poet Martial.

SECOND CENTURY

105. SILK: A LEGEND: S. Merwin; *Constable.*
Imaginary journals giving experiences in China about the year A.D. 100 or immediatey after. Illustration, in an interesting manner, of the life and thought of the period.

106. TO THE LIONS: A. J. Church; *Juv. Seeley [Eng.], Putnam [U.S.A.].*
Province of Bithynia, A.D. 112. A tale of the Early Christians in the time of the persecutions under Trajan. The author gives a favourable depiction of the Younger Pliny as Governor of the Province of Bithynia, also introducing Tacitus at one point in the story. The closing pages tell of a wonderful escape in the Amphitheatre at Ephesus.

107. VALERIUS: J. G. Lockhart; *Blackwood.*
Rome under Trajan, at the beginning of the Second Century. The hero (son of a Roman father and a British mother) relates his experiences when journeying to, and staying in, Rome. In this very " descriptive " tale one is shown the Amphitheatre, Christian persecution, etc. The Emperor Trajan himself appears.

108. *SILANUS THE CHRISTIAN: Edwin A. Abbott; *Black [Eng.], Macmillan [U.S.A.].*
Nicopolis, A.D. 118. An imaginary narrative, in which a Roman tells of hearing Epictetus lecture, and how, in order to defend his master, he obtained certain epistles of Paul, so as to compare them with the philosopher's lectures. Unexpectedly the newly-consulted teaching seemed to him superior, and he proceeded to a study of the Synoptic Gospels; a Roman friend's criticisms, however, prevented his accepting these Gospels as historical, and he was thus left with nothing more than a vague perception of the Pauline ideal. Lastly, an Athenian acquaintance lent him the recently produced Gospel of John, and here he found—while doubting its authorship and historical accuracy —a more adequate *religious* teaching than anywhere else.

109. ANTINOÜS: A. Hausrath (" George Taylor ") (trans.); *Longmans [Eng.], Gottsberger [U.S.A.].*
Rome and Egypt, round about A.D. 120. A romance of Hadrian's favourite, the youth Antinoüs, whom the author presents as a pathetic figure, and as being *intellectually*—as well as physically—endowed. Dissatisfied with the various religions (Christian and Pagan), he finally commits suicide.

110. THE EMPEROR: Georg Ebers (trans.); *Appleton [U.S.A.].*
A careful and informative study of the Emperor Hadrian, as well as of affairs in Egypt (the early Christians, etc). The book is, however, of less fictional interest than several of the author's earlier historical romances.

111. ¹MARCUS OF ROME: Elbridge S. Brooks; *Juv.* In " Young People of History "—*Putnam.*
Rome, A.D. 137: the boyhood of the Emperor Marcus Aurelius.
¹ One of the historical sketches (*fictional in part*) appearing in the single volume (" Young People of History "), which is a reissue of the books formerly published under the respective titles of " Historic Boys " and " Historic Girls." The stories, which are interesting and well-written, treat of such widely differing regions and periods as the Carthage of the Third Century B.C., and the New York of American-Revolution days.

112. NARCISSUS: W. Boyd Carpenter; *Juv.* *S.P.C.K.* [*Eng.*], *Young* [*U.S.A.*].
Athens, Alexandria, Rome, etc., about the year A.D. 160. A story of the early Christians.

113. THE UNWILLING VESTAL: Edward Lucas White; *Fisher Unwin* [*Eng.*], *Dutton* [*U.S.A.*].
Rome, A.D. 161-191. A story dealing with the time of Marcus Aurelius and his son, Commodus: both figures appear prominently. Illustrates especially the status of the Vestals. The characters converse in modern familiar language—the author insisting on this method of presenting ancient life as fundamentally truer and more illuminating than a more strained or pedantic method.

114. MARTYRS DE LYON: Antoine Baumann; *Perrin* [*France*].
An historical novel of early Christianity in Gaul about the year A.D. 177. There is a glimpse of the Emperor Marcus Aurelius in Rome.

115. *MARIUS THE EPICUREAN: Walter Pater; *Macmillan.*
This well-known masterpiece, although primarily a study of ideas, is also an imaginative presentment of Roman life in the third quarter of the Second Century. The outstanding historic figure is, of course, the Emperor Marcus Aurelius.

116. *ANDIVIUS HEDULIO: Edward Lucas White; *Fisher Unwin* [*Eng.*], *Dutton* [*U.S.A.*].
Italy (Rome, etc.) between A.D. 184 and A.D. 200. A novel which, besides being most interesting on the purely fictional side, vividly illustrates the Roman life and manners of the period. The Emperor Commodus is a prominent figure, while Severus appears towards the end of the romance.

THIRD CENTURY

117. *PYRRHO: Bartram Tollinton; *Williams & Norgate.*
Alexandria, Rome, and Britain (Roman Wall), about A.D. 200 to 212. A young man's pursuit of truth, and his final acceptance of a Platonic Christianity. The Emperor Severus, Clement of Alexandria, and Origen are among the historic figures introduced.

118. PER ASPERA: Georg Ebers (trans.); *Sampson Low.*
Alexandria within the period A.D. 211-217. A tale illustrating the conflict of religions in the Alexandria of the period. The Roman Emperor Caracalla is introduced.

119. GIANT MAXIMIN: A. Conan Doyle; In "The Last Galley; impressions and tales"—*Smith, Elder* [*Eng.*], *Doubleday* [*U.S.A.*].
A story in three parts: (1) Thrace, A.D. 210 (Emperor Severus); (2) Rhine District, A.D. 235 (Maximin proclaimed Emperor); (3) The death of Maximin, A.D. 238.

120. THE SUN GOD: Arthur Westcott; *Heath Cranton.*
Rome, A.D. 219-222. A story dealing with the time of the Emperor Elagabalus (Heliogabalus). The Christians and their rival Bishops—Hippolytus and Callixtus. In the course of the tale Tertullian appears. Ends with the Emperor's death.

121. *CALLISTA: J. H. Newman; *Longmans.*
North Africa (Sicca) about A.D. 249-250. A tale illustrating the time of the Emperor Decius and his severe persecution of the Christians. Some literary critics have classed this example of Cardinal Newman among the best efforts in historical fiction.

122. A HERO IN WOLF-SKIN: Tom Bevan; *Juv.* *R.T.S.* [*Eng.*], *Jacobs* [*U.S.A.*].
A tale of Goth *v.* Roman, A.D. 250-251: the Danubian district and Rome (Emperor Gallus).

123. ÆMILIUS: A. D. Crake; Juv. Mowbray & Co.
Antioch, A.D. 250-251: the Decian Persecution. Also Rome, Antioch, Nisibis, etc., about the period A.D. 257-269: the Valerian Persecution, and the downfall of the Emperor after his defeat by the Persians at Edessa (A.D. 260).

124. *SANGUIS MARTYRUM: Louis Bertrand; Arthème Fayard et Cie [France].
North Africa (Carthage, etc.), between A.D. 253 and A.D. 258. A tale of Cyprian, Bishop of Carthage, and the Persecution under Valerian during the period when Valerian and his son Gallienus were Joint Emperors of Rome. The author has depicted some painful scenes, the aim being—as he explains in his Preface—to illustrate the necessity for sacrifice and martyrdom in the ever-recurring struggle between evil and good.

125. LA FIN DE TADMOR: Ed. de Fréjac; Louis-Michand [France].
The Emperor Aurelian and Zenobia Queen of Palmyra, A.D. 271-272. Paul of Samosata, etc.

126. *THE LAST DAYS AND FALL OF PALMYRA (ZENOBIA): William Ware; Cassell [Eng.], Burt [U.S.A.].
Palmyra towards the end of Zenobia's reign, and up to its destruction by the Emperor Aurelian in A.D. 273. Imaginary letters of a Roman noble, " Lucius Piso," who, besides describing in a vivid manner Zenobia and her Court, deals with the events culminating in Palmyra's fall. Queen Zenobia was a woman of great talents and culture; she herself and her chief Minister, Longinus the philosopher, are the most noteworthy figures in the romance.
I may here make a brief allusion to the same author's " Aurelian "—in some degree a sequel to the book above-mentioned, but hardly of the same originality or interest (it illustrates the Rome of the Emperor Aurelian's last days).

127. A CHRISTIAN BUT A ROMAN: Maurus Jókai (trans.); Doubleday & McClure.
A tale of Christians (Rome and district) in the time of the Emperor Carinus, A.D. 283-285. Ends with the assassination of Carinus and Diocletian's election.

FOURTH CENTURY

128. FABIOLA (THE CHURCH IN THE CATACOMBS): Cardinal Wiseman; Burns [Eng.], Benziger Bros. [U.S.A.].
Rome and the " Church of the Catacombs " in A.D. 302 and following years. The Emperor Maximian is one of the historic personages introduced. The story ends with the coming of Constantine.

129. THE VICTOR'S LAUREL: A. D. Crake; Juv. Mowbray.
Southern Italy (Puteoli) and the African Deserts, etc., A.D. 302. A tale of school life during the Tenth Persecution. The Epilogue is A.D. 325.

130. THE CAMP ON THE SEVERN: A. D. Crake; Juv. Mowbray.
Roman Britain A.D. 303-304. St. Alban (as martyr) appears in the first chapter of this tale, while the Emperor Constantius is introduced in the closing pages.

131. *HOMO SUM: Georg Ebers (trans.); Sampson Low [Eng.], Appleton [U.S.A.].
Sinai and the oasis at its foot, A.D. 330. An anchorite falsely accused, accepts his punishment of expulsion—his innocence only becoming known through the real culprit's confession. A good example of Ebers as novelist.

132. FAUSTULA: " John Ayscough "; Chatto & Windus.
Rome, A.D. 340 onwards. A novel illustrating the period of the Emperor Julian, and ending with his death (A.D. 363).

133. *INGO: GUSTAV FREYTAG (trans.); In " Our Forefathers "—
Asher [Eng.], Holt [U.S.A.].
Thuringia, A.D. 357. A tale depicting the period of the coming of the Romans, when
the Franks were victorious over the Alemanni.

134. *THE DEATH OF THE GODS[1]: D. MEREZHKOVSKY (trans.);
Constable [Eng.], Putnam [U.S.A.].
Constantinople, various parts of Asia Minor, Greece, Italy, Strasburg, etc., A.D. 337
to 363. A stirring romance of the Emperor Julian from boyhood to death. Illustrates
the political and theological developments of the period in which Constantius (third
son of Constantine) and Julian ruled successively. The Arian heresy; the victory at
Argentoratum over the Alemanni and other battles in the Rhine district; the expedition
against the Persians which resulted in Julian's death—these are šome of the main
subjects with which the book deals. The portrait of Julian is a careful one, and many
other personages are brought into the story, including the Emperor Constantius and
Gregory of Nazianzen.

[1] This novel is the first volume of the author's series of historical romances, in which he seeks to
illustrate the " Pagano-Christian dualism of our nature," i.e. to show how the conception of God becoming Man is ever to be contrasted with that conception under which Man is regarded as being
essentially Divine. The remaining two volumes of this " Christ and Anti-Christ " trilogy (viz., " The
Forerunner " and " Peter and Alexis ") appear under their respective centuries—the Fifteenth and the
Eighteenth.

135. THE COMING OF THE HUNS: A. CONAN DOYLE; In " The
Last Galley; impressions and tales "—Smith, Elder [Eng.], Double-
day [U.S.A.].
Dacia, mid to late Fourth Century: the time of the Arian controversies.

136. A CAPTIVE OF THE ROMAN EAGLES (BISSULA): FELIX
DAHN (trans.); McClurg [U.S.A.].
Romans and Germans (Alemanni) in the Lake Constance region, A.D. 378. Ausonius,
the most noted Latin poet of the Fourth Century, is a figure.

137. *DESERT: A LEGEND: MARTIN ARMSTRONG; Cape.
Alexandria and the Egyptian Desert in late Fourth Century (" not so many years
since Anthony himself, the greatest of the hermits, had died "). A story well illustrating
monastic life.

138. THE DIPPING WELL: M. ELSIE GULLICK; Juv. Pitman.
Bath and the Mendip region in the time of the Roman occupation. This tale of a
boy's adventures is somewhat indefinite in date, but the period is presumably about the
middle or end of the Fourth Century.

139. EELEN OF BRINGARD: WILKINSON SHERREN; Cecil Palmer.
Britain (Durnovaria) in the time of the Emperor Gratian, c. 380. The outstanding
figure in this " romance of Wessex " is the commander, Maximus, with whose declaration as Emperor the book ends.

140. *A CENTURION OF THE THIRTIETH, ON THE GREAT
WALL, THE WINGED HATS: RUDYARD KIPLING; All three
in " Puck of Pook's Hill "—Macmillan.
Three short stories of the Romans in Britain (second half of the Fourth Century).

141. *SAINT AUGUSTIN: LOUIS BERTRAND (trans.); Constable.
N. Africa (Numidia and Carthage) and Italy (Milan and Ostia), A.D. 354-430. A
very careful and inspiring piece of fictional biography, dealing with the life of the great
St. Augustine of Hippo from birth to death. Brings out the all-round character of the
man—his intellectuality and mysticism combined with great practical ability and sense
of reality. The book shows the different stages of Augustine's career: his wild youth
and strenuous early manhood; the Platonic and Pauline influences during his time as
teacher of rhetoric in Milan, where he met Bishop Ambrose (an unfavourable depiction);
his controversies with the Manichæans and other heretical schools—especially the
Donatists. Incidentally a clear impression is given of the baseness and corruption of

the times. The later pages cover the period of the Sack of Rome by Alaric (410) and the blockade of Hippo by the Vandals in A.D. 430, during which siege the great Bishop passed away. Monica, Augustine's mother, is, of course, introduced, with the special circumstances of her death.

142. GATHERING CLOUDS: Frederick W. Farrar; Longmans.

A tale of Antioch and Constantinople about A.D. 387 to 404: the period of Alaric and the Goths. The outstanding figure in the book is St. Chrysostom, while other historic personages are the two Emperors Honorius and Arcadius, and the Empress Eudoxia.

143. *TELEMACHUS: C. Edmund Maurice; The Independent Press

The Egyptian Desert, Palestine, Constantinople, and Italy (Baiæ, Rome and Verona), A.D. 394-403. A striking tale of bygone religious life and thought, illustrating, also, social and political developments in the Roman Empire (East and West). The better side of monkish asceticism, the intolerance of certain ecclesiastics with regard to heresy (Origenism), the half-heathen, half-Christian influences of the time—all these aspects are well brought out. The career of the heroic monk, Telemachus, ending with his martyr-protest against the gladiatorial games, is presented in a manner at once interesting and moving. Other noteworthy figures are: Jerome, Theophilus the Patriarch of Alexandria, Chrysostom (sympathetically drawn), Quintus Symmachus (Roman Senator and Orator), the Latin poets Claudianus (Pagan) and Prudentius (Christian), and Stilicho the Roman General—fresh from his victory over Alaric and the Goths at Verona. There is just a glimpse of the Emperor Honorius.

144. A DUKE OF BRITAIN: Sir Herbert Maxwell; Juv. Blackwood.

Scotland and Italy in the period A.D. 397-406. Begins with an account of the Pictish people of Novantia (modern Galloway region) and their relations with the Romans; then the scene is changed to Milan during the time of Alaric's invasion of Upper Italy, A.D. 400. Flavius Stilicho, the statesman, and the Emperor Honorius appear—Stilicho's victory over the Goths (402), and the subsequent festivities at Rome (404), being covered in the story.

FIFTH CENTURY

145. *WHEN THE BOUGH BREAKS: Naomi Mitchison; in " When the Bough Breaks and Other Stories "—Cape [Eng.], Harcourt, Brace [U.S.A.].

Italy, the districts of the Danube, and other regions at the beginning of the Fifth Century. Illustrates the time of Alaric and the Goths, the Emperor Honorius, St. Jerome, etc.

146. ANTONINA: Wilkie Collins; Chatto & Windus [Eng.], Harper [U.S.A.].

Italy (Ravenna and Rome), A.D. 408. A story of the Gothic invasion, and of Alaric's first Blockade of Rome. Deals with the Christian Church and Paganism, the privations of the besieged during the blockade, etc., etc. Both the Emperor Honorius and Alaric appear.

147. *THE COUNT OF THE SAXON SHORE: A. J. Church and Ruth Putnam; Juv. Seeley [Eng.], Putnam [U.S.A.].

Southern Britain (largely Isle of Wight region) mainly in the first decade of the Fifth Century. A tale of the period when the Roman Legions left Britain to defend the Empire against the Goths, and when Count Aelius (the " Count of Saxon Shore ") was about the only remaining representative of Rome in S. Britain. Covers the murder of the British Cæsar, Gratianus, and the Election of Constantine as Emperor of Britain and the West. The troubled state of the country after Constantine's departure is depicted—British conspiracy and reversion to paganism, etc., with a hint of the Saxon advent. Besides the Count, the Emperors Gratianus and Constantine appear. The final pages tell of King Arthur's victory over the Saxons at Badon Hill, near Bath, A.D. 451.

148. THE LAST OF THE LEGIONS: A. CONAN DOYLE; in " The
    Last Galley; impressions and tales "—*Smith, Elder [Eng.], Double-
    day [U.S.A.]*.
    Thames district at the time of the departure of the Romans from Britain.

149. *HYPATIA: CHARLES KINGSLEY; *Macmillan*.
    Egypt (Nile region of the Desert and Alexandria), early Fifth Century. A very
    interesting—if sometimes historically criticized—romance of the famous woman-teacher
    Hypatia. Depicts her noble character, and reflects the conflict between the refined
    Neoplatonism which she expounded and the narrow dogmatism of Christianity as then
    developed in certain ecclesiastical quarters. Turning to a more general side, the coming
    of the Goths into the Roman Empire receives due illustration. That part of the novel
    which describes the riot and disorder culminating in the murder of Hypatia, is thrilling
    in the extreme. Other important historical figures, besides the heroine, are: Cyril
    the patriarch of Alexandria, and Synesius of Cyrene the philosophic bishop. Regarded
    as a work of fiction, and allowing for occasional modernisms reflecting Kingsley's own
    theological position, the book can hardly fail to attract, with its varied scenes and types
    of character.

150. THE BANNER OF THE WHITE HORSE: CLARENCE MARSH
    CASE; *Juv. Harrap [Eng.], Scribner [U.S.A.]*.
    Britain and Northern Europe mid Fifth Century. Primarily " a tale of the Saxon
    Conquest " (sub-title), dealing with the landing and establishment of the Saxons in
    Thanet, A.D. 449, and introducing Hengist and Horsa, as well as Vortigern and others.

151. THE FIRST CARGO: A. CONAN DOYLE; in " The Last Galley;
    impressions and tales "—*Smith, Elder [Eng.], Doubleday [U.S.A.]*.
    A short tale describing the Coming of the Saxons to England.

152. SAINT PATRICK: A NATIONAL TALE OF THE FIFTH
    CENTURY: " AN ANTIQUARY "—*Constable*. 3 vols.
    Ireland and Saint Patrick in the middle of the Fifth Century. There is an interesting
    introductory " Personal Narrative " by the author.

153. ATTILA: G. P. R. JAMES; *Routledge [Eng.], Dutton [U.S.A.]*.
    Dalmatia, the Danubian regions, etc., in the middle of the Fifth Century. A good,
    if somewhat solid, romance of the Hunnish King, ending with his death in A.D. 453.

154. *FELICITAS: FELIX DAHN (trans.); *Macmillan [Eng.], McClurg
    [U.S.A.]*.
    Juvavum (modern Salzburg) A.D. 476. A story reflecting the time of the invasion
    of the Danubian regions by the Germanic tribes.

155. OLWYN'S SECRET: " HERBERT STRANG "; *Juv. Oxford University
    Press*.
    An interesting little tale of Saxon thanes and British slaves about the end of the Fifth
    Century.

SIXTH CENTURY

156. HUMILLIMUS: WILFRANC HUBBARD; in " Orvieto Dust "—
    Constable.
    Italy in the time of Theodoric the Great and later. Life story of a man born A.D.
    500.

157. THE HOME COMING: A CONAN DOYLE; in " The Last Galley;
    impressions and tales "—*Smith, Elder [Eng.], Doubleday [U.S.A.]*.
    Constantinople, A.D. 528: the Empress Theodora. A short tale.

158. *THE STRUGGLE FOR ROME (*DER KAMPF UM ROM*): Felix Dahn (trans.); *Bentley,* 3 vols.

Ravenna, Rome, Byzantium, etc., from A.D. 526 to A.D. 553. One of the greatest of all German historical novels, depicting the Gothic Kingdom and its collapse in the years following Theodoric's death. Illustrates the restoration of the Roman Empire under Justinian, including the defence of Rome by Belisarius, and that general's other military achievements, as well as his recall and retirement; also covers the final extinction of the Gothic power in Italy by Narses. A great many historic figures appear, of whom one may specify Theodoric, Justinian, the Empress Theodora, Belisarius, Totila, and Teja.

159. *VERANILDA: George Gissing; *Constable.*

Italy (Rome and Campania) about A.D. 542 to 544. A carefully-written historical romance, illustrating the time when the Gothic King, Totila, overran Campania and a large part of Italy. Reflects the religious controversies of the period (the Arian heresy, etc.), as well as the political developments when the Roman nobles were plotting against the Empire in the Gothic interest. The tale covers Totila's blockade of Neapolis and its fall, the advance on Rome, and the siege of the latter city. The last chapter tells of the Goths still before Rome after six months' siege, with Belisarius encamped at Ravenna. There are numerous references to men of the period like Pope Vigilius, while King Totila himself is somewhat prominently introduced in the closing chapters.

160. THE STAR IN THE WEST: Mary H. Debenham; *Juv. National Society [Eng.], Whittaker [U.S.A.].*

A tale of the British Church in Wales about A.D. 550: Llancarfan district in time of the Yellow Plague, etc.

161. THE DRUIDESS: Florence Gay; *Ouseley.*

West Britain (Damnonia, North Wales, and Severn regions), and Ireland (Glendalough, etc.), A.D. 577 to 578. A short tale illustrating the struggle between Britons and Saxons, as well as the lingering influences of Paganism, and the unsettled state of affairs in both Ireland and Britain. St. Columba appears, also King Ethelbert of Kent and his Queen.

162. *DEWI SANT: Blanche Devereux; in "Star of Mercia: historical tales of Wales and the Marches"—*Cape.*

A story of St. David and Gildas in Wales, late Sixth Century (" Fifth Century " on p. 50 is clearly a misprint). Ends with the Saint's death in A.D. 601.

163. *HAVELOK THE DANE: Charles W. Whistler; *Juv. Nelson.*

Grimsby and Lincoln, end of the Sixth Century. A tale based on the legend of Grim the fisher and his foster-son, Havelok the Dane.

164. THE KING'S ORCHARD: "Marjorie Bowen"; in "The Pleasant Husband and Other Stories"—*Hurst & Blackett.*

A short story of Augustine just after the conversion of Kent, A.D. 596.

SEVENTH CENTURY

165. THE SOUL OF A SERF (*Fated to Win*): J. Breckenridge Ellis; *Juv. Lee & Laird [U.S.A.].*

Saxons v. Angles on the Baltic shores, beginning of the Seventh Century, and Britain about A.D. 616: Ethelfrith of " North Humbria," and Penda of Mercia. Also Edwin, son of Ella, just before his Northumbrian Conquest.

166. THE RED STAR: A. Conan Doyle; in "The Last Galley; impressions and tales"—*Smith, Elder [Eng.], Doubleday [U.S.A.].*

Mahomet in the Arabian Desert, A.D. 620 (*told* in Constantinople, A.D. 630).

167. THE BRIDE OF THE NILE: Georg Ebers (trans.); *Appleton.*
Egypt, A.D. 643. A romance illustrating the period of the Arab conquest.

168. KING PENDA'S CAPTAIN: Mackenzie Mac Bride; *Juv. Dent.*
Land of the North English (including the part known as Nottinghamshire to-day) about the middle of the Seventh Century. The story tells of a young Pictish hero's exploits under Penda, King of Mercia. An example of the didactic and over-descriptive type of fiction, though historically suggestive.

169. *THE CONVERSION OF ST. WILFRID: Rudyard Kipling; *Juv.* In " Rewards and Fairies "—*Macmillan.*
A short tale of Bishop Wilfrid of York and the South Saxons, late Seventh Century.

170. CAEDWALLA: Frank Cowper; *Juv. Seeley.*
A tale of the Saxons in the Isle of Wight, covering the period A.D. 680-709.

EIGHTH CENTURY

171. A PRINCE OF CORNWALL: Charles W. Whistler; *Juv. Warne.*
A well-written story of Glastonbury and the West Country at the beginning of the Eighth Century: time of the West Saxon king, Ina.

172. *THE BEAUTY OF THE PURPLE: W. Stearns Davis; *L. Parsons [Eng.], Macmillan [U.S.A.].*
Imperial Constantinople, beginning of Eighth Century. The *Proem* date is A.D. 705, but the main story covers the period A.D. 712-718. An interesting romance dealing largely with Leo the Isaurian and his successful campaign against the Saracens.

173. *INGRABAN [1]: Gustav Freytag (trans.); in " Our Forefathers " —*Asher [Eng.], Holt [U.S.A.].*
Franconia and Thuringia, A.D. 724: time of the Slavonic inroads, of Pope Gregory II., and of St. Boniface's missionary labours.

[1] This tale, and the one placed under Fourth Century (see *Ingo* on Page 16), are the only portions available in English translation, of Freytag's celebrated series of historical tales to which he gave the collective title—*Die Ahnen* (Hirzel, Leipsic, 1872-80). In this series, the history of a family is made to illustrate successive stages of German civilization. The remaining six tales, which can only be read in the original German, depict the rise (11th Century) and fall (13th Century) of Chivalry, the Reformation in the years 1519-30, the Thirty Years' War (second quarter of 17th Century), the time of Frederick—William I of Prussia covering the years 1721-40, and the Prussian patriotic revival between 1805 and 1815.

174. *STAR OF MERCIA: Blanche Devereux; in " Star of Mercia: historical tales of Wales and the Marches "—*Cape.*
A grim story of Mercia under King Offa (mid to late Eighth Century) and of the King's daughter Ethelfrith (the " Star of Mercia "). The murder of Ethelbert, King of the East Angles, is described.

175. FOR THE WHITE CHRIST: Robert Ames Bennett; *Putnam [Eng.], McClurg [U.S.A.].*
Europe mainly in the period A.D. 778-783. A somewhat elaborate fictional effort, based on history and legend. Depicts the wars of Charlemagne against the Moors and Arabs in Spain, and against the Saxons in mid-Europe. Charlemagne (Karl the Great) appears, as well as other figures—historic or legendary.

176. A KING'S COMRADE: Charles W. Whistler; *Juv. Nelson.*
Hereford about the year A.D. 792. A story illustrating the time of Offa, King of Mercia, and Ethelbert of East Anglia: arrival of the Danes.

177. A PRINCE ERRANT: Charles W. Whistler; *Juv. Nelson.*
  S.W. Wales, Cornwall, and Ireland, about A.D. 795: Saxon, Briton, Norseman, and Dane. One of the author's carefully-written tales.

---

178. *THE LIKENESS OF KING ELFWALD: W. G. Collingwood; *Titus Wilson.*
  Northumbria (Carlisle, etc.) and West Scotland (including the Islands) in the period A.D. 787 to A.D. 808. A story of the coming of the Vikings (burning of the Abbey of Iona), also illustrating the short reign of King Elfwald II of Northumbria. The author's special qualifications for depicting both the time and place of the tale are well known.

NINTH CENTURY

---

179. EDRIC THE OUTLAW: Escott Lynn; *Juv. Chambers.*
  England, France, etc., round about the year A.D. 800. Land and sea adventures (the Vikings). In the course of the story, Egbert, King of the West Saxons, is introduced during his period abroad (Charlemagne's court) before he returned to fill the throne of Wessex (A.D. 802). The Emperor Charlemagne also appears.

180. THE WANDERER'S NECKLACE: H. Rider Haggard; *Cassell* [*Eng.*], *Longmans* [*U.S.A.*].
  Jutland, Byzantium, and Egypt round about the year A.D. 800. A story in which the Empress Irene, widow of the Emperor Leo IV, is introduced.

181. THE BRAVEST OF THE VIKINGS: Beatrice Harraden; *Juv.* In "Untold Tales of the Past"—*Dent* [*Eng.*], *Dutton* [*U.S.A.*].
  A short tale of Norsemen about A.D. 824, on the eve of starting for an expedition against King Egbert of Wessex.

---

182. THE LAST OF THE PALADINS: OR THE HERITAGE OF KARL THE GREAT: Charles Deslys (trans.); *Juv. R.T.S.*
  A story of Brittany, Normandy, Rhine district, Sardinia, etc., in the second quarter of the Ninth Century.

---

183. *THE WOOING OF OSYTH: Kate Thompson Sizer; *Juv. Jarold* [*Eng.*], *Estes* [*U.S.A.*].
  East Anglia (Bures, Suffolk, etc.) in the period A.D. 850-870, and Island of Athelney in A.D. 878. A good tale of St. Osyth, who is here depicted as being St. Edmund's sister. Gives a picture of the time just before and during the Danish invasion of 866-870, covering the respective martyrdoms of Osyth and Edmund. Other historic figures are King Sighere of Essex (as he rides to wed Osyth, etc.) and King Alkmund of East Anglia (father of St. Edmund). There is slight reference to King Alfred and Guthrum in the last chapter.

---

184. THE KING'S SONS: G. Manville Fenn; *Juv. Nister* [*Eng.*], *Dutton* [*U.S.A.*].
  A very slight, but pleasing, story of King Alfred's boyhood—specially suitable for the very young.

---

185. A LION OF WESSEX: Tom Bevan; *Juv. Partridge.*
  An excellent tale of Bath, Chippenham, Berkeley, and the Welsh Border region beginning A.D. 864. The time of the Danish wars in King Ethelred's time. Alfred (as Prince) is a prominent figure.

D

186. THE KING'S PASSION: Amy J. Baker; *John Long.*
Begins Winchester A.D. 859 (Alfred appears as a boy of 10), quickly passing to East Anglia A.D. 863. A romance of Edmund, King and Martyr, ending with his painful death in the Danish invasion of 866-870.

187. THE ROOD AND THE RAVEN: Gertrude Hollis; *R.T.S.*
A tale of Scandinavia and East Anglia round about A.D. 870. The landing of the Vikings, and the murder of King Edmund.

188. *THE DRAGON OF WESSEX: Percy Dearmer; *Juv. Mowbray.*
King Alfred and Wessex in the period between A.D. 871 and 878. A tale introducing various historical personages, while, among the many Western localities touched, one may specify Exeter, Sherborne, Athelney, and Glastonbury. The book ends with the Battle of Ethandune.

189. *GOD SAVE KING ALFRED: E. Gilliat; *Juv. Macmillan.*
Various localities, including the Amesbury region, Winchester, Shaftesbury, Athelney, Arundel, and London, A.D. 885-886. A tale with King Alfred as the outstanding figure (his perfectibility is somewhat over-emphasized). Illustrates the King's progressive and improving efforts, as well as his success in repelling the Danes (Siege and Relief of Rochester). Numerous historic figures besides King Alfred and his Queen: Edward the Atheling, John Scotus Erigena the philosopher, Asser of St. Davids (Alfred's biographer), etc., etc.

190. *KING ALFRED'S VIKING: Charles W. Whistler; *Juv. Nelson.*
West County (Devon, Cornwall, Quantock region, etc.) in the late Ninth Century. A story illustrating the time of Kings Alfred and Guthrum, both of whom appear. Tells of the Norse hero's sea and land adventures, with special reference to " the First English Fleet," the Edington fight with the Danes in Wiltshire, etc.

191. THE DRAGON AND THE RAVEN: G. A. Henty; *Juv. Blackie* [Eng.], *Scribner* [U.S.A.].
A tale of the struggle between Saxon and Dane, covering, in all, the period A.D. 870 to A.D. 901. Gives a somewhat detailed account of the Danish incursions, and of King Alfred's successful resistance during his reign. The book is based on the Saxon Chronicles.

192. KEEPERS OF ENGLAND: Mary H. Debenham; *Juv. National Society* [Eng.], *Whittaker* [U.S.A.].
E. Wessex border, A.D. 878, then 893-901. A story of King Alfred and the Danes, ending with the King's death.

TENTH CENTURY

193. *THE SWORN BROTHERS: Gunnar Gunnarsson (trans.); *Gyldendal* [Eng.], *Knopf* [U.S.A.].
Mainly Iceland, with glimpses of Norway and the English and Irish Coasts, round about the year A.D. 900. A tale of Iceland and the Vikings in the period when Harold I, " the Fair-haired," was King of Norway. Love and conflict, Christ v. Odin, etc.

194. CONAN THE WONDER-WORKER [*sequel* to " Keepers of England "]: Mary H. Debenham; *Juv. National Society* [Eng.], *Whittaker* [U.S.A.].
An Irishman (" Scot ") and a Saxon youth as captives in Norway, A.D. 912-913: the Norsemen and Christianity. There are glimpses of Normandy and England.

195. *THORSTEIN OF THE MERE: W. G. Collingwood; Revised
    edition 1909—*Titus Wilson.*
   Chiefly the English Lake District, with glimpses of Scotland and Ireland, A.D. 921-
938. A very interesting and instructive tale (on saga lines), illustrating the life-conditions of the early Tenth Century in a region where people of various antagonistic
races (Saxons, Danes, Scots, Norsemen, and Celts) met in contest. There is good local
colour, and sufficient historical description and allusion to enhance the appearance of
reality.

196. *DRAGON OSMUND: Charles W. Whistler; *Juv.* *Nelson.*
   The Lincolnshire Fen districts, etc., in the early Tenth Century. A story of King
Athelstan's time, ending with the Battle of Brunanburh when he (Athelstan) completely
routed the league of Welsh, Scots, and Danes, which had been formed against him
(A.D. 937).

197. A SEA QUEEN'S SAILING: Charles W. Whistler; *Juv.*
    Nelson.
   A tale of the Vikings about A.D. 935: Northern and Irish Coasts in the time of Hakon
the Good.

198. *HIGHTOWN UNDER SUNFELL[1]: John Buchan; in "The
    Path of the King"—*Nelson* [*Eng.*], *Doran* [*U.S.A.*].
   A tale of Vikings and their disastrous raid in the Tenth Centuy.

   [1] The first of fourteen fictional sketches which admirably illustrate that persistence of the heroic,
kingly spirit which links the earliest historical periods with all those following. The remaining tales
will appear under their respective centuries. I have purposely refrained from marking any of the
tales *juvenile*, as they may be read by old and young with equal pleasure.

199. EDWY THE FAIR; OR, THE FIRST CHRONICLE OF
    AESCENDUNE: A. D. Crake; *Juv. Longmans* [*Eng.*], *Young*
    [*U.S.A.*].
   London, Winchester, Glastonbury, etc., from about A.D. 940 to 960. St. Dunstan is
the dominating historic figure, while Edwy "the Fair" (as Prince and King), his wife
Elgiva, and King Edgar, are all prominently introduced. There is a considerable
historic background, including Edwy's raid into Mercia and his defeat.

200. *THE LITTLE DUKE: Charlotte M. Yonge; *Juv.* *Macmillan.*
   Normandy, mainly in the year A.D. 943. Richard "the Fearless," just before and
after the death of his father Duke William of the Longsword. Although the tale (as
its title indicates) is primarily one about Richard's boyhood, the final chapter—passing
over some ten years or more—shows him a grown man of about 25. King Louis IV
of France appears. An excellent tale for children.

201. *EKKEHARD: Joseph Viktor von Scheffel (trans.); *Dent*
    [*Eng.*], *Dutton* [*U.S.A.*].
   Germany (Lake Constance and Rhine regions) towards the middle of the Tenth
Century. A very fine romance, illustrating the period of the Huns and their raids. The
author has purposely altered certain dates, but for the most part his tale is based on fact.

202. STYRBIORN THE STRONG: E. R. Eddison; *Cape.*
   Sweden and Denmark mid to late Tenth Century. An interesting and carefully
written novel of old Scandinavian life.

203. *THEOPHANO: Frederic Harrison; *Chapman & Hall.*
   Constantinople, Crete, Cordova, Rome, and Asia, A.D. 956 to about 970. A careful
picture of life and politics in Southern and Eastern Europe, in the third quarter of the
Tenth Century. The hero of this "romantic monograph" (as the author calls it) is
Nicephorus Phocas, and the crowning episodes of his strange career are fully described.
The conquest of Crete, the coronation of Otto II. in Rome, the attempt to reconquer
Syria and drive out the Saracens—these are a few of the subjects treated. There is an
interesting glimpse of the Spanish Caliph at Cordova. Besides Nicephorus Phocas,
several historic figures appear, including Theophano, the Emperor Constantine Porphy-
rogenitus and his successor Romanus II, and Pope John XIII.

204. *THE LOTUS WOMAN: Nathan Gallizier; *Page* [*U.S.A.*].

Byzantine Constantinople, A.D. 969. A characteristic example of the author, showing his ornate style and love of terrific situations, but also giving evidence of careful research and descriptive skill. The novel deals with some of the scenes and figures that are brought into Frederic Harrison's *Theophano*: in both stories the Emperor Nicephorus Phocas and his consort, Theophano, appear prominently, but Gallizier covers a far shorter period and a less extensive region—his novel illustrating the very last stages in the career of Nicephorus, and giving a picture of life and public events entirely within the limits of the Byzantine sphere. The half-barbaric, half-civilized atmosphere of 10th Century Constantinople is well conveyed; and its manners and customs, the corruption and license of its Court, as well as its political intrigues and discontents, are brought before the reader. Besides the Emperor and Empress, there are many personages of the time of whom perhaps the most noteworthy are John Tzimisces (proclaimed Emperor on the last page) and the Patriarch, Polyeuctus.

205. THE LOST KINGDOM: Samuel Gordon; *Shapiro, Vallentine.*

The Kingdom of Khazaria (Crimean region), A.D. 968. A novel dealing with the Varangians, etc. The sub-title is: "The Passing of the Khazars."

206. THE GRIP OF THE WOLF; "Morice Gerard"; *Juv. Marshall.*

A tale of the Free Companies in the time of the Emperor Otho, "the Reckless."

207. ELFRIDA: Lilian Hayes; in "The Thirtieth Piece of Silver"— *Fisher Unwin.*

King Edgar's family (England of the late Tenth Century): Edward the Martyr and his step-mother, Elfrida.

208. *HUGHES CAPET: Antoine Baumann; *Perrin* [*Paris*].

France, A.D. 978 onwards. A romance illustrating the period of Hugo Capet (founder of the Capetian Dynasty), Louis V. (last of the Carlovingians), and the Emperor Otho II.

209. RIQUILDA: Mrs. Kendall Park; *Murray & Evenden.*

Spain (Barcelona), A.D. 986. A story dealing with the period of the Sovereign Counts of Barcelona, and of Almanazor, the Prime Minister of the Spanish Moors.

210. *LEIF AND THORKEL: Genevra Snedden; *Juv. Harrap* [*Eng.*], *World Book Co.* [*U.S.A.*].

Norway, Greenland, and North America (discovery by the Norsemen). A capital tale of two Norse boys, and their adventures by sea and land in the time of King Trygve Olafson (late Tenth Century).

211. *THE VIKINGS OF THE BALTIC: Sir George Webbe Dasent; *Chapman & Hall.*

Jomsburg, on the shore of the Baltic, towards the close of the Tenth Century. A tale of the Vikings and their doings by sea and land in Northern Parts (Norway and Denmark). The principal historic figures, appearing at one or another point are: Sweyn, Hacon, and Olaf, Tryggvi's son.

212. THE SORCERESS OF ROME: Nathan Gallizier; *Page* [*U.S.A.*].

Rome in the year A.D. 999. There is much history of a somewhat obscure type in this elaborate and, at times, melodramatic romance of the Rome of the Millennium. The main subject which forms the story's background, is the struggle between Romans and Germans at the time of the rebellion of Johannes Crescentius, the Senator of Rome. On the more personal and romantic side, the novel is largely illustrative of the relations between the boy-emperor, Otto III, and Stephania, wife of Crescentius. The assassination of Pope Gregory V and the election of Pope Sylvester II (Gerbert of Aurillac) are among the events covered. The principal figures besides Crescentius, Otto, and Stephania, are Eckhardt, the German commander-in-chief, and Benilo, the Chamberlain. Popes Gregory and Sylvester (already mentioned) are brought into the story at different points.

ELEVENTH CENTURY

---

213. *ALFGAR THE DANE; OR, THE SECOND CHRONICLE OF AESCENDUNE: A. D. Crake; *Juv.* Longmans [*Eng.*], *Young* [*U.S.A.*].
A Wessex story (diary form) illustrating the struggle for supremacy between English and Danish Kings, 1002-1018: period of Ethelred the Unready—Edmund Ironside, and of Sweyn—Canute. An excellent blending of fiction and history; quite the most interesting of the author's *Aescendune* series, though the first and third "chronicles" (entered elsewhere) are also good examples of juvenile historical tales.

---

214. THE WARD OF KING CANUTE: Ottilie A Liljencrantz; *Juv.* McClurg [*U.S.A.*].
A tale of the struggle between Edmund Ironside and Canute in 1016, including the latter's decisive victory at Assandûn, and King Edmund's death shortly afterwards.

---

215. *FREY AND HIS WIFE: Maurice Hewlett; *Ward, Lock* [*Eng.*], *McBride* [*U.S.A.*].
Chiefly Norway in the early 11th Century. A good Saga story: King Olaf Trygvasson and his introduction of Christianity, etc.

---

216. *THE LIGHT HEART[1]: Maurice Hewlett; *Chapman & Hall* [*Eng.*], *Holt* [*U.S.A.*].
Iceland, Norway, Denmark, etc. Another of Hewlett's excellent Scandinavian Saga stories, with King Olaf prominent. Time of King Cnut in England.

[1] Several other Hewlett stories of Iceland, etc., dealing with a somewhat earlier time, are entered in the *Semi-Historical* section of this volume.

---

217. *SIGRID STORRÅDA: Selma Lagerlöf (trans.); in "The Queens of Kungahälla and Other Sketches"—*Werner Laurie*.
The Swedish Queen, Sigrid Storråda, and King Olaf Trygvason of Norway.

---

218. *ASTRID: Selma Lagerlöf (trans.); in "The Queens of Kungahälla and Other Sketches"—*Werner Laurie*.
Sweden (Upsala) and Norway. King Olaf and "Astrid," a daughter of the Swedish king by a serf mother.

---

219. *WILLIAM THE CONQUEROR: Sir Charles Napier; *Routledge*.
Normandy, Flanders, France and England, mainly in the period 1042-66. A very fair example of that type of historical romance in which there is an overweight of history. Covers much the same ground as Lytton's *Harold;* though, here, rather more stress is laid upon William's early Norman influences, and the circumstances leading up to his marriage with Matilda, daughter of Earl Baldwin of Flanders. The book touches such events as the marriage of Harold, his Coronation, and the war episodes ending with Stamford Bridge and Hastings (full account of the last-named battle). Duke William is, of course, greatly to the fore, and other prominent figures are: Matilda, Edward the Confessor, Harold, and Editha. There are, moreover, glimpses of Stigand, Archbishop of Canterbury, and other personages.

---

220. EARL SWEYN THE NITHING: Blanche Devereux; in "Star of Mercia: historical tales of Wales and the Marches" —*Cape*.
Leominster, 1047: time of Edward the Confessor, and of Earl Godwin whose eldest son, Sweyn, figures as lover in this romantic little tale.

221. *HAROLD: Lord Lytton; *Routledge [Eng.], Little, Brown [U.S.A.], and other publishers.*
England and France (Rouen), 1052-66 (Edward the Confessor—Harold). A careful and interesting historical romance dealing with the events which led to the Norman Conquest. Covers the death of Earl Godwin, Harold's visit to Duke William, the Welsh War, the Norse invasion, and the Battle of Stamford Bridge—ending with Duke William's landing and the Battle of Hastings. Besides Harold himself and the Godwins, there are a great many historic figures, including King Edward, Duke William, Bishop Alred, Lanfranc, Harold Hardrada, and King Gryffyth.

222. GYTHA'S MESSAGE: Emma Leslie; *Juv. Blackie.*
Saxon England (Bristol, London, Winchester, etc.). 1053-66. The tale ends with the coming of William and the Battle of Hastings.

223. A NORTHUMBRIAN IN ARMS: George Surrey; *Juv. Oxford University Press.*
Lincolnshire, Scotland, Cumberland and Wales, 1054-57. A tale of outlawry illustrating events that occurred some considerable time before the Norman Conquest (the last chapter jumps to the coming of William). Tells of Earl Siward's army and the victory over Macbeth, also of Malcolm Canmore (son of Duncan) becoming King of Scotland. Hereward and Harold Godwinson are among the figures introduced.

224. *FOLKE FILBYTER: Verner von Heidenstam (trans.); being Part I of " The Tree of the Folkungs "—*Gyldendal.*
Sweden about 1060: the close of the Viking Age and the suppression of Paganism by King Inge. Civil War and general disturbance.

225. *EUDOCIA: A COMEDY ROYAL: Eden Phillpotts; *Heinemann [Eng.], Macmillan [U.S.A.].*
Constantinople, 1067. A romance of the later Eastern Empire, having for its central character the then " widowed " Empress Eudocia. Although the author introduces public figures, and illustrates the political disturbances of the time (" Blue " and " Green " factions, etc.), he gives first place to the imaginative element. The Empress and the soldier Romanus Diogenes are well drawn.

226. WULF THE SAXON: G. A. Henty; *Juv. Blackie [Eng.], Scribner [U.S.A.].*
England and Rouen, 1063-66 (Edward the Confessor—Harold). A good tale of the Norman Conquest and the few years preceding it. Describes the Welsh War, Harold's accession as King, the Battle of Stamford Bridge, and the Battle of Hastings. King Edward, Harold, Duke William, and many other historic figures.

227. EDITH'S WELL: Blanche Devereux; in " Star of Mercia: historical tales of Wales and the Marches "—*Cape.*
A pretty tale of Edith, King Edward's wife, 1065.

228. RICHARD THE SCROB: Blanche Devereux; in " Star of Mercia ": historical tales of Wales and the Marches "—*Cape.*
Herefordshire immediately before and after the Norman Conquest.

229. *YOUNG MEN AT THE MANOR: Rudyard Kipling; *Juv.* In " Puck of Pook's Hill "—*Macmillan.*
A tale of the Norman Conquest, 1066.

230. *THE ENGLISHMAN: John Buchan; in " The Path of the King "—*Nelson [Eng.], Doran [U.S.A.].*
England in 1066 and 1068 (the Norman Conquest).

231. *THE RIVAL HEIRS: being the Third and Last Chronicle of Aescendune: A. D. CRAKE; *Juv. Longmans* [*Eng.*], *Young* [*U.S.A.*].

Sussex, Abingdon, the Fen district, Canterbury, and Oxford, mainly in the period 1066-72. Begins just after Harold's victory at Stamford Bridge, and passes quickly over the Battle of Senlac or Hastings. The tale specially illustrates the relations between the Normans and the conquered English: the " outlaws " and the last struggles, including Hereward's Camp of Refuge, etc. William the Conqueror and Archbishop Lanfranc are prominently introduced. The last chapters treat of the First Crusade, and Godfrey de Bouillon's taking of Jerusalem, 1099.

232. *HEREWARD THE WAKE: CHARLES KINGSLEY; *Macmillan.*

A stirring romance of the English hero, Hereward, and his career. There are many changes of scene, including England (the Fen district, etc.), Ireland, and Flanders. The later chapters of the book deal with the Norman Conquest period, 1070-71. Kingsley's imaginative treatment of Hereward is more likely to impress the reader than the somewhat vague outlines of actual history. Besides the hero himself, there are several figures of note, including King William and Earl Morcar.

233. *THE CAMP OF REFUGE: CHARLES MACFARLANE; *Constable* [*Eng.*], *Longmans* [*U.S.A.*].

A particularly good historical novel of the Norman Conquest period (Hereward, 1070).

234. IN THE NEW FOREST: " HERBERT STRANG " and JOHN ASTON; *Juv. Oxford University Press.*

England under William the Conqueror, 1066-87. An adventure story, beginning with a full account of the Battle of Hastings and ending with the King's death.

235. *A LITTLE NORMAN MAID; HERBERT STRANG; *Juv. Oxford University Press.*

Southern England, 1070 onwards. A pretty tale of Norman conquerors and English outlaws, etc. One of a series of booklets intended for children.

236. THE FOUNDLING OF THORNESFORD: MARGARET BAINES REED; *Juv. Edward Arnold.*

A short, but good, story of Eastern England (Norfolk) just after the Norman Conquest. Treats of the Saxon and Norman relationship, and introduces Prince William (the Red Prince).

237. *THE SIEGE OF NORWICH CASTLE: M. M. BLAKE; *Juv. Seeley* [*Eng.*], *Macmillan* [*U.S.A.*].

Hereford, Suffolk, Norfolk, and Brittany, 1073-96. An excellent tale illustrating the later Norman Conquest period, and—in particular—the " Bridal of Norwich " plot (Roger Earl of Hereford, Ralph Earl of Norfolk, and Waltheof). The marriage between Hereford's daughter and Norfolk was prohibited—hence the rebellion. Besides the two Earls just mentioned, William the Conqueror, Archbishop Lanfranc, Bishop Odo, and others appear.

238. MALCOLM CANMORE'S PEARL: AGNES GRANT HAY; *Hurst & Blackett.*

Malcolm III of Scotland, and his bride, Margaret (the " Pearl "). The story ends with the King's death in 1093.

239. THE PILGRIM: ARTHUR LEWIS; *Blackwood.*

A Welsh pilgrim in Rome, 1075-76 (last chapter 1084). The novel illustrates the struggle between Pope Gregory VII (Hildebrand) and the Emperor Henry IV of Germany.

240. *AUTOUR D'UNE TIARE: EMILE GEBHART; *Armand Colin et Cie* [*France*].

Italy (Rome and Canossa) in the time of the Emperor Henry IV and Pope Gregory VII, 1075-85.

241. *KNIGHTS OF ARABY: Marmaduke Pickthall; *Collins.*
Arabia in the period 1066-1120. A story of Muslim feud and battle, etc. The particular
historic atmosphere could hardly be conveyed by any novelist other than Mr. Pickthall.

242. COUNT ROBERT OF PARIS: Sir Walter Scott; *Black and
other publishers—English and American.*
Constantinople, 1098. A story of the Byzantine Empire and the First Crusade,
introducing the Emperor Alexius Comnenus and Godfrey de Bouillon. Critics are usually
agreed as to the demerits of this novel (only included here because of its somewhat
unusual historical subject, and because Scott, at his worst, is equal to some romancists
at their best). Professor Firth has gone so far as to pronounce it " unreadable," while
Andrew Lang says that it is " not a work of Scott's normal self."

243. *GOD WILLS IT: William Stearns Davis; *Macmillan.*
A romance of many localities, including Salerno, Palermo, Clermont (Auvergne),
Constantinople, Nicæa, Antioch, and Jerusalem. Opens 1085, in the *Prologue*, with
a description of Pope Gregory VII's deathbed scene, telling how he prophesied that
Godfrey of Bouillon (kneeling beside him) should lead the Christian soldiers into Jerusalem with the battle cry—" God Wills It." The story proper, covering the period
1094-99, illustrates (through the experiences of a young Norman) the manner in which
the Pope's wish was carried out. The outstanding historic events introduced, are the
preaching of Pope Urban II and Peter the Hermit with regard to the First Crusade,
and the taking of Jerusalem by Godfrey of Bouillon, with which latter episode the story
ends. The most important personages introduced, are Popes Gregory VII and Urban II,
Peter the Hermit, Godfrey of Bouillon, Tancred, and (a mere glimpse) Alexius Comnenus the Byzantine Emperor.

244. GERALD THE SHERIFF: Charles W. Whistler; *Juv.
Warne.*
A sea-tale of the English South Coast (Isle of Wight, etc.) in the time of William
Rufus, 1098.

245. A SAXON MAID: Eliza F. Pollard; *Juv. Blackie* [Eng.],
Caldwell [U.S.A.].
Abbey of Romsey, etc., in the William II—Henry I period. A good short story of
the Norman devastations. King Henry I, Archbishop Anselm, and others appear.

TWELFTH CENTURY

246. THE GARDEN OF PARADISE: Arthur Weigall; *Fisher
Unwin.*
Persia (the city of Nishapûr, etc.) end 11th Century to beginning of 12th. A pleasing
love story, in the course of which Omar Khayyám and Melik Shah, the Sultan, are
introduced.

247. *THE THREE STUDENTS: Haldane Macfall; *Knopf.*
Persia from about the last quarter of the 11th Century to the first quarter of the 12th.
The central figure is Omar Khayyám, from his student days up to his death (c. 1123).
Many public events and personages form the background of the story, while the phil-
osophical element, which one would naturally expect in an Omar novel, is not lacking.

248. *THE KNIGHTS OF THE JOYOUS VENTURE: Rudyard
Kipling; *Juv.* In " Puck of Pook's Hill "—*Macmillan.*
A short tale of maritime adventure in the year 1100.

249. *OLD MEN AT PEVENSEY: Rudyard Kipling; *Juv.* In
" Puck of Pook's Hill "—*Macmillan.*
England, beginning of 12th Century. King Henry I, Robert of Normandy, and the
Barons.

250. *THE KING'S MINSTREL: Ivy Bolton; *Juv. Mowbray.*
A good story of Rahere (" part jester, part priest, and more wizard than either ") telling in serio-comic, half-legendary fashion, how he came to be founder of St. Bartholomew's Hospital. King Henry I is prominently introduced, as well as other figures, like Lord Warwick and his son Guy Neville.

251. *THE TREE OF JUSTICE: Rudyard Kipling; *Juv.* In " Rewards and Fairies "—*Macmillan.*
King Henry I and his jester, Rahere, with backward glances at the Norman Conquest period.

252. PABO THE PRIEST: S. Baring Gould; *Methuen [Eng.], Stokes [U.S.A.].*
Westminster, and South Wales (River Towy region), c. 1115-20. An historical novel dealing largely with the Rebellion in South Wales 1115, and ending with the news of the *White Ship* disaster in which Henry I's son, William, was drowned (1120). King Henry himself is very prominent, as also are Prince Griffith (Griffith Ap Rhys) and his sister, Nest.

253. *THE SERF: C. Ranger Gull; *Greening.*
England (the Fen Country) in 1136. A somewhat uncommon and arresting story of a man whom the author presents to us under the name of Hyla, the serf: his yearnings and struggles in the direction of social freedom, etc. The book illustrates the brutality and lawlessness of Stephen's reign.

254. FOR KING OR EMPRESS?: Charles W. Whistler; *Juv. Nelson.*
A good tale of Somerset and Norwich in the time of the Civil War between Stephen and Matilda (" the Empress Maud ").

255. BRIAN FITZ COUNT: A. D. Crake; *Juv. Longmans.*
Wallingford Castle, 1139; then Oxford, Wallingford, and Dorchester Abbey, 1141-53. A story dealing with some of the principal events in the Civil War between Stephen and Matilda. The general atmosphere of the period is well conveyed.

256. A LEGEND OF READING ABBEY: Charles Macfarlane; *Constable [Eng.], Longmans [U.S.A.].*
Hardly a novel in the usual sense, as there is no plot; but the monkish narrative well illustrates the time of Stephen—the landing of Matilda, etc. Stephen, Matilda, Henry of Anjou, and others appear.

257. IN TERMS OF STEEL: W. P. Shervil; *Juv. Shaw.*
Hampshire (Southampton region) in the days of Stephen. A tale of Norwegian viking-pirates, forest outlaws, etc.

258. *L'ABBAYE DE TYPHAINES: Count J. A. de Gobineau; *Librairie Gallimard [France].*
France in the early part of the 12th Century. An interesting romance, depicting the period of Louis VI (called " le Gros "). The king himself appears in the story.

259. THE KNIGHT OF THE CAVE: W. L. O'Byrne; *Juv. Blackie.*
An informing tale of various scenes and experiences. Deals respectively with England (time of Stephen and the Civil War), Ireland, France (Clairvaux and St. Bernard) and Italy.

260. VIA CRUCIS: F. Marion Crawford; *Macmillan.*
Begins England (Faringdon), 1145: time of the wars between the Empress Maud and Stephen; then passes to Normandy, Paris, Italy, and the East. There is a picture of Bernard of Clairvaux preaching the Crusade, and some account of the Second Crusade itself (1147). Other figures in the romance are: King Louis VII and Queen Eleanor of France, as well as Henry Plantagenet.

261. *MARCABRUN: RAMON GUTHRIE; *Doran [U.S.A.].*

Mainly S. France (Poitiers) and Spain, 1135-47. A powerful, if somewhat over-tragical, novel of Troubadour days, largely based (the author says in his *Foreword*) on those poems of Marcabrun which are still extent. There is a considerable background of history (the marriage of Eleanor of Aquitaine with King Louis VII of France, etc.), while, in addition to the personages already named, King Alfonso I (" calling himself Emperor of Spain "), Bernard of Clairvaux, and Duke William of Aquitaine (father of Eleanor), are brought into the story. English readers may be reminded how Eleanor —here first introduced as a maiden of 13—eventually married Henry II of England.

262. *THE LADY OF TRIPOLI: MICHAEL BARRINGTON; *Chatto & Windus.*

Bordeaux, Blaye, Tripoli, and other regions, within the decade 1140-50. Another carefully-written romance of the Troubadour time, with Odierna Countess of Tripoli, and Rudel the Troubadour Prince of Blaye, as central figures.

263. THE WIFE OF FLANDERS: JOHN BUCHAN; in " The Path of the King "—*Nelson [Eng.], Doran [U.S.A.].*

A tale of 12th Century Bruges, illustrating early Flemish enterprise.

264 *THE DEPARTURE OF DERMOT: STANDISH O'GRADY; *Talbot Press [Ireland].*

A very slight, but arresting semi-fictional sketch of King Dermot of Leinster's preparation, in the year 1166, for sailing to Bristol.

265. "WHEN THE NORMAN CAME": MICHAEL O'HANRAHAN; [*O'Hannrachain*] *Maunsel.*

Ireland (Wexford, Dublin, etc.), 1167. A story illustrating the time of King Diarmid (or Dermot) Mac Murrough of Leinster and Strongbow (Earl of Pembroke), his Norman ally.

266. THE FALCON KING: W. L. O'BYRNE; *Juv. Blackie.*

Good semi-fictional sketches dealing with the period of Henry II. The book begins Wales, 1146; then passes to France; but culminates in the Anglo-Norman Invasion of Ireland, 1170 (Strongbow, Dermot, etc.)

267. JEHANNE OF THE FOREST: L. A. TALBOT; *Melrose.*

England (Forest of Wyre and Clee Hills district) in the early part of Henry II's reign. An interesting story of love, fighting, and adventure. The Mortimers are prominent—especially Hugh de Mortimer of Wigmore.

268. THE LOVE STORY OF GIRALDUS: ALICE CUNNINGHAME; *Griffiths.*

The French Court and the University of Paris, also the Welsh Borders, mainly late 12th Century. A story supposed to be related by " Giraldus Cambrensis " (Gerald de Barri) who, when Henry II refused to confirm his election as Bishop of St. Davids (1176), went to Paris. Eleanor of Poitou is a prominent figure.

269. *THE FOOL: H. C. BAILEY; *Methuen [Eng.], Dutton [U.S.A.].*

Begins Malmesbury, 1140 (Civil War between Stephen and Matilda), but the main story is written round Henry II in various parts of England and France from 1153 right up to his death in 1189. Altogether a very interesting, and historically-suggestive romance.

270. DOLPHIN OF THE SEPULCHRE: GERTRUDE HOLLIS; *Juv. S.P.C.K. [Eng.], Gorham [U.S.A.].*

England (Northampton, London, Canterbury, etc.), and France, 1161-70. A tale of the early part of Henry II's reign, dealing especially with the career of Becket after he had been made Archbishop of Canterbury. Covers the time of the Council of Clarendon, and Becket's exile in France (the six years there being lightly touched). Ends with the martyrdom in Canterbury Cathedral. King Henry II and Thomas à Becket are both prominently introduced.

271. THE SHADOW OF THE RAGGEDSTONE: Charles F. Grindrod; *Mathews & Marrot.*

Malvern Hills region, c. 1164. A tale in which the Religious (or Monastic) life, and the life of the World, are commingled. Illustrates the period of struggle between Church and State, when the quarrel between Henry II and Thomas à Becket was in its early stages. Both Becket and the king appear. *N.B.* This novel was first printed in 1887, but the edition of 1909 is described by the author himself as " much revised."

272. *DER HEILIGE: Conrad Ferdinand Meyer; *Haessel [Germany].*

An historical novel of great merit, dealing with Thomas à Becket. Like the same Swiss author's *Jörg Jenatsch* (given elsewhere), the present book has passed through many editions.

273. BEAU REGARD: Dorothy Brandon; *Melrose.*

Winchester, 1170. A rather sensational Troubadour story, dealing with the time of Becket and Fair Rosamond. Queen Eleanor (Eleanor of Aquitaine) is prominently introduced.

274. THE KING AND THE LADY: " E. Barrington "; in " The Gallants "—*Harrap.*

A short tale of Queen Eleanor, Rosemonde de Clifford (" Fair Rosamond "), and King Henry II.

275. ¹FAIR ROSAMOND: Bernard Capes; in " Historical Vignettes "—*Fisher Unwin [Eng.], Stokes [U.S.A.].*

Queen Eleanor and " Fair Rosamond," about 1176.

¹ The volume in which this story appears, viz. *Historical Vignettes,* contains a large number of brief fictional sketches based on history and legend. Some of the " vignettes " are distressing, others are humorous; they treat of many countries and periods—First Century Palestine, England in Saxon and later times, France, Italy, etc. Of the twenty-seven tales (each covering not more than a dozen pages) eight are given in my lists as showing the author at his best.

276. BOYS OF THE BORDER: George Bennett; *Juv. Blackie.*

A good story of the Welsh Marches (Caerleon) in the time of King Henry II (c. 1170-77).

277. IN HIS NAME: E. Everett Hale; *Juv. Seeley [Eng.], Little, Brown [U.S.A.].*

A tale of Lyons in the time of Pierre Waldo, founder of the sect named Waldenses (the " Poor Men of Lyons "). The heroine's father is presented as a relative of Waldo.

278. *THE UNHURRYING CHASE: H. F. M. Prescott; *Constable.*

An unusually fine example of historical fiction. A romance of several localities (Angoulême, Perigueux, etc.), about the period 1176-86. The outstanding figure is Richard Lion Heart, who appears as Count of Poitou and Duke of Aquitaine. The title—with its Francis Thompson reference—suggests the conflict of differing human motives which the reader will find illustrated in the book's fictional development.

279. SIR RANULF: E. K. Seth-Smith; *Juv. S.P.C.K. [Eng.], Macmillan [U.S.A.].*

Various West Country localities, including Glastonbury, 1184. A story of St. Hugh of Lincoln, in which King Henry II appears.

280. FOREST OUTLAWS: Edward Gilliat; *Juv. Seeley [Eng.], Dutton [U.S.A.].*

Another tale of St. Hugh of Lincoln in the period 1186 onwards. Many localities and historical figures. Written by a man of scholarly attainments.

281. *THE FORTUNES OF GARIN: Mary Johnston; *Constable [Eng.], Houghton Mifflin [U.S.A.].*

Mostly Southern France, and the East, in the last quarter of the 12th Century. A story dealing with the period of the Free Lances, Troubadours, etc. " Duke " Richard (i.e. Richard Lion Heart) and Saladin, are among the historical figures introduced,

282. THE WAY TO JERUSALEM: G. I. Whitham; *Juv.* In " The Shepherd of the Ocean," etc.—*Wells Gardner.*
Fictional sketches of Richard Cœur-de-Lion from boyhood to death. France (chiefly) and Palestine, etc.

---

283. THE BRETHREN: H. Rider Haggard; *Cassell [Eng.], McClure [U.S.A.].*
England (Essex) and the East (Damascus, Ascalon and Jerusalem), c. 1185-88. A story of the time immediately preceding the Third Crusade, telling of Englishmen in Syria, etc., and the special reason of their being in those parts. After recounting various fictional developments, the book leads up to the storming and capture of Jerusalem by Saladin in 1187. Saladin himself is a prominent figure in the tale.

---

284. BETWEEN TWO CRUSADES: Gertrude Hollis; *Juv. S.P.C.K. [Eng.], Gorham [U.S.A.].*
A tale illustrating the downfall of the Latin kingdom of Jerusalem in 1187 (Saladin).

---

285. *THE BETROTHED: Sir Walter Scott; *Black, and various publishers—English and American.*
A good adventure story of the Welsh Border in the time of Henry II's Welsh Wars, 1187. King Henry, Prince John, and Prince Richard are the principal historic figures.

---

286. THE KNIGHT OF RAVENSWOOD: " Mavis Warrington "; *Juv. Jarrolds.*
S. England (Hants., etc.), 1189-90. A tale in which Richard the Lionheart is the outstanding figure (his coronation, etc.). Robin Hood also appears. The book ends with Richard's departure for the East in company with Philip of France.

---

287. THE WALLS OF ACRE: Margaret Baines Reed; *Juv. Arnold.*
Palestine, 1190-91. A tale of the Siege of Acre and the Battle of Arsuf. Introduces Richard I, King Philip of France, and others.

---

288. *THE TALISMAN: Sir Walter Scott; *Black and other publishers—English and American.*
Palestine, 1191. This tale has, of course, always been among the most popular examples of Scott; it deals with the time of the truce in the Third Crusade. Richard Cœur-de-Lion is an outstanding figure, and David, Earl of Huntingdon, is greatly to the fore. Other important personages appearing in the romance are: Philip Augustus of France, Saladin, Leopold Archduke of Austria, Conrade of Montferrat, and Berengaria (wife of Richard).

---

289. A STAINLESS SWORD: J. J. Kelly; *Juv. The Talbot Press [Ireland].*
Egypt and Palestine, between 1188 and 1194. A tale of " soldier and priest," based largely on Michaud's *History of the Crusades*, and dealing with the Third Crusade. Covers the Siege of Tyre, also Acre, etc. Several historic figures, including Saladin, Richard Cœur-de-Lion and Conrad de Montferrat. There are, also, allusions to Philip-Augustus and Frederick Barbarossa.

---

290. WINNING HIS SPURS: G. A. Henty; *Juv. Sampson Low.*
A story of varied scenes. England, France, Palestine (the Third Crusade), Germany, etc., about 1190-94. This adventure tale covers many historic European events, besides touching English matters (Prince John's plots, etc.) Ends with King Richard's return in 1194.

---

291. WESTMINSTER CLOISTERS: Mary Bidder; *Wells Gardner.*
Story of a monk-artist at Westminster in 1193, introducing Richard I, Queen Eleanor, Prince John and others.

292. HENRY DE POMEROY: Mrs. Anna Eliza Bray; *Chapman & Hall.*

An old-fashioned novel of the West Country in the time of Richard I. Mrs. Bray spent a large part of her life in Devonshire, and this book contains some good local colour—Tavistock, Berry Pomeroy, and the Dartmoor region generally being touched, as well as St. Michael's Mount (Cornwall).

293. *THE LIFE AND DEATH OF RICHARD YEA-AND-NAY: Maurice Hewlett; *Macmillan.*

Richard Cœur-de-Lion in the period 1189-1199 (largely 1189-91). France (Normandy, etc.), England (a mere glimpse), Sicily, Acre, etc. A romance of unusual power, depicting Richard's character very suggestively, and illustrating the events and conspiracies of the time. Covers the two marriages of Richard, his accession on the death of his father Henry II, and his exploits in Palestine, etc. Besides the outstanding figure of Richard as Prince and King alternately, Jehanne Saint-Pol, Berengaria of Navarre, King Henry II, and Prince John are all prominently introduced; while the young King Philip-Augustus of France, King Tancred of Sicily, and others appear.

294. *MAID MARIAN: Thomas Love Peacock; *Macmillan.*

This well-known tale is described by the author himself as a " comic romance," and —like most of the Robin Hood stories—it is not properly historical. The novelist, however, fixes on the Henry II—Richard I period, introducing Lion-heart himself and Prince John.

295. IN THE DAYS OF LIONHEART: William Gandy; *Juv. Harrap.*

Wakefield and West Yorkshire in Henry II—Richard I time. The tale introduces Robin Hood, and (at the end) King Richard.

296. LION-HEART: " Herbert Strang " and Richard Stead; *Juv. Oxford University Press.*

Welsh Border (Wye Valley region), 1189; then Oxford, etc., and the period of John's plots in his brother's absence (1190-91). A large portion, however, of this short, but excellent, tale deals with the Third Crusade (Acre and the Battle of Arsuf in 1191)— Richard I and Saladin prominent. Ends with Richard's death in 1199.

297. HURRAH! FOR MERRY SHERWOOD: S. Walkey; *Juv. Cassell.*

A Forest tale, depicting Prince John plotting against King Richard in the latter's supposed absence. Richard appears (mostly in disguise).

298. *ROBIN HOOD AND THE MEN OF THE GREENWOOD: Henry Gilbert; *Juv. Jack.*

Sherwood in the Henry II—John period. Besides presenting the usual characters of Robin Hood fiction (King Richard I introduced of course), this tale has a good background of history, the author having attempted to depict the times faithfully. The book is well illustrated by Walter Crane.

299. *IVANHOE: Sir Walter Scott; *Black and other publishers— English and American.*

Leicestershire in 1194—the period being that of John's Regency in Richard I's supposed absence. This popular, and (one may say) world-famed, story illustrates general manners as well as political intrigues. In regard to the contrast here made between Norman and Saxon, historians have pointed out that the material for such a contrast no longer existed at the end of the 12th Century. Richard Lion-Heart is, of course, the outstanding historic figure. Prince John and the usual Robin Hood group are also introduced.

THIRTEENTH CENTURY

300. PHILIP AUGUSTUS: G. P. R. James; *Routledge* [*Eng.*], *Dutton* [*U.S.A.*].

France (Paris, Rouen, etc.) mainly in the period 1200-1214. An imaginative depiction of Philip II (i.e. Philip-Augustus) of France. The romance covers Philip's quarrel with Pope Innocent III; the murder of Prince Arthur Plantagenet; the Battle of Bovines (when Philip defeated Otho, Emperor of Germany)—these are some of the chief events. Besides Prince Arthur already named, King John of England appears.

301. *THE CRIMSON GONDOLA: Nathan Gallizier; *Page* [*U.S.A.*].

Constantinople 1203-4 (*Prelude :* Venice 1201). A story of the time of the Fourth Crusade, having for background the trouble between Venice and the Byzantine Emperor, Alexius III. The hero is sent on a mission from Venice to demand the release of the Emperor's ward, Eleanor, daughter of Conrad of Montferrat, and the novel tells of his experiences in Constantinople. There is some good word-painting in the description of the Byzantine capital; and the accounts of the Green and Blue factions, of the Rebellion and flight of the Emperor, and of the siege of the city by the Venetian fleet, are well written. The author's sensational tendencies are, perhaps, more under restraint than usual. The outstanding figures of the story, besides the hero, are the Emperor Alexius, the Empress Euphrosyné, the Lady of Montferrat, and Alexis Ducas Mouzzouffles the Armenian. There are many allusions to Count Baldwin of Flanders and other historic personages (the *Epilogue* briefly tells of Baldwin's coronation as Emperor of the East).

302. *THE HEART'S KEY: Maurice Hewlett; in " Fond Adventures "—*Macmillan* [*Eng.*], *Harper* [*U.S.A.*].

A tale of Southern France (Toulouse) at the beginning of the 13th Century.

303. *A SERVANT OF THE MIGHTIEST: Mrs. Alfred Wingate; *Crosby Lockwood* [*Eng.*], *Brentano's* [*U.S.A.*].

Chingiz Khan, and the Mongol Conquest of China, etc. An interesting novel based on much research (Howorth and other authorities); it spreads over a long period (1160-1227), but is mainly concerned with the years between 1203 and 1227.

304. WALDEMAR: B. S. Ingemann; trans. *Saunders & Otley*; also *Bentley*.

Denmark, 1204. The first of a series of historical novels by a Danish writer of note.

305. THE FLAME-GATHERERS: Margaret Horton Potter; *Macmillan.*

India (Mandu) 1205-50. A tale illustrating the conditions which prevailed in Mandu up to, and including, the Mohammedan Conquest in 1250.

306. THE CASTLE OF EHRENSTEIN: G. P. R. James; *Routledge* [*Eng.*], *Dutton* [*U.S.A.*].

Germany at the beginning of the 13th Century. A novel of mediæval atmosphere rather than of particular historical events.

307. ROYSTON GOWER: Thomas Miller; *Colburn,* 1838.

Sherwood Forest, mainly about 1207-13. A Robin Hood romance, reflecting the time of King John's quarrel with Pope Innocent III and the Interdict which ensued (1208-13). The tale ends with the withdrawal of the Interdict. The most important historic figures are: King John, his consort Isabella of Angoulême, and Cardinal Langton.

308. *RUNNYMEDE AND LINCOLN FAIR: JOHN GEORGE EDGAR; *Juv. Dent* [*Eng.*], *Dutton* [*U.S.A*].

England mainly 1214-17. Begins just after King John's defeat at the Battle of Bouvines (1214); and covers in turn: the great scene at Runnymede (signing of the Charter); the death of King John; the Coronation of Henry III; the naval victory over the French off Kent; the success of the Earl of Pembroke (Regent) against Louis the Dauphin at Lincoln; lastly, the Rising of the London citizens (Fitzarnulph). The tale is interesting, though somewhat over-historical; it is largely based on Roger of Wendover. A great many historical figures: King John, Isabel of Angoulême, King Philip-Augustus of France, Louis the Dauphin, Lord Nevile, William de Collingham, Hubert de Burgh, the Earl of Pembroke, etc.

309 *THE TREASURE AND THE LAW: RUDYARD KIPLING; *Juv.* In " Puck of Pook's Hill "—*Macmillan*

A Jew's tale of the England of King John's reign.

310. ROBIN HOOD AND HIS MERRY MEN: ESCOTT LYNN; *Juv. Chambers.*

Sherwood, etc., in the time of King John. The story depicts Runnymede and Magna Charta—the men of Sherwood helping the Barons against John.

311. GILBERT THE OUTLAW: D. H. PARRY; *Juv. Cassell.*

An adventure story of England at the beginning of the 13th Century. Sherwood and Robin Hood, Runnymede and King John, etc., ending in the year of John's death, 1216.

312. THE CONSTABLE'S TOWER: CHARLOTTE M. YONGE; *Juv. National Society* [*Eng.*], *Whittaker* [*U.S.A.*].

Dover, Windsor, etc., in the days of King John and Magna Charta: Hubert de Burgh and the Siege of Dover Castle by Louis, the French Dauphin.

313. THE GOOD SWORD BELGARDE: A. C. CURTIS; *Juv. Oxford University Press* [*Eng.*], *Dodd* [*U.S.A.*].

French and English in the late period of King John. A tale of the Siege of Dover (1216) and its defence by De Burgh, following the English Baron's invitation to the French Dauphin to come over and be their leader.

314. *HERE COMES AN OLD SAILOR: ALFRED TRESIDDER SHEPPARD; *Hodder & Stoughton.*

Mainly Kent and the Channel region of the Cinque Ports, late 12th to early 13th Century (John—Henry III). This very striking and original historical novel does not lend itself easily to a short descriptive note. The book presents " a tale within a tale " —the brief Part I being in the nature of a Prelude to the real story (Part II) which ends at the point where the early pages of the volume begin. Under the form of a " Lection " or series of readings to the monks of a Religious House at Reculver, the story of a Kentish family is given. The narrative, though in part legendary, is full of historical references (the Interdict, the Great Charter, the death of John, etc., etc.); moreover, besides giving these references, the author does more than allude—he actually introduces the figure of King John several times, and ends with a vivid description of the historic naval victory of the English over the French off Sandwich in 1217. The mediæval atmosphere is well conveyed in this record of great wrongs and brave deeds, of love and hate. Altogether, a novel of exceptional power, both historically and psychologically.

315. JOAN OF THE TOWER: WARWICK DEEPING; *Cassell.*

A South of England story dealing with the time of King John. Introduces the King himself, and ends with his death, 1216.

316. CROSS AND DAGGER: W. SCOTT DURRANT; *Juv. Methuen* [*Eng.*], *Lane* [*U.S.A.*].

Germany (Otto IV) and the Children's Crusade; then France, Egypt, Syria (largely), and Sicily, 1212-22. " The Old Man of the Mountain," St. Francis of Assisi, and the Emperor Frederick II.

317. THE SIGN OF TRIUMPH: Sheppard Stevens; *Juv. Chapman & Hall [Eng.], Page [U.S.A.].*
France, 1212. A tale of the Children's Crusade, and of experiences during the march to the Mediterranean.

318. THE DISTANT LAMP; Harold Begbie; *Hodder & Stoughton.*
France (Tours), 1212; also Egypt and the Holy Land. An interesting story dealing with the time of the Children's Crusade.

319. ON THE FORGOTTEN ROAD: Henry Baerlein; *Murray.*
Mainly France, 1212: time of Philip-Augustus and the Children's Crusade. The later portion of this fictional autobiography covers twenty-three years' captivity in Egypt, and ends with a glimpse of France in 1235 (St. Louis).

320. THE DIVINE MINSTRELS: Auguste Bailly (trans.); *Lee Warner [Eng.], Scribner [U.S.A.].*
Umbria in the early Thirteenth Century. A narrative dealing with the life of St. Francis of Assisi and ending with his death in 1224.

321. THE ALBIGENSES: Charles Robert Maturin; *Hurst & Blackett* also *Constable.*
A tale of France c. 1216-18. Illustrates the time of the Civil War in Languedoc which followed De Montfort's crusade against the Albigenses (this De Montfort was *father* of the great Earl of Leicester). Various historical personages appear.

322. *GREATER THAN THE GREATEST: Hamilton Drummond; *Stanley Paul.*
Rome, 1227, at the beginning of Gregory IX's pontificate; then, for the most part, Sicily (Capua), and the Court of the Emperor Frederick II. The story hinges on the feud between Pope and Emperor. One of the best examples of the author as historical novelist.

323. *LA BATTAGLIA DI BENEVENTO: Francesco Domenico Guerrazzi; *Giuseppe Maspero [Italy],* 1829.
Italy during the period of the Emperor Frederick II. One of the distinguished author's best-known historical romances.

324. THE BETRAYERS: Hamilton Drummond; *Stanley Paul.*
Lyons, Turin, and Parma in the period 1245-1248. The struggle between the Emperor Frederick II and Pope Innocent IV is the main theme. The Emperor is carefully depicted, and, if not the actual " hero " of the novel, he is the outstanding figure.

325. A SON OF THE EMPEROR: Newton V. Stewart; *Methuen.*
Germany and Italy, mainly between 1220 and 1255. A novel dealing with the Emperor Frederick II and his son Enzio, King of Sardinia. Painstaking in the historical sense, but as fiction somewhat deficient in interest.

326. THE CARDINAL: Newton V. Stewart; *Stanley Paul.*
Constantinople, and—mainly—Italy (Bologna), covering much the same period as the author's *A Son of the Emperor,* to which it is in some degree the sequel. The Cardinal of the title is Ottaviano Ubaldini, while other figures are Baldwin II, the Emperor Frederick II (just before his death in 1250), Enzio King of Sardinia, and Pope Innocent IV.

327. *THE ROUT OF THE FOREIGNER: Gulielma Zollinger; *Juv. McClurg [U.S.A.].*
Bedfordshire, the Midlands and London, 1223-24. An early Henry III tale illustrating the losing influence of those foreigners in high position who, at the beginning of the century in John's reign, had come over to England. The book ends with the Siege of Bedford. Archbishop Langton figures prominently, while Hubert de Burgh and other historic personages appear.

328. *THE EARL'S WHITE CROSS: David Ker; *Juv. Chambers.*
France, Oxford, Wales, and various localities in the period, 1252-65. A good historical story covering the Battle of Lewes, and introducing several historic figures. Simon de Montfort is specially prominent—King Henry III, Prince Edward, Prince Llewellyn, and others being also introduced.

---

329. THE HOUSE OF WALDERNE: A. D. Crake; *Juv. Longmans.*
Sussex; also Kenilworth, Oxford, etc., 1253-64. A tale of the Barons' Wars, ending with the Battle of Lewes.

---

330. A CLERK OF OXFORD: E. Everett Green; *Juv. Nelson.*
An interesting tale of Oxford, Kenilworth, etc., in the time of the Barons' Wars. The Battle of Lewes is introduced.

---

331. THE OUTLAW OF TORN: E. R. Burroughes; *Methuen.*
England (London, Derbyshire, Essex, etc.), 1243-64 (mainly 1262-64). This outlaw-and-love story is a really good example of its kind; there are thrilling fictional developments (perhaps one or two situations approach melodrama), and these are closely associated with real historic figures. The main period is that of the Barons' Wars—one of the events introduced being the Battle of Lewes. A number of real personages play important parts in the novel. The central figure is Prince Richard (youngest son of King Henry III), while among those more or less to the fore at various points in the novel are: Henry and his Queen (Eleanor of Provence), Simon de Montfort (Earl of Leicester) and Lady Bertrade his daughter, and Prince Philip of France—afterwards Philip III (" *le Hardi* "). De Montfort's sons and other figures appear to a slight extent.

---

332. THE RED SAINT: Warwick Deeping; *Cassell.*
A novel of Kent and Sussex during the Barons' Wars. The Battle of Lewes is introduced, while De Montfort and other important personages appear.

---

333. FOREST DAYS: G. P. R. James; *Routledge [Eng.], Dutton [U.S.A.].*
A good story chiefly dealing with Yorkshire and Nottinghamshire (Sherwood) round about the year 1265. Besides the Robin Hood element, there is a substantial background of history—the Battle of Evesham in particular. De Montfort, Prince Edward, and Henry III are more or less prominent.

---

334. DE MONTFORT'S SQUIRE: Frederick Harrison; *Juv. S.P.C.K. [Eng.], Gorham [U.S.A.].*
Sussex, 1264-65. A tale covering the Battles of Lewes and Evesham, and introducing Simon de Montfort, Roger Bacon, Prince Edward, and others.

---

335. THE THIRSTY SWORD: Robert Leighton; *Juv. Blackie [Eng.], Scribner [U.S.A.].*
A tale of the Norse invasion of Scotland, 1262-63. King Alexander III of Scotland, and his victory over Haco V of Norway at Largs in 1263.

---

336. THE WHITE QUEEN (formerly entitled: *Falaise of the Blessed Voice*): W. Stearns Davis; *Macmillan.*
France (Pontoise largely), c. 1237. A romantic tale of King Louis IX (St. Louis) as a young man, and his Queen, Margaret of Provence. The Queen-Mother (Blanche of Castile) is also introduced.

---

337. *EYES OF YOUTH: John Buchan; in "The Path of the King" —*Nelson [Eng.], Doran [U.S.A.].*
King Louis of France at Acre, 1249, and a Frankish knight's mission to the Tartars.

E

338. THE ORIFLAMME IN EGYPT: C. H. Butcher, D.D.; *Dent.*
England (Wiltshire) and Egypt, 1248-50. A story beginning in the England of
Henry III, but quickly passing to Egypt and the Crusade of Louis IX of France (St.
Louis)—Damietta and the disaster of Mansourah. Several historic figures, including
St. Louis, Queen Margaret of France, William Longsword Earl of Salisbury, and
Matthew Paris (" the best Latin chronicler of the Thirteenth Century ").

339. *ARNOUL THE ENGLISHMAN: Francis Aveling; *Methuen.*
Buckfast (Devon), Paris and Anagni (Papal Court), within the decade 1250-60.
Illustrates Paris in the period of Secularists *v.* Regularists, dealing largely with the
University disputes over Plato and Aristotle, Abelard and Bernard, etc. The tale begins
and ends in South Devon. King Louis IX (St. Louis) and Pope Alexander IV appear,
while Thomas Aquinas is quite prominently introduced. There is also a glimpse of
Henry III of England.

340. *THE BELLBO HERITAGE: Verner von Heidenstam (trans.);
being Part II of " The Tree of the Folkungs "—*Gyldendal.*
Sweden about the period 1250-75. Time of Valdemar and the Battle of Hofva.

341. *MESSER MARCO POLO: Donn Byrne; *Sampson Low* [*Eng.*],
Century [*U.S.A.*].
Venice, the near East, and China, late Thirteenth Century. As the title itself suggests
this romance deals with travels and experiences in the period of St. Louis of France,
the Emperor Baldwin II, Kubla Khan, etc.

342. *CASTEL DEL MONTE: Nathan Gallizier; *Dean* [*Eng.*],
Page [*U.S.A.*].
Largely Palermo, 1265-66. A highly-coloured romance of love and adventure, into
which are woven certain important historical events. Begins just before the Coronation
of Manfred, Prince of Tarentum, as King of Sicily, and reflects the political situation
which the Duke of Anjou's claim to the kingship developed. Later chapters take the
reader to the ceremony which proved to be one of papal excommunication instead of
coronation; then to the arrival of Charles of Anjou in Rome and his march southward;
lastly, to the battle of Benevento, where Manfred fell and—with him—the Hohenstaufen
Dynasty of Italy (1266). Manfred is the outstanding historic figure—his wife, Helena
of Epirus also appearing, along with several other personages.

343. THE HILL OF VENUS: Nathan Gallizier; *Page* [*U.S.A*].
Italy (various localities, including Avellino, Vallombrosa, Rome, Viterbo, and
Naples), 1266-68. Story of a youth who under compulsion takes monkish vows: his
love for a maiden at the Court of Avellino, his numerous adventures, and his breaking
of ecclesiastical bonds. The historical background is the Guelph *v.* Ghibelline struggle.
Charles of Anjou's defeat of Conradino of Swabia at Tagliacozzo is merely given as
news. Various historical figures appear, including Pope Clement IV, Charles of Anjou,
and Conradino.

344. PROVENZANO THE PROUD: Evelyn H. Gifford; *Smith,
Elder.*
Italy, 1268 onwards. The struggle between Siena and Florence; the Battle of
Tagliacozzo, etc.

345. CRISTINA: Emily Underdown; *Sonnenschein.*
Italy (chiefly Siena), in 1268. Depicts the time just after Manfred's defeat and death
at Benevento, when Charles of Anjou had entered Italy with an army, and had put
himself at the head of the Guelph, or Papal, party. In this novel we find Conradin
of Swabia—the " boy king " of the Two Sicilies—taking Manfred's place on the side
of the Ghibelline or Imperial party; successful at first, he was ultimately defeated at
Tagliacozzo (1268)—that battle being one of several military events introduced. The
Provenzano Salvani of the story is really historical, while, of the notabilities introduced,
Charles of Anjou and Conradin are the most important.

346. FLORESTANE THE TROUBADOUR: Julia de Wolf Addison;
Dana Estes.
S. France (chiefly) and Italy about the year 1270. Cimabue, the Painter, is introduced, while there are glimpses of Dante (as little boy) and of Sordello.

---

347. THE BOY AND THE BARON: Adeline Knapp; *Juv. Century.*
Germany, about 1260-80. The robber knights, and their suppression by Rudolf I of Hapsburg.

---

348. THE SAINT OF THE DRAGON'S DALE: W. Stearns Davis;
Macmillan.
Eisenach and the Thuringian forest region at the time of Rudolf I's suppression of the robber knights. A slight and somewhat indefinite tale.

---

349. *OTTO OF THE SILVER HAND: Howard Pyle; *Juv. Scribner.*
A fascinating story of a little boy in the Germany of the late Thirteenth Century. The book is charmingly illustrated by the author.

---

350. THE SWORD MAKER: Robert Barr; *Mills & Boon* [*Eng.*],
Stokes [*U.S.A.*].
A romance of Germany (Frankfort, etc.) just before and after the Emperor Rudolf I's death in 1291. Time of the Robber Barons of the Rhine.

---

351. SAN CELESTINO: "J. Ayscough"; *Smith, Elder* [*Eng.*], *Putnam*
[*U.S.A.*].
The career—from boyhood to death—of Piétro di Murrone (1215-96), who founded the Celestines, and became Pope in 1294 as Celestine V for five months.

---

352. THE GOD OF LOVE: Justin H. McCarthy; *Hurst & Blackett*
[*Eng.*], *Harper* [*U.S.A.*].
Florence about 1290. Dante and Beatrice (supposed narration by a friend of the poet).

---

353. THE BARON OF ILL-FAME: Hester Barton; *Stanley Paul.*
Florence, 1292-1302, Corso Donati (nicknamed "Baron of Ill-Fame"), and the poet Dante, are introduced along with other historic figures.

---

354. *THE PRINCE AND THE PAGE: Charlotte M. Yonge; *Juv.*
Macmillan.
England, Tunis, etc., and Acre, mostly in the period 1269-74 (Henry III—Edward I). Begins just after the Battle of Evesham, and deals to a large extent with the sons of Simon de Montfort. Describes the attempted assassination of Prince Edward during the last crusade, and, in a later chapter, his coronation. The central figure throughout is Edward, but there are other prominent historic personages, including Eleanor of Castile and the De Montforts (already named). Charles of Anjou (King of Sicily) appears.

---

355. THE NAMELESS PRINCE: Grace I. Whitham; *Juv. Blackie.*
Tale of a youth of Plantagenet blood in the closing years of the 13th Century. King Edward I is prominent. A good tale.

---

356. MORLAC OF GASCONY: Maud Stepney Rawson; *Hutchinson.*
Rye and Winchelsea in 1287, and 1293 onwards. A novel dealing with French plots in connection with the Cinque Ports. King Edward I is prominent.

---

357. A FORGOTTEN HERO; OR, NOT FOR HIM, formerly
"NOT FOR HIM: THE STORY OF A FORGOTTEN
HERO": Emily S. Holt; *Juv. Shaw.*
Cornwall and Berkhampstead, 1290-98. A tale of Edmund, Earl of Cornwall.

FOURTEETH CENTURY

358. *THE SCOTTISH CHIEFS: Jane Porter; *Juv.* Routledge, and other publishers.*

Scotland, and, to a much less extent, France and England, 1296-1305. Wallace is the outstanding figure, though Bruce is also prominent, in this famous romance of the Scottish struggle against Edward I. The story proper covers the period up to the execution of Wallace in London, though the last few pages carry the reader to Bannockburn (1314). Besides the two great Scottish patriots already named, a crowd of historic personages appear, including King Edward I of England and King Philip IV of France.

359. IN FREEDOM'S CAUSE: G. A. Henty; *Juv.* Blackie [Eng.], Scribner [U.S.A.].

Lanark, Ayr, Edinburgh, Stirling, etc., 1297-1314; there is also a glimpse of Ireland (Donegal) in the course of the tale. A number of historic occurrences are covered, including the Battles of Falkirk and Bannockburn. The principal figures introduced are Wallace, Bruce, and Edward I.

360. CASTLE DANGEROUS: Sir Walter Scott; *Black, and other publishers—English and American.*

Ayrshire and Lanarkshire, 1306. A story of the Scottish Wars (Scotland v. England) shortly before Edward I's death (1307). Some of the figures are historical, though not one is of the first importance.

361. THE CHEVALIER OF THE SPLENDID CREST: Sir Herbert Maxwell; *Blackwood.*

N.W. England and Scotland (Galloway, etc.), 1306-1314 (Edward I-II). A carefully written story with a large background of history. Covers the crowning of Robert Bruce, the death of Edward I, and the English invasion of Scotland culminating in the defeat of Edward II at Bannockburn. Edward I, Robert Bruce, and Edward II are all three introduced more or less prominently.

362. THE DAYS OF BRUCE: Grace Aguilar; *Routledge [Eng.], Dutton [U.S.A.].*

Scotland and (in much less degree) England, 1306-1314. Robert Bruce and Edward I are prominent in this old-fashioned tale, which virtually ends with the defeat of Edward II's army at Bannockburn.

363. *THE LION OF FLANDERS: Hendrik Conscience (trans.); *Lambert.*

Flanders (largely Bruges) and France (Compiègne), 1298-1302. A good tale of the Flemish Rising in the French occupation period—covering the Massacre of Bruges, and the Battle of Courtrai (the " Day of Spurs "). Also depicts the condition of affairs prior to the Rising: the pro-French attitude of the Flemish nobles as against the popular aspirations in the direction of liberty. The chief historical personages are: Robert de Bethune (the " Lion of Flanders "), Count Guy of Flanders, Charles de Valois, Philip IV of France (Philip " the Fair ") and his wife Joanna of Navarre.

364. A LADY OF FRANCE: Beryl Symons; *Stanley Paul.*

Paris, 1307 onwards. A romance depicting the life of mediæval Paris, and, on the more detailed historical side, especially reflecting the quarrel between King Philip IV and Pope Boniface VIII. Both King Philip (Philippe) and his Queen are prominently introduced.

365. A MAKER OF SAINTS: Hamilton Drummond; *Stanley Paul.*

A good tale of an Italian sculptor (one of whose two pupils is an Englishman) at the beginning of the 14th Century. Depicts Italian life in the Guelph and Ghibelline period. The poet Dante is introduced.

366. *IN THE SHADOW OF THE CROWN: Miss M. Bidder, with Introduction by Maurice Hewlett; *Constable.*
England, c. 1323-33 (Edward II-III). A really good historical romance, giving an unconventional presentment of Edward II, and introducing many important events and personages. Prince John of Eltham (Edward II's second son) may be called the hero, while his brother Edward III, Lord Roger Mortimer, and Queen Isabella (Edward II's wife) are prominent. The English victory over the Scots at Halidon Hill is one of the outstanding events.

367. *THE WHISTLING MAID: Ernest Rhys; *Hutchinson.*
A romance of Wales (various localities including Caermarthen and the Vale of Towey) in the early 14th Century. There is not much actual history, but readers are given an impressive little picture of Lord Mortimer and Queen Isabella at Bristol in 1326.

368. *THE KING'S KNIGHT: G. I. Whitham; *Juv. Blackie.*
An excellent historical tale of the Edward II-III period (Yorkshire and Durham districts). Illustrates the period of the Scottish ravages, etc. King Edward III is introduced as a young man just after his accession.

369. *THE UGLY DUCHESS: Lion Feuchtwanger (trans.); *Secker* [*Eng.*], *Viking Press* [*U.S.A.*].
The Tyrol, Bavaria, and many other adjacent regions of mid-Europe, mostly within the period between 1330 and 1360. On the ground of vigour, and knowledge of historical by-ways, this romance is little—if at all—below the standard of its very successful predecessor *Jew Süss*. Whether on the side of character-drawing and dramatic situations, the more recently published novel is to be classed below the other—*that* question is fairly debatable, though, at the time of writing this descriptive note (December, 1927), reviewers seem on the whole to have done less than justice to *The Ugly Duchess*. Undoubtedly Margareta Duchess of Tyrol is " ugly " in character and disposition, as well as in face; but the masterly account of her domestic and social insights, and of her growth in the handling of big political issues, can hardly fail to arouse interest. Of the masculine portraits, the young Duke Johann, and the three political schemers—Heinrich of Wittelsbach (Bavarian), Albert of Austria (a Habsburg), and John the blind King of Bohemia (Luxemburger)—are all more or less carefully drawn. Other noteworthy characters are the Emperors Ludwig (Lewis IV who died 1347) and Karl (Charles IV) respectively, Rudolf of Austria (Habsburger), Duke Johann the Luxemburger, and Konrad the Frauenberger. All these historical figures appear more or less prominently, but there are many sketches, or glimpses, of other real personages— Pope John XXII at Avignon (especially the vivid picture of him given on page 47), Pope Clement VI (" no theorist such as the deceased Benedict had been, but a man of the world, a splendid prince and ruler and politician "—page 123), William of Occam the schoolman (a glimpse)—these and other figures are skilfully introduced. There are, moreover, several allusions to, or descriptions of, historic events such as:—the Battle of Crécy, at which John of Bohemia—as an ally of Philip VI of France—fought and fell (this episode and the battle itself are strikingly, if briefly, given); the terrible epidemic of the " Black Death " which visited Europe about 1348; and the settlement and more or less dangerous position of Jews in German cities about this time (the Jew, Mendel Hirsch, is an arresting figure in the story). One may remind English readers that Anne, daughter of Charles IV (the " Emperor Karl " of this romance) married Richard II of England— his first wife.

370. MARCO VISCONTI: Tommaso Grossi (trans.); *Bell* [*Eng.*], *Macmillan* [*U.S.A.*].
Milan and Lake Como district in the second quarter of the 14th Century. A romance of some note in its day, illustrating the Guelph and Ghibelline period.

371. *'NEATH THE HOOF OF THE TARTAR: Baron Nicholas Jósika (trans.); *Jarrold.*
Hungary (Pest, etc.) round about 1340. An historical romance of considerable vigour, depicting the troubled period when the Tartars under Batu Khan (nephew

of the great Khan Oktai) invaded Hungary in the reign of Béla IV. The events preceding the invasion are fully described, while later chapters cover the Battle of Mohi and the Kun Massacre, etc., ending with the departure of the Mongols and the return of King Béla. The most important figures introduced are the King and Queen of Hungary, Kuthen King of the Kunok people (between the Volga and the Dnieper), and Batu Khan.

---

372. MARGHERITA PUSTERLA: Cesare Cantù; *Felice Le Monnier* [*Italy*], 1839.
A novel of Milan about 1340: it was at one time " only less popular than Manzoni's *I Promessi Sposi*."

---

373. THE WINNING OF THE GOLDEN SPURS: Percy F. Westerman; *Juv. Nisbet.*
Prologue—Winchester, 1303; main story—New Forest region and France, 1338-1347. Deals, in an interesting manner, with the Wars in France (Crécy and Calais), and introduces King Edward III, the Black Prince, etc.

---

374. *RED EVE; H. Rider Haggard; *Hodder & Stoughton.*
Suffolk Coast (near Dunwich), Windsor, France, and Italy, in the early to mid part of Edward III's reign. A tale of the Black Death. The Battle of Crécy (1346) is the principal historical incident.

---

375. THE GLORY AND SORROW OF NORWICH: M. M. Blake; *Juv. Jarrold.*
Edward III and the Black Prince at Norwich in 1340; then the French Wars, the Plague in Norwich, etc., 1340-50.

---

376. WITH THE BLACK PRINCE: W. O. Stoddard; *Juv. Appleton.*
England (Warwickshire) in the time of Edward III; also France (the Battle of Crécy, 1346).

---

377. ST. GEORGE FOR ENGLAND: G. A. Henty; *Juv. Blackie* [*Eng.*], *Scribner* [*U.S.A.*].
A story of the French Wars (Edward III) with the Battles of Cressy and Poictiers as the outstanding historic events.

---

378. WITH THE BLACK PRINCE: "Herbert Strang" and Richard Stead; *Juv. Oxford University Press.*
England and France, 1338-76. A tale covering the Sack of Southampton, the Battles of Cressy and Poictiers, etc.

---

379. *CRESSY AND POICTIERS: J. G. Edgar; *Juv. Dent* [*Eng.*], *Dutton* [*U.S.A.*].
A good example of this once favourite writer of juvenile fiction. England and France, 1344 to 1370 (passing at the very end, to 1376). The main events brought into the tale are: the Battle of Cressy (1346); the Siege of Calais; the Battle of Nevile's Cross, near Durham (1346), and the Scotch Border Wars; the Battle of Poictiers (1356); the marriage of the Black Prince; and the Battle of Navaretta (1367). The story is based, to a very large extent, on Froissart. Some of the principal figures are Edward III, Queen Philippa, the Black Prince, David II of Scotland, Lord Percy, Lord Nevile, Sir John Chandos, and the Cardinal of Perigord.

---

380. *THE SCRIVENER'S TALE OF " THE COUNTESS ALICE ": Maurice Hewlett; in " New Canterbury Tales "—*Macmillan.*
A short story of King Edward III and the Countess of Salisbury, introducing the " Garter " incident.

381. *THE GOLDSMITH'S APPRENTICE: Beatrice Harraden;
   Juv. In "Untold Tales of the Past"—*Dent* [*Eng.*], *Dutton* [*U.S.A.*].
   An excellent little tale of London (Cheapside) under Edward III; the King himself appears.

---

382. *BRAKESPEARE: George Alfred Lawrence; *Routledge.*
   England and France in the time of Edward III and the Black Prince. This once famous story of a Free Companion's doings, covers the winning of Calais, 1346-47, and the Battle of Poictiers, 1356.

---

383. *THE GATHERING OF BROTHER HILARIUS: "Michael
   Fairless"; *Murray* [*Eng.*], *Duckworth* [*Eng.*], *Dutton* [*U.S.A.*].
   A short tale of Edward III's reign, dealing with the Great Pestilence, about 1348-50.

---

384. EDGAR THE READY: W. P. Shervil; *Juv.* *Blackie.*
   An adventure story (England and France—Bordeaux, etc.) in the mid-Edward III period.

---

385. 1*SIR NIGEL: A. Conan Doyle; *Smith Elder* [*Eng.*], *McClure*
   [*U.S.A.*].
   2*THE WHITE COMPANY (sequel): A. Conan Doyle; *Smith,
   Elder* [*Eng.*], *Harper* [*U.S.A.*].
   (1) England (Surrey) and France (Brittany, etc.), 1348-56. A story of adventures by land, and, to some extent, by sea. The young hero is the "Sir Nigel Loring" who appears as a middle-aged man in *The White Company*. The record of various deeds of heroism in the French War of the period, leads up to the full and vivid account of the Battle of Poictiers (1356), with which event the book ends. Among the various historic figures introduced, perhaps the most important are: Edward III, The Black Prince, Sir John Chandos, John II of France, Philip Duke of Orleans, and the Cardinal of Perigord.
   (2) Hampshire (New Forest region), Bordeaux, Cahors, etc., and Spanish Pyrenees region, 1366-67. Though written first, this excellent historical novel is really a sequel (in point of period depicted) to the author's *Sir Nigel*—that brave knight here appearing as some 15-20 years older. A considerable portion of the story deals with life in England, but the main subject is once again the prowess of Englishmen abroad. The Hampshire hero joins an English Free Company, and, in the course of much wandering through France and the Pyrenees, meets with stirring adventures and performs many a deed of valour. The historical situation is that arising out of the Black Prince's decision to espouse the cause of Pedro the Cruel of Castile. Edward III, the Black Prince, Chandos, Sir William Felton, Bertrand du Guesclin, Don Pedro and others appear.

---

386. ERIC THE ARCHER: M. H. Hervey; *Juv.* *Arnold.*
   England, France, and Spain, mid 14th Century. A good tale of adventure, introducing Sir John Chandos, etc.

---

387. *THE LANCES OF LYNWOOD: Charlotte M. Yonge; *Juv.*
   Macmillan.
   England (Somerset), France, and Spain, mainly in the period, 1365-75 (Edward III) though the last chapter passes to the beginning of Richard II's reign. Depicts the Battle of Naveretta (1367), and introduces many leading personages of the period, such as the Black Prince and Princess Joan his wife, Bertrand du Guesclin, Pedro the Cruel (King of Castile), and Sir John Chandos. A capital story.

---

388. THE VIRGIN OF THE SUN: H. Rider Haggard; *Cassell*
   [*Eng.*], *Doubleday* [*U.S.A.*].
   Begins Hastings, with the marriage of the hero, and the death of his wife; also the attack of the French Fleet, etc. (Edward III). But the main story deals with an Englishman's experiences in Peru, mid to late 14th Century.

389. MINSTREL DICK: Christabel R. Coleridge; *Juv. Wells Gardner.*
Hertfordshire (Berkhampstead) in the last days of the Black Prince; also Chelsea and London. The tale ends with the Prince's death, 1376.

390. *GOD SAVE ENGLAND: Frederic Breton; *Grant Richards.*
Mainly Rye and Winchelsea district round about 1377: last days of Edward III, and the accession of Richard II. A romance of " atmosphere," illustrating the time of Wickliffe and the Lollards. French Admiral's descent on the English coast, etc.

391. *BERTRAND OF BRITTANY: Warwick Deeping; *Harper.*
A story of Bertrand du Guesclin and his wife, covering the earlier part of Bertrand's career up to the exhibition of his military skill at Rennes (1356).

392. BERTRAM: " Le Diamant Brut," G. I. Whitham; in " The Shepherd of the Ocean," etc.—*Wells Gardner.*
Bertrand du Guesclin from boyhood to death: a lengthy series of excellent fictional sketches.

393. *THE SWORD DECIDES: " Marjorie Bowen "; *Greening* [*Eng.*], *McClure* [*U.S.A.*].
A romance based on the true story of Giovanna (Joanna) of Naples and Andrea of Hungary, 1343-44. The chief interest is in the portrayal of individual character, but there is a general historic background (the Plague, etc.).

394. JEHANNE OF THE GOLDEN LIPS: Frances G. Knowles-Foster; *Mills & Boon.*
Naples, 1343 onwards. Another romance of Joanna Queen of Naples. Both Andrea of Hungary (her first husband whom she murdered) and Louis of Taranto (her second husband) are here presented. Boccaccio also appears.

395. THE CROSS OF PEARLS: Mrs. Catherine Bearne; *Juv. S.P.C.K.* [*Eng.*], *Macmillan* [*U.S.A.*].
France, 1344 onwards: the Hundred Years War and the Jacquerie period. A story of French family life, with history merely as a background. The French standpoint is given.

396. *RIENZI, THE LAST OF THE TRIBUNES: Lord Lytton; *Routledge* [*Eng*], *Little, Brown* [*U.S.A.*].
Italy (Rome, Florence, etc.), mainly in the period 1347-54. An historical romance of Cola di Rienzi, the Roman tribune, whose dream of a United Italy proved impossible of attainment in the conditions of the 14th Century. There are accounts of the Plague in Florence, as well as the depiction of political events. The novel ends with Rienzi's death.

397. BROKEN AT THE FOUNTAIN: Emily A. Richings; *Heath Cranton.*
Portugal (Lisbon, etc.) in mid 14th Century (the period between 1340 and 1355). A novel dealing with the love-story of Inez de Castro and Dom Pedro the Crown Prince, ending with the Civil War of 1355 which followed the murder of Inez. Besides the two outstanding figures above-named, King Alfonso IV is prominent.

398. SINGOALLA: Viktor Rydberg (trans.); *W. Scott.*
Sweden in mid 14th Century. A novel of somewhat extravagant type, with a Plague background. The sub-title is: " A Mediæval Legend."

399. THE KNIGHTS OF THE CROSS: H. Sienkiewicz (trans.); *Dent* [*Eng.*], *Little, Brown* [*U.S.A.*].
Poland and Russia, mid 14th Century. A romance illustrating the terrible struggle of Poland and Lithuania against the monk—soldiers called Teutonic Knights (or Knights of the German Order) whose aggressions and conquests extended to the Baltic.

Various localities, including Cracow and the Forest regions. The picture of the Knights is very adverse throughout. The novel ends with the great Polish victory of Grünwald-Tannenberg. One of the most important historical figures introduced is Ladislas Jagiello, King of Poland.

400. *THE LEOPARD PRINCE: Nathan Gallizier; *Harrap* [*Eng.*], *Page* [*U.S.A.*].

Venice, 1355. One of the author's most highly-coloured stories, dealing with bravo and conspirator, incantation and mystery, love and hate. Feminine influence of one kind or another is an important element. The plot largely turns on the political claims and intrigues of Hungary and Bosnia with regard to Dalmatia, etc. The outstanding figure is Zuan Castello, Prince of Lepanto, while Lucio Strozzi, the conspirator, is another prominent figure. Giovanni Gradenigo, the Doge, is also introduced.

401. THE JACQUERIE: G. P. R. James; *Routledge* [*Eng.*], *Dutton* [*U.S.A.*].

France, 1357-58. A romance of the Peasants' Insurrection—the principal figure being the Captal de Buch. The book ends with the suppression of the Revolt.

402. *THE SINGING SEASON: Isabel Paterson; *Parsons* [*Eng.*] *Boni & Liveright* [*U.S.A.*].

A striking novel of Spain in late 14th Century. The period is that of Pedro the Cruel of Castile, and Bertrand Du Guesclin is one of several historical personages introduced.

403. *AGÉNOR DE MAULÉON: Alexandre Dumas (trans.); *Dent* [*Eng.*], *Little, Brown* [*U.S.A.*].

Spain and France, 1361-69. A novel depicting Don Pedro, King of Castile (called "the Cruel"), in the blackest colours. Illustrates the period of Pedro's struggle with his brother, Henry of Trastamare, after the latter's return from France. Edward the Black Prince espoused the cause of Pedro and—as described in the romance—defeated Henry and Du Guesclin at the Battle of Navaretta (1367). The book also covers the Battle of Montiel (1369), when (after the Black Prince's retirement) Pedro was himself defeated, and ends with Pedro's assassination soon afterwards. Of the many historic figures, the following are the most important: Don Pedro and his Queen (Blanche of Bourbon), Charles V of France, Henry of Trastamare, Edward the Black Prince, Bertrand du Guesclin, and Pope Urban V.

404. *THE POPE OF THE SEA: Vincente Blasco-Ibañez (trans.); *Dutton* [*U.S.A.*].

Southern France (Avignon) and Spain, in the time of the Rival Popes—early to late 14th Century. The author describes his book as "an historical medley," and it is, perhaps, more in the nature of imaginative history than fiction in the ordinary sense. The outstanding figure is the Spaniard, Cardinal Pedro de Luna, elected Pope under the title of Benedict XIII in 1394—an opponent of the regular Pope Boniface IX, who had become Pope at Rome in 1389.

405. *THE DISCIPLE OF A SAINT: Vida D. Scudder; *Dent* [*Eng.*], *Dutton* [*U.S.A.*].

A tale of St. Catharine of Siena (1347-80) in the form of an "imaginary biography of Raniero Di Landoccio," St. Catharine's secretary. The romance is a fine piece of reconstruction, not only as regards the Saint herself, but as yielding a picture of mediæval life in the more general sense. The reader is shown Siena in Plague Time, the Papal Court at Avignon, etc.

406. THE LOVE STORY OF ST. BEL: Bernard Capes; *Methuen*.

Another story in which St. Catharine appears—the scene being Siena in the year 1374.

407. ARETHUSA: F. Marion Crawford; *Macmillan*.

Constantinople, 1376. As fiction interesting, but with little to constitute it an *historical* tale.

408. *CAPTAIN SALOMON BRAZENHEAD'S TALE OF "THE HALF BROTHERS ": Maurice Hewlett; in " New Canterbury Tales "—*Constable* [*Eng.*], *Macmillan* [*U.S.A.*].
Northern Italy in late 14th Century. A tale dealing with the time of Sir John Hawkwood.

---

409. HAWKWOOD THE BRAVE: William Beck; *Juv. Blackie.*
A story of the Free Companions in Italy, under Sir John Hawkwood, late 14th Century. Gian Visconti of Milan, etc.

---

410. *THE VIPER OF MILAN: " Marjorie Bowen "; *Alston Rivers* [*Eng.*], *McClure* [*U.S.A.*].
A romance of Gian Galeazzo Visconti, Duke of Milan, and his wars with the free towns of Northern Italy, towards the close of the 14th Century.

---

411. A MAN-AT-ARMS: Clinton Scollard; *Eveleigh Nash* [*Eng.*], *Page* [*U.S.A.*].
Northern Italy (Milan, etc), end 14th Century. Another romance of Gian Galeazzo Visconti and his times.

---

412. IN CHAUCER'S MAYTIME: Emily Richings; *Fisher Unwin.*
Forest of Arden, etc., and London, mainly c. 1365 to 1381 (Edward III—Richard II). Chaucer is, of course, the central figure (his marriage, etc.), but the story depicts many other historical personages, including Edward III and his Queen, John of Gaunt, Katherine Swynford (afterwards Duchess of Lancaster), and Wiclif. There is a glimpse of the Peasant Revolt.

---

413. IN A DESERT LAND: Valentina Hawtrey; *Cassell.*
A romance of Gloucestershire and the West Midlands, giving the history of a family in various reigns, from early 14th Century to comparatively modern times. In the course of the story many historical allusions are given—the Peasants' Revolt, Wickliffe's Preachers, etc. etc.

---

414. THE ABBOT OF KIRKSTALL: T. Walter Harding; *Heffer.*
Yorkshire, 1376; also Lincoln, London, etc. A tale of Edward III period, introducing John of Gaunt, the Black Prince, and Wiclif.

---

415. *RISING DAWN: Harold Begbie; *Hodder & Stoughton.*
England (Pevensey, London, Lincolnshire, etc.), June, 1377, to August, 1378. An adventure-and-love story, introducing such figures as John of Gaunt, John Ball, Wycliffe (prominent), and the poet Chaucer. A good picture of the time.

---

416. THE FEN ROBBERS: Tom Bevan; *Juv. Nelson.*
England (Cambridge, London, Essex Fens, Lincolnshire, etc.) in 1377. Will Langland and the Peasants.

---

417. *THE BANNER OF ST. GEORGE: M. Bramston; *Juv. Duckworth.*
Hertfordshire and Essex in the time of the Peasant's Revolt, introducing John Ball, etc. An excellent late.

---

418. *LONG WILL: Florence Converse; *Dent* [*Eng.*], *Dutton* [*U.S.A.*].
Prologue: Malvern district mid 14th Century; story proper: London and various parts of England including Kent, 1376-81 (Edward III—Richard II); and Epilogue: Malvern just after Richard II's death in 1400. A specially good tale of the period, and of the events leading up to the Peasants' Revolt. A great many historic notabilities are introduced—some of the most prominent being Will Langland, Richard II, and the Peasant Leaders: Wat Tyler, Jack Straw, and John Ball. There is a full account of the Rising itself. Besides the outstanding figures already mentioned, Chaucer, Walworth, the Queen Mother, and others appear.

419. *ROBERT ANNYS, POOR PRIEST: Annie M. Meyer; *Macmillan.*
     Ely, Bury St. Edmunds, and other localities. Another good tale of the Peasants' Revolt, introducing John Ball, etc.

420. PHILIP OKEOVER'S PAGEHOOD: Gertrude Hollis; *S.P.C.K.* [*Eng.*], *Gorham* [*U.S.A.*].
     Northamptonshire and London just before and during the Peasants' Revolt. Geoffrey Chaucer, Simon of Sudbury, and the Peasant leaders.

421. *THE KING BEHIND THE KING: Warwick Deeping; *Cassell.*
     A good historical novel of Southern England (the forests of Kent and Sussex, also London) at the time of the Peasants' Revolt. Many historical figures appear, including Jack Straw, John Ball, and King Richard II.

422. DAPPLE GREY: Margaret Baines Reed; *Juv. Arnold.*
     Sussex, Surrey, and London in the Peasants' Revolt time. The tale ends with the incident of Wat Tyler's death.

423 *A DREAM OF JOHN BALL: William Morris; *Longmans.*
     The distinguished author's imaginative presentment of Peasant Revolt days (Kent), introducing John Ball, Jack Straw, Wat Tyler, and others.

424. MASTER AND MAN: J. C. Hardwick; *Juv. Sheldon Press* [*Eng.*], *Macmillan* [*U.S.A.*].
     A tale of Kent and London in 1381 (the Peasants' Revolt). John Ball is introduced.

425. *A MARCH ON LONDON: G. A. Henty; *Juv. Blackie* [*Eng.*], *Scribner* [*U.S.A.*].
     This story, besides dealing with the Peasants' Revolt in England, illustrates the revolt of the inhabitants of Ghent, etc., under Philip van Artevelde, against the Count of Flanders (1381). The Battle of Roosbeke (or Rosebecque), in which Philip was slain (1382) is covered.

426. THE WHITE HOODS: Mrs. Anna Eliza Bray; *Chapman & Hall.*
     A tale of Philip van Artevelde's revolt, 1381-82. Mrs. Bray, who in her English stories excelled in describing those West Country scenes with which—as resident—she was familiar, has here striven, on the basis of personal observation during a visit to old Flemish towns, to furnish a genuine background.

427. *SUZANNE: Valentina Hawtrey; *Murray* [*Eng.*], *Holt* [*U.S.A.*].
     Another story dealing with Philip van Artevelde's revolt—at least in part. Begins France, 1362 (Charles V), then Flanders about 1381-82. The historical atmosphere is well conveyed.

428. THE GOLDEN QUILL: F. O. Mann; *Blackwell.*
     Southern England and London in late 14th Century. A character novel, introducing the poet Chaucer.

429. UNDER ONE SCEPTRE; OR, MORTIMER'S MISSION (formerly *The Lord of the Marches; or, The story of Roger Mortimer*): Emily S. Holt; *Juv. Shaw.*
     The Welsh Marches (Usk) and Ireland (Ulster), etc., mainly in the period 1385-99. A tale with Roger Mortimer, Fourth Earl of March (1373-99) as outstanding figure. Covers the time of his being Irish Viceroy, and ends with his death in 1399. King Richard II appears in the story.

430. *OTTERBOURNE: Edwin Duros; *Bentley,* 1832.
  Northumberland (Newcastle, etc.) and the Cheviot region (Scottish Border), 1388.
Quite an interesting historical romance of the Scottish invasion of England, leading
up to the Battle of Otterbourne, when Henry Percy (Hotspur) was defeated by Douglas.
Besides the personages just named, there are several historical figures, including the
Earl of Moray, the Earl of Northumberland, the Earls of Fife and Stratherne (sons
of King Robert II of Scotland), Sir Rafe Neville, and others.

431. WILLIAM OF WYKEHAM'S WORKMAN: Beatrice Harra-
  den; *Juv.* In " Untold Tales of the Past "—*Dent* [*Eng.*], *Dutton*
  [*U.S.A.*].
  A little tale of Winchester in 1394.

432. *THE FAIR MAID OF PERTH: Sir Walter Scott; *Black,*
  and other publishers—English and American.
  Scotland (Perth and Falkland) covering the period 1396-1402. The novel gives a
picture of the Scottish Clan feuds, and of the disturbances prevalent in King Robert
III's reign. There is an account of the imprisonment, and death by starvation, of Rothesay (Prince of Scotland), though historians say the " starvation " is no certainty. King
Robert, and his sons, the Dukes of Rothesay and Albany respectively, are prominent;
while Archibald, Earl of Douglas and others appear.

433. *THE NEW JUNE: Henry Newbolt; *Blackwood* [*Eng.*], *Dutton*
  [*U.S.A.*].
  England and Abroad (mostly England) 1396-1403: the last years of Richard II,
and the first three years of Henry IV's reign. An interesting example of imaginative
reconstruction, based on a first-hand knowledge of historic sources. Various historical
figures are introduced, and the book ends with the Battle of Shrewsbury (1403).

FIFTEENTH CENTURY

434. *THE GLEAMING DAWN: James Baker; *Chapman & Hall.*
  England (Lincolnshire, Oxford, and Norfolk), also Bohemia (Prague, etc.), mainly
in the period 1396-1420. This interesting historical novel deals almost equally with
England and Bohemia. In the first part, the hero's experiences at Oxford University
are the main theme—the theological disputes of the time (" Wicklifite " *v.* Catholic,)
etc.; while, in the book's second half, the Husite (or Hussite) War, beginning in 1419,
is the background of the fictional record. The most striking historical figures introduced
are: Fastolf, and Oldcastle (Cobham), in the English section; Cardinal Henry Beaufort,
and the great leader of the Hussites, John Zizka, in the Bohemian portion of the book.

435. RICHARD OF LYMPNE: Violet T. Kirke; *Juv.* S.P.C.K.
  [*Eng.*], *Gorham* [*U.S.A.*].
  London and Shrewsbury, 1399-1400; then France and Italy beginning of 15th Century. An interesting tale of adventure and intrigue, etc., in which both Prince Hal
and Charles VI of France appear.

436. MEN OF IRON: Howard Pyle; *Juv. Osgood.*
  England in 1400; also in 1408-18 (Henry IV—Henry V period). A tale dealing
with the time generally rather than with particular figures or events.

437. BOTH SIDES OF THE BORDER: G. A. Henty; *Juv. Blackie*
  [*Eng.*], *Scribner* [*U.S.A.*].
  A story of Henry IV's time, telling of the struggles on the Scotch and Welsh Borders.
The book, however, is one that illustrates, primarily, the Welsh War (Hotspur and
Glendower), ending with the Battle of Shrewsbury.

438. *HARRY OF ATHOL: R. H. Forster; *John Long.
Mainly Northumberland (Workworth, etc.), 1402-1408. A novel dealing with the
events which led up to the Rebellion of the Earl of Northumberland against Henry IV
(Scrope's Conspiracy). Begins with news of the victory of the Percys over the Scots
at Hamildon Hill, and practically ends with the Battle of Bramham Moor, where the
Earl of Northumberland fell. The last chapter passes to 1415. The most important
historic figures are Northumberland and his son Henry (" Hotspur "), King Henry IV
and Prince Hal.

439. HEARTS OF WALES: "Allen Raine"; *Hutchinson.
A tale illustrating to some extent the time of Owen Glendower and the Welsh Rebellion.

**440. THE SPURS OF GOLD: J. Brown Morgan and J. Rogers
Freeman; *Juv. Melrose.**
Dunstable Priory, Shrewsbury, etc., 1394, and 1402-1403. A "story of Lollard
Times "—to quote the sub-title—which leads up to the Welsh War (the Hotspur—
Glendower coalition), and the Battle of Shrewsbury.

**441. *SIMON THE COLDHEART: Georgette Heyer; *Heine-
mann.**
A well-written, exciting story of the Henry IV—Henry V period. The principal
scene in Part I is the Welsh Border region in War time, 1403-1404; while in Part II the
reader is taken to Normandy, 1417. Henry V is introduced both as Prince and as
King.

**442. FATHER FELIX'S CHRONICLES: Nora Chesson; *Fisher
Unwin [Eng.], *Wessels [U.S.A.].**
Norfolk (Norwich Priory) in the time of Henry IV. An imaginary monk's story,
reflecting to some extent the mysticism of the period, and introducing several historic
figures.

443. PERONELLE: Valentina Hawtrey; *Lane.
A novel depicting, in really interesting fashion, bourgeois life in the Paris of 1400.

**444. *OLD MARGARET: Henry Kingsley; *Ward, Lock [Eng.],
Longmans [U.S.A.].**
Ghent in the first few years of the 15th Century. An interesting story dealing with
the time of Philip Duke of Burgundy (called " the Bold "), under whose encouragement
both arts and commerce greatly developed. The Flemish painters, Hubert and John
Van Eyck, are introduced, and Duke Philip also appears.

**445. *THE DUKE OF MILAN: Maurice Hewlett; in " Brazen-
head the Great "—*Smith, Elder [Eng.], *Scribner [U.S.A.].**
A short tale of Pavia and Milan in 1402: Duke Visconti.

446. THE HOUSE OF EYES: Arthur George; *Gay & Hancock.
Milan and Lake Como, beginning of the 15th Century. A tale of the Visconti family,
dealing largely with the Lady Valentine Visconti, daughter of the Duke of Milan.
Depicts a period of conspiracy and bloodshed, covering the death of Pope Boniface IX
(1404), the coronation and excommunication of Gian Maria Visconti, and the assassination of the last-named. Louis, Duke of Orleans, is one of the figures.

**447. *BELLARION: Rafael Sabatini; *Hutchinson [Eng.], *Houghton
Mifflin [U.S.A.].**
N. Italy (Milan, etc.) in the first decade of the 15th Century, c. 1407-1409. One
of the author's exciting adventure stories, showing his usual knowledge of period and
locality. The young hero, originally intended for the Church, is adopted by the Milan

governor, who is a soldier (condottiere) of high influence. Bellarion's career thenceforward is full of surprises, and the various interests of politics, fighting, and love, are employed in the course of the fictional development. The struggle between the Ghibelline and Guelph factions is illustrated, while many names and figures of historical significance are introduced. A vivid portrait is given of the brutal young Duke of Milan, Gian Maria.

---

448. ISABELLA ORSINI: F. D. Guerrazzi; *Felice le Monnier* [*Italy*], 1884.
A story of Italy and the Medici in the early part of the 15th Century.

---

449. THE BURGUNDIAN: Marion Polk Angellotti; *Gay & Hancock* [*Eng.*], *Century Co.* [*U.S.A.*].
France (Avignon region and Paris), 1407 onwards. A story dealing with the time of Charles VI, the mad king: the relations between France and Burgundy.

---

450. *THE TORCH-BEARERS OF BOHEMIA: V. I. Kryshanovskaya [or Kruizhanovskaya] (trans.); *Chatto & Windus* [*Eng.*], *MacBride* [*U.S.A.*].
A striking historical novel of Prague and Constance, beginning 1401, but mainly in the period 1408-1419. The real hero of the book is John Hus, the Bohemian reformer (his later years and martyrdom). Other prominent personages are King Venceslas and Cardinal Brancaccio.

---

451. THE FIFTH TRUMPET: Paul Bertram; *Lane.*
A romance of Constance and the great Council, 1418. Pope Martin V and Cardinal Brancaccio are outstanding figures. A carefully-written story of a dark time.

---

452. *THE COUNTESS OF PICPUS: Maurice Hewlett; in " Brazenhead the Great "—*Smith, Elder* [*Eng.*], *Scribner* [*U.S.A.*].
A tale of Bordeaux and Toulouse in the year 1428.

---

453. UNDER KING HENRY'S BANNERS: Percy F. Westerman; *Juv. Pilgrim Press.*
England and France, 1413-17. A story beginning in the Southampton region, but mainly dealing with the two campaigns of Henry V in France (1415 and 1417 respectively). Covers the Siege of Harfleur, Agincourt, the Siege of Rouen, etc. King Henry himself appears.

---

454. JENKYN CLYFFE, BEDESMAN: Gertrude Hollis; *Juv. S.P.C.K.* [*Eng.*], *Gorham* [*U.S.A.*].
An old man relates (1440) his former experiences under Henry V. The narrative deals with Henry, first as Prince in 1409, then as King from 1413. The French Wars—Agincourt and Normandy.

---

455. *AGINCOURT: G. P. R. James; *Routledge* [*Eng.*], *Dutton* [*U.S.A.*].
Hampshire, London district, Flanders (Ghent), and France. The romance—a good example of the author—begins in the last days of Henry IV's reign, but mainly deals with the period 1413-15 (Henry V). The Coronation of Henry V, the Hussites in Ghent, the Battle of Agincourt—these are some of the more important subjects introduced. King Harry is the outstanding figure, first of all as Prince, then as King.

---

456. AT AGINCOURT: G. A. Henty; *Juv. Blackie* [*Eng.*], *Scribner* [*U.S.A.*].
Mainly France (Paris, etc.) c. 1413-15: the struggle between Orleanists and Burgundians. Charles VII of France and Henry V of England are among the several figures. The tale virtually ends with Agincourt.

457. *CORONATION: Bernard Hamilton; *originally published by Ward, Lock*; *now by Hutchinson.*
Largely Oxford and London in the second decade of the 15th Century (Henry IV—Henry V). The novel describes the persecution of the Lollards, the trial and execution of Cobham, and the Battle of Agincourt. King Henry V is well depicted.

458. CLAUD THE ARCHER: "Herbert Strang" and John Aston; *Juv. Oxford University Press.*
England and France, 1414-22: Henry V's French Wars (Agincourt, etc.) The tale ends with King Henry's death, and the hero's return to England.

459. *RICHARD DE LACY: C. Edmund Maurice; *Juv. Wells Gardner.*
An unusually good historical tale of Chichester, Oxford, London, etc., in the period 1419-50. Sir Richard Whittington and King Henry V appear in the earlier chapters; other historical personages are Bishop Pecock, Archbishop Chichele, Caxton, and Jack Cade.

460. THE CAGED LION: Charlotte M. Yonge; *Juv. Macmillan.*
Mainly England (with some foreign excursions) in the years 1421-22 for the most part. A story dealing with James I of Scotland as prisoner in England, and his friendship with King Henry V. Both kings are prominent, while Queen Catherine, Whittington, and other historic figures also appear.

461. *THE BOY KNIGHT OF REIMS: Eloise Lownsbery; *Juv. Houghton Mifflin [U.S.A.].*
Reims in early 15th Century. An attractive volume, giving the story of a young lad who—like his forbears—attains a position connecting him with the architectural growth of the famous Cathedral. Describes the craft guilds and the ways of life generally. On the directly historical side, Jeanne d'Arc appears (time of the Dauphin's coronation at Reims in 1429).

462. *JOAN OF ARC AND LITTLE PIERRE: Beatrice Harraden; *Juv.* In "Untold Tales of the Past"—*Dent [Eng.], Dutton [U.S.A.].*
A pretty tale of Joan in her Lorraine home and in Rheims, 1428.

463. *PERSONAL RECOLLECTIONS OF JOAN OF ARC, BY THE SIEUR LOUIS DE CONTE: "Mark Twain"; *Chatto & Windus [Eng.], Harper [U.S.A.].*
The supposed narrator begins with his own birth (1410) and certain portions of his childhood, but the main story deals with Joan of Arc in the period 1428-31: her "visions," her interview with Charles VII, her entry into Orleans, and her military successes generally, up to the time of her downfall, trial, and death at the stake. Many historic figures (besides those already named) are introduced—notably Cauchon, Bishop of Beauvais.

464. *A MONK OF FIFE: Andrew Lang; *Longmans.*
A Scotsman relates his experiences in France during the years 1429-31, and how he came into close contact with Jeanne d'Arc. Various localities are touched (Orleans, Paris, Compiègne, and Rouen). The Maid is, of course, prominent in the story, which ends with some account of her in prison; allusion is made to her cruel death, but no detailed description is given.

465. THE FLOWER OF FRANCE: Justin H. McCarthy; *Hurst & Blackett [Eng.], Harper [U.S.A.].*
France, 1429-31. A story illustrating the career of Joan of Arc, from the time of her "hearing the voices" up to her trial and death by fire. King Charles VII, the Queen, and Queen-Mother are among the historical figures; also Pierre Cauchon, Bishop of Beauvais.

466. THE DAYS OF JEANNE D'ARC: MARY H. CATHERWOOD; Gay [Eng.], Century Co. [U.S.A.].
Another story of Jeanne d'Arc, somewhat strikingly told, and again covering the three eventful years, 1429-31. Several historic personages are introduced—King Charles VII, Yolande Dowager Queen of Sicily, and Agnes Sorel being perhaps the most noteworthy.

467. *THE MAID: JOHN BUCHAN; in "The Path of the King"— Nelson [Eng.], Doran [U.S.A.].
A brief, but good, presentment of Jeanne d'Arc in 1429, and in 1431.

468. *LES GENS D'EPINAL: R. AUVRAY: Armand Colin et Cie [France].
An exceptionally well-written historical romance of France under Charles VII, covering the period 1423-44.

469. A KING'S TRAGEDY: "MAY WYNNE"; Digby, Long.
Scotland, 1436-37. A story dealing with the assassination of King James I of Scotland. Catherine Douglas and others are introduced.

470. ST. CLAIR OF THE ISLES: ELIZABETH HELME; Juv. Warne, also Routledge.
The Hebrides (Island of Barra), Stirling, etc., in the James I—James II period. A very old-fashioned tale, dealing—amongst other things—with the Border War in 1448.

471. *(1) THE BLACK DOUGLAS: S. R. CROCKETT; Smith, Elder [Eng.], Doubleday [U.S.A.].
    *(2) MAID MARGARET (sequel); S. R. CROCKETT; Hodder & Stoughton [Eng.], Dodd, Mead [U.S.A.].
These two novels—both interesting, though at times somewhat exaggerated in style— to a certain extent overlap. They deal mostly with events occurring 1439-60, and illustrate the strange record of the House of Douglas in the time of James II of Scotland. Taken together, the two volumes cover: The murder of William, the young sixth Earl of Douglas, and his brother David (both wrongfully beheaded in Edinburgh Castle, 1440); the murder of William the eighth Earl (stabbed by King James in Stirling Castle, 1452); King James's own death through the bursting of a cannon at Roxburgh, 1460; and the career of Margaret Douglas, called the "Fair Maid of Galloway," who married successively William the eighth Earl, and James the ninth and last Earl. Besides the above-named, and other members of the Douglas connection, several historic figures appear; King James II, Sir Alexander Livingston, Sir William Crichton, Charles VII of France, the Dauphin (afterwards Louis XI), Agnes Sorel, and others. There is a considerable French element (De Retz and Brittany in the first novel—Louis the Dauphin and Amboise, etc., in the sequel), but the more interesting and essential parts of these romances are Scottish in scene and general character. English matters (Wars of the Roses period) are slightly touched. The final chapter of the sequel passes to a time long after 1460.

472. *THE CAPTAIN OF THE GUARD: JAMES GRANT; Juv. Routledge [Eng.], Dutton [New York].
Scotland (Edinburgh, Galloway, etc.) and Flanders, 1440-52. A picture of sanguinary times, when William, sixth Earl of Douglas, was beheaded along with his brother (1440), and when the eighth Earl was stabbed in Stirling Castle by King James II (1452). There are scenes at the Court of the Duke of Gueldres, whose daughter Mary married James II. Besides King James and the Douglases, there are numerous historic figures, including Livingstone of Callander (Regent) and Crichton the Chancellor. One of Grant's best historical tales.

473. TWO PENNILESS PRINCESSES: CHARLOTTE M. YONGE; Juv. Macmillan.
Scotland (Dunbar), England, and France, in the period 1445 and the years following. A tale of the sisters of James II of Scotland: their experiences in England, and at the Court of King René of Anjou. Among the more important historic figures are Henry VI (as a young man of twenty-four), and Cardinal Beaufort.

474. BEWITCHED: Dora Mellor; *Drane's.*
Germany (Nuremburg) in the second quarter of the 15th Century. The Emperor Sigismund is an important figure in this history-laden tale of the Hussites, etc.

---

475. THE CARDINAL'S PAGE: James Baker; *Chapman & Hall.*
Begins England (Gloucestershire), but passes at once to Bohemia, 1427-30. The sub-title reads: " A Story of Adventure," and the author himself states that the book is not a sequel, but a companion volume, to his *The Gleaming Dawn* (already entered). The hero in the present case is page to Cardinal Beaufort of Winchester, and although " history is quite subordinate to adventure " (Preface), the narrative reflects the later stages of the Hussite War (the fight at Tachau, the seizing of Prague, the assault of Burgstein, etc.). Cardinal Henry Beaufort is, of course, much in evidence.

---

476. *THE BURGOMASTER OF BERLIN: " Wilibald Alexis "
(trans.); *Saunders & Otley,* 1843.
Germany, mostly 1442-48, but passing to 1470 in the last chapter. The main intention of this noted romance is twofold: to illustrate the condition of the German towns of the period, and to depict Frederick's policy of uniting the two opposing classes—the nobles and the tradesmen.

---

477. THE CAPTAIN OF THE JANISSARIES: J. M. Ludlow;
Juv. Harper.
Albania and Constantinople, 1443 onwards. A tale of considerable variety, illustrating the time of the Fall of the Byzantine Empire, and depicting Balkan life, the Turkish Wars, etc.

---

478. *FLAMES ON THE BOSPHORUS (*Fiamme sul Bosforo*): **Luigi Motta** (trans.); *Odhams Press.*
A novel giving a vivid picture of the struggle between Turks and Christians mid 15th Century (the Turkish capture of Constantinople, in 1453). There is description of both sea and land fighting. Mohammed II, son of Murad the Great, is an outstanding figure. The author is one of the best-known Italian writers of historical romance.

---

479. *THEODORA PHRANZA[1]: John Mason Neale; *Dent* [*Eng.*], *Dutton* [*U.S.A.*].
Constantinople, 1452-53. An excellent romance relating the experiences of an Englishman in the Varangians (or Lifeguards) of the Byzantine Emperor, Constantine Palaeologus. Illustrates the events leading up to the siege of Constantinople by the Turks. Besides the political developments (treasonable plot, etc.) there is a love interest —the hero seeking the hand of Theodora, the daughter of George Phranza (an intimate friend of the Emperor). The story ends with the Fall of Constantinople and the death of the Emperor. Besides Constantine and George Phranza mentioned above, the famous Genoese General, Justiniani, and Mahomet the Sultan, are both introduced.

[1] Decidedly the best of the four or five fictional attempts yet made in English to illustrate the Fall of Constantinople. Lew Wallace's long story—" The Prince of India "—is somewhat fantastic and pretentious. Dr. Neale, the author of the tale here so strongly recommended, was a prominent Anglican clergyman of Early-Victorian days, and a man of considerable literary attainments; he excelled especially as hymnologist.

---

480. HOW THE KING CAME TO BEAUFOY: Hamilton Drummond; in " The Beaufoy Romances "—*Ward, Lock* [*Eng.*], *Page* [*U.S.A.*].
A good tale of King Charles VII of France, 1456.

---

481. *A LODGING FOR THE NIGHT: R. L. Stevenson; in " New Arabian Nights "—*Chatto & Windus* [*Eng.*], *Scribner* [*U.S.A.*].
An imaginative presentment of François Villon, with the date given as 1456. One of Stevenson's short, but elegantly written, stories.

F

482. (1) IF I WERE KING: Justin H. McCarthy; *Heinemann* [*Eng.*],
        Harper [*U.S.A.*].
     (2) NEEDLES AND PINS (*sequel*): Justin H. McCarthy;
        Hurst & Blackett [*Eng.*], *Harper* [*U.S.A.*].
(1) France (Paris) c. 1463. A story of François Villon the poet, interesting enough
as fiction, but with a very slight basis of actual fact. Besides Villon, King Louis XI
is greatly to the fore. (2) France (Poitou). Villon as married man, and the troubles
accompanying this further stage of his career. Once again, Louis XI is prominent,
while his brother Prince Charles also appears.

483. FOR LOVE OF A SINNER: Robert George Anderson;
        Hutchinson.
A romance of François Villon in the time of Louis XI. The King himself appears
in the story.

484. CHATTELS: Hamilton Drummond; *Stanley Paul.*
France in the Charles VII—Louis XI period. A book illustrating the wretched
state of the peasants under their seigneurs.

485. *THE MASTIFF OF RIMINI: CHRONICLES OF THE
        HOUSE OF MALATESTA: Edward Hutton; *Second edition
        revised, Methuen;* formerly entitled " Sigismondo Pandolfo
        Malatesta, Lord of Rimini "—*Dent* [*Eng.*], *Dutton* [*U.S.A.*].
Rimini, mainly between 1430 and 1468. Semi-fictional chronicles (fictional only
in the sense of the narrative form given to them) of certain episodes in the career of
the Italian despot, Sigismondo Malatesta. Pope Pius II (Aeneas Sylvius Piccolomini) is
one of the more noteworthy figures appearing in the record. The narrative is one that
makes appeal to those with scholarly tastes rather than to the average novel-reader.

486. FRA LIPPO LIPPI: Margaret Vere Farrington; *Putnam.*
Italy, early to late 15th Century. A biographical romance based on the known career
of the famous friar-artist.

487. THE ROMANCE OF FRA FILIPPO LIPPI (THE JOYOUS
        FRIAR): A. J. Anderson; *Stanley Paul* [*Eng.*], *Stokes* [*U.S.A*].
Italy (Prato and Florence), mainly 1456-61, though the story is actually carried to
1469. A love romance of Lippi, offered by the author as a " new version " of the affair.
Among the historic figures are Cosimo de' Medici and Pope Pius II. As the author's
notes at the end of the volume show, the book is based on careful research.

488. RICHARD RAYNAL, SOLITARY: Robert Hugh Benson;
        Pitman.
A tale of 15th Century Quietism, introducing King Henry VI of England and Cardinal
Beaufort.

489. THE HERMIT AND THE KING: A FULFILMENT OF
        MONSIGNOR R. HUGH BENSON'S PROPHECY OF
        RICHARD RAYNAL: Sophie Maude; *Washbourne.*
A religious story of the Wars of the Roses period, introducing Henry VI. The author
writes from the Roman Catholic standpoint.

490. THE THREE ROSES: Enid Dinnis; *Sands.*
Yet another novel of religious character, with Henry VI as outstanding figure. Covers
the period 1425-1471, i.e., nearly the whole of Henry's life.

491. THE TRIPLE CROWN: Rose Schuster; *Chapman & Hall.*
A novel of English History in the period, 1437-60, written from the Lancastrian
standpoint. Cardinal Beaufort and Henry VI are prominent in the earlier part of the
story, while later chapters cover—and to some extent describe—Cade's rebellion, and
the Wars of the Roses (including the Battle of St. Albans, 1455, and the Battle of Wakefield, 1460). The *Epilogue* passes to Henry VI's death in 1471.

492. HELD BY REBELS: Tom Bevan; *Juv. Collins.*
England (Kent), 1450. A tale having for its historic background Jack Cade's march on London.

---

493. *BRAZENHEAD THE GREAT: Maurice Hewlett; in " Fond Adventures "—*Macmillan;* afterwards reprinted under the title " The Captain of Kent" in " Brazenhead the Great "—*Smith, Elder.*
A decidedly vivid story of considerable length, dealing with Southern England at the time of Jack Cade's insurrection (1450). Cade himself appears.

---

494. *GRISLY GRISELL: Charlotte M. Yonge; *Juv. Macmillan.*
England (Wiltshire) and Flanders (Bruges), within the period 1450-70. Tale of a young girl facially disfigured through an accident; her position in the Countess of Salisbury's household gives part of the historical element. The atmosphere of the Wars of the Roses, about the time of the Lancastrian victory at Wakefield (1460), is well conveyed. The later chapters dealing with Bruges, cover the death of Philip the Good of Burgundy, and the succession of his son Charles (1467). Among the historic figures introduced, one may specify Warwick the Kingmaker and the Duchess of Burgundy.

---

495. SIR ADAM'S ORCHARD: Margaret Baines Reed; *Juv. Arnold.*
An excellent tale of Yorkshire, 1460. Deals with the Wars of the Roses period, introducing the Earl of Warwick, Henry VI, and Queen Margaret.

---

496. THE BLACK ARROW: R. L. Stevenson; *Juv. Cassell* [*Eng.*], *Scribner* [*U.S.A.*].
A tale illustrating the earlier period of the Wars of the Roses, when Henry VI was on the point of being dethroned. The story is both historically and topographically vague, but Richard Crookback is introduced.

---

497. THE QUEEN'S MAN: Eleanor C. Price; *Juv. Constable.*
A story of the Wars of the Roses, about 1460-61. Covers the Battles of Wakefield and St. Albans, and introduces Queen Margaret and Henry VI.

---

498. JOAN OF ST. ALBANS: Beatrix Hughes; *Heath Cranton.*
St. Albans and London (Westminster) about the time of the second Battle of St. Albans (1461)—which battle is introduced. The most noteworthy of the historical figures are King Edward and Caxton (the author explains that, in her story, she has made it appear that *the introduction of printing* occurred several years earlier than History proper tells us).

---

499. *MAGIC CASEMENTS: Arthur S. Cripps; *Duckworth.*
Several short stories, dealing in a striking manner with life in South-East England, 1460-61.

---

500. MID RIVAL ROSES: H. O. M. Estrange; *Selwyn & Blount.*
A tale of the period, 1460-85 (Henry VI—Richard III). Many historical incidents and personages are introduced—the most important figures being Edward IV, Richard III, Elizabeth Woodville, and Jane Shore.

---

501. *THE MERCHANT PRINCE: H. C. Bailey; *Methuen.*
Southampton and the New Forest district c. 1460-1485. This novel chiefly illustrates the growth of commerce and the rise of the Middle Class. Warwick the Kingmaker frequently appears up to his death at Barnet, 1471, while the later chapters contain good sketches of Edward IV and Richard the Hunchback. The story ends in the year of Richard's death and Henry VII's accession. A good example of the author.

502. *IN STEEL AND LEATHER: R. H. FORSTER; *John Long.*
Northumberland (Alnwick region, Bamburgh, Berwick, etc.) and Yorkshire, mainly 1461-65. A romance of the Wars of the Roses with some good local colour. Covers the escape of Henry VI and Queen Margaret to Scotland, the siege of Dunstanburgh Castle, and the highly important Battle of Hedgeley Moor (1464). Queen Margaret, Prince Edward, Henry VI, and Edward IV are the chief historical figures.

503. MARGARET OF ANJOU: BERNARD CAPES; in " Historical
       Vignettes "—*Fisher Unwin* [*Eng.*], *Stokes* [*U.S.A.*].
A short sketch of Queen Margaret in 1463.

504. *THE LAST OF THE BARONS: LORD LYTTON; *Dent* [*Eng.*],
       Dutton [*U.S.A.*].
An example of that special type of historical fiction which puts too great a strain on the average novel-reader by an excessive introduction of real personages and events. Gives a depiction of the Wars of the Roses period, 1467 onwards—ending with a full account of the Battle of Barnet, 1471. Warwick the Kingmaker and Edward IV are the two outstanding figures; while Richard of Gloucester, Clarence, Hastings, and many others are more or less prominently introduced.

505. *FOR THE WHITE ROSE: " HERBERT STRANG " and GEORGE
       LAWRENCE; *Juv. Oxford University Press.*
Begins Burford region, 1455, but the main part of the story is concerned with London, and other localities, 1469-71. The Battles of Barnet and Tewkesbury are the two most important public events. Introduces several personages of the period (Edward IV and his Queen are prominent). An excellent tale.

506. *THE CONFESSION OF RICHARD PLANTAGENET: DORA
       GREENWELL McCHESNEY; *Smith, Elder.*
An unfinished—though in large part executed—novel of Richard Crookback, 1471-85 (Edward IV—Richard III). Many historical personages appear, including Catesby, while events of the period, like the Battle of Tewkesbury, the murder of the Princes, etc., are well presented. An interesting *defence* of Richard III.

507. MARTIN VALLIANT: WARWICK DEEPING; *Cassell* [*Eng.*],
       MacBride [*U.S.A.*].
England, late 15th Century. Mainly a forest tale of outlaw-adventure and love (the hero, originally " Brother " Martin, abandons the monastic life). The historical element is very slight, but there are allusions which indicate the period as that of the later Wars of the Roses. The book ends with news of the Earl of Richmond (Henry VII) " on the seas," i.e. just before Bosworth.

508. WHITE ROSELEAVES: EMILY RICHINGS; *Drane.*
A novel dealing with Elizabeth Wydvile (Woodville), Queen of Edward IV, and covering the period c. 1476-86. Among the many historic figures are Caxton and Henry Tudor.

509. *HOW MASTER CAXTON SHOWED TEMPER: BEATRICE
       HARRADEN; *Juv.* In " Untold Tales of the Past "—*Dent* [*Eng.*],
       Dutton [*U.S.A.*].
Caxton and his printing-press at Westminster, in 1477.

510. SANCTUARY: BLANCHE HARDY; *Philip Allan.*
England in the period 1478-86. The novel is well-written, but too crammed with historical figures and events. The murder of the Princes, the Battle of Bosworth, and other scenes, are all presented on more or less usual lines. Elizabeth Woodville (in particular), Edward IV, Richard III, Henry Tudor, and many others appear.

511. THE MERCHANT AT ARMS: RONALD OAKESHOTT; *Longmans.*
London, Corfe Castle, Nottingham, etc., as well as foreign parts (Antwerp and Bruges), end of 15th Century. Story of a man's life (told in the first person) during the Edward IV —Henry VII period. Deals mainly with the years following Richard III's coronation, 1483; describes the Battle of Bosworth, and depicts London under Henry VII (the hero becomes a Merchant Adventurer).

---

512. BEATRIX OF CLARE: JOHN REED SCOTT; *Grant Richards [Eng.], Lippincott [U.S.A.].*
Pontefract, the Midlands, London, Windsor, etc., 1482-83. An historical novel in which Richard Crookback (first as Protector, then as King) appears prominently; he is depicted as a man of strong and capable, rather than base, type. The various political intrigues and developments of the time are reflected. Many historical figures:— Richard III, Queen Anne (the Kingmaker's daughter), Catesby, Brackenbury, the Duke of Buckingham, Hastings, etc.

---

513. UNDER THE RED ROSE: ESCOTT LYNN; *Juv. Cassell.*
Herefordshire, London, etc., 1483-1485. A tale covering the Murder of the Princes and the Battle of Bosworth, with which latter event the book ends. Several historic figures.

---

514. THE WOODMAN: G. P. R. JAMES; *Routledge [Eng.], Dutton [U.S.A.].*
A very fair example of the author, depicting England in the time of Richard III. The novel ends with the landing of Richmond (Henry VII) and the Battle of Bosworth. Both Richmond and the King are prominently introduced.

---

515. *THE YOUNG LOVELL: FORD MADOX HUEFFER; *Chatto & Windus.*
A good romance of the Scottish Border (Cheviot and East Coast region), 1485-86. Bishop Sherwood of Durham and other historic figures appear.

---

516. *THE CLOISTER AND THE HEARTH: CHARLES READE; *Chatto & Windus [Eng.], Dodd, Mead [U.S.A.], and other publishers.*
Certainly one of the few historical romances to which the word *great* can be applied without hesitation. The late Sir Walter Besant (himself an historical novelist of real merit) went so far as to claim for this masterpiece of Charles Reade the position of " *the greatest* historical novel in the English language." Whether " great " or " greatest," the book is one that should be read by all lovers of historical fiction; its diversity of scene and its temporal range, are alike remarkable. Mainly Holland, Germany, France, and Italy between 1465 and 1485. An absorbing tale of love and adventure, illustrating the manners, ideas, and general circumstances of the period—a period with which the author, through study of Erasmus and other original literature, had made himself thoroughly familiar. The child born to Gerard and Margaret in the novel is, of course, the great Erasmus himself.

---

517. *THE ROYAL PAWN OF VENICE: MRS. LAWRENCE TURNBULL; *Putnam [Eng.], Lippincott [U.S.A.].*
A novel of Venice and the Island of Cyprus (mainly the latter), 1468-88. Caterina Cornaro of Venice is the chief character—her marriage to the King of Cyprus; the political schemes and developments following the King's death are illustrated in the story.

---

518. *MARIETTA: F. MARION CRAWFORD; *Macmillan.*
Murano and Venice, 1470 onwards. This interesting story, though its author himself states that it " does not pretend to be historical," is based on fact to some extent. The hero, Zorzi Ballarin, a Dalmatian waif in the service of Angelo Beroviero the glass-worker, as well as the heroine " Marietta " (Beroviero's daughter), were real people. At the same time, the facts, personages, and dates are fictionally presented, and the novel is primarily one of *atmosphere*—illustrating the days when Venice was very powerful, and when such phrases as " Council of Ten," and " Signors of the Night," were full of significance.

519. A KNIGHT OF THE WHITE CROSS: G. A. HENTY; *Juv.*
Blackie *[Eng.]*, *Scribner* *[U.S.A.]*.
A story of England and Abroad in the decade 1470-1480. The two outstanding events
are the Battle of Tewkesbury and the Siege of Rhodes.

520. HIERONYMUS RIDES: ANNA COLEMAN LADD; *Macmillan.*
A story of adventure and travel in various parts of Europe (Rhine district, Italy, and
Spain) in the period 1459 to 1493—the tale proper beginning 1472. Maximilian is the
most important of the historical figures introduced; the sub-title in itself conveys this:
" Episodes in the Life of a Knight and Jester at the Court of Maximilian, King of the
Romans " (he was elected King of the Romans in 1486, and became German *Emperor*
in 1493).

521. *THE DOVE IN THE EAGLE'S NEST: CHARLOTTE M. YONGE;
Juv. Macmillan, also *Dent* *[Eng.]*, *Dutton* *[U.S.A.]*.
One of Miss Yonge's best tales. It deals with Germany, mainly in the period 1472-
1519 (the Emperors Frederick III and Maximilian I); the latest pages of all carry the
story to 1531, i.e. two years after Charles V had been crowned Emperor. The disorders
which were so prevalent in Germany at the end of the 15th Century and the beginning
of the 16th, are here well illustrated. The portrait of Maximilian is especially interesting,
as indicative of the two sides of that remarkable man's character, viz., his strength *and*
his weakness.

522. MARY OF BURGUNDY: G. P. R. JAMES; *Routledge* *[Eng.]*,
Dutton *[U.S.A.]*.
Mainly Flanders (Ghent), beginning in 1456, but almost at once passing to a period
nearly twenty years later. The outstanding figure is, of course, Charles the Bold's
daughter Mary—the novel ending with her marriage to Maximilian of Austria, 1477.
Illustrates the political conditions about the time of Duke Charles's death, etc., and
introduces Louis XI, Margaret of York, the Duke of Gueldres, and others.

523. THE KING'S FAVOURITE: HENRY H. ATKINSON; *George Allen.*
Paris and Normandy in 1461. A tale of the French Court (Louis XI just crowned),
belonging to the " Cloak and Sword " type of fiction. King Louis is much to the fore.

524. *QUENTIN DURWARD: SIR WALTER SCOTT; *Black* *[Eng.]*, *and
other publishers—English and American.*
France and Flanders (Tours region, Peronne, and Liége) in 1468. The outstanding
figure of this famous romance is that compound of cleverness and superstition, Louis XI
of France, and Scott's portrait of the king brings to the reader an impression of his
personality which a careful study of History could hardly make more convincing. The
novel describes the revolt of the Liégois against Burgundy, and, later, the Siege of Liége
by Duke Charles and Louis XI. Besides the two personages just named, Isabella
Countess of Croye, Philip de Comines, the Bishop of Liége (Louis of Bourbon), and
William de la Marck appear.

525. FORTUNE: J. C. SNAITH; *Nelson* *[Eng.]*, *Moffatt* *[U.S.A.]*.
Spain and France (Paris) late 15th Century: time of Maximilian, and of Louis XI
of France. The adventures of an English knight—the fictional element being much
more in evidence than the historical. King Louis, however, appears (the allusion to
him as that " Flemish grocer " makes his identity unmistakable!).

526. ANNE OF GEIERSTEIN: SIR WALTER SCOTT; *Black, and other
publishers—English and American.*
Switzerland, Germany, and France, 1474-77. A novel in which Charles the Bold,
Duke of Burgundy, is prominent—covering the period which ended in his downfall
and death at the Battle of Nancy. A special feature of the book is the account given
of the *Vehm-gericht* or Secret Tribunal. Allusion is made to Louis XI's peace with
England, and among the historical figures (besides Duke Charles) one may specify
Queen Margaret of Anjou (widow of Henry VI of England), and King René of Provence,

527. IN THE DAYS OF LORENZO THE MAGNIFICENT: A. G. ANDREWES; *Foulis.*

Florence (Lorenzo de' Medici and his household) in 1475 and following years. A novel of the very historical and descriptive type. Illustrates the relations between the Medici and Pope Sixtus IV, the plot to kill Lorenzo, as well as the subsequent war between the Florentines and Papal adherents (Naples, etc.). The book ends with Lorenzo's successful treaty with Naples.

528. HIS MAGNIFICENCE: A. J. ANDERSON; *Stanley Paul.*

Florence, late 15th Century. This carefully written novel is virtually a defence of Lorenzo de' Medici, based on a thorough study of his life and times. An imaginary friend of Lorenzo " tells " the story in December, 1492, but the actual record deals with the period between 1478 (the Pazzi Conspiracy) and 1492 (Lorenzo's death).

529. *A JAY OF ITALY (BEMBO): BERNARD CAPES; *Methuen* [*Eng.*], *Dutton* [*U.S.A.*]. Also in *Dent's " Wayfarers' Library."*

North Italy (Milan, etc.), 1476. The vivid story of a youth of Christlike character, telling of his influence and experiences in a corrupt environment. Members of the Sforza family are prominent—especially Galeazzo Maria Sforza, third Duke of Milan, with whose assassination the novel ends. The mediæval atmosphere is well conveyed.

530. *RICHARD HAWKWOOD: H. N. MAUGHAM; *Blackwood.*

Italy (Florence and Rome), 1477-78. A " great-grandson to Sir John Hawkwood " is supposed to tell this story of Lorenzo de' Medici in the period of the Pazzi Conspiracy and the murder of Lorenzo's brother, Giuliano. The hero has many adventures, and there is a love element. Besides the two Medici brothers, various figures of the time appear, including Leonardo da Vinci, Sandro Botticelli, and Francesco de' Pazzi.

531. THE SWORD OF LOVE: MORAY DALTON; *Collins.*

A good romance of Florence, 1477-78, dealing—like the novel immediately above—with the intrigues against the Medici brothers, Lorenzo and Giuliano (the assassination of the latter).

532. THE HEART OF HER HIGHNESS: CLARA E. LAUGHLIN; *Putnam.*

Flanders (Bruges) and France, 1477. A tale of Duchess Mary of Burgundy, and the events leading up to her marriage with the Duke of Austria (Maximilian I). King Louis XI appears.

533. ST. LÔ: DOROTHY M. STUART; *Holden & Hardingham.*

Paris, Flanders (Ghent), and Southern France in 1483. A story illustrating the time of Pope Sixtus IV, Maximilian of Austria, and King Louis XI (the last-named is introduced as a dying man).

534. *THE JUSTICE OF THE KING: HAMILTON DRUMMOND; *Stanley Paul* [*Eng.*], *Macmillan* [*U.S.A.*].

France (Valmy and Amboise), 1483. An interesting historical romance of the time immediately preceding Louis XI's death. The hero is under secret orders from the King to carry out certain evil designs with regard to the boy-Dauphin; the record of what happens in the event, and of the manner in which feminine influence frustrates a crime, is given with much verve. Louis XI (a careful depiction), Philip de Commine, the poet Villon, and Charles the Dauphin are all prominently introduced.

535. THE RED ROSE OF LANCASTER: " MAY WYNNE "; *Holden & Hardingham.*

A tale of Brittany in 1493. The chief historical interest is to be found in the appearance of Henry Tudor—afterwards Henry VII of England.

536. KNIGHT AT ARMS: H. C. Bailey; *Methuen.*
France 1483, just after Louis XI's death and the accession of the boy-king Charles VIII. The exploits of a French Seigneur. Henry Tudor (afterwards Henry VII of England) appears prominently, as well as the young King of France himself, the Duke of Orleans, and other historical personages. The story in later chapters passes to N. Italy, and Charles VIII's expedition there in 1494 (Ludovico Il Moro, Bayard, etc.).

537. THE MARK OF VRAYE: H. B. Somerville; *Hutchinson.*
Brittany, 1485. A romance dealing with the time of the nobles' revolt against Pierre Landais.

538. *NOTRE DAME: Victor Hugo (trans.); *Dent* [*Eng.*], *Little, Brown* [*U.S.A.*] ; *and other publishers—English and American.*
Paris and the great church of Notre Dame in 1485. This celebrated example of Hugo is more in the nature of prose-poetry than historical fiction proper, though King Louis XI is somewhat prominently introduced in the later part of the book.

539. THE POPE'S FAVOURITE: Joseph McCabe; *Hurst & Blackett.*
A Borgia novel beginning Rome, 1489. Covers the election of Cardinal Borgia as Pope Alexander VI in 1492, the Campaign of Charles VIII of France, and other events. Among the numerous historic figures one may specify Lucrezia Borgia, Cesare Borgia, and Charles VIII.

540. A MAID OF BRITTANY: " May Wynne "; *Greening.*
A tale reflecting, on the historical side, the hostile feeling which existed between France and Brittany in 1491 (Charles VIII and Duchess Anne of Brittany).

541. *THE KNIGHTLY YEARS: W. M. Ardagh; *Lane.*
A particularly good romance beginning in Gomera (one of the Canary Islands), 1480, and then taking the reader to Spain (Seville) for a short time: at this point Ferdinand and Isabella are both introduced. The interest thenceforward is shifted back to the Canaries at the time of the Spaniards' Wars, 1485.

542. *THE MAGADA: W. M. Ardagh; *Lane.*
The Grand Canary, 1482-92. Another good story by the author of the preceding book; it depicts the last stand of the inhabitants of the Canary Islands against the Spaniards

543. AT THE COURT OF IL MORO: Louise M. Stacpoole Kenny; *John Long.*
Italy (Ferrara, Pavia, etc.), 1490-91. A novel illustrating the time of Lodovico Sforza's marriage with Beatrice d'Este. Leonardo da Vinci is introduced.

544. THE WOOD OF LIFE: John Buchan; in " The Path of the King "—*Nelson* [*Eng.*], *Doran* [*U.S.A.*].
France and Italy in the period just before the sailing of Columbus (the Italian Renaissance).

545. *ADMIRAL OF THE OCEAN SEA (" 1492 "): Mary Johnston; *Thornton Butterworth* [*Eng.*], *Little, Brown* [*U.S.A.*].
A very interesting story of Columbus and his voyages, ending with the great navigator's death (1506). The book mainly deals with events between 1490 and 1503. King Ferdinand and Queen Isabella both appear.

546. THE GRAIN OF MUSTARD: Hamilton Drummond; *Stanley Paul.*
Spain, 1491-93. A young woman's account of her experiences, chiefly at Santa Fé, in the siege and taking of Granada period. Queen Isabella, King Ferdinand, Torquemada, and others are introduced, as well as Christopher Columbus, just before his first great sail.

547. *HIS QUEEN: BERNARD HAMILTON; *Hutchinson.*

Genoa, Lisbon, Seville, etc., in the period 1469-93. The author has come perilously near the mistake of ultra-romanticism in this love tale of Christopher Columbus and Queen Isabella. There are, however, not a few striking scenes. The novel covers the marriage of Ferdinand of Aragon with Isabella of Castile (1469), the Fall of Granada (1482) and Columbus' Voyage West, etc. (1492-93). Besides the Explorer and Queen Isabella, King Ferdinand is prominent, while Cardinal Mendoza, Gonsalvo di Cordova, and other personages appear.

548. FAIR MARGARET: H. RIDER HAGGARD; *Hutchinson* [*Eng.*], *Longmans* [*U.S.A.*].

London, 1491 (Henry VII), but chiefly Spain under Ferdinand and Isabella. A romance of adventure, ending in Essex, 1501.

549. THE VALE OF CEDARS: GRACE AGUILAR; *Juv. Routledge* [*Eng.*], *Dutton* [*U.S.A.*].

Spain (Segovia, etc.), and to a slight extent England, 1479-1501. Experiences of an Englishman (the tale itself reveals his important identity!) in Spain after the Wars of the Roses. Illustrates the Inquisition period of Ferdinand and Isabella, and the persecution of the Jews. Ends (in England) with the marriage of Arthur, Prince of Wales (Henry VII's son) and Catherine Infanta of Aragon. King Ferdinand and Queen Isabella, as well as Torquemada, are somewhat prominently introduced. An old-fashioned tale which is still read.

550. *THE YELLOW FRIGATE: JAMES GRANT; *Juv. Routledge* [*Eng.*], *Dutton* [*U.S.A.*].

A story of Scotland in the one year 1488, but covering the end of James III's reign, and the accession of James IV. Illustrates the plots of the " English faction " in Scotland, and describes important events like the Battle of Sauchieburn and the assassination of James III. The last-named King, his son Duke of Rothesay (afterwards James IV), and Margaret Drummond are very prominent. Sir Andrew Wood, the Scottish naval commander also appears, while there is a glimpse of Henry VII in London.

551. KING HEART: CAROLA OMAN; *Fisher Unwin.*

Scotland (Stirling district, etc.) under James IV in the last years of the 15th Century. A story of the time of Margaret Drummond, Perkin Warbeck, etc. The Epilogue passes to Flodden, 1513.

552. *A TRUSTY REBEL: MRS. HENRY CLARKE; *Juv. Nelson.*

Chiefly Kent, London, and Cornwall 1495-1498. Story of a youthful follower of Perkin Warbeck. The last-named individual, who professed to be Richard, Duke of York, appears in the later chapters dealing with the rising in the West and its failure. King Henry VII also appears, and there are glimpses of Archbishop Morton and Thomas More (the latter as a young page in the Archbishop's household).

553. *A KING OF VAGABONDS: BETH ELLIS; *Blackwood.*

A romance of Perkin Warbeck: mainly England and Scotland in the period 1483-1509. The actual story begins 1495, and deals with Perkin Warbeck's claim to be the younger of the two Princes in the Tower. The claimant's short visit to Ireland (Cork), and his West Country doings, are outlined. King Henry VII appears.

554. DYNASTY: BLANCHE HARDY; *Philip Allan.*

Mainly London and the West Country, 1495-1509. An historical romance of the Perkin Warbeck period. Henry VII is an outstanding figure, while, of the numerous other historic personages, one may mention King Henry's Queen (Elizabeth of York) and Queen Margaret of Scotland,

555. *THE CARNIVAL OF FLORENCE: " MARJORIE BOWEN ";
Methuen.
Florence in the last decade of the 15th Century. Savonarola is the central figure in
this interesting historical romance, while the Medici and various other personages of
the time are prominently introduced. The novel ends with the religious reformer's
execution in 1498.

556. THE BLESSED BANDS: GERTRUDE HOLLIS; Juv. S.P.C.K.
[Eng.], Gorham [U.S.A.].
Florence in the period 1491-1504. A good tale covering many events in the period
of Savonarola, of the Borgias, and of Charles VIII's invasion. Savonarola is the outstanding figure; among the other historic personages are Lorenzo de' Medici, and (as
a boy of sixteen) Michelangelo.

557. *ROMOLA: " GEORGE ELIOT "; Blackwood [Eng.], Crowell
[U.S.A.], and other publishers.
Florence, 1492-1498 (Epilogue 1509). This famous romace has been variously estimated, but it is at least a careful (almost too careful) study of Florentine life in the
Renaissance period; again, the depiction of " Tito's " career, from the time of high
possibilities to the closing scenes of failure and downfall, cannot but impress any thoughtful reader. Turning to the historical figures introduced, Savonarola stands out most
clearly, of course, while it is interesting to meet with Niccolò Machiavelli as a young
man.

558. *THE FORERUNNER (LEONARDO DA VINCI)—also
entitled " The Resurrection of the Gods " and " The Romance
of Leonardo da Vinci "—DMITRI MEREZHKOVSKY (trans.);
Constable [Eng.], Putnam [U.S.A.].
Florence, Milan, Rome, and Amboise, etc., 1494 to 1519. A brilliant imaginative
presentment of Leonardo da Vinci and his times. The romance vividly depicts the
artistic, political, and general Renaissance conditions, while, more specifically, it deals
with: the Expedition of Charles VIII of France (1494); the later Expedition of Louis
XII; the preaching of Savonarola and the Bonfire of Vanities; the Borgian predominance;
the accession of Francis I of France, etc., etc. Although Leonardo is the outstanding
figure, there are many interesting sketches of, or allusions to, such personages as the
following: Savonarola, Gian Galeazzo Sforza, Ludovico Il Moro and his wife Beatrice
d'Este, Cæsar Borgia, Pope Alexander VI, Machiavelli, Charles VIII, Louis XII, and
Francis I.

559. SIR GALAHAD OF THE ARMY: HAMILTON DRUMMOND;
Stanley Paul.
A French knight's adventures during the Italian Expedition of Charles VIII of France
(1494-95). King Charles and Philip de Commines are much to the fore in the earlier
part of the novel, while some account of the Battle of Fornovo (1495) is given.

560. A CITY OF CONTRASTS: KATHERINE JAMES; Chapman &
Hall.
Italy (Perugia, etc.)1495 and the few years following. An interesting tale of Art, and
Political disturbance, etc. Raphael and Perugino appear; also Ludovico Sforza sur-
named Il Moro, and the Borgian Pope, Alexander VI.

561. ELENA: EVELYN B. WARDE; Simpkin, Marshall.
Italy, 1492-97, and 1507. The novel contains careful studies of Cæsar Borgia and
his sister Lucrezia.

562. THE REVELS OF ORSERA; RONALD ROSS; Murray.
A somewhat fantastic romance of Switzerland, 1495, which, however, shows both
topographical and historical knowledge.

563. OVER AN UNKNOWN OCEAN: David Ker; *Juv. Chambers.*
An English boy picked up by a Portuguese ship off the Coast of Morocco in 1497, meets the navigator Vasco da Gama. This leads to a good tale of adventure which serves to illustrate the rounding of the Cape by Da Gama, and his success in reaching the West Coast of India in 1498.

564. *KING ERRANT: Flora Annie Steel; *Heinemann* [*Eng.*], *Stokes* [*U.S.A.*].
A record, in fictional form, of the first Great Mogul in India, commonly called Baber —covering the period from 1493 (boyhood) to 1530 (death).

SIXTEENTH CENTURY

565. *THE WRONG THING: Rudyard Kipling; *Juv.* In " Rewards and Fairies "—*Macmillan.*
England, at the beginning of the Sixteenth Century. A tale reflecting the latest part of King Henry VII's reign.

566. *GABRIEL AND THE HOUR BOOK: Evaleen Stein; *Juv. Page* [*U.S.A.*].
Normandy round about 1500. A particularly charming story of a boy who helps the monks in their work as book-illuminators. King Louis XII of France and Anne of Brittany are introduced.

567. THE HONOUR OF SAVELLI: S. Levett Yeats; *Sampson Low* [*Eng.*], *Appleton* [*U.S.A.*].
Italy (Florence and Rome) in the first few years of the 16th Century. A stirring tale of adventure, introducing many historical figures: Machiavelli, Cardinal d'Amboise, the Borgias (Pope Alexander VI, Cesare, and Lucrezia), and Bayard. The book ends with the death of Pope Alexander (1503), and with Louis XII of France at Arezzo.

568. *THE COURT OF LUCIFER: Nathan Gallizier; *Hamilton* [*Eng.*], *Page* [*U.S.A.*].
Rome 1500-1503. A sensational tale of Rome in the Renaissance and Borgian period. The hero is Alfonso, Prince of Ferrara, who comes to Rome in order to investigate the charges made against Lucrezia Borgia, whom Alfonso's father Duke Ercolé, wishes him to marry. How he conducts his investigations, and with what result, is told in the novel. There are allusions to the political intrigues and wars of the time, but historical persons, rather than events, are introduced. Of the Borgias, Pope Alexander VI and Cesare are depicted very adversely, but Lucrezia appears in a much more favourable light. Among the other figures are Machiavelli, Cardinal Juliano della Rovere (afterwards Pope Julius II), Julia Farnese, Fiamma Colonna, and Paolo Orsini. There is, also, the merest glimpse of Leonardo da Vinci and Raphael at the Vatican (Jubilee Reception). The novel virtually ends with the banquet, 1503, at which the Pope and Cesare were poisoned—the first-named fatally.

569. CÆSAR BORGIA: Emma Robinson; *Routledge.*
Italy (largely Rome), 1500-1503 (the closing pages pass rapidly to the later time of Cæsar Borgias's death). A romance of adventure, love, and hate, with depictions of Carnival, Tournament, etc. Illustrates the period of the Borgian alliance with France —the War in the Kingdom of Naples, etc. Cæsar Borgia is, of course, the outstanding figure, while his sister Lucrezia, and his father Pope Alexander VI, are a good deal in evidence. Another very prominent personage is Niccolò Machiavelli, and there is allusion to " a young painter named Raffaelo Sanzio,"

570. THE GORGEOUS BORGIA: Justin H. McCarthy; *Hurst & Blackett* [*Eng.*], *Harper* [*U.S.A.*].

Rome, etc., c. 1500-1507. A somewhat melodramatic story of the Borgias. The outstanding figure is Cesare Borgia (depicted as a monster); other historic personages are Pope Alexander VI and Cardinal Rovere—the a er appearing both as Cardinal, and as Pope under the title of Julius II.

---

571. (1) *THE SHAME OF MOTLEY. (2) *LOVE AT ARMS. (3) *THE BANNER OF THE BULL—all three by Rafael Sabatini; *Hutchinson* [*Eng.*], *Houghton Mifflin* [*U.S.A.*]. Also (4) *THE JUSTICE OF THE DUKE: Rafael Sabatini; *Stanley Paul.*

Four volumes connected historically, though fictionally separate. The author takes high place among the romancists who have dealt with Borgian Italy. Not only is he fitted on the imaginative side, to reconstruct the life of that extraordinary period, but, as writer of an excellent " Life of Cesare Borgia " (Hutchinson, Eng., and Houghton Mifflin, U.S.A.), he is historically equipped. The Cesare Borgia of his books is not the unmitigated scoundrel which many other novelists have presented, but a man with at least *some* redeeming qualities—a human being, not a demon. Besides the stories here given, there is a slight fictional sketch relating to the murder of the Duke of Gandia, entitled, " The Night of Hate," in the author's *Historical Nights' Entertainment: First Series* (Hutchinson, Eng., and Houghton Mifflin, U.S.A.). (1) Italy, 1498-1503. A very interesting romance, with Cesare Borgia, Lucrezia Borgia, and Giovanni Sforza as outstanding historic figures. (2) Another interesting story of Italy and the Sforzas about the year 1500: time of Cesare Borgia's conquests. (3) " Three Episodes " dealing with Cesare Borgia and Italy round about the year 1500. Exciting in themselves, these tales, or " episodes," give a clear picture of life and manners in Borgian times. The second tale (" The Perugian ") introduces Machiavelli. (4) Collective title of seven excellent tales illustrative of Cesare Borgia and his wars, etc., in the period between 1500 and 1505 or thereabouts. The last tale (" The Pasquinade "), introducing Pope Alexander VI, is perhaps one of the best.

---

572. THE HALF-PRIEST: Hamilton Drummond; *Stanley Paul.*

A story illustrating the troubles and dangers of life in an Italian State about the year 1502, when the Borgian power was in evidence. Cesare Borgia is prominently introduced; as here depicted, he strikes the reader as being an unscrupulous, but not an utterly detestable, man.

---

573. *MY LADY LUCIA: Arthur Ritson; *Mills & Boon.*

Italy round about 1503. A decidedly interesting historical novel, giving a well-balanced picture of Cesare Borgia, who appears prominently.

---

574. *THE CHALLENGE OF BARLETTA: M. Tapparelli-D'Azeglio (trans.); *W. H. Allen.*

S. Italy, 1503. A story which has for its main background the two really historic tournays which took place when Gonsalvo di Cordova, " the Great Captain," was waiting for reinforcements before venturing out of Barletta, then in a state of siege by the Duc de Nemours. How Gonsalvo eventually sallied forth and won his great victory over the French at Ceregnola is mentioned in the author's *Preface*, but is not described in the novel itself. Besides Gonsalvo, there are numerous historic figures, of whom the most important are the Duc de Nemours, Vittoria Colonna, Bayard, and Cesare Borgia.

---

575. THE DEATH RIDER: Nina Toye; *Cassell.*

An excellent story of Italy (Rome, etc.) at the time of Julius II's Pontificate (1503-13). The Pope himself is introduced prominently, and his nephew, Francesco Maria della Rovere, also appears.

---

576. *XIMÉNÈS: " Jean Bertheroy "; *Armand Colin et Cie* [*France*].

A striking romance of Cardinal Ximénès in 1500,

577. LITTLE MADAME CLAUDE: Hamilton Drummond; *Stanley Paul.*

A tale of France, 1505, and of the child-daughter of Louis XII's Queen. A Breton gentleman goes from Blois to Amboise to recover possession of the child's person. The Queen (Anne of Brittany) appears, and there are glimpses of the King and the Cardinal of Amboise.

578. DESIDERIO: Edmund G. Gardner; *Dent.*

Italy, beginning of 16th Century (tale proper). A Renaissance novel depicting the very sanguinary period when Pope Julius II and King Louis XII of France were much to the fore in Italian politics. A glimpse of Savonarola preaching, is given in the *Prologue.*

579. FATHER MATERNUS (PETER MATERNUS): Adolf Hausrath (trans.); *Dent* [*Eng.*], *Dutton* [*U.S.A.*].

A young monk in Rome, 1511 (time of Pope Julius II). The romance depicts various aspects of the Roman life of the period—the Ghetto, etc.

580. UNDER BAYARD'S BANNER: Henry Frith; *Juv. Cassell.*

A tale by one of the older " juvenile " writers, telling of the Chevalier de Bayard, and the Battle of Ravenna (1512), etc.

581. THE ROMANCE OF THE FOUNTAIN: Eugene Lee-Hamilton; *Fisher Unwin.*

Florida, 1512-21. The quest for the " Fountain of Youth " by the Spanish adventurer, Juan Ponce de Leon, and—resulting from his search—the discovery (1512) of Florida, where he was made governor.

582. *TRUE HEART: Frederic Breton; *Grant Richards.*

An historical romance of real merit, depicting life in Switzerland (City of Basel) and Germany, 1514-25. The hero is a scholar whose experiences illustrate the intellectual and religious ferment of the period, as well as its politics. The defeat of the Switzers by Francis I of France at Marignano is one of the historical events covered. Paracelsus and Erasmus, respectively, are prominent figures in the novel, and other less eminent personages appear in the course of the story.

583. *THE FRIAR OF WITTENBERG: W. Stearns Davis; *Macmillan.*

A romance of Italy and Germany in the period, 1517-21. The outstanding figure is, of course, Martin Luther, and the main occurrences of these important years of his life are carefully presented: Tetzel's sale of Indulgences and Luther's posting of the theses at Wittenberg (1517); scenes at Leipzig, Rome, etc., and Worms (1518-21); and the chief scene of all, showing Luther at the *Diet of Worms* before the Emperor Charles V. The reader will meet with many familiar names besides those already mentioned—Melanchthon, Pope Leo X, etc.

584. *CHRONICLES OF THE SCHÖNBERG—COTTA FAMILY: Mrs. E. Rundle Charles; *Juv. Nelson* [*Eng.*], *Dodd, Mead* [*U.S.A.*].

Germany, mainly between 1503 and 1547. Many localities are touched, including Erfurt, Eisenach, Wittenberg, the Black Forest, and Eisleben. Illustrates the earlier and later periods of Luther's career—picturing him both as Reformer in the great world, and as Man in his own home. Besides the outstanding figure of Luther, other historic personages (such as Philip Melanchthon) appear.

585. THE SWORD OF THE LORD: Joseph Hocking; *Cassell* [*Eng.*], *Dutton* [*U.S.A.*].

England (Henry VIII), and—chiefly—Germany, 1517. This story of an Englishman sent on a secret mission to Germany, illustrated (as the sub-title indicates) " the time of Luther." Besides the great Reformer himself, Tetzel, Erasmus, and many others are introduced.

---

586. *DIE HOSEN DES HERRN VON BREDOW: " Wilibald Alexis "; *Janke* [*Germany*].

A romance of the Reformation period by one of Germany's most famous historical novelists.

---

587. *LICHTENSTEIN: Wilhelm Hauff (trans.); *Nister* [*Eng.*], *Dutton* [*U.S.A.*].

S. Germany (Ulm, the Swabian Alps, Stuttgart, etc.), 1519. An excellent tale of the struggle between Duke Ulrich of Würtenberg and the Swabian Union. There are, moreover, interesting fictional developments. Ends with the Swabian Union's re-conquest of Würtemberg, and the Duke's escape to Switzerland. Duke Ulrich is, of course, prominent, and the Chancellor Ambrosius Bolland is another figure.

---

588. *IN THE OLDEN TIME: Margaret Roberts; *Longmans* [*Eng.*], *Holt* [*U.S.A.*].

Germany (the Thuringian forest region—Ulm, etc.), and, in small degree, the Tyrol, 1524 onwards. A novel giving a good description of the Peasant War of 1524-25, with special reference to Duke Ulrich of Würtemberg and his struggle with the Swabian League. The Duke is favourably depicted—the influences of his exile period having already developed his character. There is a Reformation atmosphere of religious discussion, etc. Besides Duke Ulrich, his son Christopher is brought into the story.

---

589. *DIE WEISSEN GÖTTER: Eduard Stucken; *Erich Reiss* [*Germany*].

A trilogy dealing with Mexico and Montezuma in the period before and after the advent of Cortes. The last-named leader is presented as a man of strong individuality.

---

590. MONTEZUMA'S DAUGHTER: H. Rider Haggard; *Longmans*.

England, Spain and Mexico between 1515 and 1525. Autobiographical romance of an Englishman (half-English, half-Spanish) who seeks the Spanish murderer of his mother; he eventually fights with the Aztecs against the Spaniards. A distinctly sensational tale, in which the Emperor Montezuma, his brother successor Cuitlahua, Cortes, and Cacama, all appear.

---

591. BY RIGHT OF CONQUEST: G. A. Henty; *Juv. Blackie* [*Eng.*], *Scribner* [*U.S.A.*].

England (Plymouth) and Mexico, 1516-21. A tale of land and sea adventure (shipwreck), but mainly dealing with the Conquest of Mexico by Cortes. Besides the Conqueror himself, King Cacama, Montezuma, and other historic figures are introduced.

---

592. THE GOLDEN PASSPORTS: Albert Lee; *Juv. Shaw*.

Another story of the Conquest of Mexico, beginning Spain, 1518. Both Cortes and Montezuma are introduced.

---

593. THE FAIR GOD: Lew Wallace; *Warne* [*Eng.*], *Houghton Mifflin* [*U.S.A.*].

Mexico, 1519-20. A young Spaniard is the hero of this somewhat elaborate story reflecting the period of Cortes' Conquest of Mexico, and virtually ending with the death of Montezuma. Cortes, Montezuma, King Cuitlahua, and others appear.

594. THE INCA'S RANSOM: ALBERT LEE; *Juv. Partridge.*
Spain (Cadiz and Madrid), and Peru, 1529 onwards. A tale having Pizarro's Conquest of Peru as its main background. Pizarro, De Soto, and the Incas appear more or less prominently, while there is a glimpse of the Emperor Charles V in the concluding pages (Spain once again).

595. *THE CRIMSON CONQUEST: CHARLES BRADFORD HUDSON;
   Richards [Eng.], *McClure* [U.S.A.].
Panama and Peru, 1531 and the few years following. An excellent adventure romance, illustrating the Conquest of Peru by Pizarro, and introducing—besides Pizarro himself—De Soto, the Inca Atahualpa, and the young Inca Manco.

596. PERU—CHILDREN OF THE SUN: LILIAN HAYES; in "The
   Thirtieth Piece of Silver"—*Fisher Unwin.*
A short episode, or tale, dealing with Peru in the time of Pizarro.

597. *THE ARROW OF THE NORTH: R. H. FORSTER; *John
   Long.*
One of the author's North Country stories exhibiting first-hand knowledge of locality. Northumberland in the Henry VII—Henry VIII period. The romance leads up to the First Scottish War (Henry VIII), and ends with the famous Battle of Flodden, in which James IV of Scotland was defeated and slain by the English under the Earl of Surrey (1513).

598. THE CRIMSON FIELD: HALLIWELL SUTCLIFFE; *Ward, Lock.*
North Yorkshire (Wharfedale), Durham, and Northumberland, with a glimpse of Edinburgh, 1513. King James IV of Scotland appears, and the novel ends with a full account of the Battle of Flodden.

599. IN THE KING'S FAVOUR: J. E. P. MUDDOCK; *Digby.*
A romance of James IV of Scotland, in the last months (1513) of his reign, ending with an account of the disaster at Flodden.

600. THE BRAES OF YARROW: CHARLES GIBBON; *Chatto &
   Windus* [Eng.], *Harper* [U.S.A.].
A novel by one of the older writers of historical romance. Scotland, just after Flodden, in the years 1513-14. The Queen Regent, the Boy-King, and the Earl of Angus.

601. WHEN KNIGHTHOOD WAS IN FLOWER: CHARLES MAJOR
   ["E. CASKODEN"]; *Sands* [Eng.], *Bowen-Merrill* [U.S.A.].
England and France, c. 1509-1515. A love romance of Charles Brandon (created Duke of Suffolk in 1514) and Mary Tudor—Henry VIII's sister. From quite a crowd of historic figures, one may select for mention—Henry VIII, Wolsey and Louis XII of France.

602. *THE ARMOURER'S PRENTICES: CHARLOTTE M. YONGE;
   Juv. Macmillan.
London, New Forest, Calais, etc., mainly 1515-35. A tale illustrating the period of Wolsey as Cardinal, etc., up to his death, and ending with the execution of Sir Thomas More. There are several historic figures, notably: Henry VIII, Wolsey, Sir Thomas More and his family (careful depiction), the Duke of Norfolk, Colet, and Erasmus.

603. EVIL MAY-DAY: E. EVERETT GREEN; *Juv. Nelson.*
A good short tale of London, 1517: Henry VIII in the early part of his reign. The author has chosen as background, the hatred of alien artificers, and the consequent riot of the 'prentices (Newgate attacked, etc.)

604. *THE BARON'S HEIR: Alice Wilson Fox; *Juv. Macmillan.*
A story of Sir Thomas More and his young children in 1518 (Hertfordshire and London). Besides More himself, King Henry VIII is prominent, while there are glimpses of Holbein and other personages of the time.

---

605. *THE HOUSEHOLD OF SIR THOMAS MORE: Anne
Manning; *Dent [Eng.], Dutton [U.S.A.].*
Chelsea, 1522-35. A short, but striking, tale in the form of a diary by Sir Thomas More's daughter Margaret. The great man himself is, of course, the central figure in the narrative which gives a charming account of him in his family circle, and in company with his intimate friends. Many historic personages besides More are either introduced or mentioned; especially vivid is the presentment of Erasmus in the early pages of the book, while the reader is, later, offered glimpses of Henry VIII, Cardinal Wolsey, Holbein, the Duke of Norfolk, Reginald Pole (afterwards made Cardinal), and others. The story covers the fall of Wolsey, the coronation of Anne Boleyn, and, lastly, the events which led to the downfall and execution of More himself. The atmosphere of the period is most skilfully conveyed.

---

606. DARNLEY: G. P. R. James; *Routledge [Eng.], Dutton [U.S.A.].*
Mainly England (Kent and London) and France in the year 1520. An historical romance introducing many personages of the time, and describing the circumstances which led up to the famous Field of the Cloth of Gold. Among a crowd of figures, King Henry VIII, Cardinal Wolsey, and Francis I of France, are the most important.

---

607. WESTMINSTER ABBEY: Emma Robinson; *Routledge.*
Cambridge and (chiefly) London districts, 1527. The story, which suggests the atmosphere of the English Reformation, opens with a discussion between the three Cambridge Reformers, Latimer, Ridley, and Cranmer, passing quickly to Westminster. There are full descriptions of the Abbey, etc., and the fictional developments illustrate the coming of Anne Boleyn and Wolsey's loss of power. Of the numerous figures introduced (besides the Cambridge Reformers already named) the following are the most important: Henry VIII, Wolsey, Thomas Cromwell, Queen Katharine of Aragon, and Anne Boleyn.

---

608. *MY LORD CARDINAL: Charles Brunton Knight; *John Long.*
A novel chiefly of England (though there are scenes in Germany, Italy, and elsewhere), in 1530. The outstanding figure—as the title hints—is Cardinal Wolsey at the close of his career—his arrest in York, and his death at Leicester on the way south to London.

---

609 *WINDSOR CASTLE: W. Harrison Ainsworth; *Dent [Eng.], Dutton [U.S.A.].*
Windsor (Castle and Forest), 1529-36. An historical romance, mainly dealing with the period of Anne Boleyn's triumph and downfall. There is much about the Castle itself and the half-legendary stories connected with it. Of the historical figures, Henry VIII, Anne Boleyn, Catherine of Aragon, Jane Seymour, Cardinal Wolsey, the Earl of Surrey and Sir Thomas Wyatt, are the most important.

---

610. *DEFENDER OF THE FAITH: Frank Mathew; *Lane.*
York, Wharfe, and London, 1530-40. A novel of unusual character. Instead of following the conventional type of historical fiction, the author offers his readers several interesting portraits of famous men and women as they appear in a succession of quite sparkling dialogues. There are not many descriptions of events, but the account of Cardinal Wolsey's arrest is a fine piece of imaginative writing. The romance covers, in rapid survey, Wolsey's death at Leicester, More's downfall, Henry VIII's divorce from Queen Catherine, Anne Bullen's coronation and her eventual death on the scaffold, the Pilgrimage of Grace, the fall of Anne of Cleves, the coming of Catherine Howard, and the downfall of Thomas Cromwell. Most of these personages appear, as well as others—the following being particularly prominent: Henry VIII, Wolsey, Anne Bullen (the

author's spelling), the sixth Earl of Northumberland, Robert Aske, Thomas Cromwell, Lord Darcy, and Sir Henry Norris. The author explains, in his prefatory note, that *all the chief characters are real " except Lady Northumberland," while " few of the scenes are historical."*

---

611. THE KING'S MASTER: OLIVE LETHBRIDGE and JOHN DE STOURTON; *Stanley Paul.*

London and Windsor neighbourhoods, etc., 1536. The outstanding figures in this historical story, are Thomas Cromwell and Queen Anne, while Henry VIII and Sir Thomas Wyatt are the most noteworthy among the other historical personages. The novel covers the coming of Jane Seymour and the downfall of Anne.

---

612. *THE KING'S ACHIEVEMENT: ROBERT HUGH BENSON; *Pitman.*

Largely Lewes and London in the period 1533-40. A novel depicting the persecution of Roman Catholics during the supremacy of Thomas Cromwell, and the Dissolution of the Monasteries period (the destruction of Lewes Priory is a main feature). A great many historic personages are introduced, of whom the most prominent are Thomas Cromwell, Henry VIII, Sir Thomas More and Margaret Roper, Bishop Fisher, Cranmer and Latimer. Roman Catholic standpoint.

---

613. THE LADY OF BLOSSHOLME: H. RIDER HAGGARD; *Hodder & Stoughton.*

England (Eastern Counties and London), 1535-36. A tale of the Pilgrimage of Grace, introducing both Henry VIII and Thomas Cromwell.

---

614. THE CUSTOM OF THE MANOR: JOHN TREVENNA; *Mills & Boon.*

Devonshire (Dartmoor region) at the time of Thomas Cromwell's Dissolution of the Monasteries. The author can always be trusted in the matter of his special local colour (Dartmoor).

---

615. MY LORD READING: GERTRUDE HOLLIS; *Juv. S.P.C.K.* [*Eng.*], *Gorham* [*U.S.A.*].

A tale of Reading Abbey and its last Abbot, mainly 1538-39 (*ends* 1549). Tells of the Dissolution of the Abbey, etc. Elizabeth as a child-princess appears in a Windsor Forest episode. Henry VIII and Thomas Cromwell are also introduced.

---

616. THE QUEEN'S NURSE: BERNARD CAPES; in " Historical Vignettes "—*Fisher Unwin* [*Eng.*], *Stokes* [*U.S.A.*].

A tale of Jane Seymour and the birth of Edward VI in 1537.

---

617. *THE FIFTH QUEEN; *PRIVY SEAL (*sequel*): both by FORD MADOX HUEFFER; *Alston Rivers*; also—*THE FIFTH QUEEN CROWNED (*sequel*): by same author; *Eveleigh Nash.*

A well-written trilogy, depicting the rise and fall of Katharine Howard in the period 1540 to 1542. Besides Katharine herself, many historical personages are introduced— more especially King Henry VIII, Lady Mary of England, Anne of Cleves, Thomas Cromwell, and Archbishop Cranmer.

---

618. A STORMY PASSAGE: HETTIE TRAVERS; *Digby Long.*

A careful fictional study of Katharine Howard, Henry VIII's Queen, in the two years 1541 and 1542, ending with her execution. Cranmer is especially prominent.

---

619. MOOR AND MOSS: MARY H. DEBENHAM; *Juv. National Society* [*Eng.*], *Whittaker* [*U.S.A.*].

A pleasing tale of Cumberland and the Border Country (Liddesdale) in 1520 and the years following. The raids of the Armstrongs, etc.

G

620. A PRINCE OF GOOD FELLOWS: ROBERT BARR; *Chatto &*
Windus.
    A volume of stories dealing with that adventure-loving personage, James V of Scotland.

621. THE FIGHT AT SUMMERDALE: JOHN GUNN; *Juv. Nelson.*
    The Orkneys, Edinburgh, and Normandy in the second quarter of the 16th Century.
An adventure tale in which King James V of Scotland appears more than once.

622. *THE HOUR BEFORE THE DAWN: JOHN KNIPE; *Lane.*
    The Scottish Border in the late second quarter of the 16th Century. Cardinal Beaton
is an outstanding figure, and the story deals with the periods just before, and just after,
the death of James V of Scotland (December, 1542). Both the King and his Queen
(Mary of Guise) are introduced.

623. TWO DOVER BOYS: GERTRUDE HOLLIS; *Juv. Blackie.*
    A tale of adventures in the Mediterranean and N. Africa (Barbary), 1534-35. The
time is that of the corsair Barbarossa, and of the Emperor Charles V's capture of Tunis.

624. THE BATTLE BY THE LAKE: DORA BEE; *Juv. R.T.S.*
    Switzerland, Italy, and Germany, 1525-38. Zwingli the Reformer is an outstanding
figure in this interesting tale, and the Battle of Kappel, in which he lost his life, is
described. The Emperor Charles V is also prominent.

625. *THE MAID OF FLORENCE; or, NICCOLÒ DE' LAPI:
M. TAPPARELLI—D'AZEGLIO (trans.); *Bentley* [1853].
    Florence, 1529-30. An interesting romance of the period when the Florentine Republic
was defending itself against the army of the Emperor Charles V. The novel is, however,
less an account of the Siege of Florence than a picture of Florentine life just before and
during the event.

626. *THE PLOUGH OF SHAME: MARY BRADFORD WHITING;
Dent.
    Ferrara (largely), Bologna, and other localities in Italy, 1529-33. A carefully written
and interesting story of the days of the Emperor Charles V and Pope Clement VII.
There is a substantial background of history—the Peace of Cambrai (1529), the Coronation of Charles V at Bologna in the same year, the Siege and Fall of Florence, the Plague,
etc. Ariosto, Tasso, and Michelangelo appear (the last-named in a very prominent
manner).

627. WHEN THE CLOCK STRIKES TWELVE: VIOLET T. KIRKE;
Juv. In " When the Clock Strikes "—*Sheldon Press* [*Eng.*], *Macmillan* [*U.S.A.*].
    A good short story of Italy and France in the years 1534 and 1540, introducing Ben-
venuto Cellini.

628. THE RED CONFESSOR: NATHAN GALLIZIER; *Hamilton* [*Eng.*],
Page [*U.S.A.*].
    Rome, c. 1538-41. A sensational romance in which Benvenuto Cellini is prominent;
other historic figures greatly to the fore, are Pope Paul III and his infamous son, Pier
Luigi, Duke of Parma. Depicts the political scheming, as well as the social corruption,
of the time. There are some extraordinary fictional adventures, while crimes (" poison
mist " scenes, etc.) follow in quick succession. Besides the three important personages
already named, Michael Angelo is brought into the story; he is seen at the end of his
labours over *The Last Judgment.*

629. UNDER THE ROSE: Frederic S. Isham; *Ward, Lock* [*Eng.*], *Bowen-Merrill* [*U.S.A.*].

France in the second quarter of the 16th Century (round about 1540). A love and adventure story in which a ward of King Francis I, and an Austrian Duke are the prominent figures. How a "fool" turns out to be no fool, must be left to the author's own showing. Besides Francis I, several historic personages appear: Rabelais, Charles V (King of Spain and Emperor of Germany), Henry the Dauphin, and Henry d'Albert, King of Navarre.

---

630. ASCANIO: Alexandre Dumas (trans.); *Dent* [*Eng.*], *Little, Brown* [*U.S.A.*].

Paris and Fontainebleau, 1540. A romance of the French Court, especially with reference to Benvenuto Cellini's visit, and his relations with King Francis I. Besides the more properly historic element supplied by these and other figures, as well as by the allusions to the politics of France and Spain, there is much love and adventure after the author's well-known fictional style. The atmosphere of Francis' Court was, of course, more or less devoid of morals, and this is to some extent reflected in the story. Francis I and Cellini are the dominating figures, while, among the host of other personages, one may name: the Duchesse d'Etampes the King's favourite, the Dauphin (afterwards Henry II), and the Emperor Charles V.

---

631. THE TWO FLAMES: Mabel Maas (trans.); *Cape.*

Leyden and Bruges in early 16th Century. A story giving a clear picture of the religious and political developments of the time, besides showing knowledge of localities.

---

632. MARGUERITE DE ROBERVAL: Thomas G. Marquis; *Fisher Unwin.*

Canada, about 1541. A story of the time of Jacques Cartier's third voyage, when the Sieur de Roberval, a nobleman of Picardy, had been appointed Viceroy in Canada by Francis I of France. Roberval was to follow Cartier, but there was delay, and subsequent mischance.

---

633. *A FIREBRAND OF THE INDIES: E. K. Seth-Smith; *Juv.* *S.P.C.K.* [*Eng.*], *Macmillan* [*U.S.A.*].

A good tale of Francis Xavier, the "Apostle of the Indies," covering his association with Loyola in Paris (1534), his time in North Italy, his voyage (1542) as missionary to Portuguese India, and his labours in various Eastern regions. The book ends with Xavier's death (1552) in Goa, after founding a mission in Japan.

---

634. *THE STROLLING SAINT: Rafael Sabatini; *Stanley Paul* [*Eng.*], *Houghton Mifflin* [*U.S.A.*].

Italy (Milan, etc.) round about the year 1545—the time of the Emperor Charles V. The romance introduces Pier Luigi Farnese, son of Pope Paul III, and vividly depicts Italian life in those dangerous times. The reader is shown the working of the Inquisition, the political scheming, and the unscrupulous villainy of men like Pier Luigi.

---

635. A MARTYR'S SERVANT:
   A MARTYR'S HEIR (*sequel*): Arthur S. Cripps; *Duckworth.*

These two small volumes form one complete narrative told in the first person. The entire period covered is 1553 to 1594, beginning with the supposed narrator's Oxford days. The main story skilfully illustrates the early Jesuit Missions in South-East Africa: the "Proto-Martyr" of Mashonaland, etc.

---

636. THE MONASTERY: Sir Walter Scott; *Black, and other publishers —English and American.*

Melrose, and the Tweed near Abbotsford, 1547. Not usually deemed a good example of Scott. The novel reflects the time of the quarrel with England over the young Queen Mary's marriage. The Regent Murray appears, also the Earl of Morton. The *sequel* to this story, viz., "The Abbot," deals with a period twenty years later, and will be found in its correct place.

637. MARY OF LORRAINE: JAMES GRANT; *Juv. Routledge* [*Eng.*], *Dutton* [*U.S.A.*].

Scotland, 1547-48. Another story dealing with the time when the question of the little Queen Mary's marriage was to the fore; the alternative lay between the French Dauphin, or Edward VI of England. The tale covers the English invasion under Somerset, and the defeat of the Scots at the Battle of Pinkie. The Queen-Mother (Mary of Lorraine) is the outstanding figure, while the Regent Arran and others appear.

638. THE SPANISH BROTHERS: DEBORAH ALCOCK; *Juv. Nelson.*

Spain (Alcala, Seville, etc.), 1549-59, mainly from 1556, covering Philip II's victory over France at the Battle of St. Quentin. A well-written religious tale of two brothers (the one in the Church, the other in the Army), illustrating the period of the Inquisition and the two great Autos in Seville: the imprisonment and torture of Prostestants, etc. Time of Don Carlos de Seso and Juliano Hernandez. This book—which has been a favourite with more than one generation of youthful readers—is written from the Protestant standpoint.

639. *THE PRINCESS OF CLÈVES: MADAME DE LA FAYETTE (trans.); *Routledge* [1925].

A famous psychological novel, occupying an important position in the history of World Literature; it was, indeed, a departure from the unreal methods adopted by previous authors in the realm of imaginative writing or love-romance. With regard to its value as an *historical* story, its place is less assured; though, even in this respect, it does undoubtedly reflect the manners and ways of a bygone age. Originally published in the year 1678, its characters are taken almost entirely from well-known men and women of *the Louis XIV period*, but nominally it deals with the Court of Henri II, mid 16th Century.

640. *BRAVE EARTH: ALFRED TRESIDDER SHEPPARD; *Cape* [*Eng.,*], *Doran* [*U.S.A.*].

Mainly England (West Country) in the period 1529-1550 (Henry VIII—Edward VI). A very stimulating novel of the Reformation, reflecting the atmosphere of the period in a somewhat unusual manner. Illustrates, in particular, the Western Rising of 1549. Several historic Englishmen, including Henry VIII, are introduced, while an early chapter takes the reader abroad, and yields a glimpse of Rabelais at Lyons.

641. THE GIRLHOOD OF QUEEN ELIZABETH: HARRIET T. COMSTOCK; *Juv. Harrap.*

England in the Henry VIII—Edward VI period. A pleasing historical tale of Elizabeth's early years. Other prominent figures are Queen Anne and Henry VIII (earlier part of the story), Princess Mary, Lady Jane Grey, and Edward as Prince and King.

642. ENGLAND'S ELIZABETH: (JUDGE) E. A. PARRY; *Smith, Elder.*

Hertfordshire, Norfolk, and London, 1536 onwards (Henry VIII—Elizabeth). An "Elizabethan" novel in a very full personal sense. The period covered is a long one, and the author effectively introduces such events as Ket's Rebellion and the later rebellion led by Sir Thomas Wyatt. Numerous historic figures—the most important being Elizabeth as Princess and as Queen, Roger Ascham, Henry VIII, Protector Somerset, William Cecil, Gardiner, and the Earl of Leicester (the novel ends with Leicester's disgrace over dealings with Spain).

643. *THE LONELY QUEEN: H. C. BAILEY; *Methuen.*

A very careful and interesting novel of London district, etc., c. 1540 to 1566 (Henry VIII—Elizabeth). The central figure is Elizabeth both as Princess and Queen, while Sir William Cecil plays an important part in the later chapters. Among the many other historic figures, one may specify:—Henry VIII, Edward VI, Queen Mary, Lady Jane Grey, Philip of Spain, Admiral Seymour, Dr. John Dee, and Dudley.

644. *THE PRINCE AND THE PAUPER: "MARK TWAIN"; *Juv.* Chatto & Windus [*Eng.*], Harper [*U.S.A.*].

A delightful story of Edward VI—first as Prince, then as King, 1546-47 (London and district). The Prince exchanges clothes with a pauper boy who chances to be his "double," and the consequences of this act are worked out both amusingly and tragically. Illustrates the wretched condition of the poorer classes at the time. Besides Edward himself, many historic personages appear—notably Henry VIII, Princess Elizabeth, Lady Jane Grey, and Protector Somerset.

645. THE WATCH-DOG OF THE CROWN: JOHN KNIPE; *Lane.*

London (The Tower), Hampton Court, etc., in the time of Edward VI and Protector Somerset. An entertaining historical story, in which many noteworthy figures appear:—Hugh Latimer, the Princess Elizabeth, the young King himself, and (very prominently) Lord Admiral Seymour. The execution of the last-named in 1549, is covered.

646. *THE COLLOQUIES OF EDWARD OSBORNE: ANNE MANNING; *Juv.* Routledge [*Eng.*], Scribner [*U.S.A.*].

An autobiographical tale of a London 'prentice—the actual founder of the family which in 1694 attained ducal eminence (Leeds). The narrative well illustrates life in the Edward VI—Elizabeth period; there are various allusions to important personages and events—the death of Edward VI, the political and religious troubles of Mary's reign, etc. The story is quaintly and pleasantly told.

647. FOR KETT AND COUNTRYSIDE: F. C. TANSLEY; *Juv. Jarrold.*

A good tale of Norfolk in 1549, and the Rebellion headed by Robert Kett, a tanner of Wymondham, in the reign of Edward VI.

648. A QUEEN OF NINE DAYS: EDITH C. KENYON; *Juv.   R.T.S.*

A very pleasing little story of Lady Jane Grey.

649. THE DAUGHTERS OF SUFFOLK: W. J. NICOLLS; *Lippincott.*

Leicestershire, Westminster, etc., mainly in the period 1551-60. A romance of the two sisters, Lady Jane Grey and Lady Katharine Grey. Covers Lady Jane's marriage with Lord Guildford Dudley, her few days as "Queen," her imprisonment in the Tower, and her execution. One of the other events touched, is the marriage of Lady Katharine Grey with Edward Seymour, Earl of Hertford, followed by their imprisonment. Numerous personages besides those already named:—Roger Ascham, Edward VI, Queen Mary, the Duke of Northumberland, Sir John Cheke, Protector Somerset, John Aylmer, and John Heywood.

650. *THE TOWER OF LONDON: W. HARRISON AINSWORTH; *Dent, and other publishers,* [*Eng.*], Dutton [*U.S.A.*].

A really excellent historical romance of London and the Tower, 1553 (just after Edward VI's death) to 1554. The outstanding figure is Lady Jane Grey, while Queen Mary and the Princess Elizabeth are also prominent. The story covers Northumberland's execution, and Wyatt's Insurrection, as well as the chief Lady Jane Grey incidents. Besides the personages already mentioned, several others are presented: Cranmer, Ridley, Gardiner, Courtenay (Earl of Devonshire), and Roger Ascham. This novel—ending with Lady Jane's execution—shows Ainsworth at his best.

651. *THE ROYAL SISTERS: FRANK MATHEW; *John Long.*

London, 1553-56 (Edward VI—Mary). This very interesting novel, after beginning with the times immediately preceding and following Edward VI's death, covers many important events: the Duke of Northumberland's execution, Wyatt's Rebellion, Lady Jane Grey's execution, Queen Mary's marriage with Philip II of Spain, and the burning of Cranmer. Primarily, however, the romance furnishes a study of the two "royal sisters," Mary and Elizabeth.

652. "I CROWN THEE KING": MAX PEMBERTON; *Methuen.*
Sherwood Forest (Ollerton) and London, 1554. An outlaw romance, with considerable historic background. There is some account of Wyatt's Rebellion, while Queen Mary and her Chancellor Bishop Gardiner, appear more or less prominently.

653. PLOT AND PERIL: H. E. BOYTEN; *Juv. Cassell.*
An adventure story (Oxfordshire) of Queen Mary's time, with Cardinal Pole as the chief historical figure in the background.

654. *THE QUEEN'S TRAGEDY: ROBERT HUGH BENSON; *Pitman.*
Cambridge, London, Richmond, etc., 1554-58. The novel is essentially theological in tone, being primarily an apology for Queen Mary, written from the Roman Catholic standpoint. The historical background is considerable:—the Queen's marriage with Philip of Spain; the coming of Cardinal Pole; the treatment of Ridley, Latimer, and Cranmer; the conspiracies of the time; and other incidents. Mary is, of course, the outstanding figure, but Cardinal Pole, Gardiner, the Princess Elizabeth, and Latimer, are also to the fore; while Philip II, Renard, Cranmer, and many others appear.

655. CARDINAL POLE: W. HARRISON AINSWORTH; *Herbert Jenkins.*
England, 1554-58. This romance—which is a fair example of Ainsworth—begins with the arrival of Philip of Spain in England and his marriage with Queen Mary, and ends with the latter's death. Numerous historic personages are introduced—Cardinal Pole, of course, being a central figure. Bishop Bonner is, also, especially prominent.

656. THE STORY OF FRANCIS CLUDDE: STANLEY J. WEYMAN; *Cassell [Eng.], Longmans [U.S.A.],* also *Murray [Eng.].*
England (Forest of Arden district, etc.) and the Netherlands, mainly in the period 1555 to 1558. The tale illustrates religious and political disturbances generally, without introducing definite historical events. Bishop Gardiner appears as Lord High Chancellor, and the Duchess of Suffolk is prominent. As in the English section, so also in that part of the story which deals with the Netherlands, there is only a very slight historical element.

657. *THE SEA CAPTAIN: H. C. BAILEY; *Methuen [Eng.], Doran [U.S.A.].*
A romance of the Mary—Elizabeth period. Berks—Wilts region, and Bristol, 1556; then a series of sea fights and land adventures in and around the Mediterranean, the English Channel, etc. Introduces Mary Queen of Scots, and Barbarossa the pirate, telling, also, of the Spanish Fleet, and the discovery of Spain's designs against England. This lively tale of rascality and wild enterprise virtually ends with a glimpse of Lord Burghley and Queen Elizabeth at Whitehall.

658. MR. KELLO: JOHN FERGUSON; *Harrap.*
Scotland (District of the Lammermuirs and Edinburgh) in the third quarter of the 16th Century. The story well conveys the atmosphere of the period when religious superstition (witch-hunting, etc.) was rife.

659. THE ROYAL ROAD: CAROLA OMAN; *Fisher Unwin.*
France and Scotland, 1558-67. An historical tale beginning with Mary Queen of Scots' early marriage with Francis, the Dauphin of France (son of Henri II)—a boy of 14, some six weeks younger than herself. The scene quickly changes to Scotland, the novel then covering Mary's tragic experiences up to the time of her being lodged in the Castle of Lochleven. Riccio, Darnley, and Bothwell are in turn prominent.

660. MARY HAMILTON: LORD ERNEST HAMILTON; *Methuen.*
A Scottish romance of Mary Hamilton (one of the " Queen's Maries "). While historically true in atmosphere, the book is doubtfully so in the working of its main situation. Darnley, Moray, and other figures.

661. *THE QUEEN'S QUAIR: Maurice Hewlett; *Macmillan.*

A brilliant romance illustrating an important period in the career of Mary Queen of Scots. The novel begins France, 1560, just after the death of Francis II (Mary's first husband), but the main scenes are laid in Scotland during the period 1561 to 1567. Besides Mary herself, Bothwell, Moray, John Knox, Darnley, and a crowd of other historic figures are introduced. The romance practically ends with the tragedy of Darnley's death. Some critics—though not all—regard this example of Hewlett as his finest effort.

662. THE QUEEN'S MARIES: G. J. Whyte Melville; *Longmans.*

Begins Calais, but mainly Edinburgh (Holyrood), Stirling, etc., 1561-65. This pleasing tale deals with the earlier period of Mary Queen of Scots, from her arrival in Scotland up to her marriage with Darnley. Besides the Queen and her " Maries " (Beaton, Seton, Carmichael, and Hamilton), there are several historic figures: John Knox, Bothwell, Chastelâr, David Riccio, Moray, Morton, Arran, and Darnley.

663. FAIR HELEN OF KIRKCONNELL LEA: Douglas Moubray; *Hayes.*

A novel of the Scottish Border and Edinburgh, in 1565. The time is that of Darnley's marriage with Mary Queen of Scots.

664. KIRK O' FIELD: a Romance; Edward Albert; *Hodder.*

Prologue : Mary Queen of Scots and the murder of Rizzio. Book I treats of Darnley and Bothwell, 1566-67, ending with Darnley's murder; while Book II depicts Bothwell 1567-68, including his fall.

665. *THE ABBOT: Sir Walter Scott; *Black, and other publishers— English and American.*

Avenel Castle, Edinburgh, and Lochleven Castle, 1567 to 1568. A much finer novel than *The Monastery,* to which it is the sequel. The portrayal of Mary Queen of Scots is particularly striking. With regard to episodes covered, there is a description of the Battle of Langside, and the book ends with the escape of the Queen from Lochleven Castle. Besides Mary herself, there are other historical figures—the Regent Murray and George Douglas (youngest brother of Sir William Douglas) being two of the most prominent.

666. *UNKNOWN TO HISTORY: Charlotte M. Yonge; *Jun. Macmillan* [Eng.], *Harper* [U.S.A.].

England (N. Midlands, London and Richmond) 1568-87. A pretty story of Mary Queen of Scots during her captivity at Tutbury, Chatsworth, etc., Chartley and Fotheringhay. Besides the unfortunate Queen, there are several historic personages, including Queen Elizabeth, Mary Seton, Bess of Hardwicke, the Earl of Shrewsbury, Babington, and Paulet. A page or two at the end transport the reader to 1597.

667. *THE MASTER OF GRAY: H. G. Bailey; *Longmans.*

An interesting novel of Scotland, France, and England, c. 1580-87: time of the captivity of Mary Queen of Scots, etc. Many historical figures: in Scotland—James VI, the Earl of Arran, and others; in England—Elizabeth, Burghley, Walsingham, and Sir Philip Sidney. France is touched in the period of Henri III and the League.

668. *ONE QUEEN TRIUMPHANT: Frank Mathew; *Lane.*

Hampton, London, etc., and Fotheringay 1586-87. An interesting romance, though historical personages are somewhat too freely introduced. The hero, through his brother, finds himself implicated in the Babington Conspiracy and has many startling experiences (the tale is written in the first person). Among the more striking scenes are those preceding the signing (by Elizabeth) of Mary Queen of Scots' death-warrant; the interview between Elizabeth and Mary at Fotheringay; and Mary's execution. The fictional love developments are connected in a very special manner with the unfortunate Queen Mary. Both the latter personage and Queen Elizabeth are introduced most prominently, while among the numerous other historic figures may be mentioned Walsingham (greatly to the fore), Anthony Babington, Burghley, Leicester, and Sir Amyas Paulet.

669. WHERE ENGLAND SETS HER FEET: Bernard Capes; *Collins.*

An interesting romance of Elizabethan England in the period 1560-1585. The scene alternates between London district and South Devon (Ashburton, etc.). Mainly a land story, but there is a sprinkling of sea adventures. The hero's birth-mystery and his love-making are important elements. The Earl of Leicester and Sir Walter Raleigh are prominent, while Sir Richard Grenville and other historic figures appear.

670. *HENRY ELIZABETH: Justin H. McCarthy; *Hurst & Blackett.*

An excellent love and adventure tale, 1568, beginning and ending in Devon, but mostly London district (Court scenes, with Queen Elizabeth introduced). There is a noteworthy Lundy Island episode; while, in regard to historical personages besides Elizabeth, Dr. Dee makes an appearance.

671. *BY WHAT AUTHORITY: R. H. Benson; *Pitman.*

England (Sussex, London, Lancashire, etc.) in the period between 1570 and 1590. The novel takes as its background the theological controversies between Catholic and Protestant in Elizabethan times—emphasizing the hard lot of the Catholics under persecution (the martyrdom of Campion, etc.). Among the many historical figures more or less prominent, one may note Queen Elizabeth, Walsingham, Archbishop Grindal, and Campion (already named). There are many references to Drake, the Armada, etc., but the depiction of historic occurrences is secondary to the illustration of Catholic sufferings.

672. A WARWICKSHIRE LAD: George Madden Martin; *Juv. Appelton.*

A simple, but pleasantly told, story of Shakespeare's boyhood from the age of five (i.e. about the year 1569) upwards.

673. PAM THE FIDDLER: Halliwell Sutcliffe; *Werner Laurie.*

West Yorkshire, 1569. A romance dealing with the Nortons of Rylstone (Wordsworthians will recall the poem connected with this name), and the Catholic Rising. Introduces several historic figures—the most important being Elizabeth, Mary Queen of Scots (at Bolton), and Sir William Cecil.

674. UNDER THE ROSE: Felicia Curtis; *Sands.*

Windsor, Hampton Court, etc., 1569 onwards. An unambitious tale of Elizabethan times, written from the Roman Catholic standpoint. Queen Elizabeth, Leicester, John Lyly, Cecil, Walsingham, and the Duchess of Suffolk are introduced.

675. MASTER SECRETARY: James Ireland; *Hodder & Stoughton.*

A carefully written Elizabethan story of the period 1570-72. Sir William Cecil (Burleigh) is the outstanding figure, while Mary Queen of Scots and Queen Elizabeth are also prominent. Mostly England (London, Chatsworth, etc.), but there are also scenes in the Low Countries, Italy, and Spain (Philip II).

676. *DAVID ARNOT: Michael Barrington; *Crosby Lockwood.*

Italy (Padua), and—for the most part—Scotland, c. 1571-72. A student, skilled in medicine, through force of circumstances finds himself in an uncongenial Galloway atmosphere. The story of what eventually befell him, illustrates in a vivid—if somewhat too unrelieved—manner, the bigotry of the anti-necromancy period.

677. LOVE WHILE YE MAY: Henry J. Swallow; *Jarrold.*

London and Durham County, mid to late 16th Century. The London scenes are dated 1547 and 1592 respectively, but the story in its main development is connected with the Durham coast region, etc., at the time of the insurrections in the North, 1569-72.

678. RALPH WYNWARD: Miss H. Elrington; *Juv. Nelson.*

A good little tale of Elizabethan Ireland, leading up to the Sack of Youghal.

679. *MAELCHO: Emily Lawless; *Methuen* [*Eng.*], *Appleton* [*U.S.A.*].
A clever, but gloomy, story of Ireland round about 1579: period of the Desmond Rebellion.

---

680. *SIMPLE SIMON: Rudyard Kipling; *Juv.* In " Rewards and Fairies "—*Macmillan.*
A short tale of Drake in his earlier days.

---

681. WHEN HAWKINS SAILED THE SEA: Tinsley Pratt; *Juv. Grant Richards* [*Eng.*], *Brentano's* [*U.S.A.*].
A story dealing with the disastrous third voyage of Sir John Hawkins to the Spanish Main (1567).

---

682. SEA-DOGS ALL: Tom Bevan; *Juv. Nelson.*
A capital Elizabethan story of the Forest of Dean region, London, and the Spanish Main. Drake, Raleigh, and Queen Elizabeth are introduced.

---

683. WITH DRAKE ON THE SPANISH MAIN (ON THE SPANISH MAIN): " Herbert Strang "; *Juv. Oxford University Press* [*Eng.*], *Bobbs-Merrill* [*U.S.A.*].
Another " Spanish Main " story, telling of adventures among the Islands of the Caribbean Sea in the days of Elizabeth.

---

684. UNDER DRAKE'S FLAG: G. A. Henty; *Juv. Blackie* [*Eng.*], *Scribner* [*U.S.A.*].
A tale beginning Plymouth, but mostly dealing with adventures on the Spanish Main and in South America. Covers the period 1572-88, ending with the Armada.

---

685. *WESTWARD HO!: Charles Kingsley; *Macmillan, and other publishers.*
Devon (Bideford, etc.) and the West Indies in the Elizabethan period, 1575 to 1588. A deservedly popular romance of adventure, love, and fighting; covers a considerable period, and tells of varied scenes and episodes (Spaniards, Indians, the Inquisition, etc.) Towards the end of the story there are some thrilling fictional developments, which are bound up with that amazing historic event—the defeat and utter destruction of the Spanish Armada. Several great figures are introduced: Sir Richard Grenvil, Spenser the poet, Raleigh, Philip Sidney, Drake, and Hawkins.

---

686. TWO GALLANT SONS OF DEVON: " Harry Collingwood "; *Juv. Blackie.*
Begins Devonport, 1577, but is chiefly a story of sea and land adventures in the South American region (Cartagena, Cuzco, etc.) The usual Inquisition and Treasure-finding episodes.

---

687. IN THE DAYS OF DRAKE: J. S. Fletcher; *Juv. Blackie* [*Eng.*], *Rand & McNally* [*U.S.A.*].
A Yorkshire boy is carried away to Mexico and has varied experiences, 1578-80. The Spanish Inquisition is a main element, and the tale ends with the hero's release.

---

688. HIS SOVEREIGN LADY: Charles Gregory; *Melrose.*
A story of Devon, London, and the sea, round about 1581. Queen Elizabeth is prominent, while Drake is also introduced. A good specimen of the " treasure-search " romance.

---

689. *COME RACK! COME ROPE!: Robert Hugh Benson; *Hutchinson* [*Eng.*], *Dodd, Mead* [*U.S.A.*].
Derbyshire, London, etc., 1579-88. Illustrates the religious position in the period just given—the position, that is, as viewed by the able Roman Catholic author. The Jesuit martyr, Campion, is prominent, and Mary Queen of Scots' later period of captivity is an importnat background to the story. The depiction of Mary's character, and the account of Catholic sufferings, at least supplement—if they do not reverse—the more conventional assumptions of Elizabethan fiction.

690. FOR DRAKE AND MERRIE ENGLAND: S. WALKEY; *Juv.*
    Cassell.
A tale of England and the Spanish Main in the period just preceding the Armada.
Elizabeth is prominent (the hero saves her life), and Drake is also much to the fore.

691. 'GAINST THE MIGHT OF SPAIN: PERCY F. WESTERMAN;
    Juv. Pilgrim Press.
A tale of the period, 1582-88. Sea and land adventures (the Spanish Main, the
Inquisition, Pirates, etc.), ending with the Armada. Queen Elizabeth appears in the
closing pages.

692. *SIR MORTIMER: MARY JOHNSTON; *Constable* [*Eng.*], *Houghton
    Mifflin* [*U.S.A.*].
The Spanish Indies and England (Whitehall) in the years immediately preceding
the Armada (say 1583-86). This interesting tale of England's naval supremacy in Elizabethan times, covers Drake's harrying of Cartagena, etc. There is, of course, much
adventure in the way of fighting against the Spaniards—the taking of a Spanish galleon,
etc. The hero suffers from the unjust accusation of being a traitor. Queen Elizabeth,
Sir Francis Drake, and the Countess of Pembroke are prominent figures, while there
are glimpses of Philip Sidney and others.

693. IDONIA: ARTHUR F. WALLIS; *Sampson Low.*
Somerset and London about the year 1585. This " romance of Old London " (as
the sub-title describes it) is one of considerable interest and merit.

694. BY STROKE OF SWORD: ANDREW BALFOUR; *Methuen* [*Eng.*],
    Lane [*U.S.A.*].
Fife, Devon and the West Indies in the time preceding the death of Mary Queen of
Scots. A vigorous adventure story of land and sea, introducing Drake, etc.

695. *SIR LUDAR: TALBOT BAINES REED; *Juv. R.T.S.*
An excellent adventure tale of England (London, Oxford, etc.), S. Scotland (barely),
and Ireland (Dunluce and Dublin), about 1585 and the few years following. There
is a considerable background of history, including the Armada. Sir John Perrot appears
in the account of the Dublin episode.

696. *THE GATE HOUSE: MARGARET BAINES REED; *Juv. Arnold.*
An inn on the Great North Road, 1586—mainly the Highgate Hill and Hampstead
regions, as well as London proper. An¹ interesting tale dealing with Babington's
plot for the murder of Elizabeth and the release of Mary Queen of Scots. Babington
himself appears, also (at the end) Queen Elizabeth. There is just a glimpse of Shakespeare.

697. *RENÉGAT: AUGUSTIN FILON; *Armand Colin* [*France*].
A romance of England in the time of Drake and the Armada, etc. Covers the period
1586 to 1593.

698. THE GATE OF ENGLAND: " MORICE GERARD "; *Juv.*
    Arnold.
A good tale of London and Dover, c. 1587, introducing quite a crowd of historical
personages—Queen Elizabeth, Leicester, Burleigh, Drake, the Duke of Parma, etc. etc.

699. A FAIR PRISONER: " MORICE GERARD "; *Juv. Partridge.*
A tale of Drake's naval performance in the Harbour of Cadiz, 1587. Drake himself is
introduced very prominently. The fictional hero has various sea and land adventures.

700. THE BARREN WOOING: RAFAEL SABATINI; in " The His-
    torical Nights' Entertainment " *Second Series*—*Hutchinson* [*Eng.*],
    Houghton Mifflin [*U.S.A.*].
A narrative which presents an ingenious theory regarding the death of Amy Robsart.

701. *KENILWORTH: Sir Walter Scott; *Black, and other publishers—English and American.*

Oxfordshire and Warwickshire, 1575. A romance of Elizabeth and Leicester, in which the Queen is very skilfully depicted. With regard to the episode of Lady Dudley's death, Sir Charles Firth says that it is " full of inaccuracies." Amy Robsart's death really occurred in 1560, and some historians acquit Leicester of guilt. But these deviations from historical record do not lessen enjoyment of the book for most readers.

702. A LADDER OF SWORDS: Gilbert Parker; *Heinemann.*

Jersey and London in the earlier Elizabethan period. In this tale of a fugitive Huguenot both Queen Elizabeth and Leicester are much to the fore. Not one of the author's best examples.

703. *HER MAJESTY'S GODSON: " E. Barrington "; in " The Gallants "—*Harrap* [Eng.], Dodd, Mead [U.S.A.].

An Elizabethan love story, introducing Philip Sidney, Raleigh, the Queen, and others. Told in the form of supposed letters of Sir John Harington.

704. PENSHURST CASTLE: Emma Marshall; *Juv. Seeley* [Eng.], *Macmillan* [U.S.A.].

A tale of Sir Philip Sidney and Penshurst (Kent) in the few years leading up to his death at Zutphen in 1586. Numerous historic figures are introduced as well as Sidney.

705. *THE GLORY OF HIS DAY: G. I. Whitham; *Juv.* in " The Shepherd of the Ocean and other Tales of Valour "—*Wells Gardner.*

An excellent imaginative sketch of Sir Philip Sidney as boy and man (England and abroad), ending with his death. Leicester, Henry of Navarre, De Guise, Drake, etc.

706. THE QUEEN'S KNIGHT ERRANT: Beatrice Marshall; *Juv. Seeley* [Eng.], *Dutton* [U.S.A.].

S. Devon (Ottery region, etc.), London district, and Sherborne, mainly between 1580 and 1592. A story with Sir Walter Raleigh as the outstanding figure. Almost at the beginning allusion is made to Drake's return from his " Pelican " voyage, and the background of history throughout is carefully suggested and illustrated. Besides Raleigh, Queen Elizabeth and Essex appear, while there are glimpses of such notabilities as Edmund Spenser, Dr. Dee the astrologer, and Christopher Marlowe.

707. *CROATAN: Mary Johnston: *Thornton Butterworth* [Eng.], *Little, Brown* [U.S.A.].

Begins Plymouth (with a glimpse of Raleigh), 1587, but the romance mainly treats of folk sailing to Virginia and their experiences in Croatan Island—adventures among the Cherokee Indians, etc.

708. *BONAVENTURE: H. C. Bailey; *Methuen.*

England (Salisbury, New Forest, and Southampton), also Spanish Flanders (Brussels, etc.), 1586-87. A stirring romance largely dealing with certain Spanish plots against Queen Elizabeth's life. The hero " Nicholas Bonaventure "—half poet, half adventurer—is an attractive figure. The period is that of the late captivity and execution of Mary Queen of Scots, or, more precisely, the two years preceding the Armada. Sir Francis Walsingham is somewhat prominently introduced, while Queen Elizabeth, Lord Burghley, and the Prince of Parma appear in the course of the story.

709. *ROSSLYN'S RAID: Beatrice H. Barmby; in " Rosslyn's Raid and Other Stories "—*Duckworth.*

A short, but powerful, tale of fighting on the Scottish Border in Elizabethan days.

710. THE OUTLAWS OF THE MARCHES: Lord E. Hamilton; *Fisher Unwin* [Eng.], *Dodd, Mead* [U.S.A.].

Another Border tale (Liddesdale) about the year 1587.

711. LOYAL HEARTS AND TRUE: E. EVERETT GREEN; *Juv.*
     Nelson.
A fair example of this writer, dealing with Elizabeth and her Court, and introducing
Walsingham, Sidney, and other figures. The tale ends with the Armada.

712. *A FLAME OF FIRE: JOSEPH HOCKING; *Cassell* [*Eng.*], *Revel*
     [*U.S.A.*].
Hertfordshire, Cornwall, and (mainly) Spain—Toledo, the Escurial, Seville, etc.,
1587-88. The hero tells about the adventures of himself and two other Englishmen
while they were on a special search expedition in Spain. There is much about the
Inquisition, and, in the first of two interviews with Philip II of Spain, the hero is ques-
tioned about the state of the English Navy, etc. Later, when Lisbon is touched on the
voyage home, the Great Armada is seen (April, 1588), ready to start for English waters,
and the hero is enabled to give information to Drake and Hawkins as soon as he reaches
Plymouth. The story virtually ends with the defeat of the Armada (a mere sketch).
The principal historical figures are Father Parsons the Jesuit, Philip II of Spain, Drake,
and Hawkins.

713. BEACON FIRES: " MORICE GERARD "; *Juv. Hodder.*
A tale of the year 1588 (West Country), dealing more especially with the Spanish
assassination plot, and the Great Armada.

714. THE FOURTH QUEEN: ISABEL PATERSON; *Parsons* [*Eng.*].
     Boni & Liveright [*U.S.A.*].
Plymouth in Armada time (1588), and London, Windsor, etc. The central figure of
the story is the Earl of Essex whose career is illustrated up to his execution in 1601.
Various other historic personages are introduced.

715. THE SEA DEVILS: J. BLOUNDELLE BURTON; *White.*
Mainly Portugal (Lisbon, etc.), 1588. Begins with some references to the Armada,
but is primarily the story of an Englishman's experiences during captivity, and what he
endured under the Inquisition.

716. *THE BOG OF STARS AND OTHER STORIES AND
     SKETCHES: STANDISH O'GRADY; *Fisher Unwin.*
A series of stories dealing with Elizabethan Ireland (various dates between 1575 and
1602). Hardly fiction proper, but well-written imaginative history.

717. *THE FLIGHT OF THE EAGLE: STANDISH O'GRADY; *Fisher*
     Unwin.
Ireland in 1588: Sir John Perrott and Sir William Fitzwilliam. Once again history
imaginatively presented.

718. THE REBEL LADY: " JOHN BARNETT "; *Nisbet.*
A story of Western Ireland (mainly) and England, in the period 1589 to 1601. Tells
of a Spaniard saved from a sunk galleon, etc., with considerable historic background.
The Earl of Essex, Raleigh, and Queen Elizabeth appear.

719. A QUEEN OF MEN: WILLIAM O'BRIEN; *Fisher Unwin.*
Chiefly Ireland (Galway) in the Armada period. A sensational romance of Grace
O'Malley, introducing several historic figures, including Sir John Perrot. In the later
chapters Queen Elizabeth appears, and Perrot's death in the Tower (1592) is described.

720. THE SUNBEAM OF THE TOWER: BEATRICE HARRADEN;
     Juv. In " Untold Tales of the Past "—*Dent* [*Eng.*], *Dutton*
     [*U.S.A.*].
A short tale of Queen Elizabeth visiting the Tower of London about 1590.

721. THE GOLDEN GALLEON: ROBERT LEIGHTON; *Juv. Blackie*
[*Eng.*], *Scribner* [*U.S.A.*].
An adventure story introducing the famous fight of Sir Richard Grenville against the
Spaniards, in his ship *The Revenge*, off Flores, 1591. Both Grenville and Raleigh appear.

722. A KNIGHT OF GOD: EDITH MARY POWER; *Sands*.
Yorkshire, 1592. A story of Roman Catholics and their grievances under Elizabeth.

723. IN SPACIOUS TIMES: H. M. IMBERT-TERRY; *Ernest Benn.*
London, Lisbon, Spain, and Somerset (Quantock region), about 1595 or 1596. A
story of plot, Inquisition, and plague—of love and adventure, with a considerable
sprinkling, in the earlier chapters, of historic figures. Nash, Dekker, Robert Greene,
George Peele, and the Earl of Essex appear.

724. MY LORD OF ESSEX: MRS. CHARLES BROOKFIELD; *Pitman*.
Chiefly London and district; also Spain (the Capture of Cadiz), 1596. A novel
dealing largely with the Earl of Essex and Sir Robert Cecil. Other historic figures are
introduced, such as Queen Elizabeth and Raleigh.

725. (1) IN BURLEIGH'S DAYS: (2) THE SECOND CECIL
(*sequel*): E. BRANDRAM JONES; *John Long*.
Two connected historical romances. The first depicts England in the period 1588-94,
introducing Elizabeth, Burleigh, Bacon, Shakespeare, Jonson, Raleigh, Essex, etc.;
the second volume (sequel) covers 1598-1612 (the Elizabeth-James I period), with
Sir Robert Cecil as the outstanding figure. The beheading of Essex and the Gunpowder
Plot are the main events touched in this sequel, while—as before—many notabilities
appear: James I, Sir Francis Bacon, Prince Henry, and Shakespeare.

726. THE FAILURE OF A HERO: M. BRAMSTON; *Juv. S.P.C.K.*
[*Eng.*], *Gorham* [*U.S.A.*].
England, mostly in the period between 1590 and 1603, but the book ends 1612.
Hardly fiction in the strict sense, but a series of good fictional sketches strung together.
Shakespeare, Burbage, Essex, Coke, Wotton, Donne, Richard Hooker, Bacon, and
Spenser all appear. The Essex Rising is one of the historic events specially noted.

727. SPACIOUS DAYS: RALPH DURAND; *Juv. Murray*.
A well-told Elizabethan story, about the year 1599. Begins London, but mainly
describes sea adventures in the Far North (Arctic regions).

728. *THE GREAT AGE (ANNE FEVERSHAM): JOHN COLLIS
SNAITH; *Hutchinson* [*Eng.*], *Appleton* [*U.S.A.*].
Nottingham, Oxford, and London district in 1599. A love story with good historical
background. Shakespeare is really the central figure, and Burbage also appears. Queen
Elizabeth is depicted in conversation with Shakespeare himself.

729. *GLORIANA: RUDYARD KIPLING; *Juv.* In "Rewards and
Fairies"—*Macmillan*.
Queen Elizabeth "appears" (in a manner that only the tale itself can explain!)

30. THE QUEEN'S HOSTAGE: HARRIET T. COMSTOCK; *Little,
Brown* [*U.S.A.*].
Queen Elizabeth and her Court about 1590. A story of love and intrigue, introducing
Ben Jonson and Shakespeare (production of "Love's Labour Lost" at the Globe
Theatre).

731. *MASTER SKYLARK: John Bennett; *Juv. Macmillan* [Eng.],
     Harrap [Eng.], *Century* [U.S.A.].
   Stratford-on-Avon, Coventry, Northants, Herts, and London district (largely), in
1596. An excellent Elizabethan tale which many grown-ups will enjoy, as well as young
folk. The boy hero has a wonderful voice (hence his coming to be known as " Master
Skylark "), and the book tells of his adventures when he was carried off by a company
of touring players from his Stratford home to London. The mother of the hero is cousin
to Anne Hathaway of Shottery. Queen Elizabeth is well introduced, while Shakespeare
and Ben Jonson appear prominently in the last part of the story. Another prominent
figure is Thomas Heywood the playwright, and there are glimpses of Burbage, Green,
Richard Tarlton, and others.

732. *SHAKESPEARE'S CHRISTMAS: A. T. Quiller-Couch;
     in " Shakespeare's Christmas and Other Stories "—*Smith, Elder*
     [Eng.], *Dent* [Eng.], *Longmans* [U.S.A.].
   A short story of Shakespeare and his friends in 1598.

733. MIDSUMMER MORN: R. H. Forster; *John Long.*
   Tynedale and Liddesdale, 1598. A " raider " story of that Border region which the
author knows so thoroughly.

734. COURT CARDS: " Austin Clare "; *Fisher Unwin.*
   An end century tale of the intrigues between the English and Scottish Courts (Elizabeth and James VI). Covers the years leading up to the Gowrie Conspiracy in 1600.

735. *WITH ESSEX IN IRELAND: Emily Lawless; *Methuen*
     [Eng.], *Lovell* [U.S.A.].
   Dublin, Athy, Kilkenny, Limerick, Waterford, and other localities, in the year 1599.
In this story of the Earl of Essex, and his expedition for the purpose of quelling the
Irish Rebellion, the depiction of the Earl himself is really interesting. The three Earls
of Southampton, Ormonde, and Tyrone appear in the course of the narrative.

736. *THE CHARMING OF ESTERCEL: Grace Rhys; *Dent*
     [Eng.], *Dutton* [U.S.A.].
   Northern Ireland at the time of the Rebellion, end 16th Century, and covering the
withdrawal of Essex and his army in 1599. On the historical side, the Earl of Essex is
very prominent, and the opposition between him and Cecil is clearly brought out.
Another special figure in this well-written novel is O'Neil, Earl of Tyrone.

737. (1) *PRINCE AND HERETIC: (2) *WILLIAM, BY THE
     GRACE OF GOD (*sequel*): " Marjorie Bowen "; *Methuen*
     [Eng.], *Dutton* [U.S.A.].
   (1) Germany and the Netherlands in the third quarter of the 16th Century. William
of Nassau, Prince of Orange (his marriage with Anne of Saxony), the Nassau family
generally, and the Count of Egmont, are all prominent. The novel leads up to the resignation of William in 1567, the coming of Alva, and the revolt of the Netherlands; closing
with the failure of Orange's first conflict with Alva (1569).
   (2) The sequel brings to a conclusion the author's interesting fictional study of William,
Prince of Orange (" William the Silent ")—the period covered being 1572 to 1584.
The story opens when, to all appearance, the Prince had failed in his schemes; but the
reader is then shown, in a succession of pictures, how the Dutch gradually rose out of
their subjection to Spain. Besides the Prince of Orange himself, several historic figures
appear: Philip II of Spain, the Nassau brothers, the Duke of Anjou, and the Prince of
Parma.

738. *THE LEGEND OF ULENSPIEGEL AND LAMME GOEDZAK
     THE LEGEND OF THE GLORIOUS ADVENTURES OF
     TYL ULENSPIEDEL: Charles de Coster (trans.); *Heine-
     mann* [Eng.], *Doubleday* [U.S.A.]—also *Chatto & Windus* [Eng.].
   The Low Countries, Italy, etc., c. 1555 onwards. An historical novel of unmistakable
power, if somewhat coarse in tone. It gives a vivid picture of life in the Netherlands

at the time of " The Beggars," dwelling especially on the horrors of the Inquisition. Among the principal figures introduced, one may specify: The Emperor Charles V (his abdication), Philip II of Spain, and William the Silent (Prince of Orange).

739. *JAN VAN ELSELO: Gilbert and Marion Coleridge; *Macmillan.*

Paris, the Netherlands, England, and Spain, etc., 1559 (mostly), and 1572-73. A carefully written historical novel of the adventure type. The hero, a page of the Prince of Orange, after travelling on special missions (Holland and England) goes to Spain and has many thrilling experiences. The novel illustrates the Catholic schemes of Henri II of France and Philip II of Spain (the Inquisition, etc.), leading up to troubles in the Netherlands (Alva). The book closes with the success of the Sea Beggars and the resistance of Haarlem (1573). On the fictional side, a love element is introduced. Of the numerous historic figures, the most prominent, at one point or another, are: Henri II of France, Philip II of Spain, Alva, William of Orange (called " the Silent "), Egmont, and Count Horn, as well as—in the very brief English section—Elizabeth and Sir Thomas Gresham.

740. *IN TROUBLED TIMES: " A. S. C. Wallis " (trans.); *Sonnenschein.*

Netherlands (Gueldres, Brussels, etc.), 1563-72. An historical novel of unusual merit, covering the period of Margaret of Parma's Regency, the Rebellion of the Beggars, and the coming of Alva. There is some good character-drawing on the fictional side, the figure of " Meerwonde," a pessimist and cynic, being especially noteworthy. An atmosphere of theological speculation pervades a large portion of the romance, while historic personages and events are skilfully introduced. The closing pages indicate the leadership of the Prince of Orange and his brothers, and the beginning of the Beggars' success. The Regent Margaret is prominent and Alva also appears.

741. BROTHERS FIVE: Violet T. Kirke; *Juv. S.P.C.K.* [*Eng.*], *Gorham* [*U.S.A.*].

The Netherlands (Friesland, etc.), 1568-74. A tale covering several important historical events such as the seizure of Mons by Louis of Nassau, his surrender of the city to the Spaniards, and the Battle of Mookerhyde. *Epilogue*, 1579.

742. THE MASTER BEGGARS OF BELGIUM: L. Cope Cornford; *Dent* [*Eng.*], *Lippincott* [*U.S.A.*].

The Netherlands—largely Brussels—in 1568 (the last three chapters jump to the later period of 1570 onwards). A story of the " Beggars " in the time just following the triumphant entry of Alva into Brussels. Various historical allusions, including the beheading of D'Egmont and Horn (June, 1568). Louis of Nassau and others appear, while there is a glimpse of Alva.

743. *A KNIGHT OF SPAIN: " Marjorie Bowen "; *Methuen.*

A clever and interesting, but perhaps *over*-historical, novel. Don John of Austria is the outstanding figure, while his brother Philip II of Spain is considerably to the fore. One of the principal events covered is the great victory of the Holy League's fleet over the Turks in the sea-fight of Lepanto (1571). Later on, the reader is taken first to the French Court (Marguerite de Valois, etc.), and then to the Netherlands. The story ends with the death of Don John, as Viceroy of the Netherlands, in 1578.

744. LYSBETH: H. Rider Haggard; *Longmans.*

" A tale of the Dutch," beginning 1544, but the greater part of the book deals with the period 1571-74. The sieges of Haarlem and Leyden are both covered. William the Silent appears.

745. LEATHERFACE: Baroness Orczy; *Hodder & Stoughton* [*Eng.*], *Doran* [*U.S.A.*].

A tale of the Netherlands in 1572: time of the Beggars. The Prince of Orange and the Duke of Alva are prominently introduced.

746. THE WHITE HAWK: KENT CARR; *Juv. Chambers.*
North Holland in 1572. A tale of the fighting against Alva; the Prince of Orange appears.

---

747. MY LADY OF ORANGE: H. C. BAILEY; *Longmans.*
An Englishman in Holland (c. 1572) fights for William of Orange against Alva. A slight, but interesting, story, in which the Prince of Orange appears more than once.

---

748. BEGGARS OF THE SEA: TOM BEVAN; *Juv. Nelson.*
A good tale of the Revolt in the Netherlands, describing the heroic defence of Haarlem in 1573.

---

749. THE BURGOMASTER'S WIFE: GEORG EBERS (trans.); *Macmillan [Eng.], Appleton [U.S.A.].*
A story of the Siege of Leyden (1573-74), and the deliverance of the city through the cutting of the dykes. The " Beggars " were, in this way, able to sail up to the forts which Valdez had erected, and to effect their capture.

---

750. BY PIKE AND DYKE: G. A. HENTY; *Juv. Blackie [Eng.], Scribner [U.S.A.].*
A " tale of the Rise of the Dutch Republic " (sub-title), covering the sieges of Haarlem, Leyden, and Antwerp.

---

751. *RAOUL: GENTLEMAN OF FORTUNE: H. C. BAILEY; *Hutchinson [Eng.], Appleton [U.S.A.].*
Holland mainly in the period between 1573 and 1584. A romance yielding a succession of thrilling adventures in Leyden, Delft, Namur, and Antwerp. The Sieges of Leyden and Antwerp are well depicted. One of the historic figures introduced is the Prince of Parma.

---

752. *JACQUELINE OF THE CARRIER PIGEONS: AUGUSTA H. SEAMAN; *Juv. Sidgwick [Eng.], Sturgis [U.S.A.].*
A pretty tale of a girl of seventeen and her young brother in Leyden during its siege by the Spaniards, 1574.

---

753. THE " GREY FOX " OF HOLLAND: TOM BEVAN; *Juv. Nelson.*
The Netherlands (Bergen, Antwerp, etc.) and England, 1575-76. A short, but good, tale of adventure in the time of the Sack of Antwerp (Dutch revolt against Philip II of Spain).

---

754. FLOWER O' THE LILY: BARONESS ORCZY; *Hodder & Stoughton [Eng.], Doran [U.S.A.].*
The actual story deals with the year 1581, and the defence of Cambray against the Spanish army under the Duke of Parma. Queen Marguerite of Navarre and François Duke of Anjou appear.

---

755. KING STORK OF THE NETHERLANDS: ALBERT LEE; *Juv. Jarrold [Eng.], Appleton [U.S.A.].*
Described in the sub-title as " a thrilling romance of the Early Days of the Dutch Republic and the Spanish Inquisition." Leyden, Antwerp, etc., 1580-84. A tale dealing with the time of the plots against the life of William the Silent which resulted (1584) in his assassination by Balthasar Gérard. The treachery of the Duke of Anjou (" King Stork "), and the working of the Inquisition, are the principal subjects which form the background of the story.

756. SHUT IN: E. Everett Green; *Juv. Nelson.*
A story of the Siege of Antwerp, and its eventual capture by the Duke of Parma in 1585.

---

757. *THE ROMANTIC PASSION OF DON LUIS: Henri Malo (trans.) *Harrap.*
A really striking historical novel of the Low Countries (Dunkirk, etc.) in the period 1588-1620 (roughly). Begins with an account of the Great Armada, and then deals almost entirely with life in the Netherlands during the period of such men as the Duke of Parma, Cardinal-Archduke Albert of Austria, and Maurice of Nassau.

---

758. (1) *THE TWO DIANAS: (2) *THE PAGE OF THE DUKE OF SAVOY (*sequel*): Alexandre Dumas (trans.); *Dent [Eng.], Little, Brown [U.S.A.].*
(1) France, 1551 onwards, mainly in the time of Henry II and Francis II. Covers events like the defence of St. Quentin, the siege of Calais, and describes the deathbed of Francis II (d. 1560) who, as Dauphin, had married Mary Stuart. Among the principal figures are Henry II, Francis II, Diane de Poitiers, Catherine de' Medici, Mary Stuart, Duc d'Orléans (afterwards Charles IX), Marguerite de Valois, Duc de Guise, Cardinal de Lorraine, Philip II of Spain, and Queen Mary of England.
(2) France in 1555. Some of the events depicted in *The Two Dianas* are reproduced in this novel. Time of the Emperor Charles V's abdication in favour of his son Philip II of Spain, and of the troubles between the Guises and Catherine de' Medici, etc. Numerous historic figures such as Henry II, Catherine de' Medici, Diane de Poitiers, Duc de Guise, Cardinal de Lorraine, Coligny, The Emperor Charles V, Philip II of Spain, Queen Mary of England, and Cardinal Pole.

---

759. *ROYAL FAVOUR: " A. S. C. Wallis " (trans.); *Sonnenschein.*
Begins Germany (Wittenberg), but almost entirely Sweden (Stockholm, etc.), 1554-69. This story by the clever Dutch novelist, Miss Opzoomer, is of considerable psychological, as well as historical, interest. The outstanding figure is Göran Person, a pupil of Melanchthon, who in the course of the story becomes Chancellor to King Eric XIV of Sweden. Beginning his career as a student of brilliant gifts, and an idealist with lofty aims, Person is depicted as gradually succumbing to hard circumstance until the point of complete failure is reached. Of the several figures introduced besides Person, those of greatest historical significance are: Melanchthon, and the really great Gustavus Vasa of Sweden (these two in the earlier portions of the book), and the weak, passionate son of Gustavus—Eric XIV. The novel ends with the deposition of King Eric in 1569—his brother John being then elected to the throne.

---

760. THE BRIGAND: G. P. R. James; *Routledge [Eng.], Dutton [U.S.A.].*
Savoy (near the French frontier), Lyons, etc., also Paris and Fontainebleau, 1558-59. A romance of " the brigand, Corse de Leon." King Henry II of France is especially prominent, and, among other figures, one may specify Diane de Poictiers and the Maréchal de Brissac; there is, also, a glimpse of the Dauphin, Francis (Mary Queen of Scots' husband). The novel has a considerable historic background, and ends with Henry II's death.

---

761. A BOYAR OF THE TERRIBLE: F. Whishaw; *Longmans.*
A story of Ivan " the terrible " (Ivan IV) who was the first Russian sovereign to take the title of Tsar: period mid to late 16th Century. The historical background comprises the commercial treaty which Ivan concluded with Queen Elizabeth of England, and his annexation of Siberia. Ivan's earlier career is traced.

---

762. *THE TERRIBLE CZAR (PRINCE SEREBRENNI): Count Alexis K. Tolstoy (trans.); *Sampson Low and other publishers.*
Russia (Moscow region, etc.), 1565 onwards. An historical romance of high merit. The Czar Ivan IV is the central figure, but the novel gives, more especially, a *general* picture of Russian society—its manners and ideas. The horrors of the time are softened to some extent. The author (a Russian dramatist, poet, and novelist of considerable note), must not be confused with the much greater Count Leo (or Lyof) N. Tolstoy.

H

763. A KNIGHT OF ST. JOHN: F. S. Brereton; *Juv. Blackie.*
Mainly a tale of the Siege of Malta by the Turks in 1565 (from May to September), and its successful defence by Jean Parisot De La Valette, the Grand-master of the Knights of St. John.

764. *THE GOLDEN BOOK OF VENICE: Mrs. Lawrence Turn- bull; *Putnam [Eng.], Century [U.S.A.].*
A good picture of Venice, 1565 onwards. Fra Paola Sarpi is the outstanding figure of the book, which closes with his death in the early part of the 17th Century. The period depicted is that of the dispute between Venice and Pope Paul V—Sarpi becoming the chief advocate on the side of political and intellectual freedom. Another famous historical figure introduced is Veronese the artist.

765. THE MASTER MOSAIC-WORKERS " George Sand " (trans.); *Dent [Eng.], Little, Brown [U.S.A.].*
Venice, c. 1570. In this short tale of the mosaic-workers of St. Mark's, both Tintoretto and Titian appear.

766. KLYTIA: A. Hausrath [" George Taylor "]; *Sampson Low [Eng.], Gottsberger [U.S.A.].*
A story of Heidelberg, 1570, reproducing the theological atmosphere of the period (Calvinists, Zwingliites, etc.) Erastus is a very prominent figure.

767. THE SCARLET COCKEREL: C. M. Sublette; *Hodder & Stoughton [Eng.], Little, Brown [U.S.A.].*
Begins Paris 1561, but is mainly an adventure romance of the New World (Florida), based on Coligny's Huguenot Colony scheme. There is much about Spaniards and Spanish Treasure, etc. The story ends in France, 1568. The English Hawkins appears.

768. THE SWORD OF JUSTICE: Sheppard Stevens; *Gay & Bird [Eng.], Little, Brown [U.S.A.].*
A romance having as its background the struggle between Frenchmen and Spaniards for the possesssion of Florida, 1565.

769. THE LOVE OF MADEMOISELLE (formerly " In Search of Mademoiselle "): George Gibbs; *Appleton.*
An Englishman " tells " this story of England, Florida, and France (largely the two latter) in late 16th Century. This is yet another book depicting the struggle in Florida between French and Spanish colonists. Coligny and Charles IX of France are among the historical figures.

770. THE TRAITOR'S WAY: S. Levett Yeats; *Longmans [Eng.], Stokes [U.S.A.].*
France, 1560. An historical romance having for its background the Conspiracy, or " Tumult," of Amboise—a plot for removing Francis II of France from the Guise influence, and putting Condé at the head of the government.

771. THE SILENT CAPTAIN: "May Wynne"; *Stanley Paul.*
Nantes, Paris, and Amboise, 1560. Time of the Guise ascendancy, and the Catholic v. Huguenot struggle (the massacre of the Huguenots at Amboise).

772. *ABOUT CATHERINE DE' MEDICI: Honoré de Balzac (trans.); *Dent [Eng.], Little, Brown [U.S.A.].*
A somewhat " indigestible " book as fiction, though interesting as a study and defence of Catherine de' Medici. The novel proper deals with France 1560-74, ending with Charles IX's death. Besides Catherine and Charles IX, the following personages are more or less prominent: Mary Stewart, the Duc de Guise, Cardinal de Lorraine, Prince de Condé, and Henry of Navarre.

773. GASTON DE LATOUR: WALTER PATER; *Macmillan.*
   Chartres, Paris, etc., about 1562-72. Time of the Religious Wars and St. Bartholomew's Eve. Montaigne, Ronsard, Charles IX, and other figures. An unfinished philosophical romance; although merely a fragment, it has been much praised by critics of distinction.

774. UNDER COLIGNY'S BANNER: ALBERT LEE; *Juv. Morgan and Scott.*
   Mainly France (Bordeaux and Paris) between 1560 and 1575. Covers the time of the massacre of Vassy and the earlier Wars of Religion. The Cardinal de Lorraine is prominent, and many other historic personages are introduced—notably John Knox as a galley slave.

775. (1) *FOR THE RELIGION; (2) *A MAN OF HIS AGE
   (*sequel*): HAMILTON DRUMMOND; *Smith, Elder; also Ward, Lock* [*Eng.*], *Harper* [*U.S.A.*].
   Two connected romances of excellent quality, dealing respectively with: (1) France and Florida, 1562 and the few years following. The period of Coligny v. Guise, and of Coligny's Florida scheme; (2) France, 1568-72. The fierce antagonisms of Catholic and Huguenot, with Coligny and the Queen of Navarre especially prominent.

776. THE LUCKY PRISONER (*Le Prisonnier Chanceux*): J. A. DE
   GOBINEAU (trans.); *Heinemann* [*Eng.*], *Doubleday* [*U.S.A.*].
   France, 1563. A story of love and adventure, with a background of history (Catholic and Huguenot scheming, etc). A prominent historical figure is Diane de Poitiers in her retirement—the young Gascon hero of the novel being her godson.

777. A CARDINAL AND HIS CONSCIENCE: GRAHAM HOPE;
   Smith Elder.
   France round about 1565. A novel with Charles, Cardinal of Lorraine (brother of the second Duc de Guise), as central figure. Deals with the period of Catherine de' Medici's influence, and of the religious struggles in France—the Guises v. the Huguenots.

778. FOR THE ADMIRAL: W. J. MARX; *Juv. Hodder* [*Eng.*],
   Jacobs [*U.S.A.*].
   A tale of Admiral Coligny in the period 1568-72. Covers the Battle of Jarnac, the murder of Condé, the marriage of Henry of Navarre, and the massacre of St. Bartholomew.

779. ST. BARTHOLOMEW'S EVE; G. A. HENTY; *Juv. Blackie*
   [*Eng.*], *Scribner* [*U.S.A.*].
   Another tale of France in practically the same period as that illustrated in the book entered immediately above (Henty begins a year earlier). Among the principal events are the Battles of Jarnac and Moncontour, and—at the end of the tale—St. Bartholomew. Condé, Coligny, the King and Queen of Navarre, etc.

780. JOHN TEMPLE: RALPH DURAND; *Juv. Macmillan.*
   Portuguese expedition (Francisco Barreto) in South-East Africa, 1571-72. The scene is mainly the Zambesi Valley region. An Englishman, captured by the Portuguese, is the hero of the tale, which is one of sea and land adventures.

781. *COUNT HANNIBAL: STANLEY J. WEYMAN; *Murray* [*Eng.*],
   Longmans [*U.S.A.*].
   Largely a tale of Paris and Charles IX's Court in 1572: time of Henry of Navarre's marriage and of the St. Bartholomew Massacre. Besides the stirring Paris scenes, there are various provincial incidents in the Orléannais, etc. Although mainly an adventure story, the historical element is not inconsiderable, and there are two interesting depictions of Charles IX before and after " the St. Bartholomew " respectively.

782. *THE HOUSE OF THE WOLF: Stanley J. Weyman; *Longmans ;* also *Murray.*

A short, but striking, tale of France in 1572, turning on a certain incident during the St. Bartholomew Massacre. In the vivid description of the Massacre there is a glimpse of the Duc de Guise standing before the house of Coligny. In the man " De Bezers " we are given a somewhat unusual piece of character-drawing.

783. *EAUCOURT BY THE WATERS: John Buchan; in " The Path of the King "—*Nelson* [Eng.], *Doran* [U.S.A.].

A brief tale of the Massacre of St. Bartholomew.

784. *THE CHAPLET OF PEARLS: Charlotte M. Yonge; *Juv.* Macmillan.

England (slightly) and France, in the year 1572. Time of the King of Navarre's wedding, and of the Massacre of St. Bartholomew. A really good story with many historical figures such as Walsingham and Philip Sidney, King Charles IX of France, Catherine de' Medici, Coligny, and Henry of Navarre. Decidedly one of Miss Yonge's best efforts in the sphere of historical fiction.

785. *A CHRONICLE OF THE REIGN OF CHARLES IX: Prosper Mérimée (trans.); *Nimmo.*

Paris, etc., 1572-74. The well-known French writer's famous story of a French Huguenot gentleman's experiences in the period of the Bartholomew Massacre and La Rochelle. Most of the record deals with events in the one year 1572, but a few words at the end carry the reader to Charles IX's death in 1574. Among the several historical figures introduced, or to whom allusion is made, one may specially mention Coligny and Charles IX (both good depictions), while there are portrayals of Catherine de' Medici and Henry of Navarre.

786. *MARGUERITE DE VALOIS: Alexandre Dumas (trans.); *Dent* [Eng.], *Little, Brown* [U.S.A.].

France, 1572-75. A novel of love, adventure, and political conspiracy. Begins shortly before the St. Bartholomew, and then goes on to describe the terrible Massacre itself and the assassination of Coligny. The two leading figures of La Molle the Huguenot, and Coconat the Catholic, are both historical. The moral corruption of the time is reflected, and such murder devices as that of a " poisoned book," etc., are brought into the story. The conspiracy in connection with François, Duc d'Alençon, is an important feature. Ends with the death of Charles IX and the accession of Henri III. Catherine de' Medici, Marguerite de Valois and Henry of Navarre are dominating figures, and, of the many other personages introduced, the following are the most prominent:—Charles IX, the Duc d'Anjou, the Duc d'Alençon, Coligny, and the Duc de Guise (Henri of Lorraine).

787. THE WHITE PLUMES OF NAVARRE (THE WHITE PLUME): S. R. Crockett; *R.T.S.* [Eng.], *Dodd, Mead* [U.S.A.].

Paris, Southern France, and Spain, 1572 onwards. A story beginning in Paris on the Night of St. Bartholomew, and, later on, illustrating aspects of life under the Spanish Inquisition. Several historic figures, notably Henry of Navarre and Philip II of Spain.

788. ASHES OF VENGEANCE: H. B. Somerville; *Hutchinson.*

France (Paris, Tours, etc.), 1572 and the few years following. Mainly an adventure story, with a few historical allusions (the St. Bartholomew Massacre, etc.).

789. *IN THE PALACE OF THE KING: F. Marion Crawford; *Macmillian.*

Madrid in 1574. This very thrilling love and adventure story (covering a period of *hours*—not years!) is written around Don John of Austria's secret marriage at a time when his half-brother, Philip II of Spain, had schemes for his marrying Mary Queen of Scots. Besides Don John, King Philip is very prominent, while the latter's Queen also appears.

790. LOVE IN ARMOUR: Philip L. Stevenson; *Stanley Paul.*
France in the Charles IX—Henry III period, 1574. A love and adventure story,
with many historical figures, including Charles IX (an interesting depiction), Marguerite
de Valois, Henry of Navarre, and the Duke of Guise.

791. QUEST OF YOUTH: J. G. Sarasin; *Hutchinson.*
A good love story of France in 1576, with the Duc de Guise greatly to the fore.

792. THE MYSTERIES OF UDOLPHO: Mrs. Ann Radcliffe;
Routledge.
Southern France and Italy in the time of Henri III. Fault having been found with
me for the omission (deliberate) of this very famous " romance of terror," I now include
it. I would, however, warn intending readers that—whatever the tale's rightful claims
to be considered in any survey of Literature—as *historical* fiction it cannot be regarded
as of any real value.

793. *AN ENEMY TO THE KING: Robert Neilson Stephens;
Methuen [Eng.], Page [U.S.A.].
France (Paris, Guienne, etc.) 1578 and the ten years or so following. Time of the
League and the civil war between the Huguenots and the Catholics. Largely an adven-
ture story (the hero carries a letter to Henry of Navarre, etc.) Of the several personages
introduced more or less prominently, one may specify King Henry III of France, the
Duc de Guise, Marguerite of Navarre, and Henry of Navarre.

794. (1) *LA DAME DE MONSOREAU; (2) *THE FORTY FIVE
(sequel): Alexandre Dumas (trans.); *Dent [Eng.], Little, Brown
[U.S.A.].*
These two connected romances, having a gap of some years between them, may be
described separately.
(1) France in 1578: time of Henry III. This novel, under its author's usual wealth
of fictional detail, depicts the developments in connection with the League and the
Guises. King Henry III, Catherine de' Medici, François Duc d'Anjou, Henry of
Navarre, the Duc de Guise, Cardinal de Lorraine, and many others.
(2) France in 1585. This second romance (sequel) regarded historically, illustrates
for the most part the further growth of the League, and the Court of Henry of Navarre.
Both the last-named personage and Henry III are prominent as well as the Guises,
etc. etc.

795. A TRAP FOR NAVARRE: " May Wynne "; *Holden.*
A tale of Henry of Navarre's Court at Pau and Nérac, 1579. Henry himself and his
Queen are prominent. Catholic *v.* Protestant, love-making, etc.

796. *THE ADMIRABLE CRICHTON: W. Harrison Ainsworth;
Dent [Eng.], Dutton [U.S.A.].
Paris, 1579. A romance of James Crichton, son of the Scottish Lord Advocate,
Robert Crichton. He (James) was called " the Admirable " on account of his real
or supposed attainments as scholar, poet, athlete, and what not. With regard to the
novel, it is a very fair example of the author, depicting love and intrigue at the Court
of Henri III of France. Besides Crichton himself, numerous historic personages appear:
Henri III, Catherine de' Medici, Marguerite de Valois, Henry of Navarre, Chicot
the Jester, etc.

797. *A KING'S PAWN: Hamilton Drummond; *Blackwood [Eng.],
Doubleday [U.S.A.].*
One of the author's " Blaise de Bernauld " series of romances, of which *For the Religion*
and *A Man of his Age* have already appeared on another page. The present story of
France (Navarre) and Spain in 1584, tells of the hero's adventures in company with
Henry of Navarre. The time is that of the Duke of Anjou's death.

798. A CAVALIER OF NAVARRE: Charles. B. Stilson; *Hutchinson.*
France, 1587-90. A story covering the assassination of Guise, the death of Henry III,
and the Battles of Arques and Ivry. Henry of Navarre is of course introduced

799. *A GENTLEMAN-AT-ARMS: "Herbert Strang"; *Juv.*
    Oxford University Press.
Hispaniola, Normandy (Wars of the League), Low Countries, Spain, and Ireland
in the period 1587-97. There are very few English scenes in this excellent adventure
story of many lands. The historical background is well maintained, and such personages
as Henry of Navarre, Elizabeth, Raleigh, etc., are introduced.

800. THE KING'S MIGNON: J. Bloundelle Burton; *Everett.*
France, 1588. A story dealing with the assassination of the Duke of Guise, and the
few months following.

801. *A GENTLEMAN OF FRANCE: Stanley J. Weyman; *Long-
    mans*, also *Murray.*
France, 1588-89. An admirably-told and thrilling story of love, adventure, and
political intrigue. Covers the respective assassinations of the Duc de Guise (1588),
and Henri III (1589)—the romance depicting the time of the Peace between the French
king just mentioned and Henry of Navarre (both these personages are prominently
introduced). Quite one of the best examples of this deservedly esteemed writer of
historical fiction.

802. THE LOVE OF NAVARRE: Margaret Peterson; *Melrose.*
A novel illustrating the period of Henry of Navarre's campaign against the Leaguers
in Normandy, 1589, and also dealing with the events which led up to his Coronation
a few years later. King Henry is very prominent.

803. FOR FRANCE: "Morice Gerard"; *Juv. Odhams Press.*
France in 1590. The War of the League period, with Henry of Navarre as the outstanding historical figure. The tale virtually ends with the Battle of Ivry.

804. *FOR THE CAUSE: Stanley J. Weyman; in "In King's
    Byways"—*Murray* [*Eng.*], *Longmans* [*U.S.A.*].
A short, but excellent, tale of Henry of Navarre in 1591.

805. THE HELMET OF NAVARRE: Bertha Runkle; *Macmillan*
    [*Eng.*], *Century* [*U.S.A.*].
A tale of adventure and love in Paris, 1593, at the time of the City's surrender to
King Henry of Navarre. The King only appears in the closing chapters.

806. *THE ABBESS OF VLAYE: Stanley J. Weyman: *Longmans*
    [*Eng.*], *Burt* [*U.S.A.*], also *Murray* [*Eng.*]
Southern France (Lyons, etc.) 1595: a story of the peasant disturbances which occurred
in this year, when Henri IV was at the beginning of his reign. The King himself appears.
Conveys to the reader a clear impression of the time.

807. THE WARD OF NAVARRE: "Morice Gerard"; *Juv.*
    Odhams.
France (Amiens and Somme region), 1597-98. In this tale, which leads up to the
conclusion of the war with Spain, Henri IV is very prominent, while Sully and other
historic figures appear.

808. *THE GLORY OF DON RAMIRO: Enrique Larreta (trans.);
    Dent [*Eng.*], *Dutton* [*U.S.A.*].
A romance of exceptional worth, both imaginatively and historically. The scene is
Spain in 1570 (Part I), and 1591 onwards (Parts II and III). Depicts the conditions
in general, but especially the horrors of the Inquisition and the Moorish discontents.
The *Epilogue* is Peru, 1605.

809. *NOT FOR CROWN OR SCEPTRE: Deborah Alcock; *Juv.* Hodder & Stoughton.

Sweden (Upsala, Stockholm, etc.) 1570-93, and Russia (Moscow) c. 1600. A romance of Prince Gustaf Ericson Vasa, commencing *after* Eric XIV's deposition in 1569. Covers the reign of King John Vasa, the election (1587) of his son Sigismund to the throne of Poland as Sigismund III, the Regency of Duke Charles of Sodermania on King John's death in 1592, and the Great Synod at Upsala, 1593 (Protestant rights upheld). Ends in the Russia of Czar Boris Godunoff. One of the author's best tales, with the additional merit of illustrating events and characters rarely touched in fiction.

810. THE CARDINAL'S PAWN: "K. L. Montgomery"; *Fisher Unwin* [*Eng.*], *McClurg* [*U.S.A.*].

Florence and Venice (mainly the latter) about 1579. A highly-coloured romance of love and intrigue, in which members of the House of Medici (Cardinal Ferdinando and his brother Grand Duke Francesco) are greatly to the fore. An Englishman is one of the leading figures.

811. *LA PRINCESSE DE VENISE: Maxime Formont; *Lemerr* [*France*].

A good historical novel of Venice, 1597.

812. BEATRICE CENCI: F. D. Guerrazzi (trans.); *Bosworth & Harrison* [1858].

Rome and Naples, 1598-99. An historical romance dealing with the Cenci family—especially that unfortunate Beatrice of whom Shelley treats in his tragedy. The book is one of almost unrelieved gloom and horror. Pope Clement VIII and his nephew, Cardinal St. Giorgio, appear somewhat prominently.

813. JOHN VYTAL: William F. Payson; *Harper*.

Begins London under Elizabeth, but is mainly a tale of the Colony of Roanoke (island off the Coast of Virginia), 1587-98. Christopher Marlowe is introduced somewhat prominently.

814. *THE ADVENTURES OF AKBAR: Mrs. Flora Annie Steel; *Juv. Heinemann* [*Eng.*], *Stokes* [*U.S.A.*].

A tale of the great Akbar's childhood—how, as a baby-prince, he met with various adventures in the mountain region between Kandahar and Kabul. Intended for young children, but a book that will give pleasure to grown-ups also.

815. THE RUBY OF RAJAST'HAN: R. E. Forrest; *East and West, Ltd.*

A romance of Hindustan and Akbar in the third quarter of the 16th Century. Deals with the earlier part of Akbar's reign.

816. *A PRINCE OF DREAMERS: Mrs. Flora Annie Steel; *Heinemann* [*Eng.*], *Doubleday* [*U.S.A.*].

India about the decade 1580-90 (the story ends in the last-named year). A striking romance of Akbar, the great Mogul Emperor of India, illustrating his remarkable personality on its public and private sides: above all his religious tolerance, which gave Tennyson a subject for one of his latest and finest poetic efforts. Mrs. Steel's novel brings out such aspects of Akbar's reign as the unworthiness of his sons and the inevitable plots—"inevitable" seems the only word when we remember that the level of contemporary politics and religion was so far below the high aims (openly expressed) of a ruler centuries in advance of his time. The author's recognised knowledge of Indian life and manners is specially exhibited on its historical side in this book. "Akbar the dreamer, Birbal the doubter, Abulfazl the doer" (to quote Mrs. Steel's own description of them) are the principal historic figures. It may be added that the statesman, Abulfazl, left a valuable history of Akbar's reign.

817. *A NOBLE QUEEN: Philip Meadows Taylor; *Kegan, Paul.*
India (The Dekhan) between 1590 and 1600. An interesting romance of Queen Chand Beebee who defended the Dekhan in the first Moghul invasion. In the course of the story there is some account of the Portuguese missions at Goa and the Inquisition. Ends with the good Queen's death (murdered by her own people).

SEVENTEENTH CENTURY

818. THE CHEVALIER D'AURIAC: S. Levett Yeats; *Longmans.*
France round about 1600. The hero goes through many adventures, and reveals a conspiracy to Henri IV. Both the King and his Minister, Sully, appear.

819. THE DIARY OF A STATESMAN: Stanley J. Weyman; in " In Kings' Byways "—*Murray* [*Eng.*], *Longmans* [*U.S.A.*].
Three interesting tales of Henri IV and his minister, Sully. The period is, roughly, the turn of the Century (last tale 1602).

820. *FROM THE MEMOIRS OF A MINISTER OF FRANCE: Stanley J. Weyman; *Cassell* [*Eng.*], *Longmans* [*U.S.A.*], also *Murray* [*Eng.*].
France in the period 1598-1610. A series of short tales illustrating the character of Henri IV, and indicating the author's historical study of both the man and his times.

821. *THE LONG NIGHT: Stanley J. Weyman; *Longmans* [*Eng.*], *McClure* [*U.S.A.*], also *Murray* [*Eng.*].
An excellent adventure novel, having for its historical background the Savoyard attack on the City of Geneva in 1602.

822. THE GREY MAN: S. R. Crockett; *Laurie* [*Eng.*], *Harper* [*U.S.A.*].
Scotland (mostly Carrick region, but also Edinburgh) in the first year or two of the 17th Century. A tale of conspiracy, feud (Kennedy v. Kennedy), disorder and murder. The author has taken certain actual occurrences and developed them fictionally. King James VI (shortly to become " James I " of England) appears prominently at the end; while the Earl of Cassilis and other real figures are brought into the story.

823. THE HAND OF THE NORTH: Marion Fox; *Lane.*
Begins in late Elizabethan London, 1601, at the time of the Essex plot and its failure, but the more interesting part of the story is that which deals with Hexham (Northumberland) and the wild Border district.

824. QUEEN ELIZABETH: Bernard Capes; in " Historical Vignettes "—*Fisher Unwin.*
A very brief, but vivid, story of Queen Elizabeth on February 25th, 1601 (the beheading of Essex).

825. *ULRICK THE READY: Standish O'Grady; *Sealy, Bryers* [*Ireland*].
An excellent story of Ireland at the end of Elizabeth's reign. One of the principal historical events introduced is the Battle of Kinsale (1602).

826. IN SPACIOUS TIMES: Justin H. McCarthy; *Hurst & Blackett.*
A love story of London and the West Country in the last years of Queen Elizabeth (she herself appears).

827. *THE WITCH: Mary Johnston; *Constable* [Eng.], *Houghton Mifflin* [U.S.A.].

Although this novel begins with an account of Queen Elizabeth dying at Richmond (1603), there is little of the historical romance proper about it. The reader will, however, find a striking picture of English life under James I—the period when Witchcraft Trials were carried through rigorously.

828. HIS MOST DEAR LADYE: Beatrice Marshall; *Juv. Seeley.*

Sir Philip Sidney's sister, the Countess of Pembroke—Salisbury, etc., at the beginning of the 17th Century. There are many noteworthy historic figures including Shakespeare, Massinger, Lady Arabella Stuart, James I, etc.

829. FATHER DARCY: Mrs. Anne Marsh; *Chapman & Hall* [1846]; also—later—*Ward & Lock.*

Northamptonshire and London, 1580-1605 (Elizabeth—James I period). This old-fashioned historical romance begins with a depiction of Elizabeth, Cecil, and Essex, but deals largely with Catesby and Guy Fawkes in the year 1604. The novel ends with the Gunpowder Plot.

830. GUY FAWKES: W. Harrison Ainsworth; *Herbert Jenkins* [Eng.], *Dutton* [U.S.A.].

Manchester, London, the Midlands, etc., 1605-1606. A romance largely based on Lingard. Depicts the harsh penal laws against Catholics, and the development of the Gunpowder Plot. There are glimpses of the Star Chamber, as well as somewhat detailed accounts of the trial and execution of the Conspiracy leaders. Besides Fawkes himself, Humphrey Chetham, King James I, and the Earl of Salisbury are more or less prominent, while Doctor Dee the astrologer, Catesby, Lord Mounteagle and others appear.

831. WHEN LOVE CALLS MEN TO ARMS: Stephen Chalmers; *Grant Richards* [Eng.[, *Small, Maynard* [U.S.A.].

Scotland at the beginning of the 17th Century. An autobiographical romance of the Clyde district, with little historic background. Although based on the burning of a Spanish Armada ship in 1588, the genuine story begins in 1604.

832. *THE SHEPHERD OF THE OCEAN: G. I. Whitham; *Juv.* In "The Shepherd of the Ocean and Other Tales of Valour"—*Wells Gardner.*

A narrative somewhat vividly illustrating episodes in Sir Walter Raleigh's career (Elizabeth—James I period).

833. *THE HIDDEN CITY: John Buchan; in "The Path of the King"—*Nelson* [Eng.], *Doran* [U.S.A.].

Sir Walter Raleigh at the beginning of the 17th Century.

834. THE "HALF MOON": Ford Madox Hueffer; *Nash* [Eng.], *Doubleday* [U.S.A.].

A novel which, after well describing English life (Rye) in the time of James I, carries the reader to North America (Hudson the Navigator).

835. MARY PAGET: Minna Caroline Smith; *Macmillan.*

W. England (Tavistock and Dartmoor region), and the Bermudas, c. 1610. A romance of high social, as well as cultured, life in James I's reign, introducing—among other figures—the Earl of Southampton and Shakespeare; the latter is shown at the moment when the first notion of "Ariel" came to him.

836. THE FAIREST OF THE STUARTS: Winifred Brookes
Mylechreest; *Sampson Low.*
Scotland (Stirling and Edinburgh), and London, at the beginning of the 17th Century.
A pathetic tale of the early life of Elizabeth, James I's eldest daughter—her brother
Henry being also prominent. Illustrates the superstition of the age (a witchcraft trial,
etc.). Besides the two outstanding figures already mentioned, several historic personages
appear. The book ends with the death of Prince Henry, 1612.

837. THE YOUNG QUEEN OF HEARTS: Emma Marshall; *Juv.*
Seeley [*Eng.*], Macmillan [*U.S.A.*].
A tale of the young Princess Elizabeth (afterwards Queen of Bohemia), and her brother
Prince Henry, who died in 1612.

838. *THE LOST DUCHESS: J. G. Sarasin; *Hutchinson* [*Eng.*],
Doran [*U.S.A.*].
The Thames Estuary and Rochester regions, also London (the Tower, Whitehall,
etc.) between 1610 and 1615. A novel of love and adventure, with—for background—
the supposed experiences of Lady Arabella Stewart after her imprisonment (the heroine
impersonates that unfortunate individual). King James I and his Queen are both introduced somewhat prominently at certain points, while the husband of Arabella, William
Seymour, also appears.

839. *THE LANCASHIRE WITCHES: W. Harrison Ainsworth;
Herbert Jenkins [*Eng.*], Dutton [*U.S.A.*].
A tale of Lancashire (Pendle Hill, Whalley Abbey, and Preston districts) within the
1610-20 decade: the Introduction alone deals with the much earlier time of the Pilgrimage of Grace, 1536-37. There is good local colour, and county notabilities like
the Asshetons are greatly in evidence. Illustrates the period of Witch persecution, and
of the Declaration of Lawful Sports. King James I is well described, and other historic
figures are the Duke of Buckingham and the Earl of Derby.

840. *UNDER SALISBURY SPIRE: Emma Marshall; *Juv. Seeley*
[*Eng.*], Dutton [*U.S.A.*].
One of Mrs. Marshall's tenderly conceived and historically reliable tales. The out-
standing figure is the saintly George Herbert in the period 1613-33.

841. *THE FORTUNES OF NIGEL: Sir Walter Scott; *Black,*
and other publishers—English and American.
London and neighbourhood in the later part of James I's reign (c. 1620). The novel
contains a good description of Old London (the apprentices, Alsatia, etc.), and an
excellent portrait of King James himself. Buckingham is another prominent figure.

842. THE STAR CHAMBER: W. Harrison Ainsworth; *Herbert*
Jenkins [*Eng.*], Dutton [*U.S.A.*].
London and district, also Theobald's Palace near Cheshunt (Herts.), in the later
period of James I's Reign. A romance depicting, as the title indicates, the working
of the celebrated Star Chamber. There is also much illustration of the general life of
the time—the Maypole sports, the Tiltyard at Whitehall, the attitude of the Puritans
towards Sunday games, the Prisons, etc. etc. King James I, Prince Charles, and the
Earl of Buckingham are all more or less prominent.

843. JOHN O' JAMESTOWN: Vaughan Kester; *Hodder & Stoughton*
[*Eng.*], Bobbs-Merrill [*U.S.A.*].
England and Virginia at the beginning of the 17th Century. A story dealing with
Captain John Smith, and the settling of Jamestown.

844. *MY LADY POKAHONTAS: John Esten Cooke; *Houghton Mifflin [U.S.A.]*.

England and Virginia, mainly in the period 1607-17. A tale of Captain John Smith and especially of Princess Pokahontas, daughter of the Indian Chief Powhatan. Covers the period of Smith's troubles with the Company and his return to England; also the bringing of Pokahontas to Jamestown, her marriage, and her visit to England. The author touches on the supposition that Pokahontas gave Shakespeare the idea of "Miranda" (the poet is himself brought into the story). Besides the outstanding figures of the Princess and Smith, other historic personages appear—notably King James I and his Queen.

845. *BY ORDER OF THE COMPANY (TO HAVE AND TO HOLD): Mary Johnston; *Constable [Eng.]*, *Houghton Mifflin [U.S.A.]*.

Virginia (Jamestown, etc.), c. 1619-23. A very stirring tale of sea and land adventures (the Indians, etc.). The "Company" in the English title is the London Trading Company to which King James I granted a charter regarding colonization. The sending out of numerous young women to Virginia (so admirably illustrated in the early part of the romance) is historic.

846. THE HEAD OF A HUNDRED: Maud W. Goodwin; *Dent [Eng.]*, *Little, Brown [U.S.A.]*.

A tale of love and adventure in Virginia, 1619-22, dealing with the same time, and with much the same subjects, as Mary Johnston's novel described immediately above.

847. SOLDIER RIGDALE: Beulah Marie Dix; *Juv. Macmillan*.

N. America, 1620-21. A good tale of the Pilgrim Fathers, and their establishment of Plymouth Colony. Miles Standish and others appear.

848. STANDISH OF STANDISH: Jane G. Austin; *Juv. Ward, Lock [Eng.]*, *Houghton Mifflin [U.S.A.]*.

Another tale of the Pilgrim Fathers and Myles Standish, 1620-27. Love and adventure (the Indians, etc.), as well as the more serious side of those early Puritans. Readers of Longfellow will be pleased to meet once again the "maiden Priscilla." John Alden, Bradford, Winslow, and other figures.

849. THE MAID OF "THE MAYFLOWER": Albert Lee; *Juv. Morgan & Scott*.

England, and the New World (Virginia), with a glance at Leyden, in the Elizabeth —James I period. The story begins in the last years of Elizabeth, but quickly passes to a later time. Tells of the "Mayflower" voyage, and the early adventures of the Pilgrim Fathers. Ends at Salem.

850. ST. MARTIN'S SUMMER: Rafael Sabatini; *Hutchinson [Eng.]*, *Houghton Mifflin [U.S.A.]*.

A story of domestic tragi-comedy in France (Dauphiny) about 1615: period of Marie de' Medici's Regency.

851. CARDILLAC: Robert Barr; *Mills & Boon [Eng.]*, *Stokes [U.S.A.]*.

France, 1517-18. An adventure story of the beginning of Louis XIII's reign. The Queen-Mother, Marie de' Medici, at Blois.

852. ALIX OF THE CHÂTEAU: Eleanor C. Price; *Juv. Harrap*.

An excellent tale of France (Blois and Paris) in the early Louis XIII period. The Queen-Mother and the Boy-King both appear.

853. THE LAUGHING CAVALIER:
THE FIRST SIR PERCY (*sequel*): Baroness Orczy; *Hodder & Stoughton* [*Eng.*], *Doran* [*U.S.A.*].
These two connected novels depict the Netherlands (Haarlem, Leyden, etc.), 1623-24. A noteworthy historic figure in the sequel is Prince Maurice of Nassau. Most novel-readers will recognize the allusion conveyed in the title—" The First *Sir Percy !* "

854. THE WINTER QUEEN: Marie Hay; *Constable* [*Eng.*], *Houghton Mifflin* [*U.S.A.*].
The career of Elizabeth of Bohemia, daughter of James I of England, who in 1613 married Frederic V the Elector Palatine—the latter becoming King of Bohemia (for about a year only) in 1619. The author describes her work as " a romance "; while not a novel in the ordinary sense, this story of Elizabeth Stuart is a good example of fictional biography.

855. 'WARE VENICE: " K. L. Montgomery "; *Hutchinson*.
Venice at the beginning of the 17th Century. A decidedly thrilling story, having for background the Spanish Conspiracy of 1618. The most interesting historic per-sonage is Sir Henry Wotton (sent in 1604 to Venice by James I, as English Ambassador); he is introduced somewhat prominently.

856. THE SPANISH MARRIAGE: Helen Mary Keynes; *Chatto & Windus*.
A novel dealing with the incognito trip of Prince Charles (Charles I) and Buckingham to Madrid in 1623, in connection with the question of the " Spanish Match." Tells of adventures on the way to Spain viâ Paris, as well as the Madrid experiences. Both James I of England and Philip IV of Spain appear. The story begins and ends in England.

857. TOO NEAR A THRONE: Alice Wilson Fox; *Juv. S.P.C.K.* [*Eng.*], *Gorham* [*U.S.A.*].
England (Theobald's Palace, etc.) in the late James I to early Charles I period. The heroine of this tale is a daughter of Lady Arbell Stewart. Conspiracy and witch-trial are some of the more important elements introduced. James I, Charles (as Prince and King), Buckingham, and other personages, appear.

858. *A ROVER OF THE ENGLISH SEAS (being *Book II* of " The Treasure of Golden Cap ") " Benett Coplestone; *Murray*.
West Dorset and South Devon in the late James I to early Charles I period. This excellent tale is fictionally connected with the first and third parts of the volume, though these deal with 20th Century characters and scenes. The " rover " of the story, in spite of his piratical deeds, has high influences behind him; his sea fights and adven-tures make good reading—one of the most noteworthy episodes being his saving of the Breton girl whom he marries. The background is quite historical.

859. THE DUKE'S SERVANTS: S. H. Burchell; *Gay & Bird* [*Eng.*], *Little, Brown* [*U.S.A.*].
A tale of English players, 1624-28. Illustrates the period leading up to the Duke of Buckingham's assassination by Felton.

860. A HAUNT OF ANCIENT PEACE: Emma Marshall; *Juv. Seeley* [*Eng.*], *Macmillan* [*U.S.A.*].
A tale of Nicholas Ferrar and his friends after his retirement (1625) to Little Gidding, Huntingdonshire, where he founded a religious community on Quietistic lines. Introduces Dr. Donne, George Herbert, etc. The time is that preceding the Civil War (early Charles I).

861. THE MS. IN A RED BOX: John A. Hamilton; *Lane.*
Lincolnshire, 1627-28. A story which has for background the drainage of the Fens by Cornelius Vermuyden. The MS. of this novel was originally sent to the publisher *in a red box* without indication of origin—hence the title chosen for the volume. After its successful launching, the author was identified.

862. IN HIGH PLACES: M. E. Braddon (Mrs. Maxwell); *Hutchinson.*
Surrey, etc., and London, also Paris, in the period 1628-1645 (*Epilogue*, 1657). The English part of the story covers Felton's assassination of Buckingham, Strafford's Trial, etc., and the earlier stages of the Civil War. The French chapters depict the time immediately following Richelieu's death (1642), and introduce Cardinal Mazarin very prominently.

863. OLD BLACKFRIARS: Beatrice Marshall; *Juv. Seeley [Eng.],* Dutton *[U.S.A.].*
A quiet family story of the James I—Charles I period, with the artist Van Dyck as outstanding figure.

864. MAROONED ON AUSTRALIA: Ernest Favenc; *Juv. Blackie.*
A young Dutchman's imaginary narration of discoveries and adventures round about the year 1630. The story is based on tradition and history (the Wreck of the *Batavia*, etc.), though the author has for fictional purposes deliberately altered dates; for instance, Abel Janz Tasman appears " many years before his actual advent on the western coast of Australia."

865. BOYS OF BALTIMORE: A. A. B. Stavart; *Juv. Burns, Oates.*
Ireland (Cork), North Africa, and London, in 1631. The adventures of two boys carried off by pirates to Algiers, and sold as slaves. Lord Wentworth (Strafford), " Captain " Cromwell, Laud, and Charles I appear. This Roman Catholic tale is decidedly interesting and well written, but not altogether without bias.

866. THE SAPPHIRE BUTTON: Florence Bone; *Juv. Morgan & Scott.*
A tale of the Salisbury and York regions within the period 1632-42. George Herbert is an outstanding figure, while Charles I is to some extent prominent. Thomas Fairfax also appears.

867. WINIFREDE'S JOURNAL: Emma Marshall; *Juv. Seeley [Eng.],* Macmillan *[U.S.A.].*
A very fair example of Mrs. Marshall, illustrating the period in Bishop Hall's life from 1637 to his death in 1656. It was within this period that he was translated (1641) from Exeter to Norwich, and was called upon to endure many indignities and troubles.

868. *KATHLEEN CLARE: Dora Greenwell McChesney; *Blackwood.*
A good story, in diary form, of Thomas Wentworth, Earl of Strafford. Covers especially the time when—after becoming the King's personal adviser—he received his title and was made (1640) Lord-Lieutenant of Ireland. The full period of the novel is 1637-41, ending with Strafford's execution.

869. A SERVANT OF THE KING: E. Aceituna Griffin; *Blackwood.*
London, 1640-42. A tale mainly dealing, on the historical side, with the Earl of Strafford—leading up to his trial and execution. The latest pages take the story to the autumn of 1642, and the beginning of the Civil War. Besides Strafford, Charles I, Queen Henrietta, Lady Carlisle, and Pym appear.

870. *JOHN INGLESANT: J. H. SHORTHOUSE; *Macmillan.*
This famous romance not only covers many periods in the second and third quarters of the 17th Century, but also takes the reader to many localities. The story proper begins London, 1637, passing quickly to Oxford, Little Gidding, Chester, etc., and illustrating through several chapters both religious life and (in less degree) public events before and during the Civil War, up to the King's Trial and Death. In the second half of the book the scenes are abroad—Italy to a large extent, though the latest pages of all take the reader to the England of Charles II. In the Italian section there is a graphic account of the Plague in Naples. An atmosphere of religious mysticism pervades the romance throughout. Among the various historic personages are:—Queen Henrietta, Charles I, Archbishop Laud, Lord Falkland, and Bradshaw. The religious figures of Nicholas Ferrar (England) and Miguel de Molinos (Italy) are also introduced.
A remarkable article entitled " Some Truths about ' John Inglesant,' " by W. K. Fleming, appeared in the *Quarterly Review*, July, 1925. Mr. Fleming's contention (based on proofs given) is that " in many parts of the book " there is to be found " a miracle of ingenious dove-tailing into its text of a quantity of unacknowledged verbatim quotations from Seventeenth Century writers." These verbatim " liftings," he continues, " extend sometimes to paragraphs and pages "! Certainly Mr. Fleming has made out a most formidable indictment; it is, however, noteworthy that, in spite of his damaging attack on the late Mr. Shorthouse's personal integrity, he is still able to pronounce *John Inglesant* " a very remarkable book " regarded as a literary achievement.

871. THE BINDING OF THE STRONG: CAROLINE ATWATER MASON; *Hodder & Stoughton [Eng.], Revell [U.S.A.].*
Largely London and Canterbury, 1640-49. A story written round the marriage of John Milton and Mary Powell, depicting the full circumstances in a careful and suggestive manner. As to the love complications and troubles arising out of the situation —these belong to the author's own telling.

872. (1) *THE MAIDEN AND MARRIED LIFE OF MARY POWELL:
    (2) *DEBORAH'S DIARY (sequel): ANNE MANNING; *Dent [Eng.], Dutton [U.S.A.].*
(1) Oxfordshire and London, 1643 onwards. A charming tale based on the fact of John Milton's marriage (at the age of 34) with Mary Powell (aged 17). Covers the period of the married life when Mary left her husband and returned to him within two years.
(2) London and Chalfont mainly in the short period, 1665-66. The story of Milton's household at the time when removal was made to Chalfont on account of the Plague. The " Deborah " of the title is the poet's youngest child by his second wife née Catherine Woodcock.

873. *AN OLD LONDON NOSEGAY: GATHERED FROM THE DAYBOOK OF MISTRESS LOVEJOY YOUNG, KINS-WOMAN BY MARRIAGE OF THE LADY FANSHAWE: BEATRICE MARSHALL; *Seeley.*
London (Chancery Lane and other City localities), Oxford, and Bristol, 1642-49 (last chapter 1660). A tale in diary and letter form, covering the whole period of the Civil War, but—except as " news "—the battles and episodes of the period are not introduced. The atmosphere is chiefly domestic and literary, with an occasional glance at the politics of the time. Such historic figures as Sir Richard and Lady Fanshawe, Mistress Milton (Mary Powell), and Richard Lovelace, are introduced here and there; while the reader has glimpses of Pym, Hampden, Charles I, Hobbes, John Selden, Edmund Waller, Abraham Cowley, and others. It may be added that Sir Richard Fanshawe (see above) married Anne Harrison at Oxford in 1644; the latter—as Lady Fanshawe—wrote some delightful *Memoirs* which were not published until the 19th Century.

874. *WITCH WOOD: JOHN BUCHAN; *Hodder & Stoughton [Eng.], Houghton Mifflin [U.S.A.].*
Scottish Lowlands, c. 1644-45. An interesting story dealing with the period of Montrose and the Covenant. The hero—a minister of the Kirk—is a man of char-

acter and wide outlook, who sets himself against the semi-Pagan " witchcraft " prac-
tices of his time; moreover, he teaches a doctrine of mercy, when all around him are
the cruel intolerances and harsh judgments of bigots in Church and State. Hence,
charges of heresy, followed by condemnation and excommunication. Besides the
general impression of the period which the novel as a whole suggests, a more definitely
historical element is given in the picture of Montrose (he appears more than once).

875. *ENDICOTT AND THE RED CROSS: NATHANIEL HAW-
 THORNE; (in " Twice Told Tales: Second Series ")—*Dent* [*Eng.*],
 Houghton Mifflin [*U.S.A.*], *Dutton* [*U.S.A.*], *and other publishers.*
 The Colony at Salem (Massachusetts) round about 1634. One of Hawthorne's vivid
tales of the early Puritan settlers—History imaginatively presented. The central
episode is John Endicott's action in cutting with his sword the Red Cross out of the
English flag, as a protest against Prelacy and Archbishop Laud. Endicott and Roger
Williams are the two outstanding figures.

876. MERRY-MOUNT: J. L. MOTLEY; *James Munroe* [*U.S.A.*, 1849].
 A tale dealing with the early days of Plymouth Colony, written as a protest against
the gloomy side of Puritanism.

877. WITH MUSKETEER AND REDSKIN (WITH PURITAN
 AND PEQUOT): W. MURRAY GRAYDON; *Juv. Shaw* [*Eng.*],
 Penn [*U.S.A.*].
 New Plymouth, 1636. A tale illustrating the early troubles of the settlers (the Indians
—Pequots, etc.). Introduces Governor Vane, Anne Hutchinson, Roger Williams,
Winthrop, and others.

878. MISTRESS BRENT: LUCY M. THURSTON; *Juv. Little, Brown*
 [*U.S.A.*].
 A story of Maryland (" Lord Baltimore's Colony ") in the second quarter of the
17th Century.

879. ANTONIA: JESSIE VAN ZILE BELDEN; *Murray* [*Eng.*], *Page*
 [*U.S.A.*].
 A tale of the Hudson River districts (Dutch Colonists) in the period 1640-50.

880. *THE LADY OF FORT ST. JOHN: MRS. MARY H. CATHER-
 WOOD; *Sampson Low* [*Eng.*], *Houghton Mifflin* [*U.S.A.*].
 A good story of Acadie (French name of Nova Scotia and New Brunswick) in the
second quarter of the 17th Century. Illustrates the struggle between Charles de la
Tour and the Chevalier d'Aunay; also the defence of La Tour's fort of St. John by
his brave wife in his absence.

881. MONSIEUR DESPERADO: JOHN MELBURY; *Murray.*
 France (Dieppe and Paris), 1621 onwards. The story covers the La Rochelle sub-
mission, etc., and Richelieu is introduced; the love interest, however, is greater than
the historical.

882. THE CARDINAL'S PAST: MICHAEL W. KAYE; *Greening.*
 France, 1626. A good novel telling of a plot against Cardinal Richelieu, whom the
author depicts favourably. Louis XIII, Anne of Austria, and the Duchesse de Chevreuse.

883. *THE THREE MUSKETEERS: ALEXANDRE DUMAS (trans.);
 Dent [*Eng.*], *Little, Brown* [*U.S.A.*].
 France and (in very small degree) England, 1626-28. This world-famous romance,
with its exciting situations and wide range of characters, has for historical background,
the two important events—the Siege of Rochelle, and Felton's assassination of the
Duke of Buckingham. Out of the numerous historical figures, one may mention as
being especially prominent:—King Louis XIII, Anne of Austria, Richelieu, Buckingham,
and Felton.

884. MY LADY OF INTRIGUE: HUMPREY JORDAN; *Blackwood.*
Mainly France (Paris, Versailles, Nantes, etc.), 1626-29. A tale of Court intrigue,
etc., introducing many historical personages:—Louis XIII, Richelieu, Anne of Austria,
Gaston Duc d'Orléans, and Marie de Rohan (Duchesse de Chevreuse).

885. KNIGHTHOOD'S FLOWER: J. BLOUNDELLE BURTON; *Hurst
& Blackett.*
France under Louis XIII. A novel depicting persecution of the Huguenots, and,
on the historical side, covering such events as La Rochelle (1628), and the death of
Cardinal Richelieu (1642).

886. *UNDER THE RED ROBE: STANLEY J. WEYMAN; *Methuen*
[*Eng.*], *Longmans* [*U.S.A.*], also *Murray* [*Eng.*].
The author at his best. France (Paris and Béarn), 1630. A man agrees to act as
a spy in Richelieu's pay; the fictional developments thenceforward become more and
more interesting and thrilling as the story advances. The historical element is slight,
but the great Cardinal is introduced with effect at the beginning and end of the book.

887. THE BRAVEST GENTLEMAN IN FRANCE: HERBERT HAYENS;
Juv. Nelson.
France (largely Paris), c. 1631-32. A good tale of adventure and fighting, with—
for background—the rebellion of Henri, Duc de Montmorency in Languedoc. Covers
his final defeat at Castelnaudary and his execution at Toulouse (October 31st, 1632).
The Duke of Montmorency, Cardinal Richelieu, and (at the end) King Louis XIII,
are the principal historic figures introduced.

888. THE GREY FRIAR: " MORICE GERARD "; *Juv. Robert Holden.*
France (Paris region), 1631-33. Cardinal Richelieu is prominent, and there are
several other historical figures.

889. *BARDELYS THE MAGNIFICENT: RAFAEL SABATINI; *Nash*
[*Eng.*], *Houghton Mifflin* [*U.S.A.*].
Paris and Languedoc, 1632. An interesting romance illustrating the time of the
Orleanist Rebellion and the Duc de Montmorency's downfall. King Louis XIII at
Toulouse.

890. CADET-LA-PERLE: LÉO CLARÉTIE; *Ollendorff* [*France*].
Paris, 1635. A good historical novel dealing with France under Louis XIII:
Cardinal Richelieu, etc.

891. *THE MAN IN BLACK: STANLEY J. WEYMAN; *Cassell* [*Eng.*],
Longmans [*U.S.A.*], also *Murray* [*Eng.*].
France (largely Paris) about the year, 1636. A short, but extraordinarily interesting,
story of adventure, love, and hate. Louis XIII and Richelieu both appear, though
history is quite in the background.

892. THE LITTLE GREEN DOOR: MARY E. STONE BASSETT; *Juv.
Lothrop* [*U.S.A.*].
France, c. 1640. A somewhat pathetic tale of a maiden's experiences in Louis XIII's
private garden. The King himself, Anne of Austria, and Richelieu appear.

893. CINQ MARS (THE SPIDER AND THE FLY): ALFRED DE
VIGNY (trans.); *Routledge* [*Eng.*], *Little, Brown* [*U.S.A.*], also
Stanley Paul [*Eng.*].
France in the period 1639-42. This well-known historical romance of a French
writer more distinguished as poet than as novelist, has been criticised in several quarters
as being tedious and historically biased. The main subject is the fruitless Cinq-Mars
and De Thou conspiracy, in which the King's brother, Duke Gaston of Orleans, was
involved. Other historic figures appear—notably, Richelieu, Anne of Austria, and
Louis XIII. The novel exhibits strong anti-Richelieu prejudice.

894. *RICHELIEU: G. P. R. James; Dent [Eng.], Dutton [U.S.A.].
France in 1642. One of James's best efforts. The tale has for its central theme the
Cinq-Mars conspiracy. Besides Cardinal Richelieu, there are many historic personages,
of whom the following are more or less prominent: Louis XIII, Gaston Duke of Orleans,
Cinq-Mars, and Anne of Austria. The novel which is carefully written, ends with the
news of Richelieu's death.

895. A DEALER IN EMPIRE: Amelia Josephine Burr; Harper.
Spain (Madrid, etc.) in early 17th Century (time of Philip IV). The central figure
of this romance is Olivares, the Statesman. Other noteworthy figures are Velasquez,
the young King Philip, and the Queen-Mother.

896. *THE BETROTHED (I Promessi Sposi): Alessandro Manzoni
      (trans.); Ward Lock [Eng.], Macmillan [U.S.A.], also Stanley
      Paul [Eng.].
Lecco (Lake Como) and Milan, 1628-30. One of the most famous of all historical
novels—a brilliant piece of imaginative and descriptive writing. Depicts in realistic
manner the popular disturbances, the wartime famine, and the plague in Milan.

897. *THE TRIUMPH OF YOUTH: Jacob Wassermann (trans.);
      Boni & Liversight [U.S.A.].
Germany, c. 1627. An original story about a poetically-endowed youth, whose
lot was cast in an environment of religious fanaticism and witch-burning, etc., in the
early period of the Thirty Years' War. Except for an allusion here and there to Tilly,
or the War generally, the novel is purely one of historical atmosphere—neither real persons
nor actual events being introduced.

898. PHILIP ROLLO: James Grant; Juv. Routledge [Eng.], Dutton
      [U.S.A.].
Mainly a tale of the Scots in Denmark, c. 1626-27 (time of Christian IV of Denmark
and the Thirty Years' War). Covers much fighting, including the Bombardment of
Kiel and the Siege of Stralsund. King Christian IV and Tilly appear more or less
prominently, and there is a glimpse of Wallenstein.

899. A BRAVE RESOLVE: J. B. de Liefde (trans.); Juv. Hodder
      & Stoughton [Eng.], Dodd, Mead [U.S.A.].
Germany, 1628-32. A tale of the Thirty Years' War, introducing the storming of
Stralsund by Wallenstein; also Nuremberg, and the Battle of Lützen. Both Wallenstein
and Gustavus Adolphus appear—the book ending with the death of the latter at Lützen.

900. THE FORTUNE-HUNTER: Harald Molander (trans.);
      Heinemann.
Germany, 1629. Wallenstein at the Siege of Magdeburg; also Gustavus Adolphus,
etc., The novel depicts—powerfully, if not always pleasantly—the adventurer type
of the Thirty Years' War period.

901. *THE ADVENTUROUS SIMPLICISSIMUS: Hans Jacob
      Christoph von Grimmelshausen (trans.); Heinemann.
Chiefly Germany, but to a slight extent, France, Russia, etc., between 1630 and 1650.
A famous picaresque romance, illustrating in a vivid way life and manners in the time
of the Thirty Years' War. The book is written on realistic lines, and exhibits a decided
coarseness in several places.

902. A TROOPER OF THE FINNS: Tom Bevan; Juv. R.T.S.
Tale of a Scotsman serving under Gustavus Adolphus in 1630: Gustavus, Prince
Rupert, Elizabeth of Bavaria, etc.

903. *KARL OF ERBACH: H. C. Bailey; Longmans.
This excellent " tale of Lichtenstein and Solgau " illustrates the Thirty Years' War
somewhere about the year 1630: time of Pappenheimer, etc. Turenne appears.

904. THE LION OF THE NORTH: G. A. Henty; Juv. Blackie
    [Eng.], Scribner [U.S.A.].
S. Scotland and Germany, 1630-34. After experiencing sea adventures, the hero
takes part in the Thirty Years' War. The story covers the Battle of Breitenfeld, the
Siege of Nuremberg, and the Battle of Lützen. Gustavus Adolphus and Wallenstein
appear—the tale ending with the latter's assassination.

905. MY LADY'S KISS: Norman Innes; Ward, Lock [Eng.], Rand,
    McNally [U.S.A.].
Germany in 1631: the Thirty Years' War at its height. The story gives the reader
some impression of the wretched conditions prevalent at this special time of military
strife.

906. *WALLENSTEIN: Alfred Döblin; S. Fischer [Germany].
A very fine historical novel of the Thirty Years' War—depicting it in its various aspects,
and introducing (besides Wallenstein) several historic personages of the period. The
author has proved himself one of the ablest among the many writers of historical fiction
who have recently appeared in Germany.

907. *DER DEUTSCHE KRIEG (collective title of series): Heinrich
    Laube; Haessel [Germany].
A noteworthy contribution to the imaginative literature dealing with the Thirty
Years' War period.

908. *HAUS ECKBERG: Sophie Junghans; Hirzel [Germany].
Another good German romance of the Thirty Years' War.

909. *JÖRG JENATSCH: Conrad Ferdinand Meyer; Haessel
    [Germany].
The Grisons district in the Thirty Years' War. A remarkable historical novel by
the able Swiss novelist.

910. THE MERCENARY: W. J. Eccott; Blackwood.
A Scotsman's adventures in Germany and Austria, 1631. The special events covered
(Thirty Years' War) are the Sack of Magdeburg, and the Battle of Breitenfeld. Many
historical figures appear, including Wallenstein, Tilly, and the Emperor Ferdinand II.

911. THE STORY OF A CAT AND A CAKE: Mary Bramston;
    Juv. National Society [Eng.], Whittaker [U.S.A.].
A good little tale of Nuremberg and Bohemia 1631-32: Gustavus Adolphus, and the
Siege of Nuremberg by Wallenstein.

912. *THE KING'S RING[1] (Times of Gustav Adolf): Zachris
    Topelius (trans.); Jarrold [Eng.], Page [U.S.A.], also McClurg
    [U.S.A.].
Mainly Germany, 1631-35. A romance of the Thirty Years' War and Gustavus
Adolphus of Sweden. Among the principal events introduced are the Battle of Breitenfeld (1631), and the Battle of Lützen (1632). Gustavus is, of course, the outstanding
figure; another personage brought before the reader is Duke Bernhard of Weimar.

[1] This famous and excellent Swedish novel is the first, and perhaps the most interesting, of a series
covering the Seventeenth and Eighteenth Centuries. Under the general title of The Surgeon's Stories,
the remaining volumes have been published by Messrs. A. C. McClurg & Co., U.S.A.; one of them
("Times of Charles II") deals with the career of the Swedish King, Charles XII, between 1700 and
1718, covering Pultowa, etc.

913. MY LADY ROTHA: Stanley J. Weyman; *Ward, Lock* [*Eng.*], *Longmans* [*U.S.A.*], also *Murray* [*Eng.*].

Germany (Thuringia and Nuremberg) during the Thirty Years' War, 1632: Gustavus Adolphus *v.* Wallenstein. A romance of love, adventure, and fighting. Several glimpses of Gustavus Adolphus.

914. *THE BLACK CUIRASSIER: Philip L. Stevenson; *Hurst & Blackett.*

Halle, Lützen, Vienna, Prague, etc., 1632-34. A tale of the Thirty Years' War, beginning with a vivid description of the Battle of Lützen, in which General Pappenheim on the Austrian side, and Gustavus Adolphus at the head of his Swedes, both lost their lives. The chief fictional character is an Irishman, and his adventures are of a thrilling kind. The novel illustrates the political intrigues and rivalries of the time—the Emperor Ferdinand's dissatisfaction with Wallenstein, etc. Covers the Sack of Görlitz and other wild scenes, ending with the assassination of Wallenstein. The last-named General is the central figure, on the historic side, and appears very prominently. The Emperor Ferdinand II, Pappenheim (in the early chapters), and others are also introduced, while there is a glimpse of Gustavus Adolphus at the point of death (Lützen).

915. *MEMOIRS OF A CAVALIER: or, A Military Journal of the Wars in Germany, and the Wars in England. From the years 1632 to the year 1648; Daniel Defoe; *Dent* [*Eng.*], *Macmillan* [*U.S.A.*].

Fiction with the appearance of actual record. In the first part of these " memoirs," the hero tells of his birth, parentage, foreign travel, and experiences as a volunteer officer in the army of Gustavus Adolphus (Thirty Years' War)—mainly Germany, 1632-35. The second part deals with England in the period just before and during the Civil War, c. 1640-48.

916. THE WOMAN AND THE SWORD: Rupert Lorraine; *Fisher Unwin* [*Eng.*], *McClurg* [*U.S.A.*].

England and Germany, 1634. A tale of Somersetshire and London in the time of Laud and the Star Chamber; also taking the reader abroad to the Thirty Years' War. A good example of popular fiction.

917. WON BY THE SWORD: G. A. Henty; *Juv. Blackie* [*Eng.*], *Scribner* [*U.S.A.*].

The author's second tale of the Thirty Years' War, covering the period 1639-46, and describing such battles as Rocroi, Freiburg, Marienthal, and Nordlingen. Turenne and Condé are both introduced.

918. LOYALTY: Hamilton Drummond; *Nash.*

An historical romance of Spain in the second quarter of the 17th Century: Madrid and the Court of Philip IV. The King and Queen are very prominent figures in the story which is largely concerned with Court and political matters.

919. *THE DARK FRIGATE: Charles Boardman Hawes; *Juv. Heinemann* [*Eng.*[, *Little, Brown* [*U.S.A.*].

Begins and ends in England (time of Charles I), but is almost entirely a stirring tale of sea adventure about the fifth decade of the 17th Century.

920. THE DOGS OF WAR: Edgar Pickering; *Juv. Warne.*

Godmanchester, etc., 1636-45. A tale showing Cromwellian sympathies. Among the principal events covered, are the Battle of Naseby and the Storming of Bristol.

921, 922. (1)*THE DRAYTONS AND THE DAVENANTS:
    (2) *ON BOTH SIDES OF THE SEA (*sequel*): ELIZABETH
    RUNDLE CHARLES; *Juv. Nelson.*

Two connected stories, largely in diary and letter form. Both the Cavalier and the Cromwellian standpoints are presented.

(1) England (mainly the Eastern Counties) 1637-49. Illustrates the Civil War, notably such events as the Battles of Marston Moor and Naseby respectively. The book ends just before Charles I's trial, January, 1649. Hampden, Cromwell, and Milton are prominent.

(2) England and France, alternately, 1649-1666 (passing to New England 1691 in the last few pages). Covers Charles I's Execution, the Battle of Dunbar, the Capture of Dunkirk, Cromwell's death, the Restoration, the Plague, and the Great Fire. Richard Baxter (his Kidderminster period) is very prominent, and there is a good deal about the Quakers. The French portion of the story contains allusion to the Wars of the Fronde, and to the Jansenist community of Port Royal.

923. *IN SPITE OF ALL: " EDNA LYALL "; *Hurst & Blackett* [*Eng.*], *Longmans* [*U.S.A.*].

Hereford, Oxford, etc., within the period 1640-45. The historical element is large, and among the figures introduced more or less prominently, are Cromwell and Falkland (both sympathetically drawn), Charles I, Archbishop Laud, Waller, and Rupert. The standpoint is Puritan in a general way, but not unreasonably so.

924. COUSIN TIMOTHY: MARGARET BAINES REED; *Juv. Arnold.*

A somewhat indefinite adventure story of Southern England just before and during the struggle between Roundhead and Cavalier. The atmosphere of the period is conveyed, and there are allusions to historical events.

925. *WHEN CHARLES I WAS KING: J. S. FLETCHER; *Gay & Bird.*

An excellent Yorkshire tale, mainly dealing with the Civil War period. Covers Marston Moor and the Siege of Pontefract.

926. *THE GOVERNOR OF ENGLAND: " MARJORIE BOWEN "; *Methuen* [*Eng.*], *Dutton* [*U.S.A.*].

An historical novel depicting Oliver Cromwell as " Huntingdonshire gentleman "; as a Member of Parliament; as Colonel and General; and, lastly, as " Governor of England." Strafford, Pym, Lord Falkland, Charles I, and most of the leading personages of the Civil War and Commonwealth periods, are introduced; while outstanding events such as the execution of Charles, and the passing of Cromwell himself, are also brought into the story. Like most of the author's contributions to Historical Fiction, this book gives sign of being based on careful research.

927. FOLLOW THE GLEAM; JOSEPH HOCKING; *Hodder & Stoughton.*

Launceston, London, Ely, and various other localities (including Yorkshire), 1640-46. An autobiographical narrative, telling of the young hero's experiences in the service of the Earl of Strafford; of his interviews with various notabilities including Cromwell and the King: of his lengthy imprisonment for refusing to undertake a Royal mission to the Pope; lastly, of his leaving the Royalist cause altogether and becoming a devoted follower of Cromwell. The hero has more prison experiences, etc., and the Battle of Marston Moor is introduced. Earl Strafford, Archbishop Laud, Oliver Cromwell, Charles I, Prince Rupert (a pleasing depiction), Lord Essex, and others appear.

928. *THE HONOURABLE JIM: BARONESS ORCZY; *Hodder & Stoughton* [*Eng.*], *Doran* [*U.S.A.*].

Oxfordshire, 1638-45. A tale of Roundhead husband and Cavalier wife, exhibiting the difficulties arising from the alliance. The Battle of Naseby is briefly described, while Charles I, Prince Rupert, and General Fairfax appear more or less prominently.

929. ORCHARDS: WARWICK DEEPING; *Cassell.*

A novel of the Cotswold region and Oxford in 1641-42. Prince Rupert appears, but the author's aim, apparently, is less to depict historical personages or events than to convey to his readers the Royalist atmosphere of the time.

930. *MIRIAM CROMWELL—ROYALIST: DORA GREENWELL McCHESNEY; *Blackwood* [*Eng.*], *Way & Williams* [*U.S.A.*].

London, Warwickshire, Oxford, etc, 1641-45 (Epilogue 1649). The two outstanding figures of this interesting romance are Miriam Cromwell (a niece of the great Oliver) and Prince Rupert. Illustrates the general life and thought, rather than the detailed history of the period, though allusions to public events and persons are frequent. Cromwell himself is prominently introduced, and other noteworthy figures are Strafford, Falkland, Charles I and Queen Henrietta Maria.

931. *ST. GEORGE AND ST. MICHAEL; GEORGE MACDONALD; *King.*

Mainly the Welsh Border country (Raglan Castle), 1641-46. This novel, beginning in the autumn of the year in which Strafford was executed, has an interesting historical personage for its central figure, viz., Edward Somerset, the second Marquis of Worcester; covers the period when he was made General of South Wales (Civil War 1642), created Earl of Glamorgan (1644), and despatched to Ireland to secure Catholic assistance 1645. Historic events are, for the most part, given as news, but the Battle of Naseby is in part introduced, also the Siege of Raglan Castle by Fairfax. On the fictional side, the hero (Roundhead) and the heroine (Royalist) are well drawn, and their respective Causes are presented with unusual fairness. In addition to Somerset and his family circle, Charles I and General Fairfax appear. It should be noted that Edward Somerset's love of mechanical pursuits finds illustration in the story (he has been called "the inventor of the steam-engine.").

932. *TO RIGHT THE WRONG: "EDNA LYALL"; *Hurst & Blackett* [*Eng.*], *Harper* [*U.S.A.*].

Lincolnshire, etc., 1642 onwards. John Hampden is the central figure through nearly two-thirds of the tale, and several other historical personages are introduced. Covers the Battle of Edgehill and other events. The author's estimate of the Parliament side is much more favourable than that given in the conventional Civil War romance.

933. COURTENAY OF WALREDDON: MRS. ANNA ELIZA BRAY; *Chapman & Hall.*

Tavistock and district in 1642-43. An old-fashioned story of that part of the West Country which Mrs. Bray knew so well. More valuable for its local colour than for illustration of history.

934. THE ADVENTURES OF TIMOTHY: EDITH C. KENYON; *Juv. R.T.S.*

A tale of the Civil War, 1642-43, covering the Battle of Edgehill and part of the King's Oxford period. There is an interview with Cromwell, and Jeremy Taylor is also introduced.

935. *THE SPLENDID SPUR: A. T. QUILLER-COUCH; *Dent* [*Eng.*], *Cassell* [*Eng.*], *Scribner* [*U.S.A.*].

Oxford, Bristol, and the West Country, 1642-43. An historical novel of the best type, telling of the hero's stirring adventures as bearer of a royal message from Oxford to the Army in Cornwall. Princes Maurice and Rupert appear, as well as other real personages. The book is one that might well be taken as a model by any writer serving his novitiate in the sphere of historical fiction: there is history (but not too much of it), there is excellent local colour, and last—but not least—there is some good character depiction.

936. *HUGH GWYETH: A ROUNDHEAD CAVALIER: Beulah Marie Dix; *Juv.   Macmillan.*

Warwickshire, and many Midland localities (including Shrewsbury and Oxford) 1642-43. The hero is a young motherless lad brought up (in his father's absence abroad) by a Roundhead grandfather. Having heard at the beginning of the Civil War, that the long-absent father was fighting on the Royalist side, he joins the Cavalier forces. The eventual meetings (for there are several) of father and son, are of a more than strange kind, but the *dénouement* must be sought in the tale itself. The Battle of Edge-hill is introduced, and Prince Rupert appears at a later point, but history is for the most part quite in the background. The hero has some thrilling experiences (including a duel), and there is a love element.

937. MISTRESS SPITFIRE: J. S. Fletcher; *Juv. Dent [Eng.], McClurg [U.S.A.].*

Yorkshire, etc., 1642-44. The hero carries a despatch for Cromwell to Fairfax, while the latter is investing Pontefract. Both Cromwell and Fairfax appear.

938. THE LEAGUER OF LATHOM: W. Harrison Ainsworth; *Routledge.*

Mainly Lancashire in the period 1642-44, but passing in the concluding pages to the year 1651. Covers the Siege of Manchester and other Civil War events—describing especially how Lathom House was beleaguered. Charles I, Prince Rupert, the Earl and Countess of Derby, and Fairfax are prominent. A somewhat detailed account of the Earl of Derby's execution is given. Not one of Ainsworth's best stories, but it exhibits good local colour.

939. BIBLE AND SWORD: Laurence Cowen; *Hodder & Stoughton*

Ely, etc., in the period 1642-49. A story of the Cromwell Family, also introducing Milton and his runaway wife Mary. Other historic figures are: Hampden, Robert Blake, Charles I, and Queen Henrietta Maria. The author of this really interesting novel is, perhaps, over-bold in presenting long imaginary conversations between Cromwell and the King.

940. AMYAS EGERTON, CAVALIER: Maurice H. Hervey; *Juv. Arrowsmith.*

Torrington, Oxford, Worcester, etc., 1642-49. A story of the Civil War in the West of England, also covering Charles I's captivity at Carisbrooke, as well as his trial and execution.

941. *FRIENDS THOUGH DIVIDED: G. A. Henty; *Juv. Frowde [Eng], Dutton [U.S.A.], also Burt [U.S.A.].*

A good example of this popular writer for boys. Oxford, Scotland, Ireland, etc., between 1642 and 1660. The tale illustrates some of the principal events of the Civil War and Cromwellian period, covering: The wars of Montrose and the Covenanters; the Siege of Drogheda; the Execution of Charles; and the Battle of Worcester.

942. RICHARD SOMERS: H. Grahame Richards; *Blackwood.*

A story of England and France, etc., covering the long period 1642-67 (Charles I—Charles II). There are allusions to many Civil War events, but the feature of the novel is its presentment of numerous historic figures, including Cromwell, Prince Rupert, Goring, Fairfax, Richelieu, Louis XIII of France, Queen Henrietta Maria, and Charles II.

943. A BRAVE LITTLE LOYALIST: Dorothea Moore; *Juv. Nisbet.*

A mid Civil War tale of Warwickshire, etc. Adventures of a young girl in saving and carrying the King's despatches. Prince Rupert appears; also the Queen, to whom the heroine eventually delivers the packet at Oxford.

944. THE FIGHTING BLADE: Beulah Marie Dix; *Hodder &
      Stoughton [Eng.], Holt [U.S.A.].*
Oxford and the Lincolnshire Fenlands, 1643. Oliver Cromwell is somewhat prominent in this romance of a German who fights under him.

945. HAL O' THE IRONSIDES: S. R. Crockett; *Juv. Hodder
      & Stoughton.*
Begins with Cromwell at Ely, 1643. The story has many scenes in Essex and the
Eastern Counties, also showing King Charles and Prince Rupert at Oxford. The
Battles of Marston Moor (1644) and Naseby (1645) are both introduced. Cromwell
is the outstanding figure of the tale.

946. HONOUR THE KING: Helen Mary Keynes; *Chatto &
      Windus.*
Surrey, Oxford, etc., about 1643-45. This novel deals largely with the Siege and
Taking of Bristol. Charles I and his Queen are introduced, as well as other historic
personages.

947. *COLONEL STOW (COLONEL GREATHEART): H. C.
      Bailey; *Hutchinson [Eng.], Bobbs-Merrill [U.S.A.].*
England (Oxford, etc.), 1643-45. A somewhat unusual Civil War story, holding
the balance between Puritan and Cavalier. There is a good account of the Battle of
Newbury, and many historic figures appear: Cromwell (very prominent), Ireton,
Prince Rupert, Charles I, Fairfax, and Lambert.

948. THE COPERNICAN CONVOY: A. T. Quiller-Couch; in
      " Corporal Sam; and Other Stories "—*Smith, Elder, also Dent.*
A short story of Farnham and district in the Civil War, 1643.

949. WHITEHALL: Emma Robinson; *Routledge.*
England (largely Oxford) 1643-49. An historical romance of the Civil War, introducing some of the principal events like the Battles of Marston Moor and Naseby, and
Charles I's captivity (in the Wight), trial, and execution. The following are among
the chief historic figures: Charles I, Cromwell (and his family), Laud, Falkland, Waller,
Ireton, Harrison, Fairfax, Milton, Bunyan, Muggleton, Pym, Cherbury, and the
astrologer Lilly.

950. *HOLMBY HOUSE: G. I. Whyte Melville; *Ward, Lock [Eng.],
      Longmans [U.S.A.].*
Largely Northamptonshire, but also Oxford, London, etc., 1643-49. A good Civil
War story introducing the first Battle of Newbury (1643) at which Falkland was killed,
and the Battle of Naseby (1645); the latest chapters describe the trial and death of the
King. Among the principal figures are Charles I, Cromwell (a somewhat pleasing
depiction), Falkland, Goring, and Harrison.

951. THE WHITE HORSES: Halliwell Sutcliffe; *Ward, Lock.*
Yorkshire (Wensleydale, etc.) and Oxford, mid Civil War period. An adventure
story covering the Sieges of Skipton and York, also the Battle of Marston Moor (1644).
Many historic figures, including the King and Queen, Prince Rupert, Cromwell, Lambert, and Lady Derby.

952. CAPTAIN WYVERN'S ADVENTURES: A. T. Quiller-
      Couch; in " Shakespeare's Christmas; and Other Stories "—
      Smith, Elder, also Dent [Eng.], Longmans [U.S.A.].
A short tale of Cornwall (Fowey district) in 1644: the Civil War.

953. RED VELVET: A. T. Quiller-Couch; in " Corporal Sam;
      and Other Stories "—*Smith, Elder, also Dent.*
Another fictional sketch of Cornwall and the Civil War in the same year, 1644.

953a. JOHN OF THE FENS (formerly Tattershall Castle): BERNARD
     GILBERT; *Juv. Oxford University Press.*
Lincolnshire (Tattershall Castle, etc.) in the mid Civil War period. An excellent
tale of adventure and fighting. Cromwell is prominent, and Fairfax appears. Cromwellian sympathies.

954. IN ENGLAND ONCE: HUGH CHESTERMAN; *Juv. Blackwell.*
A good adventure tale of Yorkshire (mainly), in 1644. The event which forms the
background to an important part of the fictional development, is the Siege of York.
Towards the end of the book reference is made to Prince Rupert's army *starting* for the
"fatal field of Marston Moor." Charles I appears.

955. CORNET STRONG OF IRETON'S HORSE: DORA G.
     MCCHESNEY; *Lane.*
A story of the Civil War, 1644-45, covering Marston Moor, Naseby, and Bristol.
The Puritan atmosphere is well conveyed.

956. BATTLEMENT AND TOWER: OWEN RHOSCOMYL; *Longmans.*
A story of North Wales (Conway, etc.) in the Civil War, 1644-45. Deals to a large
extent with subjects of local, rather than general, interest. Ends with the Battle of
Naseby.

957. *A LEGEND OF MONTROSE: SIR WALTER SCOTT; *Black,*
     and other publishers—English and American.
Scotland, 1644-45. Depicts Montrose at the height of his success, and also illustrates
the general conditions of the Highlands in mid-Seventeenth Century (the clansmen's
blood-feuds and superstitions, etc.) Many allusions are made to the Thirty Years' War
through Dugald Dalgetty's anecdotes of his previous service under Gustavus Adolphus.
There is an account of the Battle of Inverlochy, and, besides Montrose, the eighth Earl
of Argyle is introduced.

958. *JOHN SPLENDID: NEIL MUNRO; *Blackwood* [*Eng.*], *Dodd,*
     Mead [*U.S.A.*].
A very fine novel dealing with the wars of the Campbells round about 1644-45. The
eighth Earl of Argyll is a prominent figure, the book illustrating the exact period which
Scott depicts, from another standpoint, in his *Legend of Montrose.* There is good local
colour (the Western Highlands of Scotland), while the historical atmosphere is skilfully
conveyed.

959. THE CAVALIERS: S. R. KEIGHTLEY; *Hutchinson* [*Eng.*], *Harper*
     [*U.S.A.*].
England (various localities, including Oxford and Carisbrooke), also—to a slight
extent—France, in the period 1644-48. The depiction of Civil War events is inconsiderable, but both Charles I and Cromwell are prominently introduced. In the French
scenes, Mazarin and Charles I's Queen (Henrietta Maria) appear.

960. IN THE SMOKE OF WAR: WALTER RAYMOND; *Arrowsmith*
     [*Eng.*], *Macmillan* [*U.S.A.*].
Somerset (Langport, Somerton, etc.) in 1645: the Fairfax *v.* Goring period. There
is a glimpse of Cromwell in this little story which has good fictional interest.

961. THE ROAD TO ARCADY: WALTER BAMFYLDE; *Sampson*
     Low.
Several English localities, including Gloucester, Cirencester, and Oxford, about
1645. Love story of an Irishman (Cavalier and Catholic) and an English Puritan
maiden. The period is that of the surrender of Bristol, and the siege of Gloucester.
Prince Rupert appears.

962. SILK AND STEEL: H. A. Hinkson; *Chatto & Windus.*

A story of Ireland and Abroad (chiefly the former) in Charles I's time. Covers several historical events including the Battle of Benburb, and gives a careful picture of General Owen Roe O'Neill, besides introducing other figures of importance. Written from the Irish national standpoint.

963. RUPERT BY THE GRACE OF GOD: Dora G. McChesney; *Macmillan.*

England (Bristol, Oxford, etc), 1645-46. A good tale of the Civil War in the time of the Fall of Bristol, and of Charles I at Newark. Besides the outstanding figure of Prince Rupert, there are several personages of note: Maurice (Prince Rupert's brother), Cromwell, Fairfax, Goring, Prince Charles, and others.

964. HENRY MASTERTON: G. P. R. James; *Routledge* [*Eng.*], *Dutton* [*U.S.A.*].

A young Cavalier's adventures—1646 onwards. The earlier scenes are in England (Kent, etc.), with Goring and Ireton prominent; but a large part of the story deals with Paris in the time of the Frondeur, etc., and La Rochefoucauld is one of the figures introduced.

965. PERDITA, PRISONER OF WAR: Dorothea Moore; *Juv. Cassell.*

A girl of 12 (she is seven years old in Chapter I only) is taken prisoner by the Roundheads at the end of 1647. She is brought to London, where she joins the Royal Family in their captivity (Little Princess Elizabeth, Prince Henry, etc.). Ireton, Charles I, and others appear.

966. *THE CHILDREN OF THE NEW FOREST: Captain Marryat; *Juv. Dent* [*Eng.*], *Estes* [*U.S.A.*], *and other publishers.*

The experiences of certain young folk belonging to a Royalist family, in the region of Lymington (New Forest) during the year 1647. A very old favourite with young children, though it must be confessed that, on the historical side, the tale is of slight import.

967. KING "BY THE GRACE OF GOD" (*Von Göttes Gnaden*): J. Rodenberg (trans.); *Bentley* [1871].

A novel of some note in its day, depicting the later period of the English Civil War, with Cromwell and other figures well presented.

968. THE WREATHED DAGGER: Margaret Young; *Cassell.*

An interesting story of the Civil War (begins 1642, but the time is almost entirely 1648), having for its main background the siege of Thirlsby House by Cromwell.

969. THE ROYALIST BROTHERS: E. E. Crake; *Juv. S.P.C.K.* [*Eng.*], *Gorham* [*U.S.A.*].

A good tale having for its main subject the Siege of Colchester (1648), with Sir Charles Lucas—the Royalist defender of the town—as outstanding historic figure.

970. THE STRONGHOLD: Jesse Berridge; *Melrose.*

Essex (Danbury region), 1648-49: time of the Siege and Taking of Colchester. This novel, in which Cromwell appears, conveys an atmosphere of religious mysticism.

971. THE REGICIDE: John Buchan; in " The Path of the King "— *Nelson* [*Eng.*], *Doran* [*U.S.A.*].

Cromwell in 1649: just before the execution of Charles I.

972. THE WHITE KING'S DAUGHTER: Emma Marshall; *Juv. Seeley.*

A tale of Elizabeth, second daughter of Charles I, and Carisbrooke (the princess died as prisoner in the Castle, 1650.)

973. JOHN MARMADUKE: S. H. Church; *Putnam.*
Ireland, 1649. A story of the Cromwellian Invasion, covering the taking of Drogheda. Ireton is one of the important figures, and Cromwell himself appears in a very favourable light.

974. (1) CASTLE OMERAGH:
(2) CAPTAIN LATYMER *(sequel)*: **F. Frankfort Moore;**
(1) *Constable [Eng.]*, *Appleton [U.S.A.]*; (2) *Cassell.*
These connected stories of the Cromwellian period are told from a standpoint quite other than that shown in the novel entered immediately above.
(1) W. Ireland (Co. Clare), 1649-50. Depicts the time after Drogheda, when Cromwell was marching on Wexford, etc. The story ends with Clonmel—the reader being given a glimpse of Cromwell himself.
(2) The sequel begins Ireland (Cromwell appearing), but the main interest lies in the record of the hero's sea adventures (pirates, etc.) after he has been transported to the West Indies. Prince Rupert is somewhat prominently introduced. The final scene is Ireland at the time of Ireton's death (end of 1651).

975. *NESSA: Miss L. MacManus; *Sealy, Bryers [Ireland]*, *Benziger [U.S.A.]*.
A good tale of Co. Mayo, Ireland, in the time of the Cromwellian Settlement, 1654.

976. *HARRY OGILVIE: James Grant; *Juv.* *Routledge.*
Decidedly one of Grant's best tales—regarded fictionally at least. It deals with Scotland mainly between 1638 and 1651—the principal historic background being Cromwell's invasion and the Battle of Dunbar. One of the incidents covered is the coronation of Charles II at Scone. Cromwell, Zachary Boyd, Argyle (the Eighth Earl), and Monk are among the figures introduced.

977. THE RED REAPER: John A. Steuart; *Hodder & Stoughton.*
Scotland, mainly 1644-50. A novel with James Graham, Marquis of Montrose, as hero. The chief events of Montrose's career between 1644 and 1650 are illustrated, from the day when he routed the Covenanters at Tippermuir, up to his death by hanging in the Grassmarket, Edinburgh. Of the numerous historic figures introduced, besides the " Great Marquis," the Eighth Earl of Argyle is the most important (an adverse picture). The whole book is super-Royalist in tone.

978. THE WAY TRIUMPHANT: J. M. A. Mills; *Hutchinson.*
Scotland, 1644-50, with glimpses of St. Germain and Brussels. A Royalist romance with Montrose as hero, covering the period of his victories, his later wanderings abroad, and the futile invasion of Scotland which resulted in his execution. The eighth Earl of Argyll is depicted very adversely. Other historic figures are the youthful Charles II and his mother Queen Henriette Marie.

979. (1) *MAGNUS SINCLAIR:
(2) *OF MISTRESS EVE *(sequel)*: **Howard Pease;** *Constable.*
Two connected historical romances, written with care, and presenting an interesting picture of conditions in the North of England and the Scottish Lowlands in the Commonwealth—Charles II period.
(1) The first novel deals with Northumberland and Edinburgh, etc., 1649-51. It is a story of many adventures, covering the time of Dunbar, Charles II's Coronation at Perth, and ending with the news of Worcester. The religious divisions of the sects are reflected, and there is a decided Quaker element. Cromwell and Charles II are both prominent, while Harrison, Buckingham, and others appear.
(2) The sequel offers scenes in many of the Northern Counties (Northumberland, Westmorland, Yorkshire, etc.), as well as in London (Whitehall), c. 1653-63. There is more about the Quakers and sects, while many public events like Cromwell's death and Charles II's Coronation at Westminster are touched. The fictional developments are closely connected with the Duke of Buckingham. Besides the last-named personage, Charles II, Rochester, and Nell Gwynne appear.

980. CAVALIER AND COVENANT (formerly " Anne of Argyle "):
    GEORGE EYRE TODD; *Routledge*.
Glasgow, Edinburgh, etc., 1650-51. Covers the Battle of Dunbar, and introduces
various historical personages: Charles II, the Marquis of Argyle, Dr. Zachary Boyd
the Scottish divine, and others.

981. *MAJOR WEIR: " K. L. MONTGOMERY "; *Fisher Unwin*.
Edinburgh, Loch Tay, Stirling, etc., 1650. A novel of " League and Covenant " days,
with politics and witchcraft charges as ingredients. The story begins with the account
of an interview between Weir the Covenanter and the Marquis of Montrose (James
Grahame) just before the latter's execution. Besides Weir himself and Montrose, there
are several historic figures, including the Marquess of Argyle, Charles II, the Duke of
Buckingham, and Cromwell.

982. WHEN THE KING CAME SOUTH: HELEN H. WATSON; *Juv.*
    R.T.S.
English Lake District and Midlands, 1643-51, but mainly dealing with the year 1651.
The adventures of a girl in male attire at the time of the Battle of Worcester. Cromwell
is introduced somewhat effectively.

983. THE WILD BIRD: MARGARET STUART LANE; *Juv. Oxford
    University Press*.
Dorsetshire in 1651. An excellent story of a girl just before and after the Battle of
Worcester. The fugitive Charles II is depicted up to his escape viâ Charmouth.

984. *THE TAVERN KNIGHT: RAFAEL SABATINI; *De La Mare Press*
    [*Eng.*], *Houghton Mifflin* [*U.S.A.*].
Penrith, Worcester, and East Anglia, 1651. An excellent romance of love and
adventure, beginning just before the Battle of Worcester; then covering the Battle itself
(slight description), and events immediately following. Illustrates the escape of
Charles II at one point of his adventures only, but deals fully with the experiences of
less august fugitives. Both Charles II and Cromwell appear. Ends Calais.

985. BOSCOBEL: W. HARRISON AINSWORTH; *Routledge* [*Eng.*], *Dutton*
    [*U.S.A.*].
The Battle of Worcester (1651) and Charles II's flight including the Oak Tree
episode; also his varied experiences in Staffordshire and other parts including Bristol,
Lyme Regis, and Salisbury Plain. The five Penderel brothers (foresters who guided
the King through the woods) are well introduced.

986. *OVINGDEAN GRANGE: W. HARRISON AINSWORTH; *Jenkins*
    [*Eng.*], *Routledge* [*Eng.*], *Dutton* [*U.S.A.*].
In this tale Ainsworth illustrates events in Charles II's flight subsequent to those
related in *Boscobel* (see above). A noteworthy feature of this second romance is its
striking depiction of the Southdown region about Rottingdean, Lewes, Alfriston,
Angmering, and Brighthelmstone; it is, however, doubtful whether Charles II ever
really visited Ovingdean, but the fictional interest remains on any supposition. The
story proper ends with the escape by sea from Shoreham, but the very brief Epilogue
carries the reader to the Restoration.

987. THE KING'S DOUBLE: E. E. COWPER; *Juv. S.P.C.K.* [*Eng.*],
    Gorham [*U.S.A.*].
Dorset (Melbury, Sherborne, Bridport, etc.) in 1651. A tale of Charles II's wanderings and escape, after Worcester.

988. PATRICIA AT THE INN: J. C. SNAITH; *Arrowsmith* [*Eng.*],
    Dodge [*U.S.A.*].
A brief, but exciting, tale of the period immediately following Worcester: Charles II
as fugitive.

989. *A NEST OF MALIGNANTS: Dorothea Moore; *Juv. S.P.C.K.* [*Eng.*], *Macmillan* [*U.S.A.*].

A particularly interesting tale of a girl in Worcester and in Wiltshire, 1651. The escape of Charles II after the Battle of Worcester is the main incident. Besides Charles, Cromwell is introduced (twice), and the story ends with the great Puritan generously owning himself " checkmated " by juvenile wit.

990. THE HOUSE OF THE OAK: H. A. Hinkson; *Juv. S.P.C.K.* [*Eng.*], *Gorham* [*U.S.A.*].

A short tale of Charles II's adventures after Worcester in 1651 (Boscobel).

991. *WOODSTOCK: Sir Walter Scott; *Black, and other publishers —English and American.*

Oxfordshire in 1652. A novel which holds the balance fairly well between Cavalier and Puritan in the depiction of character, though in the special case of Cromwell the famous author has perhaps attempted the impossible (Andrew Lang has wisely remarked in this connection that any attempt to " judge " men who are really great, like Cromwell and Napoleon, is " almost an impertinence "). Besides the portrait of Cromwell, there is an interesting depiction of Charles II after Worcester; historians, however, point out Scott's deviation here from the known extent of Charles's wanderings, while the author's date, 1652, is at variance with the historical time limit.

992. *THE MAKING OF CHRISTOPHER FERRINGHAM: Beulah Marie Dix; *Macmillan.*

Begins England 1652, then passes to Massachusetts. A romance of land and sea adventures (pirates, etc.)—historical chiefly in the general sense of atmosphere, and as depicting the life of the early Puritan colonists.

993. PRIDE OF THE WEST: G. I. Whitham; *Juv.* In " The Shepherd of the Ocean, and Other Tales of Valour "—*Wells Gardner.*

Adventures of Jack Granville, son of Sir Beville Granville (the " Pride of the West ") in the Civil War—Charles II period. Charles II, General Monk, etc.

994. *A DOCTOR OF MEDICINE: Rudyard Kipling; *Juv.* In " Rewards and Fairies "—Macmillan.

A tale introducing Nicholas Culpeper, the Puritan physician and astrologer, c. 1650.

995. IN COLSTON'S DAYS: Emma Marshall; *Juv. Seeley.*

Bristol in 1636, 1657, 1681, and 1710. A tale illustrating certain periods in the life of Edward Colston, the Bristol philanthropist. Not one of the author's best books, but it well conveys the religious and social atmosphere of the times covered. There is allusion to Colston's death in 1722, at the very end of the tale.

996. THE LORD PROTECTOR: S. Levett Yeats; *Cassell* [*Eng.*], *Longmans* [*U.S.A.*].

Cromwell about the year 1653. Public events are merely alluded to—the special interest being the careful picture of the Protector himself, who plays a prominent part in connection with the heroine of the tale. Ireton also appears.

997. THE KING OF CLADDAGH: Thomas Fitzpatrick; *Sands.*

Galway and the Irish West Coast islands in the period 1652-60. A story covering the Cromwellian occupation, and depicting the evils of the time from a national standpoint.

998. MY LADY'S BARGAIN: Elizabeth Hope; *Nisbet.*

Surrey, London, etc., about 1655. An entertaining story of a Cromwellian General's marriage with a Royalist lady. The strictly historical element is slight, but Oliver Cromwell is especially prominent. General Lambert is also introduced.

999. *UNA BREAKSPEAR: A. D. Martin; *James Clarke.*

Essex, London, etc., between 1648 and 1700, but mainly in the period, 1655-66 (Commonwealth—Charles II). This story well indicates the difficulties of conscientious clergymen in this time of national disturbance, as well as the religious and political conditions generally (the Fifth Monarchy Men, etc.) The later chapters quickly pass through such events as the Restoration and the Plague, but the Great Fire is described with some fullness.

1000. *SEA PURITANS: Frank T. Bullen; *Hodder & Stoughton.*

Lyme Regis, etc., and Abroad, 1643-57. A good naval story dealing with the career of Admiral Blake in the period of his fights with the Dutch, up to his victory over the Spaniards at Santa Cruz.

1001. FOR THE HONOUR OF THE FLAG: C. N. Robinson and J. Leyland; *Juv. Seeley.*

England, N. Africa, and France: a sea and land adventure story of the period 1651-53. An English lad is captured and enslaved by the Moors, but the main historical interest lies in the depiction of sea-fights with the Dutch (Blake's victory over Tromp, 18th February, 1653).

1002. THE FORTUNES OF HAROLD BORLASE: John Graeme; *Juv. S.P.C.K. [Eng.], Gorham [U.S.A.].*

West Country (England) and Abroad, 1651-55. A boy goes to sea under Blake, and has many adventures (Moors, etc.) Admiral Blake himself appears, and there are descriptions of his sea-fights with the Dutch (Van Tromp) and his bombardment of Tunis.

1003. PENRUDDOCK OF THE WHITE LAMBS: S. H. Church; *Stokes [U.S.A.].*

Holland, England, and America, 1655. A story based largely on a Royalist insurrection at Salisbury. Cromwell, Charles II, the Duke of Ormonde, and many other historical figures appear.

1004. *THE TIDE OF FORTUNE: "Morice Gerard"; *Juv. Odhams Press.*

London (chiefly) and Paris, 1657-58. A good tale of the Commonwealth period. Oliver Cromwell appears, but Richard Cromwell is especially prominent. Other notabilities are Milton (a mere glimpse), Elizabeth Claypole, Lord Goring, Mazarin, and Charles II.

1005. FAME'S PATHWAY: A ROMANCE OF GENIUS: H. C. Chatfield Taylor; *Chatto & Windus.*

A novel with Molière as hero and lover about the years 1642-43. Corneille is one of the other personages introduced. The author knows his subject, having written a biography of Molière.

1006. FLORE: Stanley J. Weyman; in "In King's Byways"— *Smith Elder [Eng.], Longmans [U.S.A.], also Murray [Eng.].*

A short tale of Mazarin's early days of State influence as the successor to Cardinal Richelieu. The date is 1643—Mazarin having himself received a Cardinal's hat about two years previously.

1007. STRAY PEARLS: Charlotte M. Yonge; *Juv. Macmillan.*

A kind of sequel to the author's *Chaplet of Pearls*, but really distinct both in period and characters. The tale well illustrates France within the period 1643-53 (Mazarin and the Fronde, etc.) Queen Henrietta of England, Prince Charles (Charles II), Anne of Austria, the young King Louis XIV, Prince de Condé, and Prince Rupert, are all introduced.

1008. THE SILVER CROSS: S. R. Keightley; *Hutchinson [Eng.], Dodd, Meads [U.S.A.].*

France, c. 1643. A love story with political background, in the earlier Mazarin period. The Cardinal himself is introduced.

1009. THE LITTLE KING: CHARLES MAJOR; *Juv. Macmillan.*
A tale of Louis XIV as a child in 1646, giving various experiences, and introducing Mazarin, the Queen Regent, and others.

1010. *TWENTY YEARS AFTER: ALEXANDRE DUMAS (trans.); *Dent* [Eng.], *Little, Brown* [U.S.A.].
The second volume of the author's great trilogy—being, of course, the sequel to *The Three Musketeers.* France and England, 1648-50. Depicts the period of Cardinalists and Frondeurs, introducing more especially Mazarin, Anne of Austria, and the young King Louis XIV. The Abbé Scarron and the Prince de Condé also appear. The English chapters deal with the surrender of Charles I in the North, as well as with his trial and execution in London. Other figures, besides the King, are: Cromwell, Harrison, Bradshaw, and Bishop Juxon. The romance, in this part of it, is decidely pro-Charles and anti-Cromwell.

1011. *MY SWORD'S MY FORTUNE: HERBERT HAYENS; *Juv. Collins.*
France, 1650-53. A story of the Fronde period when the struggle between Mazarin and his enemies was at its height. Covers the Cardinal's enforced retirement, and his return (1653) to Paris after regaining power. Besides Mazarin, such important personages as Anne of Austria, Turenne, and Condé are introduced.

1012. THE LOVERS OF YVONNE (The Suitors of Yvonne): RAFAEL SABATINI; *Pearson.*
Fictional memoirs illustrating life in Paris and Blois during the Mazarin and Fronde period.

1013. MARIE DE MANCINI: MADAME SOPHIE GAY (trans.); *Lawrence & Bullen.*
France, about 1655-59: time of Mazarin. Covers the Anglo-French alliance and the taking of the Spanish-Flemish fortress of Dunkirk by Turenne (1658). The Court scenes introduce Mazarin, Anne of Austria (the Queen-Mother), the young Louis XIV, Queen Christina of Sweden, Ninon de Lenclos and others. Marie de Mancini is herself historical.

1014. THE COMPANY OF DEATH: A. L. COTTON; *Blackwood.*
Naples in 1647. A story of the successful revolt of the Neapolitans against Spanish oppression, under the leadership of Masaniello (strictly Tommaso Aniello). Another noteworthy figure is Salvator Rosa.

1015. MAS' ANIELLO: MARIE HAYE; *Constable.*
Another good story of the Neapolitan Revolution of 1647, with Masaniello as outstanding figure. Ends with the assassination of the fisherman leader. An example of carefully written " romantic history."

1016. AMOR DEI: EIN SPINOZA—ROMAN: E. G. KOLBENHEYER; *G. Müller* [Germany]
Amsterdam, etc., early to mid 17th Century. A fictional presentment of Spinoza, the philosopher: his friendship with the brothers De Witt, etc. The novel intentionally shortens the philosopher's life.

1017. *SPINOZA: BERTHOLD AUERBACH (trans.); *Sampson Low* [Eng.], *Holt* [U.S.A.].
Largely Amsterdam, 1647-77. A novel of the great thinker, Baruch, or Benedict, de Spinoza, depicting him first of all as a youth of about 15. Covers his original connection with the Synagogue and his expulsion from it; but the depiction is less one of events than of thought-development, and readers with philosophical tastes will find an interesting account of the hero's progress towards a Monistic standpoint. The philosopher's beauty of character is emphasized. " No thinker arisen since Spinoza, has lived so much in the eternal as he did "—with this sentence the novel closes.

1018. THE MAKER OF LENSES: I. ZANGWILL; in " Dreamers of the Ghetto "—Heinemann [Eng.], Holt [U.S.A.].

A short story of Spinoza the philosopher, who (as students well know) earned his living, after expulsion from the Synagogue, as a " maker of lenses."

1019. (1) *WITH FIRE AND SWORD:

(2) *THE DELUGE (sequel).

(3) *PAN MICHAEL (sequel): HENRYK SIENKIEWICZ (trans.); Dent [Eng.], Little, Brown [U.S.A.].

A trilogy dealing with Poland, Russia, Sweden, and the Ukraine in the period 1647-1674. These remarkable historical novels present a series of vivid pictures illustrating the time when Poland was invaded by Cossacks, Russians, Swedes, Turks, and Tartars.

(1) The first volume has to do with the uprising of the Zaporogian Cossacks whose settlements were on the Dnieper, and whose normal duties, under the sovereignty of Poland, consisted in protecting the frontiers of the Ukraine against the Tartars. The novel begins on the eve of the rising, and ends with the defence of Zbaraz (the short epilogue carries the historic record to the Battle of Berestechko).

(2) The second volume deals with the invasion of Poland as a whole by the Swedes, arising out of the claims of Charles Augustus, the Swedish King, to the Crown of Poland. The earlier part of the novel shows the utter collapse of the Poles, while the later chapters describe how they ultimately repulsed and drove out the invading Swedes after tremendous fighting.

(3) Lastly, the third volume—after beginning with quieter scenes (domestic life in Warsaw)—passes to the Polish outposts in the steppes, and, towards the end, tells of the Tartar invasion of 1672-73, and of John Sobieski's great victory over the Turks and Tartars at Choczim.

In each novel a favourite Polish hero is made an outstanding figure: Prince Jeremi Wisniowiecki in Vol. I, the monk Kordecki in Vol II, and Sobieski in Vol III. Among other historic figures in the series, one may mention John Casimir and Boguslaw Radziwill. These three romances exhibit the author's wonderful knowledge as regards both history and topography—the local colour being particularly striking throughout. In his depiction of various historical personages and events, the Polish novelist makes special appeal to his fellow-countrymen; the average English or American reader will at least gain a clear general impression of dark warring days.

1020. PRETTY MICHAL: MAURUS JÓKAI (trans.); Jarrold [Eng.], Doubleday [U.S.A.].

Hungary (Kassa) round about 1650: time of George Rakoczy, Prince of Transylvania, when the Turkish Sultan's rule over the Hungarians was at its height. The romance vividly depicts the terrible state of affairs generally: fighting (Hungarians v. Turks), robbers, witches, the slave trade, etc. etc.

1021. *MARIE GRUBBE: J. P. JACOBSEN (trans.); Oxford University Press [Eng.], Amer. Scandinavian Foundation [U.S.A.].

Denmark (Copenhagen), Holland, France, etc., mostly between 1655 and 1695. A powerful novel of a tragic nature, with a considerable background of history. One of the chief events introduced is the Siege of Copenhagen by the Swedes, and their repulse. Besides the heroine—with her three marriages and two divorces—a great many other real figures appear; one may specify the three Kings, Christian IV, Frederik III, and Christian V, together with Ulrik Christian Gyldenlöve, and Ulrik Frederik Gyldenlöve.

1022. THE PRINCESS OF BALKH: MICHAEL MACMILLAN; Juv. Blackie.

Mainly India (Surat, Delhi, etc.) and the Cabul-Hindu Kush region, in the 1650-60 period. A tale of Scotsmen in India and Central Asia at the time of Aurangzebe's Wars. The final pages offer a glimpse of Charles II landing in England at the Restoration. The Emperor Shah Jehan appears in the story, and there is a glimpse of the Mogul Emperor Aurangzebe.

1023. *TARA: Philip Meadows Taylor; *Kegan Paul* [Eng.], *Scribner* [U.S.A.].

India (the Dekhan), 1657. A story dealing with the rise of the Mahrattas against the dominant Mahomedans; with the Rajah Sivaji and his raids against the Moguls and Mahomedans; and with the destruction of Afzool Khan's army.

This novel is the first of Meadows Taylor's three well-known imaginative sketches of important events in the history of India which have occurred at intervals of (roughly speaking) one hundred years. The present story, as we have seen, illustrates historical developments in the year 1657, while the two later novels—*Ralph Darnell* and *Seeta*— are written round crises associated with 1757 and 1857 respectively. Each of the two books, just named, will be found under its own century.

1024. *THE ROMANCE OF DOLLARD: Mrs. Mary H. Cather-wood; *Fisher Unwin* [Eng.], *Century* [U.S.A.].

Canada (Quebec, Montreal, etc.) in 1660. A story leading up to, and describing, the perilous French expedition up the Ottawa River, when the young officer Dollard, with sixteen Frenchmen and a dwindling number of natives, held in check the Iroquois Indians at a fort on the River. The defence was maintained for more than a week, but Dollard and his diminished garrison were at last overpowered and killed. Through this self-sacrificing act of heroism, Montreal was saved from the attack which the Iroquois had been previously contemplating.

1025. THE KING WAITS: "Morice Gerard"; *Juv.* Odhams Press.

Derbyshire, Scotland, London, and Belgium, 1651-60 (mainly the period 1658-60). A Royalist tale of adventure with General Monk's pre-Restoration activities as the chief historical background (the heroine is a niece of the General). There are glimpses of Charles II as fugitive, etc.

1026. A HEALTH UNTO HIS MAJESTY: Justin H. McCarthy; *Hurst & Blackett.*

Charles II and his small following, or "Court," at Breda (Holland) in the early part of 1660. The English scenes are very slight, The chief interest in the novel is the some-what unusual presentment of Charles as a *genuine* lover.

1027. *HIS MAJESTY THE KING: Cosmo Hamilton; *Hurst & Blackett.*

A somewhat original story of Charles II at Bruges in 1660, during the last days of his exile. Depicts the Royalist leaders (Lord Wentworth, Sir George Hamilton, Sir Edward Hyde, etc.), who had been with Charles throughout, and were now almost despairing of him. The tale ends with the calling back of the King to England. A well-balanced portrait of Charles.

1028. CHRONICLES OF A CAVALIER: J. G. Sarasin; *Hutchinson.*

Begins Northumberland, but is really a tale of Kentish localities in 1660—just before, and at the time of, the Restoration. Adventures on a secret mission, with thrilling love and spy developments.

1029. NICHOLAS THE WEAVER: Maude Robinson; in "Nicholas the Weaver and Other Quaker Stories"—*Swarthmore Press* [Eng]., *Friends Book Store, Philadelphia* [U.S.A.].

Short tale of a Yorkshireman in Sussex, 1660, after the breaking up of the Roundhead Army.

1030. THE SHADOW OF A CRIME: Hall Caine; *Chatto & Windus* [Eng.], *Caldwell* [U.S.A.].

Cumberland (Lake District and Carlisle), Commonwealth—Restoration, mainly in the latter period. An interesting story of domestic tragedy, with little history, though such a figure as Lawson the Sheriff of Cumberland, and various political allusions, together supply an element of actuality. There is a slight depiction of the early Quakers.

1031. BRAMBLETYE HOUSE: Horace Smith; *Dicks.*

Ashdown Forest region (Sussex) and London in Commonwealth—Charles II period; also Flanders and Paris. One of the older Cavalier-and-Roundhead romances, of some note in its day, but with history over-emphasized. Of the numerous personages introduced, one may mention Charles II, Rochester, the Marquess of Ormonde, Nell Gwyn, and Lilly the astrologer.

1032. *SILAS VERNEY: Edgar Pickering; *Juv. Blackie.*

England and Holland, from early Restoration time to 1666 (the last page of the book passes over many years to the supposed narrator's old age). A really interesting tale of Murder, a Will, and Kidnapping, which may be enjoyed by grown-ups as well as by the young folk for whom it is primarily intended. There are but few allusions to historic events—the most distinct being to the sea-fight off Lowestoft (1665), when the Duke of York's fleet encountered the Dutch. As to famous personages, the only one introduced is Sir Christopher Wren, of whom a glimpse is given in the closing passages. Although there are several English chapters (London and Newgate, etc.), the larger part of the story deals with adventures in Holland. A feature in the tale is some account of the early investigations into the use of steam power.

1033. HIS MAJESTY'S WELL-BELOVED: Baroness Orczy; *Hodder & Stoughton [Eng.], Doran [U.S.A.].*

London, 1662. Mainly a theatrical and social tale, with Thomas Betterton, the actor, as central figure. There is, also, a conspiracy element. Besides Betterton, a great many historical personages appear:—Lady Castlemaine, Sir William Davenant, Albemarle, Killigrew, Rochester, etc.

1034. SIR RALPH ESHER: J. H. Leigh Hunt; *Henry Colburn [1832].*

England (Epsom, etc.) mainly between 1662 and 1670. Fictional memoirs covering the period of sea-fights with the Dutch and the Great Plague. A crowd of historic figures:—Charles II and his Queen, Lady Castlemaine, Buckingham, Rochester, the Duke of Ormond, Wren, Colonel Blood, and others.

1035. *MY LADIE DUNDIE: Katherine Parker; *Gardner.*

Paisley, Edinburgh, Bath, etc., and Holland, 1662-95. A well-written fictional biography of Jean Cochrane, daughter of Lord Cochrane, who in 1684 married Colonel John Graham of Claverhouse (afterwards Viscount of Dundee). The book is not a "novel" in the usual sense, being very largely descriptive and historical; at the same time, the authoress not infrequently allows her imagination free play in the analysis of motives and feelings, as well as in her introduction of private conversations. Many historical events are covered, including the beheadal of the ninth Earl of Argyll, the Revolution of 1688, and Dundee's campaign ending with his death at Killiecrankie. Jean married again in 1693, and soon afterwards she and her husband, William Livingstone, went into exile (Holland). Death came suddenly to her and her infant boy, through the falling of an inn roof, 1695.

1036. A BORDER YEOMAN: J. Hay Colligan; *Aikman.*

A tale of Cumberland, ranging over a long period—between 1628 and 1700. George Fox is one of the historical personages introduced.

1037. *JOURNAL OF THE PLAGUE YEAR: Daniel Defoe; *Dent [Eng.], Century [U.S.A.].*

Hardly a novel in the ordinary sense; but Defoe's skill in making his narrative so realistic must not lead readers to forget that it is *imaginatively* framed.

1038. THE PURITAN'S WIFE: Max Pemberton; *Juv. Cassell [Eng.], Dodd, Mead [U.S.A.].*

Essex (Epping Forest, etc.), Windsor, and other localities about the year 1665. A love and adventure story (Puritan fugitive), ending London in Plague-time, and Oxford. Charles II appears.

K

1039. LADY JEM: Netta Syrett; Hutchinson.
London in the year 1665: time of the Plague. An engaging novel of love and adventure, in which Samuel Pepys appears very prominently. The historic atmosphere is well conveyed.

1040. FORTUNE'S FOOL: Rafael Sabatini; Hutchinson [Eng.], Houghton Mifflin [U.S.A.].
London, 1665. Another exciting love and adventure story of the Plague time. The Duke of Albemarle (Monk) and the Duke of Buckingham are introduced; there is, also, a glimpse of Pepys.

1041. A KING'S MESSENGER: C. H. Crichton; in "Tales of Love and Hate"—Mills & Boon.
A fairly long tale of England in 1665, relating to a man employed by Charles II as a spy.

1042. *OLD ST. PAUL'S: W. Harrison Ainsworth; Herbert Jenkins [Eng.], Dutton [U.S.A.].
An excellent tale of the London Plague and Fire, 1665-66. Tells of a grocer in Wood Street, Cheapside, who shut his house (after victualling it) in Plague-time. There are grim details of the terrible pestilence—the Plague Pit, etc., and the book ends with a full account of the Fire. The Earl of Rochester is a very prominent figure in the novel, while Charles II is also to the fore. Glimpses of Lily the astrologer, Pepys, and the Duke of York.

1043. CHERRY AND VIOLET: Anne Manning; Nimmo.
An example of Miss Manning that is little read nowadays. It illustrates the Plague and Fire period, 1665-66. The author's Deborah's Diary (sequel to The Maiden and Married Life of Mary Powell) also deals with the time of the Plague (see Page 98).

1044. *THE BLACK GLOVE: J. G. Sarasin; Hutchinson [Eng.], Doran [U.S.A.].
London and Hampton Court, 1666. Primarily a novel of adventure and manners, but illustrating the later stages of the Plague, and ending with some vivid sketches of the Great Fire (the burning of Newgate, etc.). John Wilmot, Earl of Rochester, the Duke of Albemarle (Monk), and the Duchess of Albemarle are very prominently introduced.

1045. WHEN LONDON BURNED: G. A. Henty; Juv. Blackie [Eng.], Scribner [U.S.A.].
A tale of London at the time of the Plague, the sea-fights with the Dutch, and the Great Fire.

1046. *MARTIN OF OLD LONDON: "Herbert Strang"; Juv. Oxford University Press.
A well-told story of a lad who saves a London goldsmith's stolen goods in the year 1666. The Great Fire is an outstanding incident.

1047. *SIMON DALE: "Anthony Hope"; Methuen [Eng.], Stokes [U.S.A.].
Hertfordshire, London, and Dover, mainly in the period 1665-70. An arresting novel, with considerable historic background (French Treaty, etc.). Charles II is very prominent throughout, also Nell Gwyn—the depiction in each case being on careful and original lines. The Duke of Monmouth and Louis XIV are also prominent, while Louise de Quérouaille, Buckingham, Rochester, and Arlington appear at one or another point.

1048. IN THE EAST COUNTRY WITH SIR THOMAS BROWNE:
EMMA MARSHALL; *Juv. Seeley.*
Norwich region, Bury St. Edmunds, and Whitehall, 1665-82. The dominating
figure is Sir Thomas Browne, author of *Religio Medici*. A glimpse of the Browne home
life is given, and the story also reflects in some measure the events of the time (news
of the victory over the Dutch, etc.). Ends London and Norwich, 1682: Browne's death.
Charles II and the Queen appear, especially the latter.

1049. *THE DUTCH IN THE MEDWAY: CHARLES MACFARLANE;
Juv. James Clarke.
A story of London, Erith, Wapping, etc., in 1667. There is a good depiction of
Pepys and his wife, while the account of the Dutch Fleet sailing up the Medway is
excellent. The tale ends with the Treaty of Breda signed, and the disappearance of
De Ruyter's Fleet.

1050. *WHITEFRIARS: EMMA ROBINSON; *Routledge* [*Eng.*], *Dutton*
[*U.S.A.*].
A spirited historical romance of London (Alsatia, etc.), 1667-83. Introduces many
events of the period, including the Great Fire, the Popish Plot, Monmouth's Campaign
in Scotland (Bothwell Brig), and the Rye-House Plot; the tale ends with Algernon
Sydney's trial and execution. Among the crowds of historic personages one may note:—
Charles II, Rochester, Buckingham, Ormonde, the Duke of York, Lord Russell,
Shaftesbury, Monmouth, Algernon Sydney, Richard Baxter, Jeffreys, Titus Oates,
Colonel Blood, Claude Duval, Pepys, and Nell Gwyn.

1051. *YESTERDAY'S TO-MORROW: DORA G. McCHESNEY; *Dent.*
Chiefly London (Whitehall, etc.), 1668. A novel which, telling of the disappointed
hopes and chequered career of a man who had served under Prince Rupert in the Civil
War of "yesterday," illustrates the religious and political intrigues of the War's
"morrow," viz., the Restoration period. Henri de Rohan, a son of Charles II, comes
as secret Catholic envoy from Rome, and it is round this theme that much of the
story turns. The Quakers constitute another important element, and George Fox
appears more than once. The King (Charles II), is prominent, while Lord Ashley
(shortly to become Earl of Shaftesbury) and Prince Rupert, are also somewhat to the
fore. Among the numerous other figures one may specify Pepys, Andrew Marvell,
Butler (of *Hudibras* fame), Buckingham, Rochester, and the Duke of Monmouth.

1052. THE GOLDEN PIPPIN: RUPERT LANCE; *Allen & Unwin.*
Eastern Counties and London, 1669-70. A novel with a very considerable historical
element, treating of plots against Charles II and an attempt upon his life. The King
himself appears prominently, and is presented in a decidedly unfavourable light. Other
historic figures are Prince Rupert, Buckingham, Evelyn, and Sir Peter Lely.

1053. LANTERN LANE: WARWICK DEEPING; *Cassell.*
London and Surrey in the third quarter of the 17th Century: a novel of love and
adventure ending with a duel. King Charles II is much to the fore in the earlier
chapters.

1054. THE GREAT ROXHYTHE: GEORGETTE HEYER; *Hutchinson*
[*Eng.*], *Small, Maynard* [*U.S.A.*].
England (London), Holland, and France, 1668-85. An historical romance crammed
with the events and figures of the time. Illustrates the English policy in regard to
Holland and France, as well as the unsettled state of Home affairs (the plots, etc.).
The marriage of William of Orange and Princess Mary of York is introduced. Among
the numerous personages are:—Charles II (a somewhat favourable depiction), the
Duke of York, Monmouth, Shaftesbury, Sunderland, William of Orange, Louis XIV,
and Colbert.

1055. *KELSTON OF KELLS: H. M. ANDERSON; Blackwood.
Scotland (Edinburgh, Galloway, etc.), England (London and Kent), and Paris, c. 1669-79. An exceptionally good example of historical fiction—interesting throughout, and vividly depicting the period when Archbishop Sharp was assassinated, and the struggle in Scotland between Episcopalianism and Presbyterianism was at its height. English politics (the King's relations with France, etc.) are also largely reflected. The number of celebrities introduced is almost bewildering, but some of the more important are:—Charles II, the Duke of York, Lady Mary of York, Princess Henrietta of Orleans. Rochester, Lauderdale, Burnet (afterwards Bishop), Nell Gwyn, Frances Stuart, Louis XIV, Bossuet and Philip Duke of Orleans. There is also a glimpse of Claverhouse.

1056. (1) *LANTERNS OF HORN:

(2) *IVORY AND APES:

(3) *MY TWO KINGS: MRS. EVAN NEPEAN; (1) Lane; (2) Bale, Sons, & Danielson; (3) Melrose [Eng.], Dutton [U.S.A.].

(1) The last published, though first in historical order, of the author's three Stuart romances; it confirms her favourable depiction of Charles II. Dover and London (Whitehall), 1670-74. The first part of the novel has for its main background the Secret Treaty of Dover and the visit of Henriette d'Orléans; the second part illustrates Court life in the time following the rise of Louise de Kéroual and her becoming Duchess of Portsmouth. Of the many historical figures, the most noteworthy are:—Charles II, Henriette d'Orléans, the Duchess of Richmond, the Duchess of Portsmouth, Monmouth, Evelyn, Sidney, and Churchill. The " Charlotte Stuart " of the previously published volumes in the trilogy, is introduced here also, but, although there is this fictional connection, each book is complete in itself.

(2) Mainly London and district, 1674-85. Nell Gwyn is extremely prominent—the central figure indeed—in this pro-Stuart and anti-Orange story, which deals largely with social and political intrigue (the Rye House Plot, etc.). Charles II appears in a favourable light, and, among the numerous other personages introduced, one finds:— the Duchess of Richmond (Frances Stuart), the Duchess of Portsmouth, Monmouth, Rochester, Buckingham, Halifax, and John Evelyn. The reader is, at one point in the romance, taken to Holland and given a glimpse of William of Orange and Bentinck. The final pages overleap some twelve years to 1687 (Nell Gwyn's death).

(3) The first published volume of the author's Stuart trilogy. The " Charlotte Stuart " (far-off cousin of the King) whose " memoirs " constitute the present novel, is the person of that name who appears in both Lanterns of Horn and Ivory and Apes. London, Windsor, and Hertfordshire, 1674-86. Imaginary memoirs—the author choosing to imply that the life of her heroine is her own former life in the 17th Century! A romance showing much careful study of the period, and depicting the " two kings "—Charles II and Monmouth—in a highly original and interesting manner. Charles II's failings are admitted, but on the whole he appears as a decidedly attractive figure. As to Monmouth, the portrait of him is much less pleasing. Besides these two outstanding personages, the Duchess of Richmond, Henrietta Wentworth, Rochester, Prince Rupert, James II, William of Orange, Churchill, Nell Gwyn, and many others appear. It may be mentioned that Mrs. Nepean has written a non-fictional study of Monmouth under the title: " On the Left of a Throne " (Lane, 1914).

1057. MY LORD WINCHENDEN: GRAHAM HOPE; Smith, Elder.
London district (Chelsea, etc.), 1672. A novel of social life, with a background of history and politics. Dr. Ken and Sir Isaac Newton are introduced, while there are the merest glimpses of Charles II, Rochester, and the Duchess of Cleveland.

1058. *WINCHESTER MEADS: EMMA MARSHALL; Juv. Seeley.
Winchester, Bath, and Wells, mainly 1672 and 1687-88 (last chapter 1703). A good tale, with Ken as central figure during his time as Prebendary of Winchester Cathedral and as Bishop of Bath and Wells. The historic episode of his refusing to give up his house for Nell Gwyn's accommodation, is introduced, while important events like the Seven Bishops' Trial, serve as background to the story. Charles II, Queen Catherine of Braganza, Nell Gwyn, and James II appear more or less prominently; there is also mention of Izaak Walton.

1059. THE BÂTON SINISTER: "George Gilbert"; *John Long*.
A supposed narration by Lady Henrietta Wentworth of events connected with the Duke of Monmouth's career in the period, 1674-85 (the tale itself ends 1686). This somewhat elaborate historical novel is written in defence of Monmouth. Charles II, Rochester, Nell Gwyn and Pepys are among the many personages introduced.

1060. *PEVERIL OF THE PEAK: Sir Walter Scott; *Black, and other publishers—English and American*.
Derbyshire, Isle of Man, and London, mainly in the year 1678. The novel hinges on the so-called Popish Plot. There are several historical figures, the most prominent being King Charles II, George Villiers Duke of Buckingham, and the Countess of Derby. The Duke of Ormond also appears. In his Preface Scott admits to having, in this romance, taken liberties with certain actualities; the Countess of Derby, for instance, is "fetched out of her cold grave, and saddled with a set of adventures dated twenty years after her death, besides being given up as a Catholic when she was in fact a zealous Huguenot."

1061. *THE PLOT: H. C. Bailey; *Methuen*.
Kent, 1678, then London and Sussex alternately. An interesting story of the "Popish Plot" time, introducing such historic figures as Shaftesbury, Buckingham, the Duke of Monmouth, Dr. Oates, the Duke of York, and Charles II.

1062. THE MARPLOT: John Buchan; in "The Path of the King"— *Nelson [Eng.], Doran [U.S.A.]*.
A short tale of Titus Oates, 1678.

1063. *THE LADY OF LYTE: Graham Hope; *Methuen*.
Paris, Hampshire, and London (Whitehall), 1678. Almost a sequel to the author's earlier Charles II novel—depicting events only four years later, and slightly introducing the figure of "Lord Winchenden." This second romance tells of a beautiful girl's experiences at Whitehall during the time of the Popish Plot. There are Puritan, Quaker, and Jesuit elements. A great many historic personages appear:—Charles II, Lord Shaftesbury, Lord Halifax, Mr. (afterwards "Sir") Isaac Newton as a Cambridge don, William Penn the Quaker, Dr. Ken, the Duchess of Portsmouth, Lord Shrewsbury and others. There are mere glimpses of Oates and Algernon Sidney.

1064. FIRE AND STUBBLE (NOBLE ROGUE): Baroness Orczy; *Methuen [Eng.], Doran [U.S.A.]*.
France and England alternately in the year 1678. A story of the Popish Plot scare, in which Lord Rochester is prominent. Other figures are Titus Oates in England, and Madame de Montespan in France.

1065. CIVIL DUDGEON: C. H. Tremlett; *Blackwood*.
England, mainly 1678-83 (Popish Plot and Rye House Plot periods). A novel crammed with historical allusions. Charles II, Shaftesbury (well depicted), Titus Oates, Buckingham, Halifax and others appear. There is, also, a glimpse of Paris and Louis XIV.

1066. THE ACCUSER: F. Arthur; *Nash*.
Kent—Sussex region and London, etc., 1678-79 (*Prologue*: The Plague 1665). A novel of the "Popish Plot"—Titus Oates being greatly in evidence. Another historic figure, though much less prominent, is Shaftesbury. The author's anti-Puritan bias is unmistakable.

1067. *ODDSFISH!: R. H. Benson; *Hutchinson [Eng.], Dodd, Mead [U.S.A.]*.
A clever and interesting romance of Charles II in the period 1678-85, written from a Roman Catholic standpoint. Charles II himself is depicted with special care, and the novel offers a comprehensive survey of the events and personages of the time. Titus Oates, the Duke of York, Jeffreys, Halifax, Nell Gwyn and many others appear,

1068. *JOHN BURNET OF BARNS: John Buchan; *Lane* [*Eng.*], *Dodd, Mead* [*U.S.A.*].

Scotland and Abroad in the late 'Seventies and early 'Eighties of the 17th Century. A Scotsman relates his experiences and adventures from early youth onwards—beginning in the year 1678. The romance shifts from Tweeddale (Peebles district), and Glasgow, to Leyden where the reader obtains a glimpse of the philosopher Leibnitz. Later, the hero returns to the Tweeddale and Clydesdale regions. The period which this novel well illustrates, is that of the Covenanters.

1069. *THE MEN OF THE MOSS-HAGS: S. R. Crockett; *Pitman* [*Eng.*], *Macmillan* [*U.S.A.*].

Galloway, Edinburgh, etc., 1679. A good example of the author, dealing with the Covenanter period, and depicting John Graham of Claverhouse at Bothwell Brig.

1070. *OLD MORTALITY: Sir Walter Scott; *Black, and other publishers—English and American.*

Scotland (Lanarkshire), 1679 and 1689. One of Scott's finest historical romances, exhibiting his intimate knowledge of both period and locality. The story begins with the *news* of the murder of Archbishop Sharpe, and on the historical side deals with the fierce animosities of the Claverhouse *v.* Covenanter time, giving vivid descriptions of the Drumclog skirmish, and the Battle of Bothwell Brig or Bridge. Besides Claverhouse, there are several historic figures, including John Balfour of Burley and the Duke of Monmouth. The last eight chapters carry the reader forward to the year 1689 (before and after the Battle of Killiecrankie).

1071. *THE CHEATS: " Marjorie Bowen "; *Collins.*

London and Italy, c. 1680. A story dealing with the tragic experiences of Jacques de Rohan, an illegitimate son of Charles II (see descriptive note on Dora McChesney's novel, *Yesterday's To-morrow*, in which De Rohan also appears). The secret influences of the Jesuits are especially illustrated in the fictional development of the present tale. The King, Buckingham, Cristina of Sweden, and other historic figures of importance appear. The hero, De Rohan, is historical—his real story being available in Andrew Lang's volume of Studies entitled: *The Valet's Tragedy, etc.*

1072. *IN STIRRING TIMES: " Herbert Strang " and Walter Rhoades; *Juv. Oxford University Press.*

S. England (Taunton, London, etc.), the Barbados, and Holland, 1680-88. A tale covering the Exclusion Bill, the Rye House Plot, the death of Charles II and accession of James II, the Monmouth Rebellion (Battle of Sedgemoor described), and the Revolution of 1688. Judge Jeffreys and Lord Churchill appear, while there are glimpses of Monmouth, William of Orange, Bishop Burnet and many others.

1073. THE RYE HOUSE PLOT: Geo. W. M. Reynolds; *Dicks.*

Hertfordshire and London, 1682-85. A fair example of this once popular author. The title sufficiently indicates its subject.

1074. WHEN THE MOON IS GREEN: Dorothea Moore; *Juv. Partridge.*

An interesting tale beginning Tangier 1680, but mainly dealing with Essex and the London region in 1682-83: time of the Rye House Plot. Many historic figures, including Charles II, Shaftesbury, Monmouth, Duke of York, Dryden, Wren, Nell Gwynne and Judge Jeffreys.

1075. *IN THE GOLDEN DAYS: " Edna Lyall "; *Juv. Hurst & Blackett* [*Eng.*], *Appleton* [*U.S.A.*].

Mostly the Eastern Midlands, London, and Penshurst, 1682-84. A tale of the late Charles II period, when fear of plots like the Rye House Plot, led to great injustice. Covers the arrest and trial of Colonel Algernon Sydney—giving an account of his execution in 1684. The hero of the story is imprisoned in Newgate, and at a personal interview with Charles II is asked, on attractive terms, to give evidence against Sydney; this, however, he refuses to do. Algernon Sydney is an outstanding figure, while the picture of Charles II is not altogether unpleasing. There are, also, glimpses of Dryden, the Duchess of Cleveland, the Duchess of Grafton, and Judge Jeffreys.

1076. DAVID MARCH: J. S. Fletcher; *Juv. Methuen.*
Yorkshire (Wakefield district), London, etc., 1683. A good tale of adventure, introducing Sir Christopher Wren, Charles II, and others.

1077. IN THE SERVICE OF RACHEL, LADY RUSSELL: Emma
Marshall; *Juv. Seeley.*
Canterbury, London, and Hampshire, mainly 1682-83, but "looking forward" to 1694 at the end. A pleasing tale, depicting the home life of Lady Russell—at the same time reflecting public events (period of the Rye House Plot). Lord Russell's downfall has, of course, an important place in the working-out of the story. Other noteworthy figures, besides the Russells, are Tillotson and Burnet.

1078. THE HOUSE OF SANDS: Lauchlan Maclean Watt; *Secker.*
The Scottish Lowlands, the Mediterranean, and Barbary (Algiers), after the Restoration. Story of a Scotsman "turned from Charles II's Court." The King himself appears in the earlier part of the book, but its main fictional interests of love, piracy, and slavery under the Moors, are set forth in later chapters.

1079. *BARNABY LEE: John Bennett; *Juv. Warne* [Eng.], *Century*
[U.S.A.].
New Amsterdam (New York) and Maryland, 1664. Introduces Peter Stuyvesant, the last Dutch Governor of New Netherland, and describes the taking of New Amsterdam by the English. In the Maryland portion of this adventure tale, Lord Baltimore and other historic figures appear.

1080. *THE OLD DOMINION (PRISONERS OF HOPE): Mary
Johnston; *Constable* [Eng.], *Houghton Mifflin* [U.S.A.].
The Colony of Virginia in the second period of Sir William Berkeley's rule as Governor (1660-76). The Governor himself appears in the story, which is quite one of the author's best examples. There is an unmistakable atmosphere of history (Puritan prisoners including a Muggletonian, Negro slaves, the Indian perils, and allusions to Charles II's Court, etc.), but the romance is essentially one of love and adventure. It is a book which, once begun, can hardly be set down until the last page has been reached.

1081. REBELS OF THE GREEN COCKADE: Escott Lynn; *Juv.*
Chambers.
The story proper begins Virginia, 1675, quickly leading up to the rising of the Indians in 1676, and General Bacon's action over this and other matters. The central theme is the popular revolt known as "Bacon's Rebellion" (1676). Bacon himself and Governor Berkeley are prominent.

1082. WHITE APRONS: Maud W. Goodwin; *Dent* [Eng.], *Little*
Brown [U.S.A.].
Another story of Virginia and Bacon's Rebellion, 1676 (there is a glimpse of England and Charles II's Court). The title of this book is taken from the fact that in the battle between Governor Berkeley's forces and the rebels under Bacon, certain women friends of the Governor were made to stand in front of the rebels. This "White Apron" device was undeservedly successful.

1083. *THE BRIGHT FACE OF DANGER: C. M. Sublette; *Hodder*
& Stoughton [Eng.], *Little, Brown* [U.S.A.].
Begins London, but deals almost entirely with Virginia, 1676. An adventure story, with a substantial historic background:—Nathaniel Bacon's war against the Indians, and the civil war following it known as "Bacon's Rebellion." The book ends with the death of Bacon. Several historic figures besides Bacon, including Governor Berkeley, and Colonel John Washington (George's grandfather).

1084. *THE HEART'S HIGHWAY: MARY E. WILKINS; *Murray* [*Eng.*], *Doubleday* [*U.S.A.*].

Virginia (Jamestown), chiefly in 1682, but ending 1688. A novel which illustrates the riots in connection with the Navigation Act; mention is made of a plot for cutting down the young tobacco plants (the colonists were forbidden by the Navigation Laws to export any tobacco other than that sent to England). Introduces the Governor of Virginia (Culpeper) and other figures.

1085. NATHALIA: F. WHISHAW; *John Long.*

A story of Russia (Moscow Court life) round about 1670. Depicts the time of Tsar Alexis—his wooing of Nathalia and their eventual marriage, followed by the birth (1672) of the child who was to become famous as Peter the Great.

1086. *STRADELLA: F. MARION CRAWFORD; *Macmillan.*

Venice, Ferrara, and Rome (chiefly Venice and Rome) about the end of Clement X's Pontificate (1670-76). A love romance of Alessandro Stradella, the singer and composer, based on some of the historical facts connected with his elopement from Venice (assassins sent to murder him, etc.). There are many thrilling fictional episodes in the story, while the historical element is increased by the introduction, at different points, of Christina the extraordinary ex-Queen of Sweden, Bernini the sculptor, Cardinal Altieri, and—at the very end—Pope Clement X himself.

1087. *L'INFANTE: LOUIS BERTRAND; *Arthème Fayard* [*France*].

Spain (Catalania and Madrid), also France, 1673-74. A novel having as its background the strained relations between France and Spain at the time mentioned, and the troubles in the Spanish frontier country. Several historic figures appear, amongst whom one may specify Marie-Anne of Austria and the little King Charles II of Spain. There are also glimpses of Louis XIV and Louvois at Versailles.

1088. THE TURBULENT DUCHESS: PERCY J. BREBNER; *Hodder & Stoughton.*

Germany, c. 1674. A romance of the time when Turenne was ravaging the Palatinate. The " Duchess of Podina " and a certain Jester are two leading characters. Frederich Wilhelm, the Elector of Brandenburg, appears (there is a plot against his life).

1089. *I WILL MAINTAIN:
          *DEFENDER OF THE FAITH (*sequel*): " MARJORIE BOWEN ";
          Methuen.

These two historical novels are the first and second volumes of the trilogy which is completed in *God and the King* (see Page 133). They deal mostly with Holland and England in the period 1672-78, depicting in particular the tragedy of the brothers De Witt, and the marriage between William of Orange and Mary Stuart. The time is that of Louis XIV's Dutch War (French-English alliance) and De Ruyter's naval successes. Of the many personages introduced, the most noteworthy are:—John and Cornelius De Witt (together with their father, Jacob), William of Orange, Bentinck, Sir William Temple, Louis XIV, Turenne, Louvois, Charles II, Princess Mary, Lord Sunderland, and the Duke of Buckingham.

1090. *THE BLACK TULIP: ALEXANDRE DUMAS; *Dent* [*Eng.*], *Little, Brown* [*U.S.A.*].

Holland, 1672-73 (i.e. the story proper). A charming romance in which, it must be acknowledged, the fictional interest is primary. At the same time, Chapters I-IV give a vivid account (from the anti-Orange standpoint) of the events which culminated in the terrible murder of the brothers De Witte by the infuriated mob at the Hague (1672). It must suffice to mention that, although the hero's connection with the De Wittes is really non-political, he is imprisoned through an intrigue. One important feature in the story, viz., the enthusiasm shown over tulip-growing, is itself suggestive of a particular time and place, but the main emphasis is on what is broadly human. Besides the early appearances of John and Cornelius De Witte, there are depictions of the Prince of Orange in both the earlier and the later portions of the book.

1091. THE PRINCE'S PAWNS: "E. BARRINGTON"; in "The Gallants "—*Harrap*.
The Dutch Court just after Charles II's death (1685): a tale of William of Orange, Mary, the Duke of Monmouth, and Henrietta Wentworth.

1092. THE ADVENTURES OF AN EQUERRY: "MORICE GERARD"; *Juv. Cassell*.
England, and (largely) Abroad, mid to late Charles II period. A tale of the early career of John Churchill up to his marriage (1675) with Sarah Jennings. Deals with Louis XIV's War in Holland (1672)—covering the Siege of Maestricht and other events. Many historic figures besides those already mentioned:—Turenne, Vauban, Louis XIV, etc. etc.

1093. *'MIDST THE WILD CARPATHIANS:
*THE SLAVES OF THE PADISHAH (*sequel*): MAURUS JÓKAI (trans.); *Jarrold* [Eng.], *Page* [U.S.A.].
Although these two novels are distinct, they may be regarded as forming one imaginative picture of Transylvania in late 17th Century (1662-66 and 1674-90). Of the numerous historic figures the most prominent are Michael Apafi, the last independent Prince of Transylvania, his remarkable consort Anna, and Teleki the Prince's chief councillor. Jókai illustrates for us the semi-barbarous and unsettled conditions arising out of the country's geographical position between East and West, i.e. between the Ottoman and the German Empires. Hungarians, Germans, Turkish pashas, Moorish brigands, etc., play their parts in these thrilling stories of fighting, adventure, and intrigue. Some of the social customs and general institutions strike the English reader as strange (for instance, a certain Martin Kuncz is "*Bishop* of the Klausenburg Unitarians"). Until the later period of the sequel, a Turkish pasha ruled over the larger part of Hungary, but—as Jókai's pages show—between 1674 and 1690 Hungary was invaded by the Transylvanian forces, and, after much fighting, the German armies were in complete possession of Transylvania itself. The descriptions of scenery constitute a special feature of these romances.

1094. THE WIZARD KING: DAVID KER; *Juv. Chambers* [Eng.], *Lippincott* [U.S.A.].
Largely the Carpathian District round about 1680. A tale dealing with the time of the Moslem invasion, and of John Sobieski's raising of the Siege of Vienna by his victory over the Turks (1683).

1095. THE FIELD OF GLORY (ON THE FIELD OF GLORY): HENRYK SIENKIEWICZ (trans.); *Dent* [Eng.], *Little, Brown* [U.S.A.].
Poland, 1682-83. A romance illustrating conditions during the Turkish Invasion of Europe, and dealing especially with the Relief of Vienna by John Sobieski. The novel is unfinished, and belongs to the author's later and less successful period.

1096. *THE VICOMTE DE BRAGELONNE: ALEXANDRE DUMAS (trans.); *Dent* [Eng.], *Little, Brown* [U.S.A.].
France, Holland, England (Scottish Border), etc., 1660-68. The third volume of the famous D'Artagnan series; some critics regard it as being not only the best volume of the series, but as taking first place in the whole of Dumas' works. The romance, though of unusual length, covers a comparatively short period—the period of Colbert's financial reforms (Colbert himself frequently appears); the latest fictional developments may be said to occur about the time of Madame de Montespan's advent. One can only mention a few of the many historic figures introduced:—Louis XIV (his marriage with Maria Theresa in 1660 and other incidents), Anne of Austria, Louise de la Vallière, Lafontaine, Marie de Mancini, Charles II and his mother Queen Henrietta, the Duke of Buckingham, and General Monk. The *Monk* episodes are especially good, and furnish an example of Dumas at his very best.

1097. *A DEMOISELLE OF FRANCE: W. J. ECCOTT; *Blackwood*.
Paris, Fontainebleau, and the road to Nantes, in 1662. A French Abbé (great-nephew of Richelieu) relates his adventures, which make entertaining reading for those who like the Dumas type of novel. Many famous personages appear: Louis XIV, Colbert, Foucquet, Madeline and Armande Béjart, Molière, La Fontaine, etc.

126   SEVENTEENTH CENTURY—continued

1098. *BLUSH-ROSE (BELLE-ROSE): Amédée Achard (trans.); Holden & Hardingham.
France in early Louis XIV period, 1663-1672. A shortened English version of Achard's popular story—one of the best examples of the " cloak and sword " type of romance which immediately followed the success of Dumas in *The Three Musketeers*. Besides the fictional ingredients of love-making, adventure, and fighting, some definitely historical events and personages are introduced. The novel deals with the War of 1667 in Franche-Comté, and the successful Invasion of Holland. Louis XIV, Louvois, the Prince de Condé, and the Duc de Luxembourg appear.

1099. THE GOLDEN FLEECE (LA TOISON D'OR): Amédeé Achard (trans.); Macqueen [Eng.], Page [U.S.A.].
France and Austria, 1664. Another romance of the once popular French novelist, again depicting the earlier period of Louis XIV. This tale of love and adventure has for background the Turkish Wars (fighting on the Bank of the River Raab, etc.). King Louis himself and Louise de la Vallière appear.

1100. HIS INDOLENCE OF ARRAS: W. J. Eccott; Blackwood.
Picardy and Paris, 1665-67. An adventure novel, similar in character to the author's romance dealing with the France of a few years earlier (see above). Introduces Louis XIV, the Cardinal Bishop of Arras, Madame de Montespan, Turenne, Louise de la Vallière, Ninon de l'Enclos, etc.

1101. *THE GREAT GAME: Hamilton Drummond; Stanley Paul.
Paris, and (largely) Auvergne, about the year 1670. An excellent novel of adventure and love in the earlier Louis XIV period. The policy and schemes of Louvois, the King's War Minister, furnish the historical background (the Minister himself is prominent in the earlier chapters).

1102. THE RED NEIGHBOUR: W. J. Eccott; Blackwood.
France (Paris, Meaux, Montmirail, etc.), 1675: De Louvois and Turenne, ending with the latter's death at Sasbach in Germany. La Fontaine appears.

1103. *LE LION DEVENU VIEUX: J. Schlumberger; Editions de la Nouvelle Revue Française [France].
Paris, 1679. An extremely able study, in fictional form, of Cardinal de Retz, about whose personality there has been so much controversy. Altogether a careful present-ment of the time (the Jansenists, etc.), though the actual period covered does not run to more than a few weeks, ending with the Cardinal's death.

1104. A DUCHESS OF FRANCE: " Paul Waineman "; Hurst & Blackett.
France in 1685. A careful depiction of Louis XIV and his Court at Versailles. The story ends at the time of the Revocation of the Edict of Nantes (October, 1685).

1105. *THE FROWN OF MAJESTY: Albert Lee; Hutchinson.
France (Paris and Seine provincial region) 1685. A tale of the anti-Huguenot period immediately following the Revocation of the Edict of Nantes, when Madame de Maintenon was at the height of her influence. There are some exciting fictional developments (Lettre de Cachet, etc.), while, on the historical side, Louis XIV, Madame de Maintenon, and the Dauphin are somewhat prominently introduced. There are glimpses, also, of Racine, La Fontaine, and others.

1106. *THE REFUGEES: A. Conan Doyle; Longmans [Eng.], Harpers [U.S.A.].
A tale of the Old World and the New, c. 1684-90. Part I depicts Paris under Louis XIV at the time of the rivalry between Madame de Maintenon and Madame de Montespan, when the latter was losing her ascendancy. Both these ladies and the King are prominent, while Louvois, de Frontenac, Condé, Bossuet, Boileau, Racine, and Corneille all appear. Part II describes the escape of Huguenot refugees from their country's intolerance; also their voyage and landing in Canada, as well as their further experiences in Quebec and inland. Time of the Iroquois troubles.

1107. THE KING'S SIGNET: Eliza F. Pollard; *Juv. Blackie* [Eng.], *Scribner* [U.S.A.].
France (chiefly), England, Holland, and Ireland, 1685-1700. A Huguenot family's experiences after the Revocation of the Edict of Nantes. Louis XIV, Madame de Maintenon, and Louvois appear. Besides the French incidents, the Battle of the Boyne is covered in the tale.

1108. *IN FURTHEST IND: " Sydney C. Grier "; *Blackwood* [Eng.], *Page* [U.S.A.].
England, and India (Surat, Goa, Agra, etc.), mainly 1664-84, though the *entire* period covered in the book is 1646-97. This interesting " narrative ", which an Englishman —" late of the Honourable East India Company's service "—is supposed to have written in the year 1697, is historical in the general sense. The author explains in her Appendix that she has endeavoured " rather to present a picture than to construct a history." Accordingly, the reader is given an account of various travels and adventures in " furthest Ind," illustrating the state of things in that Eastern region during the early days of the East India Company. The Inquisition in Goa (Portuguese Indies); the French at San Thomé; a repulse of the Dutch Fleet; an embassy to the Mogul Emperor Auren Zeeb (Aurangzib), with glimpses of the Emperor himself and his Court at Agra —these are the main features of the story. The last seventy to eighty pages deal with the hero's love experiences, etc., after his return to England in 1684. In this later part of the narrative the Revolution of 1688 is covered, but not described in detail.

1109. *BHIM SINGH: Frank R. Sell; *Macmillan*.
Rajputana (largely Udaipur), 1679-90. An excellent romance of the Rajput War (the Mughals *v.* the Rajputs), illustrating the failure of the Emperor Aurangzib's designs. Both the Emperor himself, and his son, Sultan Akbar, are introduced (the last-named personage is depicted as having no real heart in his father's War).

1110. DIAMONDS: Mrs. F. E. Penny; *Hodder & Stoughton*.
Coromandel Coast of India (Fort St. George), 1687-88. A well-written novel depicting life and ways in the early period of the Royal East India Company.

1111. *LORNA DOONE: R. D. Blackmore; *Sampson Low* [Eng.], *Putnam* [U.S.A.], *and other publishers—English and American.*
The West of England (Exmoor) mainly in the period 1673-88. This justly esteemed romance is rich in local colour, and the manner of writing adopted by the author, has given to the narrative a quaintness and charm which are peculiar to it. It can hardly be described as an " historical novel " in the full sense; it contains, however, Monmouth Rebellion allusions, besides offering glimpses of James II, Judge Jeffreys, Churchill, and others.

1112. *BEAUJEU: H. C. Bailey; *Murray* [Eng.], *Appleton* [U.S.A.].
England (Oxford, London, etc.) 1678-1688 (Charles II—James II). Begins with the Popish Plot period, and the downfall of the Whigs; then passes lightly over the Monmouth Rebellion. Largely a story of political intrigues during James II's reign. King James is himself very prominent, as also are Sunderland and Wharton; while Bentinck, Halifax and others appear.

1113. *FOR FAITH AND FREEDOM: Walter Besant; *Chatto & Windus* [Eng.], *Harper* [U.S.A.].
England and West Indies, 1662-88. The story, however, is mainly concerned with Somerset 1680-88, covering the few years before and after the Monmouth Rebellion as well as the Rebellion itself. Taunton (the " Maids of Taunton "), Sedgemoor, and the Bloody Assize. Then slavery scenes in the Barbados, and other West Indian experiences. Ends at the time of William of Orange's landing.

1114. FORTUNE'S CASTAWAY: W. J. Eccott; *Blackwood*.
England and Holland, 1683-85. A novel dealing with the Duke of Monmouth and Lady Henrietta Wentworth, at the same time reflecting the time of the Rye House Plot and the Monmouth Rebellion. William of Orange, James II and many other historic figures appear.

1115. THE PALACE FOOTBOY: Gertrude Hollis; *Juv.* *S.P.C.K.* [*Eng.*], *Gorham* [*U.S.A.*].

A tale of Wells, Glastonbury, etc., and London in the period 1683-88. Covers the Monmouth Rebellion, the Trial of the Seven Bishops, etc. The central figure is Bishop Ken. Colonel Kirke and Judge Jeffreys are both introduced.

1116. *MARTIN HYDE: John Masefield; *Juv.* *Wells Gardner* [*Eng.*], *Little, Brown* [*U.S.A.*].

Suffolk (Oulton), London, Holland, and W. England, mainly 1684-85. A fascinating tale of a young lad in the period of the Monmouth Rebellion. There are many exciting adventures both by land and by sea. Covers the landing of the Duke of Monmouth at Lyme, and the Battle of Sedgemoor (the hero is a witness of the event. Monmouth appears very prominently, and Lord Grey is another figure introduced. After the disaster of Sedgemoor, the hero gets away to the West Indies.

1117. THE BROWN MASK: Percy J. Brebner; *Cassell.*

Hampshire, Somerset, London, etc., 1685. A story of the mystery relating to a highwayman's identity. The Monmouth Rebellion is the historical background, and some of the usual figures are introduced.

1118. *THE RED SEAL: " Morice Gerard "; *Juv.* *Cassell.*

N. Somerset Coast, London, and Taunton, 1685. A good story of the Monmouth Rebellion *period*, in which James II and Judge Jeffreys are both prominent—other figures also appearing. King James is well depicted.

1119. *THE DUKE OF MONMOUTH: Gerald Griffin; *Bentley.*

An interesting tale by an early nineteenth century Irish author of considerable repute. Somerset before, during, and after the Monmouth Rebellion. Describes the series of events from the Duke's landing at Lyme Regis down to his flight after Sedgemoor and his execution. Besides Monmouth himself, Colonel Kirke is very prominent. Lady Harriet Wentworth is also to the fore, and General Feversham appears.

1120. *MICAH CLARKE: A. Conan Doyle; *Longmans* [*Eng.*], *Harper* [*U.S.A.*].

A " narrative " romance, beginning Hampshire and the hero's birth 1664, but mainly dealing with Somerset in the year 1685. Essentially a story of the Monmouth Rebellion, telling of doings at Taunton, Keynsham Bridge, and Wells. There is a full account of the Battle of Sedgemoor. Monmouth himself is prominent, while Judge Jeffreys is vividly presented.

1121. *MISTRESS CHARITY GODOLPHIN: Gladys Murdoch; *Murray.*

An interesting story of 1685. Begins West Scotland, but the scene is mainly England (West Country and Wilts—Hants region). The historic background is the Monmouth Rebellion—especially the Trial and Execution of that truly noble woman, Lady Alice Lisle of Moynes Court. The most striking passages in the book are those describing the conduct of Lady Alice before Jeffreys at Winchester.

1122. THE SWORD OF FORTUNE: Ben Bolt; *Ward Lock.*

Chiefly W. England, 1685. A novel of adventure, with the Monmouth Rebellion as background. The Duke is frequently mentioned, but does not actually appear, while there is only a glimpse of the Battle of Sedgemoor. Lord and Lady Sunderland, together with Kirke, are the prominent historic figures. The reader catches sight of Judge Jeffreys at the end.

1123. MY LADY VENTURESOME: Dorothea Moore; *Juv.* *Sheldon Press* [*Eng.*], *Macmillan* [*U.S.A.*].

A good tale of the Maids of Taunton and the Monmouth Rebellion in 1685.

1124. *THE FATE: G. P. R. JAMES; *Newby* [1851].

One of James's novels that even some readers of to-day may find interesting. The Lincolnshire—Nottinghamshire region, and Dorset, Somerset, etc., in 1685. A story of social life, but with considerable historic background (Monmouth Rebellion) in the second half. There are many allusions to public events, and several notabilities appear:—the Duke of Monmouth, Lord Churchill, the Duke of Albemarle (Monk), Judge Jeffreys (a good depiction), and the Duke of Norfolk.

1125. ANTHONY WILDING (MISTRESS WILDING): RAFAEL SABATINI; *Hutchinson* [*Eng.*], *Houghton Mifflin* [*U.S.A.*].

Somerset (largely Bridgwater) and Dorset, 1685. A love and adventure romance, with the Monmouth Rebellion as background. Deals more with the plots and general circumstances before and after Monmouth's landing at Lyme, than with actual events. The Battle of Sedgemoor is covered, but merely in the way of reference. Several historical figures are introduced besides the Duke of Monmouth: the Duke of Albemarle (Monk), Feversham, Lord Grey of Werle, and Nathaniel Wade the lawyer. There are also allusions to Sunderland, Jeffreys, Kirke, etc.

1126. BY DULVERCOMBE WATER: HAROLD VALLINGS; *Macmillan*.

This "love story of 1685" (sub-title) and the Exmoor region, verges on the semi-historic type of fiction; the atmosphere is historical, but the Monmouth Rebellion is only presented in dim fashion.

1127. A CAVALIER OF FORTUNE: ESCOTT LYNN; *Juv.   Chambers*.

Mainly London and West of England, 1685-88. A story dealing with the time of the Titus Oates flogging, the Monmouth Rebellion (description of Sedgemoor), the Bloody Assize, and William of Orange's landing. James II and his Queen, Monmouth, Jeffreys, Sunderland, and William, all appear.

1128. THE CHARIOTS OF THE LORD: JOSEPH HOCKING; *R.T.S.* [*Eng.*], *Eaton & Mains* [*U.S.A.*].

England (London, Somerset, etc.) and Holland, 1685-88. Covers the Battle of Sedgemoor, the Seven Bishops, and the coming of William. The Duke of Monmouth, Bishop Trelawny, Richard Baxter, James II, etc.

1129. (1) GALLOPING DICK:
      (2) THE HIGH TOBY (*sequel*):
      (3) THE KING'S HIGHWAY (*sequel*): H. B. MARRIOTT WATSON;
      (1) *Lane*, (2) *Methuen*, and (3) *Mills & Boon*.

A trilogy depicting the adventures and experiences of a highwayman, known as "Galloping Dick," in the Charles II—James II period. Good stories of their kind.

1130. SWORD OF THE KING: RONALD MACDONALD; *Murray* [*Eng.*], *Century* [*U.S.A.*].

A woman's narrative concerning events in England 1673-88, though mainly dealing with the year 1688 (the landing of Orange). Kirke appears in connection with the Monmouth Rebellion, while the Prince of Orange and Bentinck are prominently introduced.

1131. *THE COURTSHIP OF MORRICE BUCKLER: A. E. W. MASON; *Macmillan*.

A stirring tale of an Englishman's adventures in the period 1685-87: Holland, England, the Tyrol, Italy, and France. Not in the strictest sense historical fiction, but a romance conveying the atmosphere and general life of the time.

1132. *CAPTAIN MARGARET: JOHN MASEFIELD; *Grant Richards* [*Eng.*], *Lippincott* [*U.S.A.*].

South Devon, Cornwall, and the Spanish Main (islands off Darien) about 1685-88. A novel in which character-analysis and adventure are primary, and to which the adjective "historical" can only be applied in its more elastic sense.

1133. *CAPTAIN BLOOD: Rafael Sabitini; *Hutchinson* [*Eng.*], *Houghton Mifflin* [*U.S.A.*].
Somerset and the West Indies, 1685-89. The Irish hero gets wrongfully implicated in the Monmouth Rebellion and is transported to Barbados. The tale is essentially one of adventure and buccaneering exploits (with a love element), the reader being taken through a series of exciting scenes at Barbados, Tortuga, Jamaica and Cartagena respectively. History is, for the most part, well in the background, but there is a good picture of Judge Jeffreys in the opening chapters.

1134. *SALUTE TO ADVENTURERS: John Buchan; *Nelson* [*Eng.*], *Doran* [*U.S.A.*].
Begins Scotland (Clydesdale, Edinburgh, and Glasgow) 1685, but is mainly a story of Virginia at the end of the 17th Century. A young Scotsman goes out to manage a Virginian estate, and has many adventures with Indians, Pirates, etc.

1135. JAMES THE SECOND: W. H. Ainsworth; *Colburn.*
An historical romance of London and District in 1688. Good accounts of the Seven Bishops' Trial and the Prince of Orange's invasion. Besides James II, a crowd of historic personages appear, including George Fox, Bunyan, Richard Baxter, Sunderland, Pepys, Churchill, William of Orange, Godolphin, and Halifax.
In his useful " Bibliographical Catalogue of the Published Novels and Ballads of William Harrison Ainsworth " (Elkin Mathews), Mr. Harold Locke rightly points out that, while not one of Ainsworth's best novels, *James the Second* has had " less than justice done to it."

1136. *WINNING HIS NAME: " Herbert Strang "; *Juv.* *Oxford University Press.*
An exceptionally good tale of a lad's adventures in the Devon—Dorset region, etc., and London, mainly in the year 1688. Illustrates the time of the Seven Bishops' Trial, and the coming of William of Orange. Samuel Pepys and William are among the historic figures.

1137. THE ADVENTURES OF MARMADUKE CLEGG: " Morice Gerard "; *Juv.* *Odhams.*
London, Kent, and Holland, 1688. An adventure story, ending with the Revolution. James II, William of Orange, and Lord and Lady Churchill appear.

1138. THE SWORD OF FREEDOM: Charles Gilson; *Juv.* *Oxford University Press.*
Kent and London, also the Northampton region, 1688. An historical tale of the English Revolution, introducing—amongst other real figures—James II, Sunderland, Bishop Compton, and William of Orange.

1139. THE CHERRY RIBBAND: S. R. Crockett; *Hodder & Stoughton* [*Eng.*], *Barnes* [*U.S.A.*].
Scotland (Dumfries and the Island of the Bass) in the Charles II—James II period. A pleasing love story of Convenanter days. There is a distinct background of history, and Claverhouse, James II, and others appear.

1140. *THROUGH FLOOD AND FIRE: R. W. Mackenna; *Murray.*
Scotland (Dumfries region) somewhere about 1680. A love and adventure story, with an interesting historical background. The time is that of the Covenanters who are sympathetically drawn. Claverhouse is an outstanding figure; the author has offered a clear and suggestive presentment of his character.

1141. *FLOWER O' THE HEATHER: R. W. Mackenna; *Murray.*
Dumfries and the Galloway district generally, also Edinburgh, 1685. An Englishman's narrative of stirring adventures in the North. The romance well illustrates the sufferings of the Covenanters and the finer aspects of their religious zeal. There is an historical atmosphere throughout (Claverhouse does not appear except in a somewhat striking anecdote).

1142. MILES RITSON: Claude E. Benson; *Sampson Low.*
Cumberland (Cockermouth, etc.), also the Solway and Border regions, round about 1687. A good adventure tale with a slight historical element. Claverhouse appears.

1143. LOCHINVAR: S. R. Crockett; *Methuen* [*Eng.*], *Harper* [*U.S.A.*].
A Scottish tale of adventure and fighting. The Battle of Killiecrankie is introduced.

1144. *GRAHAM OF CLAVERHOUSE: "Ian Maclaren"; *Murray* [*Eng.*], *Cupples* [*U.S.A.*].
Holland, London, and Scotland (Edinburgh, etc.), 1674-89. As fiction this book has considerable interest and charm; on the historical side, a reader would do well to compare it with Barrington's *Knight of the Golden Sword*—the two romances reflecting opposite standpoints. There is, undoubtedly, an attempt on the part of "Ian Maclaren" to show the higher side of Claverhouse's character, but the author's sympathy with the Covenanters was probably too great to admit of his giving an impartial portrait of the novel's outstanding figure. Much is made of the unhappy division between Claverhouse and his wife (née Lady Jean Cochrane) in the days just before the Battle of Killiecrankie. This last-mentioned Battle is the event with which the book closes (Dundee's death), while in one of the earliest chapters some account is given of the Battle of Seneffe (Low Countries) where Claverhouse saved the life of William of Orange. Besides Claverhouse and his wife, many historical personages appear, the most important being William of Orange (William III) who is presented favourably more than once.

1145. *THE KNIGHT OF THE GOLDEN SWORD: Michael Barrington; *Chatto & Windus.*
France, England and to a very slight extent Ireland, but chiefly Scotland (Galloway, Edinburgh, Paisley, etc., and the Highlands), 1683-89. An autobiographical romance, in which the Roman Catholic hero (of Irish descent, though Paris-born) tells his experiences as volunteer in the service of Grahame of Claverhouse. The outstanding figure in the novel is Claverhouse himself, whose character is treated from the standpoint of almost entire sympathy; to any thoughtful reader the amount of historical research which such a careful portrait implies, must be obvious (as a matter of fact, Mr. Barrington published an excellent *biography* of John Grahame of Claverhouse in 1911). The fictional interest is well maintained throughout, while the principal historic incidents of the stormy period covered, are either suggested or described. The bigotries and rivalries of late 17th Century Scotland are illustrated in a decided, but not exaggerated, manner; perhaps justice is hardly done to the better side of the Covenanter spirit. The book ends with the Battle of Killiecrankie and the death of Claverhouse (Dundee). In the course of the story many famous personages, beside Claverhouse, are introduced:—Charles II, James II, Queen Mary Beatrice, Saints Évremond, the Duke of Buckingham, Pepys, Waller, the Duke of Hamilton, Burnet, Cameron of Lochiel, Claverhouse's brother David, etc., etc. There is a glimpse of William of Orange, and special mention of William Penn. The very brief "Afterword" is dated 1701.

1146. RINGAN GILHAIZE: John Galt; *Greening.*
This novel by the famous author of *Annals of the Parish*, deals with the Covenanters and the Battle of Killiecrankie.

1147. THE SCOTTISH CAVALIER: James Grant; *Juv. Routledge* [*Eng.*], *Dutton* [*U.S.A.*].
Scotland, France and the Netherlands, 1688-93. A tale which deals primarily with Claverhouse and the persecution of the Covenanters—describing the Battle of Killiecrankie and Claverhouse's death. There are various allusions to the English Revolution, etc. In the Foreign part of the book, the Battle of Steinkirke is an important event. The outstanding historic figure in the Scottish chapters is, of course, James Grahame of Claverhouse.

1148. *THE GLEN O' WEEPING: "Marjorie Bowen"; *Alston Rivers* [*Eng.*], *McClure* [*U.S.A.*], also *John Long* [*Eng.*].
Scotland (Argyllshire, also Glasgow and Edinburgh), and England (Romney Marsh and London), 1691-92, and 1695. A thrilling romance of the Scottish clan feuds

(Macdonalds v. Campbells), written round the historical massacre of the Macdonald clan in the wild Pass of Glencoe; the book offers an explanation of that dire event, other than the one usually accepted. The Earl of Breadalbane, Sir John Dalrymple (Earl of Stair), and William III are three of the most important figures introduced.

1149. *THE BOYNE WATER: John Banim; *James Duffy.*
N. Ireland, 1685-91. A remarkably fine historical novel, depicting events of importance which culminate in the Battle of the Boyne and William III's retreat from Limerick. The reader is taken to England (London) at one point. Among the many historic figures are General Sarsfield, General Kirke, James II, William III, Queen Mary, Tyrconnel, Schomberg, Bentinck, and Bishop Burnet. The standpoint of the author is Catholic.

1150. *THE FORTUNES OF COLONEL TORLOGH O'BRIEN: J. Sheridan Le Fanu; *Routledge,* also *Downey.*
London and Ireland (County of Limerick and Dublin), mainly 1686-1691. An important historical romance, illustrating the Wars of King James. There is a full account of the Battle of Aughrim, but, although the Battle of the Boyne and the Siege of Limerick are both covered, they are in no way described. Numerous historical figures are introduced:—James II, William III, Tyrconnel, Sarsfield, the Duke of Berwick, and others. There is some excellent local colour in the novel.

1151. ORANGE AND GREEN: G. A. Henty; *Juv.* Blackie [*Eng.*], *Scribner* [*U.S.A.*].
Ireland, 1688-91. A tale of two boys (one Protestant, the other Catholic) in the Irish Wars of the time. Covers various sieges, including that of Limerick, as well as the Battle of the Boyne (1690) and the Battle of Aughrim (1691).

1152. THE KNIGHTS OF THE WHITE ROSE: George Griffith; *Juv.* Shaw.
Ireland, England, and Abroad from 1688 to about 1696. A Jacobite tale which introduces the Irish War of 1689 (Derry and the Battle of the Boyne). Allusions to King James II, Sarsfield, Schomberg and others. A more definite appearance is that of William III, in connection with assassination schemes.

1153. *THE CRIMSON SIGN: S. R. Keightley; *Hutchinson* [*Eng.*], *Harper* [*U.S.A.*].
Ireland, 1689. A narrative story of adventures in a stirring time. In the second half of the book the attention of the reader is drawn mainly to the Siege and Relief of Londonderry. General Patrick Sarsfield and General Kirke are among the historic figures.

1154. A MAN'S FOES: E. H. Strain; *Juv.* Ward & Lock [*Eng.*], New Amsterdam Book Co. [*U.S.A.*].
A good North of Ireland tale, written from the Protestant standpoint, and having or its main historical background the Siege of Derry in 1689.

1155. *IN SARSFIELD'S DAYS (THE WAGER): Miss L. McManus; Gill [*Ireland*], Buckles [*U.S.A.*].
A striking tale of the Siege of Limerick, in 1690: the repulse of William III and his retirement. General Sarsfield is, of course, depicted, William III and the Duke of Berwick also appear, while there are glimpses of Tyrconnell and Lauzun.

1156. A REPUTED CHANGELING: Charlotte M. Yonge; *Juv.* Macmillan.
England and France (St. Germain) within the period 1680-1700 (Charles II—William III). Covers events like the Seven Bishops' Trial, the flight of James II, and the landing of the Prince of Orange. Charles II and Sir Christopher Wren are introduced in a comic episode, while James II and his family are among the other historic personages.

1157. *GOD AND THE KING: "Marjorie Bowen"; *Methuen.*
This third volume in the trilogy, of which *I Will Maintain* and *Defender of the Faith* are the first two volumes, deals with the English Revolution of 1688, and with William of Orange as King up to his death in 1702. In this historical romance the political schemes and complications at Home and Abroad during the whole of William's reign, are more or less exhaustively illustrated. Various personages like Queen Mary, Shrewsbury, Halifax, Marlborough, etc., are skilfully presented. The portrait of William himself is a very favourable one.

1158. IN THE CHOIR OF WESTMINSTER ABBEY: Emma Marshall; *Juv. Seeley.*
Mostly London, 1684-95. A tale written round the figure of the Westminster Abbey organist and composer, Henry Purcell. In the course of the semi-fictional developments the reader is made aware of several historic events, such as the Coronation of William and Mary, the Death of Mary, etc. There are glimpses of Judge Jeffreys, Mrs. Bracegirdle the actress, and others.

1159. THE KING'S CHAMPION: Bernard Capes; in "Historical Vignettes"—*Fisher Unwin* [*Eng.*], *Stokes* [*U.S.A.*].
William III just after his coronation in 1689: an incident of comic nature.

1160. THE LAST LINK: "Morice Gerard"; *Juv. Hodder & Stoughton.*
London and Suffolk, 1690. A love story with historical background. The hero is on secret service for King William III who is somewhat prominently introduced. An assassination plot is tracked, etc.

1161. (1) MY LADY BELLAMY:
(2) A LADY OF METTLE (*sequel*): Dorothea Moore; *Juv.*
(1) *Nisbet*, (2) *Partridge.*
Two connected tales of Jacobite adventure and conspiracy, together covering the period, 1689-96. Many localities are touched (London District, Edinburgh, Windsor, etc.), while several historic personages appear:—William III, Princess Anne, Thomas Wharton, etc. etc.

1162. A LADY OF QUALITY:
HIS GRACE OF OSMONDE (*sequel*): Frances Hodgson Burnett; *Warne* [*Eng.*], *Scribner* [*U.S.A.*].
Two character novels with fictional connection, illustrating English High Life mostly between 1690 and 1712 (William III—Anne period). The historical background is slight.

1163. KENSINGTON PALACE: Emma Marshall; *Juv. Seeley* [*Eng.*], *Macmillan* [*U.S.A.*].
A story of London and the West Country, 1690-94. Queen Mary is the central figure, with a general background of Jacobite plots, etc. Besides the careful depiction of the Queen and William III, there are glimpses of Bishop Burnet, Marlborough, and others.

1164. *THE BLUE PAVILIONS: A. T. Quiller-Couch; *Dent* [*Eng.*], *Cassell* [*Eng.*], *Scribner* [*U.S.A.*].
Harwich, Flanders, and France in the period 1673-91 (*mainly William III's reign*). An excellent story of sea adventures and political intrigues. King William and Marlborough appear.

1165. THE HONOUR OF A ROYALL: Herbert Hayens; *Juv. Collins.*
Begins Southampton (announcement of Queen Mary's death). A tale of England and France in the last decade of the 17th Century. A plot to murder William III is an important element in the story. James II appears at St. Germain.

1166. BY THE NORTH SEA: Emma Marshall; *Juv. Jarrold [Eng.], Whittaker [U.S.A.].*
Yarmouth, London, Bristol, etc., 1694-95. A tale introducing Mistress Bridget Bendysh, grand-daughter of Oliver Cromwell. Archbishop Tillotson, Dr. Isaac Watts, and William III also appear.

1167. SHREWSBURY: Stanley J. Weyman; *Longmans.*
England, about 1683-96 (Charles II—William III). An historical romance which, after barely touching on such events as the death of Charles II, the Monmouth Rebellion, and the Revolution of 1688, deals primarily with *Jacobite intrigues in the middle of William III's reign* (the Fenwick Conspiracy). Several noteworthy historical figures are introduced, but those appearing most prominently are the Duke of Shrewsbury, Robert Ferguson " the Plotter ", William III, Marlborough, and Sir John Fenwick. Not in some ways a good example of the author, but the book has considerable interest.

1168. THE BRACEGIRDLE: Burris Jenkins; *Lippincott.*
A story of the actress, Anne Bracegirdle, and of London under William III. The King himself is prominent (plot against his life, etc.).

1169. *THE GENTLEMAN ADVENTURER: H. C. Bailey; *Methuen [Eng.], Doran [U.S.A.].*
A good story of the William III—Anne period, beginning England 1695 (Jacobite plots). The larger part of the book, however, deals with sea and land adventures in the region of the West Indies. The hero (pirate of a kind) is at one time a prisoner in Jamaica where a shrewd Quaker befriends him.

1170. THE FIRST LIGHT ON THE EDDYSTONE: Emma Marshall; *Juv. Seeley.*
Plymouth, 1696-1703: the first Eddystone Lighthouse; then (1709) the second Lighthouse. An interesting little tale.

1171. *ROBERT CAVALIER: W. D. Orcutt; *Heinemann [Eng.], McClurg [U.S.A.].*
Paris and Versailles, also New France (Montreal, Quebec, the Lakes, etc.) and the Ohio and Mississippi regions, 1666-82. A romance of La Salle, the French explorer, and his experiences in both the Old World and the New. Tells of Jesuit plots, and of the various difficulties which had to be overcome before La Salle's discovery—described in the latest part of the tale—of the Mississippi River. Governor Courcelle, Governor Frontenac, Louis XIV, Madame de Maintenon, and Henri de Tonty are the principal figures introduced besides La Salle himself. There are glimpses of Madame de Montespan.

1172. *THE POWER AND THE GLORY: Gilbert Parker; *Hodder & Stoughton [Eng.], Harper [U.S.A.].*
Begins Quebec (Count Frontenac, newly arrived as Governor, and La Salle in 1672); then France (Louis XIV's Court at Versailles), followed by the varying fortunes of La Salle and Henri de Tonti as explorers in North America:—Fort Frontenac and the Iroquois, the reaching of the Mouth of the Mississippi in 1682, and the governorship of La Barre. After more Versailles scenes, the novel ends with the murder of La Salle in 1687.

1173. *A DAUGHTER OF NEW FRANCE: Mary Catherine Crowley; *Little, Brown [U.S.A.].*
Quebec, and (largely) the beginnings of the French settlement on the Detroit, in the period between 1687 and the early part of the 18th Century. This carefully-written romance illustrates the time of Frontenac and Sir William Phipps's siege (both these personages appear).

1174. BEYOND THE FRONTIER: Randall Parrish; *Jarrolds* [*Eng.*[, *McClurg* [*U.S.A.*].
Canada (Quebec, Montreal and the forest-river regions) in the time of La Barre's governorship (1682-85). A good tale of love and adventure, with—for historic background—the trouble between the adherents of La Salle and those of La Barre. Henri de Tonty is prominent, and Governor La Barre himself appears.

1175. THE DRUMS OF AULONE: Robert W. Chambers; *Appleton*.
Versailles, Whitehall, Dieppe, and Canada (Quebec), 1688-91. A French girl's experiences and adventures, with considerable historical background. Illustrates the anti-Huguenot measures taken under the Maintenon influence in France, the insecure position of James II in England on the eve of the Revolution, and the repulse of the English fleet at Quebec (1691). A crowd of figures:—Louis XIV, Madame de Maintenon, Louvois, James II and his Queen, Pepys, Governor Frontenac, etc.

1176. CASTLE DANGEROUS OF CANADA: Mrs. E. M. Field; *Juv. Wells Gardner*.
A good tale of New France (Canada), 1689-90. Depicts the time of Count Frontenac and of Sir William Phipps's unsuccessful attack on Quebec. Forest adventures, the Iroquois, etc. De Frontenac himself appears in the story.

1177. THE TRAIL OF THE SWORD: Gilbert Parker; *Methuen* [*Eng.*], *Appleton* [*U.S.A.*].
A romance of Canada and New York, etc., round about the year 1690. Adventures by land and sea, covering the futile naval attack on Quebec by Sir William Phipps in 1791. Governor Frontenac appears.

1178. MONTLIVET: Alice Prescott Smith; *Constable* [*Eng.*], *Houghton Mifflin* [*U.S.A.*].
A good novel dealing with the early French settlements in Canada, 1695: the Hurons, Iroquois, etc. Time of Governor de Frontenac.

1179. LE CHIEN D'OR: Walter Besant and James Rice; in " 'Twas in Trafalgar's Bay ", etc.—*Chatto & Windus* [*Eng.*], *Dodd, Mead* [*U.S.A.*].
A brief story of Quebec in 1697, and (last few pages) in 1727.

1180. THE STAR WOMAN: Henry Bedford Jones; *Hurst & Blackett*.
Hudson's Bay and other North American regions, 1697 onwards. A sea and land adventure story of Englishmen, Irishmen, Frenchmen, Mohawk Indians, Fur-Pirates, etc. There is an historical background—Iberville, Perrot, and others appearing.

1181. THE BLACK SHILLING: Amelia E. Barr; *Juv. Fisher Unwin* [*Eng.*], *Dodd, Mead* [*U.S.A.*].
Boston, England, and Boston, America, c. 1690. A tale illustrating the time of the Witchcraft trials under Cotton Mather's influence.

1182. ANNE SCARLET: M. Imlay Taylor; *Gay* [*Eng.*], *McClurg* [*U.S.A.*].
Salem (Massachusetts) about the same time as that assumed in Mrs. Barr's tale immediately preceding. Cotton Mather and his teaching with regard to witchcraft. The story shows the evils resulting from the delusion.

1183. *MAIDS OF SALEM: " K. L. Montgomery "; *John Long*.
Salem and Boston, 1691-95. Another tale illustrating the Witch craze, and depicting Cotton Mather, Sir William Phipps, etc.

1184. THE WITCH-FINDER: " MAY WYNNE "; *Jarrolds.*
Salem region (chiefly) and Boston, 1691 and a year or so following. A love story having for its background the Witchcraft mania (the hanging of Witches on " Witches' Hill," etc.). There are glimpses of Cotton Mather. The book exhibits signs of being based on careful research.

1185. *THE BEGUM'S DAUGHTER: EDWIN L. BYNNER; *Lothrop* [U.S.A.].
Old New York, 1689-90. A good story of Leisler's Rebellion, when, during the period just after the Revolution in England, Jacob Leisler (in the Protestant and anti-James interest) ousted Governor Nicholson, and eventually became for a time Governor with popular approval.

1186. IN LEISLER'S TIMES: ELBRIDGE S. BROOKS; *Juv. Lothrop* [U.S.A.].
A story of Knickerbocker New York in much the same period as that depicted in Bynner's novel. Describes Jacob Leisler's rise to popularity and power.

1187. *THE MAN THEY HANGED: ROBERT W. CHAMBERS; *Appleton.*
A romance of Captain Kidd, " the unluckiest man ever born." The scene is largely New York from 1791, but in the entire period covered (the ten years ending with Kidd's death by hanging at Wapping, England), the novel tells of many localities and sea voyages. A defence of Kidd.

1188. *IN THE DAY OF ADVERSITY: J. BLOUNDELLE BURTON; *Methuen [Eng.], Appleton [U.S.A.].*
France, 1690-92. A story of the last days of the Minister Louvois (died 1691), also covering the naval battle at Cape La Hogue (1692). Louis XIV, Admiral Rooke, and others appear.

1189. THE HONOUR OF THE HOUSE: MRS. HUGH FRASER and J. I. STAHLMANN; *Hutchinson.*
Italy (Rome, etc.), 1697: time of Pope Innocent XII. A story of social life and manners, introducing Charles of Gonzaga, 4th Duke of Mantua.

1190. TESTORE: PAT CANDLER; *Dent.*
Milan, Rome, Naples, etc., late 17th Century to early 18th. A " biographical story " of Testore, the Milan fiddle-maker, leading up to the making of a fiddle which was named " 1707 " after its birth-year.

1191. ONCE BITTEN, TWICE SHY: F. WHISHAW; *Juv. Nelson.*
A short, but good, tale of North Russia and Moscow in the period 1692-96. Peter the Great is introduced as a young man of twenty.

1192. PETER THE GREAT: A NOVEL: F. WHISHAW; *Digby, Long.*
A story of the Czar Peter within the period 1690-1710 (approximately). The strictly historical element is inconsiderable, though both Peter and his favourite, Menshikof, are much to the fore.

EIGHTEENTH CENTURY

1193. THAT WHICH HATH BEEN: DOROTHEA FAIRBRIDGE; *Sampson Low.*
A tale of Capetown in the Dutch East India Company period, 1699-1708. Governor Willem Adriaan van der Stel is the dominating figure—his bold efforts to build up the colony (agricultural development, etc.).

1194. *TOLLA THE COURTESAN: E. P. RODOCANACHI (trans.); *Heinemann.*

Rome, 1700 (the sub-title reads: " A sketch of private life in Rome in the year of the Jubilee, 1700 "). A novel written in epistolary form—a certain French Chevalier telling, in letters to his fiancée, of his own experiences in Rome, and of the general social life in that city. The author has based his work on much conscientious investigation, and the result is a really informative and pleasing record. Tolla Boccadileone (the " Tolla " of the title) is not introduced to any great extent; moreover, she was (to use the hero's own words) " worthier than her reputation," and a woman of cultivation as well as outward charm. Other historic figures who appear, more or less prominently, are:—Count Cesarini, Pope Innocent XII (including his death), the Queen of Poland, Prince Constantine Sobieski, and Cardinal Albano (his election as Pope under the name of Clement XI, etc.).

1195. A JACOBITE EXILE: G. A. HENTY; *Juv.* Blackie [*Eng.*], *Scribner* [*U.S.A.*].

England (William III—Anne), but the tale deals mainly with the hero's military service under Charles XII of Sweden in Russia and Poland about the turn of the century. Describes Charles XII's victory over the Russians at Narva in 1700—also covering the Battle of Clissow. Among the historic figures are the King of Sweden himself, the Duke of Marlborough, and Queen Anne.

1196. KIT OF THE CARABINEERS: D. H. PARRY; *Juv.* Oxford *University Press.*

England and Flanders, 1701-1704. A tale introducing William III (attempt on his life) and the Duke of Marlborough. Gives some account of the Duke's Wars up to the Battle of Blenheim.

1197. *THE SWORD OF GIDEON: J. BLOUNDELLE BURTON; *Cassell.*

Spanish Netherlands, 1702. A romance of Marlborough's early campaign in the War of the Spanish Succession (Louis XIV claimed the crown of Spain for his grandson, afterwards Philip V, while Britain, Germany, and Holland supported the rival claim of the Archduke Charles). One of the chief events brought into the story is the capture of Liége.

1198. ACROSS THE SALT SEAS: J. BLOUNDELLE BURTON; *Methuen* [*Eng.*], *Stone* [*U.S.A.*].

Another good example of the author, dealing with the War of the Spanish succession in the early stages, viz., 1702-1704. Covers the naval expedition against the French and Spanish resulting in Rooke's victory at the storming of Vigo. Later chapters tell of Marlborough and the Battle of Blenheim. Sir Cloudesley Shovel is one of the several historical personages introduced.

1199. LALLY OF THE BRIGADE: MISS L. MCMANUS; *Fisher Unwin* [*Eng.*], *Page* [*U.S.A.*].

A story of the Irish Brigade in the service of France during the Spanish Succession War (Prince Eugene in Italy). The surprise of Cremona (1702) is an outstanding event, and several historic figures appear, including Prince Eugene and Louis XIV. Essentially an adventure tale.

1200. *HUMPHREY BOLD: " HERBERT STRANG "; *Juv.* Oxford *University Press* [*Eng.*], *Bobbs-Merrill* [*U.S.A.*].

England and Abroad, end 17th Century to beginning 18th Century. A story of many adventures, in which Admiral Benbow is an outstanding figure. Illustrates the Admiral's various feats which culminated in the running fight (West Indies, 1702) against the French fleet under Du Casse.

1201. REPTON: F. KANE; *Murray.*

England, France, and Flanders mainly in the period 1702-1710. In this narrative of a young Shropshire man, Jesuit influences constitute a great feature, but there is also considerable blending of history (Marlborough's Wars, including Malplaquet)

The Duke of Marlborough and Prince Eugene appear, while—turning from military figures—St. John (afterwards Lord Bolingbroke) and the Old Pretender are brought before the reader.

1202. THE CORNET OF HORSE: G. A. Henty; *Juv. Sampson Low* [*Eng.*], *Scribner* [*U.S.A.*].
England, Low Countries, and France, 1702 to 1710. A tale of Marlborough's Wars, giving some account of Blenheim, Ramillies, Oudenarde, and Malplaquet. The Duke himself appears, also King Louis XIV.

1203. THE BRAVEST OF THE BRAVE: G. A. Henty; *Juv. Blackie* [*Eng.*], *Scribner* [*U.S.A.*].
England and (chiefly) Spain, 1703-1706. A story of sea and land adventures, with the Earl of Peterborough as outstanding figure. The capture of Montjuich (fort) and the reduction of Barcelona.

1204. A SWORDSMAN OF THE BRIGADE: Michael O'Hann-rachain; *Sands*.
Ireland and Flanders, etc., in the period 1703-1708. A story of love, fighting, and adventure, told with considerable spirit. The Duc de Vendôme appears more than once.

1205. ONE OF MARLBOROUGH'S CAPTAINS: "Morice Gerard"; *Juv. Hodder & Stoughton*.
A tale of Flanders, Germany, Austria, etc., in the period of Marlborough's Wars. The Duke and Prince Eugene both appear, and there is a somewhat lengthy account of the Battle of Blenheim.

1206. THE ADVENTURES OF HARRY ROCHESTER: "Herbert Strang"; *Juv. Blackie* [*Eng.*], *Putnam* [*U.S.A.*].
London and the Low Countries, 1704. A capital "story of the days of Marlborough and Eugene" (sub-title). Leads up to the Battle of Blenheim.

1207. FOR NAME AND NATION: Escott Lynn; *Juv. Chambers*.
Begins and ends England, but is mainly an historical tale of Marlborough's Wars 1704 to 1706. Blenheim and Ramillies are described, while Marlborough himself, Louis XIV, and the Duke of Berwick (James II's son) appear.

1208. THE HOUSE IN THE WALL: Stanley J. Weyman; in "In Kings' Byways"—*Murray* [*Eng.*], *Longmans* [*U.S.A.*].
A short story of Spanish Flanders in the year 1706.

1209. THE LAIRD'S LEGACY: Mary H. Debenham; *Juv. National Society* [*Eng.*], *Whittaker* [*U.S.A.*].
A pleasing tale of Scottish exiles in Paris and Cambrai, etc., 1707-1709 (Archbishop Fénelon); also Flanders in the time of Marlborough's Wars.

1210. DESMOND O'CONNOR: George H. Jessop; *John Long*.
France and Flanders, 1708. Love story of a Captain in the Irish Brigade (time of Marlborough's Wars). The Duc de Vendôme appears, while Louis XIV is somewhat prominent—the heroine being his ward.

1211. THE WHITE GAUNTLET: Percy J. Brebner; *Juv. Cassell*.
Hampshire, London, Windsor, etc., and the Low Countries in the Queen Anne period. An historical tale in which the Duchess of Marlborough is especially prominent—the Duke, Queen Anne, Mrs. Masham, and others, also appearing. In the foreign section of the book, the Battle of Oudenarde (1708) and the Battle of Malplaquet (1709) are both described.

1212. IN THE IRISH BRIGADE: G. A. HENTY; *Juv. Sampson Low* [*Eng.*], *Scribner* [*U.S.A.*].

Flanders, France, Scotland, England, and Spain. A tale of many scenes and many adventures, covering in particular the Battle of Oudenarde (1708) and the Spanish expedition (1710). King Louis XIV, Lord Godolphin, the Duke of Orleans, and the Duke of Berwick are among the historic figures.

1213. WITH MARLBOROUGH TO MALPLAQUET: " HERBERT STRANG " and RICHARD STEAD; *Juv. Oxford University Press.*

England and Abroad, 1701-1714. A tale of the Queen Anne period, largely illustrating the War of the Spanish Succession. Covers the Battle of Blenheim and the Capture of Gibraltar (both 1704), as well as the much later victory of Malplaquet (1709).

1214. *SIGNORS OF THE NIGHT: MAX PEMBERTON; *Pearson* [*Eng.*], *Dodd, Mead* [*U.S.A.*].

Eight short stories of Venice, mainly covering the period 1701-1706. Of these tales, one may mention as of special interest:—*A Miracle of Bells* (Conspiracy); *The Wolf of Cismon* (A Bandit's escape); and *Golden Ashes* (Depicts an alchemist, " Zuane de Franza," really based on Marcantonio Bragadino, a noted charlatan).

1215. *ISABEAU'S HERO: ESMÉ STUART; *Juv. Sheldon Press* [*Eng.*], *Macmillan* [*U.S.A.*].

Languedoc, 1702-1705. An excellent tale of Jean Cavalier and his leadership in the revolt of the Huguenot Camisards in the Cevennes. After a brave struggle Cavalier surrendered to Marshal Villars in 1704.

1216. LOUIS XIV: BERNARD CAPES; in " Historical Vignettes "— *Fisher Unwin* [*Eng.*], *Stokes* [*U.S.A.*].

A slight, but interesting, sketch of Louis XIV, August 21st, 1704.

1217. ROBIN THE PRODIGAL: " MAY WYNNE "; *Juv. Jarrolds.*

Sussex, London, and Edinburgh, 1706-1707. An interesting tale of Jacobite plots, etc., with Daniel Defoe very prominent as a secret agent to promote the Union (Scotland).

1218. RODOMONT: HENRY BEDFORD JONES; *Hurst & Blackett* [*Eng.*], *Putnam* [*U.S.A.*].

Avranches and Mont St. Michel, 1707. An adventure story, with Canadian-American element, in the late Louis XIV period.

1219. SAINT JAMES'S: W. H. AINSWORTH; *Routledge* [*Eng.*], *Dutton* [*U.S.A.*].

A tale of the Court of Queen Anne, 1707-1714. The political intrigues of the period, as well as the rivalry between the Duchess of Marlborough and Mrs. Masham (the latter is introduced mainly in her maiden state as Abigail Hill). Also covers such events as Dr. Sacheverell's Sermon at St. Paul's and his trial, and Guiscard's attempt to assassinate Harley. The Queen, Duke and Duchess of Marlborough, Robert Harley, St. John, Godolphin, Mrs. Bracegirdle, Mrs. Oldfield, Wycherley, and Steele are some of the figures.

1220. *THE HISTORY OF HENRY ESMOND, ESQ., A COLONEL IN THE SERVICE OF HER MAJESTY QUEEN ANNE; WRITTEN BY HIMSELF: W. M. THACKERAY; *Macmillan* [*Eng.*], *Dent* [*Eng.*], *Houghton Mifflin* [*U.S.A.*], *Dutton* [*U.S.A.*], *and other publishers.*

This celebrated novel is not only remarkable as a literary effort pure and simple (the style exactly reflecting that of the *Spectator* age), but, regarded as a piece of imaginative reconstruction, it presents a wonderfully vivid picture of English life and manners in Queen Anne's time. The scene is mostly laid in England, though much more than a glimpse of Flanders is furnished. The entire period extends from 1691 to 1714 (William III—Anne). The fictional interest is great, but *that* is the reader's own affair; it must suffice here to indicate that many historical events and personages are either mentioned or actually introduced. There is a general atmosphere of Jacobite influence and intrigue; the Old Pretender himself appears—providing, indeed, one of the most thrilling episodes in the romance. Again, the Duke of Marlborough and his Wars are brilliantly sketched: in this portion of the book General Webb is a prominent and striking figure. Turning from military leaders to literary chiefs, Steele and Addison (especially the former) come before the reader in fitting manner. Taking it as a whole, Thackeray's *Esmond* is incontestably one of the greatest achievements in the realm of Historical Fiction.

1221. *IN KINGS' HOUSES: Julia C. R. Dorr; *Duckworth* [*Eng.*], *Page* [*U.S.A.*].

Mostly Windsor, with digressions to Longleat, etc., about the period 1695-1709. A carefully written story, having Queen Anne as central figure, beginning with her earlier days as Princess. There is much about the little Duke of Gloucester, the only one of Anne's many children that survived infancy; his boyhood was cut short in 1700, when he was some 10-11 years old. The real interest of the novel is to be found in its account of the Queen's relations with Abigail Hill (Mrs. Masham) and the Duchess of Marlborough—both these two ladies being introduced very prominently. Many other historic figures of note either appear or are mentioned: the Duke of Marlborough, Bishop Burnet, Bishop Ken, William III, Prince George of Denmark (Anne's husband), and Lord Weymouth.

1222. THE HOUSE OF LISRONAN: Miriam Alexander; *Melrose*.

Ireland, England, and France, in the William III—Anne period (the latter's reign chiefly). The main interest of this novel is fictional—historical events and personages being sparingly depicted, though William III is introduced in a decidedly unflattering manner. There is an element of tragedy, which a certain Dutchman and his doings supply. A book of no little power on the side of character analysis.

1223. UNDER THE DOME OF ST. PAUL'S: Emma Marshall; *Juv.* Seeley [*Eng.*], *Macmillan* [*U.S.A.*].

A simple, but carefully written, story of Sir Christopher Wren's later years, covering the period from 1709 to his death in 1723.

1224. *DEVEREUX: Lord Lytton; *Routledge* [*Eng.*], *Dutton* [*U.S.A.*].

England, France, and Russia (also glimpses of Hungary, Turkey, etc.) mainly c. 1710-20. An autobiographical romance, with historic background and introducing many personages of the time; it is, however, to a large extent a character-study on something like philosophic lines. The book is nowadays neglected, but really deserves more notice than some of its author's widely-read examples. The political, social, and intellectual forces of the Queen Anne period are well suggested. St. John (Bolingbroke) is much to the fore, while Steele, Addison, Swift, Pope, Cibber, Sir Godfrey Kneller and Beau Fielden appear. In the Foreign Sections, Louis XIV and Madame de Maintenon (especially the latter), Philip of Orleans, Cardinal de Fleuri, Voltaire, Fontenelle, Anthony Count Hamilton, Peter the Great, and the Czarina Catherine, are all introduced.

1225. THE GALLANT LOVER: Henry St. John Cooper; *Sampson Low*.

Sussex (Ashdown Forest region) and London, c. 1712-14. A love and adventure romance of Queen Anne's days, with some account of highwaymen, witch-harrying, Newgate prison, etc. Lady Masham is prominently introduced—the book covering both her triumph over the Duchess of Marlborough, and—at the end—her triumph over Harley (Earl of Oxford).

1226. *ESTHER VANHOMRIGH: Margaret L. Woods; *Murray*.

England and Ireland, 1712-23. A decidedly interesting novel of Dean Swift and "Vanessa," introducing—besides the two main figures just named—Esther Johnson ("Stella") and Lord Peterborough, with glimpses of other notabilities. The story ends with Esther Vanhomrigh's death.

1227. BICKERING WITH THE DONS: PETER SCARLET; *Juv. Sheldon Press [Eng.], Macmillan [U.S.A.].*

☞ Begins Bristol in the reign of Queen Anne, but is almost entirely a brisk tale of the South Seas. There are plenty of Sea and Land adventures in the South American region—Mutiny, Spaniards, Indian Rising, etc.

1228. *THE SHADOW CAPTAIN: EMILIE BENSON KNIPE and ALDEN ARTHUR KNIPE; *Lane [Eng.], Grosset [U.S.A.].*

London, 1701 (*Prologue*), and New York, 1703. An exciting and skilfully-told romance of Captain Kidd, or, rather, of *Captain Kidd's Shadow*—the meaning of which phrase must be left for readers of the story to discover for themselves.

1229. THE BOY CAPTIVE IN CANADA: MARY P. WELLS SMITH; *Juv. Sampson Low [Eng.], Little, Brown [U.S.A.].*

Northern Vermont, chiefly 1704-1709. A tale of New England captives and their experiences among the Indians, after the attack on the village of Deerfield by the French and Indians. The time is that of Governor de Vaudreuil, who appears in the story. The last two chapters skim over many years to mid (and even late) 18th Century. One of the volumes comprising the author's *Old Deerfield Series*.

1230. THE BLACK WOLF'S BREED: HARRIS DICKSON; *Methuen [Eng.], Bowen Merrill [U.S.A.].*

A tale of France (largely), and of the Province of Louisiana in the early 18th Century period. King Louis XIV appears (as an old man nearing his end); also Philip Duke of Orleans, and Bienville the Governor of Louisiana.

1231. *THE YEMASSEE: W. GILMORE SIMMS; *Lovell [U.S.A.].*

South Carolina, 1715. A good story of the invasion of South Carolina by the Yemassee Indians and other tribes. Governor Craven (under the veiled name of " Gabriel Harrison ") is the outstanding figure of the novel.

1232. *THE CHARLES MEN: VERNER VON HEIDENSTAM (trans.); *Oxford University Press [Eng.], American-Scandinavian Foundation [U.S.A.].*

A novel of quite unusual interest and power. Charles XII of Sweden is the central figure—the period being 1697 to 1718. There are many impressive descriptions both of Charles himself and of his greatly suffering people, during the various wars. The Sieges of Pultava (1709) and Fredrikshall (1718) are introduced; at the last-named siege, Charles was killed. Among the other historic figures one may specify Peter the Great and his son; also Mazeppa.

1233. A PRINCE OF INTRIGUE: " MAY WYNNE "; *Jarrolds.*

A story of Mazeppa in the time of Peter the Great of Russia and Charles XII of Sweden, ending with the disaster of Pultava (Pultowa) and Mazeppa's death shortly afterwards.

1234. *KINGS-AT-ARMS: " MARJORIE BOWEN "; *Methuen [Eng.], Dutton [U.S.A.].*

The struggle between Sweden and Russia in the period 1700-1718. Charles XII and Peter the Great are the two outstanding figures, while Augustus (Elector of Saxony and King of Poland), Count Piper, Prince Mentchikoff and Patkul are prominently introduced. The various wars and political developments are carefully depicted—the story eventually leading up to the Battle of Poltava, Charles's exile among the Turks, and his death at Frederikshall in Norway.

1235. *AN IMPERIAL LOVER: M. IMLAY TAYLOR; *Gay & Bird [Eng.], McClurg [U.S.A.].*

Moscow, 1703-1704. A French diplomat relates the experiences of himself, his Russian wife, and his young secretary at the Russian Court, after he had been sent to Moscow on a secret mission by Louis XIV. The fictional interest—which is very considerable—arises out of the fact that the above-mentioned secretary of the diplomat falls in love with a beautiful Russian girl, whose charms also attract the Czar, Peter the Great, at a time when Catherine Shavronsky was under a cloud. The period is that following the Czar's divorce from Eudoxia, and the defeat of the Russians at Narva (1700) by the Swedes under Charles XII; while the questions of the partition of Poland and the attitude of Russia towards France and the Grand Alliance, further constitute the historical background. The most prominent historic figures are the Czar himself, Catherine Shavronsky (afterwards Catherine I of Russia), and Mentchikof (the "new favorite"). Prince Dolgoruky, leader of the anti-Mentchikof faction, appears to a much slighter extent. At the very end of the story allusion is made to the election of Stanislas to be King of Poland (1704).

1236. SHE THAT HESITATES: HARRIS DICKSON; *Ward & Lock* [*Eng.*], *Bobbs-Merrill* [*U.S.A.*].
A sensational romance of Germany (Dresden), Sweden, and Russia, c. 1710-1718. Begins at the time when Charles XII was a fugitive in Turkey, and ends with the death of Peter the Great's son, Alexis. The marriage of the last-named Prince with Princess Charlotte of Brunswick is the event round which the novel is written. Alexis is, of course, a very prominent figure.

1237. *PETER AND ALEXIS: DMITRI MEREZHKOVSKY (trans.); *Constable* [*Eng.*], *Putnam* [*U.S.A.*].
Russia (Petersburg, Moscow, etc.) and Italy (Naples), 1715-18. A novel illustrating the later period of Peter the Great, and especially dealing with the unhappy relations between the Czar and his son Alexis; the latter's flight to Breslau, etc., and sojourn in Italy (Naples), are covered, while the concluding chapters tell of his (the Tsarevitch's) return to Russia, his incarceration in the fortress of Peter and Paul, and his death (1718). Another prominent historic figure is the Tsaritsa Catherine.

1238. THE TRIUMPH OF COUNT OSTERMANN: GRAHAM HOPE; *Smith, Elder* [*Eng.*], *Holt* [*U.S.A.*].
Russia from about 1724, covering the period in which there were many changes of rule—Peter the Great, Catherine I, the boy Czar Peter II, etc. The novel depicts the political scheming of the time when Menschikoff's power was at its height. "Count Ostermann" is a German who became one of Peter the Great's Ministers.

1239. *THE GIPSY KING: "MAY WYNNE"; *Chapman & Hall.*
North Devon, 1714. The hero of this interesting story is Bamfylde Moore Carew, who actually lived 1693 to about 1770, and was known as "king of the gypsies."

1240. QUEEN ANNE IS DEAD: PATRICIA WENTWORTH; *Melrose.*
A tale of high life in London just before and after Queen Anne's death, 1714. There is some Jacobite talk, but history is greatly in the background.

1241. *THE HIGHWAYMAN: H. C. BAILEY; *Methuen* [*Eng.*], *Dutton* [*U.S.A.*].
Hertfordshire, London, etc., 1714 (last days of Queen Anne). A lively tale of adventure, with a considerable historic background of Jacobite intrigue, etc. The Queen herself is introduced (her death), and other figures are Lord and Lady Masham, the Old Pretender, Marlborough, and Sunderland.

1242. VERONICA PLAYFAIR: MAUD WILDER GOODWIN; *Warne* [*Eng.*], *Little, Brown* [*U.S.A.*].
London district and Bath at the beginning of George I's reign. A story illustrating the social, political, and literary forces of the period. The poet Pope appears at Twickenham, and Beau Nash, Bolingbroke, Swift, Lady Mary Wortley Montague and Franklin are all introduced.

1243. *DOROTHY FORSTER: WALTER BESANT; *Chatto & Windus* [*Eng.*], *Dodd, Mead* [*U.S.A.*].
England 1703-1716 (Anne-George I). An excellent story of Northumberland in the time of the first Jacobite Rebellion (1715). The Earl of Derwentwater is very prominent (his early love affair with Dorothy Forster herself, etc.), and General Forster also appears among other historic figures. There is a full account of the Earl of Mar's doings in Scotland, and of the insurgent army's surrender. Ends with Derwentwater's trial, sentence, and execution.

1244. AN ESCAPE FROM THE TOWER: EMMA MARSHALL; *Juv.*
     Seeley [*Eng.*], *Macmillan* [*U.S.A.*].
 Scotland and London, 1714-17. A tale of the '15 Rebellion, illustrating the escape
of the Earl of Nithsdale through the heroism of his wife.

1245. BALMORAL: ALEXANDER ALLARDYCE; *Blackwood.*
 A tale of England and Scotland, 1714-15. Covers the death of Anne and the coming
of George I, describing the attitude of Bishop Atterbury and the Jacobite leaders at
that time. After the early chapters, the scene shifts to Aberdeen and Deeside where the
Earl of Mar and other Jacobites are in evidence. The novel also covers Mar's march
South from Braemar at the beginning of the '15 (the later stages of the Rebellion are
merely epitomized).

1246. *ROB ROY: SIR WALTER SCOTT; *Black, and other publishers—*
     English and American.
 Northumberland (Cheviot), Glasgow, and Aberfoyle region, in 1715. A novel dealing
with Rob Roy Macgregor Campbell, the Outlaw, at the time of the '15 Rising; there
are, however, few historical details—the reader's main interest being aroused over the
love episodes, etc. The romance depicts both Highland and Lowland life.

1247. *THE LIT CHAMBER: JOHN BUCHAN; in " The Path of the
     King "—*Nelson* [*Eng.*], *Doran* [*U.S.A.*].
 A short story telling of a Cumberland incident in 1715 (Jacobites).

1248. THE BURNING CRESSET: HOWARD PEASE; *Constable.*
 Northumberland, Scotland, N.W. England, and London, 1715-16. A romance with
the Earl of Derwentwater as central figure. Gives a full account of the Rising in
Northumberland, and of the events culminating in Preston Fight and the Earl's imprisonment and death. The local colour of the story is good. Besides the Earl, Dorothy
Forster and her brother, General Forster, are prominent, while various other personages
appear.

1249. TO ARMS!: ANDREW BALFOUR; *Methuen* [*Eng.*], *Page* [*U.S.A.*].
 Scotland and France, 1715-16. The hero is a pro-George man who has many
adventures during the Mar Rising. This somewhat rousing story contains a description
of the Battle of Sheriffmuir. Both the Earl of Mar and the Pretender appear, while
in the Paris chapters the famous John Law is one of the figures.

1250. UNDER THE WOLF'S FELL: DOROTHEA MOORE; *Juv.*
     Partridge.
 N. England and London, mainly in the two years 1715-16. A tale of the '15 Rebellion
introducing the Pretender, Lord Derwentwater and Forster. In the closing chapters
the reader encounters Sir Robert Walpole and Earl Stanhope, as well as Lady Derwentwater pleading (in vain) before George I. The heroine is a Stuart with certain royal
claims undesired by herself.

1251. *BY THE POOL OF GARMOYLE: ARCHIBALD W. M. KERR;
     Northern Whig [*Ireland*].
 An interesting tale of Belfast, Cushendall, and Carrickfergus, 1715. Describes
Jacobite schemes, witch-baiting, robberies, etc., and tells how the hero finds himself
in jail on a charge of murder. The story ends in Dublin, introducing Dean Swift and
the Viceroy, Lord Sunderland.

1252. *BLIND RAFTERY AND HIS WIFE HILARIA: DONN BYRNE;
     Sampson Low [*Eng.*], *Century* [*U.S.A.*].
 Ireland (Galway and Co. Mayo) early 18th Century. A pleasing tale of a blind
poet and the Spanish lady. he marries, illustrating—among other things—the extent
to which races had become mixed in Ireland. There are allusions to personages of the

period, notably to Dean Swift and Queen Anne (an amusing anecdote is given regarding a conversation between the two); the story also reflects ways and events, such as the South Sea Company fiasco. The character of the hero " Patrick Raftery," is based on a real person, Anthony Rafter, a wandering poet; Anthony, however, lived nearly a century later than the " Patrick " of the novel.

1253. *A TORY IN ARMS: John Heron Lepper; *Grant Richards.*
Carrickfergus and Belfast region, 1715-19. This novel gives a vivid depiction of the life and movements of the period (wool-smuggling, Jacobite influences after the 'Fifteen, etc. etc.). A definitely historical element is introduced in the closing pages which describe an interview with Sir Robert Walpole in London. It may be added that the word " Tory " in the title stands for robber or outlaw.

1254. APPLES OF GOLD: Warwick Deeping; *Cassell.*
London (Covent Garden neighbourhood) in the period between 1715 and 1725 (George I). Mainly a novel of manners and character-depiction (a fencing-school and its connections high and low), with love interest. There is, however, a slight historical background—the Whig and Tory controversies and riots, etc.

1255. HIS SERENE HIGHNESS: H. C. Bailey; *Methuen.*
Two Englishmen on a Continental Tour, and their strange experiences (1717) in one of the small frontier States of the Moselle region.

1256. THE ROSE BROCADE: Mrs. Philip C. De Crespigny; *Nash.*
London and district (Leicester House, Hampton Court, etc.) in 1718. The Prince and Princess of Wales are frequently named, but the reader obtains only the merest glimpses of them. This amusing little tale of " the Road " and Court intrigue is chiefly historical in its atmosphere and implications—the financial speculation of the South Sea Bubble period, Jacobitism, etc.

1257. *A BROWN WOMAN: James Branch Cabell; in " The Certain Hour "—*McBride* [U.S.A.], also appears in the volume " Great Short Stories of the World," published by Heinemann.
Alexander Pope and John Gay in 1718. An imaginary scene in Pope's life, showing his sensitiveness over his bodily weaknesses and deformities.

1258. THE BLACKBIRD: Melville Balfour; *Hodder & Stoughton.*
Italy, Spain, and England, 1719. An exciting tale of love, adventure, and political schemes. The Old Pretender is the historic figure round which the story is written, and he is introduced very prominently. The hero is a faithful adherent of the Prince through all his wanderings and misfortunes at this special period. Bishop Atterbury appears.

1259. THE KING OVER THE WATER: Justin H. McCarthy; *Hurst & Blackett [Eng.], Harper [U.S.A.].*
Strasbourgh, Innspruck etc., 1719. A romance dealing with Princess Clementina Sobieski's flight from Germany, and her marriage with " King " James (the Old Pretender).

1260. *CLEMENTINA: A. E. W. Mason; *Methuen [Eng.], Stokes [U.S.A.].*
Italy and the Tyrol, 1719. An absorbing adventure and love story, having as its historical background the escape of Princess Clementina Sobieski from Innspruck and her flight to Italy, prior to marriage with the Chevalier de Saint George (the " Old Pretender "). The latter appears somewhat prominently in the earlier and later portions of the novel, but the outstanding figure—the heroine in fact—is Princess Clementina, while the Irishman, Charles Wogan, is the hero. The brief *Epilogue* carries the reader to a much later period.

1261. *PARSON KELLY: A. E. W. Mason and Andrew Lang; *Longmans.*

Paris, London (largely), Herefordshire, Avignon, etc., 1719-22 (last few pages 1745). A novel that has for its main background the Jacobite plot with which Bishop Atterbury was connected. There are some amusing fictional scenes, while the book as a whole shows unmistakable knowledge of the history and manners of the time. " Parson Kelly " is " secretary and right-hand man " to Atterbury, and his friend Nicholas Wogan, the retired Irish Colonel who is made to play such a leading part, was a real person. Other historic figures introduced are: Bishop Atterbury, Lady Mary Wortley Montague, John Law, Lord Sydney Beauclerk, and Lord Oxford. The " Lady Oxford " of the story is (the *Preface* informs readers) an imaginary character. In the concluding pages Prince Charlie appears. Besides these actual appearances of people more or less famous, there are numerous allusions to other notabilities of the time —Pope, Walpole, the Duke of Ormond, etc.

1262. JACK SHEPPARD: W. Harrison Ainsworth; *Herbert Jenkins* [*Eng.*], *Dutton* [*U.S.A.*].

A romance of Jack Sheppard (1702-24), the famous criminal who was executed at Tyburn, 1724. Ainsworth based his tale on facts, but in several particulars Sheppard's true record has been altered for fictional purposes (the connection with Willesden District, for instance, is imaginary). This book has often been condemned as pernicious on the ground of its idealization of a scoundrel, though certain Ainsworth authorities (see S. M. Ellis' " William Harrison Ainsworth and His Friends," 1911) deem such harsh criticism undeserved. It must, however, be said that the novel is of no great worth as historical romance, though it is an undoubtedly famous book.

1263. *THE SOUTH SEA BUBBLE: W. Harrison Ainsworth; *Dicks.*

London, 1710 (*Prologue* of some length), and 1720. An historical novel covering the time of the South Sea Company's formation (1710), and showing how—ten years later —the directors were misled (by the recent success of John Law's Paris Bank scheme) into sanctioning an absurd plan for buying up the National Debts, etc. On the fictional side, illustration is given of the way in which families and individuals were affected during the different stages of wild speculation, temporary success, and utter ruin. The titles of the three " Books " forming the story proper, neatly convey these main developments: " The Blowing of the Bubble "; " The Bubble Blown "; and " The Bubble Burst." Many historic figures: George I, George II, the Duke of Wharton, Earl Stanhope, Lord Sunderland, Walpole, Sir John Blunt (founder of the South Sea Company), the Duchess of Kendal, the Countess of Platen, and others.

1264. BUBBLE FORTUNE: Gilbert Sheldon; *Dent.*

A good tale of English life in the West Country, 1720. The fiasco of the South Sea Bubble is introduced with considerable effect. The book ends with the London coach bringing news of the Company's shares " fallen 200 and still falling."

1265. *THE RAIDERS:
     *THE DARK O' THE MOON (*sequel*): S. R. Crockett; *Fisher Unwin* [*Eng.*], *Macmillan* [*U.S.A.*].

These two connected romances of Galloway in George I's time give vivid depictions of outlawry (gipsies and smugglers), revealing the author's full knowledge of both period and locality. *The Raiders* is deemed in some quarters to be Crockett's best novel.

1266. KING COLLEY: Bernard Capes; in " Historical Vignettes "— *Fisher Unwin* [*Eng.*], *Stokes* [*U.S.A.*].

Colley Cibber and Sir Christopher Wren in 1721.

1267. *THE LION'S SKIN: Rafael Sabatini; *Stanley Paul* [*Eng.*], *Houghton Mifflin* [*U.S.A.*].

Begins Paris, but the scene is mainly London in 1721—just after the South Sea Bubble disaster. The Duke of Wharton appears in the novel, but History forms the merest background to a domestic drama.

1268. *THE GATES OF DOOM: Rafael Sabatini; *Stanley Paul* [*Eng.*], *Houghton Mifflin* [*U.S.A.*].
London and Chelsea, 1721. This excellent romance tells of a Jacobite agent at the time of the Atterbury Plot. Lord Carteret is introduced.

1269. THORNDYKE MANOR: Mary C. Rowsell; *Juv. Blackie.*
A good tale of the Gravesend district and London, round about the year 1723. Time of the Jacobite conspiracy (Bishop Atterbury). Several historic figures, including Lord Lovat, George I, Sir Robert Walpole and his wife.

1270. GEORGE I: Bernard Capes; in "Historical Vignettes"— *Fisher Unwin* [*Eng.*], *Stokes* [*U.S.A.*].
The death of George I on the road to Herrenhausen, 1727.

1271. CERISE: G. J. Whyte Melville; (*Ward, Lock* [*Eng.*], *Longmans* [*U.S.A.*], also *Appleton* [*U.S.A.*].
France (Versailles, Fontainebleau, etc.), West Indies, and England, in the first half of the 18th Century. The most important part of the tale is concerned with the period c. 1715-20—last days of Louis XIV and the advent of the Duke of Orleans as Regent during Louis XV's minority. Also covers Law's Mississippi scheme, etc. Both Louis XIV and the Regent Orleans appear.

1272. THE REGENT'S GIFT: "May Wynne"; *Chapman & Hall.*
Brittany and Paris, 1717-18: time of the Regent, Philippe d'Orléans, who is himself more or less prominent in the story. Irish Jacobite intrigues, etc.

1273. (1)*THE CHEVALIER D'HARMENTHAL:
      (2)*THE REGENT'S DAUGHTER (*sequel*): Alexandre Dumas (trans.); *Dent* [*Eng.*], *Little, Brown* [*U.S.A.*].
(1) France in 1718. The death of Louis XIV and the political developments connected therewith—notably the Spanish plot against the Regent, etc. Louis XV appears as a child of 9 or 10, while Cardinal d'Alberoni, the Minister of Spain, Philippe Duc d'Orléans, Cardinal Dubois, and Duc de Maine are more or less prominent.
(2) France in 1719. The Regent (Duc d'Orléans) and his daughter the Abbess of Chelles (Mademoiselle de Chartres) are outstanding figures. Political plots, especially in connection with the Breton nobles. The Bastille, etc. Dubois is once again greatly to the fore.

1274. THE MISSISSIPPI BUBBLE: Emerson Hough; *Methuen* [*Eng.*], *Bobbs-Merrill* [*U.S.A.*].
A romance of John Law's career, leading up to the period of his Paris residence and the disastrous Mississippi scheme.

1275. JOHN LAW, THE PROJECTOR: W. Harrison Ainsworth; *Chapman & Hall*, also *Routledge.*
London, 1705 (*Prologue*), and Paris, 1715-20. A novel of Law, the gambler and speculator, especially dealing with him during the period of his Bank and Mississippi schemes. Describes how he obtained the backing of the Regent Orleans, and how his short prosperity and popularity ended in disaster. In the closing pages he is shown escaping from Paris (1720). The brief *Epilogue* gives an outline of his later career and death (1727). In the story proper, Philippe Duc d'Orléans is a prominent figure, while King Louis XV, the Duc de Noailles, the Duc de Saint-Simon, and the Duchesse de Berri also appear.

1276. LE CHEVALIER DE PUYJALOU: H. de Charlieu; *Hachette* [*France*].
A novel of France and the Regent, 1720, illustrating the time of the Mississippi Bubble.

1277. FROM BEHIND THE ARRAS: Mrs. P. Champion de Crespigny; *Fisher Unwin.*

A good tale of adventure and family mystery in the France of 1720: time of the Regent Orleans and Cardinal Dubois. History is far in the background.

1278. SERAPHICA: Justin H. McCarthy; *Hurst & Blackett.*

Artois and Paris round about 1720. A romance of the Regency (Orleans), illustrating the profligacy of the Court in that period. Contains allusions to Law's schemes which were then in so much favour. Several personages are introduced, including the little King Louis XV, the Regent Philippe of Orleans, and the Duc de Richelieu. An unexpected appearance is that of Antoine Watteau, the Painter.

1279. A GALLANT OF SPAIN: "May Wynne"; *Stanley Paul.*

A good tale of Jacobites in Madrid about the year 1720. The time is that of King Philip V of Spain, and the statesman Cardinal Alberoni, both of whom appear.

1280. *OLYMPE DE CLÈVES: Alexandre Dumas (trans.); *Dent* [Eng.], *Little, Brown* [U.S.A.].

France, 1727-29. The romance of an actress, with a considerable element of history. King Louis XV appears as a youth of eighteen, also his Queen. The Court life and its iniquities are depicted (scenes at Rambouillet the abode of the Comte de Toulouse, etc.). The Duc de Richelieu, Mademoiselle de Charolais, Cardinal De Fleury, and numerous other figures.

1281. FRANCEZKA: Molly E. Seawell; *Grant Richards* [Eng.], *Bowen-Merrill* [U.S.A.].

Continental Europe, 1726-41. A novel of manners and tragedy, introducing Voltaire, the actress Adrienne Lecouvreur, and Marshal Saxe.

1282. *THE KING OF A DAY: "May Wynne"; *Jarrolds.*

A tale of Poland and King Stanislaus, 1733-34. Interesting, and off the beaten track.

1283. *JEW SÜSS (POWER): Lion Feuchtwanger (trans.); *Secker* [Eng.] *Viking Press* [U.S.A.].

Würtemberg, mostly in the 1730-40 period. A novel of unmistakable power and originality, revealing a marvellous knowledge of all the intricacies of mid-European politics in the second quarter of the 18th Century. Although in the full sense an *historical* novel, the book introduces few of the events and figures that belong to world-history; but the motive forces behind Würtemberg politics, as well as the more general and social side of life in the Duchy—its Court scandals, its religious animosities (Catholic, Protestant, and Jewish), its superstitions—all these different aspects are skilfully presented in the course of the story. The exact period, on a careless reading, would be somewhat difficult to fix, but now and again the affairs of the great world are touched: on Page 108, for instance, " old Prince Eugene " momentarily appears as Commander-in-Chief on the Austrian side [in the Polish Succession War of 1733-35], and as having just " retreated before the superior forces of the French " who had invaded the Duchy. Again, the " King of Prussia " [Frederick-William I] appears almost at the beginning, while, some seventy pages from the end, allusion is made to the " young King of Prussia who had just ascended the throne " [clearly Frederick II, or " the Great " as he was afterwards called, who became King May 31st, 1740]. Other references (Louis XV, etc.) strengthen the hints given in such instances as those mentioned above. Turning once again to the novel as a whole, its two outstanding figures are Josef Süss Oppenheim, the Privy Financial Councillor of Duke Karl Alexander, and the Duke himself. Both characters are analysed in a searching manner, but, while the Duke's portrait throughout yields the impression of almost unrelieved selfishness and meanness, the personality of the Jew—that unscrupulous seeker after State control and power—is presented in the closing scenes as reaching something like grandeur.

1284. HALIL THE PEDLAR: Maurus Jókai (trans.); *Jarrold*.
Stambul, early 18th Century: time of the Sultan Achmed III. The strange story
of Halil Patrona and his rebellion, etc., up to his death at the hands of the Janissaries.
To the average English reader who is unfamiliar with Turkish life and history, many
portions of the novel must appear almost farcical.

1285. THE GAMESTERS: H. C. Bailey; *Methuen [Eng.]*, *Dutton
[U.S.A.]*.
Dresden, Frankfort, etc., 1728 onwards—Frederic the Great as a youth and his
relations with an English acquaintance, etc. A novel of atmosphere and manners
(gambling, flirtation, and love-making) rather than historical romance proper, though
towards the end of the book there is a glimpse of Frederic as King of Prussia and battle-
chief (the beginning of the Austrian Succession War, 1740).

1286. *THE RED CRAVAT: Alfred Tresidder Sheppard;
Macmillan.
Prussia and Saxony, 1730, and the few years following. Story of an Englishman's
experiences in the time of Frederick William I of Prussia. The king himself is prominently introduced—the novel well illustrating his passion for giant grenadiers.

1287. A GENTLE KNIGHT OF OLD BRANDENBURG: Charles
Major; *Macmillan*.
Another story of Frederick William I of Prussia and his Court. Wilhelmina, sister
of Frederick the Great, and the latter as a youth, are the most important of the various
historical figures introduced.

1288. *THE ROAD TO VICTORY: Rose Schuster; *Chapman &
Hall*.
Germany, from about 1733 to 1741, i.e. in the period of Frederic William I of
Prussia and Frederic II surnamed "the Great." Some two-thirds of the novel
illustrate the end of Frederic William I's reign and his peculiar relations with the
Crown Prince—telling, also, of the latter's literary pursuits, marriage, etc. The later
chapters describe Frederic the Great's invasion of Silesia up to the victory over the
Austrians at Mollwitz. Besides the outstanding figures of the two Frederics, Wilhelmina
and Voltaire are noteworthy personages in the story.

1289. MADAM FLIRT: Charles E. Pearce; *Stanley Paul*.
London and Twickenham, mainly in the years 1727-28. A romance of the actress
Lavinia Fenton, leading up to her triumph as "Polly Peachum" in *The Beggar's Opera*.
John Gay is, of course, very prominent, while Bolingbroke, Pope, Dr. Arbuthnot,
Edmund Curll, the bookseller, and other notabilities appear.

1290. *THE CHASTE DIANA: "E. Barrington"; *Lane [Eng.]*,
Dodd, Mead [U.S.A.]*.
Another novel of Lavinia Fenton, covering the period from about 1727 to 1732.
Besides the actress, and John Gay author of the *Beggar's Opera*, various personages of
the time appear, including Queen Caroline and George II.

1291. *SOME ACCOUNT OF AMYOT BROUGH: E. Vincent
Briton; *Seeley*.
England—very largely Penrith, Cumberland, and Westerham, Kent; also, to a
much less extent, Flanders, Scotland, and North America. The period covered is
virtually from the beginning of George II's reign to its close. A tale of unusual charm,
slightly touching events like the '45 Rebellion, the campaign of 1747 in Flanders, etc.,
and introducing prominently (in his private and public capacities) James Wolfe of
Quebec fame. Taken as a whole, however, the story is primarily one of historical
allusion and atmosphere—fictional developments and quiet domestic scenes mostly
engaging the reader's attention; the hero and heroine are delightfully drawn. Towards
the very end of the book there is an excellent account of Wolfe at the Taking of Quebec
(in which famous military exploit the "Amyot Brough" of the story takes part, and is
wounded).

1292. *THE HEART OF MIDLOTHIAN: Sir Walter Scott; *Black, and other publishers—English and American.*

Chiefly Edinburgh and neighbourhood (the old Tolbooth Prison is central in the story's development), 1736; also London district and Dumbartonshire. In this really moving romance, although the fictional interest predominates, one is made aware of a definitely historical background. Some account is given of the Porteous Riots in Edinburgh, and there are striking depictions of the Duke of Argyle in London, and of Queen Caroline at Richmond. The character of "Jeannie Deans" is based on a real person—Helen Walker, who lies buried in a Dumfriesshire churchyard with an inscription by Scott himself. This novel, it is generally allowed, shows Scott at his best.

1293. *RODERICK RANDOM: Tobias Smollett; *Constable [Eng.], Macmillan [U.S.A.].*

A novel of sea and land (Scotland, England, West Indies, France, and elsewhere), giving a good picture of English naval matters (the Press-gang, etc.) in the second quarter of the 18th Century. The attack on Carthagena in 1841, is described.

1294. BOUNDLESS WATER: "Marjorie Bowen"; *Ward, Lock.*

A decidedly interesting murder story of the Hindhead—Haslemere district, 1733. Sir Robert Walpole appears.

1295. DICK MUNDAY: Herbert Harrison; *Sampson Low.*

Ealing village, London, and Kent in 1735. An excellent adventure story, with Jacobite schemes, a duel, and a love element.

1296. MY LADY MARY: "E. Barrington"; in "The Ladies!"— *Fisher Unwin.*

Lady Mary Wortley Montagu and her son, 1737-39.

1297. CLEMENTINA'S HIGHWAYMAN: R. Neilson Stephens and George H. Wesley; *Hurst & Blackett [Eng.], Page [U.S.A.].*

London and the Great North Road in 1742. A good tale of love and adventure—historical in the sense of conveying the atmosphere and general manners of the time.

1298. *STARBRACE: Sheila Kaye Smith; *Bell [Eng.], Dutton [U.S.A.].*

Sussex, Kent, and (in the last chapter) Scotland, mainly in the period 1743-45, though beginning in 1726. A novel of country life, in which the hero is of an unusual type. There are some rather startling scenes (a gang of robbers, etc.). The book ends with the one historical event introduced—the Battle of Prestonpans in which Sir John Cope's forces were defeated.

1299. THE MISER'S DAUGHTER: W. Harrison Ainsworth; *Routledge [Eng.], Dutton [U.S.A.].*

A somewhat sensational tale of London in 1744. There is a Jacobite element and the social life of the time is reflected, but history is quite subordinate to adventure.

1300. THE TWO-HANDED SWORD: Frank Ormerod; *Macdonald.*

Rochdale (Lancashire) and district, 1744-46. A good story of the Jacobites and the followers of Wesley.

1301. TREASURE TROVE: Samuel Lover; *Constable [Eng.], Little, Brown [U.S.A.].*

Ireland, England, Scotland, and Abroad in 1745. A novel telling of the Irish Brigade in the French and Austrian Wars, etc. There is a description of the Battle of Fontenoy, as well as some account of the '45 Rebellion in Scotland. Marshal Saxe, Prince Charles Edward, Lord Chesterfield, and Voltaire are among the figures introduced. As an historical novel the book has been severely criticized, while in humour it is decidedly inferior to the author's *Rory O' More* which appears elsewhere in my list.

M

1302. THE MOON OF BATH (THE FAIR MOON OF BATH):
Beth Ellis; *Blackwood [Eng.], Dodd, Mead [U.S.A.].*
A story of Jacobites in Bath, 1745. Beau Nash appears.

1303. THE MAN AT ODDS: Ernest Rhys; *Hurst & Blackett.*
Welsh Coast and Bristol Channel regions in 1745. A tale of piratical smugglers in and about the Channel, with good local colour and period-suggestion.

1304. AUDREY: Mary Johnston; *Constable [Eng.], Houghton Mifflin [U.S.A.].*
Virginia (Jameston, Williamsburgh, etc.), 1727. This romance, in which a Scottish Jacobite figures, has a Quaker element. It is historical chiefly in the sense of atmosphere, though Governor Spotswood appears, and there is, in one part of the story, a side glance at Colley Cibber in London.

1305. THE HOUSE ON CHERRY STREET: Amelia E. Barr; *Werner Laurie [Eng.], Dodd, Mead [U.S.A.].*
New York, 1732-34. A tale illustrating the political unrest of the period: the government party v. the popular party (the controversy over the " New York Journal ").

1306. DORIS KINGSLEY: Emma Rayner; *Dillingham [U.S.A.].*
A story of the founding of Georgia (called after George II), mostly in the period between 1730 and 1740. The Englishman, James Edward Oglethorpe, had formed the idea of a colony for poor debtors in English prisons, as well as for Protestants driven out of Germany, and the tale illustrates the carrying out of this scheme in the building of Savannah, etc. Oglethorpe took out Wesley and his brother in 1735. In 1740, after a declaration of War the previous year, he invaded Florida, but had to retire. His aim was to make Georgia a State of protection against the Spaniards.

1307. RETURN: Grace MacGowan Cooke and Alice MacGowan; *Hodder & Stoughton [Eng.], Page [U.S.A.].*
Georgia, 1739. A romance of the early days following Oglethorpe's founding of the " Debtor " Colony. An interesting and well-written book.

1308. THE HOLY LOVER: M. C. Oemler; *Heinemann [Eng.], Boni & Liveright [U.S.A.].*
Mainly N. America (Georgia), 1735-38. A John Wesley romance. After a rapid survey, in Chapter I, of Wesley's early career from childhood to manhood, the author proceeds to deal with his three years' sojourn as missioner in the Province of Georgia, and—somewhat daringly, perhaps not altogether satisfactorily—depicts him in the character of lover. As here presented, the " holy lover " can hardly be described as an attractive figure (the book's title is apparently suggested by the *Holy Club* of Wesley's Oxford days). Charles Wesley also appears prominently in the novel—Governor Oglethorpe being another historic figure of some note. The book indicates considerable research.

1309. *HETTY WESLEY: A. T. Quiller-Couch; *Harper [Eng.], Macmillan [U.S.A.].*
India, 1723 (*Prologue*); then England (London and Lincolnshire), mainly 1723-33, but the latest pages carry the story to Hetty's death in 1750. A fascinating romance, in which humour and tragedy alternate. The author's imaginative character-sketch of Mehetabel Wesley (" Hetty ") conveys the mental strength, as well as the physical charm, of this most interesting of all the six Wesley sisters. The account of her disastrous early attachment, and of her later unfortunate marriage, is given in such a way as to illustrate the domestic record of the Wesley family as a whole; in the second half of the novel the two brothers John and Charles are prominently introduced as quite young men. The wider and more human outlook gained by Hetty, is contrasted with the cramped and rigid attitude towards life which her father, and in some degree her brother John, felt constrained to adopt. The *Epilogue* gives the reader a glimpse of Wellesley (afterwards Duke of Wellington) in India, 1803, and shows the great General's indirect connection with an episode in the story proper, which of course ends several years before he was born.

1310. THE MESSENGER (THE LOVE THAT PREVAILED): F. FRANKFORT MOORE; *Hodder & Stoughton* [*Eng.*], *Cupples* [*U.S.A.*].
Yet another presentment of John Wesley in the character of lover—the scene this time being England (Cornwall) in the year 1740. The romance is sympathetic and finely conceived.

1311. BONNIE PRINCE CHARLIE: G. A. HENTY; *Juv.* *Blackie* [*Eng.*], *Scribner* [*U.S.A.*].
England, Scotland, and Abroad in the period 1728-47. A tale which, after covering the Battles of Dettingen (1743) and Fontenoy (1745) in the War of the Austrian Succession, becomes more especially a '45 Rebellion story: Prestonpans (1745) and Culloden (1746).

1312. THE GREAT ATTEMPT: FREDERICK ARTHUR; *Murray.*
A good Jacobite story of the North of England round about the year 1733.

1313. *THE NEW ROAD: NEIL MUNRO; *Blackwood.*
Scottish Highlands about the fourth decade of the 18th Century, when Wade's great *New Road* was in the making. Simon Fraser, Lord Lovat, is prominent—the clever depiction of him being very adverse.

1314. *THE LAIRD OF GLENFERNIE (FOES): MARY JOHNSTON; *Constable* [*Eng.*], *Harper* [*U.S.A.*].
Scotland and Abroad within the period 1735-50. A social and adventure novel of Jacobite times; historical events, like those connected with the '45 Rebellion, are well in the background. The hero escapes to Spain after Culloden, and has further experiences in Paris, Rome, and the Egyptian Desert.

1315. THE LITTLE LADY OF ARROCK: DAVID WHITELAW; *Chapman & Hall.*
Carlisle, the Scottish Highlands, Paris, and Edinburgh, 1716, and (mainly) 1744-45. This novel—with present day *Prologue* and *Epilogue*—is primarily one of domestic tragedy, though there is a Jacobite atmosphere. Considerable allusion to historic events, but they are hardly brought into the tale. Prince Charlie appears (a mere glimpse).

1316. *HIGH TREASON: ANONYMOUS; *Murray.*
An interesting historical romance of Kent and London in the period 1744-50. The atmosphere is more or less Jacobite, and Prince Charles Edward appears. Other historic figures are: Frederick Prince of Wales and Prince George, Henry Pelham (Prime Minister), George Selwyn, and last—but not least—Henry Fielding (the hero is brought before Fielding at Bow Street on a charge of Treason).

1317. THE LITTLE MAISTER: R. H. FORSTER; *John Long.*
A story of the Northumberland Coast and Carlisle in 1745 (mainly). Deals with the earlier part of the Rebellion, giving a good description of Prince Charlie during his Carlisle days.

1318. THE YEOMAN ADVENTURER: GEORGE W. GOUGH; *Methuen.*
A tale of the Midlands (Staffordshire, etc.) in the '45 Rebellion. Prince Charlie appears several times—notably in the chapter giving a full account of the consultation at Derby prior to the retreat. The *Epilogue* is 1757.

1319. FOR THE WHITE ROSE OF ARNO: "OWEN RHOSCOMYL"; *Longmans.*
A Jacobite tale of Wynnstay, etc., 1745, and the Welsh connection with the Derby march.

1320. *FORTUNA CHANCE: "James Prior"; *Constable.*

Sherwood Forest district of Nottinghamshire, also North Derbyshire, and South Yorkshire, chiefly in the '45 Rebellion period. A romance of atmosphere and general suggestion; but, although not historical in the full sense, the book contains reference to public events, and introduces a few real personages like William Lord Byron (the poet's great-uncle) and William Chaworth. An interesting example of the author who, since his death in 1922, has become increasingly known as essentially the novelist of Nottinghamshire.

1321. HARTLAND FOREST: Mrs. Anna Eliza Bray; *Chapman & Hall.*

A tale of domestic tragedy, beginning Exeter district, 1721, but mainly dealing with events at Hartland, North Devon, in the time of the '45 Rebellion.

1322. *MIDWINTER: John Buchan; *Hodder & Stoughton* [*Eng.*], *Doran* [*U.S.A.*].

An interesting Jacobite story, largely connected with incidents supposed to have occurred in the Cotswold—Oxfordshire and West Midland regions, 1745. Dr. Johnson, as a young man, is prominently introduced, while General Oglethorpe is another historic figure.

1323. CAPTAIN NANCY: Dorothea Moore; *Juv.   Nisbet.*

A young girl's experiences and adventures in Preston, Lancashire, also on the North Road, etc, during the '45 Rebellion.

1324. THE YOUNG CLANROY: Cosmo Gordon Lang; *Juv.   Smith, Elder.*

A tale of the Western Highlands and Crieff in the '45 Rebellion period. Prince Charlie is prominent—especially as a fugitive after Culloden.

1325. A LOYAL YOUNG REBEL: D. H. Parry; *Juv.   Cassell.*

Staffordshire and the North during the '45 Rebellion. The story depicts Prince Charlie at Edinburgh, etc., ending Culloden and immediately after.

1326. THE BRIGHT EYES OF DANGER: John Foster; *Juv. Chambers.*

A Westmorland youth's adventures 1745-46. The tale deals mainly with the earlier part of "the '45"—Cope's landing, the Prince's Edinburgh ball, etc. The Prince himself is prominent. Ends Findhorn and Spey regions.

1327. *A LOST LADY OF OLD YEARS: J. Buchan; *Lane.*

The Lowlands and Highlands of Scotland alternately, 1745-46, ending London, 1747. This historical novel of the '45 period gives only a glimpse of Prince Charlie, but the depiction of Lord Lovat is a specially careful one. The author takes a more lenient view of Lovat than that suggested in Neil Munro's *The New Road.*

1328. THE HOUSE OF DELUSION: Miss E. M. Carmichael; *Melrose.*

Scottish Highlands in the '45 Rebellion time. An interesting story mainly dealing with the character and domesticities of a certain "Lord Lochalsh," under which name the author is really giving the reader a freely-drawn picture of Simon Fraser, Lord Lovat.

1329. OUTLAWED: H. Robswood Cooke; *Hodder & Stoughton.*

A South Shields man tells how he went to Inverness on business, and became involved in the '45. The Battle of Culloden and subsequent hiding, etc. There is a carefully-balanced depiction of Simon, Lord Lovat, who appears somewhat prominently in the tale.

1330. JACK O' WINNATS: M. ANDREWS; *Juv. Heywood.*
Derbyshire (Castleton), Cumberland, etc., 1745-46. Prince Charlie's entry into Derby, and the Siege of Carlisle by Cumberland, are among the chief historical events introduced. The Prince and the Duke of Cumberland both appear—the former more than once.

1331. THE HEARTH OF HUTTON: W. J. EGGOTT; *Blackwood.*
England and Scotland, 1745-46. Story of a Cumberland squire in the '45 Rebellion, covering the march to Derby and the retreat northwards, also (at the end) the Battle of Falkirk.

1332. *WAVERLEY: SIR WALTER SCOTT; *Black, and other publishers— English and American.*
Stirling, Edinburgh, London, etc., 1745-46. This celebrated romance of the '45 Rebellion depicts more especially its earlier stages (the Battle of Preston Pans, etc.)— the later period of the Derby retreat being rapidly sketched, while the disaster of Culloden is introduced only in the shape of news. The book, even apart from its own special merits, must always hold a position of great importance as being Scott's first venture in fiction; its literary results in the hundred years following, have been enormous.

1333. *THE RED CURVE: J. G. SARASIN; *Hutchinson.*
Mainly Edinburgh, the Newcastle region, and the Inverness region, 1745-46. A very thrilling romance of the '45, in which the somewhat elusive personality of Simon Fraser, Lord Lovat, is once more presented—this time very adversely. On the strictly historical side, the only events introduced with any detail, are Prince Charles Edward's occupation of Edinburgh in the early chapters, and the Battle of Culloden at the end of the book (an excellent account); the march south to Derby and the retreat northwards, etc. are rapidly outlined—the startling fictional developments in the middle portion of the novel occupying the reader's full attention. The most important historic figures are the Prince, Lord Lovat, Marshal Wade, Lord George Murray, and Lord Balmerino.

1334. *RICROFT OF WITHENS: HALLIWELL SUTCLIFFE; *Fisher Unwin [Eng.], Appleton [U.S.A.].*
An excellent historical tale of Yorkshire (Skipton and Lancashire border region), 1745-46. Although ending with Culloden, the novel illustrates more especially that part of the '45 Rebellion which immediately preceded and followed the Derby turning point. Prince Charlie is very prominently introduced, and other figures are Lochiel, Lord George Murray, and the Duke of Cumberland. The local colour is especially good.

1335. UNDER THE WHITE COCKADE: HALLIWELL SUTCLIFFE; *Juv. Cassell.*
England and Scotland (Dunblane, Perth, and Edinburgh) in the time of the '45 Rebellion. Apart from the Battle of Prestonpans, there are not many historic scenes, but Prince Charlie is very prominent.

1336. THE OPEN ROAD: HALLIWELL SUTCLIFFE; *Ward, Lock.*
Yorkshire and the Lake District, 1745-46. A story of adventure during the Rebellion. The hero is mistaken for the Prince and taken before the Duke of Cumberland. The Prince himself is also introduced.

1337. THE LONE ADVENTURE: HALLIWELL SUTCLIFFE; *Fisher Unwin.*
Lancashire, 1745-46. Yet another of the author's tales of the '45 Rebellion. Illustrates the period of the Prince's coming south and his retreat from Derby. The Prince is fairly prominent, while Colonel Towneley may be noted among the other figures. Later chapters show the Prince in Scotland, and at the end there are glimpses of Flora Macdonald.

1338. POOR SONS OF A DAY: Allan McAulay; *Nisbet.*
Scotland, 1745-46. A tale of the '45, giving some account of Prestonpans and the earlier stages of the Rebellion, but, for the most part, rapidly sketching the incidents which culminated in Culloden, etc. Prince Charlie is prominent. Other figures are Clementina Walkinshaw, Lord George Murray, and Flora Macdonald.

1339. ALTURLIE: H. Robswood Cooke; *Hodder & Stoughton.*
France and Scotland, 1745-46. A Jacobite tale, though the hero's tendencies are not altogether on the side of the Prince. Of the historic figures introduced, one may note the Marquis D'Argenson (Louis XV's Minister) and Lord Lovat. At the end there is a glimpse of Wolfe (the future hero of Quebec).

1340. FOR BONNIE PRINCE CHARLIE: Escott Lynn; *Juv. Cassell.*
Cumberland and Scotland, 1745-46. A tale of the '45 Rebellion, covering Falkirk and Culloden. Prince Charlie, the Duke of Cumberland, and Wolfe appear; also, at the end, King George II.

1341. SCOTLAND'S HEIR: Winifred Duke; *Chambers.*
A story of Edinburgh, Derby, Stirling, and the Highlands, 1745-46. Covers the Rebellion and gives Prince Charles Edward as central figure (careful depiction). Besides the Prince, quite a crowd of historical personages appear including Lord Lovat, Lord Elcho, and Clementina Walkinshaw.

1342. *FLEMINGTON: Violet Jacob; *Murray.*
One of Mrs. Jacob's finely-written tales. Scotland (mainly the Brechin region of Forfarshire), 1745-46. The *Prologue* is dated 1727. A picture of life during, and just after, the 'Forty-Five, but the Rebellion itself is hardly introduced. The Duke of Cumberland appears.

1343. CLAYMORE: Arthur D. Howden Smith; *Skeffington.*
A Suffolk young man joins the Prince at Derby, the story then covering the Retreat, Falkirk, Culloden, and after. Prince Charlie is greatly to the fore, while Lovat and other historical personages appear. The book ends with the hero sailing to foreign parts with the Prince.

1344. CASTLE ADAMANT: Norman Dundas; *Murray.*
Stirling, Perth, etc., 1745-46. The Jacobite hero of this interesting story, after various experiences and adventures is lodged in Stirling Castle as a prisoner; he eventually escapes, and, after more adventures, attains happiness and ——. General Blakeney, Governor of Stirling Castle, is introduced, and the Duke of Cumberland appears in the last chapter.

1345. THE PORT OF DREAMS: Miriam Alexander; *Melrose.*
Paris and Ireland, 1745-47. A somewhat vigorous romance of Irish Jacobites and Prince Charlie; the Prince is prominent—notably in certain Dublin episodes.

1346. THE BLACK COLONEL: James Milne; *Lane.*
A Jacobite in Aberdeenshire after the '45 Rebellion, with some Wolfe and Quebec allusions towards the end of the tale.

1347. *MUCKLE JOHN: Frederick Watson; *Juv. Black.*
A good story of Inverness and the Highlands in 1746. The Battle of Culloden and the wandering period after it. Prince Charlie appears frequently, while Lord Lovat (adverse depiction) is another prominent figure. The Duke of Cumberland appears on two occasions,

1348. (1)*THE FLIGHT OF THE HERON:
(2)*THE GLEAM IN THE NORTH (*sequel*): D. K. Broster;
Heinemann [*Eng.*], *Dodd, Mead* [*U.S.A.*].
Two excellent Jacobite tales. (1) The Western Highlands of Scotland (Lochabar), Edinburgh, and the Inverness region, 1745. Deals more especially with the Edinburgh stage of the '45 rebellion and with occurrences round about the disaster of Culloden. The tale ends at the time of the Prince's escape by sea. Prince Charles Edward, the Duke of Cumberland, Cameron of Lochiel, Lord George Murray, and Dr. Cameron are among the figures introduced. (2) Scottish Highlands (Fort William and Loch Awe regions) and London, mainly 1752-53. The story hinges on the wanderings of the ardent Jacobite, Dr. Archibald Cameron (brother of Cameron of Lochiel), whose capture is desired by the Government. What happens eventually, after much fictional by-play, is told by the author with strict regard for historical accuracy. The Duke of Argyll appears in one of the closing chapters.

1349. I'D VENTURE ALL FOR THEE! J. S. Fletcher; *Nash.*
A story of Yorkshire (Boroughbridge, York, and the Coast) in 1746. The adventures of a Jacobite after the '45 Rebellion.

1350. THE MACDONALD LASS: "Sarah Tytler"; *Chatto & Windus.*
Flora Macdonald as heroine. The story covers the period 1746 (Charles Edward's escape) to 1750 (Flora's marriage). The *Epilogue* tells of the heroine's death in 1790.

1351. THE EXILED SCOT: H. A. Bryden; *Chatto & Windus* [*Eng.*], *New Amsterdam Book Co.* [*U.S.A.*].
Scotland, Holland, the Cape, and Mauritius within the period 1746-56. Begins with Prince Charlie's escape three months after Culloden, but mainly depicts Cape experiences (the Scottish hero is in the service of the Dutch East India Company). An expedition up country (natives, etc.) and the finding of diamonds; also sea adventures (pirates). Ends Scotland.

1352. *MR. SUFFER-LONG: Lettice Milne Rae; *Juv.* R.T.S.
Scotland, London, and Paris, mainly in the period 1745-60 (begins 1720). An excellent story of a young man who was gradually disillusioned with regard to Prince Charlie. Towards the end, the Prince and Clementina Walkinshaw are depicted.

1353. *MR. MISFORTUNATE: "Marjorie Bowen"; *Collins.*
Begins with Prince Charles Edward in the Scottish Highlands after Culloden, quickly passing to Paris. After graphically illustrating the Prince's life in Paris 1746-48, the novel gives some account of his subsequent wanderings (Avignon, Rome, Venice, etc.).

1354. BEGGARS AND SORNERS: Allan McAulay; *Lane.*
A tale of Amsterdam in 1750, but with a Scottish and Jacobite atmosphere. Prince Charles Edward is a prominent figure.

1355. *THE SLAVE SHIP: Mary Johnston; *Thornton Butterworth* [*Eng.*], *Little, Brown* [*U.S.A.*].
An escaped Scottish Jacobite's experiences and adventures in the years following the '45 Rebellion. There are many changes of scene: Edinburgh, Virginia, Africa, Jamaica, etc. The story illustrates, in a vivid manner, Slave Plantation life in Virginia, besides giving some account of the African Slave Coast trade.

1356. *THE MASTER OF BALLANTRAE: R. L. Stevenson; *Cassell* [*Eng.*], *Scribner* [*U.S.A.*].
A story of adventures beginning on the Solway shore, 1745, but almost immediately passing to 1748 and the years following. But for the early allusions to the '45 Rebellion and its connection with certain fictional characters, there is no properly historical element. Various scenes: The Bermudas, North America (New York, the Hudson, etc.), and India.

1357. O'LOGHLIN OF CLARE: Rosa Mulholland (Lady Gilbert): *Sands.*
Ireland (Co. Clare), 1746. A tale of the time when the Penal Laws were still in force, showing the extent to which the Roman Catholics suffered. The book, which is a good example of its author, is written from the Catholic standpoint.

1358. SIR RICHARD ESCOMBE: Max Pemberton; *Cassell* [*Eng.*], *Harper* [*U.S.A.*].
A story of Warwickshire in 1746, telling of matters connected with the " Hell Fire Club " at Medmenham Abbey.

1359. THE WORLD WENT VERY WELL THEN: Walter Besant; *Chatto & Windus* [*Eng.*], *Harper* [*U.S.A.*].
Deptford, Wapping, etc., and Abroad, mainly in the period 1744-62. A depiction of that mid-eighteenth century life which the author had so carefully studied. In addition to the Thames-side scenes, there are numerous sketches of nautical adventure in the Southern Seas, etc.

1360. *THE CHAPLAIN OF THE FLEET: Walter Besant and James Rice; *Chatto & Windus* [*Eng.*], *Harper* [*U.S.A.*].
London and Epsom between 1745 and 1750. An exceptionally fascinating story of mid-century life and manners. Deals partly with London prison conditions, partly with the world of fashion at Epsom.

1361. THE GOLDEN FLEECE: H. C. Bailey; *Methuen.*
Begins London, 1750, then passing to Gloucester and the Cotswold region. The story of a Jacobite heiress and of Jacobite schemes. The Pretender is prominently introduced.

1362. *PEG WOFFINGTON: Charles Reade; *Chatto & Windus* [*Eng.*], *Dodd, Mead* [*U.S.A.*].
An imaginary episode in the life of the actress Margaret Woffington (1720-60). The story deals with Peg's theatrical period at Covent Garden, and can therefore be fixed as round about 1750.

1363. THE WAYFARERS: J. C. Snaith; *Ward, Lock.*
London about 1750. A novel of manners, verging on the semi-historic type; the real figure of Henry Fielding, the novelist, is, however, introduced.

1364. *THE GOLDEN VANITY: " E. Barrington "; in " The Ladies! "—*Fisher Unwin.*
Dublin and London, 1750-52. A good short story of the beautiful sisters—Maria and Elizabeth Gunning. The marriage of Elizabeth and the Duke of Hamilton.

1365. *THE FATAL GIFT: F. Frankfort Moore; *Hutchinson* [*Eng.*], *Dodd, Mead* [*U.S.A.*].
Dublin and London, c. 1751-52. A romance of the sisters Gunning. The Duke of Hamilton who married the younger sister, and Lord Coventry who married the elder, are both introduced. Other more or less prominent figures are Sheridan, Mr. Thrale, and Whitefield the Preacher.

1366. THE BLACK MOTH: Georgette Heyer; *Constable* [*Eng.*], *Houghton Mifflin* [*U.S.A.*].
England (various localities including Bath and London), c. 1750-52. A tale of High Social life and manners, with history far in the background. One of the few allusions to a real event occurs in the *Epilogue*, where a letter contains the piece of news: " Miss Gunning is to marry Coventry."

1367. THE TWO CHIEFS OF DUNBOY: J. A. FROUDE; *Longmans* [Eng.], Scribner [U.S.A.].

France and S. Ireland, mainly in the period 1750-60. This novel by the well-known historian, biographer, and essayist of last Century, depicts Irish affairs (the schemes of French invasion, the Whiteboys, etc.) from the standpoint of an anti-nationalist.

1368. *GUY MANNERING: SIR WALTER SCOTT; *Black, and other publishers—English and American.*

Galloway and Cumberland (George II—George III). A favourite example of Scott, though less directly historical than many of his novels. Beginning in mid-eighteenth century, the story ends towards the close of the American Revolution period: it depicts gipsy life, and the smuggling due to the heavy import duties, besides illustrating the defects of eighteenth century prison discipline.

1369. (1)*KIDNAPPED:
(2)*CATRIONA (sequel): R. L. STEVENSON; *Cassell* [Eng.], Scribner [U.S.A.].

(1) Adventures of David Balfour by land and sea in 1751: Edinburgh and Queensferry; a voyage round Scotland by the Orkneys, Cape Wrath, and Skye; then Western and Mid Highlands. The Jacobite Alan Breck Stewart (banished after the '45) is greatly to the fore. An historical incident—the famous Appin murder—is woven into the tale.

(2) Further adventures of David Balfour, with more about Alan Breck and the Appin murder. The scene is largely Edinburgh, the Bass, etc., but the reader is also taken to Holland and France. The Catriona of the story is a grand-daughter of Rob Roy. Simon Fraser, Lord Lovat, is depicted in interesting fashion, and the Appin Murder Trial is well introduced.

1370. YOUNG PENNYMORE: NEIL MUNRO; in "Jaunty Jock and Other Stories"—*Blackwood.*

Scotland, 1752. A short, but good, story of a young Jacobite condemned to be hung.

1371. *SHALLOWS: FREDERICK WATSON; *Methuen.*

France, England, and Scotland, 1752 onwards. This story deals with the Flibank plot and Archibald Cameron. Prince Charles Edward is very much to the fore at various points. In the earlier chapters Condillac the philosopher is prominent, and Madame du Deffand also appears.

1372. *MOONFLEET: J. MEADE FALKNER; *Arnold.*

Adventures mainly in the Dorset Coast region, 1757-58. The finding of treasure in the Isle of Wight is the pivot of this really excellent tale.

1373. THE INFIDEL: M. E. BRADDON [Mrs. Maxwell]; *Simpkin.*

Chiefly London and district in the last years of George II's reign. The interest of the novel is chiefly in its illustration of the Methodist Revival (Wesley and Whitefield).

1374. JEMMY ABERCRAW: BERNARD CAPES; *Methuen* [Eng.], *Brentano's* [U.S.A.].

Surrey and London, 1758-60. Story of a University man turned highwayman. There is a Jacobite element, and William Pitt (afterwards Earl of Chatham) appears.

1375. A FOUNTAIN SEALED: WALTER BESANT; *Chatto & Windus* [Eng.], Stokes [U.S.A.].

London in the last *months* of George II. A story based on the dubious tradition that George Prince of Wales (about to become George III) fell in love with the Quaker maiden, Hannah Lightfoot.

1376. *THE GREAT VALLEY: Mary Johnston; *Thornton Butter-worth* [Eng.], Little, Brown [U.S.A.].
Shenandoah Valley, Virginia, mid 18th Century.   A novel telling the experiences of a Scots Minister and his family as immigrants in Virginia (the " Shenandoah Country") within the period 1735 to 1760.   There are many historical allusions, including Braddock's defeat, and the taking of Quebec; but the reader is brought nearer still to history when George Washington appears as a young surveyor, whom Governor Dinwiddie employs on a special mission (the Ohio Company matter).

1377. ROGER THE SCOUT: " Herbert Strang " and George Lawrence; *Juv. Frowde.*
N.W. England, London, and North America, 1744-60.   A tale giving in the early chapters a glimpse of the '45 Rebellion and after, but mainly dealing with New England and Canada from about 1748 onwards.   Covers the beginning of the Seven Years' War in 1756, and such events as the attack on Fort Du Quesne, the taking of Quebec (1759), and the surrender of Vaudreuil (1760).   George Washington and General Braddock are both introduced.

1378. *LADY GOOD-FOR-NOTHING: A. T. Quiller-Couch; *Dent* [Eng.], *Nelson* [Eng.], *Scribner* [U.S.A.].
Boston (Mass.) in the fifth decade of the Eighteenth Century; also Lisbon (the Earthquake, 1755).   An excellent novel based, in part, upon the true story of Sir Harry Frankland and Agnes Surriage.   The *Epilogue* passes to Bath, England, in the year 1775.

1379. FIFE AND DRUM AT LOUISBOURG: J. Macdonald Oxley; *Juv. Gay & Bird* [Eng.], Little, Brown [U.S.A.].
Boston and Louisbourg in 1745.   A tale dealing with the expedition made in " King George's War " for the capture of Louisbourg which the French had so strongly fortified. The story tells of adventures by land and sea (the colonial fleet), including the hero's capture by Indians.   Ends with the Fall of Louisbourg after six weeks' fighting.

1380. *THE GOLDEN DOG (*Le Chien d'Or*): William Kirby; *Jarrold* [Eng.], Page [U.S.A.].
A romance of Canada (Quebec) 1748-49.   Depicts the time when the Count de la Galissonière was Governor—both he and Bigot appearing.   It was La Galissonière who repulsed Admiral Byng a few years later.   The last chapter of the book passes to 1777.

1381. *FAIRFAX: John Esten Cooke; *Sampson Low* [Eng.], Carleton [U.S.A.].
Virginia (the Shenandoah Valley region), about 1748-49, though passing at the very end to 1781 (news of the surrender of Cornwallis).   A novel with some good local colour, and describing the life and ways of the time—the witchcraft delusions, etc. There is a considerable Indian element.

1382. (1)*THE FORGE IN THE FOREST:
    (2)*A SISTER TO EVANGELINE (*sequel*) (Lovers in Acadie):
    Charles G. D. Roberts; *Lane* [Eng.], Silver [U.S.A.].
F(1) A tale of Grand Pré, Acadie (now Nova Scotia) round about 1747.   The time is that of the English occupation (French *v.* English), with the " Black Abbé " as an outstanding figure.   The book is rich in local colour; it suggests—rather than describes— historic events.
    (2) Grand Pré and the " Black Abbé " once again, mainly about 1755.   The story's central theme is the expulsion of the Acadian farmers (see Longfellow's *Evangeline*). Time of Bigot in Quebec, and the French and Indian War.

1383. BEYOND THE SUNSET: Arthur D. Howden Smith; *Brentano's.*
A story of adventure among the North American Indians, mid 18th Century.   Scarcely historical in any full sense, but gives a picture of New York, etc., at the time when Canada was under French rule.

1384. *IN THE SHADOW OF THE LORD: Mrs. Hugh Fraser;
    Methuen [Eng.], Holt [U.S.A.].
England (Cookham region and London) and Virginia, 1727-54. A novel of George Washington's parents, dealing more especially with his mother, whom the reader first sees as a young maiden just arrived in England from the colony of Virginia. The marriage with Augustine Washington, the voyage to America, and the home life in Washington Manor near Fredericksburg, are described in turn. The tale conveys the religious atmosphere in which George and his sister Betty—along with three " little brothers "—were brought up; while later portions of the book cover George's early career up to his second expedition and the resignation of his commission. Besides the Washington family (including George's brother Lawrence), several historic personages are introduced or named, including Sir Robert Walpole (who appears in the English section), Lord Fairfax, and General Dinwiddie.

1385. WITH GEORGE WASHINGTON INTO THE WILDERNESS:
    Edwin L. Sabin; *Juv. Lippincott.*
North America, 1748-58. A tale illustrating the youth and early manhood of George Washington. Covers the Fort Duquesne period, and practically ends with Braddock's defeat and death.

1386. *MR. WASHINGTON (A SOLDIER FROM VIRGINIA):
    Marjorie Bowen; *Methuen [Eng.], Nelson [Eng.], Appleton [U.S.A.].*
George Washington in the period, 1753-1781. The French and Indian War (Braddock's defeat); then—passing over several years—the story rapidly reaches the Revolutionary War and Washington's command of the American Army (1775); lastly, the years of victory, ending in Cornwallis' surrender at Yorktown, October, 1781. An interesting example of fictional biography of the less comprehensive type—certain important periods in the history of Washington's career being selected by the author in preference to a continuous illustration.

1387. THE BLACK HUNTER: James Oliver Curwood; *Hodder &
    Stoughton.*
New France (the River Richelieu region and Quebec, etc.) 1754-55. A love and adventure tale, with an historical background of plotting, fighting, etc. Deals with the events leading up to the Seven Years' War (French and Indian War), and gives some account of Braddock's defeat near Fort Duquesne. The Intendant Bigot is very prominent, while Vaudreuil and others appear.

1388. *JIM MASON, BACKWOODSMAN:
    *JIM MASON SCOUT:
    *CAPTAIN JIM MASON:
    *MASON AND HIS RANGERS: Elmer Russell Gregor;
    Juv. Appleton.
These four connected adventure tales of N. America in the Colonial period, have as background the outbreak and early stages of the " French and Indian War," 1754-55. A young trader in northern New York is the hero—he and his Mohawk friends fighting under Johnson against the French and their Indian allies. Braddock's defeat is mentioned merely as news, but the Battle of Lake George is introduced in the second tale. " Jim " and his rangers disperse the marauding companies of Canadians (French) and Indians, and a perilous mission is undertaken, etc. etc.

1389. THE PATH OF GLORY: Paul Leland Haworth; *Ham-Smith
    [Eng.], Little, Brown [U.S.A.].*
North America, 1754-59. A novel of the French and Indian War period: fights and massacres, etc. Illustrates the beginnings and earlier stages of the War, besides giving —in the last pages—an account of the taking of Quebec. Montcalm, Vaudreuil, Bigot, and Wolfe appear in the course of the story.

1390. *THE HUNTERS OF THE HILLS:
      *THE RULERS OF THE LAKES:
      *THE LORDS OF THE WILD:
      *THE SHADOW OF THE NORTH:
      *THE MASTERS OF THE PEAKS:
      *THE SUN OF QUEBEC: Joseph A. Altsheler; *Juv.* *Appleton.*
These six volumes constitute *The French and Indian War Series.* They depict North America in the period 1754-63. The story is continuous—certain outstanding characters appearing throughout the series. There is a genuinely historical background, viz., the struggle between the English and the French colonists (the latter having the Indians as allies).

1391. A SOLDIER OF VIRGINIA: Burton E. Stevenson; *Duckworth* [*Eng.*], *Houghton Mifflin* [*U.S.A.*].
A story written round the events following the building of Fort Duquesne by the French, and dealing in particular with Braddock's Defeat. Braddock himself and George Washington both appear.

1392. *SCOUTING ON THE OLD FRONTIER (formerly *With Firelock and Fife*): Everett T. Tomlinson; *Juv.* *Appleton.*
North America (between Albany and Montreal), 1755. A good tale of adventure in the French and Indian War period, covering the Battle of Lake George, etc. General Johnson (afterwards Sir William Johnson) appears.

1393. *THE RED ROAD: Hugh Pendexter; *Collins* [*Eng.*], *Bobbs-Merrill* [*U.S.A.*].
¶ Virginia, and the Ohio Valley region near Fort Duquesne, 1755. An interesting romance of English v. French and of the Red Men, beginning at the time of the meeting of colonial governors at Alexandria. The tale covers Braddock's advance across the forest-clad mountains for the purpose of attacking Fort Duquesne, up to his defeat by the French and their Indian allies on the far side of the Monongahela River. There is a detailed account of the battle, and of the circumstances immediately preceding the British General's death. Many historic figures, including Braddock, " Major " Washington, Benjamin Franklin, Governor Dinwiddie, Sir John St. Clair, etc. etc.

1394. *WITH WOLFE IN CANADA: G. A. Henty; *Juv.* *Blackie* [*Eng.*], *Scribner* [*U.S.A.*].
A good tale of the French and Indian War, covering Braddock's Defeat, the Fort William Henry disaster (1757), the capture of Louisbourg (1758), Abercromby's failure at Ticonderoga (1758), and the siege and taking of Quebec (1759).

1395. *THE SEATS OF THE MIGHTY: Gilbert Parker; *Methuen* [*Eng.*], *Appleton* [*U.S.A.*].
☞ Canada (Quebec) in the period 1755-59. Begins with the announcement of Braddock's death, and ends with an account of the taking of Quebec. This excellent romance shows the author at his best. Many historic personages appear, including Governor Vaudreuil, Bigot, Montcalm, and Wolfe.

1396. WOLF-ON-THE-TRAIL: S. Walkey; *Juv.* *Cassell.*
North America, 1755. Although Braddock and Washington appear in the first chapter, this story is almost entirely one of adventure among the Redskin allies of the French, in the period just after Braddock's defeat.

1397. HOW CANADA WAS WON: F. S. Brereton; *Juv.* *Blackie* [*Eng.*], *Caldwell* [*U.S.A.*].
Colonial North America (New York, the Alleghany Mountains region, etc.) 1756-59. A tale of the fighting against the French and Indians, including the defence of Fort William Henry, the attack on Louisbourg, and the taking of Quebec. George Washington and Wolfe are among the historic figures.

1398. The FLAME OF COURAGE: GEORGE GIBBS; *Appleton*.
France (*Prologue*) and Canada in the few years leading up to Wolfe's taking of Quebec. A story of love and political intrigue in the time of Vaudreuil and Montcalm. Of the historical figures, Bigot is especially prominent, while Madame de Pompadour, Voltaire, Wolfe, Vaudreuil and Madame Vaudreuil appear at one or another point.

1399. *THE LAST OF THE MOHICANS: J. FENIMORE COOPER; *Juv. Dent* [Eng.], *Dutton* [U.S.A.]; *and other publisher—English and American*.
The second, in proper sequence, of Cooper's *Leather-Stocking Tales*. This famous story, generally deemed one of its author's best examples, illustrates the French and Indian War in 1757—dealing especially with the Massacre of Fort William Henry. Montcalm appears very prominently at certain points, and, with regard to the various historical allusions, one may make particular mention of the early reference to " a Virginian boy's coolness and spirit "—George Washington being meant.

1400. *SCOUTING IN THE WILDERNESS (formerly *The Fort in the Forest*): EVERETT T. TOMLINSON; *Juv. Appleton*.
Another tale in the author's series dealing with this period. Illustrates especially the fall of Fort William Henry in 1757.

1401. THE HEART OF A HERO: "MORICE GERARD"; *Juv. Hodder & Stoughton*.
Bath (largely), Taunton, London, and Canada, in the period 1757-59. A love story of James Wolfe and Katherine Lowther, with historical background. Covers the Bombardment of Louisbourg, and the taking of Quebec (full account of Wolfe's death). Many historical figures besides the hero and heroine: Beau Nash (" over 80 years of age "), Pitt, Lord Howe, General Amherst, and Admiral Boscawen. The last pages pass to London, 1761.

1402. A REGULAR MADAM: MRS. ALICE WILSON FOX; *Juv. Macmillan*.
England (Gloucestershire) and Canada, 1757-59. Begins with a schoolgirl's experiences, leading up to a voyage and Quebec in the time of Montcalm and Bigot, both of whom appear in the story. Tells of adventures with Indians, ending with a very brief account of the taking of Quebec.

1403. BEN COMEE: M. J. CANAVAN; *Juv. Macmillan*.
North America, mainly between 1755 and 1760, covering the period of the Fort William Henry massacre (1757), the death of Lord Howe, Abercrombie's defeat at Ticonderoga (1758), etc. The *news* of Quebec's capture is also introduced. Rogers, Major Israel Putnam, and others appear.

1404. *THE CANADIANS OF OLD (CAMERON OF LOCHIEL): PHILIPPE AUBERT DE GASPÉ (trans.); *Desbarats* [Quebec], *Appleton* [U.S.A.].
Quebec and the St. Lawrence region, 1757-67. This tale of " New France " is based on real characters to a large extent. The hero is Archibald Cameron of Lochiel, son of the Highland chieftain who lost his life at Culloden. Deals with the Indians, and depicts old ways and customs—giving a general historic impression rather than describing special events. The taking of Quebec by the English is covered, but not much more than touched. The latest chapters carry the tale to the period after the English conquest. Decidedly a novel of " atmosphere."

1405. *SCOUTING ON THE MOHAWK (formerly *A Soldier in the Wilderness*): EVERETT T. TOMLINSON; *Juv. Appleton*.
A tale of the Lake Ontario and Mohawk River regions, 1758: time of the fall of Fort Frontenac.

1406. THE STORY OF OLD FORT LOUDON: " C. E. CRADDOCK "; *Macmillan*.
North America, 1758. A story of the French and English War, illustrating especially the attitude of the Cherokee Indians.

1407. *KINDRED: Mrs. A. P. Smith; *Heinemann* [*Eng.*], *Houghton Mifflin* [*U.S.A.*].
England and (mainly) North America, 1758. An English squire who had passed his youth in a French colony, goes out to America as an unauthorized spy at the time of the Seven Years' War. He ventures under disguise among both the French and the Indians; his experiences, which are of a romantic nature, make good reading. The only point at which History is directly touched, is in the early part of the story when the hero has a fairly long interview with Pitt (afterwards Lord Chatham).

1408. *A SOLDIER OF MANHATTAN: Joseph A. Altsheler; *Juv. Smith, Elder* [*Eng.*], *Appleton* [*U.S.A.*].
North America (New York State and Canada) in the French and Indian War period. An adventure tale with historic background; the death of Lord Howe in a preliminary skirmish before Ticonderoga, the futile attack on that fortress, and the taking of Quebec, are the chief events covered. Wolfe, Montcalm, Abercrombie, and other figures are introduced.

1409. *FORT AMITY: A. T. Quiller Couch; *Murray.*
Fort Henry, Ticonderoga, and the district of the Lakes, 1758-60 (closing pages 1775 and 1818). An historical romance vividly illustrating the final stages of the struggle for Canada between French and English, and dealing largely with the Indians whose attitude at this period was a matter of considerable importance. The story is mainly illustrative of events from Abercromby's failure at Ticonderoga (1758) to the Marquis de Vaudreuil's surrender at Montreal (1760), but the last chapter passes over some fifteen years to Carlton's successful defence of Quebec against the Americans, when Montgomery (the American General) was killed. There are glimpses of, or allusions to, Abercromby, Amherst, Howe, Wolfe, Murray, Montcalm, Vaudreuil, Montgomery, and others.

1410. THE LITTLE ADMIRAL: Jean McIlwraith; *Juv. Hodder & Stoughton.*
A tale of Quebec in 1759. An English boy-prisoner among the French in the time just before the taking of Quebec; the story ends with the city's fall and Montcalm's death. The aim is to present the *French* standpoint.

1411. *THE HEROINE OF THE STRAIT: Mary C. Crowley; *Little, Brown* [*U.S.A.*]
Chiefly Detroit in the 1760-70 decade. A carefully written romance illustrating the French intrigues with the Indians which resulted in the rebellion led by Pontiac, principal chief of the Ottawas (" Pontiac's Conspiracy "). The plan was that the various tribes northwards to Ottawa and southwards to the Mississippi mouth, should join in seizing the English forts. Many small garrisons were surprised, but, through previous warning, Detroit successfully withstood attack (1763), and in the same year Fort Pitt held out and was relieved. The whole period of these schemes and various attacks is covered in the story, which introduces several historical figures.

1412. A SWORD OF THE OLD FRONTIER: Randall Parrish; *Putnam* [*Eng.*], *McClurg* [*U.S.A.*].
Fort Chartres and Detroit at the time of Pontiac's Conspiracy, 1763.

1413. THE AMULET: " C. E. Craddock "; *Macmillan.*
The British at Fort Prince George, 1763, and the Cherokee Indians.

1414. (1)*THE VIRGINIA COMEDIANS:
(2)*HENRY ST. JOHN, GENTLEMAN (*sequel*): John Esten Cooke; 1. *Appleton*, 1854; 2. *Harper*, 1858.
Two connected novels illustrating respectively the social life of Virginia in 1763-65, and in 1774-75. The old-time author, from his own actual experience as a Virginian, was able to construct his romances on a basis of double knowledge, viz., the knowledge of bygone ways and customs pertaining to his own people a few generations back, and the knowledge of local topography and general scenic conditions which were much the same in 1850 as they had been in 1750.

1415. ONE OF CLIVE'S HEROES (IN CLIVE'S COMMAND):
"HERBERT STRANG "; *Juv. Hodder & Stoughton* [*Eng.*], *Bobbs-Merrill* [*U.S.A.*].
India, 1754-57. A good tale covering the period of British struggle in India, mid 18th Century: the Black Hole atrocity (1756) and the Battle of Plassey (1757).

1416. LIKE ANOTHER HELEN: "SYDNEY C. GRIER "; *Blackwood* [*Eng.*], *Page* [*U.S.A.*].
India (Calcutta), 1755-57. Story of a young lady's experiences in the " Black Hole " period up to the retaking of Calcutta by Clive. The last-named personage appears, also Warren Hastings as a young man of about 24.

1417. *RALPH DARNELL: PHILIP MEADOWS TAYLOR; *Kegan Paul* [*Eng.*], *Scribner* [*U.S.A.*].
India and England, mainly in the period 1755-1757. The beginnings of English authority in India as opposed to the native powers (both Mohomedan and Mahratta). The novel presents an interesting depiction of great events, including the Black Hole atrocity and the Battle of Plassey. Clive is the outstanding historical figure—appearing in both the English and Indian scenes. There is a glimpse of Peg Woffington in London.

1418. TORN FROM THE FOUNDATIONS: DAVID KER; *Juv. Melrose.*
Brazil and Portugal, mid 18th Century. A tale dealing respectively with Brazilian Forests, Inquisition methods, and the great earthquake of Lisbon (1755).

1419. *SIR JOHN CONSTANTINE: A. T. QUILLER-COUCH; *Dent* [*Eng.*], *Smith, Elder* [*Eng.*], *Scribner* [*U.S.A.*].
A son's memoirs of his father, telling of home and foreign adventures (especially in Corsica) during a short period from the year 1756.

1420. (1)*FREDERICUS:
(2)*LUISE:
(3)*DAS VOLK WACH AUF: WALTER VON MOLO; *Albert Langen* [*Munich*].
A trilogy of historical novels of high quality, dealing with: (1) Frederick the Great (Seven Years' War); (2) Louisa Queen of Prussia and Frederick-William III; and (3) The German People generally, towards the end of Napoleon's occupation. The period covered by the entire trilogy is approximately 1740 to 1810.

1421. *TRENCK: ROMAN EINES GÜNSTLINGS: BRUNO FRANK; *Ernst Rowholt* [*Germany*].
Germany, round about 1744. A novel dealing with the adventurer, Trenck, and his relations with Frederick the Great's sister Amalie. Frederick himself is much to the fore.

1422. UNDER WHICH KING?: HUBERT RENDEL; *Juv. Nelson.*
France (Rouen and Paris) and Germany, in the period 1742-57; the tale, however, is chiefly one of the year 1757, being written round the two Battles of Hastenbec and Rossbach.

1423. THE WATCH NIGHT: HENRY BETT; *Stanley Paul.*
England (London, Newcastle, etc.) and Germany (Frankfort, Herrnhuth, Dresden and Berlin) mainly in the years 1744-46. John Wesley is prominent in this story of a young man's religious experiences, while some account is given of the Moravians (Germany). Readers also catch a glimpse of Frederick the Great at the time of the Silesian War.

1424. WITH FREDERICK THE GREAT: G. A. Henty; *Juv. Blackie* [*Eng.*], *Scribner* [*U.S.A.*].
Germany, etc., 1756-63. A tale of the Seven Years' War: a young Scotsman's experiences in the service of Frederick the Great. Covers the Battles of Lobositz, Prague, Rossbach, Leuthen, Zorndorf, Hochkirch, and Torgau. The hero is aide-de-camp to Marshal Keith. Frederick is, of course, very prominent in the story.

1425. THE GOVERNOR'S DAUGHTER: Norman Innes; *Ward, Lock.*
Germany (Dresden, etc.) 1757. A love and adventure tale of an Irish gentleman of fortune, at the time of the Seven Years' War. Frederick the Great appears.

1426. THE LIVELY ADVENTURES OF GAVIN HAMILTON: Molly Elliot Seawell; *Juv. Harper.*
Germany and Austria mainly in the years 1757-58: time of the struggle between Frederick the Great and the Empress Maria Theresa. Both King and Empress are very prominent in the story, while Prince Kaunitz, the great Austrian Chancellor, and General Loudon, are both introduced.

1427. IVAN DE BIRON: Sir Arthur Helps; *Isbister.*
St. Petersburg and Siberia, 1740-62 (largely 1740-41). A romance of the Russian Court, depicting the various developments in a time of conspiracy and revolution. The Duke of Courland (Ernest John de Biron), Elizabeth Petrovna (Empress in the later part of the novel), and the Duchess of Brunswick (as Regent), are outstanding figures.

1428. *CONSUELO:
    *THE COUNTESS OF RUDOLSTADT (*sequel*): " George Sand " (trans.); *Walter Scott* [*Eng.*], *Dodd, Mead* [*U.S.A.*].
These two novels of mid- to late- 18th Century depict successively the earlier and the later stages in the career of a woman singer. The localities are numerous, including Venice, Prague, Vienna, and Berlin. The atmosphere of the novel *Consuelo* in particular is more or less musical—Joseph Haydn appearing very prominently. A considerable portion of the sequel deals with theosophy and charlatanism of the Cagliostro type; most readers will find more to their liking, the many representations of social and political life which are scattered through both romances. Like Haydn, Maria Theresa is greatly to the fore at certain points, while among the crowd of other personages introduced, one may specify Baron Frederick Trenck, Frederick the Great, Princess Amelia, and Voltaire.

1429. *THE QUEST OF GLORY: " Marjorie Bowen "; *Methuen.*
A romance of Vauvenargues the French thinker and writer, covering the period, 1742-1747. The earlier chapters show Vauvenargues as a French officer in Prague at the time of its siege by the Austrians, also introducing Maréchal de Belleisle and his Retreat from the city. The remainder of the novel illustrates the Paris of Louis XV under its more cultured aspects. Besides the outstanding figure of Vauvenargues, there are several historic personages such as Duc de Richelieu, Voltaire, and Marmontel.

1430. *THE HOUSE OF DE MAILLY: Margaret H. Potter; *Harper.*
An interesting romance of France (Paris) and North America (Annapolis) in 1744. There is a careful picture of Louis XV and his Court, with the Duc de Richelieu and Madame de Châteauroux as prominent figures. D'Holbach, the philosopher and encyclopædist, also appears.

1431. PETTICOAT GOVERNMENT (PETTICOAT RULE): Baroness Orczy; *Hutchinson* [*Eng.*], *Doran* [*U.S.A.*].
A well-told story of Louis XV's Court in 1745. The year is that of the Pompadour's installation at Versailles, as well as that of Prince Charlie's departure from France for Scotland. These events may be said to furnish the background of the tale.

1432. KING MANDRIN'S CHALLENGE: "May Wynne"; *Stanley Paul.*

France, 1752-53. A Frenchman of high birth, and with a record of wild living at Louis XV's Court, falls under the Pompadour's displeasure, and becomes a forest bandit under the name "King Mandrin" of Fontainebleau. The somewhat thrilling and romantic events following this step, constitute the theme of the story. King Louis XV and Madame de Pompadour appear.

1433. THESE OLD SHADES: Georgette Heyer; *Heinemann.*

France (mainly Paris) and England, c. 1755. A romance of fictional rather than historical interest, dealing with an English Duke and his page; the latter in the course of the story becomes the Duke's ward, with mystery and love developments. Madame du Deffand and the Prince de Condé appear, while there are glimpses of Louis XV and his Queen.

1434. *THE ANCIENT RÉGIME[1] (Castelnau; or, The Ancient Régime): **G. P. R. James;** *Longman, Brown, Green, and Longmans* [1841].

Southern France, and Paris, Versailles, etc., c. 1756, and—eighteen years later—1774. Allowing for certain old-fashioned digressions of a moralizing type, this romance of Louis XV period is of quite excellent quality. There is a well-constructed plot, and the interest is maintained throughout. On the historical side there is a careful picture of King Louis, and a not unpleasing presentment of his Minister, Louvois. Illustrates the prevailing system of *espionage* (the French police), as well as the corrupt influences of the Court generally. Both Louis XV and the Duc de Choiseul are brought prominently into the story, while there are glimpses of the Duchesse de Choiseul and Madame Du Barry.

[1] Mr. S. M. Ellis in his interesting volume: "The Solitary Horseman; or, The Life and Adventures of G. P. R. James" (The Cayme Press, Kensington, 1927) tells how "Mr. Thomas Hardy, as a boy, delighted in the books of G. P. R. James and still recalls them with pleasure—particularly *The Ancient Régime.*"

1435. THE SPENDTHRIFT DUKE: "May Wynne"; *Holden & Hardingham.*

Touraine and Paris in 1761. A pleasing story, introducing the Duc de Choiseul, Louis XV, and the Pompadour (all three prominent).

1436. *LE VITRIOL DE LUNE: Henri Béraud; *Albin Michel* [*France*]

Lyons, Paris, etc., mid-to-late 18th Century. A novel illustrating the social life and political intrigues of Louis XV's time, leading up to the painful circumstances of his death in 1774. The author's style is lucid, and he gives a vivid—if somewhat unrelieved—picture of the age on its more corrupt sides. Louis XV, Madame Du Barry, and Choiseul are introduced.

1437. *LE JARDINIER DE LA POMPADOUR: Eugène Demolder; *Société du Mercure de France* [*France*].

France, mid 18th Century, passing, at the end, from 1764 to 1789 and 1792 respectively. Another well-written story of Louis XV and the Pompadour, etc.

1438. THE KING'S INDISCRETION: Michael W. Kaye; *Stanley Paul.*

France and England, 1764. A decidedly interesting love tale, having for background an intrigue of Louis XV with regard to invasion of England. King Louis, Choiseul, and that odd personage the Chevalier d'Eon, are introduced.

1439. *THE ORDER OF RELEASE: H. de Vere Stacpoole; *Hutchinson.*

Versailles, etc., 1770. A love-story, interesting in itself, and illustrating Paris in the Choiseul and Dubarry period. Various fictional developments—*Lettre de Cachet*, escape from the Bastile, etc. Several historic figures are introduced: Louis XV, Madame Du Barry, De Choiseul, Duc de Richelieu, Jean Jacques Rousseau, and others.

N

1440. *MONSIEUR DE ROCHEFORT: H. DE VERE STACPOOLE; *Hutchinson.*
Another romance of " Old Paris," 1770. Hardly a fictional sequel to the author's *The Order of Release* (see immediately above), though the two books deal with the same place and year—even with the same people to some extent. The present tale is one of adventure—the hero unintentionally getting mixed up with politics (the Du Barry and De Choiseul factions). Louis XV, Madame Du Barry, and De Choiseul appear.

1441. THE LITTLE HUGUENOT: MAX PEMBERTON; *Juv.* *Cassell*
[*Eng.*], and *Dodd, Mead* [*U.S.A.*].
Forest of Fontainebleau, 1772. A brief, but interesting, story of a young Huguenot girl in the time of Louis XV. The king himself appears.

1442. THE BURNING GLASS [1]: " MARJORIE BOWEN "; *Collins.*
Paris in the late third quarter of the 18th Century (c. 1770) : time of the Encyclopædists, Turgot, etc. In this tragic story of Julie de Lespinasse, both D'Alembert and M. de Guibert are prominent figures.

[1] Mrs. Humphry Ward's novel, " Lady Rose's Daughter " (Smith, Elder, London, 1903 ; and Harper, New York) has sometimes been entered under a French mid-18th century heading, but this is quite inaccurate ; it is a tale of mid- to late-*nineteenth* century, and the scene is England at the time of Gladstone's Egyptian policy, etc. It is true that the picture Mrs. Ward gives of High Social Life is much more French than English, seeing that her principal characters are based on French models. The heroine, " Julie le Breton," is an imitation of the historic Julie de L'Espinasse (1732–76), though an English 19th century environment is supplied for this " Julie " of Mrs. Ward's own making. Other parallels are " Lady Henry Delafield " (Madame du Deffand) and " Montresor " (D'Alembert).

1443. *THE MEMOIRS OF BARRY LYNDON, ESQ.: W. M. THACKERAY; *Macmillan* [*Eng.*], *Dent* [*Eng.*], *Houghton Mifflin* [*U.S.A.*], *Dutton* [*U.S.A.*], *and other publishers.*
Adventures—military and social—of an unprincipled Irishman, between 1750 and 1800 (Ireland, England, Germany, Italy, and other Foreign regions). A clever piece of character-drawing, the author making the imaginary writer of these " Memoirs " betray his light-hearted scoundrelism at almost every point. There are many High Society and Gambling scenes as well as Fleet Prison sketches, while the properly historical element is considerable. The narrative covers the time of Pitt (Chatham) and the Seven Years' War (Minden, etc.), also the " Whiteboy " period in Ireland. Of the several figures introduced, one may specify: The Chevalier Charles Edward at Rome (" as drunk as any porter "), Reynolds, Johnson, Goldsmith, and Samuel Foote.

1444. *THE VIRGINIANS: W. M. THACKERAY; *Smith & Elder* [*Eng.*], *Lippincott* [*U.S.A.*] a d many others.
A kind of sequel to Esmond. England, and to a less extent, North America, in the period between 1750 and 1780. The book has been pronounced " greater as an histori-cal novel than as a novel," and, be that as it may, the series of depictions of real events and personages must always strike an intelligent reader as remarkable. Illustrates the High Social Life of England in 1756 and the years immediately following; also the Colonial period in North America embracing Braddock's defeat, and the eventual English supremacy in Canada; lastly, the origin and development of the American War of Independence. The gallery of historic portraits is extraordinarily compre-hensive, including: George II, George III, Pitt (Chatham), George Washington, Braddock, Franklin, Dinwiddie, Duke of Cumberland, Wolfe, the Howes, Burgoyne, George Selwyn, Horace Walpole, Lord Chesterfield, Dr. Johnson, Reynolds, Garrick, Richardson, the Duchess of Queensbury, Dr. Hoadley, and others.

1445. *THE ORANGE GIRL: WALTER BESANT; *Chatto & Windus* [*Eng.*], *Dodd, Mead* [*U.S.A.*].
A story of London in 1760. There are King's Bench and Newgate scenes, as well as depictions of the theatrical and general life of the city in a period of which the author had a really profound knowledge. At one point in the tale we meet with Sir John Fielding, the blind Bow Street magistrate (Sir John was the half-brother of Henry Fielding the novelist).

1446. (1) THE BATH COMEDY:
(2) INCOMPARABLE BELLAIRS (*sequel*): AGNES and EGERTON
CASTLE; 1. *Macmillan* [*Eng.*], *Stokes* [*U.S.A.*]; 2. *Chapman*
[*Eng.*], *Stokes* [*U.S.A.*].
These two " Kitty Bellairs " romances depict fashionable life in Bath between 1760
and 1770 (the joint authors intentionally omit an exact date, but they clearly imply
that the period is just after George III's accession).

1447. A GENTLEMAN OF THE ROAD: HORACE BLEACKLEY; *Lane.*
S. England (Hampshire, etc., and London) in the first decade of George III's reign.
A love and adventure story, with Newgate and Tyburn scenes, etc. There is the merest
glimpse of Sir John Fielding (see note on Besant's *Orange Girl* above).

1448. *REDGAUNTLET: SIR WALTER SCOTT; *Black, and other
publishers—English and American.*
A tale largely of the Solway Firth region, 1760 or just after (Prince Charlie being, in
Scott's own phrase, " about 40 or upwards "). There is a distinctly Jacobite atmosphere,
and the Prince himself appears. Andrew Lang remarks that this novel is partly autobiographical, reproducing some of the author's earliest experiences. The oft-praised
" Wandering Willie's Tale " is introduced.

1449. *THE CASTLE INN: STANLEY J. WEYMAN; *Smith, Elder* [*Eng.*],
Longmans [*U.S.A.*], also *J. Murray* [*Eng.*].
A stirring tale of Marlborough, Chippenham, etc., in 1767. While conveying the
social atmosphere of the period, the novel is barely historical—the one historic figure
introduced being Lord Chatham (taken ill at the Marlborough " Inn " of the title).

1450. *MISS ANGEL: ANNE ISABELLA THACKERAY; *Smith, Elder.*
Venice and London, mostly between 1765 and 1768. An interesting romance of
Angelica Kauffmann, the painter, in the period leading up to her marriage with the
adventurer De Horn. Depicts the artistic and literary society of the time, introducing
Sir Joshua Reynolds, Dr. Johnson, and Mrs. Thrale. Queen Charlotte also appears,
and there are glimpses of George III, Garrick, Boswell, Hannah More, and Fuseli.

1451. INEFFECTUAL FIRES: E. M. SMITH DAMPIER; *Melrose.*
Norfolk, London, and Florence, round about 1770. An interesting, though somewhat tragic, novel, with an atmosphere of Art. There is some good character-drawing.
The period is that of Angelica Kauffmann and Sir Joshua Reynolds—Sir Joshua himself
appearing in the story.

1452. *A NEST OF LINNETS: F. FRANKFORT MOORE; *Hutchinson*
[*Eng.*], *Appleton* [*U.S.A.*].
Bath, 1771-73. A romance of Sheridan and the beautiful Elizabeth Linley, the
singer, ending with their marriage. Crowds of other notabilities (artistic, literary,
social, etc.) are introduced, of whom the following are the most important: Sir Joshua
Reynolds, Dr. Johnson, Mrs. Thrale, Goldsmith, Horace Walpole, George Selwyn,
David Garrick, and the Duchess of Devonshire.

1453. *THE JESSAMY BRIDE: F. FRANKFORT MOORE; *Hutchinson*
[*Eng.*], *Stone* [*U.S.A.*].
London in the second decade of George III's reign. A romance of Oliver Goldsmith
and Mary Horneck, giving a picture of literary, theatrical, and artistic life. Besides
the two above-named figures, Dr. Johnson, Boswell, Garrick, Reynolds, Burke, Angelica
Kauffman, the Burneys, Mrs. Bumbury, and others appear.

1454. *THE PIOUS COQUETTE: " E. BARRINGTON "; in " The
Gallants "—*Harrap.*
A Streatham tale of the Thrales and Miss Sophy Streatfield—introducing, also, Dr.
Johnson, Boswell, the Burneys, etc.

1455. LITTLE FLOWER OF THE STREET: Dion Clayton Calthorp; *Hodder & Stoughton.*
London (largely), S. Devon, etc., Algeria and France, in the third quarter of the 18th Century. A well-told love story, with historic background and many changes of scene. "Captain Coram's Hospital" and Tyburn Tree are connected with the fictional developments, while David Garrick, Sir Joshua Reynolds, and Hogarth are all three introduced.

1456. KNIGHTS OF THE ROAD: E. Everett Green; *Juv.   Nelson.*
London (Newgate), Bath, etc. A good tale written round the efforts of John Howard, the prison reformer.

1457. MY GOD-DAUGHTER: Mary H. Debenham; *Juv.   National Society [Eng.], Whittaker [U.S.A.].*
England, 1774-80. Village life, and London at the time of the Gordon Riots.

1458. PAMELA'S HERO: Dorothea Moore; *Juv.   Blackie.*
A tale of Hampstead and the Gordon Riots (1780).

1459. BARNABY RUDGE: Charles Dickens; *Chapman & Hall; and other publishers—English and American.*
London and neighbourhood, 1780. Not one of Dickens' best novels, but, nevertheless, to some extent characteristic. Sir Charles Firth thinks that "even the spirited picture of the Gordon Riots hardly makes *Barnaby Rudge* readable," while, as a presentment of men and manners, he regards the book as unconvincing. The writer of this note is inclined to endorse that judgment. The novel is, however, included in these lists as one of the comparatively few works of fiction dealing with the Gordon Riots.

1460. *THE THIRD CIRCLE OF MAPE, THE INTERPRETER: André Maurois (trans.); in "Mape"—*Lane [Eng.], Appleton [U.S.A.].*
England (London, Bath, Clifton, etc.) c. 1773-1803. An excellent short story dealing with the Kemble family and Mrs. Siddons (née Sarah Kemble); also with the latter's two daughters and their relations with Thomas Lawrence the Painter. Covers both the period of the Kembles' travelling theatrical company and the later Drury Lane successes.

1461. *THE EXQUISITE PERDITA: "E. Barrington"; *Harrap [Eng.], Dodd, Mead [U.S.A.].*
A novel with Mary Robinson, the actress, as central figure. Many of the most noted personages of late 18th Century England are introduced more or less prominently: Sheridan, Garrick, Lord Edward Fitzgerald, the Prince of Wales (George IV), Charles James Fox, and Queen Charlotte.

1462. *PERDITA: A ROMANCE IN BIOGRAPHY[1]: Stanley V. Makower; *Hutchinson.*
Bristol, London, Paris, Aix-la-Chapelle and Windsor, 1758-1800. A fictional biography of Mary Robinson (née Darby), who played "Perdita" and other parts at Drury Lane. The author has imaginatively presented the chief episodes in the career of the unfortunate *Perdita* (for by that name she came to be known eventually); the book covers her loveless marriage, her short theatrical period, her relations with George Prince of Wales (George IV), and her literary efforts. Among the principal figures are Captain and Mrs. Darby, David Garrick, George Robert Fitzgerald, R. Brinsley Sheridan, Charles James Fox, Lord Lyttelton, and the Prince of Wales—with glimpses of several other royalties.

[1] The author has explained his literary method (see *Notes* at the end of his book) in a somewhat arresting manner. He informs his readers that, "while all the persons named in *Perdita* . . . existed in fact, and while the greater number of scenes, conversations, and incidents in this book rest on historical facts," yet the presentment is mainly in the form of fiction, in order to preserve a larger truth than could be conveyed in a purely historical narrative." These words recall Charles Reade's plea for the historical novelist as *interpreter.*

1463. CASTLE MEADOW: Emma Marshall; *Juv. Seeley.*
Norwich in 1777-78, and in 1788. A tale depicting the early years of John Crome the Landscape Painter, and of William Crotch the Musician.

1464. FANNY'S FIRST NOVEL: F. Frankfort Moore; *Hutchinson.*
A novel written round the acceptance of Fanny Burney's novel *Evelina* in the year 1778. Introduces the Burney family, Garrick, Reynolds, Mrs. Thrale, and Dr. Johnson.

1465. HELD FAST FOR ENGLAND: G. A. Henty; *Juv. Blackie* [*Eng.*], *Scribner* [*U.S.A.*].
England (Putney, etc.), 1778; and Gibraltar, 1779-83, covering General Eliott's successful defence (1780-83).

1456. *AS IT HAPPENED: "Ashton Hilliers"; *Hutchinson* [*Eng.*], *Putnam* [*U.S.A.*].
Madras, England (Chester and London) and Gibraltar, c. 1778-80. A kaleidoscopic novel dealing with many people and many places. Tells at the beginning, of the Madras cabal and the mutinous council's deposition of Lord Pigot. There are many illustrations of late 17th Century life and manners in England, including a Quaker and religious element; the later chapters describe episodes in Gibraltar at the time of its successful defence by the Governor, General Eliott. At one point in the tale there is a glimpse of John Wesley, while the Duke of Queensbury ("Old Q"), and—at Gibraltar—Sir George Eliott, are both introduced, as well as other figures.

1467. *THE BOUNTIFUL HOUR: Marion Fox; *Lane.*
Olney and London (Chelsea), 1779 onwards. This social tale begins with a picture of Cowper the poet and his friend John Newton. Later chapters illustrate the period more generally (the Methodists, etc.), and there is a glimpse of the Prince of Wales (George IV).

1468. NANCY STAIR: Elinor Macartney Lane; *Heinemann* [*Eng.*], *Appleton* [*U.S.A.*].
Mainly Edinburgh 1768, and 1786-88. A romance dealing with the beautiful, talented girl, Nancy Stair, and telling in particular of her relations with Robert Burns. A murder is one of the important elements in the story. The poet Burns himself appears, and is sympathetically—if somewhat critically—drawn.

1469. A PROPHET'S REWARD: Mrs. E. H. Strain; *Blackwood.*
Scotland (Glasgow district) in the period, 1778-93. A story reflecting the political ideals before and during the French Revolution.

1470. OVER THE HILLS AND FAR AWAY: Guy Fleming; *Longmans.*
Galloway (Kirkcudbright and Solway Firth region), also Edinburgh and England, round about the year 1779. A story with a smuggling element, telling also of adventures during a journey to London by road, and of perils encountered on the return to Scotland by sea. It is through his account of the sea voyage just named that the author is able to introduce his readers to historical incidents, viz., the naval exploits of the redoubtable Paul Jones off the East Coast of Britain.

1471. *THE IMMACULATE YOUNG MINISTER: Mathilda Malling (trans.); *Constable.*
London district, Tunbridge Wells, Windsor, Paris and Fontainebleau, 1783-88. An interesting historical romance with William Pitt as the central figure. The High Society and Politics of the period are vividly presented. One of the best things in the book is the description of a debate in Parliament showing Pitt and Fox in furious antagonism. On the purely fictional side there are some exciting developments. Besides Pitt and Fox, an immense number of notabilities appear. The Prince of Wales (adverse portrait) is introduced somewhat prominently, and there are glimpses of Horace Walpole, William Wilberforce, the Duke of Queensberry ("Old Q"), Sheridan, Edmund Burke, Windham, Queen Marie Antoinette, and others.

1472. IN FOUR REIGNS: Emma Marshall; *Juv. Seeley* [*Eng.*], *Dutton* [*U.S.A.*].
Windsor, Sidmouth, Brighton, etc., in the period 1785-1842. The "four reigns" covered in the tale are: George III, George IV, William IV, and Victoria.

1473. A ROSE OF OLD QUEBEC: Anna Hollingsworth Wharton; *Lippincott.*
Quebec and London, between 1780 and 1790. An unpretentious, but pleasing, romance of Mary Thompson and Nelson—the latter being first introduced as "Captain" (1781). Other historic figures are: Fox, Horace Walpole, and the Duchess of Devonshire. There are, also, glimpses of the Sheridans, Miss Burney, Mrs. Piozzi, and Lady Hamilton.

1474. A DIANA OF QUEBEC: Jean McIlwraith; *Smith, Elder.*
Quebec, 1782-87. Nelson as "Captain" appears in this novel prominently—something in the nature of a love-affair developing between him and the heroine. The lady, however, is quite able at the end of the story to survive the news of Nelson's marriage to the widow, Mrs. Nesbit. Prince William Henry is among the personages introduced.

1475. HARTLEY HOUSE, CALCUTTA: Anonymous; *Thacker* [*India*].
India in the time of Warren Hastings. A new edition of this old work (originally published in 1789) was brought out by Thacker in 1909.

1476. *WARREN OF OUDH: Richard B. Gamon; *Erskine Macdonald.*
Bengal, etc., c. 1774-75. An autobiographical novel of India in the Warren Hastings period. There is a considerable French element (scheming agent of Louis XVI, etc.), and the whole romance shows knowledge of the historical conditions. There are glimpses of Warren Hastings himself, also of Sir Elijah Impey (recently appointed Chief-Justice of Bengal), and [Sir] Philip Francis, to whose authorship the famous *Letters of Junius* have sometimes been attributed.

1477. *THE GREAT PROCONSUL: "Sydney C. Grier"; *Blackwood.*
An able apology for Warren Hastings under the form of an imaginary diary by a lady in his family. The novel illustrates events in India during the period 1777-85, and ends in Bath a few months after Hastings' death, 1818. The leading historical figures of the time are introduced.

1478. *THE POT OF BASIL: Bernard Capes; *Constable.*
N. Italy, 1759. A very interesting romance of Isabella, eldest child of Philip, Duke of Parma, and grand-daughter of Louis XV of France. The story is written round the historic episode of the marriage-arrangement between Isabella and the young Archduke Joseph of Austria (afterwards Joseph II Emperor of Germany). But the real interest is in the fictional developments.

1479. THE ITALIAN: Mrs. Ann Radcliffe; *Routledge.*
Naples and district about 1760: the Inquisition. Considered one of Mrs. Radcliffe's best novels by competent critics.

1480. *THE WHIRLWIND OF PASSION: Edna Worthley Underwood; *Hurst & Blackett.*
Russia (St. Petersburg, etc.) mainly c. 1760-1762. An historical romance largely dealing with Catherine Alexevna (afterwards Catherine II), and depicting the Russian Court plots, etc., of an unhappy time. The earlier chapters introduce the Empress Elizabeth (Elizabeth Petrovna) at the close of her reign, while in the concluding section Gregory Orlov and Peter III (his murder) appear.

1481. *SHOES OF GOLD: Hamilton Drummond; *Stanley Paul.*
France and (chiefly) Russia, 1761-62. An exciting historical romance. A Frenchman is sent on a mission to St. Petersburg to gain Russia's friendship with France, and the description of his Russian experience illustrates the rivalries and intrigues which resulted in the murder of Czar Peter III by Alexius Orloff (the novel ends with a description of this crime). Many historical figures are introduced: Louis XV, Choiseul, and the Duc de Richelieu in the early French chapters; while, in the main part of the story, Catherine (afterwards Catherine II, called " the Great ") and Peter III are outstanding figures—as, also, are the brothers Gregory and Alexius Orloff.

1482. THE DIARY OF A YOUNG LADY OF FASHION IN THE YEAR 1764-1765, By Cleone Knox, edited by her Kinsman Alexander Blacker Kerr: Magdalen King-Hall; *Thornton Butterworth.*
The fictional diary (March, 1764 to May, 1765) of a young Irish lady who attains her 21st year within the period specified. She makes the " Grand Tour," and her diary jottings relate some of her experiences and impressions in Ireland, Derbyshire, Northampton, London, Bath, France, Switzerland, and Venice. There are many allusions to the personages of the time, such as George III and his Queen, the French Royalties, etc. The book illustrates late 18th Century " high life " on its more frivolous side.

1483. *THE REMINISCENCES OF SIR BARRINGTON BEAUMONT, BART.: Michael Barrington; *Blackwood.*
These " reminiscences " (supposed to have been written in 1812 by an Englishman of high social position) deal mainly with the period, 1778-1810, the scenes being alternately London, Paris, and Sweden. The outstanding historical figure is Count Axel Fersen, and the main episodes in his adventurous career are well illustrated. The narrative covers the period before, during, and after the French Revolution, but public events are, for the most part, lightly touched. The standpoint throughout is Royalist, Fersen's devotion to Marie Antoinette being almost the dominating theme of the book. Besides Fersen and the unfortunate Queen of France, there are numerous historic personages; George Selwyn, Horace Walpole, and C. J. Fox appear almost at once, while there are glimpses of, or special allusions to, the following: Gustavus III of Sweden, Louis XVI of France, Madame de Staël, Princesse de Lamballe, Talleyrand, and Bonaparte.

1484. *THE COMPANY OF THE MARJOLAINE: John Buchan; in " The Moon Endureth "—*Blackwood* [Eng.], *Sturgis* [U.S.A.], also *Nelson.*
An Englishman travelling in Italy late 18th Century, encounters Prince Charles Edward grown into an elderly sot.

1485. *THE VALLEY OF DECISION: Edith Wharton; *Murray* [Eng.], *Scribner* [U.S.A.]*
A novel of Italian life and manners in the period 1774-95. Count Vittorio Alfieri, the poet, is introduced.

1486. *THE CAPTAIN'S DAUGHTER: Alexander S. Pushkin (trans.); in " The Captain's Daughter, and Other Tales "—*Hodder & Stoughton.*
Russia (Province of Orenburg), 1772-74: time of Catherine II. A fairly long and decidedly striking tale of the Cossack Rising under Emilian Pougatcheff.

1487. *THE STRANGE STORY OF RAB RABY: Maurus Jókai (trans.); *Jarrold.*
Hungary in the time of the Emperor Joseph II, 1780-90. A novel telling of the hero's struggles as a social reformer.

1488. THE RED MARSHAL: LIEUT.-COL. GORDON CASSERLEY; *Philip Allan.*
France, Germany, Italy, etc., 1785. A story which deals mainly with the liberation of Carlonia, a small State in the Austrian frontier region. Introduces Louis XVI, Marie Antoinette, and a crowd of historic figures.

1489. *DER SCHILLER—ROMAN: WALTER VON MOLO; *Albert Langen* [*Germany*].
Germany in late 18th Century. A novel of the poet Schiller.

1490. THE COURTIER STOOPS: J. H. YOXALL; *Smith, Elder.*
Germany, mainly in late 18th Century (round about 1790). A romance of Goethe in Weimar. The later portions of the book pass rapidly through the French Revolution and Napoleonic War periods up to Goethe's death (1832).

1491. *THE EAGLE'S NEST: ALLAN MCAULAY; *Lane.*
Corsica, 1769, but mostly 1779-92. An interesting historical romance, introducing Napoleon as a young man, and certain other members of the Bonaparte family, viz., Charles and Letizia—Napoleon's father and mother, and his younger brother, Lucien. Another prominent figure is General Paoli, whose return to the island in the French Revolution period is one of the main events brought into the story. In the depiction of the youthful Napoleon there are some neat touches—as, for instance, where he is made to say: " I have no friends in Paris . . . also no money or very little."

1492. *THE KING WITH TWO FACES: MARY E. COLERIDGE; *Arnold* [*Eng.*], *Lane* [*U.S.A.*].
An historical novel of real distinction, dealing with Sweden and France in the period, 1788-92. Gustavus III of Sweden and Hans Axel Comte de Fersen (Swedish Marshal) are the two outstanding figures, while in the French scenes Madame de Staël is greatly to the fore. Other historic personages are Marmontel, Marie Antoinette, and Louis XVI. There is, also, a glimpse of Mirabeau.

1493. *THE OWL'S HOUSE:
*HIGH NOON (*sequel*):
*THE WEST WIND (*sequel*): CROSBIE GARSTIN; *Heinemann* [*Eng.*], *Stokes* [*U.S.A.*].
Mainly Cornwall, Morocco, West Indies, and Spain, from the middle of the 18th Century to the beginning of the 19th. A remarkable series of connected tales, depicting in realistic fashion · half-savage types of character among gypsies, smugglers, pirates, etc., and telling, more especially, of a certain family of " Penhales "—small Cornish Squires. The outstanding figure in all three romances is " Ortho Penhale," whose amazing experiences as (amongst other things) smuggler, slave in Barbary, captain of Arab lancers, seaman in the Navy, slaver captain and privateer captain, are narrated with much descriptive power as well as imaginative insight. There is a background of history—one of the most noteworthy historic illustrations being the description (in *High Noon*) of Rodney's naval victory over De Grasse and the French fleet, near the island of St. Lucia, in 1782.

1494. *THE CONQUEROR: GERTRUDE FRANKLIN ATHERTON; *Macmillan.*
West Indies and N. America, 1757-1804. A romance depicting the career of Alexander Hamilton, and illustrating both the American Revolution and the years following it. While Hamilton is the outstanding figure, there are many other historic personages, including Washington, Schuyler, Lafayette, Adams, Madison, Jefferson, and (of course) Aaron Burr.

1495. (1)*HUGH WYNNE, FREE QUAKER:
(2)*THE RED CITY (sequel): S. WEIR MITCHELL; 1. *Fisher Unwin* [*Eng.*], *Century* [*U.S.A.*]; 2. *Macmillan* [*Eng.*], *Century* [*U.S.A.*].

(1) Philadelphia, etc., mainly in the period 1763-83. Imaginary memoirs of a Quaker, telling of various experiences in the time before, during, and after the Revolution. There is a more or less rapid sketch of the War period (the " Friends of Liberty," the Declaration of Independence, etc.), and the Battle of Germantown (1777) is singled out for special notice. George Washington, Lafayette, Alexander Hamilton, and Major André appear, while there are glimpses of Patrick Henry and Jefferson.

(2) Philadelphia, 1792-95. This second novel (*sequel*), in which a French noble loves a Quaker maiden, deals with the time of Washington's Second Administration. when the Federalists led by Hamilton, were opposed by the Republicans led by Jefferson, The period was marked by wild scenes in Philadelphia (the Jacobin Clubs, etc.), and the story reflects these disturbances. Jefferson, Alexander Hamilton, Edmund Randolph, and (at the end) George Washington, all appear.

1496. *RICHARD CARVEL: WINSTON CHURCHILL; *Macmillan.*
N. America (Maryland), Scotland (Galloway), and England (London), 1765-75. An unusually interesting historical novel depicting the events leading up to, as well as the actual beginning of, the American Revolution. George Washington and Paul Jones are the outstanding American figures; while, in the somewhat lengthy section dealing with the London of 1770, Charles James Fox and Horace Walpole are prominent —Garrick also appearing.

1497. *THE GREEN MOUNTAIN BOYS: DANIEL P. THOMPSON; *Burt* [*U.S.A.*].
Vermont and other regions, c. 1768-77. This is called an " historical tale of the early settlement of Vermont," but it is really composed of two parts—the first dealing with the seven years preceding the Revolutionary War, when the land controversy (" New Hampshire Grants ") was to the fore; the second part illustrating the War of Independence (Ticonderoga and the Schuyler v. Burgoyne struggle). Benedict Arnold appears.

1498. IN THE DAYS OF POOR RICHARD: IRVING BACHELLER; *Bobbs-Merrill* [*U.S.A.*].
A tale primarily of the American Revolution, but covering the period 1768-87. The reader is shown both sides of the Atlantic, and many historic figures are introduced or glimpsed: John Adams, Franklin, Paine, Lord Howe, Edmund Burke, George Washington, etc.

1499. *GILMAN OF REDFORD: W. STEARNS DAVIS; *Macmillan.*
Boston and Harvard College, 1770-75. An historical romance, having for its hero a young student of Harvard. Depicts the life and politics of the time, covering the " Boston Tea Party," etc. Several historic figures are introduced, notably Samuel Adams and Paul Revere.

1500. *DRUMS: JAMES BOYD; *Fisher Unwin* [*Eng.*], *Scribner.* [*U.S.A.*]
North Carolina, London, Galloway, etc., 1771-80. A vivid romance of the American War of Independence period, with a considerable background of history. Introduces prominently Captain Paul Jones, and describes episodes connected with his cruising in British waters. Accounts of a sea-fight, etc. Charles James Fox appears in the London part of the story.

1501. *SPANISH BAYONET: STEPHEN VINCENT BENÉT; *Heinemann* [*Eng*], *Doran* [*U.S.A.*].
The Floridas (St. Augustine), 1774: the *Prologue* is Minorca, 1769. A decidedly original novel, illustrating life in the Southern Colonies of North America just before the War of Independence.

1502. (1)*CARDIGAN:
     (2)*THE MAID-AT-ARMS: ROBERT W. CHAMBERS; *Constable*
     [*Eng.*], *Harper* [*U.S.A.*].
These two novels are the first two volumes of the author's series depicting the Johnsons and other important families of New York Province in the American Revolution period. They are selected as likely to interest readers most.
     (1) Province of New York (northern part), also the Alleghany region and other localities including Boston, Lexington, and Albany, in the years 1774-75. Deals especially with life on Sir William Johnson's estate, and illustrates the beginning of the trouble between King and Colony. There is much about the Indians (the " Six Nations," etc.) and their attitude when the British were seeking alliance; while the Minute Men's Club and other Revolutionary movements and events are brought into the story. Sir William Johnson, Governor Tryon, Lord Dunmore, Patrick Henry, Captain Walter Butler, Paul Revere, and other historic figures appear.
     (2) Tryon County and the forests of the Kingsland district, etc., 1777. Depicts the time when the War was " sweeping towards the Mohawk Valley," and when the first serious split occurred in the Iroquois Confederacy. The principal historic event introduced is the Battle of Oriskany in which the patriots defeated the combined forces of British, Tories, and Mohawks. The whole story conveys the Revolution atmosphere and is full of allusions to Burgoyne, Clinton and other important personages. Sir John Johnson (son of Sir William), the Butlers, and General Schuyler are among those who actually appear.

1503. THE CAMP FIRE OF MAD ANTHONY: EVERETT T.
     TOMLINSON; *Juv. Houghton Mifflin* [*U.S.A.*].
A good tale of the Pennsylvania troops under Wayne (" Mad Anthony ") in the period, 1774-76.

1504. THE LITTLE RED FOOT: ROBERT W. CHAMBERS; *Hodder
     & Stoughton* [*Eng.*], *Doran* [*U.S.A.*].
North America, mainly in the period 1774-77. A novel dealing, on somewhat unusual lines, with the Indians (Iroquois). Illustrates the time of Burgoyne's Expedition and the British-Indian attack.

1505. *IN THE VALLEY: HAROLD FREDERIC; *Heinemann* [*Eng.*],
     Scribner [*U.S.A.*].
The Mohawk Valley, Albany, and the Lake Country, mainly in the period 1774-78. A new England tale of the Revolutionary War period, dealing to a large extent with the Indians, and introducing the Battle of Oriskany when the British and Indian force which had started from Oswego, was met and defeated. General Schuyler appears, and there is a considerable Johnson-Butler element.

1506. HEARTS COURAGEOUS: HALLIE ERMINIE RIVES; *Hodder
     & Stoughton* [*Eng.*], *Bowen-Merrill* [*U.S.A.*].
Virginia, Philadelphia, and York Town, 1774-81. An historical romance illustrating the period just before and during the American War of Independence up to the surrender of Cornwallis. Many historic personages appear, including Patrick Henry, Jefferson, Franklin, and Washington; also Lords Fairfax, Howe, and Cornwallis.

1507. TRUE TO THE OLD FLAG: G. A. HENTY; *Juv. Blackie* [*Eng.*],
     Scribner [*U.S.A.*].
A tale of the American War of Independence, 1774-81, covering Bunker Hill, Saratoga, etc., down to the surrender of Lord Cornwallis at Yorktown.

1508. JANICE MEREDITH: PAUL LEICESTER FORD; *Constable* [*Eng.*],
     Dodd, Mead [*U.S.A.*].
New Jersey (Brunswick), New York, and Virginia, 1774-82. A somewhat emotional novel of the American Revolution, covering—though not largely describing—the various events of the War. George Washington, Lord Cornwallis and André all three appear in the story, while there are numerous allusions to other personages of the time: Burgoyne, Gates, Tarleton, Howe, Jefferson, Lafayette, Hamilton, Wayne, etc.

1509. ERSKINE DALE, PIONEER: John Fox; *Hodder & Stoughton* [*Eng.*], *Scribner* [*U.S.A.*].
Virginia (Williamsburg) and Kentucky between 1774 and 1784. Deals with the American Revolution period, but is mainly a tale of adventures among the Indians.

1510. LIONEL LINCOLN; OR, THE LEAGUER OF BOSTON: J. Fenimore Cooper; *Juv.* *Routledge* [*Eng.*], *Putnam* [*U.S.A.*].
Boston, Charlestown, etc., 1775. A story of the early stages in the American War of Independence, covering the Battles of Lexington and Bunker Hill. General Burgoyne and other historic figures appear. There is, also, a glimpse of George Washington.

1511. AT THE SIEGE OF QUEBEC: James Otis Kaler; *Juv.* *Dana Estes* [*U.S.A.*].
A tale of Benedict Arnold's expedition to Quebec, and of the joint attack upon the city by Arnold and Montgomery (death of the latter) in 1775.

1512. PHILIP WINWOOD: R. Neilson Stephens; *Chatto & Windus* [*Eng.*], *Page* [*U.S.A.*].
New York and London, 1763-86. A romance illustrating the period named, especially the American War of Independence from 1775 up to its close. There are glimpses of George Washington and others. In the much shorter English section of the book, Sheridan is introduced (London, 1786).

1513. *POLLY TROTTER, PATRIOT: Emilie Benson Knipe and and Alden Arthur Knipe; *Juv.* *Macmillan.*
A story of New York in the earlier stages of the American Revolution, 1775-76. Reflects the general movements of the time, besides dealing with a particular plot against George Washington. Alexander Hamilton, Washington, Governor Tryon, and Nathan Hale appear more or less prominently, while there are numerous references to such men as General Charles Lee, Howe, Israel Putnam, Revere, etc.

1514. *A MAID OF '76: Emilie Benson Knipe and Alden Arthur Knipe; *Juv.* *Macmillan.*
N. America (a Massachusetts village and Boston), also England (London), 1775-76. Adventures of an American girl who, while her family favour the "loyalist" side, is herself a "patriot." Depicts the early Revolutionary period (spies, etc.), and introduces Washington and Gage, besides describing—in the English section—an interview with George III (Princess Elizabeth also appears).

1515. *THE CAROLINIAN: Rafael Sabatini; *Hutchinson* [*Eng.*], *Houghton Mifflin* [*U.S.A.*].
South Carolina (Charles Town) mainly in 1775 and 1779. A stirring romance of the time immediately preceding the War of Independence ("Sons of Liberty," etc.), *and* of the War in its later stages. A "spy" element adds to the fictional interest. Lord William Campbell, Governor of the Province of South Carolina, and other historic figures appear.

1516. (1)*HOWE'S MASQUERADE:
(2)*OLD ESTHER DUDLEY: Nathaniel Hawthorne; in "Twice Told Tales"—*Dent* [*Eng.*], *Dutton* [*U.S.A.*]; also in the separate volume, "Legends of the Province House"—*Houghton Mifflin* [*U.S.A.*].
These two stories (being the first and the fourth respectively of the *Legends of the Province House* series) have for historical background: (1) the latter part of the Siege of Boston (winter of 1775-76; (2) the departure (1776) of the British from the city, and the days following Washington's entry. Sir William Howe, the British General, appears in both tales, while John Hancock (Republican governor) is briefly introduced at the end of the second.

1517. (1)*THE LUCKY SIXPENCE:
    (2)*BEATRICE OF DENEWOOD (*sequel*): EMILIE BENSON
    KNIPE and ALDEN ARTHUR KNIPE; *Juv.   Century [U.S.A.].*
(1) England and Pennsylvania, mainly in the period 1775-78.   A girl's adventures
(both sea and land) at the beginning of the American War of Independence.   There
is a substantial background of history—Admiral Howe and George Washington being
introduced.
(2) S.E. England (Sussex, Kent and London) and N. America (Philadelphia, Mount
Vernon, etc.), 1778-81.   Continues the girlish record of *The Lucky Sixpence*, illustrating
the later developments of the American Revolution, and life on both sides of the Atlantic
in that period.   Many notabilities appear, including Charles James Fox, Horace
Walpole, and Sir Joshua Reynolds in the English chapters; George Washington, Madame
Washington, Benedict Arnold, and Lord Cornwallis in the American sections.   Virtually
ends with the surrender of Yorktown.

1518. WASHINGTON'S YOUNG AIDS: EVERETT T. TOMLINSON;
    Juv.   Wilde [U.S.A.].
New Jersey, 1776-77.   A tale illustrating Washington's highly important New Jersey
Campaign.

1519. *THE RIDER IN THE GREEN MASK: RUPERT SARGENT
    HOLLAND; *Juv.   Lippincott.*
Philadelphia, Chester (Delaware), etc., and France (Paris and Bordeaux), 1776-78.
Depicts the earlier stages of the American Revolution, including the Declaration.   The
hero saves Dr. Franklin, is taken prisoner by the British, and has further experiences with
a French privateer, etc.   The tale ends with Washington at Valley Forge and the
English leaving Philadelphia.   Franklin is the most prominent historic figure, and
Lafayette is also to the fore.

1520. *THE SUN OF SARATOGA: JOSEPH A. ALTSHELER; *Juv.*
    Appleton.
Burgoyne's Expedition, 1777.   An interesting story of the Expedition, and the events
culminating in the capture of Burgoyne and his entire army at Saratoga.

1521. *THE PILOT: J. FENIMORE COOPER; *Juv.   Routledge [Eng.],*
    Putnam [U.S.A.].
A tale of the American War of Independence—the scenes being on and off the Coast
of North-east England about 1777 (time of Paul Jones's exploits in the North Sea).
In certain portions of this romance, the author shows exceptional knowledge of matters
nautical.

1522. A VENTURE IN 1777: S. WEIR MITCHELL; *Juv.   Jacobs [U.S.A.].*
Story of three boys in Philadelphia: George Washington in Valley Forge, etc.

1523. MY SWORD FOR LAFAYETTE: MAX PEMBERTON; *Hodder*
    & Stoughton [Eng.], Dodd, Mead [U.S.A.].
Begins with France and America (War of Independence), 1777-78; then passes to
England, 1788; lastly, France and Germany during the Revolution period (Lafayette's
imprisonment by the Austrians).

1524. THE TORY LOVER: SARAH ORNE JEWETT; *Smith, Elder [Eng.],*
    Houghton Mifflin [U.S.A.].
America, France and England, 1777-78.   A story which has for its outstanding figure
the redoubtable Paul Jones.   Introduces the historic incident of his descent on the
Solway (1778).   Benjamin Franklin appears.

1525. *PATRIOT AND TORY: Edward S. Ellis; *Juv.* *Winston* [U.S.A.].
New Jersey, 1778. A carefully authenticated historical tale, having for its central event, the Battle of Monmouth, which occurred after George Washington had followed up the British forces as they were trying to cross New Jersey. The Battle was barely won by the Americans. On this occasion General Charles Lee's behaviour was such as to awaken Washington's suspicion—Lee being afterwards tried by court-martial, and, after a year's suspension, dismissed by Congress. The story touches other historical figures, besides those just mentioned.

1526. THE RED CHIEF: Everett T. Tomlinson; *Juv.* *Houghton Mifflin.*
Cherry Valley Massacre, 1778. One of several terrible massacres by Iroquois bands, under Tory captains, in the same year.

1527. LONG KNIVES: G. Cary Eggleston; *Juv.* *Lothrop* [U.S.A.].
A good tale of the difficult expedition (1778-79) made by Captain George Rogers Clark of Virginia, to Illinois; his object was to capture the British forts in the West.

1528. *THE CROSSING: Winston Churchill; *Macmillan.*
A kind of sequel to *Richard Carvel*, describing N. America (Charlestown, St. Louis, New Orleans, etc.), mainly in the period 1778-1803. Time of George R. Clark's military achievements in the West, and of Daniel Boone's Wilderness Road, etc. Shows the growth of political ideas, besides giving a picture of events and life generally in the Revolution and post-Revolution periods. Virtually ends with the Louisiana Purchase. Of the various historic figures, Clark is the most prominent. There are glimpses of Boone and Andrew Jackson.

1529. THE YOUNG TRAILERS:
THE KEEPERS OF THE TRAIL:
THE SCOUTS OF THE VALLEY:
THE FOREST RUNNERS:
THE FREE RANGERS:
THE RIFLEMEN OF THE OHIO:
THE BORDER WATCH:
THE EYES OF THE WOODS: Joseph A. Altsheler; *Juv.* *Appleton.*
These eight stories—together forming *The Young Trailers Series*—tell of juvenile adventure in the time of the Indian fighting in Kentucky, etc., late 18th Century (Revolutionary War period). The volumes of the series have a fictional connection.

1530. MARCHING AGAINST THE IROQUOIS: Everett T. Tomlinson; *Juv.* *Houghton Mifflin* [U.S.A.]
A tale of General Sullivan's expedition in the Iroquois country, 1779.

1531. THE PATHFINDERS OF THE REVOLUTION: William E. Griffis; *Juv.* *Wilde* [U.S.A.].
" A story of the Great Wilderness and Lake Region of New York " (sub-title). Another good fictional presentment of General Sullivan and the Indians.

1532. MADAM CONSTANTIA: Jefferson Carter; *Longmans.*
South Carolina, 1780. A Northumbrian Englishman relates his experiences as prisoner of war in the American Revolution period. The book is more of an interesting love and adventure story than an historical novel. There is, however, a " spy " element, and Marion, the Revolutionary leader, appears.

1533. A NEW ENGLAND MAID: Eliza F. Pollard; *Juv. Blackie.*
West Point and Benedict Arnold. A story leading up to the time when Arnold—
as Commander at West Point—turned traitor. George Washington and Major Arnold
are also introduced.

1534. MR. ARNOLD: Francis Lynde; *Methuen [Eng.], Bobbs-Merrill
    [U.S.A.].*
Virginia, 1780. A romance written round the historic figure of Benedict Arnold
(the hero of the story tries to kidnap him). Illustrates a late period in the American
Revolution, introducing, besides Arnold, Colonel Alexander Hamilton and Sir Henry
Clinton.

1535. A TRAITOR'S ESCAPE: James Otis Kaler; *Juv. Wilde
    [U.S.A.].*
A tale of the autumn of 1780, when the traitor, Benedict Arnold, was making his escape
to the British Army. Describes the various attempts to capture him.

1536. *THE SPY: A TALE OF NEUTRAL GROUND: James Feni-
    more Cooper; *Juv. Routledge [Eng.], Putnam [U.S.A.].*
N. America, 1780. The term " neutral ground " in the sub-title covered the locality
" between the royal barracks in New York City and the American outposts on the
Hudson," where a mixed population of loyalists and British sympathisers mistrusted
one another. Not many historic figures or events are introduced (though Washington
appears in the closing pages), but the tale well illustrates the later Revolution period,
and is full of allusions to such men as Burgoyne, Gates, Tarleton, Sumter, etc.

1537. *SCOUTING FOR WASHINGTON:
    *MORGAN'S MEN (sequel):
    *ON GUARD! AGAINST TORY AND TARLETON (sequel):
    *SCOUTING FOR LIGHT HORSE HARRY (sequel):
    John Preston True; *Juv. Little, Brown [U.S.A.].*
These four connected stories—called *The Stuart Schuyler Series* after the fictional youth
" Stuart Schuyler " who appears in all of them—deal with the American Revolution
from its earlier period. Taken as a consecutive narrative, these volumes cover in turn:
The early doings of the British in the time of Sumter and Tarleton; Greene's campaign
in South Carolina when a part of his men were led by Daniel Morgan at the Battle of
Cowpens (1781); the fruitless attempt of Cornwallis and Tarleton, after Morgan's
victory at Cowpens, to prevent a junction between Greene and Morgan in North Carolina,
and the Battle of Guilford Court House (British victory of a kind); lastly, the help given
to Greene by Colonel Henry Lee (father of the Civil War Confederate General) with
his " Light Horse " legion, the Taking of Fort Watson, and Lord Rawdon's victory
over Greene. Numerous historical figures appear.

1538. *THE FORAYERS[1]
    *EUTAW (sequel): William Gilmore Simms; *Lovell [U.S.A.].*
South Carolina in 1781. These two excellent novels deal with the later stages of the
American War of Independence, and the circumstances of General Nathanael Greene's
campaign in South Carolina. The various events of the famous " Dog Days " struggle
are covered, as well as the culminating blow against the British forces at Eutaw Springs,
with which battle the *sequel* virtually ends. One of the historic personages introduced
is Lord Edward Fitzgerald (in regard to whom the author raises certain points), while
Lord Rawdon, Greene, Marion, Sumter, Lee, Washington, and many other figures
appear.

[1] Two good examples of the author's series of Revolutionary Tales which have an historical connection and depict the transitional periods of the War in South Carolina. Four of the novels, viz., " The
Partisan," " Mellichampe," " Katharine Walton," and " The Scout " (originally " The Kinsman "), cover
the time from the Fall of Charleston to the Siege of Ninety-Six, introducing men like Gates, Marion,
Cornwallis, Tarleton, etc. " The Forayers " and " Eutaw " carry on the historical record, while another
novel " Woodcraft " (originally " The Sword and the Distaff ") concludes the historical sequence with
an account of the final evacuation of Charleston by the British in December, 1732. Dr. Erskine (in
Leading American Novelists) thinks that " Woodcraft " is " in many aspects the best of the series,"
but as an equal authority (Prof. Trent), when estimating the two novels here chosen, places them
" among the most interesting of all Simms' Revolutionary romances," my selection may stand. As
there is a certain sameness in the wonderful experiences described in these tales, two volumes are
more likely to please the average reader than seven.

1539. (1)*MEMOIRS OF A PHYSICIAN:
(2)*THE QUEEN'S NECKLACE:
(3)*ANGE PITOU:
(4)*LA COMTESSE DE CHARNY:
(5)*LE CHEVALIER DE MAISON ROUGE: Alexandre
Dumas (trans.); *Dent* [*Eng.*], *Little, Brown* [*U.S.A.*].

A series of connected romances covering the main events in the years preceding and
during the French Revolution.

(1) France, 1770-74. Deals with the last few years of Louis XV's reign, ending with
an account of his death. Among the more prominent of the many historic figures are
the King himself, Madame Du Barry, Choiseul, Maréchal de Richelieu, Maria Theresa,
and Marie Antoinette. Other noteworthy " appearances " are Cardinal de Rohan,
Balsamo, Swedenborg, Paul Jones, Rousseau, Voltaire, Holbach, Marmontel, and
Diderot.

(2) France, 1784-85. The famous Necklace affair (as the title indicates) is the
main historic theme round which the story turns. Louis XVI, Marie Antoinette, and
Cardinal de Rohan are much to the fore. One may specify, also, Princesse de Lamballe,
Duc d'Orléans, Maréchal de Richelieu, Madame Du Barry, Cagliostro, Lafayette,
Necker, Dr. Mesmer, Robespierre, and Marat.

(3) France in 1789. Time of the storming of the Bastille which, along with other
historic incidents, is fully described. Numerous figures of note appear, including
Louis XVI, Marie Antoinette, Philippe Duc d'Orléans, Lafayette, Necker, Madame
de Staël, Turgot, Desmoulins, Marat, and Danton.

(4) France, 1789-94. The flight of the Royal Family is one of the main incidents
introduced, and Mirabeau comes in for special mention and depiction. The usual
crowd of notabilities: The various Royalties and Princesse de Lamballe, Necker, Marat,
Robespierre, Philippe Duc d'Orléans, Rouget de Lisle, Fouquier Tinville, Cagliostro,
Thomas Paine, Barras, Desmoulins, Dr. Guillotin, " Lieutenant " Bonaparte, etc.

(5) France, 1793. A romance of the Reign of Terror, dealing with such subjects
as: Marie Antoinette in the Temple, and, afterwards, in the Conciergerie; the fate of
the Dauphin; certain attempts to rescue the captive Royalties; and, lastly, the Queen's
execution. Robespierre and Danton are among the most important historic figures.

1540. *A TALE OF TWO CITIES: Charles Dickens; *Chapman &
Hall, and numerous other publishers.*

England and France, 1775-93 (mostly 1775-76 and 1789-93). This famous story
was written largely under Carlyle's influence; it gives a general, rather than a detailed,
picture of the French Revolution period in London and Paris. The storming of the
Bastille is one of the few historical events introduced, and individual celebrities scarcely
appear. At the same time, the descriptions of the *quartier* St. Antoine and of the
Conciergerie, etc., during the Terror, yield a distinctly historical impression. Some
critics find the book rather misleading in its highly-coloured emphasis, while they admit
its interest as fiction.

1541. *THE ADVENTURES OF FRANÇOIS: FOUNDLING, THIEF
JUGGLER, AND FENCING-MASTER: S. Weir Mitchell;
Macmillan [*Eng.*], *Century* [*U.S.A.*].

France (mainly Paris), 1777-94; the tale, however, is primarily one of the French
Revolution between 1790 and 1793. As the sub-title suggests, the fictional " adventure "
interest of the book predominates over the historical, although such personages as Talma
(the tragedian) and Robespierre are introduced.

1542. OUR LADY OF DARKNESS: Bernard Capes; *Blackwood*
[*Eng.*], *Dodd, Mead* [*U.S.A.*].

England (London and Bury St. Edmunds region), Liége, and Paris, etc., mainly in
the period between 1780 and 1793. A story with the French Revolution to some extent
as background. Several historical figures appear, including David the Painter, the
Chevalier d'Eon, Madame de Genlis, the Duke of Orleans (Philippe Égalité), and
Sheridan.

1543. *THE BATTLE OF THE STRONG: Gilbert Parker; *Methuen* [*Eng.*], *Houghton Mifflin* [*U.S.A.*].
A romance of Jersey and France, mainly in the period 1781 to 1795. Besides the French invasion of Jersey described in the opening pages, there is a further historical element introduced through the hero serving in the Vendean army. The whole novel conveys the atmosphere of the French Revolution period.

1544. A ROGUE'S TRAGEDY: Bernard Capes; *Methuen*.
Savoy and Turin in 1783 and the few years following. A grim story of murder, etc., in the time of Victor-Amadeus III, titular king of Sardinia, and Duke of Savoy and Piedmont.

1545. *THE ROSE OF BÉARN: E. G. Eversleigh; *Stanley Paul*.
S.W. France (Bayonne region and Toulouse, etc.), also Paris, 1788-89. A vivid romance depicting the period just before and just after the beginning of the French Revolution. Many historic figures, including Robespierre, Mirabeau, Philippe Égalité, Danton, Louis XVI, Marie Antoinette, Madame de Lamballe, and Camille Desmoulins.

1546. *SCARAMOUCHE: Rafael Sabatini; *Hutchinson* [*Eng.*], *Houghton Mifflin* [*U.S.A.*].
Brittany (Rennes and Nantes) and Paris, 1788-92. An excellent blending of fiction and history. In the earlier chapters there is a good picture of the period immediately preceding the Revolution (Necker and the political situation generally), while later portions of the tale illustrate the Revolution itself up to the massacre of the Swiss Guard and the Jacobin Club supremacy. Danton appears, and there are glimpses of Mirabeau and Robespierre.

1547. *THE GOD OF CLAY: H. C. Bailey; *Hutchinson* [*Eng.*], *Brentano's* [*U.S.A.*].
A novel illustrating, in striking manner, the career of Napoleon from 1788 (as Lieutenant) up to his First Consul period. The scenes are various—Valence, Toulon, Paris, Italy, Egypt, etc. Depicts the Terror, and introduces many incidents connected with the politics and wars of the time (including the English naval exploits at Toulon in 1793, and at Acre in 1799). Besides Napoleon, the following appear: Lord Hood, Nelson (as " Captain "), Madame Tallien, Josephine, Carnot, Robespierre, Masséna, Marmont, Augereau, Marat, Talleyrand, and Fouché.

1548. *THE RED COCKADE: Stanley J. Weyman; *Murray* [*Eng.*], *Longmans* [*U.S.A.*].
France (Cahors and Nîmes) in 1789. A tale of Royalists in Southern France just before, and at the beginning of, the Revolution. The riots in Nîmes, etc.

1549. FOES OF FREEDOM: " May Wynne "; *Chapman & Hall*.
A good story having for background the revolt of the Belgian provinces against the Emperor of Austria (Joseph II), 1789-90.

1550. *THE THIRD ESTATE: " Marjorie Bowen "; *Methuen*.
France in the time of the States-General, 1789; then Italy and France in 1791—the coming of the " Third Estate," i.e. the popular revolutionary representatives of the States-General as contrasted with the two privileged estates. Many historic figures appear in the course of the novel: Desmoulins, Danton, Mirabeau, Marie Antoinette, etc.

1551. THE TWO CARNATIONS: " Marjorie Bowen "; *Cassell*.
Bath, London, and Paris, about 1789-92. The story of a girl driven into a loveless marriage. The later portions of the book have a French Revolution background—prison scenes (the Conciergerie, etc.) and escapes.

1552. *MADEMOISELLE MATHILDE: Henry Kingsley; *Ward, Lock* [*Eng.*], *Longmans* [*U.S.A.*].

England (Dorset) and Brittany, 1789-93. This novel begins in the Stour Valley shortly before the French Revolution, and proceeds to a depiction of life in France and England alternately in the Revolution period (Vendean conspirators, etc.). Marat is extremely prominent, while Robespierre appears to a much slighter extent. An interesting example of Henry Kingsley.

1553. JACK WITHOUT A ROOF: Charles Gilson; *Juv.* The *"Boy's Own Paper" Office.*

Paris and La Vendée in the period 1789-93. A thrilling adventure story of the French Revolution period. Deals with events in Paris up to 1793, and with the War in La Vendée (1793). In the closing pages (Paris once again) Robespierre appears.

1554. *THE CANONESS (*LA CHANOINESSE*): André Theuriet (trans.); *Nelson.*

Eastern France (Bar-le-Duc, Forest of the Argonne, Verdun, etc.), 1789 and 1791-93. The Battle or Cannonade of Valmy (1792) is described, and other events are touched. The Crown Prince of Prussia appears somewhat prominently, and there are glimpses of Frederick-William II of Prussia, and Goethe.

1555. *THE TRAMPLING OF THE LILIES: Rafael Sabatini; *Hutchinson* [*Eng.*], *Houghton Mifflin* [*U.S.A.*].

France (Picardy) just before the Revolution, 1789; then Picardy, Belgium, and Paris in 1793 (Robespierre). A really fascinating romance which may be considered one of the author's best examples.

1556. *A STORM-RENT SKY: M. Betham Edwards; *Hurst & Blackett.*

Eastern France (mainly) and Paris, 1789-94. A good depiction of provincial life (woodlanders) in the Revolution period. The novel is one of atmosphere and historical *allusion* for the most part. Towards the end of the story, however, Danton appears in his native region, and the last pages of all show him in Paris (his execution).

1557. DRAGON'S TEETH: Arthur Hood; *Cassell.*

Mainly France (Provincial château and Paris), 1789-94. A well-told story, in which the interest is almost entirely on the fictional side. There is the merest glimpse of Thomas Paine.

1558. *THE QUEEN'S FILLET: P. A. Sheehan; *Longmans.*

France (various localities including Paris, La Vendée, Vallancey, and Grenoble) c. 1785-1815, but mainly 1789-94. A romance somewhat over-crowded with historic figures and events. Book I covers the earlier Revolution developments, ending with Louis XVI's execution. Book II depicts the Temple Prison scenes (Marie Antoinette and family), certain rescue efforts, the Queen's trial and execution, and the circumstances leading up to Robespierre's downfall. The novel ends, in Book III, immediately after the shooting of Ney, December, 1814. In the volume as a whole, Talleyrand is very prominent at several points, and André Chénier, the poet, is also to the fore in the middle chapters; while, among the other numerous figures, one may specify: Louis XVI, Marie Antoinette, the Dauphin, Mirabeau, Danton, Robespierre, Tinville, David the painter, Tallien, De Batry, Cathelineau, and Larochejacquelein.

1559. *LE ROMAN D'UNE VERSAILLAISE; Augustin Billot; *Société d' Edition Française et Etrangère* [*France*].

A noteworthy historical novel illustrating the French Revolution period, 1789-97.

1560. *THE STORY OF A PEASANT: E. Erckmann and A. Chatrian ["Erckmann-Chatrian"]; *Ward, Lock* [*Eng.*], *Holt* [*U.S.A.*].

The collective title of four connected stories dealing with the French Revolution and Napoleonic times: "The States-General" (1789); "The Country in Danger" (1792);

o

" Year One of the Republic " (1793); and " Citizen Bonaparte " (1794-1815). These stories, like other excellent examples of " Erckmann-Chatrian," exhibit special originality in reflecting the attitude of *humbly placed folk* towards the great events of the period. The reader can hardly fail to realize the sympathy of the famous collaborators with Republican ideas, even though such sympathy is qualified by detestation of Revolutionary excesses; again, while imaginatively reconstructing a time of immense national enthusiasm, these stories convey a very clear distinction between *patriotism* and *militarism*.

1561. IN THE REIGN OF TERROR: G. A. Henty; *Juv.   Blackie* [*Eng.*], *Scribner* [*U.S.A.*].
England (Chelsea) and France (Paris, etc.), 1790-93. The " adventures of a Westminster boy " in Paris during the Terror (Robespierre).

1562. THE LOSER PAYS: Mary Openshaw; *Werner Laurie*.
France 1791-93. A romance of Rouget de Lisle (his son is supposed to tell the story). Bonaparte in his " twenties."

1563. *THE GIANT: Bernard Hamilton; *Hutchinson*.
France (Paris, Sèvres, etc.), 1774-94. An example of what may be called ultra-historic fiction, but, for all that, a really fine and sympathetic romance of Danton, based on careful study, and exhibiting unusual qualities as a piece of reconstruction. The *Proem* introduces Danton as a boy of 15, quickly passing to the early stages of the Revolution; but the main story opens in Paris with a picture of the Cordelier Club in 1791, and then advances to the time of the Austro-Prussian threat and the fall of the Monarchy. On the purely fictional side, there is an interesting account of Danton's love affair and marriage. The later chapters illustrate the Terror and the events culminating in the hero's arrest, trial, and execution. Besides the dominating figure of Danton, crowds of historic personages appear, including: Camille Desmoulins, Condorcet, Marat, Robespierre, Philippe Égalité, Fouquier Tinville, Fabre d'Eglantine, Couthon, St. Just, Legendre, and Tom Paine.

1564. THE LOVERS OF MADEMOISELLE: Clive Holland; *Hurst & Blackett*.
Normandy and Paris, 1792. A love and adventure story, beginning with descriptions of the attack on, and burning of, a château, and in later chapters taking the reader to Paris (the Conciegerie, the Revolutionary Tribunal, etc.). Fouquier-Tinville appears.

1565. TWO QUEENS: J. G. L. Hesekiel (trans.); *Sonnenschein*.
Denmark, 1772—Caroline Matilda, sister of George III; and France, 1792—Marie Antoinette. Based on the Memoirs of Baron Ivan M. Simolin.

1566. (1) THE SCARLET PIMPERNEL: *Greening* [*Eng.*], *Hodder & Stoughton* [*Eng.*], *Putnam* [*U.S.A.*].
    (2) I WILL REPAY: *Greening* [*Eng.*], *Hodder & Stoughton* [*Eng.*], *Lippincott* [*U.S.A.*], *Dodd, Mead* [*U.S.A.*].
    (3) THE ELUSIVE PIMPERNEL: *Hutchinson* [*Eng.*], *Greening* [*Eng.*], *Dodd, Mead* [*U.S.A.*].
    (4) THE LEAGUE OF THE SCARLET PIMPERNEL: *Cassell* [*Eng.*], *Doran* [*U.S.A.*].
    (5) THE TRIUMPH OF THE SCARLET PIMPERNEL: *Hodder & Stoughton* [*Eng.*], *Doran* [*U.S.A.*].
    (6) LORD TONY'S WIFE: *Hodder & Stoughton* [*Eng.*], *Doran* [*U.S.A.*].
    (7) ELDORADO: *Hodder & Stoughton* [*Eng.*], *Doran* [*U.S.A.*].
    (8) SIR PERCY HITS BACK: Baroness Orczy; *Hodder & Stoughton* [*Eng.*], *Doran* [*U.S.A.*].
A remarkably popular series of French Revolution tales in which the historical interest is far behind the fictional. " Sir Percy Blakeney," an Englishman with a French wife,

heads a certain *League of the Scarlet Pimpernel* comprised of English gentlemen who, by means of disguise, etc., rescue innocent Revolution prisoners.

(1) Paris, England (Kent), and Calais, 1792. The formation, and early work, of the "League," etc.

(2) *Prologue:* Paris, 1783; the tale itself deals with Paris, 1793. Time of Charlotte Corday, etc. Foucquier-Tinville appears.

(3) Paris, England (Richmond) and Boulogne, 1793: Robespierre and Tinville are introduced.

(4) Paris and Lyons, 1793. A volume of short stories, telling, yet again, of the wonderful Sir Percy; some of the stories are connected with Marat, Tinville, and Robespierre respectively.

(5) Paris and England, 1794. Begins (April) with Robespierre at the height of his power, and ends with the full story of his downfall. Several historic figures besides Robespierre, including Couthon, St. Just, Barras, and Tallien.

(6) "An adventure of the Scarlet Pimpernel" (sub-title). *Epilogue:* Nantes, 1789; Book I Bath, November, 1793; Book II Nantes, December, 1793.

(7) France (Paris, etc.) in 1794. The Dauphin is prominent, and there are glimpses of Robespierre, Danton, and Tinville.

(8) South-East France, 1794. Another "Pimpernel" story of the National Conventions period, telling of rescue (and revenge *of a kind*).

1567. *THE GIRONDIN: Hilaire Belloc; *Nelson.
France (Bordeaux, Poitiers, etc.) in 1792. A novel of adventure and politics, telling how the hero, having killed a man, wanders far afield, and at length—after fighting under Kellermann at Valmy—meets his end in an accident. Reflects the earlier Revolution movements (the speechifying of the Clubs, etc.), and conveys effectively the general atmosphere of the period.

1568. CITOYENNE JACQUELINE: "Sarah Tytler"; *Chatto & Windus* [Eng.], *Routledge* [U.S.A.].
Paris, the Luxembourg, etc., 1792-93. A good old-fashioned tale of a woman's experiences in the French Revolution. Charlotte Corday appears.

1569. CAMILLA OF THE FAIR TOWERS: Dora M. Jones; *Melrose.*
Paris and S. England, mainly from August, 1792, to January 1793. Madame Roland appears, and Tom Paine is connected with the story at certain points.

1570. NICOLE (IN THE NAME OF LIBERTY): Owen Johnson; *Macmillan* [Eng.], *Century* [U.S.A.].
Paris, 1792 and 1793. A somewhat gloomy picture of the Revolution; covers the Taking of the Tuileries, the Massacre of the Prisons, etc., and takes the reader up to the end of the Terror.

1571. THE RED CAPS OF LYONS: Herbert Hayens; *Juv.* *Chambers* [Eng.], *Appleton* [U.S.A.].
Lyons, 1792-93. Gives an account of the violent scenes in Lyons during the Convention rule—the struggle between the sections ("friends of order") and the Jacobins. Among the historic figures introduced, Challier (the sansculotte hero), Couthon, and Fouché are more or less prominent.

1572. A PATRIOT OF FRANCE: Michael W. Kaye; *Stanley Paul.*
Forest of Ardennes and Sedan regions, also Paris, 1792-93. This somewhat melodramatic story begins at the time of the Duke of Brunswick's Manifesto, soon introducing Dumouriez and De Batz as prominent figures. There is some account of the victory of Dumouriez over the Austrians at Jemappes, while plots to rescue Louis XVI constitute the main theme of later chapters. Danton and Robespierre appear.

1573. *ROSE IN THE MOUTH: Adrian Heard; *Ward, Lock.*
Mainly Paris, 1792-94. An interesting novel, introducing many of the leading figures in the Revolution period. The account of the Dauphin's supposed rescue from the Temple Prison and its sequel, supplies one more variation of this favourite theme. There is a pleasing picture of Danton, while of historical events, Marat's assassination is the most fully treated. The novel ends with Robespierre's downfall. Of the various historic figures, Robespierre, Danton, and Marie Antoinette are specially prominent; other personages are: The Dauphin, Count Axel Fersen, Bonaparte, Josephine Beauharnais, and Charlotte Corday.

1574. CHANTEMERLE: D. K. Broster and G. W. Taylor; *Murray.*
France (Paris, La Vendée, etc.) and England (Suffolk), mainly in the period 1792-94. A story illustrating the suppression of the religious orders during the Revolution, and the events leading up to the Rising in La Vendée. The Royalists and the Gironde, etc. Princess Elizabeth ("Madame Elizabeth"), Louis XVI's sister, appears, and there is a glimpse of Marie Antoinette.

1575. *A MARRIAGE UNDER THE TERROR: Patricia Wentworth; *Melrose* [*Eng.*], *Putnam* [*U.S.A.*].
France (largely Paris), 1792-94. A romance of the thrilling type, with a considerable element of history. Marie Antoinette and her family are shown during their imprisonment in the Temple, and the general atmosphere of the Terror is well conveyed. The story ends with Robespierre's fall. Besides the Royalties, many important figures are introduced, such as Danton, Marat, Robespierre, Hébert, Camille Desmoulins, and Fouquier-Tinville.

1576. (1)*THE REDS OF THE MIDI:
(2)*THE TERROR (*sequel*):
(3)*THE WHITE TERROR (*sequel*): Félix Gras (trans.); *Heinemann* [*Eng.*], *Appleton* [*U.S.A.*].
An excellent trilogy, depicting the French Revolution sympathetically, yet critically. The main localities and events, etc., illustrated in these novels, are respectively:
(1) S. E. France (Rhône district and Marseilles), also Paris in 1792. One of the incidents introduced is the singing of "The Marseillaise" for the first time, the main subject being the Marseilles Battalion (march from Marseilles to Paris).
(2) Paris and Avignon, 1792-93. The outstanding historic figure is Marat when at the height of his power, and, one notes, among the many vivid descriptions of events, an account of Louis XVI's execution.
(3) Avignon, etc., mainly in the later Revolution stages (c. 1794)—the time of "ungoverned crime." But this third novel of the series also furnishes a rapid survey of the period covering the Battles of Valmy and Jemappes, the advent of Bonaparte and his victories at Marengo, Austerlitz, etc., and even the much later downfall of the Empire at Waterloo. A feature in the final portion of the book is the narration which the soldier-hero gives of his experiences in the Retreat from Moscow, etc. General Jourdan is one of the prominent figures of the novel, while there are glimpses of Dumouriez, and others.

1577. *THE NUPTIALS OF CORBAL: Rafael Sabatini; *Hutchinson* [*Eng.*], *Houghton Mifflin* [*U.S.A.*].
Paris and the provinces, 1793. A story of the "Terror" period, with faint historical background—a glimpse of Robespierre, and allusions to Fouquier-Tinville and Camille Desmoulins respectively. The fictional developments are exciting and well presented, while, as regards character depiction, the Revolutionary "Chauvinière" is a figure of startling and half-fascinating significance.

1578. ADVENTURES OF THE COMTE DE LA MUETTE DURING THE TERROR: Bernard Capes; *Blackwood* [*Eng.*], *Dodd, Mead* [*U.S.A.*].
Mainly Paris in 1793. An adventure tale with Prison scenes (La Force), etc. Fouquier-Tinville appears, and there is a glimpse of Robespierre.

1579. *NINETY-THREE: Victor Hugo (trans.); *Dent* [*Eng.*], *Little, Brown* [*U.S.A.*].
Jersey, Paris, and La Vendée, 1793. A novel of the Royalist struggle in La Vendée, written in the gorgeously romantic style familiar to readers of the great French author. Among the historic figures introduced, one may specify Robespierre, Danton, and Marat.

1580. FOES OF THE RED COCKADE: F. S. Brereton; *Juv. Blackie.*
Largely La Vendée and Paris, 1793. A tale of adventure, fighting, imprisonment and escape, etc., at the same time illustrating the struggle in La Vendée against the Red Cockades. Robespierre appears in the Paris section.

1581. NO SURRENDER!: G. A. Henty; *Juv, Blackie* [*Eng.*], *Scribner* [*U.S.A.*].
England and France, 1791-96. "A tale of the Rising in La Vendée" (sub-title), in which Cathelineau, La Rochejaquelein, and others are introduced.

1582. *LA VENDÉE AUX GENÊTS: Marcel Batilliat; *Mercure de France* [*France*].
A good novel dealing with the Chouans, and introducing Cathelineau and La Rochejaquelin.

1583. PITY'S KIN: Robert Vansittart; *Murray.*
Nantes in French Revolution time: the rebellion in La Vendée, 1793. This somewhat intricate novel is one of historical atmosphere and ideas rather than of actual events and people; at the same time, there is a considerable fighting element, and the Royalist leaders, Cathelineau and La Rochejacquelein as well as sundry Revolutionary notabilities, either appear or have special allusion made to them.

1584. STORM AND TREASURE: H. C. Bailey; *Methuen* [*Eng.*], *Brentano's* [*U.S.A.*].
Begins Sussex coast, then France (Nantes largely) and the Rising in La Vendée, 1793. A good love story with historical background. La Rochejaquelein, Cathelineau, and General Hoche are among the more important figures introduced.

1585. *DUCHENIER; or, THE REVOLT OF LA VENDÉE: J. M. Neale; *Juv. S.P.C.K.* [*Eng.*], *Macmillan* [*U.S.A.*].
La Vendée, Paris, and London, 1793-94. This tale of the Vendéan royalists, which is considered one of Dr. Neale's best examples, introduces William Pitt the younger, Danton, and Robespierre.

1586. *SAINT MICHAEL'S GOLD: H. Bedford Jones; *Putnam.*
Paris (May, 1793), Avranches, and Mont St. Michel. The adventure and love story of a young American member of the Convention, who, finding himself suspected by the Revolution leaders as too moderate, gets away in company with a man who is after treasure in Mont St. Michel. Thomas Paine, Robespierre, Marat, Fouché, and Cathelineau (the Vendéan leader) all appear in the course of the story.

1587. QUEEN OF THE GUARDED MOUNTS: "John Oxenham"; *Hodder & Stoughton.*
Brittany and Cornwall, 1793. A story of love and adventure, mostly dealing with the two "Mounts"—Mont St. Michel, and St. Michael's Mount, and their respective regions. The historical background is the Vendéan revolt, and the English assistance given it.

1588. *MADAME THÉRÈSE: E. Erckmann and A. Chatrian (trans.); *Ward, Lock* [*Eng.*], *Holt* [*U.S.A.*].
Story of a Vosges village in the autumn and winter of 1793. A good picture of life in a stormy period, though of actual war and fighting there is little record.

1589. *THÉRÈSE OF THE REVOLUTION: Lt.-Col. Andrew C. P. Haggard; *F. V. White.*

Mainly Bordeaux, Caen, and Paris, 1793-1794. A romance of Comtesse Thérèse de Fontenay, telling how, through her influence over Tallien (afterwards her husband), she saved many lives from the guillotine. Practically all the figures in the novel are historical, and events like the assassination of Marat are treated in more or less exact fashion. Besides Thérèse herself and Tallien, one encounters Barbaroux the Girondist, Charlotte Corday, Marat, Robespierre, Bonaparte, Barras, the Painter David, Fouquier-Tinville, Madame Roland, and Josephine Beauharnais.

1590. A ROMANCE OF THREE LADIES: J. G. Sarasin; *Hutchinson.*

England (Dover and Canterbury), and Paris at the time of Danton's downfall. Mainly a novel of adventure and love in the French Revolution period, 1793-94. One of the figures introduced is the Painter David.

1591. *THE NINTH THERMIDOR: M. A. Aldanov (trans.); *Cape [Eng.], Knopf [U.S.A.].*

After a Prologue imaginatively accounting for the " stone monster " called *Le Penseur*, which is on the summit of Notre Dame, Paris, Part I opens in Russia, 1793 (Catherine II)—passing to Königsberg (Immanuel Kant appears); London where Burke, Pitt, Priestley, Talleyrand, and other historical notabilities come into view; and Brussels. In Part II the reader is shown the Paris of the later Revolution period (Marat, Danton, and Robespierre). But the main interest begins with events in that terrible month of July, 1794, leading up to the fall of Robespierre on the 27th (or " 9th Thermidor "), and his death on the day following. Barras, Fouché, Tallien, and of course Robespierre, are prominently introduced. A powerful, if somewhat gloomy, book; it forms Vol. I of the Historical Trilogy entitled *The Thinker*.

1592. *THE GODS ARE ATHIRST (*LES DIEUX ONT SOIF*): " Anatole France " (trans.); *Lane [Eng.], Dodd, Mead [U.S.A.].*

Paris, 1793-94. A novel illustrating the time when Marat and Robespierre respectively were the dominating political figures. Covers the assassination of Marat, the Fête of the Supreme Being, and the fall of Robespierre (the romance ends with the last-named event). The fictional hero is an artist who follows, with all the enthusiasm of an advanced patriot, the various movements and developments of the time: he sits on the juror's bench during the worst excesses of the Revolutionary Tribunal. The ideas and general atmosphere of the later Revolution period are skilfully conveyed, though some of the conversational discussion over politics and religion, suggests—too palpably perhaps—the author's own irony and detachment. Not many historical figures appear, but many are mentioned; Fouquier-Tinville and Robespierre are both introduced— the depiction in each case being careful and vivid.

1593. *SOUS LA HACHE: Elémir Bourges; *Armand Colin [France].*

Another novel giving an interesting and suggestive picture of the French Revolution in its later stages, from November, 1793.

1594. *LE PETIT ROI D'OMBRE: Victor Margueritte; *Librairie des Annales [France].*

Paris in the period, 1793-95. A romance dealing with the chief figures of the period, and having for one of its central themes, the mystery of the Dauphin.

1595. *THE LOST KING: Octave Aubry (trans.); *Hopkinson.*

France, mainly 1793-1803, and 1819-20. A retired Secret Agent's narrative (1841) of what happened between April 1819 and June 1820, when he was employed in the investigation of the facts relating to the Dauphin (Louis XVII). The story is remarkably well told, *and the historical implications go back to the period* 1793-1803. Louis XVIII, the Duchess d'Abrantès, Barras, the Duke of Otranto (Fouché), and the widow of Simon, the former gaoler of the Dauphin, are some of the most important figures.

1596. WHEN A COBBLER RULED THE KING: AUGUSTA H. SEAMAN; *Juv. Macmillan* [U.S.A.].

An interesting French Revolution tale, based on the tradition of the " Lost Dauphin." Begins Paris, 1792 (Louis XVI and Marie Antoinette both appear). Bonaparte is prominent, first as " Citizen," and later on as " General " (1795-6). The concluding pages pass to 1806, with " Louis XVII " on the point of sailing to America.

1597. THE MYSTERIOUS MONSIEUR DUMONT: FREDERICK ARTHUR; *Murray.*

France (La Vendée and Paris) 1793-94; also England and Prussia, 1805-1807. An adventure and love story, with historic background. Covers the period of the Vendéan Rising, Danton's fall, the Fête of the Supreme Being, and Robespierre's fall. The later chapters deal with Napoleon's Prussian Wars. La Rochejacquelein, Robespierre, Danton, Napoleon, and Marshal Lannes appear.

1598. *THE ATELIER DU LYS: MARGARET ROBERTS; *Juv. Longmans.*

A good " atmosphere " tale of the French Revolution (the Terror). There is some excellent character drawing, and the fictional developments hold the reader to the end.

1599. A DAUGHTER OF THE GIRONDE: STANLEY J. WEYMAN, in " In Kings' Byways "—*Murray* [Eng.], *Longmans* [U.S.A.].

A short story of Paris in the year 1794.

1600. *THE WHITES AND THE BLUES: ALEXANDRE DUMAS; *Dent* [Eng.], *Little, Brown* [U.S.A.].

France, 1793-99. A romance dealing with the period of the Directoire and of Bonaparte's appointment as General of the armies in Italy and Egypt. Covers Aboukir, Acre, etc., and—on the social side—offers glimpses of Madame de Staël and her Salon. Besides Bonaparte and Madame de Staël, there are numerous historic figures such as Josephine de Beauharnais, Madame Tallien, Madame Récamier, Benjamin Constant, Talleyrand, Barras, Fouché, Pichegru, Moreau, Hoche, Murat, Junot, Augereau, Masséna, and Georges Cadoudal.

1601. *THE COMPANIONS OF JEHU: ALEXANDRE DUMAS; *Dent* [Eng.], *Little, Brown* [U.S.A.].

France, 1799-1800. Time of Bonaparte's nomination as First Consul, and of the insurrections in La Vendée and Bretagne. Bonaparte, Josephine, Moreau, Bernadotte, and Fouché, are all more or less prominent, while Georges Cadoudal, the Chouan leader, is an outstanding figure. Among the many other historic personages who appear in the novel, are: Bonaparte's brothers Joseph and Lucien, Barras, Hoche, Pichegru, Cambacérès, and Eugène Beauharnais.

1602. *MAURICE TIERNAY: CHARLES LEVER; *Routledge* [Eng.], *Harper* [U.S.A.].

Mainly France, Germany, Ireland, Italy, and Austria, c. 1793-1809. Adventures of an Irish soldier of fortune. The novel deals with various regions and historical events: Paris in the Terror; the Passage of the Rhine at Strasbourg (Moreau's Army); the French invasion of Ireland and the capture of Wolfe Tone; the attack on Monte di Faccio; the arrest of the Duc d'Enghien and his death, etc., etc. Numerous historic figures appear, including Robespierre, General Humbert, Wolfe Tone, General Masséna, the Duc d'Enghien, Bourrienne, and Fouché. There is, also, a glimpse of Napoleon.

1603. THE LOST EMPIRE: CHARLES GILSON; *Juv. Frowde.*

A tale of varied scenes and events in the period, 1795-99. The Blockade of Genoa; Paris under the Directoire; the Battle of the Nile; and the Siege of Seringapatam (Tippoo Sahib). Many historic figures are introduced.

1604. BEATRICE OF VENICE: Max Pemberton; *Hodder & Stoughton* [*Eng.*], *Dodd, Mead* [*U.S.A.*].

Italy (Venice and Verona), 1796. A romance of considerable interest, illustrating the period of Napoleon's Italian Campaign. Among the historical figures are Bonaparte himself, Junot, and Moreau.

1605. *CORSICAN JUSTICE: J. G. Sarasin; *Hutchinson* [*Eng.*], *Doran* [*U.S.A.*].

The Italian Lake District (mainly Lake Maggiore), 1797. A love and adventure story, with a faint background of historical events. "General" Bonaparte is decidedly to the fore at various points—the period being that of his victories over the Austrians in Italy.

1606. *PAULINA: Max Pemberton; *Cassell.*

Venice, the Mediterranean, Paris, and London, 1797-98. Romance of an Englishman and Princess Paulina, daughter of Ludovico Manin the last of the Doges. Illustrates the period when the French entered Venice, and when the Austrian supremacy was established (the downfall of the Venetian Republic). Bonaparte is prominently introduced, and there are glimpses of Josephine, Nelson, the Prince of Wales, Sheridan, Fox, Beau Brummel and others.

1607. *VEVA: Hendrik Conscience (trans.); *Burns & Oates.*

Belgium in 1793, and (chiefly) in 1798. The first two chapters deal with the short interval between the first French occupation of Belgium and the second; in Chapter III the reader is taken on some five years to the main subject of this excellent story, viz., the Rising of the Flemish peasants against the French Republican armies. Ends with the suppression of the revolt. Some critics consider this tale the author's best effort.

1608. BARRY LEROY: H. C. Bailey; *Methuen.*

Story of an unscrupulous English spy-adventurer and his experiences, beginning Toulon, 1793. Deals mainly with his comings and goings in France, Italy, Germany, and England about the years 1797 and 1800. Bonaparte, Nelson, Lady Hamilton, Talleyrand, D'Enghien, Fox, and Pitt are among the many notabilities introduced.

1609. *THE CHOUANS: Honoré de Balzac (trans.); *Dent* [*Eng.*], *Little, Brown* [*U.S.A.*].

The Royalists in Brittany, 1799. A story of the time of Bonaparte's nomination as First Consul, also illustrating Fouché's spy system just after his appointment as Minister of Police (September, 1799).

1610. *A PRIEST IN SPITE OF HIMSELF: Rudyard Kipling; in "Rewards and Fairies"—*Macmillan.*

Talleyrand and Bonaparte round about the year 1800.

1611. BY CONDUCT AND COURAGE: G. A. Henty; *Juv. Blackie* [*Eng.*], *Scribner* [*U.S.A.*].

Adventures of a Yorkshire lad on sea and land, end 18th Century to beginning 19th. The Battles of Cape St. Vincent and Camperdown, as well as later events, are introduced. Nelson is a prominent figure.

1612. *THE KING'S OWN: Captain F. Marryat; *Dent* [*Eng.*], *Estes* [*U.S.A.*], *and other publishers.*

A tale of the sea, which, though it opens with a description of the Mutiny of the Nore in 1797, has afterwards a very slight historical element. It does, however, convey the naval atmosphere of the period in its record of experiences and adventures off the French Coast, in the Tropics, etc., etc. There is a noteworthy fight with the French.

1613. IN NELSON'S DAY: JOHN G. ROWE; *Juv. Scott.*

Norfolk (Cromer) and the sea, 1792-1805. A story of adventure by land and sea: the Press-Gang, Pirates, etc. Covers, and somewhat fully describes, the naval victories of Cape St. Vincent (1797) and Trafalgar (1805). The boy-hero saves the life of Nelson at one point in the tale—the great Admiral appearing prominently two or three times.

1614. THE MAID OF SKER: R. D. BLACKMORE; *Blackwood* [*Eng.*], *Harper* [*U.S.A.*].

S. Wales and Devonshire (with a few scenes Abroad) within the period 1782-1800. In the second half of the story there are many naval episodes, ending with the Battle of the Nile (1798). The reader is given some glimpses of Nelson, etc.

1615. *THE EXTRAORDINARY CONFESSIONS OF DIANA PLEASE: BERNARD CAPES; *Methuen.*

Mainly Brighton, London district, and Naples, 1774-99 (the birth-date of the dubious " heroine " is given as 1771 on the first page, but the story proper begins 1774 and reaches the year 1787 on the sixty-fourth page). These imaginary reminiscences of an adventuress do indeed tell of " extraordinary " experiences, some of which are decidedly painful reading. But the book is, at least, one that shows power of insight and literary skill. In the last sixty pages there is a considerable background of history; at the beginning of this final section, " Diana " leaves London in Lady Hamilton's suite (Lord and Lady Hamilton having just before that point, come into the story). Putting aside certain Paris adventures during the Revolution time, etc., related by the " editor " in a note of some five pages, the reader is quickly taken to Naples in the period of the December troubles, 1798. The historic incident of Carracciolo being hung from the yard-arm of a Neapolitan frigate is introduced. King Ferdinand and his Queen appear, as well as Lady Hamilton. There is, of course, some mention of Nelson.

1616. (1)*THE FAIR ENCHANTRESS:
    (2)*NELSON'S LAST LOVE (*sequel*): HENRY SCHUMACHER; *Hutchinson.*

These two novels depict Emma, Lady Hamilton, from about 1780 up to the time of her death in 1815.

(1) The first novel begins with " Emma Lyon-Hart " in North Wales, passing quickly to London (Drury Lane, etc.), and later still to Naples. Besides the heroine herself, George Romney, Greville, Sheridan, Prince George (George IV), and Sir William Hamilton appear, while there are glimpses of " Captain " Nelson and Goethe. The book ends with Emma's marriage with Sir William Hamilton (1791).

(2) The second story has largely to do with the Naples period from 1793, when Emma was intimate with Queen Maria Caroline, wife of Ferdinand I of Naples, and when Nelson came into close relations with her. Sir William Hamilton and Nelson are, of course, prominent among the numerous personages introduced. The latest chapters carry the reader rapidly through the period of Trafalgar, etc., to Lady Hamilton's death.

1617. *THE DIVINE LADY: " E. BARRINGTON "; *Harrap* [*Eng.*], *Dodd, Mead* [*U.S.A.*].

Mainly London and Naples, 1782-1803. The story of Lady Hamilton from her girlhood (as Emma Hart) onwards, dealing especially with the period of her relations with Nelson. Greville, Sir William Hamilton, Romney, Queen Charlotte, and, of course, Nelson, are all more or less prominent.

1618. THE NEAPOLITAN LOVERS: LOVE AND LIBERTY (*sequel*): ALEXANDRE DUMAS (trans.); *Stanley Paul.*

Naples and Sicily, 1798-99. These two connected volumes deal imaginatively with the career of Luisa San Felice, the heroine of the Neapolitan Revolution. The period covered is that between Nelson's arrival in Naples after the Battle of the Nile, and the suppression of the Revolution just mentioned. Nelson is prominent, and his part in the painful events culminating in the execution of Admiral Carracciolo, is depicted in somewhat adverse fashion. Crowds of historic figures: Nelson, Sir William and Lady Hamilton, King Ferdinand and his Queen, the Admiral Francesco Carracciolo, Cardinal Ruffo, and others. The stories originally appeared (1864) under the title, *La San Felice.*

1619. WITHIN A YEAR: FREDERICK HARRISON; *Juv.* S.P.C.K. [*Eng.*], *Macmillan* [*U.S.A.*].
England and the East, 1798-99. A story of juvenile adventure (land and sea), telling of Sir Sidney Smith at Acre and the raising of the Siege. Bonaparte and Sir Sidney both appear.

1620. *THE LOST MAMELUKE: DAVID M. BEDDOE; *Dent.*
Egypt (Cairo and district), 1789-1801: largely 1798-1801. This decidedly original novel covers Bonaparte's Egyptian expedition, up to and including the time when Kléber was left in chief command. One of the principal characters is an Englishman who identifies himself—even in the religious sense—with the Egyptians; he eventually fights with the English at Aboukir and is killed. The story ends with the departure of the French. There are numerous allusions to Bonaparte and others, but the more noteworthy figures of history scarcely appear. The Battle of Aboukir (1801) is the most important event introduced.

1621. AT ABOUKIR AND ACRE: G. A. HENTY; *Juv.* *Blackie* [*Eng.*], *Scribner* [*U.S.A.*].
A story of the French invasion of Egypt and Syria, 1798-1801. Covers the Battle of the Nile, Sir Sidney Smith's Defence of Acre, and the Battle of Alexandria. Several historical figures are introduced, of whom Bonaparte, Sir Sidney Smith and Abercrombie are the most important.

1622. *BEN BRACE: THE LAST OF NELSON'S AGAMEMNONS: FREDERICK CHAMIER; *Routledge.*
England (West Country), Central America, Canada, Italy, etc., mainly in the period 1770-1816. A deservedly famous naval story of the Nelson period, covering many sea-fights. There are full descriptions of the Battle of the Nile and the Battle of Trafalgar respectively; again, towards the end of the tale Lord Exmouth's Bombardment of Algiers is introduced. Nelson appears largely, of course—other historic figures being Hood and the Duke of Clarence (William IV); while the reader obtains glimpses of notabilities like Sir William and Lady Hamilton. There are several land scenes (the Press-gang), and there is, also, a love interest.

1623. *TOM BOWLING: FREDERICK CHAMIER; *Routledge* [*Eng.*], *Dutton* [*U.S.A.*].
England, West Indies (Martinique), the Cape, etc., 1780-1815. Another famous tale of sea-fights and naval life generally, dealing for the most part with the Nelson-Jervis-Collingwood period. There are numerous allusions to, and something like a glimpse of, the great Horatio himself, but the most important historic figure at all prominently introduced, is that of Cuthbert Collingwood, from the time when, as "Captain," he succeeded Nelson in command of the ship *Hinchinbroke.*

1624. *FROM POWDER MONKEY TO ADMIRAL: W. H. G. KINGSTON; *Juv.* *Oxford University Press.*
An old favourite among boys with a taste for stories of sea adventure. The approximate date is soon fixed in Chapter II by the statement: " England had *at that time* pretty nearly all the world in arms against her—she had managed to quarrel with the Dutch and was at war with the French and the Spaniards, while she had lately been engaged in a vain attempt to overcome the American colonies." Apart from the quotation just given, and a footnote elsewhere vouching for the exact truth of certain occurrences introduced, there are only the vaguest allusions to historical episodes. As, however, the sea-fights against the French continue till the last page or two (when " some years pass "), the tale proper may safely be described as reflecting, in a general way, Naval life from the extreme end of the 18th Century to the early years of the 19th.

1625. TO MY KING EVER FAITHFUL: "George David Gilbert"; *Nash.*

A somewhat elaborate romance of Mrs. Fitzherbert, written by way of correcting and supplementing the author's earlier novel entitled *In the Shadow of the Purple.* The story covers the period 1782-1837, and is full of allusion to events and figures of the time. Besides Mrs. Fitzherbert and the Prince (George IV), the following personages appear: George III and Queen Charlotte, C. J. Fox, Sheridan, the Duchess of Devonshire, the Duke of Cumberland, Mrs. Jordan, etc. etc.

1626. *THE PRINCE'S LOVE AFFAIR: A. H. Bennett; *Longmans.*

Mainly London and Brighton, 1785-95, but passing at the end to Windsor and London 1830. An adventure story, telling of the hero's "love affair" as well as that of the Prince of Wales (George IV). The historic background is the state of things as between the Prince and Mrs. Fitzherbert, including the secret marriage of 1785. Both these personages are very prominent, while there are glimpses of Fox and other members of the royal circle. The book presents a carefully-balanced estimate of George IV's character.

1627. *PRINCESS AMELIA: Carola Oman; *Fisher Unwin.*

Windsor, Kew, Weymouth, etc., 1786. One more example of the ultra-historical novel, but admirably written and entertaining. The central figure is Amelia, George III's favourite daughter, and the atmosphere is almost entirely that of the Royal circle. George III and Queen Charlotte, the Princesses, the Prince of Wales, the Duke and Duchess of York, and the Duke of Cumberland all appear. Other figures are Fanny Burney (as Keeper of the Robes), Mrs. Delany, and General Burgoyne.

1628. *LOVE LIKE A GIPSY: Bernard Capes; *Constable.*

Begins N. America, 1778, but deals almost entirely with England (largely Winchester, and, to a less extent Brighton), 1788 onwards. Mrs. Fitzherbert appears somewhat prominently in this original and interesting novel.

1629. PAMELA POUNCE: Agnes and Egerton Castle; *Hodder & Stoughton.*

A tale of Court and Society Life mainly in Cheltenham, Canterbury, London, and Weymouth, round about the year 1788. Queen Charlotte and the Prince appear. This book is not properly a sequel to *The Bath Comedy* and *Incomparable Bellairs,* but the "Kitty Bellairs" of those two novels here reappears as "Lady Kilcroney."

1630. LOVE GILDS THE SCENE, AND WOMEN GUIDE THE PLOT: Agnes and Egerton Castle; *Smith, Elder.*

A volume of short stories about "Lady Kilcroney" (see *Pamela Pounce* above): London, the Bath Road, Bath, and the Great North Road, late 18th Century).

1631. A POET'S YOUTH: Margaret L. Woods; *Chapman and Dodd* [*Eng.*], *Boni & Liveright* [*U.S.A.*].

A fictional study of Wordsworth, beginning (Prologue and Book I) with Hawkeshead Grammar School and St. John's College, Cambridge; then telling of his French tour in 1790 (Lyons etc.). Book II depicts his second tour (Orleans, Blois, and Paris) in 1792, especially he development of his love affair with Annette Vallon. Wordsworth's transition from Republicanism to Conservatism is sketched.

1632. THE FACE ON THE STAIR: L. Winstanley; *Hutchinson.*

N.W. England (largely the Lake District), and London, etc., 1789-1815. A story of adventure and family mystery, with only a faint background of history, though Wordsworth and Charles Lamb appear in the first half of the book.

1633. BROTHERS OF THE FLEET: Lilian M. Pyke; *Juv.* Ward, Lock.

England and Australia, mainly 1787-88. A tale of the sailing of the "First Fleet" to New South Wales, and of Captain (or Governor) Philip's sojourn at Sydney Cove. The young midshipman hero is brought into close contact with Philip from the beginning of the story. King George III appears towards the end.

1634. *A FIRST FLEET FAMILY: Louis Becke and Walter Jeffery; *Fisher Unwin [Eng.], Macmillan [U.S.A.].*
England (The Wight) and New South Wales, mainly 1786-93, though the ealier pages take the reader back to 1770. In this narrative (closely adhering to historical fact) the hero sails from England as one of the Marines guarding the convicts in the " First Fleet " Expedition to Botany Bay (1787): full accounts of the voyage, and the landing in the Bay (January, 1788). Also depicts the early colonization of N.S. Wales (the settlement at Port Jackson, etc.), and tells how escaped convicts made a voyage of some 3,000 miles down the Coast in an open boat. The story ends in England 1793.

1635. THE MUTINEER: Louis Becke and Walter Jeffery; *Fisher Unwin [Eng.], Lippincott [U.S.A.].*
A story written round the Mutiny of the *Bounty*, and the subsequent action of the mutineers in taking possession of Pitcairn Ireland (1790) under the leadership of Adams.

1636. *A BLUESTOCKING AT COURT: " E. Barrington "; in " The Ladies," etc.—*Fisher Unwin.*
Fanny Burney's retirement from Court, 1791, and her marriage with General D'Arblay, 1793. Queen Charlotte and Mrs. Piozzi (Mrs. Thrale) appear.

1637. A POOR QUAKER RABBIT-CATCHER: Maude Robinson; in " Nicholas the Weaver and Other Quaker Stories "— *Swarthmore Press [Eng.], Friends Book Store, Philadelphia [U.S.A.].*
A good short tale of the Mendip region (Cheddar, etc.) and Hannah More, 1789-92.

1638. *THE FARTHING SPINSTER: Catherine Dodd; *Jarrolds.*
London district and other parts of England, from 1789 to the present day. This " tale of five generations " well reflects the political, religious, literary, and general influences of the long period covered. Full of allusion to historical events like the French Revolution, the Coronation of Willian IV, etc., as well as to such persons as John Wesley, Hannah More, the Duke of Wellington, the Victorian authors, etc. etc.

1639. A BUSINESS IN GREAT WATERS: Julian Corbett; *Juv. Methuen.*
Brittany and Sussex, about 1794. A tale of the sea (Quiberon Bay, etc.), as well as of land adventures, with English smugglers and French conspirators (Chouans) well to the fore. There are allusions to Pitt, etc.

1640. UP AND DOWN THE PANTILES: Emma Marshall; *Juv. Seeley.*
Hampstead and Tunbridge Wells about the last decade of the 18th Century. A short tale having a Quaker element, and introducing Mrs. Piozzi.

1641. *THE JUSTICE-CLERK: W. D. Lyell; *William Hodge.*
Edinburgh, end 18th Century (1794). An interesting tale of social life and politics (" Friends of the People," etc.)—of murder and high legal circles, of riot and conspiracy. There is a theatrical tinge about the novel which is good alike in historic atmosphere and in local colour.

1642. SIR ISUMBRAS AT THE FORD: D. K. Broster; *Murray [Eng.], Heinemann [Eng.], Brentano's [U.S.A.].*
A story alternating between England, France, and the Channel Islands, 1795. The adventures of a French emigré and his child-son, followed by scenes of Chouan fighting and failure (Quiberon), and a love dénouement.

1643. *SYLVIA'S LOVERS: Elizabeth C. Gaskell; *Dent [Eng.], Dutton [U.S.A.], and other publishers.*
Yorkshire (" Monkshaven "=Whitby) in the period 1797-1800. A tale of the whaling trade and the press-gang, of Quaker shopkeepers, etc.

1644. *THE NEWELL FORTUNE: Mansfield Brooks; *Lane.*

Boston, U.S.A., London, and Sierra Leone in the last year or two of the 18th Century. A novel of some originality dealing with the Slavery Question. The young American hero inherits an enormous fortune, and has doubts as to the manner in which his father had accumulated so much wealth. He therefore determines on a thorough investigation which shall guide him towards the best way of using his fortune by way of compensation. The novel tells how he goes through varied experiences in England and the West Coast of Africa ere returning to Boston and maturing his schemes. Zachary Macaulay, the abolitionist, appears (the author more than once quotes from Trevelyan's well-known *Life* of Zachary's still more famous son, Lord Macaulay). The book is one that needs careful reading before the exact date is perceived; some half-way through, there is a misleading tombstone inscription which carries the reader forward to a time still far ahead at the end of the story!

1645. *MEMOIRS OF A PERSON OF QUALITY (FANSHAWE OF THE FIFTH): " Ashton Hilliers "; *Heinemann* [*Eng.*], *McClure* [*U.S.A.*].

Suffolk, the Midlands, Yorkshire, London, Lincolnshire, etc., largely 1797-99, but passing in the latest chapters to the first decade of the 19th Century. A novel in the form of edited extracts from certain private journals, vividly depicting the life of the period, and introducing various typical characters: Quakers, military men, the fashionable world, Church folk, the Methodists, gypsies, etc. It is in its descriptions of, or allusions to, such evils as packed juries, gambling, religious intolerance, bull-baiting, and other evils, that the book conveys to its readers the impression of a confused and difficult time. Many public men and events are mentioned, but the romance is historical in the general, rather than the particular, sense.

1646. *THE HISTORY OF MARGARET CATCHPOLE: Richard Cobbold; *Oxford University Press.*

Suffolk at the end of the 18th Century. The imaginative biography of a real woman, who lived 1773 to 1841. Stealing a horse in 1797, she was put in gaol, but escaped in 1800. She was then transported to Australia, 1801; eventually she married, and lived in Sydney from 1828 to 1841.

1647. *LORD EDWARD FITZGERALD: M. McDonnell Bodkin; *Chapman & Hall.*

A sympathetic romance of Fitzgerald's career, mostly within the period 1780-95. Begins with the time when he served in the English army during the American War of Independence (Battle of Eutaw Springs, 1781); then rapidly sketches his experiences in Dublin, in America (among the Indians), in Canada, and in London. The later portions of the novel deal with Lord Edward's domestic affairs (marriage, etc.) as well as with politics and the Irish Parliament. Many other historic figures, including Pitt, Castlereagh, Grattan, and Curran.

1648. KATHLEEN MAVOURNEEN: Randal McDonnell; *Fisher Unwin* [*Eng.*], *Sealy, Bryers* [*Ireland*].

Ireland (Co. Wicklow, Dublin, etc.), 1792-98. Covers the French Invasion (Bantry Bay) end of 1796, as well as the last French Expedition, and the outbreak of the great Rebellion. Wolfe Tone is prominent, and other leaders of the " United Irishmen " appear. There are glimpses of Lord Edward Fitzgerald, while Grattan is shown speaking in the Irish Parliament.

1649. *KILGORMAN: Talbot Baines Reed; *Juv. Nelson.*

Ireland (Derry, Dublin, etc.), Paris, and other foreign localities, mainly in the period 1793-97, though the last few pages carry the reader through 1798 and 1799. A good tale of land and sea adventures. Covers the Terror and Robespierre's Fall in France; the United Irishmen movement in Ireland in the years before the '98 Rebellion; and other public events like the Mutiny at the Nore and the Battle off Camperdown. Lord Edward Fitzgerald is introduced.

1650. NO DEFENCE: Gilbert Parker; *Hodder & Stoughton.*

Ireland (Connemara and Dublin), London, and Jamaica, mostly between 1794 and 1800. The novel illustrates, more or less directly, such events as the French Expedition (Ireland), the Mutiny at the Nore, and a Rising of the Maroons in Jamaica.

651. THE O'DONOGHUE: CHARLES LEVER; Routledge [Eng.], Duffy [Ireland].

S. W. Ireland (Bantry Bay regions) in the last decade of the 18th Century. A tale howing the author's strong Irish sympathies, and illustrating, in its later chapters, the historic event of the French Expedition of 1796, which ended so disastrously under terrible storm conditions.

1652. MY LORDS OF STROGUE: HON. LEWIS WINGFIELD; Bentley.

Ireland, mainly in the period 1795-1800, though actually beginning, 1793. Depicts the politics and manners of the time, with special emphasis on Pitt's policy towards Ireland. The author's sympathies are with the Irish, and he exhibits unsparingly the errors of English rule. The novel covers the '98 Rebellion, and introduces Curran, Wolfe Tone, the Emmets, Lord Cornwallis, Clare, and Castlereagh. William Pitt also appears.

1653. THE ISLAND OF SORROW: " GEORGE D. GILBERT "; John Long.

London, 1796 (Prologue); then Ireland (Dublin, etc.) 1797-98, and 1803. A romance dealing largely with the career of Robert Emmet—his love affair with Sarah Curran, and the " miniature " rebellion of 1803 resulting in his trial and execution. The author regards Grattan as the real Irish patriot (see *Preface*), and his depictions of Emmet, Curran, and Fitzgerald are not very pleasing. Besides the personages already named, Charles James Fox and his wife appear. The novel covers the '98 Rebellion (the sketch is based on Lecky), and virtually ends with Emmet's death.

1654. THE GREEN COCKADE: MRS. M. T. PENDER; Downey [Eng.], Sealy, Bryers [Ireland].

N. Ireland (the Belfast region), 1797-98. A tale of love and hate, of imprisonment and escape, etc., in the time of the Rebellion. The book is written entirely from the Rebel standpoint. William Putnam M'Cabe, the " Unitedman," is much to the fore, while Lord Edward Fitzgerald, Lord Castlereagh, and other historical figures are introduced.

1655. THE PIKEMEN: S. R. KEIGHTLEY; Juv. Hutchinson.

Ireland, 1798. Mainly an adventure story of the Strangford Lough region (Down), but in the later chapters the Great Rising of '98 (Battle of Ballynahinch, etc.) is depicted.

1656. *THE REBELS: M. McDONNELL BODKIN; Ward, Lock [Eng.], Duffy [Ireland], Benziger [U.S.A.].

Ireland (Dublin, Wexford, etc.) at the time of the '98 Rebellion. In some degree a sequel to the author's Lord Edward Fitzgerald (see above)—a considerable part of the present romance dealing with the tracking, capture, and death of Lord Edward. Covers the period of the Wexford troubles and the French landing at Killala. Besides Fitzgerald and his wife, Lord Clare, Sir Ralph Abercombie, Lord Camden, Henry Gratton, General Humbert, and Castlereagh appear. The book has a decided Rebel bias.

1657. UP FOR THE GREEN: H. A. HINKSON; Lawrence & Bullen.

An interesting narrative story of adventure in the time of the Irish Rebellion of 1798. The hero starts from Cork for Dublin, but only reaches the Capital after falling into the hands of the Rebels and undergoing many experiences. The reader is given a glimpse of Castlereagh, while there are allusions to Grattan and others.

1658. *RORY O'MORE: SAMUEL LOVER; Constable [Eng.], Routledge [Eng.], Dutton [U.S.A.].

Ireland at the time of the '98 Rebellion. This book is considered by some critics to be Lover's best imaginative effort. The story reflects the Rebellion to a certain extent, but can hardly be called historical in any full sense; it must be judged primarily as a work of humour.

1659. HARMLESS AS DOVES: MAUDE ROBINSON, in "Nicholas the Weaver and Other Quaker Stories"—*Swarthmore Press* [Eng.], *Friends Book Store, Philadelphia* [U.S.A.].
A short tale of Co. Wexford, Ireland: the Quakers during the troubles of 1798.

1660. *IN DARK AND EVIL DAYS: FRANCIS SHEEHY SKEFFINGTON; *Duffy* [Ireland].
Ireland (Wexford and Dublin) in 1798. A novel with a considerable historic background. Illustrates the United Irishmen Movement, and describes in some detail the actual insurrection—presenting a sympathetic, yet discriminating, picture. There are numerous historical figures, including Lord Edward Fitzgerald, Sir Ralph Abercrombie, General Lake, Lord Clare, and Lord Camden.

1661. *THE RACE OF CASTLEBAR: EMILY LAWLESS and SHAN F. BULLOCK; *Murray*.
England (Surrey, etc.) and Ireland (Dublin, West Mayo, etc.), in 1798. Adventure and politics with a good background of history. Begins with reports of French invasion, and then deals fully with the Humbert expedition. The attitude of Catholic and Protestant at this stirring time is reflected without bias, though the authors indicate the bigotry of the extreme "Orange" position. General Humbert himself is introduced.

1662. *THE NORTHERN IRON: "GEORGE A. BIRMINGHAM"; *Maunsel* [Ireland].
N. Ireland (the Portrush-Ballycastle region), 1798. A novel giving a vivid depiction of conditions in the Rebellion period—the "United Irishmen," etc. Conveys the atmosphere of high patriotic aspiration, at the same time making clear to the reader the harshness of Government methods.

1663. *TIPPOO SULTAUN: PHILIP MEADOWS TAYLOR; *Kegan Paul*.
India and England in the period, 1788-99. An excellent historical novel of the Mysore War and Tippoo. Depicts, with abundance of detail, the time when the French and the English were striving for supremacy. The book ends with Wellesley's storming of the Fort of Seringapatam and Tippoo's death in 1799.

1664. THE TIGER OF MYSORE: G. A. HENTY; *Juv. Blackie* [Eng.], *Scribner* [U.S.A.].
Southern India, 1790-99. A tale of the war with Tippoo Sahib, beginning with the period when Lord Cornwallis was governor-general of India and commander-in-chief, and ending with the capture of Seringapatam.

1665. THADDEUS OF WARSAW: JANE PORTER; *Routledge*.
Poland and England, 1792 and the few years following. The struggle of the Poles during the various intrigues of the period: their resistance to Russian, Prussian, and Austrian intervention. The Battle of Brzesc is among the events introduced. Stanislas, last King of Poland, appears.

1666. THE HUNGARIAN BROTHERS: ANNA MARIA PORTER; *Warne* [Eng.], *Lippincott* [U.S.A.].
Hungary, Vienna, Italy, etc., 1797. Archduke Charles and the Austrian Wars against the French in Italy, etc. A romance written on extremely old-fashioned lines.

1667. *THE HOUR AND THE MAN: HARRIET MARTINEAU; *Routledge*.
The Island of Hayti and France (the Jura), 1791-1803. A tale beginning with the Negro Rising in Hayti (1791), and somewhat quickly passing to much later events. The outstanding figure is the remarkable Toussaint L'Ouverture, who, originally a negro slave, was (1797) appointed commander-in-chief in the island by the French Convention. Further developments are imaginatively outlined in such a way as to bring before the reader Toussaint's nobility of character, and natural power of leadership.

The latest chapters tell how he was arrested, taken to France, and imprisoned in a dark dungeon where death released him after some months. In so far as the historical hero himself is concerned, the book may be regarded as conveying a true (if idealized) picture; but—to quote Dr. Baker's excellent Introduction to a fairly recent edition of the novel—" in drawing the portraits of his [Toussaint's] associates, and in depicting the general state of the island under his rule, Miss Martineau has given us romance of far too roseate and idyllic a character."

1668. A ROVING COMMISSION: G. A. HENTY; *Juv.* Blackie [*Eng.*], Scribner [*U.S.A.*].
Hayti, 1791-1803. A tale of the Negro Rising, etc., and the heroic Toussaint L'Ouverture.

1669. *DANIEL BOONE, WILDERNESS SCOUT: STEWART EDWARD WHITE; *Hodder & Stoughton* [*Eng.*], Doubleday [*U.S.A.*].
Pennsylvania, North Carolina, Kentucky, etc., mainly between 1760 and 1800. Daniel Boone, the Pioneer: imaginative biography rather than fiction proper.

1670. *IN THE DARK LAND: JOHN BUCHAN; in " The Path of the King "—Nelson [*Eng.*]. Doran [*U.S.A.*].
Kentucky at the end of the 18th Century: Daniel Boone and the Indians.

1671. THE HERITAGE: BURTON EGBERT STEVENSON; *Duckworth* [*Eng.*], Houghton Mifflin [*U.S.A.*].
The Ohio Valley, 1790 onwards. A story of the first Ohio settlements, and the attempts of the Indians to drive out the white new-comers. Covers the defeat of St. Clair (1791), and the victory three years later of General Wayne (" Mad Anthony Wayne," as he was called, by reason of his extraordinary daring).

1672. *PIONEER SCOUTS OF THE OHIO: EVERETT T. TOMLINSON; *Juv. Appleton.*
Ohio, 1791. An excellent tale of settlers who had come in 1790 from Massachusetts to Ohio. Tells of fishing, hunting, and the Red Men, etc. There are numerous adventures. The story, however, is not one of purely imaginary wonders, but is based on fact (" all the incidents incorporated in the tale are true," says the author in his *Preface*).

1673. THE WILDERNESS ROAD: JOSEPH A. ALTSHELER; *Juv.* Lawrence & Bullen [*Eng.*], Appleton [*U.S.A.*].
Kentucky, etc., in the last decade of the Century. An interesting story of the Indian Wars: St. Clair's defeat in 1791, and Wayne's victory in 1794.

1674. SCOUTING WITH MAD ANTHONY: EVERETT T. TOMLINSON; *Juv. Appleton.*
Ohio River regions, 1793-95. An adventure story, with good local colour, and, on the historical side, illustrating General Anthony Wayne's suppression of the Indian tribes in the Ohio country. The General himself appears.

1675. THE PRAIRIE BIRD: HON. CHARLES A. MURRAY; *Warne;* also *Routledge.*
The Ohio country and the North American Indians about four years after they had been forced by General Wayne (in 1795) to sign a treaty of peace. An old favourite which was first included in these lists on the express recommendation of the late Mr. Clement K. Shorter.

1676. *THE MINISTER'S WOOING: MRS. H. BEECHER STOWE; *Sampson Low* [*Eng.*], Houghton Mifflin [*U.S.A.*].
New England (Newport) towards the end of the 18th Century. Considered by some critics to be the author's best novel. A good picture of the New England life of the time, with its Puritanism and love of theological discussion. The historic figure of Colonel Burr is brought into the story very prominently (an adverse depiction); his earlier career is illustrated—the closing pages of the book merely glancing at the duel with Hamilton and other episodes of a later period.

1677. *BALISAND: Joseph Hergesheimer; *Heinemann* [*Eng.*], *Knopf* [*U.S.A.*].

Virginia in the 1790-1800 period. A novel reflecting largely the political developments of the time following the American War of Independence. Allusions to leading men like Washington, Thomas Jefferson, Alexander Hamilton, and John Adams are frequent, but the story on the historical side is one of general atmosphere rather than of particular events or persons. Covers Washington's Second Presidency (the Proclamation of Neutrality, etc.), and ends, after his death, with the announcement of Jefferson's election as President (Nov. 1800).

1678. *COCKADES: Meade Minnigerode; *Putnam*.

Mostly New York, Philadelphia, and New Orleans, in the period 1793-1804. An excellent romance of the Dauphin, Charles Louis Capet, based on the assumption that he did *not* die in France, but lived to have various experiences in North America. The atmosphere is thoroughly historical, and there are numerous allusions to events like the Election of Jefferson in 1801, and the Louisiana Purchase in 1803. Count Axel de Fersen is prominent in the earlier chapters, and other real personages (French and American) are more or less prominent throughout; but leading public men like Washington Hamilton, Burr, Jay, Adams, Madison, etc., are for the most part merely mentioned.

1679. *LITTLE JARVIS: Molly E. Seawell; *Juv.* *Appleton*.

The American troubles with France (c. 1798-99) regarding neutrality during the French War with England, and in the period of Adams' Administration. The tale is mainly about a lad on the American Warship " Constellation " during its cruise, and the battle with the French " La Vengeance."

1680. *THE YELLOW POPPY: D. K. Broster; *Duckworth*.

Western France (Brittany, etc.) and the neighbourhood of Paris, 1799-1800. A good tale dealing with the time of the Consulate and the Chouans. Cadoudal is introduced.

NINETEENTH CENTURY

1681. *JOHN HALIFAX, GENTLEMAN: Dinah Maria Craik née Mulock; *Hurst & Blackett* [*Eng.*], *Lippincott* [*U.S.A.*], *and other publishers.*

Mainly Tewkesbury (" Norton Bury ") and district, in the period 1794-1834. It is no wonder that this famous tale continues to attract, for Mrs. Craik's best stories exhibit much charm of style (she was a woman of exceptional culture) as well as considerable skill in character depiction. Of course this, her finest imaginative effort, *must be judged by its own non-sensational standard.* Although primarily a romance of love and the domesticities, it has, also, a distinctly historic side—reflecting English provincial conditions in the Famine year of 1800, besides illustrating the later troubles which attended the introduction of machinery, and Political Reform, respectively.

1682. RODNEY STONE: A. Conan Doyle; *Smith, Elder* [*Eng.*], *Appleton* [*U.S.A.*] *and other publishers.*

Sussex (Brighton region) and London, 1796-1803. A novel of social life in the time of the Bucks, with a distinctly pugilistic atmosphere. There are several historic figures, including the Prince of Wales (George IV), Brummell, Sheridan, Queensberry, Nelson, Lady Hamilton, and Jackson, the pugilist.

1683. A LIEUTENANT OF THE KING: " Morice Gerard "; *Juv.* *Cassell*.

W. England (Plymouth, Saltash, Lostwithiel, etc.), 1797-1805. Largely deals with a plot to take certain papers of national importance (Pitt-Bonaparte conflict). A murder conspiracy by a Frenchman adds fictional interest. The outstanding historical figure is William Pitt the Younger—at first under another name, and at the end under his own.

P

1684. *THE THUNDERER: E. Barrington; *Harrap* [*Eng.*], Dodd, Mead [*U.S.A.*].

France and Italy, 1795-1811 (the *Epilogue* gives a brief survey of later years). A romance of Napoleon and Josephine, presenting a well-considered depiction in each case. Public events are reflected rather than dealt with directly, though the Coronation at Notre Dame is fully described. Crowds of historic personages are introduced at one point or another, the most noteworthy being: members of the Bonaparte family, Hortense de Beauharnais, Junot, Barras, Madame Tallien, Duroc, Bourrienne, Talleyrand, Madame de Rémusat, Marie Walewska, and Fouché.

1685. LAZARRE: Mrs. M. H. Catherwood; *Grant Richards* [*Eng.*], *Bobbs-Merrill* [*U.S.A.*].

France and America, 1795-1815. A romance of the Dauphin—his supposed escape from prison, and his later experiences in America.

1686. *A SAILOR OF NAPOLEON: John Lesterman; *Juv.*   Cape.

Toulon, Ajaccio, West Indies, etc., 1798-1805. An excellent story of the sea, telling —amongst other things—of the friendship formed between a French naval lad (the narrator and hero in one) and an English midshipman captured at the Battle of the Nile. The Englishman only appears, to any great extent, in the first three chapters, and the story thenceforward deals with the varied and exciting adventures of the hero. There are many historical allusions—the period being that of the Directory, the Consulate, and the Empire respectively, but of history in any detailed sense there is little or none. Napoleon is introduced more than once. On almost the last page, the two " enemy-friends " meet at the English youth's Lancashire home. The book is charmingly illustrated.

1687. *LA FORCE[1]: Paul Adam; *Ernest Flammarion* [*France*].

France, Germany, and Austria, 1797-1809. An interesting historical romance of the Directory, Consulate, and Empire periods, dealing especially with Napoleon's wars against Austria (Ulm and Austerlitz, etc.). The novel touches most of the important personages and events of the time, from the Egyptian expedition down to Wagram. Napoleon is, of course, the central figure—Moreau, Ney, and Murat being also more or less prominently introduced. Familiar names are frequently encountered: Talleyrand, Barras, Madame Tallien, Madame de Staël, Pichegru, Cadoudal, Mack, and many others.

[1] This novel is chosen out of the series to which the author has given the general title : *Le Temps et la Vie ; histoire d'une idéal à travers les siècles.* " La Force " is usually considered to be a very good— f not the best—example of the author ; the other volumes in the series have scarcely the same amount of interest on the historical side.

1688. *A BROTHER OF GIRLS: " Sydney C. Grier "; *Blackwood.*

Austria (largely), Russia, Prussia, Turkey, etc., 1797 to about 1812. An Englishman on a political mission Abroad, and his varied experiences with both men and women. The story reflects very largely the political developments of the time—covering the Treaty of Amiens, the Peace of Tilsit, Napoleon's marriage with Marie Louise of Austria, and the Moscow Retreat. Besides Napoleon, such names as the Emperor Alexander I of Russia and Frederick-William III of Prussia are to be found at one or more points; while, of those more definitely introduced, one may specify: Metternich (at the end), Queen Luise of Prussia, and Lord Granville.

1689. *THE MINISTER'S DAUGHTER: Madame Hildur Dixelius (trans.); *Dent* [*Eng.*], *Dutton* [*U.S.A.*].

Lapland in the period 1798-1809. A powerful novel of character, with good local colour, but offering very few historical allusions.

1690. *A PRIEST IN SPITE OF HIMSELF: Rudyard Kipling; in " Rewards and Fairies "—*Macmillan.*

Talleyrand and Bonaparte round about the year 1800.

1691. SKIPPER ANNE: MARIAN BOWER; *Hodder & Stoughton.*
France and (largely) Yorkshire (Hull district) in 1800. A good story of Napoleon's
Secret Service in the Chouan conspiracy period. Tells how a man is compelled to
impersonate. There are some unexpected developments as the tale nears its end.
Bonaparte appears (as First Consul) and there is a glimpse of Bourrienne.

1692. *MOLL O' THE TOLL BAR: THEODORA WILSON WILSON;
Hutchinson.
Cumberland in 1801. A really excellent tale of the troubles in Napoleonic War
time (farm-burning and hunger riots; such disturbances originated in the great scarcity
of food consequent on the high price of corn). The story also depicts the manners and
character-types of the period—a cock-fighting parson, a Methodist class-leader, etc.

1693. *THE KNIGHT OF GWYNNE: CHARLES LEVER; *Chapman &
Hall.*
Ireland (Dublin, Westport, Coleraine region, etc.) and Egypt, mainly in the period
1800-1802. Although the author's sense of humour is quite apparent in this novel, a
reader will find in it a really serious treatment of Irish politics in the period of the
Legislative Union measure. The means employed (purchasing of votes, etc.) for the
carrying of said measure, are condemned in unsparing fashion. Lord Castlereagh is
prominently introduced, and the special circumstances leading up to his withdrawal are
well indicated in the course of the tale. In one of the later sections there is some account
of Abercrombie's Mediterranean Expedition and the War in Egypt (Aboukir) against
the French in 1801. The allusions to public men are numerous (Plunket, Grattan,
Pitt, George III, etc.); while, besides Castlereagh, the Duke of York and General Menou
(the French Commander-in-Chief in Egypt) are actually brought into the novel. The
fictional portrait of the " Knight " is an inspiring and attractive one.

1694. *MOONRAKER; OR, THE FEMALE PIRATE AND HER
FRIENDS: F. TENNYSON JESSE; *Heinemann [Eng.], Knopf [U.S.A.].*
Cornwall and the Island of Hayti (San Domingo), 1801-1802. Primarily an original
and startling tale of the sea, but in part, also a romance of Toussaint L'Ouverture, the
heroic negro leader whom Bonaparte treated so shamefully. The final pages pass
beyond Toussaint's death in captivity at Besancon in 1803, to the year 1822.

1695. THE STRANGE ADVENTURE OF JACK SMITH: JOHN
FINBARR; *Juv. Oxford University Press.*
Kent (Dover, Canterbury, etc.) c. 1802 or 1803, ending 1805. A thoroughly good
tale of a boy's varied experiences in the time of the Bonaparte invasion scare. There
is a glimpse of Nelson.

1696. *SPRINGHAVEN: R. D. BLACKMORE; *Sampson Low [Eng.],
Harper [U.S.A.], also Dent [Eng.], Dutton [U.S.A.].*
English South Coast (Sussex) 1802-1805. A good example of the author, and one
that can be more correctly placed under the heading of *Historical* Fiction than any of
his other novels. The dread of " Boney " at the time of his invasion projects, is reflected
in the story which gradually leads up to the great event of the period—the Battle of
Trafalgar (the book ends with an account of this momentous sea-fight). Nelson is very
prominent in the earlier chapters, as well as towards the end of the novel. Napoleon,
King George III, and Queen Charlotte also appear.

1697. *A ROMANCE OF THE FIRST CONSUL: MATHILDA MALLING
(trans.); *Heinemann.*
La Vendée and (mainly) Paris, 1800-1801. The heroine is a Royalist maiden of La
Vendée who—as a result of coming to Paris—is converted from her preconceived hatred
of the Revolution and Napoleon. Not only that, but she falls in love with the great
man himself, who speedily succumbs to her charms. The romance has a tragic ending.
The period covered is that of the second Italian campaign to which considerable allusion
is made. Bonaparte, Josephine, Madame Tallien, Madame de Staël, Madame Récamier,
Hortense de Beauharnais, Eugène de Beauharnais, Talleyrand, and other historic
figures.

1698. *THE EAGLE'S TALON (*LA SERRE DE L'AIGLE*): Georges Ohnet (trans.); *Putnam.*
France (largely Paris), 1800-1804. An interesting historical romance, beginning with the close of the Chouan insurrection (1800), but mainly dealing with the Pichegru conspiracy and the part taken in it by Cadoudal and Moreau respectively. Covers the arrest and shooting of the Duc d'Enghien, as well as Cadoudal's execution. Crowds of historic figures: Bonaparte, Josephine, Cadoudal, Pichegru, Moreau, Fouché, Duroc, Berthier, Bourrienne, Ney, Marmont, Rapp, Hortense Beauharnais, Murat, and Caroline Murat.

1699. *THE ADVENTURES OF A GOLDSMITH: M. H. Bourchier; *Mathews & Marrot.*
N. France and Paris, 1802-1804. An interesting tale of an English goldsmith (he is the supposed narrator), telling how he came to be mixed up with the Cadoudal-Pichegru conspiracy against Napoleon. Shows the First Consul's growing apprehensions with regard to England—his order for all English subjects to be arrested as prisoners of war. Although the overshadowing figure, Napoleon actually appears but little. The Chouan leader, Cadoudal, and the tragedian Talma are both prominent (Talma is shown playing *Nero* before Napoleon and Josephine), while there are allusions to Pichegru, Moreau and others. The book ends with the shooting of the Duc d'Enghien and Napoleon's assumption of the title of Emperor.

1700. A SPY FOR NAPOLEON: " May Wynne "; *Jarrolds.*
An Englishman in Normandy, 1803-1804. Illustrates especially the Cadoudal-Pichegru conspiracy against the Consulate, and the working of Fouché's spy organisation. Napoleon, Fouché, D'Enghien, Cadoudal, and Pichegru are all introduced.

1701. THE EMPEROR'S SPY: Hector Fleischmann (trans.); *Nash.*
France, 1803-1807. A sensational story of a female spy in Bonaparte's Secret Police, covering the Cadoudal-Pichegru conspiracy for the assassination of the First Consul, and telling of certain events supposed to have occurred after Cadoudal's execution in 1804. An immense number of historic figures: Bonaparte, Josephine, Pichegru, Cadoudal, Fouché, Joseph Bonaparte, etc., etc.

1702. BY NEVA'S WATERS: John R. Carling; *Ward, Lock* [Eng.], *Little, Brown* [U.S.A.].
A novel having for its historical background the events connected with the murder of the Russian Emperor, Paul I in 1801. Elizabeth of Baden, who had married Alexander (afterwards Alexander I) in 1793, is a very prominent figure in the story.

1703. *THE MOONLIGHT SONATA (*QUASI UNA FANTASIA*): John Nordling (trans.); *Melrose.*
Vienna at the beginning of the 19th Century. A romance of Beethoven as a man of 30, when the defect in his hearing (begun about 1798) was gradually approaching its final stage of complete deafness.

1704. *THE NAMELESS CASTLE: Maurus Jókai (trans.); *Jarrold* [Eng.], *Doubleday* [U.S.A.].
Hungary in the first decade of the 19th Century. An interesting story, based on the notion of a daughter of Marie Antoinette being concealed in a Hungarian castle.

1705. DIAMOND ROCK: J. Macdonald Oxley; *Juv. Nelson.*
A tale of the sea in the period 1802-1805. " Diamond Rock " is an islet (near Martinique) which the English fortified at this time. The book ends with Trafalgar.

1706. *THE OLD FOX: Lettice U. Cooper; *Hodder & Stoughton.*
S. England, c. 1803. A good story of the time when Napoleon was " waiting on the cliffs of Boulogne " (invasion of England projects). The hero (Revenue officer) and the Keswick-born heroine, are well depicted. There are no historical events or figures, but the atmosphere of French plots, smugglers, etc., suggests the period, quite apart from the mention of George III, Bonaparte, Nelson, and Collingwood. At one point allusion is made to " a book of poems by a man named Wordsworth."

1707. *THE HOUSE OF SPIES: Warwick Deeping; *Cassell.*
Sussex coast in the region of Battle, c. 1803. A story illustrating the time of the Napoleonic invasion scheme. One of the leading characters is a French spy, and there are some interesting fictional developments.

1708. 'TWAS IN TRAFALGAR BAY: Walter Besant and James Rice; *Chatto & Windus* [Eng.], *Dodd, Mead* [U.S.A.].
A slight, but interesting, example of these famous literary collaborators. The scene is Lyme Regis and district *mainly in* 1803, but the story ends in 1805. Reflects the smuggling that was so prevalent in the French War period.

1709. *THE MAYOR OF TROY: A. T. Quiller-Couch; *Dent* [Eng.], *Methuen* [Eng.], *Scribner* [U.S.A.].
Cornwall (Fowey and Looe district), Plymouth, etc., 1803-1804, and 1814. A delightfully humorous and interesting tale, largely illustrating the Napoleon Invasion Scare period. There is some good character-drawing. Except as regards general atmosphere, history is almost entirely in the background, though at one point in the story there is a glimpse of the Prince Regent.

1710. NAPOLEON DECREES: James Blyth; *White.*
English East Coast (Norfolk-Suffolk region), also Belgium and France, 1804. Story of a Frenchman in England—at once impostor and spy. Kidnapping and various adventures. Napoleon, Josephine, and Davout appear.

1711. *DEVIL DARE: THE STORY OF A TRAITOR: Alfred Ollivant; *Heinemann* [Eng.], *Doubleday* [U.S.A.].
Sussex (Eastbourne region), 1804. A novel which, though primarily one of rollicking adventure, has a distinctly historic side. Nelson never directly appears, but the reader is made aware of his *shadow* throughout; while Napoleon—newly risen to his Imperial height—actually lands on the Sussex coast, and converses with the " traitor " hero! This tale, with its subtle blend of laughter and tears, can hardly fail to hold the attention of the average reader, though the author's occasional tendency in the direction of sombre detail may not be approved in every quarter.

1712. UNCLE BERNAC: A. Conan Doyle; *Smith, Elder* [Eng.], *Appleton* [U.S.A.].
Northern France in 1805. The Camp of Boulogne, etc., and Napoleon's contemplated invasion of England. The Emperor is greatly to the fore, while Josephine and Talleyrand are more or less prominent. There are the merest glimpses of such historic figures as Ney, Murat, Lannes, Soult, etc.

1713. *THE HOUSE IN THE DOWNS: H. B. Marriott Watson; *Dent.*
Largely Sussex (Chichester district) in the time of Napoleon's invasion schemes. An exceptionally good tale, in which the hero is brought into contact with smugglers and has various adventures. There is, also, quite a substantial background of history— French plots and Admiralty despatches, the naval movements of Villeneuve and Nelson, and the announcement of the latter's arrival in English waters prior to sailing for Cadiz (1805).

1714. QUEEN'S FOLLY: Stanley J. Weyman; *Murray* [Eng.], *Longmans* [U.S.A.].
Mainly the New Forest region (Ringwood, Fordingbridge, Salisbury, etc.), c. 1805. A story of social life in the time immediately preceding Trafalgar. History is in the far background (allusions to Nelson, Bonaparte, etc.).

1715. THE GENTLEMAN: Alfred Ollivant; *Murray* [Eng.], *Macmillan* [U.S.A.].
Another of the author's tales in which the scene is the Eastbourne district (Sussex coast). The main subject is an attempt by an agent of Napoleon to kidnap Nelson a few weeks before Trafalgar, in 1805.

1716. SMUGGLER'S WAY: Dorothea Moore; *Juv.   Cassell.*
English South Coast and France, 1805.   An interesting tale of a French spy, smugglers, and preventives.   In the course of the story an English boy and girl are taken to France as prisoners (both sea and land adventures).   Ends with the *news* of Trafalgar.

1717. IN TRAFALGAR'S BAY: "Herbert Strang"; *Juv. Oxford University Press.*
A Sussex girl's adventures in the absence of her father and brother, 1805.   The press-gang, a glimpse of George III (London), and a brief allusion to Trafalgar at the end. A very slight, but pleasing, tale.

1718. ANDREW GOODFELLOW: Helen H. Watson; *Macmillan.*
Plymouth, 1805.   A tale of the time immediately preceding Trafalgar: a picture of old West Country life.   There is really little in the way of historical illustration, though the reader is at one point taken to London and shown Mrs. Jordan acting at Drury Lane before an audience which contains Nelson, the Lambs, Opie, the Prince of Wales, etc. Ends with the *news* of the Trafalgar victory.

1719. *THE INFAMOUS JOHN FRIEND: Mrs. R. S. Garnett; *Duckworth [Eng.], Holt [U.S.A.].*
Brighton, London, Hythe, etc., c. 1805.   A novel of exceptional power and interest, almost making the reader demur to the description of the chief fictional character as "infamous"—spy or what else he is made out to be.   The most important historical figures are Pitt and Napoleon.

1720. *THE TRUMPET-MAJOR: Thomas Hardy; *Macmillan [Eng.], Harper [U.S.A.].*
One of Hardy's shorter examples.   A story of George III's Weymouth and of the Dorset coast, in the period of the Napoleonic invasion scare.

1721. *TRAFALGAR[1]: Benito Pérez-Galdós (trans.); *Trübner [Eng.], Gottsberger [U.S.A.].*
The first—and to English and American readers, probably the most interesting—volume in the author's long series of historical tales published in the original Spanish under the general title of *Episodios Nacionales*; the earlier "Episodes" illustrate the Trafalgar and Peninsular War periods, but the later tales in the series, dealing with the dynastic controversies of Ferdinand VII's reign, etc., etc., become more local in interest. In this first tale, the scene is in or near Cadiz, 1805, and the young Spanish hero's naval experiences serve to indicate more or less precisely what happened immediately before and during the Battle of Trafalgar.   It is shown how Villeneuve committed a fatal error in leading the combined French and Spanish fleets out of the Bay of Cadiz, while an excellent account is given of the great sea-fight which followed.

[1] A full list of the *Episodios Nacionales* is to be found at the end of L. B. Walton's carefully written volume: "Pérez-Galdós and the Spanish Novel of the Nineteenth Century" (Dent, Eng., and Dutton, U.S.A.).

1722. PETER THE POWDER BOY: Walter Wood; *Juv.   Routledge.*
Portsmouth, Gibraltar, Tangier, etc., 1805.   A good adventure story telling of a young lad's sea and land experiences.   Covers Trafalgar and the time immediately following. Pirates, Moors, Robbers, etc.   Nelson appears.

1723. *THE SPANISH PRISONER: Mrs. Philip C. De Crespigny; *Nash.*
Begins in the Navarra Province (N. Spain), with the *news* of Trafalgar, quickly passing to Valladolid; the reader is then taken to England and back to Spain, 1805-1806.   An interesting story of a Spanish girl whose cousin-fiancé, as prisoner of the English, breaks his parole; the girl is disgusted, and—driven by an accumulation of circumstances—goes in male attire to England with other prisoners, impersonating her now unattractive lover.   During the time in England (Portsmouth region) certain unexpected developments occur, which must be left to the author's own telling.

1724. *THE ADVENTURES OF A TRAFALGAR LAD: JOHN
LESTERMAN; *Juv. Cape.*
West Indies, etc., 1805. A good sea tale beginning five days after Trafalgar. The
youthful hero is put in charge of a captured French privateersman used for conveying
prisoners to England; this incident is the prelude to dangers and adventures innumerable—fights, mutinies, escapes, Spanish slave-trader experiences, etc. The historical
element is very slight (a few backward glances at Trafalgar in the opening pages).

1725. *TRUE MAN AND TRAITOR: M. McDONNELL BODKIN;
Fisher Unwin [Eng.], *Duffy* [Ireland].
Ireland (mostly Dublin) and Paris, c. 1800 to 1803. A romance of the Irish patriot,
Robert Emmet, beginning with him in the Debating Society of Trinity College. Covers
in turn: His falling in love with Sarah Curran; his visit to Paris and the interview with
Napoleon; the preparations for a Rising on his return to Ireland; the actual Rising;
and, lastly, his flight, capture, trial and execution. Many historic personages, besides the
central figure of Emmet, are introduced: Tom Moore, Curran, Sarah Curran, Lord
Clare (prominent), Castlereagh, Napoleon, and others.

1726. *ROBERT EMMET; STEPHEN GWYNN; *Macmillan.*
Chiefly Dublin, 1803. A carefully written novel of Emmet's conspiracy, and the
events leading up to the Rising and its lamentable sequel. The Curran family is, of
course, largely in evidence. There is a good description of Emmet's trial (Lord Norbury,
etc.), while, in regard to the whole circumstances of the Rising, the author has furnished
some interesting notes at the end of the volume.

1727. AT THE POINT OF THE BAYONET: G. A. HENTY; *Juv.*
Blackie [Eng.], *Scribner* [U.S.A.].
India in the period 1779-1804, "A tale of the Mahratta War," covering in particular
the Battles of Assaye and Laswari (1803), and introducing Holkar and Scindia the
Mahratta leaders.

1728. PANDURANG HÀRI: W. B. HOCKLEY: *Chatto & Windus.*
Supposed memoirs of a Hindu, relating to life among the Mahrattas in the first two
decades of the 19th Century (1801 onwards). A careful imaginative sketch of the
disturbed period just named: last years of the Peeshwas' rule.

1729. *A FREELANCE IN KASHMIR: LIEUT.-COL. G. F. MACMUNN;
Smith, Elder.
Kashmir, 1804. A story of adventure, fighting, and love, with a young Scot as hero
(his mother was an Afghan lady). The book shows considerable knowledge of North
West Indian localities, and illustrates the lawless time when Lake and Wellesley were
breaking up the Maratha Confederacy. There is the merest glimpse of Lord Lake at
the end of the story.

1730. *DECATUR AND SOMERS: MOLLY E. SEAWELL; *Juv.*
Appleton.
A tale with Stephen Decatur (the American naval commander) as principal historical
figure. The period is mostly between 1798 and 1804. Deals largely with the war
against Tripoli (1801-1805) which originated in the trouble with the Governor of Tripoli
over increased tribute for the protection of vessels from pirates in the Mediterranean.
Decatur's achievement of burning the warship *Philadelphia* off Tripoli, is one of the
most important historic events introduced. Another striking incident is the blowing-
up (by Lieutenant Somers and those under him) of the specially loaded *Intrepid.*

1731. *THE MAGNIFICENT ADVENTURE: EMERSON HOUGH;
Hodder & Stoughton [Eng.], *Appleton* [U.S.A.].
Virginia, etc., mainly 1803-1809. An interesting romance illustrating Lewis and
Clark's Exploration of the Far West. Period of the Louisiana Purchase and of Aaron
Burr's Conspiracy. Burr's daughter, Theodosia, plays a prominent part in the story.
The two most important historic figures are Thomas Jefferson (as President) and Burr—
both of them appearing at several points.

1732. *LEWIS RAND: Mary Johnston; *Constable [Eng.]*, *Houghton Mifflin [U.S.A.]*.
Virginia (Richmond, Charlottesville, etc.) 1790, then 1804-1808. Story of a lawyer-politician: his varied sympathies and his personal ambitions. The historic background is well conveyed throughout, especially the circumstances of Aaron Burr's conspiracy (Burr's trial is described in some detail). One important incident is an election in which Federalist and Democrat-Republican meet in contest. On the purely fictional side there is a domestic and love element. Among the large number of public men either mentioned or actually appearing, one may specify Jefferson and Burr as by far the most prominent.

1733. OPENING THE WEST WITH LEWIS AND CLARK: Edwin L. Sabin; *Juv.* *Lippincott.*
Lewis and Clark's Expedition in the New Territory of Louisiana, and the Columbia Country, 1804-1806. Fictional history of an interesting kind, telling of wonderful exploits and adventures (the Indians, etc.). This expedition was sent out by Jefferson Davis the year after the Louisiana Purchase.

1734. LOST WITH LIEUTENANT PIKE: Edwin L. Sabin; *Juv.* *Lippincott.*
Arkansas River districts, and the Mountains of Southern Colorado, etc., 1805-1807. A tale based on the explorations of Zebulon Montgomery Pike (soldier-explorer). Adventures with Indians and Spaniards, etc.

1735. *A SON OF THE REVOLUTION: Elbridge S. Brooks; *Juv.* *Wilde, Boston [U.S.A.]*.
Ohio, Tennessee, the Mississippi and Alabama regions, etc., mainly 1805-1807 (the closing pages pass quickly from 1808 to 1836). A good story of a young lad and his close relations with the famous Aaron Burr (the latter fascinates the boy at first, but gradually appears in his true colours). The events leading up to Burr's conspiracy, as well as the circumstances of his arrest and trial on the charge of treason, are fully illustrated in the tale. The hero has many exciting adventures as the bearer of despatches to General Jackson, etc. etc. Besides Burr, and General Jackson, both Henry Clay and Thomas Jefferson appear.

1736. BLENNERHASSETT: C. F. Pidgin; *Clark [U.S.A.]*.
The Ohio region, etc., mainly about the period 1805-1807. A story of the Burr-Blennerhassett conspiracy, leading up to the trial and acquittal of Burr. The scheme was—broadly stated—to raise a force for the purpose of conquering Texas (then Spanish territory), and also with the intention, said Burr's enemies, of setting up an independent nation.

1737. *THE GOLDEN LADDER: Rupert Hughes; *Hurst & Blackett [Eng.]*, *Burt [U.S.A.]*.
Providence, New York, and Paris, 1794-1865, but mainly 1800-1836. A romance dealing with Betty Bowen who, after becoming Madame Junot in the first instance, as a widow married the notorious Aaron Burr. The atmosphere of the tale is largely political, and many historical events are touched—notably the duel between Burr and Hamilton, in which the latter was mortally wounded. There are many allusions to the celebrities of the time (John Adams, James Monroe, Jefferson, etc.), while the following appear more or less prominently: Aaron Burr, Alexander Hamilton, Mrs. Hamilton (as widow), and Elizabeth Patterson (the " Belle of Baltimore ") who married Jerome Bonaparte. In the brief Paris section, Fouquier-Tinville is introduced. The book ends with a rapid survey of the events following Burr's death up to Betty's own death in 1865.

1738. *REZÁNOV: Gertrude Atherton; *Murray [Eng.]*, *Authors' and Newspapers' Assn. [U.S.A.]*.
Mainly San Francisco, 1806. A novel of manners and local colour, in which a plenipotentiary on a political and trading mission to California, plays an important part. On the historical side, the story reflects certain Russian aims at the time.

1739. *THE MUTINEERS: Charles Boardman Hawes; *Juv.* Heinemann [*Eng.*], Little, Brown [*U.S.A.*].
Begins New England, 1809, but is mainly a thrilling sea romance, describing a series of adventures on an eastward voyage, and in the China sea, etc.

1740. *AT ODDS: Baroness Tautphoeus; *Macmillan* [*Eng.*], *Lippincott* [*U.S.A.*].
S. Germany and the Tyrol, 1800-1809. A novel with a strong Irish element, though dealing with mid-European regions and events. There is considerable illustration of history—the Capitulation of Ulm (1805), and the expulsion of the French and Bavarians by the Austrians and Tyrolese (1809). A very favourable depiction is given of Andreas Hofer who is quite prominently introduced; Napoleon also appears (at Ulm).

1741. WITH THE RED EAGLE: William Westall; *Chatto & Windus.*
The Tyrol in 1809. Adventures of an English (or, rather, half-Irish) Captain during the patriotic struggles of the Tyrolese against the Bavarians. Covers the Battle of Berg Isel, etc. Andreas Hofer, Spechbacher, and others appear.

1742. *A RED BRIDAL: William Westall; *Chatto & Windus.*
This novel is expressly stated by the author to be a " supplement "—not a sequel proper—to *With the Red Eagle* (see above). The Tyrol, Bavaria, and Vienna, 1809-1810. Beginning on the eve of Hofer's revolt, the story proceeds to cover both the actual revolt and the events succeeding it. Ends with the shooting of Hofer. The hero is an Austrian with a Scottish mother.

1743. *ANDREAS HOFER[1]: " Louise Muhlbach " (trans.); *Appleton.*
Vienna and the Tyrol, 1809-1810. An historical romance of Hofer, the peasant leader of the Tyrolese. Describes in full detail the successful Rising against the Bavarians and the French (the fighting by the Bridge of Laditch, etc.). Also covers the various Austrian political developments in the period of the Battle of Wagram and the Treaty of Schönbrunn, and shows how, under the last-named Treaty, the Tyrol was sacrificed. The novel ends with an account of the betrayal and death of Hofer. The Emperor Francis, the Empress Ludovica, Metternich, Count Andréossi the French Ambassador, and Princess Esterhazy are more or less prominently introduced.

[1] I have chosen this book out of the author's numerous historical romances, because it is a very fair example in itself, and also because it deals with certain interesting historic events and figures which are not very often touched by writers of fiction. As to the other romances of " Louise Muhlbach " (Klara Mundt), they are doubtless praiseworthy and careful productions, but their historical superfluity, their " improving " footnotes, and their hyper-introduction of notabilities, can hardly appeal to the modern reader of novels.

1744. *PONCE DE LEON: William Pilling [" An Estanciero "] *Werner Laurie,* 1910, and *Chapman & Hall,* 1893 [*Eng.*], also *Mitchell's Book Store* [*S. America*].
Argentina (Buenos Aires), 1806-1810. This excellent novel illustrates the period in which the people of Argentina successfully withstood the British expeditions; it also shows how, in the revolution of 25th May, 1810, the Spanish domination came to an end. Among the historic figures introduced, one may specify General Beresford (afterwards Viscount Beresford).

1745. A SHEAF OF BLUEBELLS: Baroness Orczy; *Hutchinson* [*Eng.*], *Doran* [*U.S.A.*].
Département de l'Orme (Normandy) about 1805-1807. A tale of Royalist plots in the period of Napoleon's victories in Prussia and the Peace of Tilsit. Fouché appears in the opening pages, where, also, the reader obtains the merest glimpse of Napoleon.

1746. *THE STRONG HAND:
*OUT OF PRISON (*sequel*): " Sydney C. Grier "; *Blackwood.*
Two connected novels of Germany (Molzau), Paris, and Fontainebleau in the period 1806 to 1814: the family alliances of a German State, and the intrusion of Napoleon

who is presented in a distinctly unfavourable light.   The two books, taken as one story, illustrate an important period—Vol. I beginning with the news of Jena (1806), and Vol. II ending with the entry of the allies into Paris (1814).   Public events, however, are but lightly touched for the most part; on the other hand, historic personages abound, and, of these, one may specify as being prominent: Napoleon and Josephine; the Electress Louisa Frederica; the young Elector Bernard and Princess Alexandrine Napoléon; Princess Magdalene of Weldart and her husband; Hortense Queen of Holland; Jerome Bonaparte and his wife; Talleyrand; Caulaincourt; Cambacérès; and the Empress Marie Louise.

1747. *FRIEDRICH OF MÜNSTER[1]: C. Edmund Maurice; being Part I of " Unquenched Fires "—*Birrell & Garnett* [*Eng.*].
Westphalia, Saxony, Berlin, etc., 1802-19.   An interesting story which well illustrates the disturbed state of affairs in Westphalia during Jerome Bonaparte's reign.   The author's knowledge of Westphalian conditions at the time, is made evident; he brings before his readers the great figure of Baron von Stein, also introducing Queen Louisa of Prussia, the philosopher Fichte, Marshal Blücher, Jerome Bonaparte, and others.

[1] The late Mr. C. E. Maurice was the author of " Bohemia " in *The Stories of the Nations* series, and so recently as 1926 he published a " Life of the Great Elector of Brandenburg." From 1871 to 1885 he was lecturer in history at Queen's College, London.

1748. (1)*RUHE IST DIE ERSTE BÜRGERFLICHT:
        (2)*ISEGRIMM: " Wilibald Alexis " [Georg Häring]; *Janke* [*Germany*].
Prussia at the time of Napoleon's invasion.   Two good examples of the famous author.

1749. *DEUTSCHE MÄNNER: W. Jensen; *Grethlein* [*Germany*].
A novel of Germany in the Napoleonic period, especially dealing with the year 1809.

1750. *A FIDDLER OF LUGAU: Margaret Roberts; *Juv.   Hatchards* [*Eng.*], *Whittaker* [*U.S.A.*].
A story of life in Saxony during the Napoleonic Wars, by one of the older writers of tales for the young (she was known widely as " the author of *Mademoiselle Mori* ").   Miss Roberts specialised in fiction illustrating the history of such countries as Italy, France, and Germany.

1751. THE ADVENTURES OF AN AIDE-DE-CAMP: James Grant; *Juv.   Routledge* [*Eng.*], *Dutton* [*U.S.A.*].
Italy, 1808 and the year or two following.   A story of the English campaign in the Calabrias against the French: the Battle of Maida and the Siege of Scylla.   Various adventures (bandits, etc.) and love affairs.

1752. *THE EMPRESS-MIGHT-HAVE-BEEN: Octave Aubry (trans.); *Cape* [*Eng.*], *Harper* [*U.S.A.*].
France and Poland, mainly 1808-10; *Epilogue:* Elba, 1814.   Imaginative history in the form of a novel dealing with the Polish beauty, Madame Walewska, and her love for Napoleon.   Reflects the period of Josephine's divorce and the preparations for the Emperor's marriage with the Archduchess Marie Louise of Austria.   There are frequent allusions to public events.   Besides the two outstanding figures, crowds of more or less famous men and women appear: Josephine, Fouché, Duroc, Talleyrand, Madame de Rémusat, the Queen of Holland (née Hortense de Beauharnais), etc. etc.

1753. *THE TRAVELLER IN THE FUR CLOAK: Stanley J. Weyman; *Hutchinson* [*Eng.*], *Longmans* [*U.S.A.*].
Germany (Wittenberg, Hamburg, Berlin, etc.), 1809.   Tells how an Englishman of the Foreign Office who is on a political mission to Austria, loses and regains the confidential despatches entrusted to him.   There are some exciting developments (murder, hairbreadth escapes, etc.), with a substantial background of history—the story illustrating the state of affairs in Germany just after Napoleon's victory over the Austrians at Wagram.   Davout, the French Marshal, appears somewhat prominently.

1754. SCHÖNBRUNN: J. A. Cramb; *Putnam.*
Austria (Vienna region), 1809. A novel with an ultra-historic atmosphere. Depicts Napoleon at the height of his power in the days just before and after the Treaty of Schönbrunn (October, 1809). The author rashly attempts in some degree to analyse the Emperor's mind. The book is *crammed* (the pun comes unintentionally!) with allusions to persons and events of the period. Beethoven appears, while Rapp, Duroc, and Savary are more or less prominent, but Napoleon is the one outstanding figure.

1755. *TOM BURKE OF " OURS ": Charles Lever; *Downey [Eng.], Little, Brown [U.S.A.] and other publishers.*
Mainly France, Austria, and Germany in the period 1800-1814. An Irishman serves under Napoleon, and the account of his career illustrates some of the chief events of the Consulate and the Empire respectively—the Chouan conspiracy, and the great victories of Austerlitz and Jena. The novel concludes with a more or less rapid sketch of Napoleon's Russian failure, and the resulting changes in France. Napoleon is very prominently introduced (a highly favourable depiction), while Talleyrand, Cadoudal, Pichegru, Moreau, Murat, Bernadotte, Duroc, and Eugène Beauharnais all appear.

1756. *CHARLES O'MALLEY: Charles Lever; *Routledge [Eng.], Little, Brown [U.S.A.], and other publishers.*
One of Lever's best novels, with humorous scenes, adventures, duels, fighting, etc. Ireland, Portugal, Spain and Belgium, c. 1805-1815. In the earlier chapters there is much about Dublin (Trinity College, Phœnix Park, etc.), as well as glimpses of other Irish localities; later, comes a depiction of the Peninsular War—the Passage of the Douro, and the Battles of Talavera, Fuentes D'Onoro, and Ciudad Rodrigo, etc. etc. The book ends with the Duchess of Richmond's Ball (Brussels), Quatre Bras, and Waterloo (*a good description*). Wellington is very prominent, while Napoleon and Sir Thomas Picton are among the other historic figures.

1757. FLEUR-DE-CAMP: A. Godric Campbell; *Chatto & Windus.*
France, Germany, and Austria, 1805-15 (*Prologue* 1792). Tale of a French girl, illustrating many important events throughout the period of the First Empire. There is a good description of the Battle of Austerlitz, while Eylau, Dresden, and Leipsic are also touched. The novel virtually ends with Waterloo. There is frequent change of scene—the reader being taken to such widely-distant places as Nordlingen, Elchingen, Ulm, Vienna, and Paris. Napoleon, Rapp, Murat, Ney, and Berthier appear.

1758. A BOY OF THE FIRST EMPIRE: Elbridge S. Brooks; *Juv.* Fisher Unwin [Eng.], Century [U.S.A.].
Mostly France, and other Continental regions in slight degree, 1806-15 (final pages 1840). An amusing and interesting tale, though not to be taken too seriously on the historic side. The hero—a page in Napoleon's household—almost worships his master, who is presented in a very favourable light. Allusions to most of the leading events of the period, ending with Napoleon at St. Helena. Besides the Emperor, Marie Louise of Austria, Fouché, Josephine, Blücher, and Davout appear.

1759. *DEMI-ROYAL: " Ashton Hilliers "; *Methuen.*
England (Cheshire and London, etc.), Germany, Spain, and the Low Countries, 1805-1819. An autobiographical novel of life and adventure in many regions. There is a large Quaker element (the Ellwood family and Stephen Grellet, etc.), while both the social and military life of the period are reflected. On the side of actual events, some description is given of the Battle of Jena, as well as a few sketches of Peninsular War experiences. The story ends with the announcement of Queen Victoria's birth. Mrs. Fitzherbert and the Prince Regent are prominent (the fictional developments being closely connected with these personages); and, of the many other figures, the most noteworthy are: Wellington, Lord Liverpool, Lord Eldon, the Duke of Cumberland, and Bernadotte. There are, also, passing glimpses of Sir Francis Burdett, " Gentleman " Jackson, the Dukes of York and Kent respectively, the Duchess of Kent, and Prince Metternich.

1760. *THE STOOPING LADY: MAURICE HEWLETT; *Macmillan* [Eng.], *Dodd, Mead* [U.S.A.].

London, 1809-1810. A love story illustrating English High Social Life and Radical Politics. Cobbett is an outstanding figure, while " Orator " Hunt, Sir Francis and Lady Burdett, and the Prince of Wales appear. There are, also, allusions to Tom Moore, Sidney Smith, Rogers, Greville, and other personages of the time.

1761. THE BEAU AND THE LADY: " E. BARRINGTON "; in " The Gallants"—*Harrap*.

Mrs. Fitzherbert, Beau Brummell, and the Prince of Wales (George IV). Sheridan, also, is prominent in this imaginative sketch.

1762. *TWISTED EGLANTINE: H. B. MARRIOTT WATSON; *Methuen* [Eng.], *Appleton* [U.S.A.].

Hampshire (Lymington, New Forest, and Winchester), and London, c. 1809. A really excellent story of a Beau and his doings, reflecting the life and manners of the period. The Prince of Wales appears.

1763. *GOSSIP'S GREEN (THE BATTLE OF THE WEAK): MRS. HENRY E. DUDENEY; *Cassell* [Eng.], *Dillingham* [U.S.A.].

A well-written and altogether charming story of English South Coast life, which begins 1790, but quickly passes to 1810 and the years following. There are many allusions to public men and events of the time, though the book is not an historical novel in the full sense.

1764. HURDCOTT: " JOHN AYSCOUGH "; *Chatto & Windus* [Eng.], *Herder* [U.S.A.].

Wiltshire (" Chalkshire ") in the second decade of the 19th Century. A story of country life, with a distinctly Roman Catholic atmosphere. On the historical side, there are merely a few allusions to events, but the early chapters contain an unfavourable sketch of Hazlitt, and a pleasing little picture of Charles Lamb and his sister Mary.

1765. A PRINCE OF ROMANCE: STEPHEN CHALMERS; *Grant Richards* [Eng.], *University Press* [U.S.A.].

West Scotland, largely in the years 1812-13. A Jacobite love tale on somewhat startling and original lines, which it would be unfair to give away. Great events of the period, like Napoleon's Moscow Campaign, the Battle of Leipsic, and the American War of 1812, are more or less *reflected* in the story, but history is quite in the background. The Duke of Argyll, Cameron of Lochiel, and others appear.

1766. THE BAYMOUTH SCOUTS: TOM BEVAN; *Juv.* R.T.S.

Dorset, and Havre, Caen, etc, 1811. Two English lads are captured by the French, and put in prison at Havre. The story tells of their escape, etc. Bonaparte appears, and there is a faint glimpse of George III and his Queen at Weymouth in the last page or two.

1767. A HUNDRED YEARS AGO: HORACE BLEACKLEY; *Nash*.

Lancashire, 1812. A story illustrating chiefly the Luddite Riots against the introduction of Machinery, but also in some degree exposing the bad forgery laws then in force. There is an allusion to the assassination of Perceval, the Prime Minister, in May, 1812.

1768. *STRONG MAC: S. R. CROCKETT; *Ward, Lock*.

Scottish Lowlands, and (in small degree) Spain, 1812-13. A story of rough Lowland life, showing the author's general knowledge of time and place. The properly historical element (Peninsular War) is very slight.

1769. *" MR. ROWL ": D. K. Broster; *Heinemann* [*Eng.*], *Doubleday* [*U.S.A.*].
Huntingdonshire, various Midland localities and South Devon, 1813. An interesting novel about a young French prisoner, and his experiences in England. Presents a good picture of early 19th Century conditions.

1770. *WEIR OF HERMISTON: R. L. Stevenson; *Chatto & Windus* [*Eng.*], *Scribner* [*U.S.A.*].
Edinburgh and the Scottish Lowlands, 1813-14. This unfinished romance of the unhappy relations between a father and son, was suggested by the character of the hard-hearted Scottish judge, Lord Braxfield (1722-99). Stevenson, however, fixes his fictional incidents some fifteen years after the date of the Judge's death. Professor Hugh Walker has expressed the opinion that this mere fragment has " a grandeur which few complete novels possess."

1771. THE MOSS-TROOPERS: S. R. Crockett; *Hodder & Stoughton.*
Galloway and London district, c. 1812-16. Queen Charlotte is rather prominent at one point in this story, and there are glimpses of other Royalties (English and Foreign); but the primary interest is in the direction of love and smuggling, etc., on Solwayside.

1772. *THE AMERICAN PRISONER: Eden Phillpotts; *Methuen.*
A stirring tale of Dartmoor (the Princetown War Prison for American and French prisoners) in 1814: time of the " 1812 War " with America. The author is here dealing with the region which novel-readers have learnt to regard as in a very real and special sense *his own.*

1773. SMITH BRUNT: Waldron K. Post; *Putnam.*
A story of naval engagements (England *v.* America) in the period 1806-1815. One of the outstanding events presented, is the encounter between the *Shannon* (English frigate) and the *Chesapeake* American frigate in 1813.

1774. OUT OF THE CYPRESS SWAMP: Edith Rickert; *Methuen* [*Eng.*], *Baker & Taylor* [*U.S.A.*].
Louisiana, 1808; then the War period, 1812-15. A good story in which the chief historical event is the successful defence of New Orleans by General Andrew Jackson against Sir E. Pakenham, in January, 1815.

1775. D'RI AND I: Irving Bacheller; *Grant Richards* [*Eng.*], *Bobbs-Merrill* [*U.S.A.*].
N. America (Western frontier) and the War of 1812. The tale proper covers the period 1810-12, but there is a glimpse of President Monroe in 1817 at the very end of the book.

1776. MIDSHIPMAN FARRAGUT: James Barnes; *Juv. Appleton.*
A tale based on the early life of David Glasgow Farragut, the American Admiral. At the age of nine (1810) he entered the navy, and served under Captain David Porter in the War of 1812. This story covers the period of Porter's naval successes 1812-14.

1777. *A LOYAL TRAITOR: James Barnes; *Juv. Harper.*
Another tale of the sea by James Barnes, dealing with the War of 1812 period. The hero starts as a Connecticut village waif, 1809; afterwards—in the four or five years following—he has various experiences and adventures, first of all on board a privateer, then during his time of imprisonment in England (Dartmoor), and eventually in the days following his escape.

1778. *THE CIRCUIT RIDER: Edward Eggleston; *Scribner*; also *Grosset Kelly* [*Eng.*] and *Grosset & Dunlap* [*U.S.A.*].
Southern Ohio (Cincinnati) c. 1810-12. A story of Methodism and social life among the Early Westerners. Gives an interesting picture of the circuit preachers who " brought order out of chaos." The period is the beginning of Madison's Administration (he was elected President in 1809), while, at the end of the tale, allusion is made to the outbreak of " the War with Britain " (1812).

1779. *A HERALD OF THE WEST: Joseph A. Altsheler; *Juv.*
Appleton.*
Washington, Philadelphia, New York, Boston, New Orleans, etc., 1811-15. A tale
illustrating the strong anti-British feeling in the War of 1812 period, and ending with
General Andrew Jackson's defence of New Orleans at the beginning of 1815. Clay,
Clinton, Madison, and Jefferson appear.

1780. WITH PORTER IN THE *ESSEX:* James Otis Kaler; *Juv.*
Burt [U.S.A.].
Captain David Porter's cruise in the Pacific and his captures of property and men
in 1812; also his Valparaiso encounters with two British Men-of-War in 1814.

1781. MIDSHIPMAN PAULDING: Molly E. Seawell; *Juv.*
Appleton.
Northern New York, etc., 1813-14. A tale having Lieutenant Hiram Paulding, of
the United States Navy, as hero. Deals with naval experiences to a large extent
(Americans v. British), and ends with a full description of the Battle of Lake Champlain,
September 11, 1814.

1782. THE ERRAND BOY OF ANDREW JACKSON: W. O.
Stoddard; *Juv. Lothrop [U.S.A.].*
Mobile and New Orleans, 1814-15. A tale of events at the end of the War of 1812
—General Andrew Jackson being (as the title indicates) the outstanding historic figure.

1783. *THE SCARLET SASH: John M. Elson; *Dent.*
Canada (Niagara frontier), 1812-14. A novel of love and social life, with a considerable element of history. The period is that of the War of 1812, and one of the principal
events introduced, is the Battle of Queenston in which General Sir Isaac Brock met his
death. The General is quite prominent in a large part of the story.

1784. IN THE DICTATOR'S GRIP: John Samson; *Juv.   Blackie.*
Begins W. England, 1806, then S. America (the Pampas and Paraguay) in the period
1806-14. Covers the surrender and escape of Beresford at Buenos Aires; the later
successes of the Paraguayans, leading up to the end of Spanish rule and the declaration
of independence (1811); and the rise of the famous dictator, Dr. Francia.

1785. LOVE AND HONOUR: M. E. Carr; *Smith, Elder [Eng.], Putnam
[U.S.A.].*
Chiefly Westphalia under Jerome Bonaparte, 1807-13. A novel in which the fictional
developments far outweigh the historical. There is, however, some reflection of the
period in which Napoleon's career was at the turning-point. King Jerome appears,
and towards the end of the story the reader is given a glimpse of the Battle of Leipsic—
so fatal in its results to both Jerome and his greater brother.

1786. *IF YOUTH BUT KNEW: Agnes and Egerton Castle; *Smith,
Elder [Eng.], Macmillan [U.S.A.].*
Westphalia (Border region) and Cassel, 1813-14. A pleasing love story of the forest,
etc., illustrating the last months of Jerome Bonaparte's evil rule as King of Westphalia.
Jerome himself appears. The authors are seen to advantage in this romance of their
earlier literary period.

1787. *A DAUGHTER OF THE LEGION: Violet M. Methley;
Juv.   Cassell.
France, 1812. An amusing tale of a schoolgirl who comes into close contact with
Napoleon more than once; she discovers a plot against the Emperor, and is able to
send him a message of warning. The book itself must be allowed to tell how she was
rewarded.

1788. *SONS OF THE SWORD: Margaret L. Woods; *Heinemann* [Eng.], *McClure* [U.S.A.].
Spain (Madrid, Medina, etc.), 1808: time of the French occupation, and Sir John Moore's advance. An unusual romance of the Peninsular War, having little to do with the actual fighting; the Emperor Napoleon, however, is very prominent in this story of an Irish girl, and Sir John Moore is pleasantly introduced. The novel ends with Napoleon in Austria (1809).

1789. *BOYS OF THE LIGHT BRIGADE (THE LIGHT BRIGADE IN SPAIN): " Herbert Strang "; *Juv.* *Blackie* [Eng.], *Putnam* [U.S.A.].
A tale of the Peninsular War, 1808-1809, covering Sir John Moore's Retreat from Astorga to Corunna, and the Battle at the last-named place (Moore's death in the moment of victory); also the Defence of Saragossa by Palafox from July, 1808, to February, 1809.

1790. *DOÑA YSABEL: Mathilda Malling; *Ernst Bejesen.*
A novel of the Peninsular War, 1808-10, dealing with Ney, Masséna, etc.

1791. *WITH MOORE AT CORUNNA:
*UNDER WELLINGTON'S COMMAND (*sequel*): G. A. Henty;
Juv. *Blackie* [Eng.], *Scribner* [U.S.A.].
These two Peninsular War stories constitute a single record, having the same hero, and exhibiting an unbroken historic sequence. Spain and Portugal in the period 1808-1812. Time of Soult's invasion of Portugal, and the English army's passage of the Douro, etc. In addition to his account of Sir John Moore's Retreat, the author describes such battles as Corunna, Talavera, Torres Vedras, Ciudad Rodrigo, and Salamanca. Wellington appears many times—first as Sir Arthur Wellesley, then as Lord Wellington.

1792. *THE KING'S REVOKE: Margaret L. Woods; *Smith, Elder* [Eng.], *Dutton* [U.S.A.].
Spain, England (London), and France, 1808, and the few years following. Story of an Irishman and his adventures in the period when Joseph Bonaparte was transferred to the throne of Spain by his brother. The historic event with which the novel is mainly concerned, is the imprisonment of Ferdinand VII and Don Carlos in the Castle of Valençay—the country home of Talleyrand. Ferdinand and Talleyrand both appear prominently in the novel.

1793. *THE SPY: Captain Charles Gilson; *Juv.* *Oxford University Press.*
Imaginary memoirs of an English Baronet, beginning with his experiences in London, etc., but, after the first hundred pages, dealing entirely with the Peninsular War in the period 1808 to 1812. A tale of exciting military adventures, covering several important events, but more especially describing in turn, Roleia, Talavera, the retreat on the lines of Torres Vedras, and the storming of Badajoz (the tale virtually ends with this last episode, 1812). Not many historical figures are introduced—apart from Wellington who appears at first as " Sir Arthur Wellesley," but there are plenty of *allusions* to such personages as Napoleon, Massena, Soult, Picton, Craufurd, etc.

1794. THE YOUNG BUGLERS: G. A. Henty; *Juv.* *Griffiths & Farran* [Eng.], *Dutton* [U.S.A.], *Burt* [U.S.A.].
Eton, 1808, and the Spanish Peninsula, 1809-1814. A tale illustrating the greater part of the Peninsular War, and covering all the more important battles from Talavera to Vittoria and Toulouse.

1795. RAIN OF DOLLARS: A. T. Quiller-Couch; in " Shakespeare's Christmas, and Other Stories "—*Dent* [Eng.], *Smith, Elder* [Eng.], *Longmans* [U.S.A.].
Sir John Moore's Army and the retreat upon Corunna, 1809. A short tale.

1796. *THE SNARE: Rafael Sabatini; *Martin Secker* [*Eng.*], *Houghton Mifflin* [*U.S.A.*].

Portugal (Lisbon, etc.) in 1810. An interesting story of the Peninsular War at the time when Wellington constructed his " lines of Torres Vedras." The principal character is an Irishman (officer), and there are many exciting developments on the fictional side, while the novel as a whole illustrates, historically, the intrigues and troubles with which Wellington had to contend at this point in the War. The great General himself appears.

1797. WITH WELLINGTON IN SPAIN: F. S. Brereton; *Juv.* *Blackie.*

London, Portugal, and Spain, 1810-12. A good tale, beginning with the Press Gang and sea adventures, but mainly dealing with the Peninsular War (the hero is eventually an ensign on Wellington's staff). Ciudad Rodrigo, Badajoz, and the Battle of Salamanca.

1798. *THE TWO SCOUTS: A. T. Quiller-Couch; in " The Laird's Luck; and Other Fireside Tales "—*Dent* [*Eng.*], *Cassell* [*Eng.*], *Scribner* [*U.S.A.*].

Chapters from supposed memoirs relating to the Peninsular War campaigns 1808-1813. The three selected pieces cover the short period March-April, 1812, and tell of spying on Marmont's movements, the strategy shown in beating Marmont at Cabeca Negro Mountain behind Almeida, and Marmont's attack on Guarda. Wellington, General Wilson, etc.

1799. *THREE MEN OF BADAJOZ: A. T. Quiller-Couch; in " The Laird's Luck; and Other Fireside Tales "—*Dent* [*Eng.*], *Cassell* [*Eng.*], *Scribner* [*U.S.A.*].

Scotland, 1808, and Spain 1812. A tale containing a full description of the Badajoz assault, April 12th, 1812. Passes, at the end, to Scotland, 1829.

1800. *THE LAMP AND THE GUITAR: A. T. Quiller-Couch; in " Shakespeare's Christmas, and Other Stories "—*Dent* [*Eng.*], *Smith, Elder* [*Eng.*], *Longmans* [*U.S.A.*].

A short story dealing with Wellington, 1811-12: the Battle of Salamanca.

1801. *THE YOUNG LOVERS: H. C. Bailey; *Methuen.*

Passes from West Sussex (1810) to the Peninsular War. A good historical novel covering the Battles of Fuentes d'Onoro (1811), Salamanca (1812), and Vittoria (1813). Wellington, Fitzroy Somerset, and other historical figures are introduced.

1802. *ALICE LORRAINE: R. D. Blackmore; *Sampson Low* [*Eng.*], *Harper* [*U.S.A.*].

Sussex and Kent, also Spain, 1811-14. A good example of Blackmore, mainly dealing with life in the region of the South Downs, but also depicting some of the Peninsular War battles such as Ciudad Rodrigo and Badajoz.

1803. *THE SILVER DRUM: Neil Munro; in " Jaunty Jock and Other Stories "

A short tale of Spain, 1812. A sculptor who had once been a drummer, tells of certain episodes at the Sack of Ciudad Rodrigo, ending with an account of what happened subsequently.

1804. *A YOUNG MAN MARRIED: "Sydney C. Grier"; *Blackwood.*

Spain, 1812-13. An entertaining story of a young English officer's marriage with a beautiful Spanish girl. Begins the day after the Storming of Badajoz—a day of discreditable excesses on the part of certain British troops. The primary interest is fictional, viz., the machinations of the heroine's family, and her own adventures; but in the background are the military movements leading up to the Battles of Salamanca and Vittoria respectively. Lord Wellington is introduced in a somewhat amusing manner in the earlier part of the book.

1805. *THE ADVENTURES OF HARRY REVEL: A. T. QUILLER-COUCH; Dent [*Eng.*], Cassell [*Eng.*], Scribner [*U.S.A.*].
Largely a social novel of the West Country at the beginning of the 19th Century: an unjust charge of murder, etc. The later chapters of the book deal with the Peninsular War (Ciudad Rodrigo). There is a glimpse of Wellington.

1806. *THE ROMANCE OF WAR: JAMES GRANT; *Juv.* Routledge [*Eng.*], Dutton [*U.S.A.*].
Scotland, Spain (mostly), Flanders, and France, 1812-15. A popular tale of adventure, love, and fighting. Describes (amongst other events) the Battles of Albuera, Vittoria, Orthes, Quatre Bras, and Waterloo. The outstanding historic figures are Wellington, Sir Rowland Hill, and Cameron of Fassifern.

1807. *THE SPANISH LADY: MARGARET L. WOODS; *Cape.*
Spain (Cadiz) in 1813. A story dealing with Lord Wellington's attachment to a beautiful Spanish girl, and the plots and complications arising out of it. How a rupture came about, and how Wellington's conduct affected some of the characters in the novel, is told with much force and humour. Besides Wellington, Sir Thomas Picton and Lord Fitzroy Somerset (afterwards Lord Raglan) are introduced.

1808. *CORPORAL SAM: A. T. QUILLER-COUCH; in " Corporal Sam, and Other Stories "—*Smith, Elder.*
A good short story of the Peninsular War (San Sabastian) in 1813.

1809. *WAR AND PEACE: COUNT LYOF N. TOLSTOY (trans.); *Scott* [*Eng.*], Heinemann [*Eng.*], Crowell [*U.S.A.*], McClure [*U.S.A.*] and others.
A really great piece of literature, which is universally recognised as one of the world's finest examples in the way of historical fiction. The scene is chiefly Russia (Moscow, St. Petersburg, etc.) in the period 1805 to 1820. Readers are shown the social life of the big cities as well as the horrors and privations endured by the soldier in wartime. There are vivid accounts of the battles of Austerlitz (1805) and Borodino (1812); of Napoleon at Moscow; and of the famous Retreat. At various points one is brought into contact with historical figures like the Emperor Alexander, Napoleon, Murat, Davout, etc. The book is of extraordinary length, and has been well described as a " panoramic novel." Again, it is one of those few examples of what may be termed *openly didactic* fiction which can be praised equally as works of art and as admonitory pronouncements; for, besides recognising the novel's merits under the aspect of imaginative literature pure and simple, readers may consider it as the unmistakable embodiment of Tolstoy's protest against War.

1810. *PAN TADEUSZ[1]: ADAM MICKIEWICZ (trans.); Dent [*Eng.*], Dutton [*U.S.A.*].
Lithuania, largely 1811-12. This famous historical *epic poem* is here presented to English readers in a form not unlike the novel proper. It gives a vivid picture of life and manners among Polish gentlefolk in the period just before Napoleon's invasion of Russia. There are allusions to such historic events as Dombrowski's march from Italy, the Hayti insurrection (Polish forces), Jena, the Peace of Tilsit, and the Declaration of War between France and Russia, 3rd August, 1811.

[1] A specially good English translation of this poem was made by Maude Ashurst Biggs, and published by Trübner in 1885 under the title : " Master Thaddeus," with a Preface by W. R. Morfill.

1811. *MOSCOW IN FLAMES: G. P. DANILEVSKI (trans.); *Stanley Paul.*
Russia in 1812. An historical romance giving a good picture of Russian life and patriotism in the period of Napoleon's Moscow expedition. Two of the principal historic events introduced, are the Battle of Borodino, and the Burning of Moscow. Napoleon, Murat, Berthier, Davout and Rapp are among the figures introduced. The closing pages of the novel look onward as far as 1843.

1812. *THE GREAT WHITE ARMY: Max Pemberton; *Cassell.*
Russia (Moscow, etc.), 1812. This story—" told " by a Surgeon-Major—begins just after Borodino, and describes the deserted state of Moscow on the French arrival, the burning of that city, and its abandonment by Napoleon. The remaining and larger part of the tale deals with experiences (mainly in the Grand Army's rearguard) during the Retreat, introducing the Battle of Krasnoë and Napoleon's narrow escape there, as well as the terrible losses at the River Bérézina. Napoleon and Marshal Ney both appear.

1813. THROUGH RUSSIAN SNOWS: G. A. Henty; *Juv.* *Blackie* [*Eng.*], *Scribner* [*U.S.A.*].
Russia, 1812. A tale illustrating Napoleon's invasion of Russia—especially the Battles of Smolensk and Borodino, and the disastrous Retreat from Moscow.

1814. *THE WARRIOR'S SOUL: Joseph Conrad; in " Tales of Hearsay "—*Fisher Unwin;* also *Nash.*
A short but graphic story of Napoleon's Russian Campaign, 1812.

1815. *BARLASCH OF THE GUARD: " H. Seton Merriman "; *Smith, Elder* [*Eng.*], *McClure* [*U.S.A.*].
Prussia (mainly Dantzig) and Russia, 1812-13. A somewhat vivid story, describing the experiences of a Dantzig family at the time of the French occupation and the Comte de Rapp's governorship. The novel illustrates the Borodino and Moscow Retreat period. There is a glimpse of Napoleon watching the burning of Moscow.

1816. KENNETH; OR, THE REAR-GUARD OF THE GRAND ARMY: Charlotte M. Yonge; *Juv.* *Parker* [*Eng.*], *Appleton* [*U.S.A.*].
Russia, Prussian Poland, etc., 1812-13; also Paris and England, 1815. A tale well illustrating the horrors of the French Retreat from Moscow. Marshal Ney is a prominent figure, and there is a glimpse of Murat.

1817. (1) THE SWORD HAND OF NAPOLEON:
(2) THE EAGLE OF THE EMPIRE: Cyrus Townsend Brady *Juv.* *Hodder & Stoughton* [*Eng.*], *Dodd Mead* [*U.S.A.*].
These two connected novels (the second is hardly a sequel in the strict sense) deal with Russia, France, etc., in the period 1812-15. The Battle of Borodino (Napoleon's victory over the Russians), and the Moscow Retreat, are outstanding events in the first volume, while the second covers the Hundred Days and Waterloo. In both tales the dominating historic figure is, of course, Napoleon, and, of the many other personages, Ney is perhaps the most prominent. There are glimpses of the Czar Alexander I, Murat, Davout, Junot, Marmont, Berthier, and others.

1818. *THE EXPLOITS OF BRIGADIER GERARD: A Conan Doyle; *Smith, Elder* [*Eng.*], *Appleton* [*U.S.A.*].
Eight stories of France, Spain, England (Dartmoor), Germany, etc., told by the amusingly self-confident French officer, Gerard. They illustrate events in the period of Napoleon's Wars, etc., between 1807 and 1813. In several tales Napoleon appears (notably in the second, seventh, and eighth), while Masséna is introduced in the fifth story, and the poet Körner in the sixth.

1819. *ADVENTURES OF GERARD: A. Conan Doyle; *Smith, Elder* [*Eng.*], *McClure* [*U.S.A.*].
Another batch of eight Gerard tales dealing with various regions (Venice, Saragossa, England, Russia, etc.), mostly between 1808 and 1815, though the last story is 1821. There are glimpses of Soult and the Emperor in the seventh narration (Waterloo), while in the eighth (St. Helena) Gerard sees Napoleon lying dead.

1820. THE GREAT SHADOW: A. Conan Doyle; in "The Great
     Shadow, and Other Napoleonic Tales"—*Arrowsmith.*
  Tweedmouth region, and Belgium, 1813-15. A tale of love and political plotting
(an aide-de-camp of Napoleon is in the hero's home). Covers the period of the Battle
of Leipzig and Napoleon's retirement in Elba, while later portions of the story lead up
to Waterloo (an account of the battle). There is a glimpse of Bonaparte.

1821. *THE SHADOW OF THE SWORD: Robert Buchanan;
     Chatto & Windus [*Eng.*], *Appleton* [*U.S.A.*].
  France (Brittany), and, to a small extent, Belgium, 1813-15. This romance so depicts
the life of humble folk in a Breton village as to convey, throughout, the martial influences
of the time. The author was a genuine poet (though a minor one), and this particular
novel contains descriptions of coast scenery which show that he could write prose of
the kind that is akin to poetry. Buchanan's book (like the much greater work of
Tolstoy—*War and Peace*) is clearly written as a protest against War, and, though the
emphasis is occasionally made too evident, the reader's interest can hardly fail to be
retained up to the end. Perhaps the later chapters—especially those which give a
glimpse of Napoleon on the eve of Waterloo—at times verge on melodrama; but here
again there is some genuinely fine writing. Taken altogether, the novel is a striking
example of romantic fiction, which—now that realism and romanticism are coming
to be regarded as *complementary*—should have a good chance of once again finding
recognition and even popularity.

1822. (1)*FACE TO FACE WITH NAPOLEON:
     (2)*IN THE YEAR OF WATERLOO (*sequel*): O. V. Caine;
     Juv. *Nisbet* [*Eng.*], *Bradley* [*U.S.A.*].
  Two interesting stories dealing with events of much importance.
  (1) North Germany, 1812-13. The youthful son of a Prussian soldier (by an English
wife) and his English boy-cousin, have some thrilling experiences during the German
struggle against Napoleon. The tale illustrates the fighting in the Elbe district, etc.,
and ends with an account of the great Battle of Leipzig. Napoleon, Blücher, Frederick-
William III of Prussia, Scharnhorst, Stein, Metternich, and others appear.
  (2) The sequel begins with the Congress of Vienna, February, 1815, and ends with
Waterloo. The same two heroes carry despatches from Wellington, meeting with many
adventures in Italy and France. The book covers Napoleon's return from Elba and the
Battle of Ligny, etc., while the Battle of Waterloo is described with some fullness.
Napoleon, Wellington, Talleyrand, the Duke of Otranto (Fouché), and Queen Hortense
are more or less prominently introduced.

1823. *TOM CRINGLE'S LOG: Michael Scott; *Juv.* *Sampson Low*
     [*Eng.*], *Dodd, Mead* [*U.S.A.*] *and other publishers.*
  Jamaica, Cuba, and the West Indies, c. 1813. A deservedly famous story of an
English midshipman's adventures (pirates, slavers, etc.). The period can be fixed with
some precision through Davout being introduced at Hamburg (he was Governor-General
of the Hanse Towns, 1813-14).

1824. *ST. IVES: R. L. Stevenson; *Heinemann* [*Eng.*], *Scribner* [*U.S.A.*].
  Edinburgh, various English districts, and a glimpse of Paris, 1813-14. Story of a
French prisoner of war in Edinburgh Castle: his escape from the Castle and his many
experiences afterwards. The novel ends with the news of Napoleon's departure from
Elba. Of the thirty-six chapters, the *last six* were written by A. T. Quiller-Couch on
the basis of certain definite information as to outline given by R. L. S.'s amanuensis.

1825. *SUSPENSE: Joseph Conrad; *Dent* [*Eng.*], *Doubleday* [*U.S.A.*].
  Italy (mainly) and England in the period of Napoleon's retirement in Elba. This
posthumous novel, though left unfinished, was sufficiently advanced to reveal both
imaginative power and historical knowledge. The author has managed to convey to
his readers the impression (suggested in the book's title) of *all Europe waiting in anxiety.*

1826. LAURISTONS: "John Oxenham"; *Methuen.*
  England (London and district) and France, 1800-1815, but emphasizing the "Hundred
Days" period, and ending with Waterloo—the first conveyance of the news to London.
The story of a London Banking House, offering glimpses of Burke, Fox, Pitt, the Duke
of Kent, Bonaparte, Talleyrand and others.

1827. STORIES OF WATERLOO: W. H. Maxwell; *Routledge* [*Eng.*],
    Dutton [*U.S.A.*].
England, Ireland, and Abroad, mostly 1812-1815. The title of this book is somewhat
misleading, as the Peninsular War period (Badajos) is reflected to some extent, *as well as*
the time just before, during, and after Waterloo. In a sequence of sketches (middle
of volume) Quatre Bras, Ligny, and Waterloo are respectively described in considerable
detail.

1828. (1)*THE HISTORY OF A CONSCRIPT:
    (2)*WATERLOO (*sequel*): E. Erckmann and A. Chatrian (trans.)
    Ward, Lock [*Eng.*], *Holt* [*U.S.A.*].
    (1) Phalsbourg, Frankfort, Leipsic, etc., 1813. A tale of Napoleon's later wars
culminating in the disaster at Leipsic. There are glimpses of Napoleon, Ney, etc.
Well illustrates the horrors of conscription. Both this book and its sequel are valuable
as showing the attitude of people in a humble position.
    (2) France and Belgium, 1814-15. Begins with Louis XVIII's return, passing to
the period of the "Hundred Days." Vivid descriptions of the road to Waterloo, as well
as of the Battle itself. The tale as a whole exhibits the differences of political opinion in
the France of that time.

1829. *THE BLOCKADE: E. Erckmann and A. Chatrian (trans.);
    Ward, Lock [*Eng.*], *Holt* [*U.S.A.*].
Another good example of "Erckmann-Chatrian," dealing with the late Napoleonic
period. As this tale describes the Blockade of Phalsbourg in 1814, and ends with
Napoleon's abdication, its position in strict historical sequence is between the two books
entered above.

1830. *REGINA (*DER KATZENSTEG*): H. Sudermann (trans.);
    Lane.
Eastern Prussia, 1814-15. This domestic and psychological novel—striking rather
than pleasing—covers the period between the Peace of Paris and Ligny. Allusion is
made to Frederick William III, but history is quite in the background.

1831. DRAWN FOR THE MILITIA: Maude Robinson; in "The
    Time of Her Life, and Other Stories"—*Swarthmore Press* [*Eng.*],
    Friends' Book Store [*U.S.A.*].
Chelmsford in 1814. A short story of a Quaker conscientious objector.

1832. AN EMPEROR'S VISIT: Maude Robinson; in "The Time of
    Her Life, and Other Stories"—*Swarthmore Press* [*Eng.*], *Friends'
    Book Store* [*U.S.A.*].
A Quaker family entertain the Emperor Alexander I of Russia in their Sussex home,
1814.

1833. *THE WOUNDED NAME: D. K. Broster; *Heinemann* [*Eng.*],
    Doubleday [*U.S.A.*].
An interesting story of a young French Royalist's adventures and courtship, beginning
Devonshire, 1814, but mostly dealing with France (Brittany), 1815—the Hundred Days
period.

1834. *THE BRONZE EAGLE: Baroness Orczy; *Hodder & Stoughton*
    [*Eng.*], *Doran* [*U.S.A.*].
France (Grenoble, Lyons, and Paris) and Belgium, 1814-15. An interesting novel,
covering Napoleon's return from Elba and the Hundred Days period. Tells of Royalists
v. Bonapartists in connection with some "millions of francs" originally seized by
Talleyrand during the flight of the Empress Marie Louise. The book virtually ends
with an account of Waterloo. Napoleon appears, and there are glimpses of Berthier,
Wellington, and others.

1835. ON THE FIELD OF WATERLOO: F. S. Brereton; *Juv.*
  Blackie.
   Paris, 1793; then England (Devon), France, and Belgium, 1814-15. Two English
lads are taken by a French frigate to Brest and imprisoned in a fortress. Eventually
they escape, and, after returning to England, enter the Guards in time to serve with
the Allied Army in Belgium. There are descriptions of Quatre Bras and Waterloo.
Napoleon and Wellington both appear.

1836. *THE LAIRD'S LUCK: A. T. Quiller-Couch; in "The
  Laird's Luck; and Other Fireside Tales"—*Dent* [*Eng.*], *Cassell*
  [*Eng.*], *Scribner* [*U.S.A.*].
   Scotland, September, 1814, then Brussels in the second quarter of the year, 1815.
A tale containing a full description of Quatre Bras.

1837. CORPORAL VIOLET: L. T. Meade; *Juv. Hodder & Stoughton.*
   Chiefly Devonshire, also Paris, London, and Brussels, 1814-15. A duel, described
in the opening pages as occurring in 1809, has an important bearing on this tale. The
historical element is chiefly to be found in the later chapters which illustrate the Hundred
Days period. There is a brief account of Waterloo.

1838. *THE HUNDRED DAYS: Max Pemberton; *Cassell* [*Eng.*],
  Appleton [*U.S.A.*].
   S. France (Grasse, Nice, Grenoble, etc.) and Paris, 1815. An historical romance of
Napoleon's reappearance after Elba in the period known as the "Hundred Days."
The fictional development is mostly connected with events *before* the final struggle in
Belgium—the latest pages giving little more than a rapid sketch of Quatre Bras and
Waterloo. Napoleon appears prominently.

1839. *THREE FEET OF VALOUR (formerly "Brown"): Dorothea
  Moore; *Juv. Nisbet* [*Eng.*], *Eaton & Mains* [*U.S.A.*].
   A really fascinating little story of a small boy in the Cambridge district, 1815. An
important part of the tale deals with smuggling in the Essex fen-land. The Duke of
Wellington appears.

1840. *JACKANAPES: Mrs. Juliana Horatia Ewing; *Juv. Dent*
  [*Eng.*], *Dutton* [*U.S.A.*] *and other publishers.*
   Quite a juvenile classic (indeed, the qualifying adjective "juvenile" might be omitted,
seeing that the book appeals to older readers as well as to the young people). A very
charming little tale of English life in the early 19th Century, virtually beginning 1815
(the news of Waterloo).

1841. *THE CHARTERHOUSE OF PARMA (*LA CHARTREUSE
  DE PARME*): Marie-Henri Beyle ["De Stendhal"]; *Chatto &
  Windus* [*Eng.*], *Heinemann* [*Eng.*], *Boni* [*U.S.A.*].
   Begins Milan, 1796 (Bonaparte's entry), and in two chapters passes lightly over
nineteen years to the Battle of Waterloo. The early chapters of this famous novel
constitute its sole claim to be entered under the heading of historical fiction proper;
the main portion of the book presents a study, in fictional form, of high social behaviour
and mentality, end 18th Century to early 19th Century. The scene is almost entirely
Northern Italy, more or less in the region of the Lakes.

1842. *VANITY FAIR: W. M. Thackeray; *Dent* [*Eng.*], *Dutton* [*U.S.A.*]
  and other publishers.
   This brilliant novel, though primarily a study of high social life and manners in the
early 19th Century (George III-George IV), has certain definitely historical elements.
There are, for instance, the very brief, but wonderfully impressive, passages dealing
with events before, during, and after the Battle of Waterloo—passages rarely equalled,
as regards dramatic intensity, in the whole range of imaginative literature. Again,
it is generally understood that the titled "Steyne" of the novel is intended to represent
the unprincipled Marquis of Hertford of that day.

1843. *LES MISÉRABLES: Victor Hugo (trans.); Dent [Eng.], Little, Brown [U.S.A.].
Another celebrated novel which, although not usually classed under the heading of historical fiction, in no small degree illustrates definite events in France, as well as that country's life and politics generally, in the period 1815-48 (the dates throughout the book go backwards and forwards in most confusing fashion, but the full period is that here given). The Battle of Waterloo is finely treated under several aspects, and at considerable length, while the Revolution of 1830 (Louis Philippe), the 1832 disturbances, and the insurrection of 1848, are also brought before the reader in the course of the tale—or, rather, series of tales.

1844. THE BLACK OFFICE: Agnes and Egerton Castle; in " The Black Office and Other Chapters of Romance "—*Murray*.
Paris and London, 1815. An interesting story of some eighty pages, indicating the methods pursued by the *Bureau Secret*, acting under the Duc d'Otrante (Fouché) the Minister of Police.

1845. FOR LOVE AND RANSOM: Esmé Stuart; *Juv.   Jarrold*.
Mainly S. Italy (Apulia and Naples), 1814-15: last chapter England, 1816. An interesting tale covering Murat's overthrow by the Austrians and subsequent flight; also leading up to his eventual capture and death (October, 1815).

1846. *YEOMAN FLEETWOOD: " M. E. Francis "; *Longmans*.
Lancashire (near Ormskirk and Liverpool), also Brighton, within the 1810-15 period. A delightful tale of social life, only becoming distinctly historical towards the end, when the Prince of Wales (George IV), Mrs. Fitzherbert, and Brummell are brought before readers in the Brighton scenes. The novel is somewhat indefinite as regards date, but, as Beau Brummel fled to Calais in 1815 and never afterwards returned to England, the year named must be taken as the time-limit for the story proper.

1847. *RUNNING HORSE INN: Alfred Tresidder Sheppard; *Macmillan [Eng.], Lippincott [U.S.A.]*.
Kent (Herne, Canterbury, etc.) and London, in the Regency. A novel which, besides its excellent qualities on the purely fictional side, offers a vivid depiction of the miseries and general state of unsettlement which characterized the post-Waterloo period from the end of 1815. There is a good account of the conspiracy which resulted in the Spa Fields Riot of 2nd December, 1816.

1848. *TRAVELLING MEN: W. G. Dowsley; *Simpkin [Eng.], Talbot Press [Ireland]*.
Co. Tipperary, Ireland, 1816. A serio-comic tale of two youths at school together, one of whom the author chooses to present as George Borrow in the budding stage! A portrait of Robert Emmet suggests to young Borrow a startling piece of audacity at a school prize-giving (Toler, the Lord Chief Justice of Ireland, appears on the occasion). Turning to the novel's more serious side, it reflects the wretched state of affairs in the time following Waterloo (the " Ejectment Act," etc.). Besides Borrow, another literary figure is introduced, viz. Tom Moore.

1849. SIR DAVID'S VISITORS: " Sarah Tytler "; *Chatto & Windus*.
One of the author's simple but good stories of a bygone time. It tells of Kensington in Regency days, introducing Sir David Wilkie, and his friends Sir Thomas Lawrence and Mrs. Siddons.

1850. THE PIRATE CITY: R. M. Ballantyne; *Juv.   Nisbet*.
Algiers, 1816. A story well illustrating the iniquities of the Algerine Pirate system under Achmet Pasha. Ends with the famous Bombardment by Lord Exmouth. The Dey of Algiers (i.e. Achmet) appears prominently.

1851. THE QUIET LADY: Agnes Mure Mackenzie; *Heinemann*.
The Outer Hebrides, 1816-17. A novel of character analysis rather than of incident. There are, however, some definitely historical *allusions*.

1852. THE WATERLOO LASS: Mary H. Debenham; *Juv.* *National Society* [*Eng.*], *Whittaker* [*U.S.A.*].
English North Country life (Tees district) in 1816 and in 1825. Last chapter 1838. An unpretentious, but pleasing, little tale.

1853. TRANSPORTED: Maude Robinson; in " Nicholas the Weaver, and Other Quaker Stories "—*Swarthmore Press* [*Eng.*], *Friends Book Store* [*U.S.A.*].
A short story of Elizabeth Fry and Newgate, 1817.

1854. *JACK O' PETERLOO: Theodora Wilson Wilson; *Labour Publishing Co.*
" A novel in three episodes," with the respective dates: 1793, 1805, and 1819. The scenes are for the most part in N. W. England. The unsettled state of the country, and the social injustices of the time, are forcibly illustrated. In the third *episode* there is some account of the Massacre of Peterloo (Manchester). Henry Hunt (" Orator " Hunt) is prominently introduced.

1855. *STARVECROW FARM: Stanley J. Weyman; *Hutchinson* [*Eng.*], *Murray* [*Eng.*], *Longmans* [*U.S.A.*].
Windermere District and Kendal, mostly in the autumn of 1819. A decidedly thrilling story of a young impetuous girl's adventures and love affairs. Reflects the suffering and discontent which prevailed among the working classes after the Napoleonic Wars. The exact time is that immediately following the Peterloo Massacre at Manchester (the short account of this event which is given in Chapter III, is *retrospective*). No historical figures of any great note are actually introduced, but there are allusions to such personages as Lord Liverpool, the " mad Sovereign and the dissolute Regent," Cobbett, Orator Hunt, " that queer half-moithered Mr. Wordsworth at Rydal," Southey, and Samuel Rogers.

1856. *THE MANCHESTER MAN: Mrs. G. Linnaeus Banks; *Abel Heywood.*
A noteworthy tale of Manchester, mostly covering the period 1799-1831. The book is full of local colour, revealing intimate knowledge, while many celebrities of the time are introduced—Samuel Bamford for example. The outstanding feature of the story on its historical side is the account given of the Peterloo Massacre (1819), and of " Orator " Hunt's connection therewith.

1857. *THE REVOLUTION IN TANNER'S LANE: W. Hale White; *Fisher Unwin* [*Eng.*], *Doran* [*U.S.A.*], *and other publishers*).
London, Manchester, and Cambridgeshire, mainly between 1814 and 1824. A novel of exceptional power, depicting the Radical Politics and Religious Nonconformity of the period, as well as the really terrible condition of the working classes after Waterloo. Illustrates the time of Bamford and the Manchester Clubs, and deals with the attempted march of the " Blanketeers " to London (1817) for the purpose of presenting a People's Petition to the Prince Regent. Soon after the account of the last-named episode, four years are passed over, and the scene changes to a small town on the Great North Road, where the interest is chiefly connected with a certain " Tanner's Lane Chapel." The fictional developments, however, are beyond the scope of this note.

1858. THE QUEEN CAN DO NO WRONG: Herbert Compton; *Chatto & Windus.*
A novel with Caroline of Brunswick as central figure (a defence). The book is divided into three parts, covering respectively—1796 to 1806; 1814; and 1820 to 1821. Besides the Queen herself, several personages appear, including Princess Charlotte and Lord Brougham.

1859. *A LADY OF THE REGENCY: Mrs. Maud Stepney Rawson; *Hutchinson* [*Eng.*], *Harper* [*U.S.A.*].
Chiefly England (London District, Northumberland, Windsor, Weymouth, etc.) in the period 1813-21. A romance of Court life, having for its central figures Princess

Charlotte, and her mother, Caroline of Brunswick. The fictional heroine is a young girl-in-waiting who attends in turn the above-mentioned Royal personages. The story illustrates very fully the later years of the unfortunate Caroline, and an immense number of historic figures are introduced besides those already named: Queen Charlotte, George IV (first as Prince Regent, then as King), various other Royalties, Lord Castlereagh, George Canning, Brougham, Orator Hunt, etc. etc.

1860. *SCHWAMMERL: RUDOLF HANS BARTSCH; *Staackmann* [*Germany*].
An imaginative presentment of Franz Schubert. Another great figure appearing in this clever novel, is Beethoven.

1861. *THE SILVER SKULL: S. R. CROCKETT; *Smith, Elder.*
S. Italy (Apulia), mainly in the 1815-20 period. A somewhat thrilling romance of the years immediately succeeding the reinstatement (by the Congress of Vienna, 1815) of Ferdinand I, who in 1816 united his two States into the Kingdom of the Two Sicilies. The story covers the final suppression of the brigands by the Englishman, Richard Church (afterwards *Sir* Richard Church), who acted as General in Ferdinand's service.

1862. *THE MURDER OF MONSIEUR FUALDÈS: ARMAND PRAVIEL (trans.); *Collins.*
Rodez (French provincial town), 1817-18. A novel based on the real murder of M. Fualdés (ex-public prosecutor). Deals with the discovery of the murder and the investigations, accusations, and trial following it. The political atmosphere of the time is cleverly suggested in the course of the story.

1863. *EL SUPREMO: EDWARD LUCAS WHITE; *Fisher Unwin* [*Eng.*], *Dutton* [*U.S.A.*].
An historical romance of Paraguay in 1816, with the Dictator, Dr. Francia, as outstanding figure. An extremely interesting and forcible presentment of a remarkable man. Less a depiction of events and special conditions—though these are reflected—than a sympathetic character study.

1864. *A CAPTAIN OF IRREGULARS: HERBERT HAYENS; *Juv.* *Nelson.*
Chili and Argentina, 1816-18. A good example of the author, dealing with the struggle of Chili against Spanish rule. There is variety on the fictional side as well as on the historical. An Englishman tells of his experiences as officer in the Chilian army. Some account is given of the Battle of Chacabuco, and other fighting—especially the Battle of Maipo, San Martin's great victory over the Spaniards in 1818. The outstanding historical figure is General José de San Martin, whose exploit of leading an army across the Andes (1817) is introduced. General O'Higgins (the Irish-born South American leader who became Dictator of Chili) is the most important of the other historic figures.

1865. IN THE GRIP OF THE SPANIARD: HERBERT HAYENS; *Juv.* *Nelson.*
Venezuela and New Granada, 1818-21. A good story of the War of Independence, and the important victory (Carabobo) over the Spanish troops in June, 1821. Deals with the English volunteers, etc. The outstanding historical figure is the famous Simon Bolivar, " the Liberator."

1866. *WITH COCHRANE THE DAUNTLESS: HERBERT HAYENS; *Juv.* *Blackie* [*Eng.*], *Scribner* [*U.S.A.*].
Another interesting tale of South America by Mr. Hayens. The historical element in this instance is the part played by Cochrane (afterwards Earl of Dundonald) in helping Chili and Peru to secure their independence, as well as his later services on behalf of Brazil. The period covered is 1818-25.

1867. AT THE POINT OF THE SWORD: HERBERT HAYENS; *Juv.* *Nelson.*
South America, mainly between 1820 and 1824. Another Simon Bolivar tale, dealing with that part of the War of Liberation which resulted in the Spaniards being driven out of Peru (1824). Various historical figures.

1868. THE MAID OF ATHENS: LAFAYETTE McLAWS; *Sampson Low* [*Eng.*], *Little, Brown* [*U.S.A.*].

Athens, Stamboul, England, and Missolonghi, mainly 1811-15, but begins 1796 and ends 1824. A romance of Lord Byron, dealing with the period of his sojourn in Greece and his marriage with Miss Milbanke a few years later. The book is to some extent an apology for Byron. Sheridan and Hobhouse appear.

1869. *GLORIOUS APOLLO: " E. BARRINGTON "; *Harrap* [*Eng.*], *Dodd, Mead* [*U.S.A.*].

A fictional study of Lord Byron, based on the various authorities, but somewhat elastic in regard to dates. Begins with Byron taking his seat as a young peer in the House of Lords; covers the time of " Childe Harold " and other literary periods; describes the feminine influences (Lady Caroline Lamb, his marriage with Miss Milbanke, etc.); introduces many literary and other notabilities; and ends with Byron's death in Western Greece, 1824.

1870. *ARIEL: ANDRÉ MAUROIS (trans.); *Lane* [*Eng.*], *Appleton* [*U.S.A.*].

Eton, Horsham, Oxford, London, Edinburgh, etc., also Switzerland and Italy, 1809-22. Fictional biography, giving the main events in Shelley's career, and introducing — besides the poet himself—his family and friends. Some of the more prominent figures are Harriet Grove, the Godwins, Lord Byron, Harriet Westbrook, Thomas Jefferson Hogg, Leigh Hunt, and Trelawny. The book ends with Shelley's death by drowning off the coast of Italy.

1871. *MORTAL IMAGE (THE ORPHAN ANGEL): ELINOR WYLIE; *Heinemann* [*Eng.*], *Knopf* [*U.S.A.*].

A novel which pictures Shelley as not really drowned in 1822, but as having been picked up by a Boston vessel off Leghorn (Italy), revived, and taken to America, where —under the name " Shiloh "—he had varied experiences and wanderings. The book is fantastic in conception, but quite absorbing as fiction.

1872. THE LION OF JANINA: MAURUS JÓKAI (trans.); *Jarrold* [*Eng.*], *Harper* [*U.S.A.*].

Janina, Stambul, etc., 1819-26. A highly-coloured historical romance which will hardly appeal to readers who have little taste for scenes of bloodshed and horror. The " Lion " of the title is Ali, pasha of Janina, who almost throughout is the outstanding figure. Another historical personage introduced prominently is the Sultan Mahmoud. The story covers Ali's downfall, and in the closing pages the reader is given a description of the massacre of the Janisaries by Ibrahim Pasha, when twenty thousand of them fell in one day (1826).

1873. (1)*THE VINTAGE:
    (2)*THE CAPSINA (*sequel*): E. F. BENSON; *Methuen* [*Eng.*], *Harper* [*U.S.A.*].

(1) Greece—the Morea (Nauplia, Corinth, etc.), 1820-21. A novel illustrating events just before and during the Greek War of Independence. Some of the principal developments in the story are connected with the siege and taking of Kalamata, the occupation of Valtetzi, the siege and fall of Tripoli, and the massacre of the Turks at Monemvasia. There is more than enough dash and colour to satisfy lovers of romantic adventure—some of the scenes indeed might be deemed almost gruesome. Mehemet Salik, the Turkish governor of Tripoli, is somewhat prominent, while Archbishop Germanos and others appear.

(2) The Islands of the Aegean Sea, and the town of Nauplia in the Morea, etc., mainly 1821-22. A story of female valour in the struggle against the Turks. There are many stirring, not to say sanguinary, scenes—the whole book presenting a succession of fights (mostly naval) and daring deeds of one kind or another. The later chapters tell of events culminating in the siege and taking of Nauplia by the Greeks; on the fictional side, the novel ends tragically. Constantine Kanaris is among the figures introduced.

1874. *LOUKIS LARAS: Demetrios Bikelas (trans.); *Macmillan*.
Smyrna, Chio (the island), and various other localities, 1821-22. A well-written and well-translated novel of the narrative type. A Chiote merchant relates his experiences in the Greek War of Independence—conveying a series of vivid historical pictures. There are numerous adventures (sea and land), and the terrible massacres and outrages by the Turks are introduced realistically.

1875. IN GREEK WATERS: G. A. Henty; *Juv. Blackie [Eng.]*, *Scribner [U.S.A.]*.
A story of adventure illustrating the Greek War of Independence, 1821 onwards.

1876. *TAKEN FROM THE ENEMY: Henry Newbolt; *Chatto & Windus*.
London and the sea in the year, 1821. A story telling of exciting adventures in connection with a plot to rescue Napoleon from St. Helena. There is, also, a love element. The tale, which is full of verve and can be read with pleasure by young and old alike, practically ends with the news of the ex-Emperor's death.

1877. THE LOADSTONE: Violet M. Methley; *Hurst & Blackett*.
Largely St. Helena at the time of Napoleon's captivity. The story deals with plots for the ex-Emperor's escape, etc. The great man is himself prominent, while Sir Hudson Lowe (Governor of the island) and General Bertrand are among the other personages introduced.

1878. *SAINT HELENA, LITTLE ISLAND: M. A. Aldanov (trans.); *Jarrolds*.
This volume forms Part III of the Russian author's Trilogy entitled *The Thinker*; the novel forming Part I (" The Ninth Thermidor ") has already appeared in these lists. The present story (St. Helena, beginning of the 'Twenties) is quite brief, and has little or no plot; it is, however, a clever—if somewhat dismal—imaginative sketch. In the first half, a cynical Russian adventurer marries an English girl; in the second half, Napoleon's last illness and death constitute the main interest.

1879. CORINTHIAN JACK: Charles E. Pearce; *Stanley Paul*.
Bristol, Bath, etc., and London, 1823. A tale of the Ring, introducing Tom Cribb and other pugilists.

1880. *ROMANCE: Joseph Conrad and Ford Madox Hueffer; *Smith, Elder ; also Nelson*.
Kent, Jamaica, Cuba and London, mostly between 1820 and 1830. A stirring tale of adventure (pirates, bandits, etc.). The hero is son of a man whose money had been wasted in Regency days, and who had retired to his wife's dowry farm in Kent. The novel tells of the young lad's thirst for " romance "—how it was engendered, and to what results it eventually led; and, although the historical element is of the slightest, there are sufficient references to public events to make the reader sure of the exact period. George Canning's Government is mentioned in an early chapter, while, in the last two chapters, Lord Stowell, the admiralty judge, is introduced; again, there are allusions to the uproar in London over the Pirate Question and Slave Question in connection with West Indian trade.

1881. *JAMES WILSON AND HIS FRIENDS: C. Edmund Maurice; (being Part II of " Unquenched Fires "—*Birrell & Garnett*.
England (Shrewsbury, Bury, Manchester, London, etc.) and Ireland (Co. Clare), between 1822 and 1832. This tale, though almost complete in itself, is really the concluding part of the author's excellent novel, of which the first part (*Friedrich of Münster*) dealing with Westphalia in 1802 onwards, has already been described. The scenes now are in England and Ireland alternately. The reader is given a vivid account of the struggles over the Combination Laws, Catholic Emancipation, and the Reform Bill. Many famous names are encountered, and there are glimpses of Cobbett and other progressive leaders.

1882. DORCAS BROWN'S SCHOOL: Maude Robinson; in "The Time of Her Life, and Other Stories "—*Swarthmore Press* [*Eng.*], *Friends' Book Store* [*U.S.A.*].
A quaint little Sussex story based on fact; it deals with a lady's pioneer work in Education, 1825.

1883. *OVINGTON'S BANK: Stanley J. Weyman; *Murray* [*Eng*], *Longmans* [*U.S.A.*].
English West Midlands (Welsh Border), about the early second quarter of the 19th Century. One of the author's best novels. Although not historical in the full sense, it admirably reflects the period when railway and commercial developments were greatly in evidence, while the allusions to literature (Wordsworth) and politics (Cobbett) further enhance the general impression of early 19th Century life and thought. The heroine is delightful, and her father, the Squire, is both amusingly and convincingly drawn.

1884. *GLENANAAR: P. A. Sheehan; *Longmans*.
An interesting novel depicting the Doneraile Conspiracy Trial at Cork, 1829 (the Whiteboy period), as well as Irish life generally in the eighteen-thirties. The reader is also taken to events connected with the years 1848 and 1867. Daniel O'Connor is the principal historic figure introduced.

1885. *DROMINA: "John Ayscough"; *Arrowsmith* [*Eng.*], *Putnam* [*U.S.A.*].
S. Ireland, Italy, France, etc., and the Island of San Diego (Hispaniola), mostly 1820-30. A romantic tale in which the Dauphin (son of Louis XVI), who is speedily introduced as a gypsy-king, plays an important part. Except for its allusions to real people and events, the book is not properly historical, and makes its appeal chiefly to those who can appreciate fiction of the highly imaginative, semi-religious type. Various historical personages are mentioned at one point or another, and Pope Pius VIII makes a quasi-appearance as writer of a letter of condolence.

1886. *THE GREEN BOOK: Maurus Jókai (trans.); *Jarrold* [*Eng.*], *Harper* [*U.S.A.*].
Russia (St. Petersburg, etc.), 1825. One of Jókai's best novels, alike in style and interest. Vividly illustrates both Court life and the life of the people generally, in a year of revolutionary conspiracy. The romance contains some thrilling accounts of particular incidents—notably in those pages which describe the methods adopted for the assassination of the Czar Alexander I. On the side of individual portraiture, the personality of the Czar is impressively conveyed. The book exhibits more restraint, and is less melodramatic in tendency, than some of its author's earlier examples in fiction; moreover, the descriptive writing (in the first and last chapters, for instance) is of a high order.

1887. *DECEMBER THE FOURTEENTH: Dmitri Merezhkovsky (trans.); *Cape*.
Russia in 1825: the accession of the Tsar Nicholas I. The novel tells (Book I) of the revolutionary disturbances of *December 14th*, 1825; and in Book II gives a picture of Nicholas I's harsh suppression of revolution and liberty, *after* the Fourteenth.

1888. THE HONOUR OF HENRI DE VALOIS: David M. Beddoe; *Dent*.
Egypt and Syria, 1828-34. A love romance having for its main historical background the conquest of Syria by Ibrahim (the adopted son of Mahomed Ali) in the early 'Thirties. Both Mahomed and Ibrahim appear more or less prominently.

1889. THE TIGER OF THE PAMPAS: Herbert Hayens; *Juv. Nelson*.
La Plata, 1829. A tale dealing with the time of the Argentine dictator, Juan Manuel de Rosas, and having as its central figure the leader of the Gauchos, Quiroga (called " The Tiger "). The story depicts the Civil War and ends with Quiroga's death.

1890. PRINCE ROMAN: Joseph Conrad; in "Tales of Hearsay"—
Fisher Unwin; also *Nash*.
A short tale of Poland in the time of Nicholas I of Russia. The Rebellion of 1830.

1891. *THE DAY OF WRATH: Maurus Jókai (trans.); *Jarrold* [*Eng.*],
McClure [*U.S.A.*].
Hungary in the second quarter of the 19th Century. A highly coloured romance, illustrating the semi-feudalism and generally bad conditions prevailing in the Hungary of the period. Popular discontent and uprising, crime and pestilence—these are some of the main subjects dealt with. The translator of the novel, Mr. Nisbet Bain, tells in his introduction how Jókai here wrote under conditions of a depressing nature (the failure of the Magyar Revolution, 1848-9), and this accounts, doubtless, for some of the gloomy pictures given. At the same time, the book is considered one of its author's best fictional efforts.

1892. *BENDISH: A STUDY IN PRODIGALITY: Maurice
Hewlett; *Macmillan* [*Eng.*], *Scribner* [*U.S.A.*].
London and neighbourhood (Golder's Green), 1830. The central figure is "George, Lord Bendish"—a reflection more or less of Byron; but, besides depicting the character of an individual, the novel conveys a vivid impression of the general literary and political life of the time. Leigh Hunt and Tom Moore are introduced, also "Orator" Hunt the Radical politician.

1893. ST. PATRICK'S EVE: Charles Lever; *Chapman & Hall* [1825].
Ireland (Lough Corrib and Galway region) between 1825 and 1835. The story is fairly short, but it gives a picture of the Cholera ravages of the period, besides illustrating the political discontent. In his account of farm ejectment, etc., the author is clearly revealed as one who recognised the need of more direct, personal oversight on the part of Irish landlords.

1894. UNDER THE MENDIPS: Emma Marshall; *Juv.   Seeley* [*Eng.*],
Dutton [*U.S.A.*].
English West Country, 1831. A tale of William IV's reign, dealing especially with the Bristol Riots.

1895. *CHIPPINGE (CHIPPINGE BOROUGH): Stanley J. Wey-
man; *Smith, Elder* [*Eng.*], *McClure* [*U.S.A.*], *Murray* [*Eng.*].
London, Chippenham region, and Bristol, 1831-32. A novel admirably illustrating the Reform period. There are several exciting and well-depicted scenes (an election, etc.); but the most important historical presentment is that of the famous Bristol Riots. There is an interesting sketch of Lord Brougham in the early pages of the book, and *Lady* Landsdowne is somewhat prominently introduced in the course of the story.

1896. *MATTHEW HARGREAVES: "S. G. Tallentyre"; *Smith,
Elder* [*Eng.*], *Putnam* [*U.S.A.*].
An excellent story of English Middle Class and Business Life (Kent and London), mainly between 1830 and 1840 (William IV—Victoria). Full of allusions to such matters as the "newly-opened railway to Greenwich," and to notabilities of the time— "the new little girl Queen" (1837), etc. etc.

1897. MARIE[1]: H. Rider Haggard; *Cassell*.
South Africa, 1836. A tale of "Allan Quartermain" as a very young man. Illustrates the period of the Great Trek, when the Dutch at the Cape were almost in rebelli n, and the Boers went northward in search of homes. The story tells of the embassy to the Zulu king, Dingaan, and the resulting massacre. Retief, the Boer general, and King Dingaan are both introduced.

[1] The first novel in the triolgy, of which "Child of Storm" (see Page 234) and "Finished" (see Page 251) are the second and third volumes respectively.

1898. *THE PATIENCE OF JOHN MORLAND: Mary Dillon; *Nash* [*Eng.*], *Doubleday* [*U.S.A.*].

Washington, between 1820 and 1830, i.e. during the administrations of Monroe, J. Quincy Adams and Andrew Jackson. A story illustrating American politics in the period, just mentioned, and introducing a great many historical figures. Besides the three Presidents already named, the following politicians appear: Henry Clay, John C. Calhoun, Thomas H. Benton, John Randolph, and James Buchanan. Amongst the various other personages, one may specify Robert E. Lee (as a West Point cadet), Mrs. Calhoun, and Mrs. Madison. The hero and heroine of the tale are based on real people whose names are changed, and whose characters, moreover, are treated fictionally.

1899. LITTLE ABE LINCOLN: Bernie Babcock; *Lippincott.*

Kentucky and Indiana, mostly in the second decade of the 19th century (*begins* 1809). A story of the childhood of Lincoln and his sister Sarah. The cabin in the wildwoods.

1900. *THE LAST STAGE: John Buchan; " The Path of the King "— *Nelson* [*Eng.*], *Doran* [*U.S.A.*].

A short imaginative sketch of Abraham Lincoln as a boy of nine in 1818.

1901. *THE SOUL OF ANN RUTLEDGE: Bernie Babcock; *Lippincott.*

New Salem, Illinois, 1831-35. Largely the love romance of Abraham Lincoln and Ann Rutledge, but also illustrating the future President's early pursuit of knowledge, his free theological leanings, and his first attempts as a political speaker. He is depicted as Captain of a company formed at the time of the Indian invasion (Black Hawk War), and as eventually going into the " Store business." Peter Cartwright, the Methodist preacher, appears.

1902. A MAN FOR THE AGES: Irving Bacheller; *Constable* [*Eng.*], *Bobbs-Merrill* [*U.S.A.*].

New Salem, Illinois, etc., mostly in the period 1831-42. Abraham Lincoln is the outstanding figure—the tale illustrating his early experiences, first at New Salem, and then at Springfield. The Rutledges and others appear. In the closing pages of the book a rapid survey is made of events up to 1865.

1903. THE DEVIL'S OWN: Randall Parrish; *Jarrolds* [*Eng.*], *McClurg* [*U.S.A.*].

N. America (Fort Armstrong), 1832. A good adventure tale of the Black Hawk War—" Black Hawk " being the name of the Indian chief who tried to prevent emigrants from settling in Illinois, and the Iowa and Wisconsin territories.

1904. THROUGH SWAMP AND GLADE: Kirk Munroe; *Juv. Blackie* [*Eng.*], *Scribner* [*U.S.A.*].

Florida, 1835 onwards. A story of the Second Seminole War; this war against the Indians (led by their chief, Osceola) lasted almost seven years, but the Indians were eventually conquered, and—most of them—went west. The swamps and thickets of Florida made the work of conquest difficult.

1905. *THE MAGNIFICENT IDLER: Cameron Rogers; *Heinemann.*

Long Island, 1816 (Ch. I); also Long Island and other localities, 1823-1892. A fictional biography of Walt Whitman, covering his teaching and press experiences, as well as the nursing of his brother in War time and his other hospital activities. There is, of course, much illustration of the period when *Leaves of Grass* appeared (Emerson's opinions in regard to that book, etc. etc.) The first chapter deals with Walter Whitman, the father, a few years before the poet's birth.

1906. *THE NIGHTINGALE: Marjorie Strachey; *Longmans.*

Warsaw, Paris, etc., mainly in the period 1835-49. The life of Chopin, the composer and pianist, fictionally presented. " George Sand " (Madame Dudevant) is, of course, especially prominent, and numerous other personages appear.

1907. *WITH SAM HOUSTON IN TEXAS: Edwin L. Sabin; *Juv.* *Lippincott.*
Arkansas River region, etc., and Texas, mainly in the period 1832-36. A tale illustrating the struggle in Texas against Mexican rule, and covering the declaration of independence, the Alamo massacre, the Battle of San Jacinto, and the eventual capture of Santa Anna, the Mexican General. The outstanding historical figure is General Sam Houston, commander-in-chief of the Texan army.

1908. *THE SHE-WOLVES OF MACHECOUL: Alexandre Dumas (trans.); *Dent [Eng.], Little, Brown [U.S.A.].*
France, largely in the period 1832-43, though the *full* period, including the Epilogue, is 1795-1843. A tale illustrating the Duchesse de Berri's attempted Vendean rebellion, from her landing at Marseilles (1832) to her arrest at Nantes. It is a book very suitable for young folk. Besides the Duchesse, several historic figures are introduced at one point or another: Louis XVIII, Louis Philippe, La Rochejacquelin, and others.

1909. *THE FIERY DAWN: Mary E. Coleridge; *Arnold [Eng.], Longmans [U.S.A.].*
France (Lyons, La Vendée and Nantes), 1832-34. A romance of the Duchess of Berri's Vendean plots. Besides the outstanding figure of the Duchess, there are many historic personages including: Thiers (as Minister of the Interior); the writers Balzac, Théophile Gautier, and Gerard de Nerval; and the artist, Corot. There is, also, considerable mention of Victor Hugo.

1910. EARNCLIFFE OF ERRINGTON: F. B. Forester; *Juv.* *Sheldon Press [Eng.], Macmillan [U.S.A.].*
N. England (Cumberland) and Spain, 1835-36. An adventure story, telling of a young fellow who goes to Spain in search of his father, and falls into the hands of Carlist guerillas. The Carlist Rising forms the historical background.

1911. WITH THE BRITISH LEGION: G. A. Henty; *Juv.* *Blackie [Eng.], Scribner [U.S.A.].*
Spain, 1835-37. A tale of the British Legion, commanded by Sir George De Lacy Evans for the child-Queen Isabella II (her mother Christina acting as Regent) against the Carlists. Several historic figures.

1912. *THE BRITISH LEGION: Herbert Hayens; *Juv.* *Nelson.*
Spain, 1835-37. A story of the Carlist War and the British Legion's share in it. The English hero has many adventures, and there is much fighting between the Christinos and the Carlists. The Carlist leader, Cabrera, is prominent in the tale, while Espartero, General Chichester, and other personages appear.

1913. *IN KEDAR'S TEXTS: " H. Seton Merriman "; *Smith, Elder [Eng.], Dodd, Mead [U.S.A.].*
N. England and Spain (Algeciras, Madrid, Toledo, etc.), 1838-39. A good story mainly dealing with Spain at the time of the struggle between the Queen Regent (Christina) and Don Carlos. The Queen Regent herself is introduced prominently, and the Captain-General Vicente is another figure. The book ends in the period of he Carlist defeat and the flight of Don Carlos to France.

1914. *THE SENTRY: Nicolai Lyeskov (trans.); in " The Sentry and Other Stories "—*Lane.*
Russia (Petersburg), 1839. A short, but excellent, story of a young highly-cultured officer, with humane tendencies, and of a sentry under his command who leaves his post to save a drowning man. Illustrates the military despotism and harsh measures under Tzar Nicholas I.

1915. THE POMP OF THE LAVILETTES: GILBERT PARKER;
Methuen [Eng.], Appleton [U.S.A.], Harper [U.S.A.].
Lower Canada in 1837. A story of the time when Louis Papineau, the French
Canadian, led a rebellion; it broke out in November, 1837, but was quickly suppressed.

1916. IN TREATY WITH HONOR: MARY CATHERINE CROWLEY;
Little, Brown.
A tale of Quebec and the Canadian Rebellion of 1837-38, the outcome of which was
the famous Report issued by Lord Durham in 1839.

1917. *JOHN CHARITY: H. A. VACHELL; *Murray [Eng.], Dodd, Mead
[U.S.A.].*
S. England (Winchester, Oxford, etc.) about 1815-37, but mostly California in the
late 'Thirties. An interesting love and adventure story, with a background of civil
war and politics.

1918. (1)*THE HERO OF HERAT:
(2)*THE JUDGMENT OF THE SWORD (*sequel*): MAUD
DIVER; *Constable [Eng.], Putnam [U.S.A.].*
(1) The first of these two connected novels deals with Afghanistan and India in the
period 1837-41; it is a good example of fictional biography, having Major Eldred
Pottinger as central figure. It begins with Pottinger on an exploring mission, and
leads up to the defence of Herat (First Afghan War). Introduces—besides the historic
hero—Yar Mahomed Khan of Herat, Burnes, Mc Neill, Lord Auckland, and other
figures.
(2) The sequel is a romance of the Afghan War generally, rather than a one-man
novel (though Pottinger still appears prominently). The period covered is 1841-43,
and there is a graphic account of the many errors which characterized the manage-
ment of military affairs at this crisis. Covers the Siege of Kabul, and the terrible scenes
in the Khurd Kabul Pass (Elphinstone's army). The final pages tell of Pottinger's death
in Hong Kong, 1843. There are a great many historic figures, of whom the following
are perhaps the most important: Major Pottinger, General Elphinstone, Sir William
Macnaghten, Sir Robert and Lady Sale, and the Sirdar Mahomed Akbar Khan.

1919. *CLEVELY SAHIB: HERBERT HAYENS; *Juv. Nelson.*
The Punjab (time of Ranjit Singh, called " The Lion of the Punjab "), and Afghanistan
(Cabul, Jellalabad, etc.), mainly in the period 1838-42. An exciting tale of the supposed
narrator's adventures, having largely for its historic background, events just before and
during the first Afghan War. Deals with the primary cause of the War (the British policy
of dethroning Dost Mohammed in favour of Shah Soojah), and covers the Cabul revolt,
the terrible slaughter in the Khoord Cabul Pass, and the coming of General Pollock's
" avenging army." Sir William Macnaghten appears in the time shortly before his death,
while there are many references to other historic personages like Sir Robert Sale, Dost
Mohammed (his surrender), Akbar Khan, etc.

1920. TO HERAT AND CABUL: G. A. HENTY; *Juv. Blackie [Eng.],
Scribner [U.S.A.].*
Afghanistan, 1838 and few years following. A story of the First Afghan War, describ-
ing the annihilation of the British troops in the mountain passes between Cabul and
Jellalabad, and the relief of the last-named place where Sale had been invested. Intro-
duces Sale, Pottinger, and other figures.

1921. WHEN VALMOND CAME TO PONTIAC: GILBERT PARKER;
Methuen [Eng.], Macmillan [U.S.A.].
A French Canadian village, mostly c. 1842. The hero of this short and highly romantic
story, is a supposed son of the great Napoleon, born in St. Helena. There are various
allusions to bygone events, as well as to such personages as Napoleon himself, Count
Bertrand, and Lucien Bonaparte (mentioned as dead " two years ago "). Moreover,
in the *Epilogue* the reader learns the news: " Louis Napoleon enters the Tuileries."
Apart from these references, the novel is only historical in the sense of conveying the
French-Canadian life of the time.

1922. * "THE MEN WHO FOUGHT FOR US " IN THE " HUNGRY
      FORTIES ": Allen Clarke; *Co-operative Newspaper Society, Ltd.*
Rochdale, 1842, and the year or two following. A story well illustrating the original
efforts of the " Rochdale pioneers " which resulted in the great Co-operative Movement.
Begins with the news of the arrest of Thomas Cooper, the Chartist, in connection with
the Pottery riots, and describes the influences of the period in the direction of Owenite
Socialism and Co-operation. The later chapters (or " pictures " as the author calls
them) tell of the occurrences leading up to the actual starting of the Co-operative Stores
—also touching on the factory troubles, etc. The local colour is good, and many real
figures are introduced. Two personages of note outside the Rochdale groups also appear,
viz. Sam Bamford the Radical, and G. J. Holyoake.

1923. *THE GREAT HOUSE: Stanley J. Weyman; *Murray [Eng.]*,
      Longmans [U.S.A.].
Begins Paris, but quickly passes to Staffordshire (Valley of the Trent) in the 'Forties.
A novel well depicting the life and politics of the period. The historical background
is the controversy over the Corn Laws (the Corn Law League, etc.), and Sir Robert
Peel's *volte face* in 1845. There are some amusing descriptions of political meetings.
Ends with the announcement of the Repeal of the Corn Laws. No historic figures
appear, though there are many allusions to Peel and others.

1924. THE GATE-OPENERS: " K. L. Montgomery "; *John Long.*
Carmarthenshire, 1843-44. A tale of the Turnpike (or " Rebekah ") Riots, with
some account of that strange practice connected with Welsh funerals which was known
as the Sin-Eating.

1925. *THE SHEEP STEALERS: Violet Jacob; *Heinemann [Eng.]*,
      Putnam [U.S.A.].
The Welsh Border district (Black Mountain and Wye Valley), mainly " Crishowell,"
i.e. Crickhowell, Breconshire. Time of the Highway Act regarding Tolls and the
consequent Rebecca Riots (1843). This really fine and moving tale begins with the
Riots, and the murder of a toll keeper; the chapters which follow tell of certain fictional
developments which are described as covering a period of some twelve months.

1926. *MAGIC OF DAWN: Henry A. Doudy; *Hutchinson.*
Australia and (in small degree) England, 1839-44. A well-told story of Adelaide
in early days as the " Forest City," and of Captain Charles Sturt's explorations (he
was the discoverer of South Australia and the River Murray). Both Captain Sturt
and his wife are introduced.

1927. THE NEXT TIME: Louis J. Walsh; *Gill [Ireland]*.
Ireland (Dublin, Tipperary and other localities) in the period 1829-1848, mainly
between 1841 and 1848. A novel with a considerable background of history. It begins
with the news of the Catholic Emancipation Act being passed, and in later chapters
depicts in turn: the founding of *The Nation* as organ of the " Young Ireland " Party
(1842); the Repeal agitation of 1843; the break between the Young Irelanders and
O'Connell; and the founding of *The United Irishman* (12th February, 1848) which resulted
in John Mitchel's trial and transportation. Lastly, there is some account of the insurrection of 'Forty-Eight. In the course of the story many noted figures appear besides
O'Connell and Mitchel already named; of these, one may specify William Smith O'Brien
and John Blake Dillon—both prominent young Irelanders.

1928. MONONIA: Justin McCarthy; *Chatto & Windus [Eng.]*, *Small,*
      Maynard [U.S.A.].
Southern Ireland, 1848. A love story with historic background: the Young Ireland
movement and the politics of the time. Illustrates the failure of the attempted Nationalist
Rising of '48.

1929. THROUGH THE SIKH WAR: G. A. Henty; *Juv.* *Blackie*
      [Eng.], *Scribner [U.S.A.]*.
A tale of India in the period 1845-49, covering the conquest of the Punjaub in the
two Sikh Wars. Hardinge and Lawrence are important figures.

1930. SWORD AND ASSEGAI: Anna Howarth; *Smith, Elder*.
A story of South Africa dealing, on the historical side, with the Kaffir risings of 1846 and 1851.

1931. THE MANTLE OF THE EMPEROR: L. Black and R. Lynd; *Griffiths*.
Italy, France, England, and Switzerland, 1830-46. An entertaining story of an Irishman's adventures, with a considerable background of history. Louis Napoleon (afterwards Napoleon III) is a very prominent figure, and the portrait of him here given is unconventional and more or less favourable. Covers the revolt against pontifical rule in Italy, Louis Napoleon's abortive attempts to reach the throne of France, his imprisonment in the fortress of Ham and his escape therefrom. Several historic figures, including Queen Hortense, Cardinal Fesch, the Duchesse de Berri and Talleyrand.

1932. *BETWEEN TWO THIEVES: " Richard Dehan "; *Heinemann* [Eng.], *Stokes* [U.S.A.].
France, England, Russia, and Turkey, mainly in the period 1845-55. A somewhat rambling story with a considerable historical element. Deals largely with France, especially in the time of the 1848 revolution, Louis-Philippe's abdication, and the coming of Napoleon III. The later chapters illustrate the Crimean War, more on the general side than in any detailed manner. An enormous number of notabilities are introduced in the course of the novel; some real people are thinly disguised under names like " Lord Dalgan," Lady " Stratclyffe," etc. etc., while others appear openly like Louis-Napoleon, Victor Hugo, De Morny, Gortchakoff, and the Tsar Nicholas. The depiction of Napoleon III is distinctly adverse.

1933. THE FLOWER OF DESTINY: William Dana Orcutt; *McClurg* [U.S.A.].
France, 1846-52. A romance of the period between Louis Napoleon's escape from the fortress of Ham and his assumption of the Imperial title just a year after the *coup d'état* of 1851. Louis Napoleon and Eugénie de Montigo (favourable depiction) appear, as well as a few other notabilities.

1934. THE MADONNA OF THE BARRICADES: J. St. Loe Strachey; *Cape* [Eng.], *Harcourt* [U.S.A.].
New Forest, Oxford, London, and Paris, 1847-48. Imaginary memoirs, giving a more or less accurate picture of the time, but hardly satisfactory on the fictional side. The Oxford of 1847-48, the Carbonari (secret society), and the Paris revolution of 1848, are subjects that enter largely into the narrative in its earlier and later stages. Louis-Napoleon, Karl Marx, and other personages appear.

1935. JOURNEYMAN LOVE: Maud Stepney Rawson; *Hutchinson*.
Largely Paris in the period just before and during the Revolution of 1848. A novel of music and politics. Of the various historic personages, George Sand and Chopin are the most prominent. There is some mention of Heine, and slight allusions are made to Guizot, Louis Blanc, Louis Philippe, and other figures of the period.

1936. ISHMAEL: M. E. Braddon; *Maxwell* [Eng.], *Harper* [U.S.A.].
France (Brittany, Paris, etc.) in the period 1848-68. Depicts the Paris of 1850 and the *coup d'état* of December, 1851, as well as the later political developments of the Second Empire. Napoleon III is shown in an unfavourable light. Victor Hugo is one of the several historic figures introduced.

1937. THE LAST HOPE: " H. Seton Merriman "; *Smith, Elder* [Eng.], *Scribner* [U.S.A.].
England (Suffolk) and France, 1850-51. A tale of the supposed Dauphin (Louis XVII). Some connection is made to appear between the fictional dénouement and the historic *coup d'état* of Louis Napoleon (Napoleon III).

R

1938. BEYOND MAN'S STRENGTH: M. HARTLEY; *Heinemann*.
N. Italy (largely Turin), 1814–24, and 1847–1849. Story of the Irish-Welsh wife of an Italian, with an atmosphere of politics throughout. Illustrates (Book I) the Piedmontese Rising of 1821, and (Book II) the War with Austria 1848-49. The outstanding figure is King Carlo-Alberto, whose moderation was condemned by the Mazzinists. Cavour also appears. The names of other historic personages like Victor Emmanuel, D'Azeglio, Garibaldi, etc., are encountered at various points, while there are two separate glimpses of Byron, and a single glimpse of Shelley. The novel ends with mention of the Battle of Novara (no description) and the death of Carlo-Alberto.

1939. *MADEMOISELLE MORI: MARGARET ROBERTS; *Juv.* Longmans [*Eng.*], *Munro* [*U.S.A.*].
Story of a patriotic girl-singer in Rome between 1846 and 1850. Illustrates the early hopes in connection with Pope Pius IX, and, later, the Italian Revolution of 1848-49: Charles Albert (King of Sardinia) v. the Austrians, and Garibaldi v. the Neapolitans. The author's reputation was established by this book which reveals historical and topographical knowledge in an unusual degree.

1940. *VITTORIA: GEORGE MEREDITH; *Constable* [*Eng.*], *Scribner* [*U.S.A.*].
Northern Italy (largely Milan), 1847-49. This stirring romance of an operatic singer depicts the " Young Italy " movement and the national uprising against the Austrians in Lombardy. The book ends with the Fall of Vicenza, and the Austrians once more established in Milan. As that specialist in Italian history, Prof. G. M. Trevelyan, has pointed out (in a lecture at Cambridge, 1920), *Vittoria* is " partly an historical novel looking back to the past like ' Waverley ' or ' Westward Ho! '; partly a work of contemporary fiction that has by process of time become historical, like Chaucer or Miss Austen." In the same section of this Cambridge address, one reads the following particularly interesting tribute: " *Vittoria* contains the finest and truest picture of Mazzini that has ever been drawn."

1941. *ADRIA: A TALE OF VENICE: ALEX. NELSON HOOD; *Murray*.
England (early chapters) and Venice in the late Eighteen-Forties—mainly 1848 and 1849. A novel of the " descriptive " type, but having both fictional and historical interest. The English hero is sent by Lord Palmerston on a secret mission to Venice—the inhabitants of that city being on the eve of revolt against Austrian oppression. After considerable fictional developments, the book, in its later portions, introduces the heroic Daniele Manin as the outstanding historical figure; the successful revolt, the Austrian evacuation, the proclamation of the Venetian Republic (with Manin as President), and, lastly, the re-taking of the city by the Austrians after a five months' siege—these events are all in turn covered. Besides its presentment of Manin, the novel affords a glimpse of Palmerston (already named), and there are allusions to Carlo Alberto, Pope Pius IX, and others.

1942. *DIE VERTEIDIGUNG ROMS: RICARDA HUCH; *Deutsche Verlags-Anhalt* [*Germany*].
Garibaldi and Mazzini, 1848-49: an " imaginative history."

1943. *THE LAME ENGLISHMAN: WARWICK DEEPING; *Cassell*.
Rome in 1849. An interesting novel dealing especially with the defence of the city against the French. Mazzini, Garibaldi, etc.

1944. (1)*THE PATRIOT:
       (2)*THE MAN OF THE WORLD:
       (3)*THE SAINT: ANTONIO FOGAZZARO (trans.); *Hodder & Stoughton* [*Eng.*], *Putnam* [*U.S.A.*].
A trilogy having a certain historical sequence, though each novel is more or less complete in itself. While conveying the impression of a mid- to late-nineteenth century atmosphere, and containing allusions to famous events and persons, these three romances are not historical novels in the strictest sense; they illustrate primarily the author's

advocacy of social and religious reform—at the same time having genuine interest on the purely fictional side, as well as in their descriptions of Italian scenery.

(1) The first novel depicts life in N. Italy (Lake region) largely in the year 1851, when Cavour and his policy were to the fore, and when the gloom of Austrian oppression hung over the country.

(2) The second novel is descriptive of life in the Province of Venice in the 'Eighties. A model priest is the outstanding figure, while there are good domestic scenes, and some excellent character-drawing.

(3) The last volume in the trilogy (N. Italy and Rome about the end of the 19th Century) conveys—through its striking fictional developments—the author's teaching in regard to a real Christian democracy and Religion in its essence. It should be added that the love-story in this third novel is central in its significance.

1945. BARRICADE: "John Presland"; *Philip Allan.*
Vienna and Olmütz, 1848. A tale of the revolutionary troubles in Vienna, and of the bombardment of the city by Prince Windischgraetz. A number of the Hapsburg Royalties appear, including the Emperor Ferdinand, and his nephew, the Archduke Francis-Joseph, in whose favour the Emperor abdicated after the insurrection. Other figures are Windischgraetz (already mentioned) and Blum, the revolutionary leader.

1946. *RED, WHITE, AND GREEN: Herbert Hayens; *Juv. Nelson.*
Austria and Hungary (Vienna, Pesth, etc.), chiefly 1848-49. Decidedly a tale of war, having for most of its principal figures (fictional as well as historical) military men, and introducing a succession of battle scenes almost throughout. The book illustrates in careful manner the period of the Vienna insurrection (1848), the abdication of the Emperor Ferdinand I in favour of his nephew Francis-Joseph, and the revolt in Hungary. A large portion of the story is devoted to the struggles of Hungarians against Austrians and Russians respectively—Russia supporting Austria. The dissensions between General Görgei and Kossuth are emphasized (the last-named personage being somewhat unsympathetically depicted). Many historical figures are introduced or mentioned, of whom Prince Windischgrätz, Kossuth, Görgei, Klapka, and Field-Marshal Paskevitch (Russian) are more or less prominent at one point or another.

1946a. *THE STRONGER WINGS: A. Jeans; *Elliot Stock.*
Austria (rural districts and Vienna), 1848-49. An interesting novel of the liberal movements against Metternich's despotism, and of the revolutionary outbreak in Vienna. Shows the influences of culture and new ideas among the University students, etc., at the same time giving a picture of ignorant extremists. Prince Metternich is very prominently introduced, and the Austrian Field-Marshal Windischgrätz also appears.

1947. *THE GENIUS: Margaret H. Potter; *Harper.*
Moscow, Petersburg, etc., mid to late 19th Century. A novel beginning 1840, but mainly covering the period 1855-90. The hero ("Ivan Gregoriev") is more or less identifiable with Tchaikowsky, the musical composer. Like the real man, the fictional "genius" studies under Anton Rubinstein. Altogether a careful and interesting presentment—at once historical and psychological.

1948. THE LIGHT IN THE CLEARING: Irving Bacheller; *Collins [Eng.], Grosset [U.S.A.].*
America (the Northern States region) 1831-44. A story with Silas Wright, the high-minded American statesman, as dominating figure on the historical side. The scene ultimately shifts to Washington—Wright then appearing in his capacity as Senator. Politics and religion are the novel's main elements.

1949. THE ISSUE: George Morgan; *Lippincott.*
A novel dealing with the question of Slavery in the Southern States of America, and covering the period 1831-61, when Daniel Webster, Henry Clay, and J. C. Calhoun (the "great triumvirate" of orators) were the outstanding figures in American politics, prior to Abraham Lincoln's advent in the few years immediately preceding the Civil War.

1950. *CONISTON: Winston Churchill; *Macmillan.*
Boston, Washington, etc., in the second and third quarters of the 19th Century. This interesting novel begins soon after General Jackson had become President (1829), and illustrates the developments in politics and social life in the long period ending with Grant's Presidency (1869-77).

1951. *FALSE DAWN: Edith Wharton; *Appleton.*
The first and most interesting story in Mrs. Wharton's *Old New York* series. Although quite short, this fictional sketch conveys a clear impression of New York *and Europe* in the Eighteen-Forties. The young American hero on his European tour meets, and talks with, John Ruskin in the Italian Alps region; he also encounters some of the Pre-Raphaelites in London.

1952. WITH CARSON AND FRÉMONT: Edwin L. Sabin; *Juv.*
    Lippincott.
N. America, beginning in 1840, but mainly dealing with the period 1842-44. An adventure story based on Frémont's exploration (under Government authority) of the Rockies and of an overland route to the Pacific.

1953. *FIFTY-FOUR FORTY, OR FIGHT: Emerson Hough;
    Hodder & Stoughton [Eng.], Bobbs-Merrill [U.S.A.].
Washington, Montreal, etc., about 1844-46. A story with a considerable background of history. The atmosphere is largely political, the outstanding subject being the dispute between the United States and Great Britain over Oregon. The cry in 1846 was " The Whole of Oregon, or none "—in other words that the British were to give up the entire country below 54° 40′ (" 54-40, or fight "). Later in the year a Treaty was made between the States and Great Britain. John Calhoun appears, and there are glimpses of President Tyler, Henry Clay, Edward Everett, and Sam Houston.

1954. RIO BRAVO: E. L. Sabin; *Juv. Hutchinson [Eng.], Macrae Smith
    [U.S.A.].*
St. Louis, New Orleans, and N. Mexico (Texas border), 1846. A story of love and adventure, with General Zachary Taylor's campaign in Mexico as the historic background. A beautiful Spanish girl adds interest on the fictional side. Several historic figures, including General Taylor himself, Jefferson Davis, and Robert E. Lee (as " captain ").

1955. FIGHTING WITH FRÉMONT: Everett McNeill; *Juv.*
    Chambers [Eng.], Dutton [U.S.A.].
A tale of the Conquest of California, 1846. The time is that of General Taylor's two victories—Palo Alto and Resaca de la Palma (May 8th and May 9th respectively). The outstanding historical figure in the story is Colonel (afterwards General) Frémont, the explorer, who did great service after the outbreak of the Mexican War.

1956. *THE QUEST OF THE FOUR: Joseph A. Altsheler; *Juv.*
    Appleton.
New Orleans, etc., and Mexico, 1846-47. A good adventure story leading up to the War in Mexico under General Taylor. The Pass of Angostura, and the Battle of Buena Vista (1847). General Taylor himself appears, as also does Santa Anna, the Mexican President and Commander-in-Chief.

1957. THE TEXAN STAR:
    THE TEXAN SCOUTS:
    THE TEXAN TRIUMPH: Joseph A. Altsheler; *Juv. Appleton.*
These three stories, which together form *The Texan Series*, tell of a youth and his friends in the Mexican War of 1846-48.

1958. **INTO MEXICO WITH GENERAL SCOTT*: EDWIN L. SABIN: *Juv. Lippincott.*
Mexico, 1847. A tale of the Mexican War and General Winfield Scott's two hundred miles' march (after taking Vera Cruz) to the City of Mexico, near which a succession of battles were fought. Scott's army was a small one for the task undertaken, but he eventually entered the city, and brought the War virtually to an end. U. S. Grant appears as " Second Lieutenant."

1959. **TRAIL-MAKERS OF THE MIDDLE BORDER*: HAMLIN GARLAND; *Lane.*
State of Maine (New England border-line), Boston, the Great Lakes, and Wisconsin, etc.; also the Civil War region (Vicksburg); 1837-1863 (mostly 1842-63). An interesting story of early pioneers and life in the period of first railway enterprise and the opening of the West. There are allusions to the Mexican War, the finding of gold in California, and the political controversies of the time; while special reference is made to men like William Lloyd Garrison, " the young poet " Whittier, and Wendell Phillips. The second part of the book tells of the outbreak of Civil War—the later chapters leading up to the Siege and taking of Vicksburg. Throughout this part of the story, Grant is the outstanding historical figure; he is introduced effectively at more than one point.

1960. **EBEN HOLDEN*: IRVING BACHELLER; *Fisher Unwin* [Eng.], *Lothrop Publishing Co.* [U.S.A.].
A much-read story of N. America (Valley of the St. Lawrence, and, later, New York) within the period 1845-65. Besides the descriptions of early days in St. Lawrence County, there are interesting pictures of New York journalism in 1860, followed by a rapid survey of the Civil War. Horace Greeley of *The Tribune* is prominently introduced, while there are glimpses of Abraham Lincoln and of the " Prince of Wales " (Edward VII) as a young man of 19.

1961. **THE COVERED WAGON*: EMERSON HOUGH; *Appleton.*
N. America: the Missouri region and the Western States, 1848. An excellent adventure tale, illustrating the emigration westward over an immense region, which took place in 1848 (the " great wagon train "). The troubles with the Indians, etc.

1962. *GOLD SEEKERS OF '49*: EDWIN L. SABIN; *Juv. Lippincott.*
St. Louis, the Isthmus of Panama, and California, 1849. An adventure story of the Gold Rush Year, telling what happened to the " seekers " on their long journey, as well as in San Francisco, etc., when their destination was reached.

1963. **GOLD*: STEWART EDWARD WHITE; *Hodder & Stoughton* [Eng.], *Doubleday* [U.S.A.].
Panama and California, 1849. A tale vividly depicting the gold rush which followed the discoveries made in California: adventure and the lawless conditions which prevailed generally.

1964. **THE GREY DAWN*: STEWART EDWARD WHITE; *Hodder & Stoughton* [Eng.], *Doubleday* [U.S.A.].
California (San Francisco), 1852 onwards. A good picture of the rough times when some of the best citizens of San Francisco organized a Committee of Vigilance to deal with the disorders.

1965. **THE PURCHASE PRICE*: EMERSON HOUGH; *Hodder & Stoughton* [Eng.], *Bobbs-Merrill* [U.S.A.].
Washington and various localities, 1850-51. An excellent story of American politics (the Slave Question) and life in the middle of the century. There are several allusions to public men like Clay, Webster, Garrison, Beecher, etc., as well as to such European contemporaries as Louis Napoleon and Kossuth.

1966. *MARTIN RIVAS: Alberto Blest-Gana (trans.); *Chapman & Hall.*
Chili (Santiago), 1850-51. A clever novel of Business, Politics, and Social Life, giving an interesting picture of mid-nineteenth century conditions in South America. Introduces the revolutionary fighting which took place in Santiago on the twentieth of April, 1851.

1967. *UNDER THE LONE STAR: Herbert Hayens; *Juv.   Nelson.*
Begins San Francisco, 1854, but mostly Nicaragua 1855-57. An English-born youth's story, telling the peculiar circumstances under which he went with an expedition into Nicaragua having for its purpose military help to the " Liberals " in that country in their struggle against the " Serviles." Much fighting and numerous adventures. The outstanding figure is William Walker, the organiser of the above-named expedition (both the man and the event are historical). Walker had a chequered career—being lawyer, journalist and filibuster alternately. In the period covered in this tale he assisted the Democrats in Nicaragua (as we have seen), and fought against Costa Rica; he was actually made lawful President of Nicaragua (as in the story).

1968. CHILD OF STORM: H. Rider Haggard; *Cassell [Eng.], Longmans [U.S.A.].*
Zululand, mainly 1854-56. An " Allan Quartermain " tale, which describes the quarrel between the two Princes, Cetewayo and Umbelazi, and the Battle of Tugela (December, 1856). King Panda appears as well as the Princes.

1969. THE COIL OF CARNE: " John Oxenham "; *Methuen [Eng.], Lane [U.S.A.].*
England and the Crimea, mainly between 1835 and 1855. A novel of life in the 'Thirties (Book I); then, passing over some ten years (Book II), depicting the Early Victorian period before and up to the Crimean War. The last part of the book gives some account of Alma, Balaclava, Inkerman, and Sevastopol.

1970. *MARMADUKE: Mrs. Flora Annie Steel; *Heinemann [Eng.], Stokes [U.S.A.].*
Scotland (Aberdeenshire coast), London, and the Crimea, 1848-55. An excellent Early Victorian tale, suggesting the atmosphere of the period, and having a slight background of history. The Crimean scenes have more to do with the hospitals of the War than with its actual battles.

1971. *RAVENSHOE: Henry Kingsley; *Ward, Lock [Eng.], Longmans [U.S.A.].*
A fine novel beginning West England, 1831, but quickly passing to Oxford and London respectively about 1852-53. Depicts the manners and life of the time (University Boot-Race, the Derby, etc.), also reflecting political discussion during the Aberdeen Coalition Ministry. The later portion of the book treats of the Crimean War in 1854 (Battle of Alma and the Siege of Sebastopol); these war scenes are vividly, if somewhat briefly, presented.

1972. TRUE UNTO DEATH: Eliza F. Pollard; *Juv.   Partridge.*
An interesting tale of a young English girl in Russia (St. Petersburg and Moscow) in the period 1851-55. Ends in the Crimea during the War.

1973. THE INTERPRETER: G. J. Whyte Melville; *Ward, Lock [Eng.], Longmans [U.S.A.].*
A romance of various localities including Hungary and the Danubian Principalities, Turkey, London, Vienna, Constantinople, and the Crimea, c. 1853-55. The historical background is largely Omar Pasha's successful resistance to Russia, and the later chapters give some account of the Crimean War.

1974. BLAIR OF BALACLAVA: Escott Lynn; *Juv.* *Chambers.*
England and the Crimea, 1853-57. The young hero of this story takes part in the famous Charge of the Light Brigade. Alma, Sevastopol, Balaclava, and Inkermann are all covered, while Sir Colin Campbell, Lord Raglan, Lord Lucan and Lord Cardigan appear.

1975. *SEVASTOPOL: Count Lyof N. Tolstoy (trans.); *Walter Scott* [*Eng.*], *Crowell* [*U.S.A.*] *and other publishers.*
Three striking fictional sketches illustrating, in realistic fashion, military life during the Siege of Sevastopol (Crimean War). The sketches are respectively headed:— December, 1854; May, 1855; and August, 1855.

1976. THE PATH TO HONOUR:
THE KEEPERS OF THE GATE (*sequel*): " Sydney C. Grier ";
Blackwood.
Two connected novels of India in mid-nineteenth century. The first story deals with troubles (revolt of Granthi regiments) c. 1850, while the sequel illustrates the earlier part of the Mutiny, beginning with the news of the outbreaks at Meerut and Delhi. There is a substantial background of history, but it is, perhaps, chiefly by its imaginative reproduction of the Mutiny *atmosphere* that the novel can be termed historical.

1977. A STAR OF THE EAST: Charles E. Pearce; *Stanley Paul.*
Delhi (mainly), Simla, Calcutta, etc., and England (slightly), 1851-57. A novel depicting the conditions in India during the years preceding the Mutiny, as well as at the actual outbreak. The book ends with the Delhi massacre.

1978. THE DEVIL'S WIND: Patricia Wentworth; *Melrose* [*Eng.*], *Putnam* [*U.S.A.*].
London and India, 1854-58. A story of the Indian Mutiny—Cawnpore and district being the region, more or less, throughout. Sensational but interesting. Nana Sahib is introduced.

1979. FLOTSAM: " H. Seton Merriman "; *Longmans.*
India (Calcutta and Delhi), England, and Ceylon, mostly between 1854 and 1860 (actually begins 1831). A story which to some extent illustrates the Indian Mutiny. There are glimpses of Nicholson.

1980. WHEN NICHOLSON KEPT THE BORDER: J. Claverdon Wood; *Juv.* Office of *The Boy's Own Paper,* London.
N. W. India, c. 1856-57. A good adventure tale of the time just before the Mutiny, and presenting John Nicholson as the central historical figure. Tells of Nicholson's success with the savage border tribes, and of his death at the taking of Delhi after the Mutiny had actually broken out. Lieutenant Roberts (afterwards Lord Roberts) also appears.

1981. *ON THE FACE OF THE WATERS: Mrs. F. A. Steel; *Heinemann* [*Eng.*], *Macmillan* [*U.S.A.*].
This most impressive novel of the Indian Mutiny period begins Lucknow, March, 1856, but nearly the whole of the story is connected with Delhi from September, 1856, up to its siege and taking by Nicholson in September, 1857. The reader is given a series of vivid pictures, including an account of the outbreak at Meerut (10th May, 1857). Of the many historic figures introduced, Hodson of Hodson's House and John Nicholson (especially the latter) stand out prominently. The book ends with Nicholson's death—the result of wounds received when leading the storming party at Delhi.

1982. *SEETA: Philip Meadows Taylor; *Kegan Paul* [*Eng.*], *Scribner* [*U.S.A.*].

The author himself describes this tale of the Indian Mutiny as a " general impression " which excludes painful details for the most part.   The whole book is clearly indicative of first-hand knowledge, and readers will gain a good general impression of the conditions just before, and during, the Mutiny, i.e. from about 1856 down to the end of 1858. This novel completes the author's trilogy illustrating the history of India in (roughly) 1657, 1757, and 1857.

1983. RED REVENGE: Charles E. Pearce; *Stanley Paul.*

India (mainly Cawnpore), 1857.   The author states in his preface that in this novel he has " given the leading place to *fact*," and certainly the horrors of Cawnpore are depicted in a painfully realistic manner (Sir Hugh Wheeler's entrenchment and the massacre of the boats, etc.).   Ends with Havelock's entry into the city.   Nana Sahib is prominently introduced.

1984. EIGHT DAYS: R. E. Forrest; *Smith, Elder.*

India, May 8th to 15th (both inclusive), 1857.   A story of the eight eventful days in the course of which the Indian Mutiny began.   The ancient city of Khizrabad (close to Delhi) is the scene of the novel, which reveals the author's special knowledge of both period and locality.

1985. BARCLAY OF THE GUIDES: " Herbert Strang "; *Juv. Frowde* [*Eng.*], *Doran* [*U.S.A.*].

Largely Delhi, 1857.   An adventure story of Lumsden's Guides and the Indian Mutiny, up to the storming of Delhi.   There are several historic figures, including Hodson, Nicholson, " Lieutenant " F. Roberts (Lord Roberts) and John Lawrence. The *Epilogue* passes to 1863.

1986. A HERO OF THE MUTINY: Escott Lynn; *Juv.   Chambers.*

Delhi, Meerut, Cawnpore, and Lucknow, 1857.   A tale of two English lads in the Indian Mutiny, or—as the author prefers to call it—the " Sepoy Revolt " (the sepoys of the Bengal army being the chief mutineers).   Covers the period from the outbreak to the Fall of Lucknow.   Sir Henry Havelock, Major Hodson, Nicholson, Sir Colin Campbell, Nana Sahib, and the King of Delhi are all introduced.

1987. SECRET BREAD: F. Tennyson Jesse; *Heinemann* [*Eng.*], *Doran* [*U.S.A.*]

West England (Cornwall and Devon) and London, mostly between 1857 and 1900. A story carefully illustrating life and manners in the second half of the 19th Century. Reflects both religious and political developments, and, though a novel of historic atmosphere rather than one dealing with particular events or persons, it contains allusions to public men like Gladstone, Disraeli, and Rosebery, and also refers to the South African War.

1988. *THE FLAME IN THE SOUTH: Luke Hansard; *Hutchinson.*

London (Chelsea), Paris, and Italy, mainly in the period 1851-1867 (the latest pages pass to 1914).   A novel with a considerable background of history.   Begins with London in the days of the " young Queen and Prince Albert," then taking the reader to Paris at the time when Orsini was being tried for his share in the attempt on Napoleon III's life (1858).   There is also an excellent account of Garibaldi and The Thousand in Sicily (Calatafini and Palermo), 1860.   The later portions of the novel deal yet again with London and Italy in the 'Sixties—covering Garibaldi's defeat by the papal troops at Mentana (1867).   Mazzini and Garibaldi are prominently introduced, and Jules Favre appears as making the speech for the defence in Orsini's trial.

1989. *THE PILLAR OF FIRE: H. C. Bailey; *Methuen.*

London in the late 'Fifties (Lord Palmerston, Mazzini in exile, etc.); Paris (Napoleon III); then Italy and the War with Austria 1859 (Cavour, Victor Emmanuel, and Louis Napoleon again); ending with Garibaldi's conquest of Sicily in 1860.   A novel showing the author's knowledge of the period.

1990. *FOR FREEDOM: Tighe Hopkins; *Chatto & Windus.*
An excellent story, having for its background the War of Italian Liberation in 1859. The fictional developments are interesting, while, on the historical side, there are good accounts of the storming of Palermo and other fighting. Garibaldi is, of course, the outstanding historical figure.

1991. AVANTI!: James M. Ludlow; *Juv. Revell* [U.S.A.].
Sicily, 1860. A story of two brothers—one a patriot, the other a priest. Tells of the events leading up to the Rising in which Garibaldi took such an important part. The atmosphere throughout is one of political scheming and discontent under the Bourbon tyranny. The latest chapters deal with the freeing of Sicily—the landing of the Thousand, and the Battle of Palermo. Garibaldi and General Bianci both appear.

1992. ONE OF THE RED SHIRTS: Herbert Hayens; *Juv. Nisbet* [Eng.], Jacobs [U.S.A.].
Naples, the Island of Caprera, and Sicily, in 1860. A young Englishman serves under Garibaldi as one of "The Thousand" who helped the Mazzinists to throw off the Bourbon tyranny in Sicily. Covers the Battle of Calatafini, the storming of Palermo and the entry into Naples. Garibaldi is the outstanding historic figure.

1993. *ONE CROWDED HOUR: "Sydney C. Grier"; *Blackwood.*
Genoa, Naples, and Sicily, 1860-61. Two Englishmen fight for Garibaldi—the novel giving a full account of the expedition from Genoa and the overthrow of Bourbon rule in Sicily. The entry of Garibaldi into Naples, the siege by the Royalists, and the arrival of the Sardinian army (Victor Emmanuel) are also covered. The political atmosphere of the time is well conveyed. Besides Garibaldi, Francis II King of the Two Sicilies, and Queen Marie Sophie (especially the latter), are prominently introduced.

1994. *PIETRO THE GARIBALDIAN: Anna Maxwell; *Parsons.*
Italy (Brindisi neighbourhood, Genoa, Naples, etc.) and Sicily, mainly 1860-61. A novel which admirably reflects the history of the time. Covers the freeing of Sicily and the entry into Naples, ending with the disbandment of Garibaldi's forces, and the news of Cavour's death. The stimulating influence of Mazzini is well brought out at various points, while allusions to the more cautious Cavour are frequent. Garibaldi and Victor Emmanuel are introduced prominently.

1995. AMONG HOSTILE HORDES: Bessie Marchant; *Juv. Gall & Inglis.*
China, 1863-64. A story illustrating the rebellion of the Taîpings, when Charles George Gordon was in command of a Chinese force; both he and Tien Wang, the leader of the Taîpings, appear.

1996. THE GREENSTONE DOOR: William Satchell; *Sidgwick & Jackson.*
New Zealand (Auckland, etc.), mid-nineteenth century. An interesting story of New Zealand and the Maoris in the 'Fifties and 'Sixties. The later chapters carry the reader to the end of the War in Waikato. Sir George Grey appears, and there is a glimpse of Bishop Selwyn.

1997. MAORI AND SETTLER: G. A. Henty; *Juv. Blackie* [Eng.], *Scribner* [U.S.A.].
A good tale of New Zealand in the late 'Sixties. Depicts the second period of the Maori struggle, covering the Massacre of Poverty Bay.

1998. *MARCHING ON: Ray Strachey; *Cape* [Eng.], *Harcourt, Brace* [U.S.A.].
Kansas, Pennsylvania, Virginia, etc., 1845-1861. A novel depicting the period before the Civil War, and especially dealing with the Anti-Slavery Movement. Gives an interesting picture of the religious and political discussions of the time, also of the various developments consequent on the coming of the railways. But the culminating historic events round which the story is written in the later chapters, are: The desperate struggles in Kansas following the passing of the Kansas-Nebraska Bill in 1854; the riots and

murders at the time when Charles Sumner was assaulted; the slave-running scheme of John Brown and his famous raid into Virginia (Harper's Ferry); and, lastly, the capture, trial, and execution of Brown (1859). The final pages carry the tale to 1861 (War declared). Many leading Abolitionists, besides John Brown, appear, including Garrison, the Motts, and the Childs. There is a glimpse of Colonel Robert Lee.

1999. (1)*THE FORTUNES OF OLIVER HORN: *Newnes* [*Eng.*], *Scribner* [*U.S.A.*].
(2)*KENNEDY SQUARE: F. Hopkinson Smith; *Werner Laurie* [*Eng.*], *Scribner* [*U.S.A.*].
    These two connected novels (there is a " Horn " element in the second book, though it is not exactly a sequel) both deal with Southern life in the States about the 'Fifties, but the first novel depicts, in addition, artistic life in the New York of the Early 'Sixties, i.e. during the Civil War. Of the two novels, *Kennedy Square* has a more distinctly historical interest; not only are the allusions to noted men and women more frequent (Henry Clay, N. P. Willis, Longfellow, Margaret Fuller, Hawthorne, Emerson), but Edgar Allan Poe is actually brought into the tale at one important point, where he presents a somewhat pitiful figure.

2000. *WESTWAYS: S. Weir Mitchell; *Fisher Unwin* [*Eng.*], *Century* [*U.S.A.*].
    America (Northern States) in the period 1855-65. An interesting novel, dealing, in its greater portion, with life in a rural community during the five or six years before the Civil War. Admirably reflects the bitter politics of the time (the Frémont and Buchanan contest of 1856, etc.). The later chapters tell of scenes in Washington during the Civil War, and, to a slight extent, depict the War itself (Vicksburg). Abraham Lincoln and General Grant appear at different points in the story.

2001. *THE BATTLE GROUND: Ellen Glasgow; *Constable* [*Eng.*], *Doubleday* [*U.S.A.*].
    Virginia within the period 1855 and 1865. A story dealing in its longest portion—Books I and II—with Virginian High Life (domestic scenes) in the old Slavery and Abolitionist days. Book III tells of the early Civil War time, but, while there are battle references, the main interest is directed towards non-combatants. In Book IV the reader is offered glimpses of the War itself (the campaign into Maryland, etc.), and several historic personages are mentioned, such as Lee, Jackson, Stuart, McClellan, and Sheridan; allusion is also made to Fredericksburg and other battles, leading up to the Fall of Richmond and the Confederate surrender. The standpoint is fair and impartial, showing appreciation of the Southern sufferings at the end of the struggle. The novel as a whole is one that yields a *general impression*, and in this way differs from those Civil War romances of a more detailed, and directly historical, character.

2002. *THE CRISIS: Winston Churchill; *Macmillan*.
    St. Louis and various localities, 1857 to 1865—the period before, during, and immediately after the American Civil War. Describes the beginning of the War at Fort Sumter, the capture of Vicksburg, etc. The novel favours the cause of the North, but shows the fine qualities of men on the other side. The most conspicuous historical figures are Lincoln, Grant, and Sherman. Albert Edward, Prince of Wales, appears at the St. Louis Agricultural Fair (1860).

2003. *O GENTEEL LADY: Esther Forbes; *Heinemann* [*Eng.*], *Grossett & Dunlap* [*U.S.A.*].
    America (Boston), Italy, and England in the middle of the century. A very interesting novel reflecting the literary life of Boston and Concord. Among the many noted authors introduced, one may specify Emerson, Thoreau, Whittier, Holmes, Longfellow, and the Alcotts. In the English chapters George Eliot and Tennyson, respectively, appear.

2004. HE KNEW LINCOLN AND OTHER BILLY BROWN STORIES: Ida M. Tarbell; *Macmillan* [*Eng.*], *McClure* [*U.S.A.*].
    Illinois, mid-nineteenth century. An old man tells anecdotes of Lincoln, mostly covering the period between 1858 and 1865. Interesting, though possibly too emotional to suit all tastes.

2005. THE SOUL OF ABE LINCOLN[1]: Bernie Babcock; *Lippincott.*
Virginia, etc., 1860-65. Begins with Lincoln just nominated for the Presidency, and proceeds to his election, and the beginning of the Civil War. The novel is, on the fictional side, the love-story of a certain " Belle of Mississippi " and a Union officer. The historical background is considerable—the whole of Lincoln's fine speech after Gettysburg being introduced, as well as other war-time incidents. The scene in the latest stages is Washington (the White House), and the book ends with Lincoln's assassination. There is a glimpse of Walt Whitman.

[1] The author in another story entitled, " Booth and the Spirit of Lincoln," deals with the escape of John Wilkes Booth, the actor, after shooting the President.

2006. THE VICTIM: Thomas Dixon; *Appleton.*
Kentucky, Virginia, etc., 1814-53 (*Prologue*), and 1860-67 (main story). An historical romance of Jefferson Davis, written from the Southern standpoint. The author claims to have drawn his hero's " real character unobscured by passion or prejudice." In the *Prologue* of some 60 pages, Jefferson Davis appears as a Lieutenant of the U.S. army (time of Black Hawk Rising), while in the novel proper he is seen mostly as President of the Confederacy during the Civil War. Many historic figures are introduced besides Jefferson Davis and his wife: Colonel Zachary Taylor, Stonewall Jackson, Lee, Grant, etc. etc.

2007. *FOREVER FREE: Honoré Willsie Morrow; *Cape* [*Eng.*], *Morrow* [*U.S.A.*].
Washington (the White House), March, 1861, to January, 1863. An interesting depiction of Abraham Lincoln in the days just preceding the Civil War, and during the first two years (or nearly so) of the actual War. A scheming woman-spy (Confederate) is prominent in the story, and the account of her doings is amusing and startling by turns; perhaps a few of the situations connected with her will strike some readers as verging on melodrama. The War serves as background merely, but the politics of the time are clearly presented; the list of " books consulted," given at the end of the volume, shows that the novel is based on careful research. It is, however, on the side of Lincoln's private life (in the picture of him, his wife, and his family) that the main charm of the book is to be found. With regard to the outside world, famous names and figures appear almost continuously: John Hay (Lincoln's private secretary), General Scott, William Russell the war correspondent, Charles Sumner, Seward, Lord Lyons, Horace Greeley, Chase, McClellan, Frémont, Stanton, Stoddard, Walt Whitman, E. C. Stedman, and many others.

2008. THE SOUTHERNER: Thomas Dixon; *Appleton.*
Washington (the White House), 1861-65 (*Prologue* deals with the woodland home of Lincoln in his earliest years, 1809-18). A romance of Abraham Lincoln in the Civil War period; the idea which the author intends to convey is that in character and general disposition the great American President was essentially a " Southerner." In the early part of the book there is a glimpse of Henry Clay, while in the White House chapters (main story) Lincoln, Mrs. Lincoln, Major John Hay, Sherman, McClellan, Lee, Jefferson Davis, and many others appear.

2009. *THE END OF THE ROAD: John Buchan; in " The Path of the King "—*Nelson* [*Eng.*], *Doran* [*U.S.A.*].
A striking little sketch of Abraham Lincoln in 1842, and (mainly) in the 'Sixties, ending with his death.

2010. *THE LONG ROLL: Mary Johnston; *Constable* [*Eng.*], *Houghton Mifflin* [*U.S.A.*].
A carefully detailed and suggestive historical novel of the Shenandoah Valley Campaign in the American Civil War. Begins Virginia, 1860, and ends with the death of General Jackson (" Stonewall Jackson ") 1863. Of the many battles described, one may specify Bull Run, Gaines's Mill, Cedar Run, Manassas, Antietam, and Fredericksburg. The outstanding figure is Stonewall Jackson, but other historic personages appear, including Jefferson Davis and Lee.

2011. KINCAID'S BATTERY: George W. Cable; *Hodder & Stoughton* [Eng.], *Scribner* [U.S.A.].
New Orleans, etc., 1860-65. A story of the Civil War period, showing strong Confederate sympathies. Historical events are not introduced to any large extent, though there is some account of Faragut's destruction of the Confederate Fleet, besides allusions to such battles as Vicksburg, Port Hudson, and Gettysburg. Largely a picture of social life during the War, with a love element.

2012. WITH LEE IN VIRGINIA: G. A. Henty; *Juv.* Blackie [Eng.], *Scribner* [U.S.A.].
Virginia, 1860-65. Begins with a Plantation scene in Virginia and the sale of a negress at a Slave Auction; but the tale is mainly one of the American Civil War. The Battles of Bull Run (First and Second), Fredericksburg, Chancellorsville, and many other War incidents are described. The story ends with Lee's surrender in 1865. Lee himself is, of course, the outstanding historic figure.

2013. DAD: Albert Payson Terhune; *Methuen* [Eng.], *Grossel* [U.S.A.].
Mexico, 1847, and Virginia, Maryland, etc., 1861-62. Story of a man dismissed from the army in the days following Scott's entrance into the City of Mexico. The greater portion of the story deals with the hero's experiences in the American Civil War—one of the most important events introduced being the Battle of Antietam. Several notabilities appear, including Winfield Scott, Grant, McClellan, and Lincoln (the last-named in an anecdote).

2014. THE SHEPHERD OF THE PEOPLE: Sidney Herbert Burchell; *Gay & Hancock*.
Washington, 1861-63. A story of social life in Washington during the earlier stage of the Civil War. The outstanding figure is Lincoln, and the opening pages give an amusing account of an imaginary conversation between him and a little girl. William Lloyd Garrison is another historic figure introduced, while Stanton (Secretary of War), Horace Greeley, General McClellan, and others are in the background. Ends with the news of Gettysburg.

2015. *THE PATRIOTS OF THE SOUTH (THE PATRIOTS): Cyrus Townsend Brady; *Cassell* [Eng.], *Dodd, Mead* [U.S.A.].
America (Richmond, Washington, etc.) mainly 1861-65. A tale of the Civil War, beginning with its outbreak, then passing to the Army of Northern Virginia and the Battle of Gettysburg (1863), and in later chapters describing the Southern Army's hardships, the Battle of Spottsylvania Court House (1864), and Lee's surrender to Grant at Appomattox (April 9th, 1865). The novel is written in a manner that indicates careful research; moreover, while Lee is—in the second half of the book—the real hero (" the Bayard of the South "), the author has also given a very pleasing picture of Lincoln in the short account of an interview. These two great men are the principal historic figures introduced; there are many references to Grant, but he does not actually appear.

2016. *THE CORTLANDS OF WASHINGTON SQUARE: *THE SMITHS (sequel): Janet A. Fairbank; *Arrowsmith* [Eng.], *Bobbs-Merrill* [U.S.A.].
These two very interesting novels cover the whole period of the Civil War and the decades following it. Regarding the two volumes as, to a certain extent, one story, the principal localities are New York in Abraham Lincoln's time, and Chicago during the Fire and the financial crisis, etc. Although these novels reflect, in the main, Nineteenth Century manners and events, the latest chapters of the sequel depict American life in the early years of the Twentieth Century. Several historical personages are introduced, notably Walt Whitman.

2017. *TWO LITTLE CONFEDERATES: Thomas Nelson Page; *Juv. Fisher Unwin* [Eng.], *Scribner* [U.S.A.].

Virginia, 1861-65. An excellent story of two boys left at home in Virginia, when the whole male population, between the ages 17 and 50, had gone to the Civil War. Told from the Confederate standpoint, the book shows the many troubles that came on those left unprotected at home in war time. The book ends with the news of Richmond evacuated, and Lee's surrender at Appomattox Courthouse.

2018. WHO GOES THERE? THE STORY OF A SPY IN THE CIVIL WAR:
A FRIEND WITH THE COUNTERSIGN (*sequel*): Blackwood K. Benson; *Macmillan*.

These two carefully written novels cover the American Civil War period 1861-65, from Bull Run to Gettysburg, and the time after Gettysburg, respectively. The author describes, or (more often) alludes to, so *many* important events and personages that his volumes will hardly succeed in holding the attention of the ordinary present-day reader of fiction.

2019. *THE GUNS OF BULL RUN:
***THE GUNS OF SHILOH:**
***THE SCOUTS OF STONEWALL:**
***THE SWORD OF ANTIETAM:**
***THE STAR OF GETTYSBURG:**
***THE ROCK OF CHICKAMAUGA:**
***THE SHADES OF THE WILDERNESS:**
***THE TREE OF APPOMATTOX**: Joseph A. Altsheler; *Juv. Appleton*.

These eight volumes together form *The Civil War Series*, covering the American Civil War, 1861-65. As the titles of the books suggest, some of the principal battles and events are described. In four of the stories a lad fights for the North, while in the remaining four stories his cousin fights for the Confederates (South). Lincoln, Jefferson Davis, Grant, Lee, and many other historic figures are introduced. An excellent series, worthy of the author's high reputation.

2020. THE CAPTAIN: Churchill Williams; *Lothrop Publishing Co.*

A novel having for its main historical background the achievements of General U. S. Grant in the Fort Henry, Fort Donelson, and Shiloh (Pittsburg Landing) period, 1862.

2021. THE RED MIST: Randall Parrish; *Nash* [Eng.], *McClurg* [U.S.A.].

Maryland, 1862. Story of a Confederate spy, in which the fictional and love elements predominate, though there is a distinct Civil War background, and both "Stonewall" Jackson and Lee appear.

2022. *IN CIRCLING CAMPS: Joseph A. Altsheler; *Juv. Appleton*.

A tale of the American Civil War, giving careful descriptions of the Battle of Shiloh (1862) and the Battle of Gettysburg (1863). The full period covered in the book is 1861-65, from Lincoln's election up to General Lee's surrender.

2023. *THE CHALLENGE TO SIRIUS: Sheila Kaye Smith; *Nisbet* [Eng.], *Dutton* [U.S.A.].

England (Sussex) and America in the period 1840-64. A novel illustrating Early Victorian life in Sussex—largely in the 'Fiftees during the Crimean War. On the definitely historical side, however, the fullest depiction is to be found in the many chapters which deal with the hero's experiences when fighting on the Southern or Confederate side in the American Civil War (Battles of Shiloh, Vicksburg, Chattanooga, Missionary Ridge, etc.). There is considerable mention of Bragg, the Confederate General.

2024. ON THE OLD KEARSAGE: CYRUS T. BRADY; *Juv. Scribner.*
A story of naval adventures in the American Civil War, from the sinking of the *Cumberland* in 1862, up to the *Alabama* and *Kearsage* fight, when the latter vessel (under Captain Winslow) attacked and sank the famous Confederate warship off the Northern Coast of France in 1864.

2024a. *CEASE FIRING: MARY JOHNSTON; *Constable [Eng.], Houghton, Mifflin [U.S.A.].*
Mississippi, Virginia, and Tennessee, December, 1862, to April, 1865. An historical novel in the fullest sense, covering a large portion of the Civil War period, and introducing an immense number of important men and events. The book is written from the Southern standpoint, and the local colour—as one would expect from the author—is particularly good. Of the many war-pictures, one may specify those which represent the Siege of Vicksburg, and the Battles of Gettysburg, Chickamauga, Missionary Ridge, Spottsylvania, and Cedar Creek. The story ends with the march towards Appomattox. Jefferson Davis, Lee, Grant, Sherman, Bragg, Stuart, J. E. Johnston, Pemberton, and other leading figures appear.

2025. *THE RED BADGE OF COURAGE: STEPHEN CRANE; *Heinemann [Eng.], Appleton [U.S.A.].*
Virginia, 1863. A young American soldier tries to analyse his feelings on the eve of his first battle (Chancellorsville)—wondering how he will stand the coming ordeal; and, as he thus looks ahead, he is seized with a " panic fear." The pages that follow describe, with much insight and power, the man's actual experiences in the battle, and the mental processes to which they give rise.

2026. EMMELINE: ELSIE SINGMASTER; *Juv. Houghton Mifflin [U.S.A.].*
A good little tale about a girl's experiences in and around the small town of Gettysburg during the great battle of 1863.

2027. *THE HEART OF HOPE: NORVAL RICHARDSON; *Dodd, Mead [U.S.A.].*
A novel having for its main historical background the Siege of Vicksburg by Grant and Sherman, and its eventual surrender (July 4, 1863), after great privations and sufferings on the part of the besieged.

2028. THE CAVALIER: GEORGE W. CABLE; *Murray [Eng.], Scribner [U.S.A.].*
The American Civil War in the Mississippi region up to the time of Sherman's raid from Vicksburg to the town of Meridian (Feb., 1864). More a novel of atmosphere and character-drawing than historical fiction in the full sense; many references to fighting and military movements, but little or no description of definite battles. Confederate standpoint.

2029. THE ROCK OF CHICAMAUGA: GENERAL CHARLES KING; *Dillingham [U.S.A.].*
A story dealing with General George H. Thomas (called by his men " The Rock of Chicamauga "). Introduces his repulse of the Confederates under General Bragg at the Battle of Chicamauga (September, 1863) prior to the retreat to Chattanooga; also the victory gained by him (Thomas) at Nashville (December, 1864) which ended the war in Tennessee.

2030. *MOHUN: JOHN ESTEN COOKE; *Huntington [U.S.A.].*
Virginia, 1863-65. Fictional memoirs of a staff Officer, dealing with the Army of North Virginia in the Civil War. The standpoint is Confederate. There are full accounts of the Battle of Gettysburg and of the Campaign of October, 1863, as well as of later events. Gives a graphic description of Lee's ragged regiments (" Lee's Miserables ") in the Autumn and Winter of 1864. Covers the Fall of Richmond, December, 1864, and ends with Lee's surrender at Appomattox Court-House, 9th April, 1865. Epilogue, 1868. A murder, and the trial following it, are incidents on the fictional side.

2031. *THE SWORD OF YOUTH: James Lane Allen; *Macmillan* [*Eng.*], *Century* [*U.S.A.*].

Kentucky, 1863, and N. Virginia, 1865. A lad left at home to look after the farm, hankers after fighting in the Civil War. The second half of the book tells how, after becoming a soldier, he is summoned to a dying mother, and has to choose whether he shall remain at his post, or—following his affectionate instincts—return home. What decision he arrived at, together with the consequences of such decision, must be left to the author's own skilful telling. There is a glimpse of Lincoln, and an interview with Lee.

2032. ROLAND BLAKE: S. Weir Mitchell; *Houghton Mifflin* [*U.S.A.*].

New York, etc., and Philadelphia, 1864. A tale which is for the most part social rather than historical, though the Civil War (Wilderness Campaign) is lightly touched in the earlier part.

2033. THE LOST DESPATCH: Natalie Sumner Lincoln; *Appleton.*

Largely Washington, 1864-65. A secret-service story of Civil War time. Tells of a woman suspected of being a spy and of having murdered a secret-service officer.

2034. MY LADY OF THE NORTH: Randall Parrish; *Putnam* [*Eng.*], *McClurg* [*U.S.A.*].

Virginia, 1864-65. A love-story, telling of a Confederate captain's adventures as bearer of a despatch from General Lee, and illustrating the time of Sheridan's Raid in the Shenandoah Valley. Covers Sheridan's successes at Winchester and Fisher's Hill, etc. Several historical figures appear.

2035. *CICELY: Sarah Beaumont Kennedy; *Hodder & Stoughton* [*Eng.*], *Doubleday* [*U.S.A.*].

Georgia (Atlanta), etc., 1864-65. This love romance of the latest Civil War period, begins with Sherman's order, on the occupation of Atlanta, that non-combatants should leave; in the further development of her story, the author well describes the time of Sherman's march and his occupation of Savannah (December 21st, 1864). The book ends with the news of Appomattox and Lincoln's assassination respectively (there is a generous tribute to the hero of the North).

2036. *BEFORE THE DAWN: Joseph A. Altsheler; *Juv.* *Hutchinson* [*Eng.*], *Doubleday* [*U.S.A.*].

A story of the Confederates in the later stages of the American Civil War. Deals with the period of the Wilderness battles and the Fall of Richmond in 1865. There are glimpses of Lee and Grant, and other historic figures appear.

2037. *THE CARLYLES: Mrs. Burton Harrison; *Appleton.*

Richmond and Washington at the very end of the American Civil War and the time immediately following it, 1865-66 (also Egypt). This domestic novel begins with the President of the Confederate States (Jefferson Davis) receiving in church the news that Lee " could not hold Petersburg any longer." Covers the evacuation of Richmond by the Confederates, and the entry of Grant's forces. General Lee's actual surrender and the assassination of Lincoln are respectively given as " news." The book—which is written from the Confederate standpoint—depicts the troubles of the Southern families during this trying period. There is a glimpse of Lee just before the surrender.

2038. (1) THE LEOPARD'S SPOTS:
    (2) THE CLANSMAN:
    (3) THE TRAITOR[1]: Thomas Dixon; *Doubleday, Page* [*U.S.A.*].

A trilogy dealing with the Race Conflict in the United States in the years following the Civil War.

(1) The first novel has for its scenes the Foothills of North Carolina, Boston, and New York, 1865-1900. It begins with General Lee at Appomattox, and covers (to use the author's own words) the time " from the enfranchisement of the Negro to his disfranchisement."

(2) The second novel (Washington and the Foothills of the Carolinas, 1865-70) describes the Ku Klux Klan conspiracy in detail. The names of many real people are changed, but Grant and Lincoln are openly brought into the story.

(3) The third volume returns to the Foothills of North Carolina, in the period 1870-72, and illustrates the downfall of the Ku Klux Klan. Grant appears as President.

¹ Mr. Dixon has written another novel entitled, "The Black Hood," in which the scene is North Carolina, 1871; it has to do with much the same events as those covered in *The Traitor*, but, having been written seventeen years later, its author claims for it a truer perspective.

2039. *RED ROCK: THOMAS NELSON PAGE; *Heinemann* [*Eng.*], *Scribner* [*U.S.A.*].
The Southern States mainly in the late 'Sixties. A novel of social life, illustrating the time after the Civil War—the period of the "Carpet-bagger," the Ku Klux Klan, etc. There is a rapid survey, in the first three chapters, of the days just before and during the outbreak of the War, but in Chapter IV there is a jump of four years; accordingly, the story—as already indicated—is almost entirely one of the Reconstruction period in the South.

2040. *SEWARD'S FOLLY: EDISON MARSHALL; *Juv.* *Little, Brown* [*U.S.A.*].
Washington and Alaska (Sitka), 1866-67. An historical tale of the period just after the American Civil War, when the question of Russian America (Alaska) was uppermost. A Southern lad is employed (at first somewhat against his inclination) by William H. Seward, the Secretary of State, over a mission for the purpose of stopping the Russian American—Hudson's Bay Company Treaty. The story describes his adventures among Russian and Indian surroundings in the Alaskan region. Eventually the Czar sells the whole of Russian America to U.S.A. (1867). The statesman, Seward, appears somewhat prominently.

2041. THE ROARING U. P. TRAIL: ZANE GREY; *Hodder & Stoughton* [*Eng.*], *Harper* [*U.S.A.*].
Western American States, mainly in the period 1865-69. This interesting novel illustrates the building of the Union Pacific Railway. The Sioux Indians and their "doom."

2042. *THE MISSOURIAN: EUGENE P. LYLE; *Heinemann* [*Eng.*]' *Doubleday* [*U.S.A.*].
City of Mexico, etc., mainly about 1865-67. The hero is an ex-Confederate officer sent as emissary to the Emperor Maximilian. Another prominent character is a certain French Marquise who is on a mission from Napoleon III of France. There is some account of the fighting between imperialists and republicans—the tale ending with the Emperor's capture and execution (he was shot June, 1867). Maximilian is the outstanding historic figure, while the Empress, Marshal Bazaine, and Benito Juarez also appear. The Daniel Boone introduced must not be confused with the famous hunter and pioneer who died in 1820.

2043. AN EMPEROR'S DOOM: HERBERT HAYENS; *Juv.* *Nelson.*
Mexico, 1865-67. A good tale of the Mexican War of Independence and the Emperor Maximilian. The closing pages describe how Maximilian was eventually shot (1867).

2044. *THE HOUSE OF THE FIGHTING COCKS: HENRY BAERLEIN; *Parsons* [*Eng.*], *Harcourt, Brace* [*U.S.A.*].
State of Veracruz, Mexico, 1866-67. Tale of a Spanish student in the time when Maximilian was Emperor of Mexico. Largely a character novel, with an element of philosophical and theological discussion. Decidedly a well-written and interesting book. Ends with the revolution.

2045. *NORTH OF 36: EMERSON HOUGH; *Appleton.*
Texas in 1867. An excellent story illustrating the impoverishment in the Texas region during the Reconstruction Period. Tells of the trail-making on the Plains up north from Texas to Kansas, of cattle-grazing and cow hunting, of cattle rievers and Indians (the Comanches).

2046. THE GRAVES AT KILMORNA: P. A. Sheehan; *Longmans.*
Ireland, and Dartmoor (Princetown prison), 1866-67 and the years following. This
" story of '67 " (sub-title) depicts the Fenians and their aims with much sympathy.

2047. *THE DUNFERRY RISIN': J. J. Moran; *Digby, Long* [*Eng.*],
Lalor [*Ireland*].
W. Ireland, mostly 1867-68. A brightly-written tale of the Fenians and an attempted
insurrection. Some of the characters are well drawn (a Methodist shopkeeper and his
fear of Popery, etc.), while the political situation in the period is skilfully presented.
Conspiracy, betrayal, imprisonment, and a sentence to ten years penal servitude—these
are some of the book's main subjects.

2048. *THE REBEL: H. C. Bailey; *Methuen.*
England, Ireland (County Galway), Italy and France in the 1866-71 period. The
defeat of the Garibaldians at Mentana (1867) is an outstanding event in the novel, while
the Franco-German War of 1870-71 is lightly touched in the latest chapters. Among
the historic persons introduced, at one point or another, are Disraeli, Mazzini, and
Garibaldi.

2049. THE DRUMS OF WAR: H. de Vere Stacpoole; *Murray* [*Eng.*],
Duffield [*U.S.A.*].
A novel of Germany and France in the Second Empire period, 1860-70: Bismarck
and Napoleon III. The book ends with the scenes in Paris on war being declared.

2050. THE DAYSPRING: Dr. William Barry; *Fisher Unwin.*
Paris in the Napoleon III—Commune period. A book of somewhat elusive character,
but best defined as a novel of ideas. Beginning in the late 'Sixties (Second Empire),
it does little more than dimly reflect the events culminating in the Franco-German War
and the Commune. There are a few glimpses of historical personages.

2051. *THE NABOB: Alphonse Daudet (trans.); *Heinemann,* also
Greening.
Chiefly Paris (in small degree S. France and Corsica), 1864 and the year or two
following. A story of Parisian Society in the days of the Second Empire. Depicts,
after the way of satire, the profligacy and cynicism of the time, introducing a great
many historical figures under disguised names. It has been maintained, for instance,
that the " Nabob " himself is based on a real individual who, having made a fortune
in Egypt, startled Paris in 1864; that the " Duc de Mora " is the noted Duc de Morny
(under whom Daudet at one time acted in a secretarial capacity); and that " Felicia
Ruys " is Sarah Bernhardt.

2052. A GLORIOUS LIE: Dorothea Gerard; *John Long.*
Eastern Austria (Carpathian region), Bohemia, etc., 1866-70. A novel of domestic
tragedy for the most part, but containing a vivid description of the Prussian victory over
the Austrians at Sadowa (Königgratz) in two of the early chapters.

2053. JOHN OF GERISAU: "John Oxenham"; *Hurst & Blackett,*
also *Hodder.*
Prussia v. Austria, 1866, and the Franco-German War (Gravelotte, etc.), 1870. Several
historic figures are introduced, and there is some account of Prussian political aims and
developments, especially in the 'Sixties.

2054. THE STORY OF THE PLÉBISCITE (THE PLÉBISCITE):
E. Erckmann and A. Chatrian (trans.); *Smith, Elder* [*Eng.*],
Scribner [*U.S.A.*].
A story of the Vosges region in the time leading up to the Franco-German War. The
book is written from the standpoint of the ceded Provinces, and shows the state of
insecurity, as well as the bad conditions generally, of pre-War France.

s

2055. *THE FRONTIERS OF THE HEART: Victor Margueritte (trans.); *Heinemann* [*Eng.*], *Stokes* [*U.S.A.*].
France and Prussia: mainly Paris, Amiens, and Marburg, 1867-68, and 1870-71. A novel of considerable interest and power. A French girl marries a Prussian of cultured, scientific type, and the main point of the story is the strain put upon their domestic relationship when the Franco-German War comes. The author skilfully shows how—in spite of their genuine love for one another—patriotic feeling more and more erects a barrier between them; eventually, the question as to the " nationality " of their infant son accentuates the division, and they separate (after the War)—the wife returning to France with the child until he shall become five years old. Incidentally, the chief events of the War are introduced—for the most part as " news." There is a glimpse of Gambetta.

2056. THE TWO OF DIAMONDS: Anthony Wharton; *Collins*.
The tale proper deals with Paris in the 'Sixties—depicting life under the Second Empire in the time just before its downfall. Napoleon III appears, and there are glimpses of Flaubert, Zola and Verlaine. Towards the end of the book the reader is taken rapidly through the later decades of the 19th Century up to the beginning of the 20th Century. The scene shifts to London.

2057. (1)*THE SCHOOL FOR SAINTS:
(2)*ROBERT ORANGE (*sequel*): " John Oliver Hobbes ";
Fisher Unwin [*Eng.*], *Stokes* [*U.S.A.*].
(1) France (Brittany and Paris), England, and Spain in 1869. A novel with a considerable historical element. The hero, " Robert Orange," becomes a Roman Catholic, and there is much discussion over theological matters. He has long chats with Disraeli (time of the Irish Church Bill), stands for Parliament, and fights on behalf of Don Carlos in Spain. The book ends with his marriage, October 17, 1869. Disraeli, and Prim the Spanish General, are the two principal historic figures.
(2) The scene of the sequel is mostly England towards the end of the year 1869, with " Robert Orange, M.P." as the all-important figure. Although scarcely equal to the first volume, the present story well reflects the mid-Victorian influences, especially on the religious side. One of the subjects introduced is Gladstone's nomination of Temple to the see of Exeter, and the fuss which resulted through the latter having been a contributor to the famous *Essays and Reviews* volume. The atmosphere is largely Roman Catholic. Disraeli again appears, but much less prominently; the book closes with a letter supposed to be written by him in 1879—ten years after the events of the novel.

2058. *THE IRON YEAR: Walter Bloem (trans.); *Lane*.
Prussia and France, 1870. A novel of the Franco-German War period, containing some vivid descriptive writing as well as good character-drawing. Describes the politics of the time immediately before the War (the vacant Spanish throne, Benedetti, etc.), and proceeds to the actual outbreak. A considerable portion of the tale may be said to centre in Saarbrücken (or Saarbrück, as it is sometimes spelt), though Gorze Rezonville, Nancy, and Strasbourg are also touched. The closing pages carry the reader no further than September 30th, 1870. King William I of Prussia appears, while there are many allusions to Prince Frederick Charles and other personages.

2059. *THE GARDEN OF SWORDS: Max Pemberton; *Cassell*.
Chiefly Strasbourg in 1870. A story that well illustrates the early stages of the Franco-German War, telling of the fears and sufferings of non-combatants, etc. On the definitely historical side, there is a description of the Battle of Wörth, and the book ends with some vivid scenes in Strasbourg, during its siege by the Germans.

2060. *THE ATTACK ON THE MILL (*L' ATTAQUE DU MOULIN*):
Émile Zola (trans.); *Heinemann* [*Eng.*], *Stokes* [*U.S.A.*].
The Prussians in Lorraine, 1870. A short story realistically depicting the horrors of war.

2061. *VALENTIN: A FRENCH BOY'S STORY OF SEDAN: Henry Kingsley; *Ward, Lock* [*Eng.*], *Longmans* [*U.S.A.*].
The sub-title sufficiently indicates the subject of this book. The author was himself present at the Battle of Sedan " in the capacity of his own war correspondent " when editing *The Edinburgh Daily Review.*

2062. THE VIRGIN FORTRESS: Max Pemberton; *Cassell.*
Metz, 1870. A story of the Siege in the Franco-German War, and of an Englishman fighting on the German side. Deals with such subjects as German spies in the city, etc., and ends with capitulation. Bazaine appears, also Frederick-Charles (the " Red Prince ").

2063. THE ISLE OF UNREST: " H. Seton Merriman "; *Smith, Elder* [*Eng.*], *Dodd, Mead* [*U.S.A.*].
Corsica and France, 1870-71. A romance primarily of Corsica, in the period just before, and during, the Franco-German War. In the French section of the novel there are glimpses of the Army of the Loire.

2064. *JÖRN UHL: Gustav Frenssen (trans.); *Constable.*
N. Germany, largely in the period 1870-71. An intensely realistic and moving story of German provincial life just before, during, and after the Franco-German War. There is a brilliant sketch of the Battle of Gravelotte, as well as other war allusions, so the book—though primarily depicting the mental and spiritual development of the young peasant hero—is well entitled to a place among novels illustrating the life and events of the period.

2065. THE CRIMSON WING: H. C. Chatfield Taylor; *Grant Richards* [*Eng.*], *Stone* [*U.S.A.*].
Germany and France, 1870-71. A novel of the Franco-German War, chiefly dealing with the period from the days immediately preceding the Declaration of War up to Sedan. Describes Wissembourg, Wörth, and Sedan. Various historic personages appear, including the King of Prussia, Count Benedetti, the Crown Prince of Prussia, Moltke, Bismarck, Napoleon III and Sheridan the American General.

2066. A HERO OF SEDAN: F. S. Brereton; *Juv. Blackie* [*Eng.*], *Caldwell* [*U.S.A.*].
This " tale of the Franco-Prussian War " mainly illustrates two great events: the Battle of Sedan and the Siege of Paris, 1870-71.

2067. *THE DOWNFALL (*LA DÉBÂCLE*): Émile Zola (trans.); *Chatto & Windus* [*Eng.*], *Macmillan* [*U.S.A.*].
A novel of the Franco-German War period, 1870-71, but dealing especially with the Battle of Sedan. The later portion of the book covers the Siege of Paris and the Commune. Full of allusions to historic events and personages (there are glimpses of Napoleon III and King William of Prussia). The author emphasises the horrible side of War.

2068. *UNE ÉPOQUE: Paul and Victor Margueritte; *Plon-Nourrit et Cie* [*France*].
Collective title of the four striking novels: " Le Désastre," " Les Tronçons du Glaive," " Les Braves Gens," and " La Commune "; they virtually cover the entire War period, though dealing more particularly with such events and times as Bazaine's capitulation at Metz, the Siege of Paris, and the Commune. Only two novels in the series, and part of a third, have yet (end 1927) been translated into English: " The Disaster " (Chatto & Windus), " The Commune " (Chatto & Windus), and " Strasbourg: an Episode of the Franco-German War " (Smith, Elder). The last-named volume contains one of the four " episodes " which together form the third novel in the series (" Les Braves Gens ").

2069. *ROBERT HELMONT: Alphonse Daudet (trans.); *Dent* [*Eng.*], *Macmillan* [*U.S.A.*].

France (River Seine region, not far from Paris), 1870-71. An imaginative sketch in diary form (scarcely a novel in the full sense), exhibiting the experiences and thoughts of a man who, on the eve of the Franco-German War, broke his leg, and was compelled to lead a life of almost complete solitude. The diary begins September 3rd, 1870, and ends January 30th, 1871. In spite of its brevity and the absence of a regular plot, the book well illustrates the conditions of wartime (especially during the Siege of Paris period), and is delightfully written. A human, even tender, element is at times very noticeable. Although the scene is more or less *near* Paris, the description—" a portrayal of the siege " (given in a recent bibliography), is entirely misleading.

2070. THE MAN OF IRON: " Richard Dehan "; *Heinemann* [*Eng.*], *Stokes* [*U.S.A.*].

England, Germany, France and Belgium, 1870-71. An historical romance dealing more especially with Bismarck and the Franco-German War. Covers the chief battles (Wissenbourg, Wörth, Saarbrück, Metz, Gravelotte, etc.), ending with Paris beleaguered, 27th January, 1871. The novel shows the author's knowledge of the period, but it is somewhat marred by its prolixity and an occasional coarseness of tone. The following are some of the historic personages introduced: Bismarck, Moltke, Von Roon the War Minister, King Wilhelm, the Crown Prince, Prince Frederick-Charles (the " Red Prince"), Prince Imperial, Bazaine, Thiers, and Jules Favre.

2071. (1)*LORRAINE: *Putnam* [*Eng.*], *Harper* [*U.S.A.*].
(2)*ASHES OF EMPIRE: *Macmillan* [*Eng.*], *Stokes* [*U.S.A.*].
(3)*THE RED REPUBLIC: Robert W. Chambers; *Putnam*.

A trilogy covering the whole period of the Franco-German War and the Paris Commune, 1870-71.

(1) The Moselle Valley, etc. Covers the Declaration of War, Saarbrück (full description), and Sedan. Napoleon III and the Prince Imperial appear.

(2) Paris from the announcement of Sedan up to the siege and surrender of Paris. Describes Gambetta's proclamation of the Republic, the privations of the siege, etc. There is a glimpse of the Empress escaping.

(3) Paris, March 1871 onwards. A full account of the events resulting in the Commune and its horrors. The outstanding figure is Monsignor Darboy, Archbishop of Paris, with whose murder the novel practically ends.

2072. UNDER THE IRON FLAIL (FLOWERS OF THE DUST): " John Oxenham "; *Cassell* [*Eng.*], *Wessels* [*U.S.A.*], *Fisher Unwin* [*Eng.*].

France (Brittany, Metz, Paris, etc.), and—to a very slight extent—England, 1870-71. An English surgeon's story, beginning before the Franco-German War, then covering the Sieges of Metz and Paris respectively, and finally giving some illustration of the Commune. There is a glimpse of Napoleon III, and several allusions to noted people are made in the course of the story.

2073. A WINDOW IN PARIS: " Marianne Farningham "; *Juv. James Clarke*.

Prologue: Paris, 1867. The main story is one of Paris 1870-71, depicting the scenes on the Declaration of War, and the period leading up to the Siege and the Commune. Ends just after the Commune.

2074. IN TIME OF WAR (originally *Workman and Soldier*): James F. Cobb; *Juv. Frowde* [*Eng.*], *Dutton* [*U.S.A.*].

Brittany and Paris, 1870-71. This interesting tale, though covering the whole War period, is primarily what the sub-title indicates: " A tale of Paris life during the Siege and the rule of the Commune."

2075. A TATTER IN SCARLET: S. R. Crockett; *Juv. Hodder & Stoughton*.

Southern France, chiefly under the Commune. Two youths (Scottish and Irish respectively), after fighting in Garibaldi's Italian Corps in the last stages of the Franco-German War, January, 1871, have various adventures in the Rhône Valley district.

2076. *THE GERMAN LIEUTENANT: August Strindberg (trans.); in "The German Lieutenant and Other Stories"—*Werner Laurie* [*Eng.*], *McClurg* [*U.S.A.*].
France and Switzerland, 1870-72. A remarkable tale of an episode in the Franco-German War, and the consequences issuing from it in the life of a German officer. Shows the contrary feelings which War evokes in Man.

2077. *BROKEN SHACKLES: "John Oxenham"; *Methuen.*
France and Switzerland, 1870-76. A story of Bourbaki's command of the Army of the East, and his attempt to break the Prussian line at Belfort, followed by the disastrous Retreat to Switzerland. The second half of the novel deals with matters of domestic interest, etc. Several historic figures appear, including Gambetta, Bourbaki, and the "Red Prince."

2078. *KINGS IN EXILE (*LES ROIS EN EXIL*): Alphonse Daudet (trans.); *Dent.*
Paris, 1872, and the few years following. A novel having for its background what may be called history *in little*. The author here tells, with much feeling and imaginative power, of the exiled King Christian II of Illyria, his Queen Frédérique, and their little son Leopold—the time being just after the above-named state had become a republic. The Queen of Palermo (cousin of the Queen of Illyria) also appears, but the specifically historical side of the novel is quite subordinate to its universal aspect as a presentment of human character-types.

2079. THE VELVET GLOVE: H. Seton Merriman; *Smith, Elder* [*Eng.*], *Dodd, Mead* [*U.S.A.*].
Spain (Saragossa and the region of the Pyrenees), 1870-71. A story which has for its historical background the political intrigues and general unsettlement of Spain, just before the second Carlist War proper (1872-4). At one point there is direct reference to Amadeo of Savoy (Duke of Aosta) who had just been declared King of Spain. There are glimpses of General Pacheco, and some account of fighting (Captain Zeneta's retreat), but the fictional developments constitute the main interest.

2080. *THE ARROW OF GOLD: Joseph Conrad; *Nash.*
Marseilles in the mid-Seventies (time of the Second Carlist War in Spain). This novel is somewhat rashly allowed place in these lists, but—in a quarter deserving serious attention—it has been classed among "the very few fine *historical novels* in English"! One may venture to suggest that the true import of the book is to be found in its subtle character analysis; for, while the time is more or less definite, and there are allusions to real people and events, the background of the narrative is "historical" only in a very dim sense. The hero is connected with Spanish politics through no enthusiasm for either Carlos or Alphonso; certain fictional developments result in his joining an organization for the smuggling of arms and ammunition to the Carlists. Again, some attention must, surely, be given to the express declaration in the "First Note" of the book itself: "*History has nothing to do with this tale.*"

2081. *MAINWARING: Maurice Hewlett; *Collins* [*Eng.*], *Dodd, Mead* [*U.S.A.*].
Mainly London, but to some extent Marseilles, Venice and other localities, in the 'Seventies and 'Eighties. The hero, "Mainwaring," is an Irish-born man who, after experiences abroad, enters English politics. He takes up an advanced position on the popular side, is imprisoned on account of his share in a Trafalgar Square riot, and becomes a Member of Parliament. There are glimpses of Disraeli ("Isaac Bentivoglio") and Gladstone ("William Hardman"). The novel has a somewhat tragic ending.

2082. *THE HORSEMEN OF THE PLAINS: Joseph A. Altsheler; *Juv. Macmillan.*
The Rocky Mountains district in the late 'Sixties. A good adventure story, having for its historical background the Cheyenne War, and General George A. Custer's victory in the Battle of the Washita River (1868).

2083. MOLLY McDONALD: RANDALL PARRISH; *Jarrolds* [*Eng.*], *McClurg* [*U.S.A.*].

Kansas plains, Arkansas river region, etc., 1868. A love and adventure story, with Custer's Indian War as historic background. There are scenes introducing the Cheyennes and other Indians, while the book ends with the Battle on the Washita. General Custer and General Sheridan both appear.

2084. *ON THE PLAINS WITH CUSTER: EDWIN L. SABIN; *Juv. Lippincott.*

Chiefly Kansas, Nebraska, and Dakota, 1866-76. Another good adventure tale, with General George Armstrong Custer as the outstanding historical figure. Depicts the fighting with the Indians (the Cheyennes and the Sioux) during some ten years, and ends with the Battle of the Little Big Horn (1876) in which Custer was killed. Two other noted figures are introduced, viz., General Sherman, and (as a " young scout " with a reputation as baffalo hunter) Bill Cody.

2085. SOFTFOOT OF SILVER CREEK: ROBERT LEIGHTON; *Juv. Ward, Lock.*

N. America (Western States) in the 'Seventies. A story of adventure and fighting with the Sioux, etc. In the later chapters General Custer appears—his death and the destruction of his forces on the Little Big Horn (Montana) being covered.

2086. THE LAST OF THE CHIEFS: JOSEPH A. ALTSHELER; *Juv. Appleton.*

Adventures in the Rockies once again (survivors from a wagon train massacre), and an " outside " view of the Little Big Horn disaster in which Custer and his men were destroyed (1876).

2087. *THE WATCHERS ON THE PLAINS: RIDGWELL CULLUM; *Chapman & Hall* [*Eng.*], *Jacobs* [*U.S.A.*], *and other publishers.*

Dakota and South Nebraska at the time of the Indian Rising in the 'Seventies. One of the author's many stories of rough life in North American regions.

2088. BY SHEER PLUCK: G. A. HENTY; *Juv. Blackie* [*Eng.*], *Scribner* [*U.S.A.*].

Story of a youth's English upbringing, his adventures in Central Africa, and—second half of book—his experiences in the Ashanti War (Wolseley) up to the capture of Coomassie in 1874.

2089. WITH WOLSELEY TO KUMASI: F. S. BRERETON; *Juv. Blackie.*

" A Story of the First Ashanti War," telling of a young Englishman appointed manager of a gold mine near Kumasi (or Coomassie)—his escape, and his falling in with the British expedition under Wolseley. The capture of Kumasi is introduced.

2090. *THE BAD TIMES: " GEORGE A. BIRMINGHAM "; *Methuen* [*Eng.*], *Doran* [*U.S.A.*].

A story of West Ireland, beginning in 1800, but soon passing to 1875 and the years following. Depicts the period of the earlier Home Rule movement, giving various character types by way of illustration. The standpoint is that of an independent Home Ruler.

2091. *CASTLE CONQUER: PADRAIC COLUM; *Macmillan.*

Ireland about the late 'Seventies and early 'Eighties. This finely-told story by the Irish poet, illustrates the time of the Land Question—of Coercion Acts and Evictions, etc. Some of the later chapters are written round a murder and the trial following it.

2092. HER MAJESTY'S REBELS: S. R. Lysaght; *Macmillan.*
Ireland about the 'Eighties. A novel dealing with the " Nationalist Party " period,
though historical in a general sense only. While the author disclaims any identification
of his fictional characters with the actual men of the time, he makes the admission that
his hero's career is not unlike that of Parnell in certain respects.

2093. IN THE TRACK OF THE TROOPS: R. M. Ballantyne; *Juv.*
Nisbet.
England, Danubian regions, Turkey, etc., in the 'Seventies. A tale of the Russo-
Turkish War of 1877-78. The English hero acts as surgeon in the Russian army. The
Fall of Plevna is one of the chief incidents covered. General Skobeleff and Osman
Pasha are the two most important names mentioned in the story. The author is at
special pains to show the horrid side of War rather than its " glory."

2094. *THE VULTURES: " H. Seton Merriman "; *Smith, Elder.*
London, Poland (Warsaw), and St. Petersburg, c. 1881. An interesting novel, which
illustrates Secret Service and Conspiracy. The outstanding historical event is the
assassination of the Czar Alexander II near his palace on March 13th, 1881.

2095. THE WHITE TERROR AND THE RED: A. Cahan; *Hodder
& Stoughton* [Eng.], *Barnes* [U.S.A.].
Begins Germany, 1874, but the scene is mostly Russia in the years following. A
story of Nihilist plots against the Czar Alexander II, whose eventual assassination is
fully described. In the later part of the book there is much about the anti-Jewish riots
under Czar Alexander III. Both the Czars are brought into the novel, which is carefully
written.

2096. FROM CADET TO CAPTAIN: Colonel J. Percy-Groves;
Juv. Frowde.
England, France, and South Africa, mainly c. 1869-79. A tale of military life, dealing
largely (in the first half) with Sandhurst College in the 'Sixties, then passing to Aldershot,
etc. The last eighty pages of the book tell of the hero's part in the Zulu War following
the Isandlwana disaster; the March to Ekowe for the relief of Colonel Pearson, and the
Battles of Ginghilovo and Kambula, 1879, are more or less fully described.

2097. A ROMANCE OF THE CAPE FRONTIER: Bertram Mitford;
Heinemann.
South Africa (King Williamstown region, etc.) in the late 'Seventies. A distinctly
sensational tale of the Cape frontier in the period of the Kaffir Rising (1877-78).

2098. THE WORD OF THE SORCERESS: Bertram Mitford;
Hutchinson.
South Africa, 1878-79. A novel of Zululand leading up to the war with the English;
though somewhat melodramatic, it exhibits good local colour. There is a description
of Cetewayo's defeat of the British at Isandhlwana, and Cetewayo himself is a prominent
figure in the story.

2099. WITH SHIELD AND ASSEGAI: F. S. Brereton; *Juv. Blackie.*
Zululand (Cetewayo) in the 'Seventies. " A tale of the Zulu War " in the main
covers the disaster of Isandhlwana, the defence of Rorke's Drift, and the defeat of the
Zulu army at Ulundi. Lord Chelmsford, etc.

2100. *FINISHED: H. Rider Haggard; *Ward, Lock* [Eng.], *Longmans*
[U.S.A.].
Transvaal and Zululand, 1877-84. The concluding novel of the Quartermain Trilogy,
in which " Marie " and " Child of Storm " are the first two volumes. The present tale
depicts the events leading up to the Zulu War, as well as the actual War and the period
following it. Isandhlwana is introduced, and Cetewayo is the outstanding figure (the
book ends with his death).

2101. FOR NAME AND FAME: G. A. Henty; *Juv.   Blackie [Eng.],
Scribner [U.S.A.].*
A tale which, beginning in England and the Eastern Seas (Malays), deals chiefly
with the Afghan War (1878-80).   Covers the forcing of the Afghan position on Peiwar
Kotul by Roberts, the siege of Cabul, and, lastly, the famous march from Cabul to
Kandahar, where Roberts defeated Yákúb Khan.

2102. *OLD FOR-EVER: Alfred Ollivant; *Allen & Unwin [Eng.],
Doubldeay [U.S.A.].*
N. W. Frontier of India (Peshawar, Kohat, etc.), 1879.   A good story of the Afghan
War period, dealing with the experiences of an English Major and his wife.   The
fictional interest outweighs the historical, and cholera proves the worst foe.   General
Roberts appears.

2103. WITH ROBERTS TO CANDAHAR: F. S. Brereton; *Juv.
Blackie.*
" A tale of the Third Afghan War " (sub-title), 1880.   The special events illustrated
in this story are the Siege of Cabul and the Relief of Candahar.

2104. *BILLETS AND BULLETS: Hugh St. Leger; *Juv.   Griffith,
Farran.*
England, Ireland, and Egypt, c. 1880-82.   This adventure story deals mostly with
" billets in Ireland and bullets in Egypt " (to use the author's words) or, more explicitly,
with military duty in such places as Limerick, Listowel, Tralee, Cork, etc., and, later
on, with Arabi Pasha's rebellion in Egypt.   The hero is carried off to sea by an Egyptian,
taken to Alexandria, and there remains during the bombardment by Admiral Seymour
(July, 1882).   Tel-el-Kebir and the March to Cairo are also covered.   General Drury
Lowe and other figures.

2105. A CHAPTER OF ADVENTURES: G. A. Henty; *Juv.   Blackie
[Eng.], Scribner [U.S.A.].*
England (Essex), and—mainly—Alexandria, in the Early 'Eighties.   Tells of the
young hero's adventures at sea (a wreck) and in Alexandria, where he is a prisoner, at
the time of the Arabi Pasha troubles.   The Bombardment by the British Fleet (1882)
is described, with the scenes of fire and confusion following it.   Ends with more sea
experiences and India.

2106. WITH GORDON TO KHARTUM: Eliza F. Pollard; *Juv.
Blackie.*
England (Berkhampstead), and Egypt (Alexandria, Cairo, and the Soudan) in the
period 1882-98.   A tale covering the Arabi Pasha rebellion, as well as the later events
connected with the supremacy of the Mahdi.   There is a careful picture of the latter
(or Mohammed Ahmed, to give his real name)—his encouragement of the Slave Trade,
his religious fanaticism, etc.   General Gordon is also prominently introduced, with
details concerning his last stand and death at Khartum.   The book ends with the
announcement of the Mahdi's death.

2107. THE DASH FOR KHARTOUM: G. A. Henty; *Juv.   Blackie
[Eng.], Scribner [U.S.A.].*
India, England (Gloucestershire), and—mainly—Egypt, c. 1883-85.   A tale leading
up to the Nile Expedition for the relief of Khartoum (the fall of the city and Gordon's
death are given as " news " in the middle of the story).   Describes the three battles—
El Teb (February, 1884), Tamai (March, 1884) and Abu Klea (January, 1885).

2108. THE CURSE OF THE NILE: Douglas Sladen; *Nash.*
Egypt and the Sudan, 1884-98.   " A story of love in the desert," having a substantial
background of history: The Siege and Fall of Khartum (1885); the period of Mahdist
rule; and Kitchener's reconquest of the Sudan, ending with the Battle of Omdurman
and the entry into Khartum (4th September, 1898).   General Gordon, the Mahdi, the
Khalifa, and many other figures.

2109. *VERDI: Franz Werfel (trans.); *Jarrolds* [*Eng.*], *Simon &
Schuster* [*U.S.A.*].
Venice in the 'Eighties. A novel having Verdi, the Italian composer, as its central
figure, and depicting him in a favourable light. Much of the book deals with the
musical rivalry of Verdi and Wagner—the latter appearing in the opening pages. Another
musical composer introduced is Boito. The Venetian life of the time is well illustrated.

2110. (1)*CAPTAIN DESMOND, V.C.: *Blackwood* [*Eng.*].
(2)*DESMOND'S DAUGHTER: Maud Diver; *Blackwood* [*Eng.*],
Houghton Mifflin [*U.S.A.*].
Although these two volumes are here placed together as being in some degree connected,
they can be regarded as two almost independent novels.

(1) The first volume deals with Anglo-Indian life in the late nineteenth century
period, well illustrating the Border fighting in Northern India—the Punjab Frontier
force and the Afridis. This more or less historical element is a mere background to the
purely fictional developments.

(2) The second volume is, perhaps, more definitely historical. Beginning in Cornwall,
the story quickly passes to Upper India (Kashmir), and leads up to Sir William Lockhart's Tirah Campaign (1897). The local colour is good, while the atmosphere of the
book as a whole is typically Anglo-Indian.

2111. *THE WAR TRAIL OF BIG BEAR: William Bleasdell
Cameron; *Duckworth*.
Canadian North-West Territories (Fort Pitt and the Saskatchewan River district),
mainly 1884-85. A story dealing with the rebellion of the Wood Cree Indians, and
the Frog Lake Massacre. Begins with the Fort Pitt trading difficulties which led up
to the outbreak—the Fort being an important trading-post of the Hudson's Bay Company.
The later chapters tell of captivity in the Indian Camp, etc., and of release, ending with
the Battle of Frenchman's Butte and the suppression of the Rising. There is a glimpse
of Louis Riel, the rebel leader, in the last chapter.

2112. *MICHAEL FORTH: Mary Johnston; *Constable* [*Eng.*], *Harper*
[*U.S.A.*].
Largely Virginia and the States, but in some of its later chapters the novel touches
Africa, England, Switzerland, Italy, etc.; the *main* period is between the late 'Sixties
and the late 'Eighties. Reflects some of the hard life-conditions and business developments in the South after the Civil War. Primarily, however, the author is here concerned with ideas rather than events, and those to whom religious mysticism makes
appeal will find her special presentment of it very interesting. There is little or no
history in the strict sense, though glimpses of General Lee and Queen Victoria respectively are given in different parts of the story, while allusions to Blaine and Cleveland,
as well as to the writers of the day, suggest a background of real events.

2113. *A SON OF THE MIDDLE BORDER: Hamlin Garland;
Lane [*Eng.*], *Macmillan* [*U.S.A.*].
Wisconsin, Dakota, New England, and California, mainly in the 1865-90 period.
A novel of real charm telling of a farming family and Westward expansion; the book
is, also, one that largely reflects the literary tastes of the period (the allusions to famous
books and authors are numerous). There is a glimpse of Edwin Booth in *Hamlet*.

2114. *THE MAN OF PROPERTY:
*IN CHANCERY: (being Parts I and II of *The Forsyte Saga*):
John Galsworthy; *Heinemann* [*Eng.*], *Scribner* [*U.S.A.*].
England (mainly London) from the mid 'Eighties to the beginning of the Twentieth
Century. A wonderfully vivid portrayal of English Upper Middle Class life—conveying
in particular that sense of "family" and "property" which has served so largely as a
motive in circles of inherited wealth. There is a well-defined historical background
throughout; for, not only do these early portions of the *Saga* give the general impression
of a late-Victorian atmosphere, but they contain excellent accounts of the situation in
London on the announcement of Kruger's Ultimatum, the wild scenes of Mafeking
night, and the special circumstances of Queen Victoria's funeral.

2115. DOOMSLAND: Shane Leslie; *Chatto & Windus.*
Ireland (Ulster, Maynooth, Dublin, etc.), and—in much less degree—England and Abroad, mainly in the period from the 'Eighties of the Nineteenth Century to the first decade of the Twentieth Century. A novel of Irish life and politics with considerable change of scene and time. There is a glimpse of Parnell in the chapter describing an election, but the historical element in the story as a whole is very slight.

2116. HOLY ROMANS: Aodh De Blácam; *Maunsel* [*Ireland*].
London and Ireland (Donegal), late 19th Century to early 20th. Story of a young Irishman's upbringing in London, and the influences that moulded him politically and religiously (much discussion in both these directions). The novel spreads over a wide period—the later chapters, in Book III, covering the Great War, but the more important sections illustrate *late 19th Century politics* about the time of Parnell's defeat.

2117. *THE PRESIDENT'S SCOUTS: Herbert Hayens; *Juv. Collins.*
Chili (Santiago, Valparaiso, etc.), 1890-91. Story of an Englishman in the Chilian Revolution, when the Balmacedists (or followers of President Balmaceda) were opposed to the Congressional Party. Describes the sinking of an ironclad, and various battles, including the battle of Placilla fought August 28th, 1891. There are some exciting mob scenes (Santiago) at the end. Balmaceda himself appears.

2118. THE EDGE OF EMPIRE: Joan Sutherland; *Mills & Boon.*
Kashmir, London, Paris, etc., in the 1890-1900 period. A novel of social life, having as historical background in the second half, the Chitral Expedition (1895). The properly historic section ends with the Siege of Chitral and its Relief.

2119. WITH KITCHENER IN THE SOUDAN: G. A. Henty; *Juv. Blackie.*
Egypt, 1882-1899. A tale beginning with the troubles in Alexandria and Admiral Seymour's bombardment; then, after some account of the Soudan campaign of 1883-85, passing to the later Kitchener period (1898) when he routed the Dervish forces at Atbara, and won the victory of Omdurman (both battles fully described). Lord Cromer, Kitchener, and others appear.

2120. ONE OF THE GRENVILLES: Sidney Royse Lysaght; *Macmillan.*
England, North Africa, and Ireland (Kerry), about the last two decades of the 19th Century. A novel spread over a fairly long period, and with the scenes continually shifting. One part of the book deals with an Englishman's strange experiences during some ten years as a captive of the Arabs—the time being that of the Mahdist Rebellion; he is brought into contact with the Khalifa, etc.

2121. THE WHITE TRAIL; Alexander Macdonald; *Juv. Blackie* [*Eng.*], *Caldwell* [*U.S.A.*]
Yukon district, Canada (Dawson City, etc.), 1897. The story of a young Scot's adventures, illustrating the rush which followed the discovery of gold in the Klondike, 1896. The author states that his tale " deals with an actual journey and with an actual people."

2122. THE GREAT GOLD RUSH: W. H. P. Jarvis; *Murray.*
Canadian N.W. Territory, 1898. A story of the immigration following the discovery of the Klondike Gold Fields in 1897. The early days of Dawson City: prospectors and miners, official corruption, conspiracy and uprising, etc.

2123. *THE LONG TRAIL: Hamlin Garland; *Juv. Harper.*
Begins Minnesota, passing north of Vancouver to the North-West Territory, 1898-99. A tale of youthful adventures on a long journey to the Klondike, also of experiences after arrival in the gold-mine region.

2124. CONTRABAND OF WAR: M. P. Shiel; *Richards.*
America, England, Cuba, and various parts of the world, 1897-99. A highly-coloured tale of finance and international politics in the period just before and during the Spanish-American War. The two outstanding fictional figures are an American financier and a Venezuelan millionaire (Spaniard), who begin as enemies and end (after the War) as friends. There are many startling developments, and a good deal of fighting (the Battle of Santiago is included). Lord Salisbury appears, as Prime Minister of England, also President McKinley.

2125. THE CRUISE OF THE THETIS: " Harry Collingwood "; *Juv. Blackie.*
London, Cuba, etc., 1894-99. A good tale dealing with the Cuban uprising (1895), and the events leading up to the Spanish-American War. The young English hero and his friend (the son of a Cuban tobacco planter) together work out a plan for helping the insurrection in Cuba; as the outcome of this scheming, they put out to sea in a steam yacht and have varying adventures—sailing in Cuban waters, etc. The story ends with the loss of the *Maine* reported, and the outbreak of the Spanish-American War.

2126. *THE PRICE OF HARNESS: Stephen Crane; in " Wounds in the Rain "—*Methuen* [*Eng.*]; *Stokes* [*U.S.A.*].
Cuba, 1898. A striking little tale of the Spanish-American War, written in the author's realistic manner.

2127. CRITTENDEN: John Fox; *Constable* [*Eng.*]; *Scribner* [*U.S.A.*].
N. America (largely Tampa) and Cuba, 1898. Story of a Kentuckian in the Spanish-American War time; he goes to Cuba and is badly wounded. There is a good description of the fighting.

2128. THE CODE OF THE MOUNTAINS: Charles Neville Buck; *Methuen* [*Eng.*]; *Watt* [*U.S.A.*].
Kentucky in the last decade of the 19th Century, also the Philippine Islands at the time of the Spanish-American War. The first part of the tale illustrates life in Kentucky (blood feuds), while the later chapters deal with the period in which the battleship *Maine* was destroyed by explosion (1898), and the American Navy made its victorious attack on Manila.

2129. *VAN CLEEVE: Mary S. Watts; *Macmillan.*
New York, etc., and Port Tampa (Florida), also Cuba, mostly in the 'Nineties. A story of social life and finance before, during, and after the Spanish-American War. Covers the *Maine* disaster, Dewey's capture of Manila, and the destruction of the Spanish fleet. The last pages of the book carry the fictional record some ten years farther.

2130. UNDER THE SPANGLED BANNER: Captain F. S. Brereton; *Juv. Blackie.*
Birmingham, America, and Cuba (Havana and Santiago), c. 1897-99. A tale of youthful adventure in the Spanish-American War period. Covers the loss of the *Maine*, and the destruction of Cervera's squadron, ending with the fall of Santiago and the departure of the Spanish forces from Cuba. Various sea and land episodes, including capture of lads by the Spaniards and their escape into the safety of the American Fleet.

2131. *SENATOR NORTH: Gertrude Atherton; *Lane* [*Eng.*], *Dodd, Mead,* [*U.S.A.*].
Washington in the late 'Nineties. One of the best novels of American politics, with an abundance of fictional interest. The book is historical in the general sense—reflecting the period when the questions relating to Cuba and the Spanish-American War were uppermost.

2132. *THE TORCHBEARERS: MARY BRADFORD WHITING; *Dent.*
N. Italy (the Pisan district, Siena, Florence, etc.), 1898-1900. A novel dealing with Italian politics, mostly in the period between the Milan Bread Riots (1898) and the assassination of King Humbert (1900); both the riots and the assassination are merely given as " news," and do not form part of the story. An Englishman, spending a year or two in Italy, is persuaded to act under the Secret Service of Police—at the same time getting mixed up, against his will, with one of the popular " Leagues of Resistance." There are some exciting developments, and the political atmosphere of the period is well conveyed.

2133. THE SWORD OF WEALTH: HENRY WILTON THOMAS; *Putnam.*
Italy (Lombardy), c. 1898-1900. A novel reflecting the troubled state of affairs in Northern Italy (Milan, etc.) at the end of King Humbert's reign. The story covers both the Bread Riots and the assassination of the King by an anarchist.

2134. THE JUDGMENT HOUSE: GILBERT PARKER; *Methuen.*
England (largely) and S. Africa, c. 1896-1902. A novel dealing with the period between the Jameson Raid and the end of the Great Boer War. The author, however, specially disclaims the term " historical "—explaining in his *Preface* that the story " does not present a picture of public or private individuals living or dead." Still, in spite of this disclaimer, the reader will find such names as Jameson, Rhodes and Kruger mentioned at various points, while the story is clearly intended to convey the atmosphere of the period. On the actual war side, the presentment is made in a series of sketches that are, for the most part, somewhat indefinite. The standpoint adopted is that of British Imperialism.

2135. NORA LESTER: ANNA HOWARTH; *Smith, Elder.*
England and S. Africa (Colesberg, etc.), in the 'Nineties. The story of an Englishman with Dutch blood in his veins. Illustrates life on the Dutch and English farms in the South African colonies at the outbreak of war. Gives an interesting picture of the relations between English and Dutch, and describes the hardships undergone by refugees after the war had begun. The first thirteen chapters depict life in England, and hardly prepare the reader for the much more vivid writing of the South African section.

2136. ALETTA: BERTRAM MITFORD; *White.*
S. Africa, 1899. A tale covering the period just before the South African War, as well as its early stages. The novel shows more first-hand knowledge than the majority of tales dealing with the Boers; they are depicted in a not altogether unpleasing light. The English hero has some romantic and other experiences amongst his Boer captors. " Oom Paul " (Kruger) appears.

TWENTIETH CENTURY

2137. WITH BULLER IN NATAL: G. A. HENTY; *Juv. Blackie* [*Eng.*], *Scribner* [*U.S.A.*].
S. Africa (Johannesburg, Dundee, etc.), 1899-1900. Story of a lad's experiences in the South African War (taken prisoner, etc.). Elandslaagte, the Siege of Ladysmith, Colenso, Spion Kop, and—at the end—the Relief of Ladysmith.

2138. *HUGH GORDON: ROSAMUND SOUTHEY; *Duckworth.*
S. Africa, 1899-1900. A good novel of the South African War, beginning just before the Boer Ultimatum. Covers the Siege of Ladysmith, Buller's landing, Colenso, Spion Kop, and the Relief of Ladysmith.

2139. WITH ROBERTS TO PRETORIA: G. A. Henty; *Juv.*
Blackie [*Eng.*], *Scribner* [*U.S.A.*].
Begins England (Somerset), then S. Africa (Capetown, Kimberley, Bloemfontein, etc.), 1899-1900. A tale of the War, covering the battles of Belmont, Graspan, and Modder River; dealing, also, with the Magersfontein disaster. There are special accounts of the Relief of Kimberley, Cronje's surrender at Paardeberg, and the Relief of Mafeking. Ends soon after the entry into Pretoria (June, 1900). Roberts, Methuen, and Cronje appear.

2140. SCOUTING FOR BULLER: Herbert Hayens; *Juv. Nelson.*
S. Africa, 1899-1900. The experiences of an English Colonial youth in the South African War (a prisoner in the hands of the Boers, etc.). The tale covers Dundee, the Siege of Ladysmith, Colenso, Spion Kop, and the Relief of Ladysmith. Buller and Sir George White both appear.

2141. OLD FIREPROOF: Owen Rhoscomyl; *Duckworth.*
S. Africa, 1899-1900. A novel of the South African War, reflecting it in a general way rather than depicting historic events or persons. The story is supposed to be told by an Army Chaplain—his record dealing largely with the heroic figure of a certain Welsh Captain, whom he prefers to call " Old Fireproof " throughout (the name is that by which the Captain is known amongst his own men).

2142. MAJOR GREVILLE, V.C.: G. G. Munik; *Sampson Low.*
S. Africa (Durban, Pretoria, Capetown, etc.), 1899-1902. A tale of the South African War written by a Boer, but, although revealing the enemy standpoint, it gives a fair depiction of men and events. The hero is an Englishman, and the dedication is " to the memory of the Brave Men of Two Nations, once enemies, now friends." The story covers and describes various battles, including Belmont, Graspan, Modder River, Magersfontein, Spion Kop, and Abraham's Kraal (an excellent battle plan in each case). President Kruger and Cronje are both favourably introduced, while mention is made of Methuen, De Wet, Botha, and others.

2143. *ONE OF THE FIGHTING SCOUTS: F. S. Brereton;
Juv. Blackie.
S. Africa (Orange Free State), 1900. An excellent story of the guerrilla fighting at the end of the South African War. The hero is an Englishman, while an Irishman is also prominent; the account of their many desperate adventures can hardly fail to appeal. One may specify, among the several historic figures: ex-President Steyn, and Generals Louis Botha and Christian De Wet.

2144. ABRAHAM'S SACRIFICE: Gustaf Janson (trans.); *Methuen.*
S. Africa, c.1900-1901. A story beginning at the point in the South African War when Cronje had just been captured. The book, however, presents no detailed picture of the War, and in the second half deals with the state of things after the British conquest. Well written, and not without considerable force and interest as a peace-lover's protest against war in general. At the same time, the Swedish author would have strengthened his case had he more fairly held the balance as between Boer and Briton. Historically, the novel reflects the unfriendly feeling towards the English, which existed in most European countries at the time of the South African War.

2145. *IT HAPPENED IN PEKING: Louise Jordan Miln; *Hodder
& Stoughton* [*Eng.*], *Stokes* [*U.S.A.*].
China, 1899-1900. An excellent story of the Boxer Rising, with good local colour, and showing the Chinese character in a much more favourable light than the usual estimate allows. There is an interesting picture of " Legations' Society " (English and American), while, on the historic side, the siege of the Legations and their eventual relief, as well as the general conditions before and after the Rising, are skilfully presented. A Manchu girl plays an important part, and the Empress Dowager is very prominently introduced (an original portrait).

2146. WITH THE ALLIES TO PEKIN: G. A. Henty; *Juv.*
    Blackie.
      China (Pekin, Tientsin, Taku, etc.), 1900. The Rising of the Boxers against all
foreigners and Western reform. The story describes the two months' attack on the
European Legations in Pekin, telling, also, how Admiral Seymour marched to their
relief after the siege of Tientsin. Sir Claude Macdonald appears.

2147. THE DRAGON OF PEKIN: F. S. Brereton; *Blackie.*
      China, 1900. A story of thrilling adventure, covering the period of the Boxer
Rebellion: the attack on the Legations (Pekin), Admiral Seymour at Tientsin, and
the march thence to Pekin, etc. There is a glimpse of the Boy-Emperor.

2148. THE LOST COLUMN: Charles Gilson; *Frowde.*
      China, 1900. Another good story illustrating the Boxer Rebellion. Begins just
before the outbreak, and leads up to scenes in Tientsin and Peking after the trouble
had begun. The Siege of Tientsin, and Admiral Seymour's march to the relief of the
Peking Legations. The Admiral himself appears.

2149. *THE TREASURE OF HO: L. Adams Beck; *Collins [Eng.]*,
    Dodd, Mead [U.S.A.].
      China (Peking and the Northern hilly wilds), c. 1900-1901. A strange, but fascinating,
story of an Englishman who has a long Anglo-Chinese family record behind him (the
tale hinges on certain bygone episodes in the life of an 18th century ancestor). One
of the important figures is a Buddhist priest whose early appearance introduces the
reader to that element of clairvoyance or " inner knowledge," which is brought into
the story at many points. Intermingled with this unusual element, are the hero's
thrilling adventures in Peking during the time of the Boxer Rebellion and Admiral
Seymour's relief expedition. The famous Dowager Empress is very prominently introduced, and several members of the imperial family (Manchu Dynasty) appear. The
hero finds himself mixed up with a conspiracy against the Manchus, though in the end
he marries a Manchu lady!

*NOTE.—It is sometimes urged that occurrences of a year or two ago should be reckoned as " history."
    Of course there is justification of a kind for such a claim, but the same reasons, which seemed
    to forbid extending my lists beyond the Early 'Seventies when preparing the first edition of this
    " Guide " in 1902, appear now to demand a parallel limit. Accordingly, I have taken the first
    two years of the Twentieth Century as my farthest reach, and this decision is additionally
    supported by the fact that my time limit exactly coincides with the end of the Victorian Age.
    An interval of some thirty years between events and their narration is about the time needed,
    in my opinion, for genuine historical perspective. Surely we see events more truly, in one sense,
    after the lapse of years, even though exact details tend to fade away; we then reach, if not the
    stage of impartial judgment, at least the approximation to such.*

SEMI-HISTORICAL NOVELS AND TALES

" Many corresponding circumstances are detected by readers, of which the author did not suspect the existence. He must, however, regard it as a great compliment, that in detailing incidents purely imaginary, he has been so fortunate in approximating reality, as to remind his readers of actual occurrences."

Sir Walter Scott in his " Additional Note to ' Guy Mannering.' "

" Any narrative which presents faithfully a day and a generation is, of necessity, historical."

Owen Wister, in " The Virginian."

" Historical fiction proper looks backward by the help of imagination and antiquarian study. But there is another class of work which we may call ' contemporary ' historical fiction: that is, the epic, drama, or novel of contemporary manners, which acquires historical value only by the passage of time. . . . Homer, Shakespeare, and Fielding copied from the life of their own day. . . . They give evidence, not indeed as to particular events, but as to the manners, thought, and customs which they knew so well."

G. M. Trevelyan in the Sidgwick Memorial Lecture.

SUPPLEMENTARY LIST OF
SEMI-HISTORICAL NOVELS AND TALES

Which, while not strictly "Historical," in some way represent bygone periods.

NOTE.—Nothing like exhaustiveness is claimed for this Semi-Historical List; the method of study which it indicates, might be carried much further, but the books given will, it is believed, be found at once carefully chosen and fairly large in number. It may be objected that in this section I have not always been consistent in following the distinction made in my Introduction between genuinely historical fiction and fiction that is semi-historical. The difficulty of placing certain borderland books exactly, must be offered as excuse in such cases. With regard to the annotations, these—generally speaking—are necessarily brief and more or less vague, seeing that the very fact of a story being "semi-historical," implies the absence of historical detail.

2150. *THE LONG JOURNEY: FIRE AND ICE.[1]
. *THE CIMBRIANS. THE LONG JOURNEY II.
*CHRISTOPHER COLUMBUS. THE LONG JOURNEY III.
JOHANNES V. JENSON (trans.); *Gyldendal [Eng.], Knopf [U.S.A.].*
A series of imaginative sketches of Man's Life in Northern Europe (Scandinavia) and elsewhere, from prehistoric times to a comparatively modern period. Hardly fiction in the usual sense, but constituting a fine example of imaginative re-creation, based on Science, Legend, Saga, and History. Deals with the old Northern roving, seeking impulse, ending on a note of something like philosophic mysticism.

[1] Strictly speaking, of course, books of this kind are not even "semi" historical: the people whom Messrs. Jensen, Roberts, "Ashton Hilliers," Begoüen, etc., have, with such power of imagination, tried to reproduce for us, lived in the far-off unrecorded periods of our planet. At the same time it must be borne in mind that, through the study of Science, we are able to trace, if not the detailed history of races long passed away, at least the general outline of their manner of living; hence it may be claimed that even romances dealing with Primitive Life, are based—as regards their framework—on certain *bygone facts* which Nature has recorded for us.

2151. ALLAN AND THE ICE-GODS: H. RIDER HAGGARD; *Hutchinson.*
One of the author's backward-looking tales in the "Allan Quartermain" series. Here Allan is presented as "Wi the Hunter," living in the Ice Age.

2152. *IN THE MORNING OF TIME: CHARLES G. D. ROBERTS; *Dent [Eng.], Hutchinson [Eng.], Stockes [U.S.A.].*
A story beginning in "the World without Man," but passing quickly to some two hundred or three hundred thousand years later when the real fictional interest begins: Early Man and Woman in primeval days (the great beasts, etc.).

2153. *THE MASTER GIRL: "ASHTON HILLIERS"; *Methuen [Eng.], Putnam [U.S.A.].*
A really fascinating story of Man and Woman in the Stone Age.

2154. *BISON OF CLAY: MAX BEGOUËN (trans.); *Longmans.*
The Pyrenees region some 25,000 years ago (the Stone Age). A striking novel of the "Magdalenians" whose finger marks and drawings in the ancient clay of the Tuc d'Audoubert cavern were discovered by the author and his brothers in 1912.

2155. *A TALE OF THE TIME OF THE CAVE MEN (formerly
"The Story of Ab"): STANLEY WATERLOO; *Juv. Black* [*Eng.*],
Doubleday [*U.S.A.*].
A vivid adventure tale of the Stone Age and the Cave-men.

2156. *DWIFA'S CURSE: "BLUE WOLF"; *Robert Scott.*
A well-written and interesting tale of the Stone Age. The volume has good illustrations.

2157. *WELAND'S SWORD: RUDYARD KIPLING; *Juv.* In "Puck
of Pook's Hill"—*Macmillan.*
A short tale of Prehistoric Britain (the Flint Men, etc.).

2158. *HELEN: EDWARD LUCAS WHITE; *Cape* [*Eng.*], *Doran* [*U.S.A.*].
The romance of Helen of Troy, told in seven tales. The author writes:—"These
tales are the outcome of years of pondering on the possible historical events out of which
grew the legends embodied in the Homeric tale of Troy."

2159. *THE PRIVATE LIFE OF HELEN OF TROY: JOHN ERSKINE;
Nash [*Eng.*], *Bobbs-Merrill* [*U.S.A.*].
Sparta, after the return of Menelaus from Troy in company with Helen. This clever
imaginative character-sketch is included here on the same ground as the book immediately preceding it—viz., that these Troy legends grew out of certain "possible
historical events."

2160. *THE SPLENDOUR OF ASIA: L. ADAMS BECK; *Collins* [*Eng.*],
Dodd, Mead [*U.S.A.*].
N. India in the period between the 7th Century B.C. and the 5th Century B.C. An
imaginative portrayal of Siddartha, the Buddha; the romance aims at giving an ex-
position of his teaching. A moving and carefully-executed piece of work.

2161. *THE PILGRIM KAMANITA: KARL GJELLERUP (trans.);
Heinemann.
India between the 7th Century B.C. and the 5th Century B.C. A "legendary
romance" of the Buddha, based on considerable study, and showing imaginative
power.

2162. CHILDREN OF THE DAWN: MARY CARBERY; *Heinemann.*
A tale of Druidic Ireland, based on ancient legends concerning the coming of "sun-
worshippers from . . . Hellas who taught the arts of peace and brought light into
dark places." There are some references to Athens and its worship of the "Unknown
God," to Egypt, and to peoples of the East (Jews, etc.).

2163. *THAÏS: "ANATOLE FRANCE"; *Greening.*
A story of Early Christian life in Egypt: time of the anchorites. A psychological
study, from the standpoint of a modern sceptic.

2164. *UTHER AND IGRAINE (UTHER AND YGRAINE):
WARWICK DEEPING; *Cassell* [*Eng.*], *Outlook Co.* [*U.S.A.*], *Knopf*
[*U.S.A.*].
Britain in the time of the early Saxon Conquests, about 490 A.D.: Winchester, Wales,
and Tintagel. A love romance of King Arthur's parents, written in a style at once
forceful and graceful.

2165. SIR MARROK: ALLEN FRENCH; *Juv. Century.*
A tale of the Forest of Bedegraine (Sherwood) in the times of King Uther and King
Arthur respectively.

2166. THE CLUTCH OF CIRCUMSTANCE: DOROTHY SENIOR;
    Black [Eng.], Macmillan [U.S.A.].
A good story of Britain in the time of King Arthur and the Round Table: Cormac,
King of Leinster, etc. Suggested by Malory.

2167. *GALAHAD: JOHN ERSKINE; Nash [Eng.], Bobbs-Merrill [U.S.A.].
An extremely clever adaptation of Arthurian legend.

2168. *QUEEN'S KNIGHT: CHESTER KEITH; George Allen.
S. Britain about the middle of the Sixth Century. A good Arthurian romance, or
—as the author himself calls it—" prose epic." King Arthur, Queen Guenever, Lancelot,
Gawaine, Bedivere, etc. etc.

2169. THE SONS OF AETHNE: J. M. REID; Blackwood.
A story of West Scotland, etc., about the 8th Century. Exhibits full knowledge of
Celtic traditions.

2170. *PASSE ROSE: ARTHUR SHERBURNE HARDY; Houghton Mifflin.
A romantic tale of Maestricht, Aix, the Ardennes district, etc., in the 8th Century.
There is so little in Mr. A. S. Hardy's pleasing story which can be said to approach
history proper, that it is now (5th edition of Guide) brought into the semi-historical
section.

2171. (1)*A LOVER'S TALE: MAURICE HEWLETT; Ward, Lock [Eng.],
        Scribner [U.S.A.].
    (2)*THORGILS OF TREADHOLT: MAURICE HEWLETT;
        Ward, Lock [Eng.], Dodd, Mead [U.S.A.].
    (3)*GUDRID THE FAIR: MAURICE HEWLETT; Constable
        [Eng.], Dodd, Mead [U.S.A.].
    (4)*THE OUTLAW: MAURICE HEWLETT; Constable [Eng.],
        Dodd, Mead [U.S.A.].
These four independent novels deal with Iceland, Norway, Greenland, etc., about
the 9th and 10th Centuries. They are based on the Sagas, and are consequently not
without historical elements of a vague type (in Gudrid the Fair, for instance, the first
discovery of America is illustrated). The author has had no hesitation in depicting
his characters as having, fundamentally, very much in common with the men and
women of to-day; the clear implication of these stirring tales is that, be the changes
of outward condition what they may, Human Nature has certain abiding qualities.

2172. ERIC BRIGHTEYES: H. RIDER HAGGARD; Longmans.
A tale of Iceland " before the year 999," based on the Sagas.

2173. *THE KING'S FOOL : MICHAEL BARRINGTON; Blackwood.
A really moving story of Troubadour days. There is nothing to indicate exact time
or place, but one may infer that the book is intended to illustrate life about the 12th
Century.

2174. *THE FOREST LOVERS: MAURICE HEWLETT; Macmillan.
A delightful romance of Mediæval Life (England). Some critics are disposed to class
this book as Maurice Hewlett's greatest literary achievement; certainly it is one of his
finest imaginative productions, and at least must be ranked with The Queen's Quair,
Richard Yea-and-Nay, The New Canterbury Tales, and those masterly Saga stories of Iceland
and Norway which he gave us in his later career of authorship.

2175. A LITTLE SHEPHERD OF PROVENCE: EVALEEN STEIN;
        Juv. Page [U.S.A.].
One of the author's pleasing stories, telling of a crippled lad in Mediæval Provence.

2176. *THE MERRY ADVENTURES OF ROBIN HOOD: Howard Pyle; *Juv. Newnes* [Eng.], *Scribner* [U.S.A.].
Mediæval Nottinghamshire: an excellent adaptation of the Robin Hood legends, with good illustrations by the author.

2177. THE BOY KINGS: Margaret Baines Reed; *Juv. Edward Arnold.*
A good mediæval story, historic only in the sense of having a 13th Century atmosphere.

2178. BELTANE THE SMITH: Jeffery Farnol; *Sampson Low* [Eng.], *Little, Brown* [U.S.A.].
Mediæval England about the 13th or 14th Century. Romance of an " outlaw and rebel," quite indefinite in date.

2179. A MEDIÆVAL GARLAND: Mrs. J. Darmesteter; *Lawrence & Bullen.*
Italy and France, mostly late 13th Century, to late 16th Century. A volume of short but illuminating tales of such cities as Assisi (1290), Cherbourg (1429), Chalons (1446), Milan (1496), Metz (1518), and Ferrara (1535 and 1595).

2180. (1)*YOUTH WENT RIDING: C. E. Lawrence; *Collins* [Eng.].
(2)*LASS OF THE SWORD: C. E. Lawrence; *Murray* [Eng.], *Dutton* [U.S.A.].
These two mediæval tales are in some degree connected—" Palentyre " and the " Imperial city of Dornivaulx " being scenes in both. There is much charm in these pictures of knight-errantry and tournament, of girl-knight and man-knight, of chivalry and love.

2181. *THE GARLAND (THE BRIDAL WREATH):
*THE MISTRESS OF HUSABY (sequel):
*THE CROSS (sequel): Sigrid Undset (trans.); *Gyldendal* [Eng.], *Knopf* [U.S.A.].
A remarkable triology of the highly esteemed Norwegian novelist, in which the career of a woman (" Kristin Lavransdatter ") from childhood to death is depicted with much feeling and power. The scene is Norway in mediæval times, but the main interest is psychological rather than historical.

2182. GOLDEN HAWK: Edith Rickert; *Arnold* [Eng.], *Baker & Taylor* [U.S.A.].
A story of 14th Century Provence: time of the Popes at Avignon.

2183. THE CASTLE OF TWILIGHT: Margaret H. Potter; *McClurg* [U.S.A.].
Brittany, 1380. A novel well illustrating the position of women under Feudalism.

2184. *LITTLE NOVELS OF ITALY: Maurice Hewlett; *Macmillan.*
Stories of Italian Life and Manners, early 14th to late 15th Century. Finely told, and exhibiting the author's knowledge of time and place.

2185. *SPRINGTIME (UNDER CASTLE WALLS): H. C. Bailey; *Murray* [Eng.], *Appleton* [U.S.A.].
Italy (Lombard plain) in the Early Renaissance period.

2186. HERE COME SWORDS: Coutts Brisbane; *Lane* [Eng.], *Dodd, Mead* [U.S.A.].
A story of Italy in late 15th Century: about the time of Lorenzo the Magnificent.

2187. THE LOVE CHASE: Maurice Hewlett; in "Fond Adventures"—*Macmillan* [*Eng.*], *Harper* [*U.S.A.*].
Italy (Mantua) in the time of the Sforzas, late 15th Century. A somewhat dark story, in which the psychological interest predominates.

2188. *SILVER CROSS: Mary Johnston; *Thornton Butterworth* [*Eng.*], *Little, Brown* [*U.S.A.*].
A story of English religious life in Henry VII's reign.

2189. *THE GOD SEEKER: Peter Rosegger (trans.); *Putnam.*
The Styrian Alps, 1493. An unusual tale showing considerable power, with good local colour.

2190. RAOUL THE HUNCHBACK: H. B. Somerville; *Hutchinson*
Provence in the early 16th Century. Love, intrigue, and desperate adventure.

2191. *TARAS BULBA: Nicolai V. Gogol (trans.); *Scott* [*Eng.*], *Crowell* [*U.S.A.*].
A powerful story of the Zaporogian Cossacks in the late 16th Century.

2192. *THE SEA-HAWK: Rafael Sabatini; *Martin Secker* [*Eng.*], *Houghton Mifflin* [*U.S.A.*].
Cornwall and the Mediterranean in Elizabethan times. The Barbary Corsair of this exciting tale is not after the conventional type of piratical fiction.

2193. CAPTAIN RAVENSHAW: Robert Neilson Stephens; *Ward Lock* [*Eng.*], *Page* [*U.S.A.*].
A good adventure romance of late Elizabethan London.

2194. *THE HISTORY OF DON QUIXOTE DE LA MANCHA: Miguel de Cervantes Saavedra (trans.); *Various publishers —English and American.*
Southern Spain at the beginning of the 17th Century. One of the world's great books which, although primarily a satire on high flown chivalry romances, has special value for readers of a later time as bringing before them bygone ways and manners. It has been well said that from *Don Quixote* " we get a better idea of life in Spain three hundred years ago than any history book could give us."

2195.* CAPTAIN FRACASSE (*LE CAPITAINE FRACASSE*): Théophile Gautier (trans.); *Duckworth* [*Eng.*], *Page* [*U.S.A.*], and other publishers.
A famous story of strolling players in the reign of Louis XIII, illustrating to a large extent the French life of the time, and containing passages of brilliant descriptive writing.

2196. *THE AMBER WITCH: Johann Wilhelm Meinhold (trans.): *David Nutt* [*Eng.*], *Scribner* [*U.S.A.*]. Also *Oxford Univ. Press.*
North Germany in the period of the Thirty Years' War. A graphic tale of superstition which, in its realistic detail, must strike some readers as conveying almost too painful an impression. The author—a Lutheran pastor and writer of the second quarter of last century—is best known by this book.

2197. BLACK BARTLEMY'S TREASURE: MARTIN CONISBY'S VENGEANCE (*sequel*): Jeffery Farnol; *Sampson Low* [*Eng.*], *Little, Brown* [*U.S.A.*].
England (Kent), and—chiefly—the Spanish Main, mid-17th Century. These two books together form one highly-coloured story of adventure by land and sea (Pirates, the Spanish Inquisition, etc.).

2198. THE RED AXE: S. R. CROCKETT; *Dent* [*Eng.*], *Harper* [*U.S.A.*].
Prussia—Poland region (largely Thorn) in the first half of the 17th Century. A highly-coloured romance of adventure and love in the wild days of the Thirty Years' War.

2199. *THE LIFE AND ADVENTURES OF ROBINSON CRUSOE: DANIEL DEFOE; *Various editions—English and American.*
A world-famous romance suggested by the actual experiences of Alexander Selkirk who from the year 1704 lived a solitary life for some four years or more on the island of Juan Fernandez in the Pacific Ocean. *Defoe's story* begins with the hero's birth in York, 1632, quickly passing to 1651 and a thirty-five years' absence from England. There is some account of adventures off the African Coast, but the great interest of all is aroused in that portion of the book which deals with the sojourn of over twenty-eight years on a small island, up to the end of the year 1686.

2200. WOLVES OF THE SEA: RANDALL PARRISH; *Jarrolds* [*Eng.*], *McClure* [*U.S.A.*].
Narrative of a man's experiences after he had been condemned to slavery in Virginia for taking part in the Monmouth Rebellion. The story is almost entirely one of sea adventures.

2201. THE HONEST MAN: UNA L. SILBERRAD; *Hutchinson.*
London and Kendal, etc., late 17th Century. A middle-aged man " comes into a fortune, and finds romance." The chief merit of the book is its fictional interest.

2202. *THE SCARLET LETTER: NATHANIEL HAWTHORNE; *Numerous publishers—English and American.*
A great piece of literature. Puritan life and morals at the end of the 17th Century. This famous novel, though conveying an historical atmosphere, is essentially a study of human mentality—how the consciousness of guilt, under certain special conditions and influences, may completely overshadow life.

2203. *LOST ENDEAVOUR: JOHN MASEFIELD; *Nelson.*
London (Black Heath, Deptford, etc.), Spanish Main, and Virginia, beginning in 1690, but chiefly 1693 onwards. An excellent tale of kidnapping and adventure (sea and land): Pirates, Spaniards, Indians, etc.

2204. SAMPSON RIDEOUT, QUAKER: UNA L. SILBERRAD; *Nelson.*
A tale of Southern England (Salisbury, Shaftesbury, etc.) round about the year 1700.

2205. *THE PIRATE: SIR WALTER SCOTT; *Black, and other publishers —English and American.*
Shetland and the Orkney Islands in 1700. The story is really based on facts which occurred in 1725.

2206. *THE BLACK DWARF: SIR WALTER SCOTT; *Black, and other publishers—English and American.*
A tale of the Scottish Lowlands in 1708, dealing with Jacobites, etc.

2207. *THE BRIDE OF LAMMERMOOR: SIR WALTER SCOTT; *Black.*
The Lammermoor district of Berwickshire round about the year 1710 (see the allusion to Harley's victory over the Whigs, at the beginning of Chapter XXVII). This fine example of Scott is based on an incident gathered from the first Earl of Stair's family records, though the scene is changed in the novel from Wigtownshire to Berwickshire.

2208. *THE SPECTATOR: Joseph Addison and Richard Steele; *Various publishers—English and American.*

English life and manners at the beginning of the 18th Century (Queen Anne period). Although the famous literary compositions which form the " Spectator " collection, are generally described as papers or essays, they contain such well-conceived figures (Sir Roger de Coverley, Sir Andrew Freeport, Will Honeycomb, Moll White, etc.) that, in spite of the lack of plot, they may be regarded as having some claim to be classed under the heading of imaginative, or fictional, literature. In presenting these types of the men and women of their day, and in conveying social ways and influences, Addison and Steele have furnished later generations with the means of reconstructing a past age.

2209. SIR ROGER'S HEIR: F. Frankfort Moore; *Hodder & Stoughton.*

A tale of English country life in the time of Queen Anne, based—as the title suggests —on the *Spectator* character types.

2210. OUR ADMIRABLE BETTY; Jeffery Farnol; *Sampson Low* [Eng.], *Little, Brown* [U.S.A.].

One of the author's breezy love and adventure stories of bygone England: a duel, a highwayman, etc. The date is soon fixed as 1716 by the statement that Ramillies was fought *ten years previously.*

2211. *THE FOOL ERRANT: Maurice Hewlett; *Heinemann* [Eng.]. *Macmillan* [U.S.A.].

The experiences of an English gentleman of somewhat fantastic disposition, during his wanderings in Italy (Padua, Florence, Lucca, Siena, etc.), 1721-41. There is allusion at the very end of the book, to the hero's death in 1759.

2212. *CAPTAIN SINGLETON: Daniel Defoe; *Dent* [Eng.], *Macmillan* [U.S.A.].

An imaginary record of adventure (the crossing of Africa by marooned sailors) in George I's time.

2213. *ROGER MALVIN'S BURIAL: Nathaniel Hawthorne; in " Mosses from an Old Manse "—*W. Scott* [Eng.], *Houghton Mifflin* [U.S.A.].

New England in 1725. One of Hawthorne's powerful imaginative sketches, conveying an early-18th Century atmosphere, and exhibiting that sense of locality which was peculiar to his genius.

2214. *AT THE SIGN OF THE QUEEN PÉDAUQUE: " Anatole France " (trans.); *Lane & Gibbings.*

French life and manners in the first half of the 18th Century. A critical study rather than romance proper: the author portrays, with keen satire, the life of an unprincipled Abbé of the period.

2215. *MONSIEUR BEAUCAIRE: Booth Tarkington; *Murray* [Eng.], *McClure* [U.S.A.].

Bath in the days of Beau Nash. A literary critic of repute has alluded to this little story as being a " delightful miniature historical romance," but the word " historical " might well be replaced by " *semi*-historical."

2216. *MORTALLONE AND AUNT TRINIDAD: A. T. Quiller-Couch; *Arrowsmith;* also *Dent.*

Bristol and the Spanish Main. A volume containing the two stories given in the title, and a slight fictional sketch entitled: " Captain Knot "; the tales deal largely with sea-adventure in the first half of the 18th Century. " Mortallone " (or, to give the full title, " The Keys of Mortallone ") is a particularly entertaining piece of fiction.

2217. GABRIELLE TRANSGRESSOR: Harris Dickson; *Lippincott.*
New Orleans in mid-18th Century.

2218. FRENCH NAN: Agnes and Egerton Castle; *Smith, Elder.*
Story of a Versailles Court Beauty married to an English Squire, mid-18th Century.

2219. *SOPHIA: Stanley J. Weyman; *Murray.*
London and Sussex in 1742. A good tale of social life and adventure.

2220. *TRUE AS STEEL: " Herbert Strang "; *Juv. Oxford University Press.*
Dorsetshire in 1746, 1747, etc. Connected tales, the same principal character appearing throughout; they deal in interesting fashion with such subjects as a Jacobite fugitive, a highwayman, etc., and the atmosphere of the period is well conveyed.

2221. *TREASURE ISLAND: R. L. Stevenson; *Cassell* [Eng.], *Scribner* [U.S.A.].
A world-famous tale of adventure in the mid-18th Century, which is almost sufficiently described in the title; hardly any reader—*young or old*—who begins the book, will be able to leave it unfinished.

2222. THE LADY OF LYNN: Walter Besant; *Chatto & Windus* [Eng.], *Dodd, Mead* [U.S.A.].
King's Lynn, Norfolk, mid-18th Century. The manners and life of a time which the author was so peculiarly qualified to reconstruct.

2223. THE ROAD OF DESTINY: Ellis Middleton; *Mills & Boon.*
London, Huntingdonshire, and Yorkshire in mid-18th Century. An interesting story of gambling and Jacobite days.

2224. HAZARD: A ROMANCE: John Overton; *Melrose.*
Southern England in George II's time. A love story with Jacobite element.

2225. *THE OLD CHELSEA BUN-HOUSE: Anne Manning; *Juv. Routledge* [Eng.], *Scribner* [U.S.A.].
A quaintly-worded depiction of English mid-18th Century life (a letter in the tale is dated " 1749 ").

2226. *NO OTHER WAY: Walter Besant; *Chatto & Windus* [Eng.], *Dodd, Mead* [U.S.A.].
The London of 1750-53: King's Bench Prison, Newgate, St. James's Square, Vauxhall, etc. Another good example of Besant's 18th Century fiction. The story is one that grips the reader from first to last.

2227. *OIL OF SPIKENARD: E. M. Smith-Dampier; *Melrose.*
Norfolk (Breckland) and London, mostly 1752-53, but ending 1756. An interesting novel of mid-Century life and manners. The primary interests of the book are character development and love.

2228. *SIR CHARLES GRANDISON: Samuel Richardson; *Chapman & Hall* [Eng.], *Lippincott* [U.S.A.], *and other publishers.*
Northamptonshire, London, and Italy, mid-18th Century. A good example of the author, especially valuable as depicting life and manners from the standpoint of a contemporary.

2229. *CLARISSA HARLOWE: Samuel Richardson; *Chapman & Hall* [*Eng.*], *Lippincott* [*U.S.A.*], and *other publishers.*
A picture of English Middle Class Life in mid-18th Century. The novel of sentiment *par excellence.*

2230. *TOM JONES: Henry Fielding; *Dent* [*Eng.*], *Macmillan* [*U.S.A.*], and *other publishers.*
A realistic (at times coarse) presentment of English life generally, in the middle of the 18th Century. One of the greatest of all English novels. Fielding's characters are typical in the largest sense rather than mere individual creations. "Sophia," it is said, was based to a considerable extent upon the personality of the author's own first wife.

2231. *HUMPHREY CLINKER: Tobias G. Smollett; *Constable* [*Eng.*], *Macmillan* [*U.S.A.*], and *other publishers.*
To some extent a satire on the Methodists, but interesting mainly for its faithful illustration of English Town and Country Life (including the domesticities), mid-18th Century.

2232. *THE VICAR OF WAKEFIELD: Oliver Goldsmith; *Dent* [*Eng.*], *Dutton* [*U.S.A.*], and *other publishers.*
English Rural Life about the middle of the 18th Century. This famous tale has a tender simplicity which, in its own way, has never been surpassed.

2234. THE HONOURABLE ROGER: Charles A. Brandreth; *Hutchinson.*
Lincolnshire, 1755. A good picture of Methodists, Jacobites, Whigs, Tories, etc. The account of an Election at Lincoln is noteworthy.

2235. *DOOM CASTLE: Neil Munro; *Blackwood* [*Eng.*], *Dodd, Mead* [*U.S.A.*].
A French Count's experiences on a visit in the Western Highlands of Scotland (country of the Argyll), mid-18th Century.

2236. THE LAWLESS LOVER: N. W. Byng; *Methuen.*
An excellent story of English highwaymen about the middle of the 18th Century.

2237. MY LADY APRIL: John Overton; *Werner Laurie.*
Bath in the time of the Beaux, mid-18th Century.

2238. BESS OF THE WOODS: Warwick Deeping; *Cassell* [*Eng.*], *Harper* [*U.S.A.*].
A good tale of English country life (squire, parson, etc.) in mid-18th Century.

2239. *THE PASSIONATE ELOPEMENT: Compton Mackenzie; *Secker* [*Eng.*], *Putnam* [*U.S.A.*].
A novel illustrating life at a fashionable English Inland Spa ("Curtain Wells"), mid- to late-18th Century.

2240. THE STRANGE ADVENTURES OF MR. FRANCIS: M. C. Reynolds; *Juv.* *Blackie.*
Yorkshire, London, and the Caribbee Islands, 1765. A good story of pure adventure (treasure finding.)

2241. *THE SMUGGLER: G. P. R. James; *Routledge* [*Eng.*], *Dutton* [*U.S.A.*].
Kent (the Folkestone-Hythe and Romney Marsh regions) in the early part of George III's reign. Custom-House officers and smugglers, etc. A good example of the author.

2242. *THE PRIDE OF JENNICO: Agnes and Egerton Castle; *Macmillan.*

Part I, Moravia, end 1771; Part II, England, 1772; and Part III, Moravia, 1773. A love and adventure romance.

2243. CAPTAIN QUALITY: E. A. Wyke Smith; *Lane.*

London and Southern England, mid- to late-18th Century. A tale of Social Life and the Road, of Vauxhall and the Old Bailey, etc.

2244. *JOHN MAXWELL'S MARRIAGE: Stephen Gwynn; *Macmillan.*

A powerful story of life in Northern Ireland (Donegal), 1761-79. Depicts religious animosities and touches on the history and politics of the period. There is a glimpse of America.

2245. *HIS GRACE OF GRUB STREET: G. V. McFadden; *Lane.*

An interesting story of a Journalist in London, 1773: time of Horace Walpole and Garrick (allusions only).

2246. DEAN'S HALL: Maude Goldring; *Murray.*

A tale of Yorkshire and the Quakers in the second half of the 18th Century.

2247. BACK O' THE MOON: AND OTHER STORIES: Oliver Onions; *Hurst & Blackett.*

Late 18th Century life in the West Riding of Yorkshire: weavers, coiners, etc.

2248. THE McBRIDES: John Sillars; *Blackwood.*

A tale of smuggling, etc., in the Isle of Arran, late 18th Century.

2249. *EVELINA: Fanny Burney [Madame D'Arblay]; *Dent* [*Eng.*], *Dutton* [*U.S.A.*], *and other publishers.*

A novel, in epistolary form, of English fashionable life in late 18th Century: a satire on vulgarity. The famous novelist herself explains the plan of the work:—" To draw characters from nature, though not from life, and to mark the manners of the time " —as these appeared to a young and beautiful girl of seventeen during the " first six months after her entrance into the world." The novel was originally sold for £20, and published anonymously in 1778 under complete secrecy. It is said that when her father, Dr. Burney, came to read the tale, he at once discovered the author's identity.

2250. *CASTLE RACKRENT: Maria Edgeworth; *Dent* [*Eng.*], *Dutton* [*U.S.A.*], *and other publishers.*

Perhaps the best of Miss Edgeworth's tales depicting Irish Life and Character. The story is given under the form of reminiscences by an old family retainer (" Thady "), in which he tells of those owners of the " Castle Rackrent " estate whom he has known and served. The record has been well termed an " ironic presentation." Bibliographers seem puzzled as to the period which Miss Edgeworth has here illustrated; " Latter half of the 17th Century," and " Earlier half of the 18th Century," are two of the descriptions given. There can, however, be no doubt as to the main period being *the end of the 18th Century*. In a passage to be found in that part of the " Memoirs " which is far the longest and most important (the part dealing with " Sir Condy Rackrent "), we find this little bit of dialogue:—" What is it you're reading there, my dear? " asks Sir Condy of his Lady, and she replies—" *The Sorrows of Werter*." That settles the question of approximate date.

2251. *JOHN INGERFIELD: Jerome K. Jerome; *Simpkin.*

A very pathetic, well-written tale of East London (Limehouse) in late 18th Century. An admirable example of the " short story."

2252. GOD'S PROVIDENCE HOUSE: Mrs. G. Linnæus Banks; *R. Bentley*, also *Paul*.
Chester and Delamere Forest in 1791. The general atmosphere of the period is well conveyed.

2253. THINGS AS THEY ARE; or, THE ADVENTURES OF CALEB WILLIAMS (Caleb Williams; or, Things as they are): William Godwin; *Robinson [Eng.]—2nd edn. corrected 1796;* also *Routledge*.
A novel which embodies the author's protest against the English Penal Laws at the end of the 18th Century. The period when Holcroft, Horne Tooke, and others were charged with high-treason (Godwin defended them powerfully in the *Morning Chronicle*).

2254. *THE LOST LAND: Julia M. Crottie; *Fisher Unwin*.
A fictional autobiography depicting in powerful though somewhat gloomy fashion, life in an Irish town (province of Munster), 1780-97.

2255. A KING'S WOMAN: Katharine Tynan; *Hurst & Blackett*.
Ireland (Dublin, etc.) in the time of the United Irish Society, and the '98 Rebellion. The story is supposed to be related by a Quakeress. Historical chiefly in the sense of atmosphere.

2256. *THE ANNALS OF THE PARISH: John Galt; *Dent [Eng.]*, *Dutton [U.S.A.]*, *and other publishers*,
Scottish village life (Ayrshire) 1760-1810. A deservedly famous novel reflecting, with wonderful cleverness, the manners and thought-tendencies of the period.

2257. *THE ANTIQUARY: Sir Walter Scott; *Black, and other publishers—English and American.*
The " north-eastern coast of Scotland " (see Chapter II) in the last decade of the 18th Century. Considered by many lovers of Scott to be one of his finest novels; it gives—to quote the author's own words—" an imitation of the shifting manners " of the time, depicting scenes " the originals of which were daily passing around." In other words, he was, in this case, not writing historical fiction of his usual kind, but a novel of *contemporary* life, which for us of a later age has become an instructive presentment of old, far-off days. Here indeed (as an esteemed critic has recently said) is one of those novels by the author whom all of us regard as the " historical novelist " *par excellence*, which show that, in order properly to estimate his genius, " the emphasis should be thrown not upon ' historical ' but upon ' novelist.' "

2258. *THE TRAMPING METHODIST: Sheila Kaye Smith; *Bell [Eng.]*, *Macmillan [U.S.A.]*, *Dutton [U.S.A.]*.
Sussex and Kent, 1799. A novel depicting the rural life and thought of the time.

2259. THE INIMITABLE MRS. MASSINGHAM: Herbert Compton; *Chatto & Windus*.
Gretna Green, London, and Botany Bay, 1799. Story of girl who becomes an actress; a careful picture of end-century ways.

2260. ARTHUR MERVYN: Charles Brocden Brown; *McKay [U.S.A.]*.
A novel of some note in its day, depicting life in Philadelphia, 1793 (Yellow Fever Year).

2261. *THE CHOIR INVISIBLE: James Lane Allen; *Macmillan*.
Kentucky, 1795. A tale of atmosphere and character-depiction.

2262. KITWYK: Mrs. J. Lane; *Lane.*
Imaginative sketches of Dutch village life round about 1800.

2263. *DESTINY: Susan Ferrier; *Dent [Eng.], Macmillan [U.S.A.].*
This somewhat noted work of fiction cleverly depicts Scottish life and manners about the beginning of the 19th Century.

2264. THE INTERLOPER: Violet Jacob; *Heinemann.*
An interesting tale of life in the S.E. Coast region of Scotland at the beginning of the 19th Century.

2265. *PRECIOUS BANE: Mary Webb; *Cape.*
Welsh Border life and ways (sin-eating, etc.) at the beginning of the 19th Century: time of the Napoleonic Wars. A novel of real power and originality.

2266. *JIM DAVIS: John Masefield; *Juv. Wells Gardner [Eng.], Stokes [U.S.A.].*
A tale of the English South Coast (Devon, etc.) and the sea, in the early years of the 19th Century. Smugglers, a French spy, etc.

2267. *SWALLOW BARN: J. P. Kennedy; *Putnam.*
A well-known novel of Virginian life in the early part of the 19th Century.

2268. MARGARET: Sylvester Judd; *Ward, Lock [Eng.], Roberts [U.S.A.].*
An old tale of no little power, depicting New England life in early 19th Century.

2269. *FRENCHMEN'S CREEK: A. T. Quiller-Couch (in "Shakespeare's Christmas; and Other Stories"—*Dent [Eng.], Smith, Elder [Eng.], Longmans [U.S.A.].*
A short story of Falmouth district about the first decade of the 19th Century.

2270. *YE SEXES GIVE EAR! A. T. Quiller-Couch (in "Shakespeare's Christmas; and Other Stories")—*Dent [Eng.], Smith, Elder [Eng.], Longmans [U.S.A.].*
Another short tale of Western England (Plymouth and Saltash) in the same period as the author's story given above.

2271. *THE GRANDISSIMES: George W. Cable; *Hodder & Stoughton [Eng.], Scribner [U.S.A.].*
New Orleans in early 19th Century. One of the author's vivid depictions of Creole life.

2272. *EL OMBÚ: W. H. Hudson; *Duckworth.*
"El Ombú" is used as the collective title of four short stories, but properly it is the title of the first and longest story only. This last-named novelette of the southern pampas of Buenos Ayres, touches History in a very slight degree; it is, however (the author tells us) "mostly a true story." At the beginning of the *narrative* (for it is an old gaucho's tale), the reader catches a mere glimpse of the army under Lieut-General Whitelocke, during the English invasion of Argentina in 1807; there are, also, a few references to historic personages. But the value of the story lies in its literary quality, and in vivid presentment of fearful crime and tragedy. The period covered is considerable —the narrative passing from the English invasion year to a much later time.

2273. A LAD OF KENT: Herbert Harrison; *Juv. Macmillan.*
Canterbury region, 1808. The story of a lad who goes through various experiences of a thrilling nature. Smuggling, sheepstealing, the Press-Gang, etc.

2274. COUSIN HUGH: "Theo. Douglas"; *Methuen.*
English South Coast, c. 1809. Traffic in the escape of French prisoners, and the importation of false coin, etc.

2275. *THE WESTCOTES: A. T. Quiller-Couch; *Dent [Eng.], Arrowsmith [Eng.], Coates [U.S.A.].*
Chiefly South Somerset, with a glimpse of Prince Town, Devon, 1810-11. A story of much humour and interest, illustrating the later Napoleonic time when the conduct and general bearing of French prisoners on *parole*, were questions of some importance in the West Country.

2276. *SHIRLEY: Charlotte Brontë; *Dent [Eng.], Dutton [U.S.A.], and other publishers.*
Yorkshire in the time of the Luddite troubles. This novel, with its fine character depiction and good local colour, is generally considered one of Charlotte Brontë's best examples—if not the best of all.

2277. *FOREST FOLK: "James Prior"; *Heinemann [Eng.], Dodd, Mead [U.S.A.].*
Nottinghamshire in the Luddite period. A novel of outstanding merit, descriptively and analytically. The author (his real name was James Prior Kirk) has been called "the literary interpreter of Nottinghamshire," while a critic of distinction has pronounced his books to be "a permanent contribution to literature."

2278. *IN THE YEAR '13 (*UT DE FRANZOSENTI'D*): Fritz Reuter (trans.); *Sampson Low [Eng.], Munro [U.S.A.].*
One of the famous German humorist's later novels, illustrating Mecklenburg life during the French occupation.

2279. TWO MEN O' MENDIP: Walter Raymond; *Longmans [Eng.], Doubleday [U.S.A.].*
Rustic life in the Cheddar district, 1813. One of the author's excellent Somersetshire tales.

2280. *POISON ISLAND: A. T. Quiller-Couch; *Dent, [Eng.], Smith, Elder [Eng.], Scribner [U.S.A.].*
Cornwall (Falmouth) and the West Indies, 1813-14. West Country life and manners in two-thirds of the story, then a treasure-hunt in the West Indies.

2281. *OUR MR. DORMER: R. H. Mottram; *Chatto & Windus [Eng.], Dial Press [U.S.A.].*
Eastern England, 1813-1920. Life in a county town, as exemplified in the hundred years' history of certain families connected with a Quaker Banking Establishment. Altogether a novel of exceptional power and interest.

2282. *PRIDE AND PREJUDICE:
    *EMMA:
    *PERSUASION: Jane Austen; *Macmillan, and other publishers —English and American.*
English Provincial Society at the beginning of the 19th Century. These three disconnected books (indeed all Miss Austen's tales) vividly reflect the life and ways of the period. They exhibit a power of microscopic observation, as well as a sense of humour that in its quiet way has never been excelled. One sometimes encounters people who are unable to recognise any charm or interest whatever in Jane Austen; they are to be pitied, for the admission shows either lack of perspective, or lack of humour. It is perfectly true that the outlook implied in these stories is a very limited one, but we may sometimes learn from the microcosm what the macrocosm has failed to convey to us.

2283. (1) THE BROAD HIGHWAY:
(2) THE AMATEUR GENTLEMAN:
(3) THE LORING MYSTERY:
(4) THE HIGH ADVENTURE: JEFFERY FARNOL; *Sampson Low* [*Eng.*], *Little, Brown* [*U.S.A.*].
Four novels of Regency Days, all framed somewhat after the picaresque model of an earlier literary period.
(1) The first novel of the author, and one which may still be classed among his best examples. The scenes are in Kent (Sevenoaks and Tonbridge regions): a rattling love and adventure story, telling of coach and highway, and presenting typical figures of the time, such as buck, or pugilist, or " Peninsular " soldier.
(2) Kent again (largely) and London: a young Kentish man's experiences in the fashionable world after coming in for a fortune; also his love affair.
(3) This is a tale dealing with a murder, etc., and having its scenes in Sussex.
(4) Another story of South-East England, in which conspiracy, adventure, and prize-fighting are important elements.

2284. *THE BLACK PROPHET: WILLIAM CARLETON; *Lawrence & Bullen* [*Eng.*], *Sadleir* [*U.S.A.*].
One of Carleton's best novels. Ireland in the terrible year of 1817, when the fever epidemic and the famine were at their worst. The condition of the Irish people at this time, is described in graphic manner.

2285. *TRAITS AND STORIES OF THE IRISH PEASANTRY: WILLIAM CARLETON; *Dent* [*Eng.*], *Macmillan* [*U.S.A.*], *and other publishers*.
Irish Peasant Life in the first quarter of the 19th Century. A wonderfully impressive and vivid depiction, occasionally marred (some critics aver) by unsympathetic treatment of the Catholic clergy. Carleton was born in Co. Tyrone of peasant birth—his father being a tenant farmer; developing literary tastes, he took to journalism and authorship.

2286. *FAITH TRESILION: EDEN PHILLPOTTS; *Ward, Lock* [*Eng.*], *Macmillan* [*U.S.A.*].
Cornwall about the second decade of the 19th Century. A story of smugglers, etc.

2287. LORDS OF THE NORTH: AGNES C. LAUT; *Heinemann*.
Canada about the second decade of the 19th Century. A story illustrating the struggle between the Hudson Bay Company and the North-West Company: time of Lord Selkirk's Red River Settlement.

2288. THE BRONZE COLLAR: JOHN FREDERICK; *Putnam*.
A striking romance of Spanish California in 1818. A French soldier and an English nobleman figure largely in the tale.

2289. (1)*SO SPEED WE:
(2)*THE TRUSTY SERVANT:
(3)*THE ROMAN WAY:
(4)*THE HONEST LAWYER:
(5)*MAUMBERY RINGS:
(6)*THE PREVENTIVE MAN:
(7)*SHERIFF'S DEPUTY:
(8)*THE TURNING SWORD: G. V. McFADDEN; 1-4 *Lane*, 5, *Hodder & Stoughton* [*Eng.*], *Doran* [*U.S.A.*], 6-8, *Lane*.
These excellent novels of Dorsetshire are placed together, because, although not fictionally connected, they cover in the aggregate the period between 1810 and 1835 (roughly).
(1) A story of social life in Dorsetshire (Sherborne and Shaftesbury district) in the early 19th Century days of coaching and hard-drinking, etc.

(2) A particularly interesting novel of the Wool and Dorchester regions, depicting life in the Regency period.

(3) Another interesting tale of the Dorchester district, beginning 1797, but mainly dealing with the supposed events of twenty years later. Good local colour.

(4) A novel of Wareham and Dorchester, about the third decade of the 19th Century.

(5) Dorchester region yet again: a story told round a horse-stealing episode in the time of George IV.

(6) Dorsetshire coast, 1829. Smuggling, and the tracing of a murder, with some excellent character-drawing and good local colour.

(7) Dorchester and neighbourhood: a romance dealing with the time of the Machinery Riots.

(8) Essentially a novel of character depiction and love—the Poole of 1833 being the locality.

2290. *SILAS MARNER: "GEORGE ELIOT"; *Blackwood* [*Eng.*], *Dent* [*Eng.*], *Lippincott* [*U.S.A.*], *Dutton* [*U.S.A.*], *and other publishers.*
North Warwickshire about the year 1820. A small yet "great" book, presenting an imaginative re-creation of English rural life and manners at the end of George III's reign.

2291. MERVYN CLITHEROE: W. HARRISON AINSWORTH; *Routledge* [*Eng.*], *Dutton* [*U.S.A.*].
A novel of Manchester about 1820. Mainly of interest as furnishing some good local colour.

2292. ALL FOOLS TOGETHER: CHARLES E. FORREST; *Collins.*
English rural life (Eastern Counties) round about the year 1820: poaching, politics, etc.

2293. *THE APPRENTICE: MAUD STEPNEY RAWSON; *Hutchinson.*
Sussex (Rye) and Kent, in the short period between George III's death and the coronation of George IV. A good example of Mrs. Rawson's "local-colour" fiction of the semi-historical type. In the development of the story, considerable prominence is given to the controversy between advocates of a new harbour for Rye on the neighbouring Marsh (with a view to reviving the town's ancient importance as a seaport), and those favouring agricultural schemes of reclamation.

2294. CLAD IN PURPLE MIST: CATHERINE DODD; *Jarrolds.*
Isle of Man (mainly), Liverpool, and Australia, between 1820 and 1840. A story of Middle Class life.

2295. MADAME DELPHINE: GEORGE W. CABLE (in "Old Creole Days")—*Hodder & Stoughton* [*Eng.*], *Scribner* [*U.S.A.*].
New Orleans, 1821-22. A good and fairly long story of Creole life.

2296. THE CAPTAIN OF THE WATERGUARD: E. E. COWPER; *Juv. Sheldon Press* [*Eng.*], *Macmillan* [*U.S.A.*].
Cornwall, 1822. Smugglers and the Preventive Waterguard for the district. A tale of love and adventure.

2297. *LAVENGRO:
*THE ROMANY RYE (*sequel*): GEORGE BORROW; *Dent* [*Eng.*], *Dutton* [*U.S.A.*], *and other publishers.*
Semi-romances describing a wanderer's experiences and impressions (Gipsy life) within the first quarter of the 19th Century. In at least the opening part of "Lavengro," the author depicts his own early days, and, in this connection, it has been well said that his narrative "bears the same relation to autobiography as the historical novel bears to history."

2298. A HUNGARIAN NABOB: Maurus Jókai (trans.); *Jarrold*
[*Eng.*], *Doubleday* [*U.S.A.*].
Hungary in 1822. A novel of atmosphere and of provincial life generally.

2299. *GÖSTA BERLING'S SAGA: Selma Lagerlöf (trans.);
Oxford University Press [*Eng.*], *American Scandinavian Foundation*
[*U.S.A.*].
This unmistakably powerful, if somewhat fanciful, Swedish novel depicts life in a
region described as " towards the forests of Finland," about 1820 onwards.

2300. SIR WATERLOO: Alfred E. Carey; *Selwyn & Blount.*
Sussex and London in the 'Twenties and 'Thirties of the 19th Century. A story of
early railway development and life generally in the period of George Canning, Catholic
Emancipation, etc., ending 1837.

2301. *PETER SIMPLE: Captain Frederick Marryat; *Dent* [*Eng.*],
Dutton [*U.S.A.*], *and other publishers.*
British naval life about the beginning of the second quarter of the 19th Century.
This book is deemed by many critics the author's best example.

2302. *MR. MIDSHIPMAN EASY: Captain Frederick Marryat;
Dent [*Eng.*], *Dutton* [*U.S.A.*], *and other publishers.*
Another of Marryat's famous tales which, in spite of its distinctly farcical elements,
gives a clear picture of naval life in the early part of the 19th Century.

2303. *THE SEMI-ATTACHED COUPLE: Hon. Emily Eden;
Mathews & Marrot.
A novel first published in 1860, and now reappearing as it well deserves to do. Not
only a clever and amusing story in itself, but one that gives a clear depiction of English
life and manners as exemplified in High Whig circles about the third decade of the
19th Century, when " Bowood " and " Chatsworth " were names of huge import.
Here and there the author's satire has affinities with that of Jane Austen.

2304. *PENDENNIS:
*THE NEWCOMES: William Makepeace Thackeray;
Macmillan [*Eng.*], *Dent* [*Eng.*], *Houghton Mifflin* [*U.S.A.*],
Dutton [*U.S.A.*] *and other publishers.*
These two great works of fiction which are to some extent connected, together cover
the Late Georgian—Early Victorian period, and illustrate manners among the fashionable and well-to-do classes. Various character-types are presented; not only do the
more elaborate depictions remain in the reader's memory, but many of the thumb-nail
portraits are almost equally unforgettable. Both novels introduce figures which are
more or less clearly identifiable with real people, and " Pendennis " has a semi-
autobiographical element.

2305. *THE HISTORY OF AYTHAN WARING: Violet Jacob;
Heinemann [*Eng.*], *Dutton* [*U.S.A.*].
The Welsh Border and River Wye region (Breconshire-Herefordshire) in the third
decade of the 19th Century. A novel of real power, with good character-drawing and
local colour. The trouble over the excise laws towards the end of George IV's reign,
constitutes the slight historical background.

2306. *SCARLET AND BLACK: Marie-Henri Beyle (trans.)
[" De Stendhal "]; *Chatto & Windus* [*Eng.*], *Boni* [*U.S.A.*].
The Besançon and Jura district, 1830. Mainly a psychological study, but reflecting
the politics of the time.

2307. MISTRESS BARBARA CUNLIFFE (MISTRESS BARBARA):
HALLIWELL SUTCLIFFE; *Fisher Unwin* [*Eng.*], *Crowell* [*U.S.A.*].
A story of the Yorkshire Wool Combers in 1830.

2308. TREWERN: R. M. THOMAS; *Fisher Unwin.*
Wales, 1831-34. A Welsh squire with Whig sympathies, and his environment, in the Reform period.

2309. KINGS OF THE MISSOURI: HUGH PENDEXTER; *Bobbs-Merrill* [*U.S.A.*].
St. Louis, etc., 1831. A tale of fur-traders on the Missouri River.

2310. *MIDDLEMARCH: " GEORGE ELIOT "; *Blackwood* [*Eng.*], *Collins* [*Eng.*], *Little, Brown* [*U.S.A.*], *and other publishers.*
Though some readers find this great novel lacking in fictional interest, others maintain that the character-drawing and large mental scope of the book more than atone for any deficiency of plot. It gives a wonderful picture of English provincial middle-class life in the Early 'Thirties, i.e. in the period between the Roman Catholic Relief Bill (1829) and the Great Reform Bill (1832), the social and domestic aspects rather than the political, and touching upon many subjects of general and special interest. It has been too much the fashion of late to decry " George Eliot," but one may venture the surmise that, when many of the popular novels of to-day have passed into permanent oblivion, the book here under notice will be increasingly estimated at its true value.

2311. *FELIX HOLT: " GEORGE ELIOT "; *Blackwood* [*Eng.*], *Dent* [*Eng.*], *Dutton* [*U.S.A.*], *and other publishers.*
Not generally considered one of the author's best examples, though to a few readers it makes special appeal. The novel offers a picture of life in the English Midlands in the year after the Reform Bill of 1832. The early struggles for liberty.

2312. *CONINGSBY: BENJAMIN DISRAELI [Lord Beaconsfield]; *Longmans* [*Eng.*], *Dent* [*Eng.*], *Dutton* [*U.S.A.*].
England in the period 1832-41. A clever political novel, written with the object of presenting Toryism as a popular movement. A great many contemporary figures appear under disguised names (the full " revised key of 1845 " is given at the end of the *Everyman's Library* edition).

2313. *SYBIL: BENJAMIN DISRAELI [Lord Beaconsfield]; *Longmans;* also *Oxford University Press.*
England, 1837-42 (Chartist Days). Deals with labour conditions at the time, and emphasizes the need for a better understanding between rich and poor. This book (like " Coningsby ") is in the first rank of *Political Fiction proper.*

2314. EARLY VICTORIAN (BASSET): " S. G. TALLENTYRE "; *Smith, Elder* [*Eng.*], *Moffat* [*U.S.A.*].
An amusing sketch of English village life in the late 'Thirties.

2315. *LIFE AND ADVENTURES OF MICHAEL ARMSTRONG:
MRS. FRANCES TROLLOPE; *Henry Colburn* [*Eng.*], *1840.*
Lancashire (" Ashleigh "=Ashton-under-Lyne), Derbyshire, and—to a slight extent —Westmorland, in the second quarter of the 19th Century. A novel illustrating the conditions of child-labour in factories. Mrs. Trollope (the mother of the famous Anthony), was a woman of great pluck as well as ability; she originally turned to authorship when her barrister-husband had fallen into serious financial difficulties. Several books of travel, in addition to novels, came from her pen.

U

2316. (1)*TOM BROWN'S SCHOOLDAYS:
(2) TOM BROWN AT OXFORD (*sequel*): THOMAS HUGHES;
*1, Macmillan [Eng.], Dent [Eng.], Dutton [U.S.A.], and other
publishers. 2, Macmillan.*
English Public-School and University life in the late 'Thirties and early 'Forties.
With regard to the first story (one of world-wide fame), the author himself stated:—
" Dr. Arnold is the only portrait "; but this assertion has not prevented investigators
from identifying certain characters with Dean Stanley and other real persons who,
as boys, were educated at Rugby. N.B. Readers are recommended to consult Mr.
Stanley T. Williams' interesting essay—" The Parent of School-Boy Novels," in his
book entitled: *Studies in Victorian Literature* (Allen and Unwin).

2317. *THE STORY OF SUSAN: MRS. HENRY DUDENEY; *Heinemann
[Eng.], Dodd, Mead [U.S.A.].*
Life in a small Sussex market-town in the period 1839-45. An admirable tale, full
of humour and insight.

2318. *HERRIDGE OF REALITY SWAMP: WILLIAM HAY; *Fisher
Unwin.*
Australia in the early 'Thirties. A powerful story of Convict Life.

2319. *THE ESCAPE OF THE NOTORIOUS SIR WILLIAM
HEANS: WILLIAM HAY; *Fisher Unwin.*
Tasmania, about 1840-43. Another of the author's vivid romances depicting the
Convict period.

2320. *FOR THE TERM OF HIS NATURAL LIFE: MARCUS
CLARKE; *Macmillan [Eng.], Munro [U.S.A.], and other publishers.*
A novel that may be termed a classic example in the sphere of Colonial Fiction. The
scene is Port Arthur, Tasmania, in the second quarter of the 19th Century, and the
subject—illustrated in a most striking and realistic manner—is the Convict Life of
early days.

2321. JACK THE OUTLAW: J. KEIGHLEY SNOWDEN; *Simpkin.*
Yorkshire (Nidderdale), 1841. Tale of a poacher, reflecting the bad Game Laws
of the time.

2322. MY UNCLE THE CURATE: MARMION W. SAVAGE; *Chapman
& Hall.*
This novel—originally published anonymously in 1849—begins Cambridge, but is
really a story of Ireland (Donegal and Dublin) in the 'Thirties. It well reflects the
politics of the time.

2323. A DAUGHTER OF THE MANSE: " SARAH TYTLER "; *John
Long.*
A good tale of Scottish village life in the 'Thirties and 'Forties (the Disruption of
1843).

2324. THE HOOSIER SCHOOLMASTER: EDWARD EGGLESTON;
Routledge [Eng.], Orange Judd [U.S.A.].
An interesting picture of New England in the 'Thirties. A dialect novel (the " Hoosier
folk-speech ").

2325. *THE DOOMSWOMAN: GERTRUDE ATHERTON; *Lane.*
One of Mrs. Atherton's clever novels of California, depicting the Spanish life of the
'Forties.

2326. *THE GORGEOUS ISLE: GERTRUDE ATHERTON; *Doubleday, Page* [U.S.A.].

A story of life in the island health-resort of Nevis (Leeward group of the West Indies) 1842.

2327. *THE BLITHEDALE ROMANCE: NATHANIEL HAWTHORNE; *Dent* [Eng.], *Dutton* [U.S.A.], *and other publishers.*

A novel based on the Brook Farm socialistic experiment which George Ripley started in 1841 with the assistance of certain fellow-Transcendentalists (Emerson, Margaret Fuller and others). Hawthorne himself joined this group, though hardly as an enthusiast, and the romance partially reflects his experiences; at the same time, the leading figures of the author's imagination do little more than faintly suggest this or that real personage under a veiled name.

2328. CAPTAIN FLY-BY-NIGHT: JOHNSTON McCULLEY; *Jenkins.*

California in the second quarter of the 19th Century (Mexican days). A tale of uprising, adventure, and love.

2329. THE PRODIGAL JUDGE: VAUGHAN KESTER; *Methuen* [Eng.], *Bobbs-Merrill* [U.S.A.].

The Carolinas, Tennessee, etc., in the second quarter of the 19th Century. Reflects bygone conditions, with murder and a slave-insurrection plot as important elements in the story.

2330. *PROBLEMATIC CHARACTERS: *THROUGH NIGHT TO LIGHT (*sequel*): FRIEDRICH SPIELHAGEN (trans.); *Leypoldt & Holt* [U.S.A.] *1869 onwards.*

The second of these two books is the *completion* of the novel rather than a sequel in the ordinary sense. Taking, therefore, the two parts together, they may be described as depicting German social life and political conditions in the Eighteen-Forties, and leading up to the time of the revolutionary disturbances of 1848. Spielhagen's *Problematische Naturen* is the first of several novels by him, dealing with life in Germany from the 'Forties to the 'Eighties; they reflect social movements and politics in successive periods, but are scarcely historical novels in the full sense. They have all—at one time or another—been translated into English.

2331. *CRANFORD: MRS. GASKELL; *Macmillan* [Eng.], *Dent* [Eng.], *Dutton* [U.S.A.], *and other publishers.*

This well-known book presents some delightful fictional sketches of English Provincial Life in the second quarter of the 19th Century. The "Cranford" of the story is, of course, the Cheshire market-town of Knutsford, where Mrs. Gaskell was herself brought up by an aunt.

2332. *DAVID COPPERFIELD: CHARLES DICKENS; *Chapman & Hall* [Eng.], *Dent* [Eng.], *Dutton* [U.S.A.], *and other publishers.*

This universally esteemed novel, though exhibiting many of the author's characteristic touches of humour, may to some extent be taken more seriously than many of his equally famous stories. The reader here finds himself living in a *real* Early-Victorian England —not in a "strange realm situated somewhere between Victorian England and Elfland" (as Mr. J. B. Priestley well puts it). There are some excellent depictions of life and manners among the English Middle Classes in the second quarter of the 19th Century.

2333. *MARY BARTON: MRS. GASKELL; *Dent* [Eng.], *Dutton* [U.S.A.], *and other publishers.*

Mrs. Gaskell's knowledge of locality, and her clear appreciation of the general conditions under which men and women worked in the factories of the early Victorian period, are strikingly exemplified in this novel of Manchester. A really moving story.

2334. *ALTON LOCKE: Charles Kingsley; *Macmillan* [*Eng.*], *Dent* [*Eng.*], *Dutton* [*U.S.A.*].
England in the Chartist period. This novel depicts sympathetically the position and aims of working-men in the 'Forties. Kingsley associated himself whole-heartedly with the movement known as " Christian Socialism," in which Frederick Denison Maurice took such a leading part; *Alton Locke* was, therefore, the natural expression of his reforming zeal.

2335. *CATHARINE FURZE: W. Hale White ["Mark Rutherford"]; *Hodder & Stoughton* [*Eng.*], *Doran* [*U.S.A.*].
A psychological tale, primarily, but one that conveys a distinctly historical atmosphere. The scene is England (Eastern Midlands) in the Eighteen-Forties, and market-town life at the beginning of Queen Victoria's reign is presented in a manner at once graphic and humorous.

2336. *COUSIN PONS (*LE COUSIN PONS*): Honoré de Balzac (trans.); *Dent* [*Eng.*], *Dutton* [*U.S.A.*].
Paris mostly in the 'Forties. A novel of charm and power, connected with the author's " Cousin Betty " (*La Cousine Bette*) by way of contrast. A mania for collecting bric-à-brac, and musical enthusiasm, are central themes in " Cousin Pons "; but the novel as a whole has the additional interest of conveying to readers the author's intimate sense of atmosphere which unmistakably reveals him as a man belonging to the time he illustrates. It is because of this " contemporary " advantage, that some literary authorities describe the stories of Balzac (also the best examples of our own early writers of fiction in the 18th Century, etc.) as invaluable *historical* novels. Certainly, in the sense indicated, they may be so called, but, seeing that most people define " historical novel " in a less comprehensive manner, it appears the wiser course to place books of the above-mentioned kind under the heading: *Semi-Historical*.

2337. *DEBIT AND CREDIT (*SOLL UND HABEN*): Gustav Freytag (trans.); *Constable* [*Eng.*].
A novel of Silesia and Posen in the Eighteen-Forties. Illustrates business development as well as the general social movement, and depicts the evil conditions giving rise to the troubles of 1848. This realistic example of the well-known 19th Century German author, was generally deemed his greatest literary achievement.

2338. THE WAY OF THE WINEPRESS: W. Riley; *Jenkins*.
Yorkshire (West Riding): a story depicting a small industrial town in early Victorian times.

2339. *JOSEPH VANCE: William De Morgan; *Heinemann* [*Eng.*], *Holt* [*U.S.A.*].
A picture of Victorian life and manners mainly in the period from the 'Forties to the 'Eighties. The first, and perhaps the best, of the author's vivid romances.

2340. *SUSSEX GORSE: Sheila Kaye-Smith; *Nisbet* [*Eng.*], *Knopf* [*U.S.A.*].
An interesting novel of Sussex rural life (farming, etc.). The *Prologue* is dated 1835, but the actual story covers the long period—1840 to 1905. There are many allusions to public events and politicians, almost justifying the book's entry in the properly historical section.

3 41. *CASTLE RICHMOND: Anthony Trollope; *Chapman & Hall*.
A tale of S.W. Ireland in the Eighteen-Forties giving some graphic descriptions of the Irish Famine.

2342. *KNOCKNAGOW: Charles J. Kickham; *Duffy* [*Eng.*], *Benziger* [*U.S.A.*].
Ireland (Tipperary) in mid-19th Century. A character novel illustrating " the power of capricious eviction " by landlords in the period.

2343. *HARD TIMES: Charles Dickens; *Chapman & Hall* [*Eng.*], *Dent* [*Eng.*], *Dutton* [*U.S.A.*], *and other publishers.*
A novel of mid-19th Century England, embodying a protest against the anti-social attitude which at that time was adopted through false views on Political Economy.

2345. *NORTH AND SOUTH: Mrs. Gaskell; *Dent* [*Eng.*], *Dutton* [*U.S.A.*]. *and other publishers.*
The English Industrial Revolution in the 'Fifties: the novel illustrates the contrast between the " manufacturing North " and the " rural South."

2346. *FAR FROM THE MADDING CROWD:
*THE MAYOR OF CASTERBRIDGE: Thomas Hardy: *Macmillan.*
Two of the most widely-read and valued novels in Hardy's famous Wessex series, each in turn offering a vivid depiction of Dorsetshire and its agricultural interests in the middle of the 19th Century. Besides emphasizing human aspects, they exhibit in marked degree that poetic sense of Nature which is peculiar to the author's genius. The identification of the novelist's disguised place-names is quite superfluous here, seeing that so many books and magazine articles have dealt fully with the subject. " Casterbridge," at any rate, cannot need any key among those who read standard fiction at all!

2347. *BEAUCHAMP'S CAREER: George Meredith; *Constable* [*Eng.*], *Scribner* [*U.S.A.*].
One of the author's best novels, reflecting English Radicalism about the middle of the 19th Century. Meredith never drew a more attractive figure than that presented in the hero of this fascinating, if somewhat tragic, romance.

2348. *IT IS NEVER TOO LATE TO MEND: Charles Reade; *Chatto & Windus* [*Eng.*], *Collins* [*Eng.*], *Scribner* [*U.S.A.*].
England and Australia, mid-19th Century. A famous " novel of purpose," dealing first of all with Convict Life, and exposing the brutality in the gaols of the period; also giving a picture of life in the districts of the new Australian goldfields.

2349. *THE RECOLLECTIONS OF GEOFFREY HAMLYN: Henry Kingsley; *Dent* [*Eng.*], *Collins* [*Eng.*], *Dutton* [*U.S.A.*].
England and Australia. A novel chiefly illustrating life in the Australian Bush region about the middle of the 19th Century. Generally deemed one of the author's best examples.

2350. *ROBBERY UNDER ARMS: " Rolf Boldrewood "; *Macmillan.*
A very interesting adventure-story of Australia about the middle of the 19th Century. The book has long taken high place in Australian literature.

2351. THE SCARLET MASK: Charles Rodda; *Nelson.*
Australia in early days: the story of a bushranger, supposed to be told by himself.

2352. THE COASTLANDERS: Bernard Cronin; *Hodder & Stoughton.*
Life in Tasmania, about the middle of the 19th Century. The opposition of older settlers to new ways and general development.

2353. (1)*BARCHESTER TOWERS:
(2)*DR. THORNE: Anthony Trollope;   Bell [Eng.], Dent
[Eng.], Dutton [U.S.A.], and other publishers.
Two of the most interesting novels in Trollope's famous Barsetshire Series. This
limited selection must not be taken as meaning that readers with ample time should
be satisfied with the two stories here given (*such* readers ought to begin with " The
Warden " and only rest satisfied when " The Last Chronicle of Barset " has been
thoroughly digested).

(1) This second story of the Series is one indicating great humour and powers of
observation, besides admirably illustrating life in an English Cathedral City during the
mid-19th Century period. There is no searching character-analysis in the book, and
life on its highest and lowest sides is barely touched, but we find here—as in all the
author's best novels—a naturalness and ease of presentment that convey to the reader
an impression of *real life*. Here and there one encounters fictional exaggeration, but
that defect is the exception.

(2) Perhaps the most delightful tale of the whole series. The tendency to " exaggeration " to which allusion was made above (in the case of " Barchester Towers "), is
here entirely absent, and we seem throughout the story to be veritably living in that
environment of High County-Family exclusiveness so specially indicative of Early-
Victorian days. This historical aspect is what has to be emphasised in the present
note, but one cannot refrain from alluding to " Mary Thorne "—surely one of the
most charming heroines in the whole range of English Fiction.

2354. SUNNINGWELL: F. Warre Cornish;   Constable [Eng.], Dutton
[U.S.A.].
A well-written story, or, rather, series of fictional sketches, dealing with mid-19th
Century Church matters—" High Church " and " Broad Church." Shows knowledge
and humour.

2355. *HARD CASH: Charles Reade;   Chatto & Windus [Eng.],
Collins [Eng.], Dana Estes [U.S.A.].
English manners and ways (Oxford, Henley Regatta, etc.), about the middle of the
19th Century. Besides the considerable financial element, there are some nautical
adventures and glimpses of foreign parts; but the novel has one dominating idea or
purpose—that of so illustrating the evils then connected with private asylums as to
expedite measures of reform.

2356. *LITTLE WOMEN: Louisa M. Alcott;   Juv. Dent [Eng.],
Dutton [U.S.A.], and other publishers.
New England, c. 1850. A world-famous story of young American life in mid-19th
Century. Certain characters are said to be based on real people (Miss Alcott's own
grandfather, etc.). Though here marked " *juvenile*," the tale is one which makes appeal
to the grown-ups as well as to the young. Altogether a masterpiece in its own
unpretentious line of imaginative writing.

2357. *UNCLE TOM'S CABIN: Mrs. Harriet Beecher Stowe;
(Dent [Eng.], Dutton [U.S.A.] and numerous other publishers—
English and American.
The slave-trade in North America (States) c. 1850. A book which—no matter what
the doubts cast in some quarters upon either its historical veracity or its literary merits
—must always be granted an important position in the records of mid-19th Century
authorship. After appearing serially in a newspaper, it was first published in volume
form at Boston 1852, when it immediately caught the popular taste, and was sold in
America alone to the extent of half a million copies; in England, also, the sales of the
book were enormous, while translations appeared in various languages. The political
influences of the story were acknowledged as having been of the first importance, notably
by the great Lincoln himself.

2358. THE SPLENDID ROAD: Virginia Roe;   Cassell.
Valley of the Sacramento, California, 1850-52. A tale of the pioneers, and the Great
Road running between Oregon and California (the Oregon Trail). The time is that
of the gold diggings. There is some good descriptive writing on the topographical
side.

2359. *THE LUCK OF ROARING CAMP AND OTHER SKETCHES: Bret Harte; *Dent* [*Eng.*], *Dutton* [*U.S.A.*], *and numerous other publishers.*
Justly celebrated tales, giving a wonderfully vivid picture of Californian Mining Life in the Eighteen-Fifties.

2360. *A KENTUCKY CARDINAL:
*AFTERMATH (*sequel*): James Lane Allen; *Macmillan.*
Two of the well-known author's most popular stories (both have been illustrated by Hugh Thomson): they reflect life and manners in Kentucky, 1850.

2361. OLDFIELD: Nancy H. Banks; *Macmillan.*
Another good tale of mid-19th Century Kentucky. Life in a small town.

2362. CUDJO'S CAVE: J. T. Trowbridge; *Juv. Lee & Shepard* [*U.S.A.*].
An interesting tale of Tennessee and the Slavery Question, round about 1860.

2363. *ISABEL STIRLING: Evelyn Schuyler Schaeffer; *Nash* [*Eng.*], *Scribner* [*U.S.A.*].
New England, Arizona, etc., between the 'Fifties and the 'Seventies. The widening of religious ideas illustrated in a woman's life-history.

2364. KATRINA: A TALE OF THE KAROO: Anna Howarth; *Smith, Elder.*
South Africa at the time of the great smallpox epidemic, 1859.

2365. *SAÏD, THE FISHERMAN: Marmaduke Pickthall; *Methuen* [*Eng.*], *Doubleday* [*U.S.A.*].
An adventure story illustrating Muslim life and character from the early 'Sixties onwards (Damascus, etc.). The author's unusual knowledge of the East, which this book so clearly indicates, has been confirmed by his later imaginative productions.

2366. *TATTLEFOLD: Lawrence Pilkington; *Warne.*
A Lancashire Colliery Village in the third quarter of the 19th Century. The tale admirably illustrates the manner in which new ideas and methods in industrialism and politics, were coming to the fore in the mid-Victorian period; it also reflects the widening of religious thought. There is good character-drawing and much quiet humour.

2367. *UNCLE PIPER OF PIPER'S HILL: "Tasma" [Jessie C. Couvreur]; *Trübner, 1888.*
Victoria (near Melbourne) in the third quarter of the 19th Century. An excellent novel of Australian life in the period named.

2368. *THE PLEASANT WAYS OF ST. MÉDARD: Grace King; *Constable* [*Eng.*], *Holt* [*U.S.A.*].
A particularly good story of New Orleans, 1865, illustrating the conditions just after the Civil War.

2369. (1)*THE CALIFORNIANS:
(2)*AMERICAN WIVES AND ENGLISH HUSBANDS:
(3)*DORMANT FIRES (SLEEPING FIRES): Gertrude Atherton; *1, Lane, 2, Service* [*Eng.*], *Dodd, Mead* [*U.S.A.*], *3, Murray* [*Eng.*], *Stockes* [*U.S.A.*].
Three distinct novels in which Mrs. Atherton illustrates Californian Society as it had developed in the second half of the 19th Century. The third book here entered ("Dormant Fires," etc.) is an especially striking tale of social life in the San Francisco of the 'Sixties, though the reader is carried at the end, to the winter of 1878-79.

284 SEMI-HISTORICAL NOVELS AND TALES—continued

2370. THE VOICE OF THE PEOPLE: Ellen Glasgow; *Heinemann* [*Eng.*], *Doubleday* [*U.S.A.*].
A well-written Virginian story of the Reconstruction Period.

2371. *PHINEAS FINN:*
***PHINEAS REDUX* (sequel):** Anthony Trollope; *Bell* [*Eng.*], *Ward, Lock* [*Eng.*], *Dodd, Mead* [*U.S.A.*].
These two closely-connected stories are taken from Trollope's series of Political Novels. They are interesting in themselves, and together form an almost distinct story of the one man Finn, " the Irish Member "; it is true that he appears slightly in the author's later novel, " The Prime Minister," but in this last-named book the central figure (a very attractive one) is the " second Duke of Omnium." The two novels now recommended, deal with a period which one may assume to be the Eighteen-Sixties, and they illustrate, in a general way, *the inner and social side of Politics* rather than the more serious and controversial side. The characters and scenes are typical—not real; accordingly, of political history proper, and of its great mid-Victorian personalities, we do not learn anything explicit in these tales.
Of course, those of us who are lovers of Trollope (and we have the satisfaction of knowing that we form a large company nowadays) cannot rest content with two examples of the series only; and, for the sake of those finding genuine interest in the " Finn " books, it may be well to make bare allusion to the remaining novels. " Can You Forgive Her?" is the first story of all, while—following the two books specially noticed here—we come to " The Prime Minister " (already mentioned), and " The Duke's Children." A sixth novel, " The Eustace Diamonds," is sometimes given under the *Political* heading, but, although having a certain fictional connection, its chief interest may be regarded as isolating it. It is worthy of mention that Mr. Michael Sadleir deems the last book of the group, viz., " The Duke's Children," to be " in some ways the best."

2372. *PICCADILLY*: Lawrence Oliphant; *Blackwood.*
A novel of considerable brilliance, depicting English Society and Politics in the 'Sixties. The book had a great vogue in the years following its first appearance (1870). Oliphant's own career was a varied and somewhat strange one (a good biography of him was written by that versatile Victorian author, Margaret Oliphant).

2373. *THE PRINCE OF LISNOVER*: Grace Rhys; *Methuen.*
A very pleasing fictional treatment of Irish life in the 'Sixties.

2374. *WHEN WE WERE BOYS*: William O'Brien; *Longmans* [*Eng.*], *Maunsel* [*Ireland*].
Ireland about the mid-'Sixties. A novel of recognised force and interest, dealing with the Fenian movement, and showing—as we should expect from the author's personal record—strong Nationalist sympathies.

2375. *THE OLD WIVES' TALE*: Arnold Bennett; *Chapman & Hall* [*Eng.*], *Doran* [*U.S.A.*].
One of the author's finest achievements on the side of imaginative writing—some critics go so far as to rank it above all his other novels. It gives a realistic depiction of life in the English Midlands (Staffordshire), covering the Mid and Late Victorian periods, i.e. from the 'Sixties to the 'Nineties.

2376. A GENTLEMAN ADVENTURER: Marian Keith; *Hodder & Stoughton* [*Eng.*], *Doran* [*U.S.A.*].
Canada (Red River Region) in the Eighteen-Sixties. A tale of adventure, with a Scotsman as hero, illustrating the time just before and during the transfer of land from the Hudson Bay Company to the Dominion. There is some mention of Louis Riel and his rebellion.

2377. *AN INTERNATIONAL EPISODE: Henry James; in
" Daisy Miller, and Other Tales "—*Macmillan.*
New York and Newport in 1874. American life and manners reflected through the
experiences of two young Upper-Class Englishmen visiting the States. A short, but
remarkable, example of the famous author, showing his powers of general observation,
as well as his insight and wit.

2378. *BOY LIFE ON THE PRAIRIE: Hamlin Garland; *Juv.*
Macmillan.
Northern Iowa about the time of the Early 'Seventies. Interesting fictional sketches
illustrating the old methods of haying, harvesting, and threshing, etc.

2379. *A SPOIL OF OFFICE: Hamlin Garland; *Arena Publishing
Co.* [*U.S.A.*].
Iowa, Kansas, and Nebraska region in the 'Seventies An excellent novel, depicting
the Politics of the " Middle West."

2380. *DEMOCRACY: Henry Adams; *Fisher Unwin* [*Eng.*], *Holt*
[*U.S.A.*].
Washington: a depiction of American Politics in the Eighteen-Seventies. The book
appeared first (1880) as an anonymous production, and has been highly estimated as
an example of that somewhat difficult literary method—the imaginative reflection of
the politician's world. Moreover, the novel is essentially one of purpose, furnishing
" an arraignment of the ' Spoils System '."

2381. THROUGH ONE ADMINISTRATION: Mrs. Frances
Hodgson Burnett; *Warne* [*Eng.*], *Osgood* [*U.S.A.*].
Washington and political life about the late 'Seventies—much the same period as
that of Henry Adams' " Democracy " (see above).

2382. *YOUTH RIDES WEST: Will Irwin; *Cape* [*Eng.*], *Knopf*
[*U.S.A.*].
Colorado (the Rocky Mountain region) in the 'Seventies. The novel presents an
excellent picture of a Mining Camp.

2383. *THE VACATION OF THE KELWYNS: William Dean
Howells; *Harper.*
New England life (the Shakers, etc.): " an idyll of the Middle Eighteen-Seventies."

2384. *THE VIRGINIAN: Owen Wister; *Macmillan.*
Wyoming between 1874 and 1890. A story vividly depicting the life of the "real
West " in the period named. The book won for its author an enduring fame.

2385. THE BLAIZED TRAIL:
THE RIVERMAN (*sequel*): Stewart Edward White; *Constable*
[*Eng.*], *McClure* [*U.S.A.*].
Pioneer life in Michigan, late 19th Century. The lumbering business, logging
operations, etc.

2386. *ROBERT ELSMERE: Mrs. Humphry Ward; *Smith, Elder*
[*Eng.*], *Macmillan* [*U.S.A.*].
English intellectual life—especially the influences of the Oxford liberal movement
in religion—about the late 'Seventies to early 'Eighties. Several leading men of that
period suggested to the author the characters of her novel; for instance, the fictional
figure of " Gray " is very largely based on Professor T. H. Green, of Oxford, whose
high character, wide interests, and mental gifts combined to make him a " teacher of
teachers " (this T. H. Green the *philosopher*, must not be confused with his contemporary,
J. R. Green, the *historian*).

2387. *GOD'S FOOL: " Maarten Maartens "; *Constable.*
An original novel of Dutch life (wealthy mercantile circles) in the late 19th Century. On the whole, the most striking example of this once popular novelist. Although a Dutchman, " Maartens " (or, rather, Van der Poorten-Schwarz, to give him his correct name) wrote all his novels in really excellent English.

2388. BLACK JACK DAVY: John M. Oskison; *Appleton.*
Oklahoma, late 19th Century. A story of early pioneers in the Indian Territory. Oklahoma was purchased from the Indians in 1889.

2389. LITTLE HOUSES: George Woden; *Methuen.*
A tale of life in the English West Midlands in the 'Eighties and 'Nineties.

2390. *ORIENTAL ENCOUNTERS: Marmaduke Pickthall; *Collins.*
Palestine and Syria, 1894-96. Fictional impressions of Oriental life and its environment.

2391. THE TRAGEDY OF THE KOROSKO: A. Conan Doyle;
      Smith, Elder [Eng.], Lippincott [U.S.A.].
North Africa (Nubian Nile and the Desert), 1895. An entertaining story, telling of a mixed party of travellers (English, French, and American) on a steamer excursion, and of an attack by Bedouin Arabs.

2392. *THE CATHEDRAL: Hugh Walpole; *Macmillan [Eng.],*
      Doran [U.S.A.].
Life in an English Cathedral-City at the end of the 19th Century (last decade). Writing in a well-known weekly newspaper a few years ago, Mr. Walpole himself alluded to the " Polchester " of this novel as follows:—" Something of Truro is in it, something of Durham, but in truth it is nakedly Polchester and nowhere else at all." Turning to the story as a whole, it is one of genuine power, alike in its analysis of character, and in its *sense of locality and period.* Besides the one outstanding tragedy (so convincingly and impressively presented), there are cleverly-sketched minor tragedies. But, although gloom more or less pervades the book, there are some intensely humorous scenes, while the interest of the reader is continuously maintained up to the final catastrophe.

BIBLIOGRAPHY

BIBLIOGRAPHY

Although I have adopted the heading "Bibliography," it should be understood that, in offering the subjoined list, I do not claim for it absolute comprehensiveness. There are, of course, almost innumerable Biographies, Literary Studies, Histories of Literature and Fiction, etc., in which *indirect* references to our subject may be traced. Moreover, in preparing this volume, it has been found necessary to consult largely "The Dictionary of National Biography," the Encyclopædias (the Britannica, Chambers', etc.), "Appleton's Cyclopædia of American Biography," and other Standard Works of the Dictionary type. I confine myself below to noteworthy writings which deal more or less *directly* with the subject of Historical Romance.

Article on Historical Romance in *The Quarterly Review*. Vol. XXXV., page 518 (March, 1827.)

Article on Historical Romance ("Sir Walter Scott and his Imitators,") in *Fraser's Magazine*. Vol. V., pages 6 (Part I.) and 207 (Part II.). (February and March, 1832.)

Article on "The Picturesque Style of Historical Romance " in *Blackwood's Magazine* Vol. XXXIII., page 621. (April, 1833.)

Article on "Historical Romance in Italy," by G. W. Greene, in *The North American Review*. Vol. XLVI., page 325. (April, 1838.)

Article on Historical Romance in *Blackwood's Magazine*. Vol. LVIII., page 341. (September, 1845.)
   [Afterwards appeared in Vol. III. of Sir Archibald Alison's " Essays."]

Article on Historical Romance, by G. H. Lewes, in *The Westminster Review*. Vol. XLV. page 34. (March, 1846.)

Article on "History in Fiction," in *The Dublin Review*. Vol. XLV., page 328. (December, 1858.)

Lecture III. ("Scott and his Influence ") in David Masson's " British Novelists and their Styles." (Macmillan, 1859.)

Article on "Historical Novels," by H. James, jun., in *The Nation*. Vol. V., page 126. (August 15th, 1867.)

Article on Historical Romance in *The Argosy*. Vol. XVII., page 364. (May, 1874.)

The Historical Sections in the Boston Public Library Catalogue of "English Prose Fiction." (Boston, 1877.)
   [The brief Preface by Justin Winsor has some interesting remarks on the Historical Novel.]

Chapter X. ("The Waverley Novels ") in R. H. Hutton's " Sir Walter Scott." (Macmillan's *English Men of Letters* Series, 1878.)

The Essay on "The Waverley Novels " in Vol. II. of Walter Bagehot's " Literary, Studies." (Longmans, 1879.)

"A descriptive Catalogue of Historical Novels and Tales. For the use of School Libraries and Teachers of History. Enlarged from the List in the 'Journal of Education,' March, 1882." Compiled and described by H. Courthope Bowen, M.A. (Edward Stanford, 1882; and Scribner & Welford, U.S.A., 1884.)

The section on "The Historical Novel," in Bayard Tuckerman's "History of English Prose Fiction." (S. Low & Co.; and G. P. Putnam's Sons, U.S.A., 1882.)

The Essay on "Historical Fiction" in W. F. Allen's "Essays and Monographs." (Geo. H. Ellis, Boston, 1890.)
[An extremely interesting essay by one who was well qualified to treat of the subject.]

Essay VI. ("Alexandre Dumas") in "Essays on French Novelists," by George Saintsbury. (Percival & Co., Eng., 1891; and Scribner, U.S.A.)

The essay on "Sir Walter Scott," in Vol. I. of Leslie Stephen's "Hours in a Library." (Smith, Elder & Co., 1892; and Putnam, U.S.A. New edition, with additions.)
[Sir Leslie Stephen is one of the most formidable critics with whom the lover of Historical Romance has to deal. That which it is possible to say against such fiction is said more forcibly by him, perhaps, than by anyone else.]

Article on "The Historical Novel," by Prof. A. J. Church in *Atalanta* for April, 1893.

The useful and partially-selective lists of Historical Tales given in "The Intermediate Textbook of English History," by C. S. Fearenside and A. Johnson Evans. (W. B. Clive, University Tutorial Press, Ltd., 1893, etc.)

The short selective list of Historical Tales given in the appendix to John Fiske's "History of the United States for Schools." (James Clarke & Co., 1894; and Houghton Mifflin & Co., U.S.A.)

Article on "The Historical Novel as illustrated by Sir Walter Scott," by Edwin Lester Arnold, in *Atalanta* for March, 1894.

The essay on "The Historical Novel" in W. P. James's "Romantic Professions and other papers." (Elkin Mathews and John Lane, 1894.)
[A reprint, in somewhat revised form, of the suggestive article appearing in *Macmillan's Magazine*, November, 1887.]

Chapter X. ("Sir Walter Scott") in Prof. Raleigh's "The English Novel." (John Murray, 1894; and C. Scribner's Sons, U.S.A.)

The essay on "Le Roman Historique" in "La Vie et les Livres" (First Series) by Gaston Deschamps (Armand Colin et Cie, Paris, 1894.)
[A brief survey of certain modern French Novelists as represented in the excellent "Bibliothèque de Romans historiques" (Armand Colin); the introductory remark are suggestive and possess some general interest.]

Chapters X., XI., and XII. in Prof. Saintsbury's "Essays in English Literature, 1780—1860. Second series." (J. M. Dent & Co., 1895; and C. Scribner's Sons, U.S.A.)
[Originally appeared in *Macmillan's Magazine*, August, September, and October, 1894. A contribution to the subject of quite exceptional brilliance and value.]

"A descriptive List of Novels and Tales dealing with the History of North America," by W. M. Griswold. (Cambridge, U.S.A., 1895.)

The Section headed "Historical Tales" in "Guide to the Study of American History,' by E. Channing and A. B. Hart. (Ginn & Co., 1896.)

A Letter on "Historical Novels, Past and Present," by "Mazarin," in *The Bookman* (English), October, 1896.

Article on "The Indian Mutiny in Fiction," in *Blackwood's Magazine*, February, 1897.

Article on "The Importance of Illustrating New England History by a series of Romances," by Rufus Choate, in *The New England Magazine*, November, 1897.
[Reprint—somewhat abridged—of an Address delivered at Salem in 1833. See also the volume "Addresses and Orations" (Little, Brown, & Co., 1878).]

Paper read before the College of Preceptors on " The Use of Historical Romances in
    the Teaching of History," by R. F. Charles, in *The Educational Times*, November,
    1897.

Article on " The American Historical Novel," by Paul Leicester Ford, in *The Atlantic
    Monthly*, December, 1897.
    [In this article a definition of the " Historical Novel " at variance with my own,
has been suggested. In spite of Mr. Ford's argument, I am still of opinion that the
line of demarcation between the Historical Novel proper and the Novel of Character
or Adventure can be more clearly drawn than he allows. I was careful, when dealing
with this question in my Introduction, to avoid making the test one of actual historical
accuracy; but there are, I have implied, certain readily-verifiable personages and events
which form a basis amply sufficient for purposes of distinction. The pirates of " Treasure
Island " are taken (as Mr. Ford says) from actual figures of the 18th Century, but under
my definition Stevenson's novel is not thereby constituted " historical " in the strict
sense.]

Chapter II. (" The Novel—Scott and Miss Austen ") of Book X., and Chapter II.
    (" The Victorian Novel ") of Book XI. in " A Short History of English Literature '
    by George Saintsbury. (Macmillan, 1898.)
    [" Scott created the historical novel after some thousand years of unsuccessful
attempt."]

Article on " The Neo-Romantic Novel," by G. R. Carpenter, in *The Forum*, March, 1898.

Article on " Historical Novels Past and Present," by Harold Frederic, in *The Bookman*
    (American), December, 1898.
                [An admirably-written, stimulating article.]

List of Historical Novels, etc., illustrating the Period 1066 to 1815, in the volume " Work
    and Play in Girls' Schools," by Dorothea Beale, Lucy H. M. Soulsby, and Jane
    Frances Dove. (Longmans, 1898.)

" Le Roman Historique à l'Époque romantique," by Louis Maigron. (Hachette et
    Cie, Paris, 1898.)
                [Contains a fine tribute to Scott, and much interesting matter.]

Chapters III. and IV. of " The Development of the English Novel," by W. L. Cross.
    (Macmillan, 1899.)
    [A very full treatment. In the Appendix are some useful lists of the earlier Historical
Novels.]

Article on " Three American Historical Romances," by W. E. Simonds, in *The Atlantic
    Monthly*, March, 1900.

Article on " The Reading of Historical Novels and the Study of History," by Ada
    Shurmer, in *The Scots Magazine*, April, 1900.

Chapter III. (" The Historical Novel ") in F. H. Stoddard's " The Evolution of the
    English Novel." (Macmillan, 1900.)
                [A highly important contribution.]

The two sections on Historical Fiction, relating to Greece and Rome respectively, in
    Arthur L. Goodrich's " Topics of Greek and Roman History." (Macmillan, 1900).

Article on " Historical Novels and their uses in teaching," by C. S. Fearenside, in *The
    School World*, November, 1900.
    [An exceptionally good article. The writer states his case clearly and forcibly, and
his argument is all the more convincing by reason of its moderation.]

Article on " The New Historical Romances," by W. D. Howells, in *The North American
    Review*, December, 1900.

The Essay on " The Historical Novel " in Prof. J. Brander Matthews' " The Historical
    Novel and other Essays." (C. Scribner's Sons, 1901.)
    [Originally appeared in *The Forum*, September, 1897. Represents that School of
Criticism which is most adverse to Historical Romance. Some of the Professor's remarks
convey the impression that he disbelieves in *any* reconstruction of the Past ; such an
article is, surely, unfavourable to *History itself*, which is always more than any mere
statement of " facts."]

Article on " Great War Novels," by Jane H. Findlater, in *The National Review* for July,
    1901 (also appeared in *The Living Age*, August 24).
[Sienkiewicz, Tolstoy, and Zola compared as representing three different schools—
the Epic, the Emotional, and the Realistic. Incidentally the authoress ably defines
the province of Historical Romance.]

" A History of German Literature," by John G. Robertson.   (William Blackwood &
    Sons, Eng., 1902 ; and Putnam, U.S.A.).

The list of Historical Tales given in J. S. Lindsey's " Certificate Note-Book of European
    History, 1814-1848." (Heffer & Sons, Cambridge, 1902.)

" History of English Romanticism in the Nineteenth Century," by Henry A. Beers.
    (Kegan, Paul, & Co., 1902; and Henry Holt & Co., U.S.A.).
        [Contains some valuable direct criticism. See especially Chapter I.]

Article on " The Novel of American History," by Annie Russell Marble, in *The Dial*
    (Chicago) for the first half of June, 1902.
            [An extremely interesting, well-balanced article.]

Article on " Venice in Recent Fiction," by Louise Closser Hale, in *The Bookman*
    (American) for February, 1903.
[Marion Crawford, Mrs. Turnbull, and Max Pemberton compared. A good plea
for Venetian History as " material."]

Article on " Battles in Fiction," by Eveline C. Godley, in *The National Review* for March,
    1903.
[The authoress knows her subject well; in a brief but distinct survey she takes her
examples from Tolstoy, Erckmann-Chatrian, Zola, etc.]

Studies in German Literature in the Nineteenth Century," by John Firman Coar.
    (Macmillan Co., New York, 1903.)

The useful classified lists of Historical Novels given in J. S. Lindsey's " Problems and
    Exercises in British History," Parts I.—IV.   (Heffer & Sons, Cambridge, 1903-4.)

Article on " History in Fiction," by Philip Sidney in *The Gentleman's Magazine* for
    December, 1903.
[Urges accuracy in Historical groundwork; it is contended that this may be effected
" without wearying the reader with dryasdust . . . information," and " John Inglesant "
is cited as a crowning instance.]

Article on " Maurus Jókai and the Historical Novel," by H. W. V. Temperley, in *The
    Contemporary Review* for July, 1904; also appears in *The Living Age* (Boston, U.S.A)
    of August 13, 1904.

Article on " Mr. Stanley Weyman's Novels," in *The Church Quarterly Review* for January,
    1905.
[Contains a strong plea for Historical Romance in the opening sections.]

Chapter V. (" The Waverley Novels "), Chapter VI. (" Scott's Greatness "), and
    Chapter XIII. (" Charles Reade ") in " The Makers of English Fiction," by W. J.
    Dawson. (Hodder & Stoughton, Eng.; and Revell, U.S.A.)
[Some acute remarks on Historical Romance are to be found in each of the three
chapters specified above.]

Dr. Richard Garnett's *Introduction* in the new edition of " The Household of Sir Thomas
    More," by Anne Manning (De La More Press, 1905).
[A well-balanced estimate of the Historical Novel by one whose knowledge and
literary judgment were really wonderful. This short essay has a special value as
embodying some of a great scholar's reflections at the end of his long life.]

The second edition, " revised and greatly enlarged," of H. Courthope Bowen's " De-
    scriptive Catalogue of Historical Novels and Tales. For the Use of School Libraries
    and Teachers of History." (Stanford, 1905.)
[It is a great pity that, in this later edition of his Catalogue, Mr. Bowen—who was
a pioneer in his own line of Bibliography—did not do more to improve his original work

(published 1882). Apparently ignoring what had been done by others, he allowed glaring mistakes to remain, and his lists as they now stand, are most inaccurate as well as most incomplete. Several well-known romances are *re-entered under their sub-titles* as separate books! Indeed, there can have been no serious attempt at verification in numerous cases.]

" History in Fiction: a Guide to the Best Historical Romances, Sagas, Novels, and Tales," by Ernest A. Baker. Vol. I. English Fiction; Vol. II. American and Foreign Fiction. (Routledge, Eng.; and Dutton, U.S.A., 1907.)
[The author's wide reputation is well sustained by these really excellent lists, which for the most part are fully annotated, and conveniently arranged under Countries. Perhaps it would have been better if the entry of *exact dates* had only been attempted where a book was known at first-hand. On the side of Juvenile Tales, these lists seem to me less satisfactory: the notes, besides being often meagre, are not always reliable, while a great many of the best tales—published before " History in Fiction " was compiled—do not appear at all. A good feature in each volume is the Index.]

Article on " The Growth of the Historical Novel," by Rowland E. Prothero, in *The Quarterly Review* for January, 1907.
[A very valuable contribution. The origin and growth of Historical Fiction are dealt with at considerable length.]

The essay on " A Historical Romance " in John Morley's " Miscellanies, 4th Series." (Macmillan & Co., 1908.)
[Some extremely interesting remarks on Historical Romance in general, as well as on the particular book—Mr. Frederic Harrison's " Theophano "—which occasioned the essay. Appeared first in *The Nineteenth Century* for October, 1904.]

Chapter VI. (" Background ") in " The Technique of the Novel," by Charles F. Horne, Assistant Professor of English in the College of New York City. (Harper & Brothers, 1908.)
[There is a well-written section on " The Historical Novel," in the chapter above-mentioned. I quote one passage: " Historic novels may do far more for history than make it ' pleasant medicine.' They may vivify, they may interpret it, as the sober historian never can."]

Chapter VI. (" Modern Romanticism: Scott ") in " Masters of the English Novel," by Richard Burton, Professor of English Literature in the University of Minnesota. (George Bell & Sons, Eng.; and Henry Holt & Co., U.S.A., 1909.)
[A fair and thoroughly sane estimate of Historical Romance, and of the true relation between " the story of truth and the story of poetry."]

The chapter on " Scott and Romanticism," in Part II. of " A History of Story-telling," by Arthur Ransome. (T. C. & E. C. Jack, Eng.; and F. A. Stokes & Co., U.S.A., 1909.)

The " Introduction " by Arthur James Grant, Professor of History in the University of Leeds, in the volume of " Scott " selections which forms one of the *Masters of Literature Series*. (George Bell & Sons, 1909.)

Part III. (" Sea Stories, Novels," etc.) in " The British Tar in Fact and Fiction," by Charles Napier Robinson, Commander R.N. (Harper, 1909.)

The sections on " Setting in Historical Fiction " and " The Question of Anachronism " in Chapter IV. (" The Study of Prose Fiction ") of William H. Hudson's " Introduction to the Study of Literature." (George G. Harrap & Co., Eng.; and D. C. Heath, U.S.A., 1910.)

" Leading American Novelists," by John Erskine, Ph.D. (Henry Holt & Co., 1910.)

The section on " Creative Art: *Prose Fiction* " in " The Literature of the Victorian Era," by Hugh Walker, LL.D., Professor of English in St. David's College, Lampeter (Cambridge University Press, Eng.; and G. P. Putnam's Sons, U.S.A., 1910).
[Especially interesting and noteworthy, for readers of Historical Romance, are the remarks on Scott and his imitators (pp. 619-621); those on Thackeray (pp. 704-706); those on Reade (pp. 763-765); and those on the Later Fiction (pp. 753-755).]

Article on " The Importance of the Historical Novel," by J. F. Harris, in *The Journal of Education* for August, 1910.
[A forcible plea for the uses of Imaginative Literature in the training of youth.]

The annotated lists of " Historical Novels " and " Stories of Irish Life in the Past," in " A Readers' Guide to Irish Fiction," by Stephen J. Brown, S.J. (Longmans & Co., Eng.; and U.S.A., 1910.)
[Wonderfully comprehensive lists of novels and tales which in some way illustrate Irish life and history. The descriptive notes—often of considerable length—are interesting, and commendably free from bias. Naturally, some of the romances included can hardly attract the non-Irish reader; on the other hand, a few tales of general interest might still be added. The book contains useful notes on authors.]

" Two Centuries of the English Novel," by Harold Williams. (John Murray, 1911.)
[Contains—among other good things—some excellent remarks on Scott's " intuitive, sense for historical atmosphere and situation " (see p. 158).]

" A Guide to British Historical Fiction," by J. A. Buckley and W. T. Williams. (Harrap, 1912.)
[A little book which, within its comparatively narrow limits, is quite excellent.]

" The English Novel," by George Saintsbury in the *Channels of English Literature* series. (J. M. Dent & Sons, Eng.; and E. P. Dutton & Co., U.S.A., 1913.)

" A Guide to Historical Fiction," by Ernest A. Baker, M.A., D.Lit. (Routledge, Eng.; and Macmillan, U.S.A., 1914.)
[Much more than a new edition of the author's " History in Fiction " (1907) which has been already noticed. The present large volume contains an interesting Introduction, and is, taken altogether, a most valuable and useful work of reference. The Index (Authors, Titles, Historical Names, Places, Events, Allusions, etc.) is a special feature. Dr. Baker's " Guide " is undoubtedly the best of all the larger bibliographical works dealing with Historical Fiction which have hitherto been published—being not only superior to those preceding it, but also (apart from the inherent defect of having appeared 14-15 years ago) superior to all later productions. There are, however, not a few serious errors of description, and the criticism with regard to " exact dates "—made in my note upon the author's previous work, " History in Fiction "—must be repeated in the case of the present volume. Again, one may venture the surmise that the extraordinarily full book-lists include a very large number of novels and tales which a literary critic of Dr. Baker's high standing would hardly have admitted in his most catholic mood, had his knowledge of them been direct. In other words, the lists need much sifting.]

The account of English Fiction contemporaneous with the Revolution in France, given in the volume: " The French Revolution and the English Novel," by Allene Gregory, Ph.D. (G. P. Putnam's Sons, New York and London, 1915.)

The two articles on " Irish Historical Fiction," by Stephen J. Brown, S.J., appearing in the September, 1915, and March, 1916, issues of the *Irish Quarterly Review : Studies* (The Educational Co. of Ireland, Dublin.)
[Informative and interesting articles written by a highly-qualified expert.]

" A History of the French Novel to the Close of the 19th Century," by George Saintsbury (Vol. I., Macmillan, 1917; Vol. II., Macmillan, 1919.)

" A History of English Literature," by Arthur Compton-Rickett (T. C. & E. C. Jack, 1918)—especially the section: *Sir Walter Scott—Characteristics of His Work.*

The study of " Charles Reade " in " Studies in Literature," by Sir Arthur Quiller-Couch. (Cambridge University Press, Eng.; and Putnam, U.S.A., 1918.)
[One remark in this study calls for special notice:—" If there must be a first place among historical novels, *The Cloister and the Hearth* and *Esmond* are the great challengers for it."]

" Motives in English Fiction," by Robert Naylor Whiteford. (G. P. Putnam's Sons, New York and London, 1918.)

The lists of Fiction given under the heading: " References " at the end of each chapter, and the " List of Important Books " (Appendix E), in " School History of the United States," by Prof. Albert Bushnell Hart, LL.D. (American Book Company, U.S.A., 1918.)

" Ireland in Fiction: a Guide to Irish novels, tales, romances and folklore," by Stephen
  J. Brown, S.J. (New Edition: Maunsel, Dublin and London, 1919; and Herder,
  U.S.A., 1920.)
  [A greatly improved and enlarged edition of the author's " A Reader's Guide to
Irish Fiction," published in 1910, and already noticed on a previous page. Appendix
C contains a select list of *Irish Historical Fiction*—the descriptive note in the case of each
book appearing in the body of the work. There is, also, a useful bibliography (Appendix
A), as well as—amongst other good features—an Index of Titles and Subjects (Authors,
being arranged alphabetically, are not indexed). For all interested in Irish Fiction,
this work is indispensable.]

The Chapters dealing with Fiction (General and Individual) in " A History of American
  Literature," Vols. I—IV., Edited by W. P. Trent, John Erskine, S. P. Sherman,
  and Carl Van Doren. (Cambridge University Press, Eng.; and G. P. Putnam's
  Sons, U.S.A., 1918-21.)

" Historical Fiction: Chronologically and Historically Related," by James R. Kaye
  Ph.D. (Snowdon Publishing Company, U.S.A., 1920.)
  [This large and handsome volume undoubtedly bears many signs of scholarship and
careful research, but it is questionable whether the method adopted is one calculated
to satisfy either the Teacher of History or the average Reader. The author's aim is
to supply—under topographical and historical headings, as well as in chronological
order—a series of brief historical résumés, with illustrative historical stories (sometimes
annotated, sometimes not) attached. It is hoped that, in this way, " the necessity of
resorting to the historical treatise for the facts " will be obviated. But most intelligent
folk (old and young) who are lovers of historical fiction, will in all probability continue
to supplement their novel-reading by a direct study of this or that standard History;
indeed, where *young people* are concerned, the reading of historical tales is usually
encouraged either for the purpose of *leading them to history proper*, or with a view to *illustrating whatever History Book they may just have been reading.* Turning to the examples of
fiction specified by Dr. Kaye, the somewhat limited selections often strike one as being
quite arbitrary. Why, for instance, is John Buchan's short tale, " The Lemnian,"
given the preference over all his more important early stories? Why, out of the many
inviting examples of a front-rank historical romancist like Sir Arthur Quiller-Couch,
select only *one?* Why specify J. M. Neale's " The Farm of Aptonga," and ignore his
best story of all—" Theodora Phranza "? Why include Miss Yonge's slight production,
" The Constable's Tower," and exclude her two charming tales: " The Dove in the
Eagle's Nest," and " The Chaplet of Pearls "? Why altogether omit such exceptionally
able writers of historical fiction as Neil Munro and Alfred Tresidder Sheppard—
especially when a great many quite inferior novelists have been included? These and
several other questions must occur to lovers of historical romance who consult the
recommendations in this book. Turning to a really satisfactory feature, Dr. Kaye has
carefully indicated the main historical illustration which certain well-known novels
and tales provide; unfortunately, he has been content, in far too many cases, either
with a very brief and indefinite annotation, or with the mere insertion of title and
author without any accompanying note whatsoever. There is a good Index. Publishers'
names are not given in any part of the volume, and novels of an advanced type are
recommended by the side of juvenile tales, without guidance. Some of the short
biographical sketches of authors are very interesting.]

Article on " Historical Novels," by G. P. Gooch, in *The Contemporary Review*, February,
  1920. (No. 650.)
  [An extremely interesting contribution by an historian of established reputation.]

The Chapters dealing with Fiction (General and Individual) in Vol. XII. Second
  Impression, 1920, and Vol. XIII. Second Impression, 1921, of " The Cambridge
  History of English Literature," edited by Sir A. W. Ward and A. R. Waller.
  (Cambridge University Press, Eng.; and G. P. Putnam's Sons, U.S.A.)

Article: " Une Évolution nouvelle du Roman Historique," by Louis Bertrand, in *La
  Revue de Paris*, 15 May, 1921.
  [Suggestive and interesting remarks by one who is himself a distinguished writer of
historical novels.]

" The American Novel." by Carl Van Doren. (Macmillan, 1921.)

" The Tale of Terror: a study of the Gothic Romance," by Edith Birkhead, M.A.
  (Constable, 1921.)

"Contemporary American Novelists 1900-1920," by Carl Van Doren. (Macmillan, 1922.)

"Historical Novels," by Sir C. H. Firth, being Leaflet No. 51 (March, 1922) in the Historical Association's series of leaflets.
[Of unusual interest as stating quite candidly Sir C. H. Firth's own preferences in the region of historical fiction, and also as expressing his view—based on wide experience —with regard to the place of historical novels and tales in the education of the young.]

Article: "History and Fiction," by G. M. Trevelyan, in *The Cornhill Magazine*, May, 1922, and in *The Living Age*, June 3rd, 1922.
[Another very interesting testimony to the value of historical fiction by a well-known historian.]

Article: "The Character of an Historical Novelist," by H. Belloc, in *The London Mercury*, November, 1923 (Vol. IX., No. 49).

"The Political Novel: its development in England and in America," by Morris Edmund Speare. (Oxford University Press, Eng. and U.S.A., 1924.)

The essay entitled: "A Romantic Novelist (Jane Porter)" in the volume: "These Were Muses," by Mona Wilson. (Sidgwick & Jackson, 1924.)

The very brief, but valuable, remarks on historical fiction in "The English Novel of To-day," by Gerald Gould. (John Castle, London, 1924.)

Chapter II. "The Waverley Novels" (especially Section IV.), in "Sir Walter Scott," by Dr. Oliver Elton (Edward Arnold, 1924)—the whole essay consisting of two chapters, and a portion of another, revised for separate issue, from the writer's *Survey of Literature, 1780-1830*. (Edward Arnold, Eng., and Longmead, U.S.A.)

"The Historical Novel: an Essay," by H. Butterfield. (Cambridge University Press, Eng.; and Macmillan Co., U.S.A., 1924.)
[The Le Bas Prize Essay for 1923. An able and useful contribution to the study of the subject.]

The various lists of historical tales in Books III., IV. and V. of "The Grip-Fast History Books"—being books on British History "for use in Catholic Schools." (Longmans, Green & Co., 1924-25.)

The remarks on Scott and other more recent writers of historical romance in "A Century of the English Novel," by Cornelius Weygandt. (Brentano's, Eng.; and Century Co., U.S.A., 1925.)

"The Cowboy and His Interpreters," by Douglas Branch. (Appleton, 1926.)

The section: "General Fiction" (in Chapter XI.), and the section: "Historical Narratives" (in Chapter XIII.), appearing in "Children's Reading: a Guide for Parents and Teachers," by Lewis M. Terman, Ph.D., and Margaret Lima, M.A. (D. Appleton & Company, N. York and London, 1926.)
[Unpretentious, but useful, lists (briefly annotated), giving some of the best historical tales which are suitable for children. Against each book is entered the age at which it may be read most profitably ("12-14," "9-12," etc., etc.). Best books are starred. The author's name, the title of the book, the American publisher's name, and the American price are all given. The volume has an Author Index and a Title Index.]

"The Story of the World's Literature," by John Macy. (George G. Harrap & Co., Eng.; and Boni & Liveright, U.S.A., 1927.)

"The Light Reading of Our Ancestors: Chapters in the Growth of the English Novel," by Lord Ernle. (Hutchinson, 1927.)
[On page 286 of this volume will be found the following passage:—"In spite of its absurdities, *The Castle of Otranto* (1764-5) was the real starting-point of the English historical novel. As burlesques contained the germ of modern novels of real life, so the seed of modern historical romance was sown in a work of serious trifling."]

" Historical Fiction suitable for Junior and Senior High Schools," compiled by Hannah Logasa, University of Chicago High School. With an Introduction by A. F. Barnard, University of Chicago High School (Philadelphia: McKinley Publishing Company, February, 1927)—being No. 1 of the Publications of the National Council for the Social Studies.

[A noteworthy feature in this booklet is the Introduction—" The Historical Novel: Comments on Its Use in Schools," which contains some interesting remarks likely to prove helpful to school-teachers and educationists. It must be confessed, however, that Mr. Barnard's assertion that the lists of novels and tales are " carefully prepared," is hardly borne out by an examination of them, since many of the very brief descriptive notes (especially the attempts at exact dating) appear to show either carelessness or second-hand knowledge. To take a few examples relating to well-known books and authors only. D. P. Thompson's " The Green Mountain Boys " is described as dealing with " the Capture of Ticonderoga and Burgoyne's invasion, 1775-77 "; now, this famous old American romance *deals in the second part only with the Revolutionary War*, the whole of the first part illustrating the land controversy (" New Hampshire Grants ") in the seven years before the Revolution. Again, Mary Johnston's " Lewis Rand " is dated " 1800-06," the correct dates being *1790, then 1804 to 1808*. In the case of Mary Dillon's " The Patience of John Morland," the novel is dated: " 1830-50," when *the authoress herself* has definitely stated (at the beginning of the volume) that the time is " the third decade of the last century," i.e. 1820-30. Turning to history other than American, there is similar misdating. Stanley Weyman's " The Abbess of Vlaye " should be: *The Year 1595*—not " 1589—1610." Again, Mrs. Craik's " John Halifax, Gentleman " should be dated 1794-1834, instead of the misleading " 1798-1815." George Macdonald's " St. George and St. Michael " is strangely dated " 1649," when the whole story covers events *between 1641 and 1646*. Mary Johnston's " Foes " (*The Laird of Glenfernie* in England) is dated: " 1714-19," instead of *about 1735-50*, and described with singular infelicity and inaccuracy: " Stuart tyranny in Scotland. Fight for James Stuart "—the romance actually dealing with the *period* of the '45 Rebellion. Worse still, John Buchan's " Midwinter "—a Jacobite tale of 1745 introducing Dr. Johnson as a young man—is described: " Wars of the Roses, 1455-85 "; while Marion Crawford's novel depicting the events of some *hours'* duration in 1574 (" In the Palace of the King ") is made to cover the lengthy period " 1556-98 "! Many other examples of inaccuracy could be given, but these must suffice. It is quite true that other bibliographies of Historical Fiction show similar errors of description, but in this special case, *where the expectation of accuracy is raised by the fact of the book's issue under high educational authority*, much more than the usual care over verification should have been taken. It may be added that the book—regarded as a selective catalogue presenting authors and titles under a few general headings—is useful and good, though some of the inclusions and exclusions are surprising; where the compilation seriously fails is in the insufficiency and unreliability of its annotations.]

The List of " British Historical Fiction," compiled by Jonathan Nield, and approved by the National Home Reading Union, in *The Reader*, July, 1927 (Vol. II, No. 10).

The leading article on " Dumas: History and Romance," in *The Times Literary Supplement*, September 1st, 1927.

The leading article: " What is Truth? " by Henry Seidel Canby in *The Saturday Review of Literature* (New York), December 31st, 1927.

[This lengthy article—in some degree a review of Feuchtwanger's " The Ugly Duchess "—is primarily a most interesting examination of the motives underlying the older and the newer types of Historical Fiction. Beginning with a reference to Sir Walter Scott (the true father of the modern historical novel), and alluding to his romantic standpoint as that of one who " saw the Middle Ages in a golden haze," Dr. Canby proceeds to a comparison between Hewlett and Feuchtwanger: the former regarded the past as revealing " a conflict of nobility with barbarous instincts "—the latter regards it as presenting " a stew of politics, sensuality, greed, and stupidity." These differences of attitude arise through one author having written at the end of last century, and the other in the Nineteen-Twenties. In " Richard Yea-and-Nay " and in " The Ugly Duchess " each author reflects—as he must—the special influences of his own time (" each age does best what most interests it "); and yet there is, in these recent books of Feuchtwanger, " the same fabric of historical romance that Hewlett worked over, only with different threads uppermost and a different design. Each view is implied in the work of the other, but apparently you cannot get both in one. . . . The material world of Feuchtwanger and the moral world of Hewlett (or Shakespeare for that matter) will not coalesce. But there is only one world, one human society. Hence neither book is true altogether, and both must be read, which is the argument of this essay."]

NOTE.—*It is interesting to see what Novelists themselves have said on the subject of Historical Romance, and in this connection I would specially refer to the Dedicatory Epistle in Scott's " Ivanhoe," the very brief but exceedingly suggestive opening section in Chapter I. of Reade's " The Cloister and the Hearth," the Preface to Scheffel's " Ekkehard," Maurice Hewlett's excellent Introduction to Miss Bidder's tale " In the Shadow of the Crown," and Miss Yonge's Preface to her own " The Chaplet of Pearls." Quite recently, J. Schlumberger has offered some wise remarks on historical fiction in the Preface to his clever book : " Le Lion Devenu Vieux." Lastly, although one can hardly class Wilkie Collins among those authors who have succeeded in revivifying the Past, the Preface to his " Antonina " shows an acute perception as to the best method of blending imagination and history.*

INDEX OF AUTHORS AND TITLES

INDEX OF AUTHORS AND TITLES

The numbers refer to the items, not to the page.

NOTE.—The Birth and Death dates of Authors have been given where possible. It should be noted that the book-dates refer to *original* publication. Translation dates are ignored, but with regard to a few books it has been found necessary to rest content with the approximate date of issue.

A

Y

C

CHESSON, Nora
442   Father Felix's Chronicles (1907)
CHESTERMAN, Hugh, b. 1884
954   In England Once (1926)
CHURCH, Rev. Alfred John, 1829-1912
41   Patriot and Hero (formerly *The Hammer*) (1890)
45   Lords of the World (1898)
49   Two Thousand Years Ago (Lucius) (1886)
87   The Burning of Rome (1892)
106   To the Lions (1889)
CHURCH, Rev. A. J. and Ruth Putnam
147   The Count of the Saxon Shore (1887)
CHURCH, Samuel Harden, b. 1858
973   John Marmaduke (1889)
1003   Penruddock of the White Lambs (1903)
CHURCHILL, Winston, b. 1871
1496   Richard Carvel (1899)
1528   The Crossing (1903)
1950   Coniston (1906)
2002   The Crisis (1901)
" CLARE, Austin " (Miss W. M. James)
734   Court Cards (1874)
CLARÉTIE, Léo, b. 1862
890   Cadet-La-Perle (1908)
CLARKE, Allen
1922   "The Men Who Fought for Us " in the " Hungry Forties " (1914)
CLARKE, Mrs. Henry
552   A Trusty Rebel (1905)
CLARKE, Marcus (1846-1881)
2320   For the Term of His Natural Life (1874)
COBB, James F.
2074   In Time of War (originally " Workman and Soldier ") (1880)
COBBOLD, Richard, 1797-1877
1646   The History of Margaret Catchpole (1845)
COLERIDGE, Christabel R.
389   Minstrel Dick (1896)
COLERIDGE, Hon. Gilbert J. D., b. 1859, and Marion (*née* Darrock)
739   Jan Van Elselo (1902)
COLERIDGE, Mary Elizabeth, 1861-1907
1492   The King with Two Faces (1897)
1909   The Fiery Dawn (1901)
COLLIGAN, I. Hay
1036   A Border Yeoman (1922)
" COLLINGWOOD, Harry " (William J. C. Lancaster)
686   Two Gallant Sons of Devon (1913)
2125   The Cruise of the Thetis (1910)
COLLINGWOOD, W. G., b. 1854
178   The Likeness of King Elfwald (1917)
195   Thorstein of the Mere (1895)
COLLINS, Wilkie, 1824-1889
146   Antonina (1850)
COLUM, Padraic
2091   Castle Conquer (1923)
COMPTON, Herbert
1858   The Queen Can Do No Wrong (1903)
2259   The Inimitable Mrs. Massingham (1900)
COMSTOCK, Harriet T.
641   The Girlhood of Queen Elizabeth (1914)
730   The Queen's Hostage (1906)
CONRAD, Joseph, 1857-1924
Tales of Hearsay (1925):—
1814   The Warrior's Soul
1890   Prince Roman
1825   Suspense (1925)
2080   The Arrow of Gold (1919)
CONRAD, Joseph, and Ford Madox Hueffer
1880   Romance (1903)

GARLAND, Hamlin, b. 1860
　1959　Trail-Makers of the Middle Border (1926)
　2113　A Son of the Middle Border (1914)
　2123　The Long Trail (1907)
　2378　Boy Life on the Prairie (1899)
　2379　A Spoil of Office (1892)
GARNETT, Mrs. R. S.
　1719　The Infamous John Friend (1909)
GARSTIN, Crosbie, b. 1887
　　　　⎧ The Owl's House (1923)
　1493 ⎨ High Noon (1925)
　　　　⎩ The West Wind (1926)
GASKELL, Mrs. Elizabeth Cleghorn (*née* Stevenson), 1810–1865
　1643　Sylvia's Lovers (1863)
　2331　Cranford (1853)
　2333　Mary Barton (1848)
　2345　North and South (1855)
GASPÉ, Philippe Aubert de
　1404　The Candians of Old (Cameron of Lochiel) (1864)
GAUTIER, Théophile (1811–1872)
　2195　Captain Fracasse (1863)
GAY, Florence
　161　The Druidess (1908)
GAY, Madame Sophie, 1776–1852
　1013　Marie de Mancini (1839)
GEBHART, Émile
　240　Autour D'Une Tiare (1894)
GEORGE, Arthur
　446　The House of Eyes (1913)
GERARD, Dorothea (Madame L. de Longgarde), b. 1858
　2052　A Glorious Lie (1912)
" GERARD, Morice " (Rev. John Jessop Teague), b. 1856
　206　The Grip of the Wolf (1900)
　698　The Gate of England (1914)
　699　A Fair Prisoner (1912)
　713　Beacon Fires (1915)
　803　For France (1923)
　807　The Ward of Navarre (1920)
　888　The Grey Friar (1924)
　1004　The Tide of Fortune (1922)
　1025　The King Waits (1921)
　1092　The Adventures of an Equerry (1905)
　1118　The Red Seal (1906)
　1137　The Adventures of Marmaduke Clegg (1920)
　1160　The Last Link (1911)
　1205　One of Marlborough's Captains (1912)
　1401　The Heart of a Hero (1913)
　1683　A Lieutenant of the King (1904)
GIBBON, Charles, 1843–1890
　600　The Braes of Yarrow (1881)
GIBBS, George, b, 1870
　769　The Love of Mademoiselle (formerly " In Search of Mademoiselle ") (1926)
　1398　The Flame of Courage (1926)
GIFFORD, Evelyn H.
　344　Provenzano the Proud (1904)
GILBERT, Bernard
　953A　John of the Fens (formerly " Tattershall Castle ") (1924)
" GILBERT, George David " (Miss Arthur)
　1059　The Bâton Sinister (1903)
　1625　To My King Ever Faithful (1909)
　1653　The Island of Sorrow (1903)
GILBERT, Henry
　298　Robin Hood and the Men of the Greenwood (1912)
GILKES, A. H.
　33　Four Sons (1909)
　38　Kallistratus (1897)

z

N

INDEX OF TITLES

INDEX OF TITLES

The numbers refer to the items, not to the page

C C

SUBJECT INDEX

SUBJECT INDEX

The numbers refer to the items, not to the page

Countries are given occasionally, but provinces, towns, and local topography have received preferential indication. Pertinent single entries, rather than grouped entries, have been adopted. Semi-historical references are denoted thus*

E E

I have likewise refrained from giving many tales dealing with Early-Christian times. We are here, it must be admitted, on controversial ground, and under the First Century heading I have endeavoured to insert romances of the highest quality only. For instance, I think that Dr. Abbott's "Philochristus" and Wallace's "Ben Hur" ought to satisfy two different types of readers. And this is the place, doubtless, to say that in my lists will be found books of widely differing merit and aim. School teachers, and others in like capacity, ought to discriminate between authors suitable for juvenile or untrained tastes, and authors whose appeal is specially to those of maturer thought and experience.* Differing as much in method and style as in choice of period and character type, Thackeray's "Vanity Fair" and George Eliot's "Romola" have at least this in common—they require a very high degree of intelligence for their due appreciation. Who, among those of us with any knowledge of such works, would dream of recommending them to a youthful reader fresh from the perusal of Miss Yonge's "Little Duke," or Captain Marryat's "Children of the New Forest?"

Naturally in a list of this kind there is bound to be very great inequality; certain periods have been wholly ignored by writers of the first rank, while in others we have something like an *embarras de richesse*. Consequently, I have been compelled, here and there, to insert authors of only mediocre merit. In other cases, again, I have not hesitated to omit works by writers of acknowledged position when these have seemed below the author's usual standard, and where no gap had to be filled. I would instance the James II.—William III. period. Here "Edna Lyall" might have been represented, but, there being no dearth of good novels dealing with both the above reigns, I did not deem it advisable to call in this popular writer at the point which has been generally considered her lowest. I mention this to show that omissions do not necessarily mean ignorance, though, in covering such an immense ground, I cannot doubt that romances worthy of a place in my list have been overlooked.

I think many will be surprised to find how large a proportion of our best writers (English and American) have entered the domain of Historical or Semi-Historical Romance. Scott, Peacock, Thackeray, Dickens, Hawthorne, George Eliot, Charlotte Brontë, George Meredith, Thomas Hardy, R. L. Stevenson, Charles Kingsley, Henry Kingsley, Charles Reade, George Macdonald, Anthony Trollope, Mrs. Gaskell, Walter Besant, Lytton, Disraeli, J. H. Newman, J. A. Froude, and Walter Pater—these are a few of the names which appear in the following pages; while Tolstoy, Dumas, Balzac, "George Sand," Victor Hugo, "De Stendhal" (Henri Beyle), De Vigny, Prosper Mérimée,

* Since these words were written, I have—in later editions—tried to help in the work of discrimination, by specially marking a large number of books which are more or less likely to appeal to the young. (See Note immediately preceding the Main List, page 1).

Martinique, 1623
Martinique, islet near ['Diamond Rock' in the novel], 1705
Marvell, Andrew, 1051
Marx, Karl, 1934
Mary, the Virgin, 73
Mary i (of England), 649, 650, 758
Mary (queen of Scots), 637, 651, 652, 653, 654, 655, 657, 659 [marriage with Francis], 661, 663 [marriage with Darnley], 664, 665, 666, 667, 673 [at Bolton], 675, 689, 694, 696, 708
Mary [wife of Maximilian i], 522, 532
Mary [queen of William iii], 1091, 1149, 1157, 1158
Mary of Guise [queen of James v of Scotland], 622
Mary of Magdala, Saint, 74
Mary de Poictiers, 758
Mary Tudor [sister of Henry viii], 601, 617
Mary of York, lady, 1055
Maryland, 878 [Lord Baltimore's colony], 1079, 2021
Masaniello see Aniello, Tommaso
Masham, lady Abigail, 1211, 1219, 1220, 1221, 1225, 1241
Massachusetts, 992
Masséna, André (duc de Rivoli), 1547, 1600, 1602, 1790, 1793
Massinger, Philip, 828
Mather, Cotton, 1181, 1182, 1183, 1184
Matilda (of England; "empress Maud"), 254, 255, 256
Matilda [wife of William i], 219
Matthew Paris, 338
Mauplia, 1873
Maurice, Prince [royalist], 935, 963
Maurice of Nassau (prince of Orange), 757, 853
Mauritius, 1351
Maximian (Roman emperor), 119, 128
Maximilian i (emperor), 520, 521, 533
Maximilian (emperor of Mexico), 2042, 2043
Maximus (Roman emperor), 139
Mayflower, voyage of the, 849
Maypole sports, 842
Mayo Co. (Ireland), 975 [The Cromwellian settlement]
Mazarin, cardinal, 862, 959, 1004, 1006 [early days], 1007, 1008, 1009, 1010, 1011, 1012, 1013
Mazeppa, Ivan [Cossack hetman], 1232, 1233
Mazzini, Giuseppe, 1938, 1940 [prominent], 1942 [and Garibaldi, main theme], 1943, 1988, 1989, 1994, 2048
Mazzinists, the, 1938
McClellan, George Brinton, 2001, 2008, 2013
McKinley, William, 2124
McNeill, sir John [diplomatist], 1918
Meaux, 1102
Mecklenburg during French occupation, 2278*

Mediæval life (England), 2174*, 2177*, 2178*
Mediæval life (Europe), 2179*, 2180*
Medici, Catherine de, 758, 772 [title and main theme], 777, 784, 785, 786, 796
Medici, Cosimo, 487
Medici, Guiliano, 530, 531
Medici, Lorenzo il Magnifico, 527, 528, 530, 531, 556
Medici, Marie de, 851, 852
Medici family, 448, 527, 555
Mediterranean, the 623, 657
Mehemet Salik [governor of Tripoli], 1873
Melanchthon, 583, 759
Melik (shah of Persia), 246
Melrose, 636
Memphis, 44, 59
Menander, 35
Mendip hills, 138
Mendip region, 1637
Mendoza, cardinal, 547
Menelaus, 2159*
Menenptah ii [Egyptian king], 8
Menou, baron Jacques François de [French general], 1693
Menshikoff, prince, 1134
Menshikoff, Alexander [Russian statesman and general], 1192, 1235
Mentana, Garibaldi's defeat at, 1988
Mentchikoff see Menshikoff
Mercia, 163, 165, 168, 174, 176, 199. [Edwy's raid]
Mesmer, Friedrich Anton, 1539
Messalina, 78, 79
Methodism in America (c. 1810), 1778
Methodist revival, 1373
Methodists, 1467, 1645, 2231*
Methuen (Paul Sanford Methuen, 3rd baron), 2139, 2142
Metternich-Winneburg, Clement, prince of, 1688, 1743, 1759, 1822, 1946, 1946a
Metz, siege of, 2062, 2070, 2072
Mexican war (1846-48) the, 1955, 1956, 1957, 1958, 1959
Mexican war of Independence, 2043
Mexico, 590, 591, 687
Mexico, conquest of, 591, 592, 593
Mexico City, 2042
Michelangelo, 556, 626, 628
Miguel de Molinos, 870
Milan, 141, 144, 370, 372, 411, 445, 446, 447, 529, 558, 634, 896
Milbanke, Anna Isabella [afterwards lady Byron], 1868, 1869
Milton, John, 871, 872, 939, 949
Milton, mistress see Powell, Mary
Mining camp (Colorado), 2382*
Mining life in California, 2359*
Minoan civilisation see Ægean civilisation
Minute Men's club, the, 1502
Mirabeau (Honoré-Gabriel de Riquetti) count, 1492, 1539, 1545, 1546, 1550, 1558
Missionary Ridge, battle of, 2023, 2024a
Mississippi, 2024a
Mississippi river, 1171

temp cd